THE MASTER GAME

UNMASKING THE SECRET RULERS OF THE WORLD

GRAHAM HANCOCK
&
ROBERT BAUVAL

disinformation®

BY THE SAME AUTHORS

BY GRAHAM HANCOCK

The Sign and the Seal
Fingerprints of the Gods
Heaven's Mirror (WITH SANTHA FAIIA)
Underworld
Supernatural

BY ROBERT BAUVAL

Secret Chamber
The Orion Mystery (WITH ADRIAN GILBERT)
The Egypt Code
Black Genesis (WITH THOMAS BROPHY)

BY GRAHAM HANCOCK AND ROBERT BAUVAL

The Message of the Sphinx

www.grahamhancock.com
www.robertbauval.com

To my mother, Yvonne Bauval.

Robert Bauval

For my father. Your warmth and wise advice are sorely missed.

Graham Hancock

◘ disinformation®

Library of Congress Control Number: 2011933032

ISBN: 978-1-934708-64-4

eISBN: 978-1-934708-75-0

Designed by Greg Stadnyk

Attention colleges and universities, corporations and other organizations:
Quantity discounts are available on bulk purchases of this book for educational
training purposes, fund-raising, or gift giving. Special books, booklets, or book
excerpts can also be created to fit your specific needs. For information contact the
Marketing Department of The Disinformation Company Ltd.

10 9 8 7 6 5 4

Printed in the United States of America

CONTENTS

CONTENTS

EPILOGUE: THE MASTER GAME

ACKNOWLEDGEMENTS

The making of this book has a long and chequered history. It began in 1992 and was finally brought to a close in 2011. The time-span reflects not only the complex nature of the subject matter but also the strong and enduring working relationship and friendship that I have with my co-author, Graham Hancock, a master of the trade *par excellence*. It also highlights, yet again, the power of teamwork and the old but true axiom that 'two heads are better than one.'

I would like to thank the many colleagues and friends who, through the many years, have helped me directly or indirectly with this book. My foremost thanks go to my wife, Michele, who always gave me unflinching support. It is not easy to live with someone whose mind is often engrossed in solving historical puzzles. I also would like to pay special tribute to Mary Bruck of Edinburgh who sadly passed away recently. She was a very dear friend and she will be sorely missed. Much thanks also go to my friends all over the world, not least Hoda Hakim (Cairo), Chafik and Racha Kotry (Alexandria), John and Josette Orphanidis (Athens), Gouda Fayed (Giza, Nazlet El Salman), Javier and Eva Sierra (Malaga), Adriano Forgione (Rome), Sandro Mainardi (Florence), Linda and Max Bauval (Hawaii), Christopher and Caroline Knight (UK), Alan Butler (UK), Juliano Fernadez (Uruguay), Jean-Paul and Valentina Tarud-Kuborn (Chile), Jeanne Ribeiro (Brazil), Ryan Gilmore (Canada), Gary Evans (UK), Hillary Raimo (USA) and Sherif el Sebai (Cairo). My gratitude to my literary agent and friend Bill Hamilton of A. M. Heath & Co. Ltd., who is always there to encourage and advise me, and to listen to my over-enthusiastic oratory. The same gratitude also goes to my editor and friend Gary Baddeley of The Disinformation Company in New York for his patience, dedication, support and invaluable help. Much appreciation to Ralph Bernardo for his diligence and dedication in putting this book together. As always I give thanks to all my readers, old and new, and hope that they will find *The Master Game* as enjoyable as it was for me to co-write.

Robert Bauval
Malaga, Spain

ACKNOWLEDGEMENTS

Thank you to my wife Santha and to our six children Sean, Shanti, Ravi, Leila, Luke and Gabrielle, who have given me so much solidarity, love and support over the 19 years this book has been in the making. I'm really grateful to my Dad, too, who read the whole manuscript during what turned out to be his last summer and took the trouble to give me many helpful comments and suggestions. He passionately disagreed with many of my views on the Christian Church, but we agreed equally passionately that life has a spiritual meaning and that it does not end with the grave.

Graham Hancock
Bath, England

LIST OF ILLUSTRATIONS

The Master Game

Man is born free, but everywhere he is in chains.

Jean-Jacques Rousseau, *Le Contrat Social*

There is one thing stronger than all the armies in the world; and that is an idea whose time has come.

Proverb

"What is the Master Game?"

"Who is playing it?"

"Where? How? Why?"

"And which side is winning?"

THE GAME OF GAMES

For a very long time there has been a belief, sometimes widely held and proclaimed, sometimes held only by persecuted minorities, that we humans are here on this planet to nurture and perfect our souls – and thus to equip ourselves for immortality.

Those who hold such beliefs usually also believe that negative spiritual forces are at work amongst mankind – evil angels who seek to lead us astray and divert us from our true path.

It is irrelevant whether any of this is ontologically true. All that matters is that it has been and continues to be believed. Such beliefs, built around a concept of antagonistic forces – Darkness and Light, Good and Evil – battling for the human soul are bound to have been acted upon by those who held them strongly.

In this book we will explore a number of mysterious ancient documents, prominent amongst them the so-called *Hermetic Texts*, written down in Latin and Greek in the early centuries of the Christian era. In one of these texts the god Hermes (the Greek counterpart of the ancient Egyptian wisdom god Thoth) delivers a prophecy to his pupil Asclepius:

> Do you know, Asclepius, that Egypt is an image of heaven, or to speak more exactly, in Egypt all the operations of the powers which rule and work in heaven are present in the Earth below? In fact it should be said that the whole Kosmos dwells in this our land as in a sanctuary.
>
> And yet, since it is fitting that wise men should have knowledge of all events before they come to pass, you must not be left in ignorance of what I will now tell you.
>
> There will come a time when it will have been in vain that Egyptians have

honored the Godhead with heartfelt piety and service; and all our holy worship will be fruitless and ineffectual.

The gods will return from earth to heaven; Egypt will be forsaken, and the land which was once the home of religion will be left desolate, bereft of the presence of its deities.

O Egypt, Egypt, of thy religion nothing will remain but an empty tale, which thine own children in time to come will not believe; nothing will be left but graven words, and only the stones will tell of thy piety.

And in that day men will be weary of life, and they will cease to think the universe worthy of reverent wonder and worship ... Darkness will be preferred to light, and death will be thought more profitable than life; no one will raise his eyes to heaven; the pious will be deemed insane, the impious wise; the madman will be thought a brave man, and the wicked will be esteemed as good.

As for the soul, and the belief that it is immortal by nature, or may hope to attain to immortality, as I have taught you – all this they will mock, and even persuade themselves that it is false.

No word of reverence or piety, no utterance worthy of heaven, will be heard or believed.

And so the gods will depart from mankind, – a grievous thing! – and only evil angels will remain, who will mingle with men, and drive the poor wretches into all manner of reckless crime, into wars, and robberies, and frauds, and all things hostile to the nature of the soul.[1]

Against the onset of such dark times – and there have been many dark episodes in the past two millennia – we demonstrate in this book that certain groups and individuals have always stood prepared to act. These daring and valiant people knew from the outset that their resistance might put them in extreme danger and would require much sacrifice, even the willingness to die. They also knew that their task might take a very long time, spanning several generations, centuries, perhaps even millennia. But it was the only game really worth playing for upon the outcome depended nothing less than the spiritual redemption of mankind.

THE MASTER GAME

Today covertly directed from Washington, DC, the 'Master Game' as we have come to see it has evolved into nothing less than a grandiose scheme played on the world stage to bring about a 'new world order'. Let us be very clear from the outset, however, that this book is neither a 'conspiracy theory' nor a compilation of such theories. Our objective is solely to make sense of historical events, particularly events of recent times, that have rocked the very soul of humanity.

Yet the Master Game was not easy to recognize and comprehend, not least because it drew inspiration from a distant golden age set in far away places. This was when groups of carefully selected men and women, neophytes and adepts, were carefully initiated into a high *gnosis* to equip them with great intellectual powers that would enable them to guide and direct society along the path of virtuosity and enlightenment. This is why it will be necessary for the reader to journey with us to the very source of the 'Game' and unhurriedly be ushered through the secret routes and alleyways that infiltrate great social and religious reforms, the birth of the state of Israel, and finally the hideous episode of 9/11 and the ongoing military and political mayhem that it set in motion.

As investigative writers with one foot in the Western world and the other in the Arab world, and also as historians opting to dig deep under the veneer of established history, we have become increasingly and disturbingly aware that the Master Game has taken a rather strange twist over the last sixty years or so. Indeed it is our conclusion that it has now lost sight entirely of its original objective and, far worse, could be leading mankind towards an Armageddon of biblical proportions. To put it bluntly, there is a very dangerous and extremely strong social and political undercurrent in one part of the world that is building up largely unnoticed, and that is about to blow, like an overheated giant pressure cooker, into a gruesome clash of civilizations.

For hundreds of millions of Muslims (and even in some Christian and Jewish communities) there is a weird perception that a Masonic-Zionist-American plot, hatched back in the early 1900s (but not implemented until the 1940s), has been devised to take over and control the Arab world from Washington, London and Tel Aviv. This perception on the one side, whether based on facts or falsehoods, is perilously misunderstood on the other side by the Western world as a whole. Our findings show that the Master Game is not only being played by a set of new players having very different rules of engagement but also using very different game-boards. In simple terms, the Master Game has stopped being a battle between oppressed and oppressors, between the forces of evil and the forces of good, and has transmuted itself into a dangerous collision of two cultures who see the future of the world in very different ways.

From the time of the Italian Renaissance in the 15th century, the Master Game began to change from direct physical confrontation with the powers that be (of the kind that took place during the Cathar 'experiment' – see *Part I: The Secret Faith*) to something much more subtle and insidious – a form of symbolic warfare that would assail the establishment secretly and stealthily from within. This new approach would not use conventional weaponry, or military forces, but rather a *special gnosis* known only an elect few. Like camouflaged commandos operating under the cover of darkness these elite, initiated insiders would place powerful 'intellectual time-bombs' in the very heart of their unsuspecting oppressors, set to detonate at propitious moments. Continuing through the Enlightenment of the 17th century, the great social upheavals of the French and American Revolutions of the late 18th century and finally down to our own times, it is not an accident that top architects, town planners, and even sculptors and artists have been busily changing the urban landscapes of major cities – principally in Rome, London, Paris and Washington, DC – by strategically locating monuments and buildings that seemingly evoke 'Masonic' ideologies and symbolism. Their objective or, more aptly, that of the Masters has been to erode and finally eliminate the iron-hold of the Church and the monarchies and to establish a new world order based on seemingly 'Masonic' ideals.

We have made it our task to understand whence these ideas originated and also to attempt to define the true purpose of these strange urban developments. To this end we have found it necessary not only to undertake a sort of 'intellectual archaeology' of history but also to *self-initiate* ourselves into an ancient and very potent way of thinking which, for want of better terms, we have dubbed *talismanic thinking*.

In our many years of research into ancient cultures and, more specifically, their powerful symbolic art and architecture, it has slowly dawned on us that the true language of humans is not, as we previously thought, the spoken word but the 'silent language' of symbols and signs that 'speak' directly to the mind and the soul of a person. And although everyone knows that a symbol is an image or an object that represents something, few are aware that some symbols can be converted into extremely powerful intellectual instruments that can have devastating effects on large huge numbers of people by *charging* them with intoxicating ideologies and stirring emotions. When a symbol, whether a tangible object, monument or building, or whether an intangible idea or logo is thus *charged*, then it becomes a *talisman*. Think of the Christian Cross, the Star of David, the Islamic Crescent or the Nazi Swastika and the disturbing effects such talismans have had throughout history and you will begin to get the gist of this elusive Master Game.

To have a full understanding of how talismans work, and knowledge of exactly where, how and when to apply them for maximum effect, is to be in possession of a potent arsenal of intellectual weaponry that can be used to change, reform, transform or, as the case may be, overthrow entrenched social and cultural systems ... and also replace them with new ones. Kingdoms, empires, whole civilizations have been brought down with such intellectual weaponry, and the amazing thing is that in the most successful assaults not a single shot was fired or a single bomb exploded; furthermore the intellectual war was fought with one side entirely oblivious of where the attacks came from and unable to assess the damage inflicted until it was too late.

In 2009 the American novelist Dan Brown published his latest thriller, *The Lost Symbol*, which purported to unmask the true 'Masonic' mission and the meaning of the strange city layout of Washington, DC. Although the plot was largely fictional, the historical and urban settings he used were rooted in reality. The initial result of such wide popularization in semi-fictional blockbusters is that several millions of people are now aware of a possible covert mission to turn the capital of the United States into a Masonic 'experiment' using talismanic symbolism in the layout of streets and positioning of stately buildings and monuments. Another, more pertinent result, is that some residents of Washington, DC have become preoccupied by the real possibility that they live, eat, work and play inside a giant 'Masonic temple' that is their city. Yet neither Dan Brown nor anyone else as far as we know has been able to explain exactly why such a strange city plan was created in the first place nor, too, what ultimate function such a scheme might truly serve.

But as we emphasized earlier, to get to grips with this conundrum one must go back to the very roots of the ideologies that fired such a scheme and track its evolution and transmission across the ages. It is an intellectual journey that is truly worth the effort because at its end of the voyage, as happened with us, a veil will be lifted to reveal a strange world that was always there and yet is *invisible to the uninitiated eye*.

Prologue:
The Sacred Cities

The boat of Isis, a feast which was celebrated in Rome with great pomp, was known as Navigium Isidis; *after it had been launched in the water, it was brought back to the Temple of Isis and prayers were made for the prosperity of the emperor, for the empire and for the Roman people ...*

François Noël, *Dictionnaire de la fable*

No one ignores that Paris was originally enclosed in the island [the Île de la Cité]. *It was thus, since its origins, a city of navigation ... As it was in a river rife with navigation, it took as its symbol a boat, and as tutelary goddess, Isis, goddess of navigation; and this boat was the actual one of Isis, symbol of this goddess.*

Antoine Court de Gébelin, *Monde primitif analysé et comparé avec le monde moderne*

CHAPTER ONE

BEHIND THE VEILS

On 14 July 1789 a furious crowd ran riot on the streets of Paris and stormed the great prison known as the Bastille. Less than an hour later the fate of France hung in the balance and European history seemed set on a new and alarmingly unpredictable course.

Contemporary engravings of the Bastille show a forbidding rectangular structure flanked by eight tall towers. It does not look easy to storm. Built in the late 14th century as a fortress to protect eastern Paris, it was converted in the 17th century into a squalid and ghastly prison for dissidents. By the time of the Revolution it was firmly established in the public mind as an instrument of tyranny and as a powerful symbol of the despotism of the French crown.

The day after the storming of the Bastille an enterprising local contractor, Monsieur Pierre-François Palloy,[1] took it upon himself to mobilise a workforce of 800 citizens to dismantle the hated prison stone by stone.[2] The work was so well done that within a month most of the structure had been reduced to rubble with only a small part of the perimeter wall and foundations still intact.

At this point something curious occurred. The suggestion was made, and for a while taken seriously, that the stones of the Bastille should be salvaged in order to construct a replica of an ancient Egyptian pyramid on the site.[3] And although the project later stalled for lack of funds, the core idea of making a symbolic connection with ancient Egypt persisted behind the scenes. If a pyramid could not be managed something less would have to suffice. Thus it was that on 10 August 1793 a group of revolutionaries ceremoniously installed a large statue of the ancient Egyptian goddess Isis where the Bastille had formerly stood. Depicting the goddess seated on a throne flanked by two lions, the statue had been conceived by Jacques-Louis David, the famous artist and propagandist of the revolution. It was to be one of the props in a macabre republican feast hastily put together in order to celebrate the decapitation of King Louis XVI six months previously and the forthcoming guillotining of Queen Marie-Antoinette still two months ahead.

The sculptors, François Marie Suzanne and Pierre Cartelier, did not have sufficient time to cast the statue in the preferred medium of bronze so they simply moulded it in plaster and coloured it with bronze paint.[4] From the bare nipples of the 'goddess Isis' could be seen water being ejected into an open basin below the statue. Known as the 'Fountain of Regeneration', the general idea was for the crowd of people to pass in procession in front of 'Isis' and drink 'from her fertile breasts the pure and salutary liquor of regeneration'.[5]

De-Christianisation

Everyone knows that philosophical ideas, notably those of Jean-Jacques Rousseau and Voltaire, were part of the ferment that led to the French Revolution. Still it is hard to explain why an overtly *religious* ritual – such as the Isis ceremony described above – should have received official sponsorship from the revolutionary government as early as 1793. That it did so, moreover, on a site so powerfully symbolic as the Place de la Bastille, raises an interesting question. Is it possible that spiritual and even 'religious' beliefs could have played a greater role than has hitherto been recognised in precipitating and sustaining the changes that gripped France after 1789.

For example, although the matter has been little studied, it became clear in the early days of the Revolution that its core objectives included not only the eradication of the monarchy and a radical readjustment of the social and economic order, as might be expected, but also another, even more far-reaching goal: the eradication, no less – one might almost say the *extirpation* – of Christianity from the soil of France. This objective was adopted as official policy in the winter of 1793, a few months after the Isis rituals at the Bastille, and set in train an intense and systematic national campaign of 'de-Christianisation'.[6] As French historian Michel Vovelle sums up, this now almost forgotten facet of the Revolution was not some passive and progressive attempt at conversion, but a methodical and forceful enterprise imposed though violence and intimidation.[7]

Why this sudden rush to stamp out Christianity?

Was it just that the Revolutionaries saw Christianity as a rival for the loyalty of the masses and hated and resented the ancient ties between the monarchy and the Church?

Or was there another, deeper game being played?

Very Christian Kings beheaded by the Cult of the Supreme Being

The kings of France liked to trace their origins back to the *Merovingians*, a Frankish dynasty of the fifth to the eighth centuries AD. Nothing is known about Merovech, the semi-legendary founder of the dynasty, but his son Childeric I is a historical figure who ruled a tribe of Salian Franks from his capital at Tournai *circa* AD 470. In AD 481 or 482 Childeric was succeeded by his son Clovis I who united almost of all of Gaul and converted to Christianity around AD 496.

Clovis died *circa* AD 511, but the Merovingian dynasty continued to rule much of what is now France until AD 750. It was succeeded by the Carolingian dynasty which gained great renown *circa* AD 800 with the dramatic coronation by Pope Leo III of Charlemagne as the very first 'Holy Roman emperor'. Thereafter all kings of France were regarded as the protectors of the Roman Church and to this effect bore the title *Roi Très Chrétien* – 'Very Christian King'. Indeed so pious were France's medieval kings that one of them was actually canonised as a saint – Louis IX, a hero of the Crusades, who we will meet in Part I.[8]

Meanwhile to return to that terrible year of 1793–4 – the year, in fact, of the revolutionary 'Terror' with its unruly orgy of beheading – a different kind of religious phenomenon was suddenly widely observed in France: Catholic priests began to 'abdicate' their positions in droves[9] and a new, officially-sponsored cult was launched by the *Convention* (the Revolutionary government) within recently 'de-Christianised' churches and cathedrals all across the land. Sometimes referred to as the 'Cult of Reason' but more commonly as the 'Cult of the Supreme Being', it seems that this new religion was the brainchild of the revolutionary leader Maximilien Robespierre and that its establishment was masterminded once again by the artist Jacques-Louis David (who had previously been involved in the Isis/Bastille stunt).

The tricolor goddess with the Phrygian cap

In street festivals staged during the French Revolution, the 'goddess Reason' was routinely personified by an actress garbed with a *tricolor* red, white and blue veil and wearing the so-called *Phrygian cap*. This same little red cap was in great vogue with the general public in the early part of the Revolution and was worn especially by the *sans-culottes* ('without culottes'), the most zealous faction who partook in the thousands of guillotine executions in Paris and throughout the country.

The Phrygian cap is the typical headwear of two well-known pagan deities: the goddess Cybele and the god Mithras.

Cybele was the one of the great mother goddesses of antiquity and, more particularly at one stage of Roman history, whose 'republic' the French revolutionaries tried to emulate. As the name of her cap suggests, her cult origins were in ancient Phrygia (modern Turkey). In statuary she was routinely associated with two lions, either depicted harnessed to her chariot or flanking the ceremonial throne used by the high-priests of her cult. Medieval and Renaissance scholars frequently identified her with the ancient Egyptian goddess Isis. It therefore seems unlikely to be an accident that a Cybele-like goddess was to figure so prominently in the iconography of the French Revolution – for example in the so-called *Génie de La République*, a marble sculpture by the artist Joseph Chinard, made in the aftermath of the fall of the Bastille, which shows '*République*' as a young woman in Graeco-Roman garb wearing the Phrygian hat.[10]

In the strange and terrible year of 1793–4 the so-called *Cult of Reason* spread like wildfire in the French provinces alongside the de-Christianisation process. It became common to witness large processions, or street theatres, in which the 'goddess Reason' wearing the Phrygian cap was towed on a cart to the nearest church or cathedral. Such events might look like nothing more than excuses for men and women to get drunk together, yet in France there were always more serious undertones. On 7 November 1793 for example no less a figure than the bishop of Paris, was forced by the Convention to recant his faith. Three days later, on 10 November, huge celebrations were organised at his cathedral in honour of the alternative Cult of Reason.

As the highlight of the celebrations a certain Mlle Aubry, a beautiful and popular actress wrapped in a white veil and blue tunic and wearing the red Phrygian cap, emerged from a 'temple' dedicated to 'philosophy' and was sat on a throne while the crowds came to pay homage to her. The procession then marched to the Convention, where Citizen Chabot, a zealous revolutionary and one of the co-architects of the new cult, decreed that henceforth the Cathedral of Notre Dame in Paris, the oldest and most revered Christian sanctuary in the land, was to become the 'Temple of Reason'. Several ceremonies then followed where the role of the 'goddess' was assumed by various Parisian beauties, among them Mlle Maillard, Mlle Lacombe and Mme Momoro.[11]

The obelisk and the painting

In 1813, twenty-six years after the storming of the Bastille, the great culture-changing momentum of the French Revolution seemingly came to a grinding halt with the defeat of Napoleon. Seizing the moment, the exiled Count of Provence, Louis-Stanislas-Xavier, elder brother of Louis XVI, promised the French people that he would uphold some of the tenets of the Revolution in a new form of monarchy. Then, advised by the brilliant statesman Talleyrand, he entered Paris in May 1814 where he was received with open arms by the war-weary French and, amid much jubilation, was installed on the throne as Louis XVIII.[12]

Louis XVIII ruled for ten years. He was a Freemason – on his death in 1824 he was succeeded by his brother, the Count of Artois – also a Freemason – who took the name Charles X. Both monarchs showed a marked preference for ancient Egyptian symbolism in their public works and two projects of Charles X are of particular interest in this regard. The first involved transporting an intact ancient Egyptian obelisk to Paris. The second called for the commissioning of a gigantic painting in the Louvre.

The obelisk

In 1827, Jean-François Champollion (dubbed the 'father of modern Egyptology' for his breakthrough decipherment of ancient Egyptian hieroglyphs) was commissioned by Charles X to arrange for the importation to Paris of a 3,500-year-old obelisk – one of a pair – that stood at Alexandria in Egypt.[13]

The obelisk was destined for the Place de la Concorde, a prestigious location of great personal significance to Charles X. It had originally being named in honour of his father, Louis XV, an equestrian statue of whom had once graced it. But the statue had been pulled down and destroyed during the 1789 Revolution and the site renamed by the Convention as 'Place de la Concorde'. Here also the guillotine had been erected that had beheaded Louis XVI in January 1793 and Marie-Antoinette in October of the same bloodstained year. May we speculate that the installation of the obelisk was to commemorate the idea of a reborn and restored monarchy, with the ancient solar symbol of the divine kings of Egypt rising in the heart of the Parisian skyline like a 'phoenix'?

The painting

Charles X's second noteworthy project was to commission the artist François-Édouard Picot to decorate the ceiling of his personal museum at the Louvre with a specific 'Egyptian' theme.

Picot, like many promising artists of the time, had studied under the master, Jacques-Louis David – the man responsible for the statue of Isis in the Place de la Bastille. We should not be surprised, therefore, that the very same 'Isis' is found on Picot's painting for Charles X.

Still decorating a ceiling of the Louvre, the great work was completed in 1827 and measures roughly 5 x 4 meters. Its title is *L'Etude et le Génie dévoilent à Athènes l'Antique Egypte* ('Learning and Genius Unveil Ancient Egypt to Athens'). The figure of Isis dominates the scene and is depicted seated on a throne flanked by two lions – as was the case with David's earlier Isis of the Bastille. The viewer, however, is immediately drawn to contemplate the sky above the goddess, where can be seen flying two angels in the act of 'unveiling' the secrets of Isis.

We catch a tantalising glimpse of a haunting landscape containing in the far distance an obelisk and a group of pyramids at which Isis languidly casts her gaze. From the clouds next to the angels, the Greek goddess Athena appears with an owl at her feet symbolising initiation and wisdom. To the left of Athena is a winged-goddess wearing a laurel wreath symbolising 'Learning' (*l'Etude*). To the right of Athena is the so-called *Génie de Paris*, a naked winged youth brandishing a torch in order to illuminate and reveal to Athena the Egyptianised landscape below.

After the abdication of Charles X in 1830, Louis-Philippe I became the new ruler of France. Also known as the 'Citizen King', he commissioned a monument to commemorate the *Trois Glorieuses*, those three days of 26, 27 and 28 July 1830 that marked France's Second Revolution. This monument, which was completed in 1836, is a tall pillar erected in the Place de la Bastille on the very spot where David had positioned his statue of Isis in August 1793. On top of the pillar is a close replica of the winged youth with the torch seen in Picot's painting in the Louvre.

Is Picot reminding us that here, below the winged *Génie de Paris*, had once been a statue of Isis as also seen in his painting?

Coincidence, or blueprint?

Let us imagine ourselves in Paris today, riding in a helicopter above the Bastille pillar and looking westward, along the line of sight of the *Génie de Paris*. We are hovering over the city's oldest and most sacred quarters. Sprawled beneath us are some of the most impressive buildings and monuments that Paris has to offer. To our left runs the Boulevard Henri IV leading to the River Seine. The river itself runs roughly from east to west, and thus parallel to our westward line of sight, while beyond Boulevard

Henri IV is the old Pont Sully arching over the eastern edge of the Île St. Louis with its famous abbey of the same name. The western tip of the island is linked by a pedestrian bridge to the much larger Île de la Cité, site of the celebrated Cathedral of Notre Dame and the impressive Palais de Justice.

Across the Seine is the tall bell tower of the Abbey of Saint-Germain-des-Prés – the latter, as we shall later see, intriguingly once a sanctuary dedicated to the goddess Isis. Yet all these wonders will pale when we focus our eyes along our line of sight westwards with the *Génie de Paris*, for before us will unfold the most enchanting urban landscape that Europe has to offer. Shooting straight like an arrow is the Rue de Rivoli leading to the Church of Saint-Germain l'Auxerrois – the oldest in Paris, where the ancient kings of France were traditionally baptised. Immediately beyond the church is the crab-shaped *Grand Louvre*, perhaps Europe's most wonderful museum and, until 1663, the main palace of the kings of France.

And there is yet more to feast our eyes upon. Today an imposing glass Pyramid – commissioned by President Mitterrand for the bicentennial celebration of 1989 – looms like a giant diamond in the central courtyard of the Louvre. This out-of-place pyramid seems to define for us an open vista westward leading through Napoleon's Arc du Carrousel and towards the impeccably-groomed Tuileries Garden. Our line of sight further takes in the wide and perfectly straight Avenue des Champs-Élysées, the backbone of Paris that was once known as the *Axe historique* – the 'Historical Axis'. At this point it is impossible not to see the tall Egyptian obelisk that rears up towards the sky in the Place de la Concorde at the entrance of the Champs-Élysées. And nor can we ignore the way in which the whole layout that we observe from the high vantage point of the *Génie de Paris* bears an uncanny and striking similarity to the layout and general scheme suggested in Picot's painting. For if we examine this painting more closely and try to imagine ourselves now alongside the other winged *Génie de Paris* which hovers over the mysterious Egyptianised landscape of Picot's masterpiece, something immediately becomes clear. The obelisk and the various pyramids that Picot included not only seem to define the central axis of the painting but, if transposed to the layout of Paris, will correlate with the Concorde Obelisk and the Louvre Pyramid that define the central or 'Historical' Axis of the city!

Charles X's decision to send Champollion to Egypt to bring back the obelisk was taken during the year 1826–7 *while Picot was in the process of painting his masterpiece at the Louvre*. We also know that Picot was deeply involved in the furbishing of Charles X's Egyptian museum at the Louvre

Palace and that he would almost certainly have been privy to the discussions surrounding the importation and positioning of the obelisk. Even though it was not until 1836 that it was finally raised up in the Place de la Concorde, therefore, its easy to understand why the artist might have been inspired to put an obelisk in his 1827 painting – and in the right place.

Much harder to explain is the relationship between the pyramids Picot shows in the painting and the Louvre Pyramid visible in our aerial view. This is because the latter is a modern work, less than 20 years old at time of writing, designed by architect I. M. Pei and completed in 1984.

So the question is, how could Picot have anticipated I. M. Pei's pyramid? Or – more conspiratorially – did the 1827 painting allude to some sort of occult plan or blueprint for Paris that has continued to be implemented over more than 150 years? Or is it just a huge coincidence that the Egyptianised landscape being unveiled in the painting has been reproduced in the architecture of Paris?

Was Freemasonry behind the French Revolution?

We have already seen how during the 1789 Revolution it was proposed to raise a pyramid at the site of the Bastille – something that Picot would certainly have known of. Picot is also likely to have been aware of a number of other grandiose 'pyramid' projects that were planned before and after the Revolution but that had been stalled because of shortage of funds.

There had been, for example, a massive 'pyramid tomb' planned in Paris in honour of the scientist Sir Isaac Newton who was a hero of the Enlightenment and, consequently, of revolutionary ideals. The 'pyramid' was designed by the French architect, Joseph-Jean-Pascal Gay, in 1800, and was to have had a great perimeter wall with four gates modelled on the Temple of Karnak in Upper Egypt, and an alley of 18 sphinxes leading to the 'pyramid'.[14]

There were too, the various pyramids proposed by the architect Étienne-Louis Boullée. One of his surviving sketches is of a group of pyramids closely resembling the pyramids in Picot's painting – where they are seen enveloped in clouds and haze with their capstones missing.[15] The historian Jean Starobinski in his study of the emblems and symbols of the 1789 Revolution, explains that the 'language of the Revolution' was intensely 'symbolic'. Starobinski also speaks of a mood that seems to have seized architects in the immediately pre-revolutionary period: a novel need to use basic geometrical shapes – cubes, spheres, pyramids – on a monumental scale and to transform Paris into some sort of 'utopian city':

... [there was a] need to add images to ideas, and to design the plans of an ideal city. This city, like all other utopic cities, would be governed by the laws of a simple and strict geometry ... All these grand architectural styles in line with simple principles of geometry presented as projects remained unrealised. [And although] a harmonious city, a city for a new age ... existed in the portfolios of certain architects, well-before the storming of the Bastille ... the Revolution would have neither the time, nor the resources, nor perhaps the audacity to ask them to undertake these great civic projects ...[16]

But why an *Egyptianised* utopian vision for Paris? Why pyramids and pseudo-Egyptian landscapes? Where did such strange ideas come from? And who was promoting them?

Such obsessions with symbolism, architecture and particularly geometry once again suggest the influence of Freemasonry. Yet the authorities are divided on the matter. Scores of historians argue that an important role was indeed played by Freemasons in the French Revolution while, on the other hand, equal numbers argue that Freemasonry had nothing or little to do with it. This state of affairs is adequately expressed by the French historian Jacques Godechot, an expert on the subject:

There is a whole genre of literature, with shows no sign of abating, which attributes the responsibility of the Revolution, and especially the days of 1789, to the Duc d'Orléans [the first Grand Master of the *Grand Orient*, the supreme body which regulates Freemasonry in France]. According to this literature, it was the Duc d'Orléans who was responsible for the riots of the *Réveillon*, those of the 14th July, those of the night of the 4th August, and those of the days of October. The Duc certainly attempted to profit from these events but whether he was the cause of them seems highly doubtful. In any case, if he did play this game, his efforts constituted a small influence compared to the much larger forces that pushed the people, France and even all of the Western world towards Revolution ...[17]

The truth is that no historian, however thorough his or her research, can really know what 'forces', visible or occult, moved the French people to erupt in total revolution against the monarchy and the Church in 1789. By definition such 'forces' are impossible to gauge and sometimes may not be 'visible' or 'documented' at all. It is a similar problem attempting to catalogue the forces behind the Crusades in the Middle Ages or behind the

Holocaust in Nazi Germany – or indeed those 'forces' that launched the United States on its 'War on Terror' at the beginning of the 21st century. No single force, occult or otherwise, can be deemed solely responsible for any of these events; rather a combination of forces has in every instance been at play.

In the case of the French Revolution, it is clear that one of the main forces was generated by the terrible oppression of the people and the abuse of power by the monarchy. Yet no historian will deny that there was also a strong philosophical and/or intellectual undercurrent to the Revolution which exerted a powerful influence on the behaviour of key figures such as Maximillien Robespierre, Jean-Paul Marat and George Jacques Danton, as well as others such as the painter Jacques-Louis David and the sculptor Jean-Antoine Houdon. At this stage of our investigation Freemasonry remains as good a candidate as any for the source of this undercurrent.

Meanwhile, across the Atlantic in America, another 'sister' Revolution had taken place a decade earlier. There, too, a strong philosophical/ intellectual undercurrent can easily be detected which moved the main players such as Benjamin Franklin, Thomas Jefferson, Thomas Paine and George Washington. And there, too, a utopian city was, quite literally, in the making – to an esoteric plan far less veiled than that of Paris.

Franklin, Freemasonry and Revolution

That the American Revolution or War of Independence was much influenced by Freemasons and Masonic ideologies and principles is a well-accepted thesis. There are several good works on this topic[18] that leave little doubt that Freemasonry was one of the driving forces behind the ideals and tenets, and the attachment to republicanism, of the American Revolution. What is less well known is the fact that there was a very close connection between the French and American Masonic lodges at that time.

It is not clear whether or not Freemasonry might have entered North America before the establishment of the Grand Lodge of England in 1717, but the earliest surviving records of formal Masonic lodges in America are from Boston and Philadelphia in the early 1730s.[19] The spread of Freemasonry in America occurred through the so-called *military lodges*, and by the eve of the War of Independence in 1775 it had become extremely popular among the ranking officers and gentry.

One of the first American Freemasons was Benjamin Franklin, who was initiated in February 1731 and became Master of the *St. John's* lodge in the city of Philadelphia, where he 'produced the oldest draft of

American lodge by-laws still in existence'.[20] Franklin, who had founded the *Pennsylvania Gazette* in 1729, is also renowned in Masonic circles for printing (in December 1730) the very first article in America which referred to Freemasonry.[21]

In those days Freemasonry in America was regulated by the Grand Lodge of England which appointed 'Provincial Grand Masters' in various regions of the North American continent. In 1749 Franklin was appointed Provincial Grand Master of Pennsylvania. An intellectual, a brilliant politician and, above all, a cunning *agent provocateur*, Franklin was to become the key figure in the American revolt against Britain and, of course, the most renowned 'Founding Father' of the United States.

Both as a young man and later in his adult life, Franklin passed three sojourns in England – a total of 15 years accumulated between 1724 and 1726, 1757 and 1762, and 1765 and 1775. During these lengthy stays no one disputes that he gravitated in his choice of friendships towards influential Freemasons and radical intellectuals. On his return visits to America he became notorious for stirring up dissent against British colonial rule – so much so that the Privy Council of London found it necessary to summon him and severely warn him not to rouse anti-British sentiment in the colonies.

It was Franklin who, while in England, had encouraged rejection of the Stamp Act imposed by the British on the American colonies (which required settlers to pay a tax to certify all legal documents and transactions). Franklin managed to intercept a series of letters written by Thomas Hutchinson, the British governor of Massachusetts, in which several important American political figures were spoken of in very hostile terms. Franklin dispatched copies of these letters to friends in America who had them published, causing such an outrage that the British had to appease the situation by repealing the act.

By the spring of 1775 the pressure was mounting against Franklin in England, and he decided it was time to return to America. He arrived there on 5 May. While he had been at sea, war had broken out between the British and the American revolutionary forces at Lexington and Concord on 19 April 1775.

On his arrival in Pennsylvania, Franklin was immediately appointed as a delegate to the Second Continental Congress, the body that was soon to become the Congress of the United States of America. Other newly appointed members were Thomas Jefferson and George Washington. Among the first decisions that the Congress made (on 15 June 1775) was the appointment of Washington as commander-in-chief of the revolutionary armed forces.

Washington was 43 years old in 1775 and Franklin 69. Like Franklin, Washington was a Freemason. He had been initiated into the brotherhood in 1752 at Fredericksburg, Virginia, and had been raised a Master Mason the following year.[22] John Hancock, a rich Harvard gentleman, was president of the Congress at the time. He, too, was a prominent Freemason, later to be remembered for his large signature on the Declaration of Independence.

In September 1776 the Congress agreed to send a commission to France in order to seek military and financial support for the war against Britain. Franklin was a member of the three-man commission. He arrived in Paris just before Christmas that year. Although France was not at war with England at the time, it was regarded as its natural enemy and, therefore, sympathetic to the American cause.

Franklin immediately struck up friendships with important figures in French society and, particularly, among the elite and the Freemasons. To the French he personified the unsophisticated nobility of the New World, and he quickly became the darling of French society and the hero of the intellectuals and military gentry. A sort of 'Franklin cult' was to emerge, and his portrait was seen everywhere, from snuffboxes to chamber pots. His company was in great demand by artists, intellectuals and high-society ladies. Spies and informers infested his house.

Franklin was to engage in secret negotiations with the Count of Vergennes, Louis XVI's minister for foreign affairs. These negotiations lasted several years, and eventually treaties were signed in 1778 in which France pledged military and economic support to the revolutionary cause in America.

Meanwhile in Paris Franklin pursued his social and intellectual interests with gusto by joining the illustrious Masonic 'Nine Sisters' lodge.[23] This famous lodge was founded in 1776 by Jérôme Lalande and the Abbé Cordier de Saint-Fermin, the latter the godfather of Voltaire. This was the same year that the Declaration of Independence was signed in America, with Franklin being the most senior of the signatories. Lalande was France's most respected astronomer, and wielded much influence amongst Parisian intellectuals.

Nine Sisters lodge

The *Loge Les Neuf Sœurs*, the 'Lodge of the Nine Sisters', named after the nine muses of Greek mythology, was in fact the successor of an older lodge, *Les Sciences*, which Lalande had founded in 1766 with the philosopher and mathematician Claude Adrien Helvétius. Helvétius was a staunch advocate of absolute atheism whose political and philosophical ideas would much influence the 1789 Revolution. After the death of Helvétius in 1771, his wife, Anne Catherine Helvétius, joined forces with Lalande and Saint-Fermin in the creation of the Nine Sisters lodge. Her own elite salon in the Rue Sainte-Anne in Paris was famous throughout Europe, and was dubbed 'the general headquarters of European philosophy'.[24] Another of her salons in Auteuil near Paris maintained very close links with the Nine Sisters lodge.[25]

Not surprisingly, Franklin was a regular visitor to Mme Helvétius's salon. Another was the Marquis de Lafayette, a young officer in the French army. Lafayette belonged to a Masonic lodge, *Le Contrat Social*, which was linked to other important lodges throughout France. Notable amongst these was the lodge *La Société Olympique*, with its membership of young officers such as the Count de Chambrun, the Count-Admiral François Joseph Paul de Grasse, the Count-Admiral Charles Hector d'Estaing and the buccaneer John Paul Jones – all of whom would fight for the American cause a few years later.[26]

In 1777 Franklin became the 'Venerable Master' of the Nine Sisters lodge and in 1778 he was given the ultimate honour of assisting in the initiation of the 84-year-old Voltaire. It is said that the aging Voltaire was supported on the arms of Franklin and Antoine Court de Gébelin, the Swiss-French inventor of the modern esoteric Tarot.[27]

In April 1777 Franklin's agent in Paris, the diplomat Sileas Deane, succeeded in recruiting the young Marquis de Lafayette, then only 19 years old, and dispatching him to America to serve under Washington.[28]

All in all therefore there is ample evidence of Masonic activity – in France focussed on the care and nurture of the American Revolution and centred around Franklin and the Nine Sisters lodge. Such evidence is suggestive but does not permit us to deduce that the Nine Sisters lodge and/ or Freemasonry in general were also responsible for the violent eruptions in Paris on 14 July 1789 with the storming of the Bastille and the total revolution that followed.

Still, the suspicion lingers. As the French historian Bernard Fay explains:

> The revolutionary impulse, the revolutionary funds, the revolutionary
> leaders, during the first two years of the Revolution, came from the

privileged classes. If the Duc d'Orléans, Mirabeau, Lafayette; if the Noailles family, the La Rochefoucauld, the Bouillon, the Lameth and other liberal nobles had not deserted the nobility in order to join the cause of the people and the Revolution, the revolutionaries would have been deprived of this advantage which allowed them to triumph from the outset. Now, all these nobles who rallied in haste to the cause of new ideas, although at the end they lost their fortunes, their situation, their ranks, and their lives, were Freemasons and we cannot attribute this to hazard, unless we ignore the evidence.[29]

Not surprisingly, Bernard Fay also sees the Nine Sisters lodge as being the focus of the activities that marked the early years of the French Revolution. This lodge, as we know, harboured not only several key players in both the French Revolution *and* the 'sister' American Revolution, but also writers, intellectuals, politicians and artists who used their talents to extol the virtues of the Republic. 'It is certain', writes Masonic historian Jean-André Faucher, that:

> ... the Freemasons [of the Nine Sisters lodge and other lodges] who contributed to the collapse of the monarchy and to the success of the Revolution were in great numbers.[30]

Another alleged member of the Nine Sisters lodge was the brilliant trained orator, lawyer and self-made politician George Jacques Danton. He is credited by many scholars with the pivotal role in toppling the French monarchy and in the creation of the First Republic in September 1792. He was also the founder of the infamous *Club des Cordeliers*, an ultra-radical revolutionary society officially known as the *Society of the Friends of the Rights of Man and of the Citizen.*

Robespierre and the Cult of the Supreme Being

Danton was one of the so-called *Triumvir*, contesting the control of the Republic with two other revolutionary leaders, Robespierre and Marat – the latter a Freemason. It has never been conclusively established that Robespierre was a Freemason too. Nevertheless, his intellectual ideals and obsession with the 'virtues', as well as his promotion of the Cult of the Supreme Being, all reek of Masonic influence.

In Freemasonry God is often described as the 'Grand Architect of the Universe'. His symbol is either a five-pointed star – the 'Blazing Star', in which is depicted the letter 'G' – or a glowing pyramid or triangle with the all-seeing-eye, (the 'Eye of Providence') inscribed within it. This symbol can still be seen on the 1789 Declaration of the Rights of Man and of the Citizen and appears quite obviously to have been modelled on the 'Supreme Being' of the Freemasons – likewise symbolised by the all-seeing-eye in the glowing pyramid.

English Freemasonry in particular has gone to great lengths to assert that belief in a Supreme Being is a precondition of membership.[31] Thus in an official statement by the 'Board of General Purposes', ratified by the United Grand Lodge of England, it was confirmed that:

> The Board has given the most earnest consideration to this subject, being convinced that it is of fundamental importance to the reputation and well-being of English Freemasonry that no misunderstanding should exist on either side of the Craft. It cannot be too strongly asserted that Masonry is neither a religion nor a substitute for religion ... On the other hand, its basic requirement that every member of the Order shall believe in a Supreme Being and the stress laid upon his duty towards Him should be sufficient evidence to all but the willfully prejudiced that Masonry is an upholder of religion since it requires a man to have some form of religion before he can be admitted as a Mason ...[32]

The above statement was, in fact, construed from the *Constitutions of Freemasons*, drafted in 1723, where in the so-called *First Charge*, which is entitled 'Concerning God and Religion', the following statement appears:

> Let a man's religion or mode of worship be what it may, he is not excluded from the Order, provided he believe in the Glorious Architect of Heaven and Earth ...[33]

The term 'Supreme Being' is widely used in the information literature of the United Grand Lodge where, for example, an official leaflet declares that 'members must believe in a Supreme Being, but there is no separate Masonic God'.[34] In other Masonic pamphlets the term 'Grand Architect of the Universe' is also extensively used. Clearly no distinctions are made between terms like 'Glorious Architect of Heaven and Earth', 'Grand Architect of the Universe' and 'Supreme Being'. All are, quite obviously, considered appropriate and interchangeable epithets for the Masonic idea of 'God'.

Taking into account that most of the main players of the French Revolution were Freemasons (including fellow *Triumvir* members Danton and Marat), and giving thought to the terminology used by Robespierre for his republican cult, it is difficult to avoid the conclusion that his Supreme Being was one and the same as the Masonic 'Grand Architect of the Universe'. Indeed, the historian Michel Vovelle, an expert on cults of the French Revolution, quite readily equates the 'Supreme Being' of Robespierre with the 'Grand Architect' of the Freemasons.[35]

Rousseau and the *Contrat Social*

It is well known that Robespierre was much influenced by the work of Jean-Jacques Rousseau (1712–1778), the writer and philosopher whose *Contrat Social* (a political tract which extolled the virtues of social equality and the dignity of man), set the foundation for the Declaration of the Rights of Man and of the Citizen, the natural successor to the American Declaration of Independence.

Although Rousseau was not a Freemason, French Masons took many of his philosophical and political ideas as gospel – so much so that one of the most important and influential pre-revolutionary Masonic lodges, *La Loge du Contrat Social*, was named in his honour. It must be remembered that both Voltaire and Rousseau were – and still are – regarded as having been the intellectual dynamos behind the Revolution. It would be going too far to say that they actually *caused* it, but it is fair to say that they provided the moral framework upon which the Revolution rested.

Thus it is not at all surprising to find that the two most important Masonic lodges in France in the years immediately preceding the 1789 Revolution were the Nine Sisters and *Le Contrat Social*, the former linked to Voltaire and his godfather, and the latter to Rousseau's political masterpiece bearing the same name. It was at these lodges that many of the protagonists of both the French and American Revolutions would gather.

Le Loge du Contrat Social was founded in Paris in 1776 at the same time as the Nine Sisters lodge. Originally going under the name of *Loge Saint-Lazare*, it had taken over the function of an older lodge, *La Loge Saint-Jean d'Écosse de la vertu persécutée* based at Avignon, the latter acting as the 'Mother Lodge' for one of Freemasonry's elite orders, the so-called *Scottish Rite*, also known as the Supreme Council of the 33rd Degree.[36]

Almost as popular as the Nine Sisters lodge, *Le Contrat Social* recruited its members from the very best of the liberal nobility, the intellectuals and the military. Under its warrant other lodges were set up all over France, the most notable being the lodges *Saint-Alexandre d'Écosse* and *l'Olympique de la Parfaite Estime*.[37] The name of the *Contrat Social* lodge had, in fact, been chosen by one of Jean-Jacques Rousseau's intimate friends, the Baron d'Astier[38] who, like Robespierre and many other intellectuals of the Revolution, practically deified Rousseau. In April 1794 Robespierre even had Rouseau's body exhumed and reburied at the Pantheon in Paris next to other national heroes.[39]

Designer Cult

Robespierre's Cult of the Supreme Being was officially installed in France on 7 May 1794, a little more than a year after the beheading of Louis XVI. By then the de-Christianisation process had taken its toll, with the clergy abdicating *en masse*, and many Christian places of worship converted into 'temples' for the new revolutionary cult.

Although a staunch anti-clerical, Robespierre was not an atheist. He was to present a report to the Convention on the 'principles of political morality which must guide the Convention in the administration of the internal affairs of the Republic' in which he stated:

> ... the idea of the Supreme Being and the immortality of the soul is a perpetual reminder of Justice. It is thus social and republican.[40]

The Convention agreed, decreeing soon after:

> The People of France recognise the existence of the Supreme Being and the Immortality of the Soul.[41]

'A deist in the mould of Rousseau',[42] Robespierre firmly believed that at the true basis of the new democratic state should be a *natural* religion, one that was intrinsic to the human condition, one that could root the virtues of the nation onto 'eternal and sacred foundations'.[43] It was proposed that the cult would consist of celebrations and gatherings throughout the year – Robespierre wanted 36 festivals in all[44] – devoted notably to the important events of the Revolution (such as 14 July), to various entities and concepts such as the Supreme Being, Nature, Liberty, and Equality, and finally to the 'virtues most useful to man' such as Truth, Patriotism and so forth.

As part of Robespierre's cult, the old Gregorian calendar was abandoned in favour of a 'Republican' calendar with the months given 'natural' names. This new calendar was divided into 36 *decadi* of 10 days each, producing a year of 360 days to which were added 5 'complementary' days to commemorate 'virtue, genius, labour, opinion and rewards'.[45]

It is indeed odd to discover that this Republican calendar appears to have been modelled on the ancient Egyptian solar calendar – which was divided into 36 *decans* each of 10 days, producing a year of 360 days to which five additional days were added to commemorate the virtues of Osiris, Isis and other divinities.

Lalande and Sirius

The task of developing the Republican calendar was given to Charles-Gilbert Romme, a respected mathematician and president of the Committee of Public Instruction. According to Masonic historian Charles Sumner Lobingier, Romme was a prominent Freemason of the Nine Sisters lodge.[46] Romme was assisted in technical matters by the mathematician Gaspard Monge and the mathematician-astronomer Joseph-Louis Lagrange. Monge, too, was a staunch Freemason and a prominent member of the Nine Sisters lodge which in turn had been founded by the astronomer Jérôme Lalande, who had served as director of the Paris Observatory since 1768.

Lalande, and the astronomer-historian Charles-François Dupuis, sat on the committee established by Romme to create the new Republican calendar. Dupuis was a firm believer that all religious ideas stemmed from ancient Egypt and, more particularly, that the city of Paris was somehow associated with the Egyptian goddess Isis. We shall return to this later. Meanwhile, David Ovason, in his intriguing book *The Secret Zodiac of Washington DC*, makes this most revealing comment concerning Lalande during the obituary ceremony for Voltaire at the Nine Sisters lodge in November 1778:

> The French astronomer Joseph [Jérôme] Lalande, so used to standing in the darkness while looking up at the stars, would probably have thought of only one star as he stood in the darkened Parisian room on 28 November 1778. In his capacity as Master of the Lodge of Nine Muses [Sisters], Lalande was mourning with his Brothers [of which one was Benjamin Franklin] the passing of the writer Voltaire ... Among the symbols guarded by the 27 Brothers was a pyramid ... As he gazed at the Pyramid. Lalande would almost certainly have been drawn to thinking about the star Sirius. An astronomer who had shown great interest in ancient orientations, he could not help realising the importance

assigned to this star by the ancients. If the Egyptian Pyramids themselves were not aligned to it, he knew fully well that a large number of Egyptian temples had been, and that an entire Egyptian calendar was regulated by it. In his four-volume study of stellar lore, Lalande had listed six alternative names for Sirius, and gave its position in 1750 with remarkable accuracy. His interest was almost personal: he would have known that in the horoscope of his own birth, the sun and Mercury had bracketed this powerful star.[47]

Ovason also points out that Lalande's involvement with and deep admiration for Voltaire make it very likely that he would have been familiar with Voltaire's book *Micromégas* published in 1752. In this curious work of fiction Voltaire set the home of the hero in the star Sirius and prophetically noted that this star also had a satellite – a fact only discovered to be true in 1844 by the Prussian astronomer Friedrich Bessel.[48] Sirius, of course, was also the star identified by the ancient Egyptians with the goddess Isis – and again Lalande would have known this.[49] Indeed, so interested were Lalande and Dupuis in the goddess Isis that one of their colleagues at the *Académie des Sciences* could not help commenting:

> '*MM. Dupuis et de Lalande voient Isis par-tout!*' ['Messrs. Dupuis and Lalande see Isis everywhere!']'[50]

Monge, Isis and Osiris

There is another connection with Egypt and the Republican calendar which needs to be mentioned. The mathematician Gaspard Monge, who worked out the mechanics of the calendar, was a keen student of Egyptology. Through his close friendship with Napoleon Bonaparte, whom he accompanied to Egypt in 1798, he was to found the *Institut d'Égypte* in Cairo.

Like many Freemasons of his time, Monge believed that Masonic rituals had originated in ancient Egypt and that modern Freemasons had inherited ancient Egypt's secret system of initiation and symbolic language. Even today, confirms a Masonic historian:

> Many Freemasons consider that the Masonic Order draws much of its mysteries from Pharaonic Egypt. It is thus that they refer themselves to Osiris and Isis, symbols of the supreme being and universal nature ...[51]

Celebrations and iconography

The first official celebrations held in honour of the Supreme Being under France's new Republican calendar took place on 8 June 1794.

At the heart of the proceedings, organised by Robespierre's close friend the artist Jacques-Louis David, was a huge amphitheatre in the Tuilleries Garden in front of the Louvre Palace. There the official congregation gathered to listen to a sermon preached by Robespierre in honour of the Supreme Being. At the close of the sermon, David had arranged for the dramatic burning of a Hessian cloth statue representing 'Atheism' – from which emerged, like a phoenix from the flames, a stone statue representing 'Wisdom'.

Next the choir of the Paris Opera sang:

Father of the Universe, Supreme Intelligence, Benefactor unknown to mortals. You will reveal your existence to those who alone raise altars in your name.[52]

'Those who raise altars' were, of course, the Republicans; and the 'altar' in this particular case turned out to be a massive artificial mountain (historian Jean Kerisel calls it a 'pyramid') in the heart of the Champs de Mars, where today stands the Eiffel Tower.[53] Representatives of the 48 districts of Paris as well those of the Convention with Robespierre at the helm, made their way to the pyramid/mountain and ascended its flanks. Robespierre then was raised on the summit next to a symbolic 'Tree of Liberty', while patriotic hymns were sung by the Paris Opera choir.

Let us note that in the iconography of the Revolution the all-seeing-eye (or 'Eye of Providence') was often shown above the 'Tree of Liberty' while at other times it was also seen within a glowing triangle or pyramid hovering above the scene, much like the symbol seen today on the US one-dollar bill. This symbol, in fact, was originally designed for the so-called *Great Seal of the United States* in 1776 by a committee that included Benjamin Franklin and Thomas Jefferson.[54] The very same symbol was also to appear in 1789 on the frontispiece of the Declaration of the Rights of Man and of the Citizen drafted by the Marquis de Lafayette, a close friend of both Franklin and Jefferson. The symbol clearly represents the Supreme Being of the Republicans and, by extension, the Masonic 'Grand Architect of the Universe' – also depicted as a pyramid with the all-seeing-eye or 'Eye of Providence'. In one propaganda poster which has survived from the 1789 Revolution, the all-seeing-eye is portrayed above the words *'Être Suprême'*, i.e. 'Supreme Being', which confirms the link between the two ideas.[55] In this poster the 'eye' is not within a pyramid but inside a solar disc from which shoot down golden rays of light on the 'People' and the 'Republic'. There are two figures on the bottom of the poster, the one on the left is the aging Voltaire, and the one on the right is Jean-Jacques Rousseau, the two intellectual heroes of the Revolution.[56]

This sort of iconography and rhetoric is strongly suggestive of an attempt to push forward some sort of deist-cum-Masonic 'religion' as an alternative to Christianity. And as British historian Nigel Aston remarks in his book *Religion and Revolution in France*, the 'belief in the Supreme Being permitted enough variations to accommodate many tastes.'[57] Aston quotes the patriot Lazare Carnot, a Freemason and also a member of the Convention, who, made a speech in 1794 extolling the many virtues of mankind, and explained:

> ... these are things to be found in the *Supreme Being*; he is the *seal* of all thoughts which make for the happiness of man.[58]

Meanwhile, on the other side of the Atlantic ...

This perhaps unpremeditated association of the 'Supreme Being' with the idea of a seal brings to mind the Great Seal of the United States, which not only displays the 'Supreme Being' with the symbol of the glowing pyramid and the all-seeing-eye, but also is an icon of the individual's constitutional right to the pursuit of happiness.

On 18 September 1793, just a few weeks after the festivities that were staged at the Place de la Bastille by David, another sort of ceremony, this time blatantly Masonic, took place across the Atlantic at the site of the future Capitol in Washington, DC. Wearing a Masonic apron given to him by the Marquis de Lafayette, George Washington laid the cornerstone of the Capitol on Jenkins Heights during a ceremony attended by hundreds of Freemasons. The Masonic apron worn by Washington, which had been embroidered by Mme de Lafayette, contained an assortment of well-known Masonic symbols, but its centrepiece is undoubtedly the all-seeing-eye emblazoned by a radiating sun disc. Interestingly, author David Ovason, a Freemason who has conducted extensive research into the meaning of this Masonic ceremony, concluded that it was, among other things, primarily intended to consecrate both this building as well as the Federal City to the zodiacal constellation of Virgo:

... The idea of Virgo plays an important role in the astrological symbolism which dominates the city. I have also examined two foundation ceremonials in which the Virgoan element was of considerable importance. By taking this approach I might have given the impression that the sole Masonic concern in these early years of the building of the Federal City was with Virgo ... The importance of Virgo, and her connection with the goddess Isis, has been recognised in Masonic circles from the very early days of American Masonry. The French astronomer Joseph [Jérôme] Lalande had been an important Mason, and his writings were widely read by Americans of the late 18th century. As early as 1731, Lalande had recognised that: 'The Virgin is consecrated to Isis, just as Leo is consecrated to her husband Osiris ... The sphinx, composed of a Lion and a Virgin, was used as a symbol to designate the overflow of the Nile ... they put a wheat-ear in the hand of the Virgin, to express the idea of months'...[59]

In his book *Inside The Brotherhood*, Masonic researcher Martin Short has this to tell us about George Washington's affiliation to Freemasonry:

His [Washington's] funeral in 1799 had been conducted according to Masonic rites. The coffin had been draped with a Masonic apron given to him by a brother revolutionary and Mason, the Marquis de Lafayette, and the many Masons present each cast a sprig of acacia, to symbolise both Osiris's resurrection and Washington's own imminent resurrection in the realm where Osiris presides.[60]

It is perhaps significant that the national memorial later built in Washington, DC in honour of George Washington was in the form of a huge Egyptian-style obelisk, and that on its eastern entrance was displayed the ancient Egyptian symbol of the solar disc. It is reported that during the dedication ceremony a prominent Mason read a speech and, after extolling the virtues of Freemasons, added those strange words:

Their minds enlightened with divine love, their hearts radiant with discovering of pure love, their souls cherishing – like the ancient Egyptian worshippers of Osiris – the hope of immortality.[61]

We shall see later how many of the symbols involved with the cornerstone ceremonies of the Capitol and the Washington Monument were

THE MASTER GAME

veiled with symbolism involving the 'star of Isis' i.e. Sirius. Meanwhile we hope that it has become fairly evident that, for reasons and motives not yet too clear, the ceremonies, festivities, and city monuments associated with the 'sister' American and French Revolutions display Masonic ideas and imagery and, perhaps even more intriguing, are heavily tinged with 'Egyptian' connotations and symbols.

Part I:
The Secret Faith

CHAPTER TWO

LOST WORLD

Mixed with the many other currents and forces that are acknowledged to have driven the French Revolution we've tried to demonstrate in Chapter One that powerful religious and spiritual energies were also at play. These energies surfaced visibly in an aggressive de-Christianisation campaign that saw great cathedrals, including the famous Notre Dame in Paris, reconsecrated as temples of the 'Supreme Being'. Throughout the land, ancient Egyptian and other 'pagan' images were substituted for Christian symbols, notably the cross, and even ancient Egyptian deities such as the goddess Isis were venerated. The Convention was thus not referring to the God of the Christians, or to the Christian vision of the afterlife, when it affirmed in 1794 that the 'People of France recognise the existence of the Supreme Being and the Immortality of the Soul.'

Strange and startling though these developments were, the late 18th century was not the first time that a religion utterly opposed to Christianity, showing signs of an ancient Egyptian influence, and deeply interested in the fate of the soul, had taken root in the land we now know as France. In the 12th century, more than 600 years before the Revolution, just such an alternative religion had materialised in Provence and Langeudoc – seemingly out of nowhere – already deeply entrenched in the hearts and minds of large sectors of the population. It was also present in force in adjoining districts of eastern Spain and northern Italy, and scattered in smaller communities throughout the rest of Europe as far afield as Belgium, northern France and Germany.

The name of this religion that had so rapidly and successfully displaced the Roman Catholic Church in areas so close to the seat of its own power was … Christianity.

At any rate its practitioners called themselves 'Good Christians', but the Church, labelled them heretics from the moment they first came to its attention. Their contemporaries in the 12th, 13th and 14th centuries frequently called them *Manichees* (after the ancient dualist heresy of Manicheism, supposedly wiped out in Europe hundreds of years previously). And they were known by a wide variety of other epithets including, most commonly, *Albigensians* (after Albi, a prominent city of Languedoc), and *Cathars* (derived from the Greek word *katharos* and meaning the 'Pure').[1]

These Cathars (the name that we will generally use here) venerated Jesus Christ every bit as much as the Catholics did. That was why they called themselves 'Good Christians'. But the place that he occupied in their religion was radically different. In the Catholic view Christ was the 'Word … made flesh' who 'dwelt among us'.[2] The Cathars repudiated this utterly and worshipped him as a being of pure spirit – an emanation from the 'Good God', a projection or an apparition. They categorically denied his material incarnation as the 'Son' of God, born in a human body to 'dwell among us'. They also forcefully rejected the Catholic teaching of Christ crucified to redeem our sins. How could he have been crucified, they asked, if he had never existed physically in the first place? Far from revering the central spiritual symbol of Christianity, therefore, the Cathars denied the significance of the cross. For them it was an obscene instrument of torture that the Church of Rome had misled millions into worshipping as an idol.

Turning the most cherished symbols, doctrines and dogmas of Christianity upside down like this was a Cathar speciality that infuriated and repeatedly challenged the medieval Catholic Church.

The source of the problem was that unlike the single all-powerful and all-good God of the Christians, the Cathars were *dualists* who believed in the parallel existence of two deities – a *God of Good* and a *God of Evil*. Each was powerful only in his own domain and nearly impotent in the realm of the other. The domain of the God of Good was entirely spiritual, intangible, immaterial and filled with Light. It was here that human souls had originated – the creation of the Good God. The domain of the God of Evil was the earth itself, the material world and all physical life upon it – an infernal place of pain and punishment filled with Darkness and iniquity. In the Cathar scheme of things it was the God of Evil, the maker and ruler of the material world, who had fashioned the bodies (though not the souls) of mankind out of 'mud and water'. And it was towards this same Evil God, Cathar preachers argued, that the worship of the Roman Catholic Church was directed.

The pope, in other words, was not a servant of the Good God but the Devil's representative on earth. And the purpose of the Catholic Church was not to transmit our souls to the spiritual and light-filled domain of heaven after death, but to trick us into returning again and again – in one human incarnation after another – to the hell-realm of the material world. Only a lifetime of self-denial culminating in the special *gnosis* – or inspired knowledge – attained on initiation into the highest grade of the Cathar faith could save us.

It was a revolutionary teaching and, in 12th century Europe, an extremely dangerous one.

Hesitating at the crossroads

During the period of world history for which written records have survived – most of the last 5,000 years – no scholar would seriously argue with the proposition that religions have played a fundamental role in shaping the character of civilisation and directing its course. Likewise few would dispute that the human race during this period has consistently been divided not only by different languages and cultures but also by the competing spheres of influence of different religions. Some ancient faiths that once commanded absolute obedience across vast areas have withered away and vanished. Others that were insignificant have risen to prominence. Others still are almost forgotten in their original homelands but have flourished in distant lands. Against the recent background of rampant secularism in many rich countries, and rampant religious fervour in many poor ones, we are left today with four great faiths commanding distinct socio-geographic spheres of influence, that still collectively claim the allegiance of roughly nine of every ten of us:

- *Hinduism* is strong only in the Indian subcontinent but there it has over 800 million adherents.

- *Buddhism* sprawls from Sri Lanka to Tibet, and from China to Southeast Asia and Japan.

- *Islam* has hundreds of millions of followers in Indonesia, Bangladesh, Pakistan, Iran, Turkey, the Levant and North Africa, but its heartland and historical home is in the Arabian peninsula.

- *Christianity* has a near-monopoly in the Americas, having obliterated or utterly marginalised all the New World's indigenous faiths during the past 500 years. It also predominates in Australia, New Zealand, sub-Saharan Africa and other areas of former

European colonial expansion. It's historical home is in the eastern Mediterranean. However, after the triumph of Islam in the Middle East and North Africa more than a thousand years ago, Christianity's heartland moved to Europe itself.

Today, as a result, it is a habit of mind to think of Europe as a region locked so firmly and for so long within the Christian sphere of influence that no other faith need be considered to have shaped its destiny. For scholars prepared to look hard enough there are, of course, faint traces of earlier, pagan beliefs in the European heritage, but these are rarities and throwbacks – quaint exotica with no mainstream impact. Whether we travel to Austria, Belgium, Britain, France, Germany, Greece, Holland, Ireland, Italy, Portugal, Spain or Switzerland, the reality is that all the countries of Europe confront us with very long unbroken traditions of Christianity. In some cases these traditions substantially predate the fourth century AD when the Roman Empire under Constantine adopted Christianity as its state religion and established Rome (where a persecuted Christian community had already existed for 250 years[3]) as the headquarters of the newly empowered Catholic Church.

Almost immediately after coming into imperial favour the formerly persecuted church fathers themselves turned persecutors. They sought to impose their control on Christians throughout the Roman Empire, to suppress schisms and to distil a universally agreed doctrine out of the great variety of teachings that the faith had previously encompassed. To this end, as we will see in later chapters, they promulgated dogmas and defined and declared anathemas upon a whole series of heresies. These were then systematically hunted down and obliterated over the next three centuries.

Notable among the forbidden faiths was the great dualist heresy of Manicheism (to which no less a figure than Saint Augustine, one of the four most revered 'doctors of the Church', had belonged for nine years before converting to Christianity in AD 386).[4] Claiming to lead to direct and personal knowledge of the divine, all forms of Gnosticism were also persecuted to vanishing point. Influenced by elements of the ancient Egyptian religion, Asian and Middle Eastern mysticism, Greek philosophy, and alternative interpretations of Jewish and Christian teachings, Gnosticism was as profoundly dualistic as Manicheism and was for some centuries the chief rival to Roman Catholic hegemony.[5]

By the seventh century, however, Manicheism had been expelled to the distant East, and the numerous Gnostic sects that had confronted the early church seemed to have been obliterated.[6] No longer facing any organised spiritual competition, Catholicism was able to see out the remainder of the Western Dark Ages with its defences relaxed. The result, by the early 11th century, was that churchmen had no living experience of heresy. Those who sought to remind themselves of its dangers could only turn to books – amongst them Saint Augustine's agonised account of his own 'errors' as a 'Manichee' written 700 years earlier.[7]

It therefore came as a something of a jolt when a heresy (looking very much like Manicheism) suddenly resurfaced in the 12th century in the form of Catharism in areas at the very heart of Western culture. Moreover it proved to be no transitory movement linked to the lives of a few charismatic leaders but the most deadly threat ever to confront the Catholic faith. Appearing as though from nowhere it was a well-organised 'anti-Church' that claimed an antiquity even greater than that of Catholicism itself. It also had the temerity to recruit its new members directly from Catholic ranks.

What made Catharism such a threat and outrage to the Catholic Church, however, was not just its embarrassing success at converting Catholics, nor the challenge of its doctrines – radical though they were. Nor was it simply the shock of confronting a dualist heresy that seemed to have conjured itself up out of the past like a ghost. Nor was it the heresy's obvious dynamism, nor the uncomfortably rapid spread of its sphere of influence ever closer to Rome during the 12th century. The real problem was that as well as winning over large numbers of ordinary people, Catharism had succeeded in attracting the tacit and sometimes even the overt support of some of the most powerful noble families in southwestern Europe. These included, most notably, the Counts of Toulouse, the Counts of Foix, and the Trencavel viscounts who ruled the walled cities of Albi, Béziers and Carcassonne. With their knights and castles and strength of arms concentrated in the Languedoc and surrounding areas, such men had transformed Catharism into something that the Church of Rome had never faced before. Here was a heresy that could fight back, that would not easily be crushed by the use of secular force, and that might conceivably, if allowed to grow further, push the Catholic religion out of Europe altogether.

For more than a century, with consequences that reach us today, European civilisation hesitated at the crossroads of two competing spiritual systems and confronted the choice of two very different ways forward into the future. Let's take a closer look at the key players and events during this decisive period of history.

A language in which 'oc' means 'yes'

Languedoc today is part of the colourful mosaic of southern France. It adjoins Provence to the east and is separated from Spain to the west by the Pyrenees mountains. In the 12th and 13th centuries it was famed for the romantic poetry of its troubadours, for its 'Courts of Love',[8] for the fiercely independent character of its people, and for its unique culture.

Underlining this sense of difference was the basic fact that the people of Provence and Languedoc had never been French subjects and did not even speak French. Indeed at that time what the word 'France' conjured to mind for most was just the Ile de France, the region immediately around Paris. More broadly defined, 'France' also included the territories lying between the Loire, the middle part of the Meuse and the Scheldt. But the lands to the south of the Loire and south of the Massif Central, as well as the whole of the Mediterranean coast, were excluded. As late as the 14th century travellers heading north from Toulouse or Avignon thought of themselves as journeying *to* 'France' rather than within it.[9]

Together with the regions of Limousin and old Aquitaine, and the southern part of the French Alps, Languedoc and Provence were known in medieval times by the collective name of *Occitania*. They by no means formed a 'state' or a 'country' as we understand those concepts today. On the contrary, other than to family, friends and neighbours, the primary loyalties of the majority of the inhabitants were to the town or city in which they lived or to the aristocrats whose fields they ploughed. Still they had much more in common with each other than they did with the cultural and political community of northern states that were in the process of becoming 'France'. And above all else these 'Occitanians' were united by their common language, literally the *langue d'oc* – that is to say the language in which the word for 'yes' is *oc* (as opposed to the *langue d'oil*, the 12th century language that was to evolve into modern French, in which the word for 'yes' was *oil* – later to become the more familiar *oui* of today).

Medieval scholar Joseph Strayer points out that the French of the north and the Occitan of the south are separated by one of the sharpest breaks in the whole family of Romance languages and are mutually incomprehensible. Occitan is, however, very close to Catalan and quite close to Castilian. The result is that in the 12th century:

> A merchant from Narbonne would have been easily understood in
> Barcelona, while he would have needed an interpreter in Paris ... A baron
> of the Ile de France would have found more men to talk to in London, or

even in Cologne, than he would have in Toulouse. Now a language barrier is not an impassable obstacle, but it is a real one, and it is the kind of barrier that creates misunderstandings and suspicions.[10]

The mailed fist of Occitania

Power in Occitania was in the hands of a feudal aristocracy dominated by the three great families of Foix, Trencavel and Toulouse.

Described at the time as 'the peers of kings, the superiors of dukes and counts',[11] the princes of the house of Toulouse ruled a domain extending from Toulouse itself to Nimes in the east, and from Cahors in the north to Narbonne on the Mediterranean coast.[12] They also enjoyed, and could sometimes call upon, an impressive range of international alliances. Raymond VI, Count of Toulouse from 1194–1222, for example, was a cousin of the king of France and brother-in-law to the kings both of England and of Aragon.[13] He also tolerated and sometimes even promoted Catharism and travelled with a Cathar holy man.[14]

The Counts of Foix, lords of the high Pyrenees along the border with Spain, were renowned for their military prowess, stubborn ruthlessness, and strong Cathar connections. In 1204 Raymond-Roger, Count of Foix from 1188–1223, witnessed the reception of his widowed sister Esclarmonde into the *perfecti* (literally the 'perfect'), the highest rank of Cathar initiates.[15] Two years later his own wife, having born him six children, was also received into the *perfecti* and retired from the world to preside over the Cathar equivalent of a nunnery.[16] Though never avowedly a Cathar himself, Raymond-Roger was staunchly anti-Catholic all his life. On one occasion it seems that soldiers in his employ chopped a canon of the Church into pieces and used 'the arms and legs of a crucifix to grind up spices with, in lieu of a pestle.'[17] In a lengthy essay on 'the barbarity and malignity of the Count of Foix' a contemporary pro-Catholic chronicler wrote:

> His wickedness exceeded all bounds ... He pillaged monasteries, destroyed churches, excelled all others in cruelty.[18]

The Trencavel dynasty, controlling lands that stretched from the Tarn to the Pyrenees, added their own combination of wealth, hereditary influence, military might and pro-Cathar sympathies to the equation of power in Languedoc. Raymond-Roger Trencavel, who ruled from 1194 until his capture and murder by Catholics in 1209, had been tutored by the well-known Cathar scholar Bertrand de Saissac. The latter had once shown his contempt for the laws of Catholicism when a monk he disliked was elected abbot at the monastery of Saint Mary of Alet. Bertrand's response was to have the corpse of the former abbot exhumed and placed, mouldering, in the abbatial chair to supervise a new election. Not surprisingly the abbot elected on this occasion did meet with Bertrand's favour.[19]

Support for and involvement with the Cathars, combined with a rejection of the Church, were not confined solely to the upper levels of the aristocracy. In the Lauragais, the populous area between Toulouse and Carcassonne, the minor nobility are reported to have been almost solidly Cathar. The same was also the case for their counterparts in the Corbières between Carcassonne and Narbonne.[20] Tellingly it has been calculated that 30 per cent of all Cathar *perfecti* were of noble birth.[21] Moreover even the remaining Catholic nobility of Occitania often proved to be at least sympathetic to the Cathars – and at times were openly supportive of them. An indication of their dilemma is to be seen in the reply given by the Catholic knight, Pons d'Adhémar of Rodelle when he was asked by Foulkes, the bishop of Toulouse, why he and his co-religionists had not expelled the heretics from their lands:

> We cannot. We have grown up amongst them. We have relatives amongst them, and we see them living good, decent lives of perfection.[22]

Weaving the threads of the Great Heresy

Thus sheltered by the aristocracy of the region on both sides of the religious divide, the Cathars also found strong support at all other levels of Occitanian society. Large numbers of them were skilled craftsmen and artisans. A list of Cathars present in the city of Béziers in 1209 includes:

> ... one noble (*baronus*), four doctors, five hosiers, two blacksmiths, two pelterers, two shoe-makers, a sheep-shearer, a carpenter, a weaver, a saddler, a corn-dealer, a cutler, a tailor, a tavern-keeper, a baker, a wool-worker, a mercer, and a money-changer.[23]

Martin Barber, professor of history at the University of Reading, observes that the Béziers list includes no less than 10 individuals employed in the textile industry, and that a great many other primary documents from the period likewise link weavers (*textores*) to the heresy.[24]

This is true both within and outside the borders of Occitania. In France the general name by which Cathars were known was simply *Texerant*, the 'weavers'.[25] In 1145 the renowned French ecclesiastic Bernard of Clairvaux undertook a preaching tour to warn against a 'heresy of weavers'.[26] It had supposedly sprung up fully formed 'from the suggestions and artifices of seducing spirits'[27] and was so successful at winning conversions that:

> Women have quitted their husbands, men have deserted their wives ...
> Clerks and priests ... often abandon their flocks and their churches, and
> are found in the throng, among weavers male and female.[28]

Likewise in 1157 Archbishop Samson of Rheims was almost certainly complaining of Cathar missionary activity when he spoke of a 'Manichean plague' that had recently infected the greater part of Flanders[29] (we noted earlier that 12th century churchmen commonly referred to the Cathars as Manicheans – after the dualist sect of that name that had supposedly been stamped out hundreds of years previously). This new outbreak of the heresy, Samson said, was being spread by itinerant weavers and cloth-merchants.[30]

The explanation is simple. Employment as weavers and in other sectors of the medieval cloth trade – with its extensive international connections – was chosen as 'cover' by Cathar *perfecti*. They needed cover to avoid early detection by Church authorities because they were mounting what can only be described as a large-scale and well-thought-out missionary campaign. The rather gentle, patient and systematic methods that they used to win local trust, and eventually conversions to the heresy, have been nicely described by the Canadian historian Stephen O'Shea:

> On the paths and rivers of the Languedoc of 1150 there were not only traders
> and troubadours but also pairs of itinerant holy men, recognisable by the
> thin leather thong tied around the waist of their black robes. They entered
> villages and towns, set up shop, often as weavers, and became known for
> their honest hard work. When the time came, they would talk – first in the
> moonlight, beyond the walls, then out in the open, before the fireplaces
> of noble and burgher, in the houses of tradespeople, near the stalls of the
> marketplace. They asked for nothing, no alms, no obeisance; just a hearing.
> Within a generation these Cathar missionaries had converted thousands.
> Languedoc had become host to what would be called the Great Heresy.[31]

The *Perfecti* and the *Credentes*

The missionaries were all Cathar *perfecti*, and, as Stephen O'Shea rightly observes, it was their custom – like modern Mormons or Jehovah's

Witnesses – to travel and evangelise in pairs.[32] Their black robes would have given them something of the look of Christian monks or priests. Other than their appearance, however, there was really no similarity at all between the lifestyles of these *perfecti* and the lifestyles of the typical Catholic clergy of the period. As even their most bitter opponents were willing to admit, the distinguishing characteristic of the *perfectus* was that they lived exemplary lives of chastity, humility, great poverty and simplicity throughout the whole period of Catharism's rise and fall.[33] Meanwhile the Church of the 11th and 12th centuries had already become decadent and disreputable. It was widely despised because of the rampant sexual licence of so many of its ministers. In some areas it was openly hated because of its vast wealth, corruption, greed, and unnecessary ostentation. Doubling as large-scale feudal landlords most bishops enjoyed lives of profligate, scandalous luxury. No wonder, then, that they were unpopular in their own dioceses where they were reviled for their indifference to the privations of the poor.[34]

To understand the extreme asceticism for which the *perfecti* were renowned, one need only recall the teaching that lay at the core of Cathar dualism. The material world was the wholly evil creation of a wholly Evil God. All contact with matter was therefore also evil and could only inhibit Catharism's primary project. This was the gradual purification and eventual release of immortal human souls from their cycle of rebirths in mortal human bodies. 'O Lord, judge and condemn the imperfections of the flesh,' went one of their prayers:

Have no pity on the flesh, born of corruption, but show mercy to the spirit, which is imprisoned.[35]

The *perfecti* were active participants in what they saw as a cosmic struggle between utterly incompatible powers – spirit and matter, good and evil.[36] Success in the struggle required them to lead lives in strict accordance with their beliefs and teachings. Since flesh was 'born of corruption' it followed that any foodstuff thought to have originated from processes of coition and reproduction was absolutely forbidden to them. This meant, in practice that they could eat neither flesh nor fowl, nor any of the derivatives from these creatures such as eggs, milk, cheese, cream or lard.[37] Their diet consisted of bread, vegetables, pulses, fruits and nuts. Inconsistently (to the modern mind) fish were also allowed. This was because of a medieval misconception that fish did not issue from sexual reproduction but were somehow spontaneously generated in water or mud.[38]

The same anti-reproductive, anti-coital logic meant, of course, that the *perfecti* must themselves be totally celibate – even an 'unchaste' kiss was believed sufficient to destroy their ritual purity. All other bodily needs and desires brought the same peril and were likewise to be shunned.[39] To harden their resistance to the desire for nourishment they not only rigorously followed the already sparse diet outlined above but also subjected themselves to lengthy fasts amounting to more than 70 days a year on bread and water alone.[40] The purpose of all these privations was to loosen the bonds that imprisoned the soul within the body.[41]

In pursuit of the same objective, and in order further to minimise their contacts with the snares and lures of the material world, the *perfecti* renounced all property and personal possessions except the clothes they stood up in.[42] Many other austerities were also required of them. Despite these, however, there was no shortage of candidates for the *perfectus* grade and the Cathar religion in fact made it very difficult for anyone to achieve it. Aspiring *perfecti* underwent a period of training and direct exposure to the full rigours of the life that they would lead after initiation. Known evocatively as the *abstinentia*, this typically involved three years of full-time attachment to a senior *perfectus*. Only at the end of the *abstinentia*, if they had conducted themselves satisfactorily, would they become eligible for the ritual known as the *consolamentum* ('consoling') that completed their own elevation to *perfectus* status.[43]

Though often referred to as the 'priests' of the Cathar religion, several researchers have noted that the *perfecti* were in reality much closer in terms of their austerities, their personal comportment and their function within the faith to the:

> ... ascetic teachers of the East, the bonzes and fakirs of China or India, the adepts of the Orphic mysteries, or the teachers of Gnosticism.[44]

This impression is enhanced by contemporary reports which seem to describe *perfecti* in trancelike or meditative states. One eyewitness speaks of the 'extraordinary sight' of a Cathar *perfectus* seated on a chair 'motionless as a tree trunk, insensible to his surroundings.'[45]

But the Cathar authorities knew very well that a life of meditation, total chastity, austerity and withdrawal from the material world was beyond the reach of the average mortal. Moreover their society did not – and could not – consist solely of *perfecti* and candidate *perfecti* whose celibacy would provide them with no successors. What was needed was a much wider pool to draw on. This was supplied by a second grade or rank, far more numerous than the *perfecti*, known as the *credentes* ('believers'). It was they, in their tens of thousands, who constituted the vast majority of all Cathars. It was they who contributed the social and economic energy – to say nothing of the military muscle – that made this religion such a threat to the Church of Rome.

What the *credentes* believed in were the fundamental tenets of the dualist faith concerning the existence of two gods, the evil nature of matter and the imprisonment of the soul in flesh. They might even aspire, ultimately, to becoming wandering gurus of *perfectus* rank themselves. But the reality was that most *credentes* never took up the challenge. Instead, wherever Catharism was established, we know that its *credente* class lived ordinary lives of no great self-denial. They married, produced children, owned property, ate well and generally enjoyed the world. They certainly attended the simple services and gatherings led by *perfecti* that were part of the Cathar calendar. Along with all other *credentes* they likewise accepted and took with extreme seriousness a general duty to accommodate the impoverished *perfecti* on their travels and to provide them with a strong network and support system. They were also required to offer a ritual salute to any *perfectus* they might encounter. Called the *melioramentum* this involved triple genuflections and greetings to the *perfectus* and culminated in the following exchange:

> *Credente*: 'Pray God for me, a sinner, that he make me a good Christian and lead me to a good end.'

> *Perfectus*: 'May God be prayed that he may make you a good Christian.'

The exchange, explains medieval historian Malcolm Lambert, was standardised and had a special meaning:

> To be a Good Christian, or a Christian at all, in Cathar belief was to become a Perfect. To come to a good end was to die in possession of the *consolamentum*, not having forfeited it by lapse. In the exchange and genuflection, Perfect and adherent reminded each other of their own status, the one waiting, not yet freed from Satan, the other outside his power, in a unique position.[46]

Credentes were taught that it was particularly important for them to find a *perfectus* and to perform the *melioramentum* if they had in any way

THE MASTER GAME

been exposed to the contamination of Catholic influences. This was so at least partly because obeisance – amounting almost to worship (and referred to in some contexts as 'adoration') of the *perfectus* represented a direct and public denial of the Catholic Church.[47] When the prominent *credente*, the Lady Fidas of St. Michel, travelled to Rome with Countess Eleanor of Toulouse, she cheekily took a Cathar *perfectus* with her: 'to worship him in the very chapel of the Pope.'[48]

Whether they were nobles or peasants, however, the majority of *credentes* would postpone until their deathbeds the moment when they felt ready to summon a *perfectus* to confer upon them the dualist baptism of the *consolamentum*. It was an act of momentous importance that filled the recipient with a charge of the Holy Spirit, and, for some, could open the door to the Kingdom of Heaven. Though it amounted, on the surface, to nothing more than a short ritual accompanied by prayers and a laying on of hands, the *consolamentum* was considered to be so powerful that it was sufficient, *by itself* – even without years of itinerant austerity – to initiate the dying *credente* into the ranks of the *perfecti*. He or she would thereafter consume only bread and water, avoiding any further contamination from the evil world of matter. The hope for those thus consoled, and in a state of ritual purity, might not have been that death would this time bring a final release from the cycle of rebirth in human form, but that it would, at the very least, bring 'progress on the chain of being towards it.'[49] On occasions when patients unexpectedly recovered after being consoled they could always return to the normal life of a *credente* and to full involvement with the world. In that case they would have to receive the *consolamentum* and enter a fast once again when death approached or whatever progress their souls might have made in this incarnation would be lost.

It was by no means certain that the next incarnation would bring the soul to a body that would again receive the Cathar teaching (or even, necessarily to a human body at all – rather than, say, the body of a donkey – let alone to the body of a Cathar). *Credentes* were therefore provided with a strong incentive to receive the *consolamentum* in this life (where they knew it was definitely available) but to so juggle things that they did not have to go through with it until their deathbed. During the late 12th century when there were large numbers of *perfecti* on the roads and living in every village, town and city of Occitania this was not usually difficult to accomplish. But during the 13th century, as we shall see in Chapters Six and Seven, Catharism became a persecuted faith throughout Europe – with the greatest attention paid to Occitania. There, amidst demonic scenes from the lowest circles of hell, the populations of entire cities were put to the sword by soldiers of the Church of Rome. The papal inquisitors followed and as they went about their work the numbers of *perfecti* fell into an ever more catastrophic decline with each new mass burning. By the early 14th century there are only known to have been three *perfecti* still at work in the whole of the Languedoc, once the very epicentre of the faith. Surviving *credentes* faced great uncertainty as to whether they would be able to obtain the *consolamentum* at all. The desperate solution of many Cathars nearing the end of their natural lives in these last days was the *endura* – an Occitan word meaning 'fasting' or 'hungering' applied to the bread and water fast that normally followed deathbed consolings.[50] Now, however, those who had received the ritual preferred not to risk breaking their fast even if they later began to show signs of recovery. The consequence was that the *endura*:

> ... came to have the precise and technical meaning of fasting to death after receiving the *consolamentum*.[51]

Abolishing superstition and the Fear of Hell

When extensive persecution of Catharism began in the 13th century the fundamental difference in lifestyle between the consoled and the unconsoled – between *perfecti* and *credentes* – was sometimes seized on by the latter to try to persuade their accusers that they weren't heretics at all. In the bourg of Toulouse in 1223 for example Jean Teisseire, a *credente* in the prime of life who had no interest in an early *consolamentum*, was arrested and accused of heresy. 'I have a wife and I sleep with her,' he protested, 'I have sons, I eat meat and I lie and swear'[52] (along with marriage, sex, reproduction and meat-eating, lying and the swearing of oaths were forbidden to *perfecti*).[53] Convicted on the evidence of witnesses, Tessiere's arguments were ignored by the court. He was sentenced to burn at the stake and placed in the bishop's prison to await execution. The procedure now allowed him to recant and go free but he stubbornly continued to profess his innocence and remained on death row. There he fell into conversation with several Cathar *perfecti* and a few days later accepted the *consolamentum* at their hands. Still refusing to recant beliefs that he now acknowledged he held he was 'burnt with the rest.'[54]

There are many reports of courage and extreme self-sacrifice from the era of persecution. They tell us that Catharism was capable of inspiring its adherents with profound and strongly-held beliefs concerning the progress and afterlife destiny of the soul. Indeed these beliefs were so strong that again and again *perfecti* and *credentes* like Teisseire were prepared to suffer death in the utmost agony rather than recant and jeopardise their imminent release from the evil world of matter.

There are several well-attested accounts of the condemned rushing *en masse* towards the pyres that had been prepared for them and flinging themselves joyfully into the roaring flames. Whether we think of them as credulous fools, therefore, or as exalted martyrs, it seems that Catharism had liberated these people from the paralysing fear of hell that the Catholic Church had used for centuries to terrify and close the minds of medieval Europeans. Indeed such a liberation would have followed more or less automatically from conversion to Cathar dualism – which proposed no lower hell than the earth itself, 'the lowest plane of consciousness to which we sink'[55] – a place of trial and torment in which our souls were *already* undergoing fierce penances and had remained trapped for countless prior incarnations. Hell, in other words, was not an unknown destination, to which we would be sent for sins defined by the Catholic Church, but a known one in which we were already present but which it was our destiny one day to escape.

In this way, at a stroke, the Cathars not only abolished all fear of death in their initiates but also sundered bonds of superstition and demonology that had stalled the progress of Western civilisation throughout the Dark Ages. Seeking to sweep the cobwebs away from all aspects of habitual religious behaviour they said that chanting in church 'deceived simple people', and ridiculed as an irrational waste of money the Catholic practice of paying alms for souls in purgatory.[56]

By giving exposure and prominence to such ideas – albeit for just a brief period of history – the Cathars encouraged a new freedom of thought and a new spirit of flexibility and openness to change. The psychologist Arthur Guirdham believes that this was 'perhaps their most significant contribution to the emancipation of the common man'[57]:

> Not to understand this is to fail to realise that Catharism was not only an enlightened but an optimistic creed. Some of the contemporary defenders of Catharism regard it as a dour, Calvinistic and basically pessimistic religion. Sir Steven Runciman who is, on the whole, very fair in his assessment of the Cathars, regards the religion as foredoomed because of its built-in pessimism. Those holding such views are at a loss to explain how such a repressive and pessimistic creed could have spread like wildfire through the most sophisticated and sceptical region of Europe ...[58]

A Renaissance ahead of its time?

Catharism's sudden flowering took place at a time when Europe, stimulated by the contact with the East that the Crusades had brought, was shaking off the slumber of the Dark Ages and rediscovering ancient wisdom in the classical texts. Often described by historians as the 'Renaissance of the 12th century', this period of 'change, experimentation and broadened horizons'[59] ended hundreds of years of intellectual stagnation. It saw the birth of many new philosophical and scientific ideas, witnessed the rise of the first towering Gothic cathedrals, and experienced far-reaching social and economic changes.

Together with the neighbouring parts of eastern Spain and northern Italy where the Cathar religion was also strong, the 12th century civilisation of Occitania – urbanised, sophisticated, cosmopolitan – was 'indisputably ahead of anywhere else in Europe'.[60] It lay at the epicentre of what promised to become a great upheaval in Western values marked by a spirit of inquiry and the introduction of a gentler, more cosmopolitan and more tolerant world view. Moreover, had Catharism succeeded in all its aims, we can be certain that there would have been no place, in this new age, for the Catholic Church – which, as the church of Satan, had for so long led so many souls astray. Far from succeeding, however, the Cathar heresy was crushed by a series of violent and genocidal 'crusades', unleashed by the Catholic Church in the first half of the 13th century. The last of the resistance was then slowly and methodically finished off by the papal Inquisition which was officially established in 1233 specifically for the repression and extirpation of Catharism.[61] Had it not been for the destruction and dislocation wrought by these so-called *Albigensian Crusades* some believe that the culture of the Languedoc could have anticipated the Renaissance in Italy by more than two centuries.[62]

Such speculations are frowned on by mainstream historians.[63] As a result questions like – 'what would have happened to the West if Catharism had won its struggle against the Catholic Church?' – are rarely given any serious scholarly consideration. An exception was the French social philosopher and activist Simone Weil. She died in 1943 as a result of voluntary starvation in sympathy with her compatriots then under German occupation. Aged only 34 at the time of her fatal *endura* Weil had spent the last few years of her life cultivating a deep interest in the unique culture of 12th century Occitania. She believed Catharism to have been the source of all its inspiration. By crushing the Greeks more than 2,000 years ago, she argued, the Roman Empire had 'brought sterility to the Mediterranean basin'. Only once since then had another civilisation raised its head in the same region which might have had the capacity to attain 'a degree of freedom and spiritual creativity as high as that of ancient Greece.' Snuffed out in the 13th century by the Church of Rome, this was the lost Occitanian civilisation of the Cathars – which, in Weil's analysis, had somehow plugged itself into much older currents of thought:

> Little as we know about the Cathars, it seems clear that they were in some way the heirs of Platonic thought, of the esoteric teachings and mysteries of that pre-Roman civilisation which embraced the Mediterranean and the Near East ...[64]

Weil was one of those for whom Occitanian civilisation in the 12th and 13th centuries had conceived the true Renaissance. Its potential had been greater even than that of the Italian Renaissance in the 15th century. Because Languedoc was the heartland of this precocious civilisation, the brutal engine of the Albigensian Crusades smashed not just the Cathars but Europe's last living link with the ancient wisdom traditions of India, Persia, Egypt and Greece. By contrast the centuries that followed the destruction of Languedoc 'were an essay in totalitarian spirituality.'[65]

Cosmopolitan cities

Occitanian society under the influence of the Cathars was anything but totalitarian. It was far ahead of the rest of Europe in the process of urbanisation. Its rapidly-expanding cities like Narbonne, Avignon, Toulouse, Montpellier, Béziers, and Carcassonne proudly guaranteed the freedom of thought and the economic and political independence of their citizens. Even in his own city, for example, the Count of Toulouse lacked any executive legal authority over the citizens and was only obeyed so long as he respected local common law.[66] Narbonne, Avignon, Montpellier and Béziers were hives of intellectual activity – in every sense university cities even before their universities had officially been founded. The most advanced course on Aristotle in Europe, which took account of the latest work by Arab scholars, was taught at Toulouse.[67]

Arab merchants and doctors had long found their way to Occitania across the Pyrenees from those parts of Spain then under Muslim control, or by sea from the East. They had been welcomed by the Cathars – who were inclined to see the Roman Catholic Church, not the 'infidel', as the natural enemy. Besides, for the Cathars, all human bodies, whether Muslim,

Christian or Jew, were the prisons of entrapped souls. Since all suffered the trials and rigours of the material world equally, and since only Catharism offered a way out of it, the oppression of one man by another on grounds of race or creed was absurd.

Such ideas spilled over into civic life and resident aliens in the cities of Occitania enjoyed full citizens' rights, regardless of their nationality or creed.[68] Moreover while Catharism maintained its resolute antipathy to the Church of Rome it was open-handed and liberal with other faiths that were willing to co-exist peacefully with it. This was a time when possession of land by non-Christians was a criminal offence in northern France. It was a time when mobs of Catholics throughout Europe could frequently be worked up into frenzies of anti-Semitic prejudice. Yet in Occitania large and long-established Jewish communities owned land, worshipped openly in synagogues, and prospered unmolested throughout the 12th century.[69] They, too, seem to have been going through a period of creative intellectual and spiritual enquiry, just as the Cathar communities were. Indeed it was in the coastal cities of Languedoc in this same period that Jewish savants elaborated the occult philosophy of the Cabala and began to explore its implications.[70] A system of mysticism rooted in ancient Judaic traditions, Cabala laid claim to secret knowledge and divine revelation. It also exhibited strong dualistic tendencies in which the 'left side' and 'right side' of the cosmos were envisaged in constant opposition and conflict.[71]

It is notable that acclaimed schools of Talmudic law flourished at Narbonne, Lunel and Beaucaire in the 12th century and that there is a report from 1160 of Jewish students from 'distant lands' studying there.[72] Intriguingly the same source – Rabbi Benjamin of Tudela – also describes an encounter with a Jew at Lunel who had 'discarded all worldly business, studied day and night, kept fasts, and never ate meat.'[73] This suggests the possibility that Cathar ideas about how we should live in the world and what we are doing here had begun to have an impact not only on the large number of former Catholics it had freed from the fear of hell but also on the followers of other faiths as well.

Cathars and troubadours

It was in the 12th and 13th centuries that Catharism briefly lit up people's minds in Occitania. In the same period another extraordinary intellectual phenomenon also appeared and disappeared in precisely the same region now encompassed by southern France, northern Spain and northern Italy. This parallel phenomenon was the lyric poetry of the troubadours – a form that was invented in Occitania and composed in the Occitan language. Judged by literary experts today as 'one of the most brilliant schools that ever existed', it is accepted as an influence on all later European lyrical poetry.[74] Of much greater consequence however, is the fact that troubadour poetry also had an unprecedented *social* impact. Indeed it brought about what has been described as 'a revolution in thought and feeling, the effects of which are still apparent in Western culture.'[75]

The revolution had to do with attitudes towards women in society. The troubadours themselves were favoured at the many noble courts of Occitania – where they enjoyed high status and exceptional freedom of speech (sometimes even intervening in political matters). Launched from this position of eminence their poetry focussed respect-filled eyes upon women in general (including such lowly figures as shepherdesses), and upon the ladies of the courts in particular, bestowing an exalted, almost saintly, status on the female gender. These poems promulgated the idea of courtly love in which the male protagonist existed to worship his lady and to serve her faithfully. Such love was adulterous, in the sense that the lady was almost always married, but also pure in the sense that it was not to be consummated physically.[76] The essence of the whole exercise was self denial and frustration, longing from afar and the ennoblement of chastity. In the process the man who must love and yet not touch, must desire and yet never be fulfilled, was raised above the common herd.[77] What was really being celebrated, suggests Zoé Oldenbourg, was 'nothing else, surely, but the urge to proclaim a triumph of self-will?'[78]

Is it a coincidence that Cathar *perfecti*, too, sought to impose their will over every physical need and desire, and believed it necessary for their bodies to pass through suffering, protracted vigils, deprivation of the senses and many deaths before that goal could be achieved? For these and other reasons, Oldenbourg believes that there must have been a considerable degree of overlap between the troubadour movement and Catharism. She goes so far as to argue that on many occasions when:

> ... the troubadours ... mention God and Jesus Christ it is very probable that they are speaking as Cathars, and that their deity is the 'Good God' of the Manichean faith.[79]

But Oldenbourg is out of line. It is the concensus of medieval historians and literary scholars that the ideas diffused through Occitania by the troubadours in the 12th and 13th centuries had very little and perhaps even

nothing at all to do with Catharism.[80] We may only comment, with Arthur
Guirdham, that this simply makes no sense:

> How could two such startling manifestations of culture occur at the
> same time and in a limited area without their being related to each
> other? To hold such an opinion is equivalent to saying that the teachings
> of Freud swept London in the 1920s but had no influence on medicine or
> literature.[81]

Women hold up half the sky

In tandem with the poetry of the troubadours, the basic organisation
and beliefs of Cathar religion also had the effect – whether by accident
or by design – of elevating the status of women in Occitanian society.
Catholicism had done nothing to dismantle the gross inequalities of the
sexes that prevailed in the European Middle Ages and explicitly forbade
woman to become priests. Catharism, on the other hand, regarded the
souls of men and women as absolutely equal. It saw no reason why the
material envelopes that they were imprisoned in – namely their bodies,
which by chance could be either male and female – should be treated with
any less equality.

For this reason membership of the Cathar *perfectus* class was
not restricted by sex and both men and women could and did become
perfecti. On the highways and byways of these dangerous times Cathar
perfectae preached and travelled less than their male counterparts[82] – for
understandable reasons of physical security. Nor do we find any women
among the relatively few 'bishops' and 'deacons' at the top of the simple,
low-maintenance and minimally hierarchical structure by which Catharism
was administered in Occitania. Nevertheless there is no doubt that women
were highly esteemed and enjoyed great influence in their communities[83]
where they often established group homes for 'the daughters, widows and
dowagers of the local petty nobility and artisan classes'.[84]

In practice it is thought that the cadre of active *perfecti* present in
Occitania at any one time is likely to have included rather more males than
females (perhaps on the order of 6:4), but this resulted from individual
choices, not policy, and was compensated by a higher ratio of women
amongst the *credentes*.[85]

In summary, by contrast with anything the Catholic Church had to
offer, the status of women within the Cathar faith was high and their role
both important and recognised. This liberation, too, must have played its

THE MASTER GAME

part in the great awakening of ideas and human potential that took place in Occitania in the 12th century.

The revolution and the new world order

The point we wish to make here is that although Catharism was a system of inspired spiritual knowledge and, in every sense a religion, it was also a great deal more than that.

We've seen that it was, at one level, a social programme anticipating by centuries the modern recognition that human potential can never be fully realised without 'women's liberation'. Likewise we've seen how the Cathar doctrine of the equal predicament of souls – and the basic irrelevance of the sex, race or creed of the bodies in which they happen to be trapped – lent itself naturally to the refreshing liberalism, open-mindedness, cosmopolitanism and democratising tendencies of Occitanian society.

Catharism was also a comprehensive philosophy of anti-materialism that offered all who adhered to it a choice of two very clear ways forward in this life – a 'high' road and a 'low' road. The high road was the way of solitary meditation and renunciation of the world – the suppression through willpower of all physical needs, attachments and desires – that was followed by the *perfecti*. The low road was the way of engagement in the world followed by ordinary *credentes* until they received the *consolamentum* on their deathbeds. They hoped to make solid progress in this incarnation in the great project of freeing their souls from the trap of matter but understood that they might need to return again and again to the material plane before that objective would finally be achieved.

Had it been allowed to become widespread and to win dominance over the Catholic Church throughout Europe we cannot say what the long-term political and economic consequences of such a philosophy might have been. Simple logic suggests that it would have been most unlikely to have led to either of the two great political and economic systems – capitalism and communism – that were ultimately to dominate human affairs in the 19th and 20th centuries. Both are entirely materialist in their outlook and their disagreement is only over the manner in which the riches of the world are to be extracted and divided up. We can suppose that the very different concerns of Catharism, and its horror of material entrapment, would have led during the course of history to very different arrangements concerning 'production', the ownership of its 'means', and the uses and exploitation of the masses.

Already in 12th century Occitania there is evidence that the Cathars had begun to meddle with the feudal economic order through programmes of adult education and practical training for the poor and disenfranchised. For example workshops run by skilled *perfecti* were set up to provide apprenticeships in leather, paper-making and the textile trade.[86] One of the objectives of these workshops was undoubtedly to turn out missionaries who could be self-sufficient as they wandered from town to town making conversions (as we noted earlier, surviving records show a particularly strong concentration in Cathar areas of weavers and other workers in the textile trade). But the long-term effects of such an education programme, leading as it did to the foundation of an instructed artisan class, might have been literally revolutionary if it had been allowed to continue. Little wonder, therefore, that the French philosopher Voltaire seized on the memory of the suppression of Catharism to rabble rouse against the evils of the Church and of feudal oppression of the masses.[87] Initiated as a Freemason in 1778, as we saw in Chapter One, Voltaire's ideas were amongst the cocktail of influences that precipitated the French Revolution in 1789.

Pacifism was another central value in the ethical system of the *perfecti* and a resolute commitment to nonviolence was part of the regime of self-control over the baser bodily instincts and desires that their initiation required of them. There are cases on record of *perfecti* who chose to be burned at the stake rather than satisfy the Inquisition that they were innocent of heresy by killing even as lowly a creature as a hen.[88] Yet surprisingly for people with such apparent contempt for their own lives – and for the pains of death – it has been observed that the *perfecti*:

> ... retained an absolute respect for the fact of life itself; they would not allow any violent intervention by the human will (which they regarded as invariably evil and arbitrary) in the fate of a soul pursuing its road to salvation.[89]

The same reasoning explains why the *perfecti* were utterly opposed to the use of the death penalty, even for capital offences. They also claimed that common criminals should not be punished but instead educated to become better citizens.[90] Such *avante garde* doctrines were of course denounced by the Church as scandalous.[91]

Equally controversial was the strident insistence of the Cathars – quite contrary to the spirit of the times and the teachings of Catholicism – that preachers of crusade were 'murderers'.[92] Had the Cathars continued to win

THE MASTER GAME

converts at the rate they achieved in Occitania, instead of themselves being stamped out (significantly by a crusade), what might the consequences have been? Isn't there every likelihood that they would have transformed the international landscape of the Middle Ages – again with incalculable but quite possibly very positive consequences for the subsequent course of world history?

Fighting back

But the world is the way it has been, not the way it might have been, and the Cathars did not win. As we will see in Chapters Six and Seven, they lost everything – their lands, their culture, their freedom and their lives – in the blood-drenched horror of the Albigensian Crusades. Ravaging Occitania between 1209 and 1244,[93] these were 35 years of virtually unremitting war – a brutal war of sieges and burnings and fearful massacres. Despite belonging to the 'church of Love', therefore, which 'did violence to no man',[94] the very fact that a nation of vegetarian pacifists were able to resist the papal armies for so long tells us that they did not simply lie down and surrender when they were attacked. They fought back – tooth and nail.

This is by no means the only such paradox that Catharism offers. We've noted already that its doctrinal horror of sex (as the production-line that delivers new material incarnations for trapped souls to be reborn in) did not result in a concomitant change in reproductive behaviour in Occitania during the Cathar heyday. On the contrary Cathar families went on producing children in large numbers and the region enjoyed rapid population growth. The solution to the apparent paradox lies in the very different standards of behaviour expected of *credentes* and *perfecti*. The former adhered to the beliefs of Catharism but were not required to emulate the practices of its adepts.

We've seen how this system left *credentes* free to marry, make babies and eat meat as they chose. By the same token, despite its pacifism, it also left them free to resist persecution, and to defend their country and their faith with force of arms – even if doing so required them to commit acts of 'violent intervention in the fate of other souls'. The *perfecti* themselves seem always to have stood back from the fray, leaving the actual job of fighting the enemy to the *credentes*. Still there is evidence, in the face of pitiless Catholic aggression and mounting atrocities against Cathars, that even the *perfecti* found reason to qualify their philosophy of absolute pacifism and nonviolence. Since this world was the creation of the Evil God, and the material realm was fully in his power, it followed that he could create beings of pure evil – demons who merely looked like humans but had no souls – to destroy the Good Men and Good Women of the Cathar faith. To fight against such beings, who were numerous in the crusading armies and amongst the inquisitors, was hardly a crime.[95]

The ancient enemy

So in defending themselves against the murderous assault of the Albigensian Crusades, Cathars came to feel vindicated in their beliefs. The Catholic Church was the instrument of an Evil God who had created the material world as his personal fiefdom of suffering and horror, pain and misery. Now day by day in Occitania there was ever more compelling evidence for the accuracy of this proposition: the massacres repeatedly unleashed upon the civilian population; the tortures and the informer culture devised by the Inquisition; the endless holocaust of the Cathar faithful.

The scale, ferocity and sheer thoroughness of the Crusades are of course a measure of the threat that the Church perceived in Catharism. We already knew that the military support given to the Cathars by the great lords of Occitania had triggered this perception of danger. But as we looked through the heresiological literature of the period, we could not fail to note that something else, perhaps almost equally potent, seemed to have been at work at well.

For although the scale of the Church's response was new – indeed unprecedented – the Catholic authorities clearly recognised Catharism as an old and deadly enemy. It was for this reason that they so often referred to the Cathars as 'Manichees', a heresy over which Rome had supposedly triumphed centuries before. For their part, though they would never have identified themselves as 'Manichees', the Cathars claimed that their religion had come down to them from antiquity, 'passed from Good Man to Good Man'. It was, they said, the true faith that the Church had usurped in the early days of Christianity.

Most medieval scholars today prefer to argue that Catharism was essentially a new phenomenon and very much the product of its times. But neither of the protagonists in this affair, Catholics or Cathars, thought this was the case. They believed themselves to be caught up in the latest episode of an ancient struggle of profound consequence for the future of mankind.

In the next chapters, with due respect to the opinions of the experts, we will investigate the possibility that the protagonists could have been right.

CHAPTER THREE

WHERE GOOD
AND EVIL MEET

These are they who ... fell from Paradise when Lucifer lured them thence,
with the lying assurance that whereas God allowed them the good only,
the Devil (being false to the core) would let them enjoy both good and evil;
and he promised to give them wives whom they would love dearly; and
that they should have authority over one another, and that some amongst
them should be kings, or emperors, or counts; and that they would learn
to hunt birds with birds, and beasts with beasts.

Cathar Prayer[1]

U p till now we have been able to treat the problem of the Cathars as if their heresy existed in isolation. Of course this was not the case. They posed a massive threat to the Church of Rome on the basis of their success in nearby Occitania and northern Italy. But they were in fact part of a much larger heresy that threatened the entire Christian establishment in Europe – not only the Roman Catholics in the West but also the Orthodox Church of the East based in Constantinople (ancient Byzantium, known today as Istanbul).

The Catholic/Orthodox schism had been developing for centuries and became official in AD 1054. By that date the former bishops of Constantinople had already long been in the habit of calling themselves *ecumenical patriarchs* – literally 'patriarchs of the entire inhabited world'.[2] Since this seemed to challenge the pope's own claim to the top job it was a source of great mutual hostility. Nevertheless both churches were of one mind on the subject of heresy – which was to be stamped out.[3] And just as Rome faced the heresy of Catharism in the West in the 12th and 13th centuries, so too, and for rather longer, the patriarchate in Constantinople confronted the heresy known as *Bogomilism* in the East which began its period of expansion some 200 years earlier and survived until the end of the 14th century.

It was called 'Bogomilism' after its supposed founder whose name in Greek was *Theophilis* and in Slav *Bogomil* – meaning 'Beloved of God'.[4] Active in Bulgaria in the first half of the tenth century, this enigmatic individual preached a form of dualism that was identical, in almost every detail, to the creed that would later be introduced into Western Europe as Catharism. Hand in hand with these spiritual teachings, he is also remembered as the organiser of a political rebellion that gave the persecuted Slav peoples a voice and incited them to withdraw their labour and fealty from their Graecized Bulgar overlords.[5]

Although the Bogomil heresy endured in the East for three centuries longer than Western Catharism there is little reliable information about Bogomil himself. Not a single contemporary reference to him has come down to us and we know nothing about where or when he was born or died, who his teachers were, or how widely he preached.[6] The earliest-surviving report to mention him by name (although it is not the earliest to notice the heresy he started[7]) appears in a book written at some point between AD 977 and AD 990.[8] The work of a hostile Christian monk named Cosmas, this tract tells us only that:

> In the days of the Orthodox Tsar Peter [AD 927–969] there lived ... a priest called Bogomil (Loved of God), who in reality was not loved of God (*Bogu ne mil*), who was the first to sow heresy in the land of Bulgaria.[9]

Though it supplies no more information about the man himself, Cosmas's book was written specifically to denounce the faith that Bogomil had founded. His purpose was to draw the attention of the Orthodox Church to the threat it faced, and to upbraid Church authorities for the lapses that had permitted such a heresy to flourish.[10]

Close to the sources of power

In the years following the death of Tsar Peter in AD 969 Bogomilism spread rapidly westwards out of Bulgaria into the Balkan principalities of Serbia and Bosnia (where it fared so well that it was frequently the official state religion).[11] Equally influential in Croatia, Dalmatia and Macedonia, it also extended its grip into the heart of the great city of Constantinople itself,[12] headquarters of the Orthodox Church of the East. The first account of Bogomilism being practiced within the walls of Constantinople dates

THE MASTER GAME

from 1045. It is found in a letter written by the monk Euthymius of Periblepton – who even claimed to have discovered a heretical 'cell' in his own monastery.[13]

Cosmas I (1075–81) was the first emperor of Constantinople to take stern action against the Bogomils.[14] His successor, Alexius I Comnenus (1081–1118) was even more vehement in his attacks on the heresy. At an uncertain date between 1097 and 1104 he ordered the arrest of a known Bogomil named Diblatus who was tortured for information about key figures in the movement. The trail led to Basil, a renegade monk from Macedonia, now living under cover at a monastery in Constantinople, who was said to have been a Bogomil evangelist for more than 40 years.[15]

Next Comnenus set a trap for Basil. Pretending only to know of him as a respected Orthodox monk, the emperor innocently asked for enlightenment about the Christian faith. Human nature being what it is Basil could not pass up this apparently golden opportunity and set out to try to convert Comnenus to Bogomilism. A series of meetings followed in which the emperor thoroughly debriefed the unfortunate Basil, getting him to reveal not only the central doctrines of the heresy but also compromising details of its organisation and membership in Constantinople.[16]

Basil and his associates were then arrested and contemporary accounts tell us that Comnenus reasoned in person with the Bogomils, trying to win them back to the Orthodox faith. Those who recanted were pardoned and released. Those who would not recant were imprisoned for life. Only Basil, on this occasion, suffered the extreme penalty – so much favoured by heresy hunters in the West – of being burnt to death. His stake was set up in Constantinople's Hippodrome for the edification of a large crowd.[17]

Surviving records from Constantinople say nothing more about Bogomilism until the 1140s when there are reports of more heresy trials.[18] Then in 1145 we learn that no less a figure than Cosmas Atticus, patriarch of the Orthodox Church, has fallen under the spell of a certain Niphon, a Bogomil. When – horror of horrors – the heretic was allowed to take up residence in the patriarchal palace other ecclesiastics began to agitate against him. Eventually they took their complaints directly to Emperor Manuel I (himself later rumoured to have had covert 'Bogomil tendencies') and in 1147 Cosmas was deposed and Niphon arrested.[19] Still the episode indicates that by the mid-12th century, at about the time that Catharism was first detected in the West, Bogomilism had grown from a minor cult started by an unknown priest into a major religion that could position itself close to the sources of power in the East.

Papa Nicetas

This sense of a big faith on the move, taking shape, growing in confidence and building up structure before our eyes, is heightened 20 years later in 1167. In that year, seemingly out of the blue, Nicetas, a senior Bogomil bishop from Constantinople, suddenly turned up in the West. He arrived first in Lombardy in northern Italy where he persuaded the local Cathar bishops to adopt important doctrinal changes and to be 'reconsoled' at his hands.[20] Then he moved on to the Languedoc.

The entire Cathar administration of Occitania had gathered to await his presence at the small town of Saint-Félix-de-Caraman near Toulouse. Under his guidance routine matters such as boundary disputes amongst the existing Cathar bishoprics were resolved and three new dioceses of Toulouse, Carcassonne and Agen were established.[21] As in Lombardy, however, the primary purpose of Nicetas' visit seems to have been to urge important doctrinal changes upon the Cathars and to reaffirm what were clearly by this stage well-established links between the Cathar and Bogomil churches.[22] Indeed the immense respect shown to Nicetas, and the fact that he once again 'reconsoled' all the *perfecti* present, tell us very clearly that the relationship between these two churches was that of a senior to a junior, or a father to a son. The Cathars of 1167, in other words, clearly regarded Bogomilism as the 'home church' to which they owed their allegiance.

This conclusion is endorsed by modern historians who have amassed persuasive evidence that the Catharism of the West was indeed a direct offshoot of Bogomilism.[23] Although northern Italy is closer to Constantinople the heresy seems to have been brought to northern France and even to Germany first (a report has survived of the trial of a Cathar bishop in Cologne as early as 1143).[24] When it reached the Languedoc, and by what route, is not certain but it had clearly been present long enough by 1167 for bishoprics to have been established and boundary disputes to have broken out.

It seems, however, that there must also have been some doctrinal lapse amongst the Western Cathars which the doctrinal changes introduced by 'Papa' Nicetas were designed to correct. These brought Catharism into line with his own powerful faction of the Bogomil church which believed in the absolute opposition of the 'two powers' of Good and Evil.[25] By contrast there were other Bogomils, and prior to 1167 many Cathars too, whose beliefs compromised this pristine polarity. These so-called *mitigated dualists* contemplated linkages, and even family relationships, between the

Good God and the God of Evil, something that absolute dualists were not prepared to do.

Another objective of Nicetas's visit was to organise further missionary activity throughout Europe, using Occitania as a bridgehead. There is evidence that delegates left the 1167 Council of Saint-Félix invigorated and actively anticipating the prospect.[26]

Social engineering

In the decades after Nicetas at the close of the 12th century the Cathar and Bogomil churches begin to look increasingly as though they are involved in a well-planned and coordinated plot.[27] The purpose of this plot could not have been more revolutionary: to compete with and eventually to overthrow the Church of Rome and the Orthodox Church of the East. The absurd worship of the Evil God who had made this world was to be undermined – not all at once but slowly, city by city, region by region. The true dualist religion of the Cathars and the Bogomils was to be introduced in its place. The fundamental aim of the project was to free the souls of all mankind from the prison of matter and allow them to return to the heavenly realm of the Good God who had made them. Since this would require an attitude towards material things radically different from the dominant interests of the times it was obvious that permanent changes in the structure of society would also be necessary.

For us as researchers, this issue was clarified when we discovered that the Cathars in Occitania had involved themselves quite extensively in what we described in the last chapter as 'meddling with the feudal economic order'.

It seemed unlikely to be a coincidence when we learned that the Bogomils did exactly the same thing. From the earliest references in 10th century they are linked with social, economic and political upsets. 'They teach their followers not to obey their masters', warned the monk Cosmas in his expose of the abominations of this seemingly new heresy:

> ... they scorn the rich, they hate the Tsars, they ridicule their superiors, they reproach the Boyars, they believe that God looks in horror on those who labour for the Tsar, and advise every serf not to work for his master.[28]

Confronted by material like this it is little wonder that many historians have judged Bogomilism to be 'at base ... a social movement, directed against feudal oppression.'[29] Others disagree and argue that we should 'beware of attributing too much importance to the social anarchism of the Bogomils or of seeing in them Slavonic communists of the Middle Ages.'[30] In our opinion neither view is quite correct. The Bogomils were not early communists – or any such thing – since communism is a wholly materialist ethic concerned only with the material world. Neither were they 'at base' a social movement. Exactly like Catharism, the evidence convinces us that the Bogomil religion was first and last a spiritual movement, interested exclusively in the liberation of souls. It was the efficient pursuit of this spiritual objective, rather than any of the normal characteristics of a 'social movement', that led the Bogomils inevitably towards revolutionary behaviour in the material world. It inspired a critical attitude towards earthly hierarchies and put a new mood of intelligent rebelliousness into the air.

The same phenomenon of 'social engineering' running alongside dualist heresy was observed in other parts of Europe as well. In Occitania and France we showed in the last chapter how the Cathars busied themselves in the education of a skilled artisan-class – notably weavers and others involved in the cloth and paper trades. In this way empowerment of the poor through skills-training went hand-in-hand with the spread of the faith. We were therefore not surprised to learn that researchers in Italy have unearthed proof of significant links there between Catharism and the trade of pursemaking. Like weaving, this was an occupation that could provide suitable cover for missionary activities enabling Cathar evangelists to travel incognito 'making and selling their wares and at the same time making heretical contacts.'[31]

So, although the dualists professed to hate this world, such strategies show that they did not hesitate to use rather worldly and 'street-wise' methods to win converts from the established Christian Churches. After travelling amongst the Italian Cathars in the early 13th century Ivo of Narbonne reported that they routinely:

> ... sent to Paris capable students from nearly all Lombard and some
> Tuscan cities. There some studied logic, others theology, with the aim of
> strengthening their own error and overthrowing the Catholic faith.[32]

Such evidence of calculation and strategy seem less discordant with the Cathars' ethereal central purpose when we remember that they believed themselves to be locked in an elemental struggle – often literally to the death – for the soul of man. If the Catholic Church were allowed to crush out the light of Catharism forever then the soul of man would likewise be lost forever. With the stakes so high and the enemy so diabolical, any means, fair or foul were reasonable to bring him down.

School of heresy

Further evidence that Cathars and Bogomils were involved not only in social agitation but in a coordinated 'plot' to overthrow established Christianity comes from study of the methods they used to win conversions. The field missionaries of both sects appear to have followed the same procedures in the same order so closely that it is obvious they must have shared the same training. In this, once again, we have the sense of confronting people who were not in any way ethereal but, on the contrary, rather down-to-earth, calculating and strategic.

They also demonstrated a good basic knowledge of psychology in ensuring that the course of instruction they gave as missionaries began with easily-acceptable generalities and moved on only very slowly to reveal the more deeply heretical – and thus conventionally shocking – aspects of their faith.[33] Euthymius Zigabenus, who interrogated the monk Basil in Constantinople while he was awaiting his execution in the Hippodrome, was told that the Bogomils began by instructing their followers in those beliefs and practices which they shared with the Orthodox:

> ... preserving the fouler doctrines for later, and entrusting them to the more initiated in impiety as mysteries.[34]

The objective, in other words, was to detach potential converts as far as possible from the beliefs they had been raised in before attempting to substitute the alternative dualist system.

Another technique used by both Bogomil and Cathar preachers was to capitalise on the common-sense scepticism of ordinary people to demystify elaborate Church rituals – and therefore, by association, the whole religious edifice that lay behind them. The Mass was a favourite target of the Cathars who asked churchgoers to think very carefully and objectively about each of its details. When they partook of the wafer and the wine of Holy Communion, for instance, how could they possibly imagine – as Catholic priests had taught them – that they were consuming the *actual* body and blood of Christ? Wasn't this contrary to reason, if not just plain stupid? All the Catholics that had ever existed had been performing the Mass and guzzling the Holy Communion for hundreds and hundreds of years. If what they had been consuming were really the physical body and blood of Christ then he must have been absolutely enormous – at least the size of a mountain, with veins like rivers – which clearly had not been the case. Moreover, coming at the problem from a different direction, Cathar evangelists would frequently add an unpleasant reminder about digestive processes and their end products. Did decent people who loved God really want to pass his body and blood through their intestines?[35] What kind of religion was it that would require them to participate in such bizarre and frankly cannibalistic practices? So logic, reason and good taste were all against the Church being right about this basic issue long before the time came to introduce more 'touchy' Cathar doctrines like the non-physical nature of Christ.

The next step in the conversion process was often for the missionary to provide concrete examples of how far the Church had strayed from the true path. Favoured object lessons were the notorious sins of the clergy and their extravagant lifestyles. These were then graphically compared to the simple, decent, unostentatious lives advocated in the New Testament for Christians. After contemplating the glaring contradictions thus revealed, most right-thinking citizens in the audience would have needed little further convincing that there was something rotten in the heart of the Church.

In a similar way, further still down the road of conversion, the method for introducing the dualist doctrine of the evil nature of material creation was to illustrate it with numerous practical examples that anyone could easily grasp. Earthquakes might be cited, or volcanic eruptions, or lightning strikes, or snakes, along with many of the other noxious evils that we all know do stalk the material world.[36] As before, New Testament texts would be extensively quoted, this time to show that the true teachings of Christ and his apostles endorsed the dualist rejection of material things.[37]

Malcolm Lambert, a modern scholar with decidedly pro-Catholic sympathies, claims that the heretics usually achieved these effects by dishonest manipulation of the relevant passages which were 'wrenched out of context' to reinforce the dualist message.[38] The end result, most efficacious in winning conversions, was that the typical unsophisticated audience for a dualist sermon would be convinced that they had received 'an exhortation by good men based on the words of the founder of Christianity and of his followers.'[39]

It is little wonder, therefore, that for a long while the Cathars and the Bogomils enjoyed enormous success in their respective spheres of influence. By the end of the 12th century they had together created what Sir Steven Runciman describes as 'one great confederate Dualist Church … stretching from the Black Sea to Biscay.'[40] At its core were sixteen bishoprics positioned in areas of influence and high population all the way from Constantinople in the East to Toulouse in the West.[41] Since the heretics had, from the beginning, commanded great influence in the countryside as well as in the cities – and had generally worked from the bottom of society up in their programme of conversions – they entered the 13th century occupying an astonishingly strong position in Europe. Not even 250 years had passed since Bogomil himself had first appeared in Bulgaria to preach the doctrine of the Good and the Evil God. Yet in that short time an international infrastructure had been laid down and enough popular support won for medieval dualism to begin to think of itself as an established religion and to proclaim its own 'universality and supra-national unity'[42] over and against that of the established Church.

The Portrait of Dorian Gray

Accepting as all scholars do that Bogomilism was simply 'Bulgarian Catharism',[43] or, more accurately, that 'Catharism was in origin a Western form of Bogomilism',[44] what were the most important beliefs at the core of this heretical, pan-European religion?

We've seen that a belief in duality was fundamental – that is to say, a belief in two Gods, one Good, one Evil, with the latter depicted as the creator of the earth, of mankind, and of all material things. This in turn led the dualists to the conclusion that Christ, as an emanation of the Good God, could not have existed 'in the flesh' – which was by definition evil. Likewise he could neither have been born nor crucified (both of which call for a physical body) – and therefore could not have redeemed our sins by dying on the cross.

The reader is also familiar with the notion, again shared in full by the Bogomils and the Cathars, that the Holy Spirit had been brought to earth by the non-physical Christ and transmitted ever since – 'from Good Man to Good Man' – through the ritual of the *consolamentum* and the laying-on of hands. In both branches of the religion the ritual was the same and in both it served as an instrument of initiation at which a sacred *gnosis* was acquired that raised the candidate from the class of the neophytes to the class of adepts.[45]

Such beliefs and behaviour, on their own, clearly delineate key differences between mainstream Christianity on the one hand and the Bogomil/Cathar religion on the other. But there are many more – as might be expected given the genuinely Gnostic and essentially non-authoritarian character of the heresy. Like all earlier forms and expressions of Gnosticism it honoured the power of individual revelation over and above established doctrine. The result, part of the life of the religion, was a luxuriant jungle of speculation by both Cathars and Bogomils around their key concerns. These were the origins of evil, the essential goodness and immortality of souls, and the cause of their repeated incarnations in human bodies here on wicked planet Earth. It was the encouragement given to such individual creativity and freedom of expression that led to the principal schism in the heretical Church – that between so-called *absolute* and *moderate* dualists, which in turn proliferated into numerous smaller subdivisions. These seem to have competed for conversions – 'although they may have differing and contrary opinions'[46] – but they also apparently recognised one another and co-existed in a spirit of mutual tolerance.[47]

Despite the state of intellectual anarchy that prevailed amongst the heretics we thought it was possible to make out certain fundamentals of their religion on which all or most seem to have agreed. When we compared these with the fundamentals of established Christianity it was difficult to avoid the eerie feeling that each was a weirdly distorted reflection of the other. Like Dorian Gray and his portrait in the attic they were the same but opposites, near but very far apart.

The journey of the soul

One matter of great common interest and wildly dissimilar treatment was the origin and ultimate fate of the soul and its relationship to the human body.

Established Christian teaching is extremely clear:

> Each individual soul is a new creation of God, infused into the body destined for it.[48]

At death the soul is separated from the body, though not permanently as the two will be reunited at the Second Coming of Christ and the resurrection of the dead. Then:

> ... departed souls will be restored to a bodily life and the saved will enter in this renewed form upon the life of heaven.[49]

Said to be a 'fundamental element' of Christian doctrine it was a dominant view amongst medieval theologians that:

... the resurrection will involve a collection and revivifying of the particles of the dead body.[50]

Naturally the Cathars and Bogomils did *not* believe in the resurrection of the body. They regarded it as a truly impractical and actually rather hideous idea. Their interest was exclusively in the soul which they saw as an immortal non-physical intelligence that entered the human body at conception and thereafter wore it like a 'tunic'[51] until the body died. They pictured the soul as a time traveller on an immense journey towards perfection. Rather than the one-off 'resurrection' of billions of mouldering corpses on Judgement Day, their view was that each soul would be reborn many times on earth, in many different bodies – both human and animal[52] – before attaining its goal. Very much as in Buddhism, the objective was to progress to the advanced state of detachment, purity and self-control, obtainable only in human form,[53] that was believed necessary to release the soul forever from its imprisonment in the world of matter. The price was a life, perhaps many lifetimes, of severe asceticism and meditation. Moreover, though austerities were regarded as absolutely necessary, the reader will recall that they were not on their own held to be sufficient to obtain the soul's release. For that was also required the power of the Holy Spirit transmitted through the laying on of hands in the *consolamentum*.

So, in the dualist scheme of things, the destiny of the soul after death depended on what it had done with its period of physical incarnation just completed:

- If, through efforts made in this and previous lives, it had been born in the body of a man or a woman who would become a Cathar or Bogomil *perfectus*, and if the *perfectus* concerned died in a fully-consoled state without having lapsed, then the soul's term of imprisonment on earth would end. Released from the snares of matter it could rise back at last to its true home in the furthest and highest heaven – the realm of pure spirit ruled by the God of Good.

- If on the other hand the soul had incarnated in a body that did not have the opportunity to encounter Cathar or Bogomil teachings – and thus to be consoled – then it would born again in yet another body, and another, and another, until it did, finally, come to 'the understanding of God.'[54]

A doctrine of karma is not explicitly spelled out in the fragments of the dualist teachings that have come down to us. Still it is clear that goodness and personal austerity were thought to be beneficial to the progress of the soul while a lifetime of wickedness and self-indulgence would have profoundly negative consequences. Punishments of a 'karmic' nature could take the form of rebirth in particularly ghastly circumstances, or as an idiot, or even as a dumb animal – which, since it could not speak or reason, would only further frustrate the progress of the soul caged within it.[55]

Jehovah (aka the Devil) and the Old Testament

For Cathars and Bogomils the earth, and all material things in the perceptible universe, were the work of the Evil God. And while they worshipped the God of Good they acknowledged that he existed in an entirely separate dimension and had no direct influence in the Devil's playground.

By way of stark contrast, Christians believe in only one God, depicted as omnipotent and universally good, who created the material world and with it the human body and soul. He also established a spiritual heaven somewhere 'above' and outside the material dimension. There the souls of his elect, restored to their bodies, are to be sent on the Day of Judgement while for the remainder of mankind – sinners all – it is well known that God has prepared a suitable hell.

For mainstream Christians the books of the Old Testament, just like those of the New Testament, are regarded as inspired texts that form an integral part of their canonical scriptures.[56] Much is made of the continuity between the old 'Law', shared with the synagogue, and the new Law brought by Jesus. Likewise when Roman Catholics or Orthodox Christians speak of God as the 'Father' and Jesus as the 'Son' they clearly understand the 'Father' to be none other than Yahweh (Jehovah), the God of the Old Testament. Nothing compels us to believe that he has become some completely different or even radically transformed deity. Jesus brings a 'New Covenant', certainly, but you don't have to read the small print to realise that the God Christians go to church to worship today *is* still Jehovah.

The heretics adopted the same general scenario but their take on it was radically different. Far from being the object of their worship, Jehovah for them was synonymous with the 'Devil', or 'Satan', or 'Lucifer' – just another of the many names by which the Evil God who had made the material world was known. They judged him by his deeds which were well known and had always been arbitrary, vengeful, violent and cruel. The Old Testament, in describing these deeds, was simply an extended paean to Jehovah's unmitigated wickedness and was seen by the Cathars and the Bogomils as an irredeemably evil text – evil through and through – that had been written to flatter this evil deity. To adopt it as scripture, as the established Christians had done, was to capitulate entirely to the Devil. They therefore exorcised the Old Testament from their lives and would accept no argument based on its authority.[57] They relied instead upon the New Testament, and in some extreme cases on just a few specific books within the New Testament.

To this extent, though they were not Christians, theirs was a new Testament religion. However they also reverenced several other texts, as we shall see later, that were neither known nor accepted by the mainstream Church.

The creature of mud and the Hole in Heaven

If the basic dualist perception is of the separation and complete incompatibility of the realms of spirit and matter then how is it possible that souls – though wholly spiritual and the creation of the Good God – could have ended up imprisoned in human bodies created by the Evil God?

Cathar and Bogomil missionaries had a varied collection of myths at their disposal to help confront such paradoxes and answer questions arising from them in graphic and engaging ways.[58] The myths weren't 'dogmas' or even 'doctrines' and it would be foolish to think that they were taken literally. Rather they were storyboards used as teaching devices – the point being for different teachers to bring different listeners in different circumstances to their own independent understanding of the mystery.

In brief, what the dualist myths tell us is that the paradoxical mixing of good and evil in the heart of the human creature came about after the Evil God/Jehovah/Satan had created the material earth as described in the Old Testament. Some of the myths state that he was not satisfied with this achievement so he attempted to create a man, moulding the body out of mud or clay, like a potter.[59] But try as he might he was unable to breathe the spirit of life into the body he had made – for the spirit of life is in the gift of the Good God alone. In desperation therefore:

> He sent an embassy to the Good Father, and asked Him to send His breath, saying that the man would be shared if he were to be endowed with life … Because God is good, He agreed and breathed into what [Jehovah/Satan] had moulded the breath of life; immediately man became a living soul, splendid in his body and bright with many graces.[60]

A quaint sidelight comes from a vernacular form of the myth, repeated to the Inquisition in Toulouse in 1247. A witness reported having been told by a Cathar how the Devil made the body of the first man, Adam, and God gave it a soul. But then:

The man leaped up and said to the Devil, 'I do not belong to you'.[61]

So we are to envisage an independent-minded creature here, one who is aware of the good within himself and capable of subduing the evil material inclinations of his body. The natural impulse of this 'Living Soul' is to return to the realm of the Good God yet it cannot do so without purification because it has now been thoroughly contaminated by matter. Worse, far from sharing Adam, as he had promised, it is the intention of the Evil God to monopolise the man, drawing him ever deeper into the realm of this world and causing him to forget his spiritual origins. Eve is suddenly (sometimes confusingly) on the scene, also a 'Living Soul', and she and Adam are impelled by the Devil:

... towards that carnal union that finally consummated their position as creatures of matter.[62]

The original gift of Spirit breathed by God into the parents nevertheless is transmitted through the act of reproduction to their descendants, and their souls, now enchained to matter, are reborn again and again on the Devil's earth.

Another myth tells a different story to make essentially the same points. In this case the Evil God starts out not so much as a completely separate principle but as an emanation from the Good God – a heavenly being of the type that we might think of as an angel. Like Satan in Christian cosmology his pride, arrogance and avarice corrupt him and he must leave the good heaven. In the momentum of his Fall he draws down with him:

... a great crowd of souls who had been created by God and were living close to him in a state of beatitude. It was from this inexhaustible reserve of fallen or captive angels that human souls derived.[63]

In other recensions the God of Good and the God of Evil may be portrayed as equal and opposite powers, or the latter may again be a fallen emanation of the former. Having created the material world, the God of Evil lures a host of angels out of heaven. This he does by promising them:

> ... possessions, gold, silver and wives, till they fell like rain upon the earth for nine days and nights to be shut up in bodies by Satan.[64]

Many accounts say that a third of all the angels in heaven,[65] due to their own 'weaknesses', were thus tempted to descend to earth to animate the zombie bodies that the God of Evil had prepared for them. Meanwhile the God of Good notices the radical decline in the angel population and discovers that the departure of so many has ripped a hole in heaven. He prevents further losses by jamming his foot in the hole and tells those who have already fallen that they will remain on earth, encased in bodies 'for the moment and for now.'[66] Through the cycle of reincarnation, harnessed to the sex impulse that ensures an endless supply of new bodies to replace those that wear out, the Devil believes that he has imprisoned the fallen angels in the human race forever. But the enigmatic words 'for the moment and for now' lead us to understand that the God of Good has a plan that will frustrate the Devil and restore the lost souls to heaven.[67]

Christ's Holographic mission to the realm of an alien God

Since the dualist perspective makes the God of Good powerful only in the spiritual realm, and the God of Evil powerful only in the material realm, it does not easily provide a mechanism for either to operate on the other's home turf. Perhaps this is why it takes a very long time – thousands of years we're told, in all the Cathar and Bogomil cosmologies[68] – for the Good God to implement his plan to frustrate the Devil.

It is a plan conceived out of compassion for the imprisoned souls of the angelic host – because their life on earth, isolated from the Holy Spirit that had filled them before their fall, is one of 'unimaginable suffering'.[69] Denied the radiance of the Spirit, and all that is good, they are trapped far from their true home in a dimension to which they do not belong. A Cathar prayer expresses their grief:

> We are not of this world, and this world is not of us, and we fear lest we meet death in this realm of an alien God.[70]

The prayer goes right to the heart of the problem. How is the God of Good to project his spiritual power into the material realm of the God of Evil in order to rescue the souls trapped there?

The dualists all gave the same answer to this question – Jesus Christ. But their Christ was a very different figure from Jesus the 'Son of God', born a man, later crucified and resurrected from the dead, who is worshipped by Roman Catholics and Orthodox Christians. The reader will recall that the Cathars and Bogomils believed Christ to have been non-human – an emanation from the Good God who could never have been 'born' into evil flesh but who had manifested in our material dimension as a particularly convincing yet 'non-physical' apparition. Indeed it might even be helpful in explaining what the dualists had in mind here to say that their Christ figure was a sort of *avatar* – not a created, material being, but an emission or radiation or instrument of the Good 'sent forth to deal with the created world.'[71]

Christ's mission was threefold.

First he was to preach a religion, and transmit a *gnosis*, that would lift the scales from the eyes of mankind and provide high initiates with insight into the meaning of death, the true character of existence and the fate of the soul.

Secondly, he was to offer instruction as to how humans might best live together through their vast cycle of incarnations in the hell called the earth. In the long-term project of cleansing souls contaminated by matter and preparing them to return to heaven there was no doubt that certain social arrangements and personal commitments were more conducive to the success of the 'mission' than others. For example if humanity could be persuaded to organise itself according to principles of love, nonviolence, kindness, frugality, tolerance and mercy then this would obviously be better for all concerned than hate, bloodshed, cruelty, excess, dogmatism and vengeance. Since the God of Evil sought every opportunity to urge us on to all of the latter – and to every other ugly and wicked impulse of which we are capable – the purpose of the teachings of Jesus was to provide a counter-balance. Though in fact he was a phantasm, the perfect 'life' that he would appear to live on earth would also serve as an example to show others the way.

The third and by far the most important objective of Christ's holographic mission was to bring down with him from heaven a blazing fragment of the Holy Spirit. For those souls who succeeded in purifying and perfecting themselves on earth it would provide the final necessary burst of sacred energy that would break the bonds of matter and return them to heaven.[72] We might envisage it as a flaming torch, lit from the main fire of the Spirit in heaven and now able to transmit its revivifying flame to souls marooned in the material world below.

THE MASTER GAME

Before his feigned death upon the cross, the Cathars and the Bogomils believed that Jesus had passed custody of this spiritual flame to the apostles through the laying on hands – the original ritual of the *consolamentum* – and thence to the primitive church.

A short excursion to parallel worlds

For some years our own long-term research interest has been in religious systems that give special emphasis to the dualisms of 'heaven-earth', 'sky-ground' and 'above-below'. We have argued in previous books that such systems were once prominent in the ancient world – most notably amongst the Egyptians.[73] There are, for instance, funerary texts 3500 years old (and older examples of the same type of material could be cited) that instruct the pharaoh to make a copy on the ground, and gain knowledge – *gnosis* – of a region of the sky called 'the hidden circle of the *Duat*'.[74] He is to do this so that he may become a 'spirit' after death and be:

> ... well-equipped both in heaven and earth, unfailingly and regularly and eternally.[75]

The source of this passage is the 11th division of the *Book of What is in the Duat* (written on the walls of the tomb of Thutmosis III, 1479–1425 BC). A little later in the same text – in the 12th division – the pharaoh is instructed for a second time to make a copy on the ground of the hidden circle of the *Duat* so that it may:

> ... act as a magical protector for him, both in heaven and upon earth.[76]

We have argued that such dualistic sky-ground thinking was a key element in the religion of ancient Egypt for at least 3,000 years from the beginning of the Old Kingdom to the time of Christ. And we've tried to show how that religion inspired the pharaohs to undertake great construction projects – the Pyramids of Giza, for example, or the Temples of Karnak and Luxor – which in a variety of different ways sought to 'copy' or 'reconstitute' the perfection of the heavens in the land of Egypt.[77]

We were therefore intrigued to discover that surviving texts, traditions and inquisitional records from Occitania, Italy and Constantinople contain not only copious illustrations of the well-understood 'spirit-matter', 'good-evil' dualism practiced by the Cathars and the Bogomils but also rarer examples of a distinctly 'ancient Egyptian' heaven-earth dualism.

For example, when Euthymius Zigabenus interrogated the Bogomil evangelist Basil in Constantinople around the year 1100 he was told one of the versions of the 'fallen angel myths' often used to explain how souls created by the God of Good had come to be in bodies created by the God of Evil. In this variant both Satan and Jesus are 'Sons' – emanations – of the Good God. Satan, the elder 'Son' covets the father's kingdom and rebels against him. The rebellion fails and Satan is expelled from heaven. Yet through pride and envy he still yearns to possess a realm where he might be God. He therefore creates the earth and '*a second heaven*' (our emphasis), moulds his zombie humans from mud and water and persuades the Good God to breathe souls into them.[78] The reader knows the rest of the story.

Another hint of the same kind of thinking comes in reports, collected by the Inquisition, of Cathar teachings concerning 'the truth of the Upper and Lower Worlds'.[79] Here we read about the God of Good 'preaching in the sky to his people', and how he sent Satan down to 'this world' and how afterwards Satan desired:

> ... to have a part of the Lower and Upper possessions, and the Lord did not wish it, and on this account there was war for a long time.[80]

Striking and colourful reference was also made to a Cathar teaching that:

> Oxen ... grazed and ploughed the soil and worked on the sky as on the earth.[81]

Rather than outlining actual 'beliefs' it seems to us that such teachings are best understood as simplified illustrations or mental images to assist neophytes in the analysis of difficult concepts. Embedded in all of them is the fundamental dualist idea of two parallel worlds, one all spirit, one all matter, but here visualised in terms of graphic sky-ground metaphors. It was in the same vein that the Cathars would often speak of the 'earthly earth' and the 'heavenly earth'[82] – the former being our planet, this underworld or hell-world on which human incarnations are served out; the latter to be understood as a parallel celestial or heavenly realm.[83]

There was a text that was held in the highest regard by the heretics. Known as the *Vision of Isaiah* it reached the Cathars in the late 12th century from the Bogomils, being translated in the process from Greek or Old Slavonic into Latin. However it is believed by scholars to have 'deep roots in the past, probably finding its origins among the Greek Gnostics towards the end of the first century AD.'[84] In it we read how Isaiah (a prophet generally exempted by the dualists, for reasons that need not detain us here, from their general hatred of the Old Testament) is given a great privilege by the God of Good. He sends an angel from heaven to take the prophet by the hand and lead him on a journey through both the earthly and the celestial realms, crossing the barrier between the two – something that 'no one who desires to return to the flesh' has ever before been permitted to do. As they ascend through the heavens they see tremendous battles raging on all sides between the emanations of the God of Evil and the emanations of the God of Good:

> For just as it is on earth, so also it is in the firmament, because replicas of what are in the firmament are on earth.[85]

Rainier Sacconi, a relapsed Cathar *perfectus* who turned inquisitor in the mid-12th century, reported significant discussion of such ideas amongst his former co-religionists. They believed, he said, that certain of their sacred books had been *written in heaven and brought down to earth* (our emphasis) by Christ who entrusted them to the primitive church on the completion of his mission.[86]

It was to this primitive church, 'which alone could offer true consolation to the souls dwelling in exile,'[87] that the dualists claimed to belong. Through an unbroken chain of consolations, they said, their *perfecti* had preserved and passed down the flame of the Holy Spirit undimmed from the time of Christ. The only problem was that they had been forced to preserve it in secret because the God of Evil, absolute master of this world, had substituted a false Church for the true Church one century before and endowed it with immense material power. This imposter Church masqueraded as 'Christian' but actually served the Devil.[88] By working for its downfall, therefore, the Bogomils and Cathars claimed that they only sought to restore the *status quo ante* that had prevailed at the time of the apostles.

Ancient legacy or medieval invention?

It sounds like blatant propaganda. Of course heretics would like us to believe that only their Church was the authentic descendant of the church of the apostles. Even if they'd only invented themselves yesterday, why settle for anything less? Surprisingly, however, several leading scholars in this field are convinced that such claims are solidly based and that the Cathar and

Bogomil Churches somehow did manage to preserve genuine traditions from the earliest days of Christianity.

The pro-Catholic scholar Martin Lambert doesn't want to make too much of it when he admits that.

> By a strange chance the rite of the *consolamentum* that appears in the 13th century texts does seem to have been based on a rite for baptism and on practices connected with the catechumenate [those who were candidates for baptism] much earlier than the contemporary Catholic rites of baptism or ordination.[89]

But Steven Runciman points out that this is by no means the only close resemblance. In his view, whether we think them 'strange' or not, there are far too many similarities for us to put them all down to 'chance':

> The Ritual Feast of the Cathars [which involved a simple breaking-of-bread ceremony] is, if we equate the Perfect with the Early Christian priest, exactly the same as the Early Christian Communion Feast. The Kiss of Peace terminated Early Christian services as it did those of the Cathars ... The *consolamentum* in its two aspects was closely akin to the adult baptism administered by the Early Church to the dying and to the ordination or initiation into its ministry. The very details of the service are similar. In the Early Church [as was the case with a prospective Cathar *perfectus*] the catechumen was tested by a long and stern probationary period [prior to] his initiation ceremony ... The actual ordination was identical, consisting of the laying on of hands and of the Gospel upon the catechumen's head ...[90] ... While polemical churchmen in the Middle Ages denounced the heretics for maintaining a class of the Elect or Perfect they were denouncing an Early Christian practice, and the heretic initiation ceremony that they viewed with so much horror was almost word for word the ceremony with which Early Christians were admitted to the Church.[91]

> Such similarity cannot be fortuitous. Obviously the Cathar Church had preserved, only slightly amended to suit its doctrines of the time, the services extant in the Christian Church during the first four centuries of its life.[92]

Runciman notes that everywhere they went – whether it was amongst the oppressed Slav peasants of Bulgaria or amongst the free-thinking burghers of Occitania – the heretics were able to exploit pre-existing social and economic conditions in order to gain a foothold. But, he concludes, 'the political impulse was not everything':

> Behind it there was a steady spiritual teaching, a definite religion, that developed and declined as most religions do, but that embodied a constant tradition.[93]

It is his view that this tradition is in one sense as old as human speculation about the nature of evil in the world – dating back, long before Christianity, to whatever prehistoric age it was when men first asked 'why God, if there be a God, could permit it?'[94] From there Runciman is willing to trace the same primordial religion very tentatively into the historical period, seeing elements of it drawn together from 'Egyptian, Zoroastrian and even Buddhist ideas.'[95] Three centuries after Christ it was likewise notable how:

> Stoics and Neoplatonists each in their own way condemned the world of matter; and Jewish thinkers of Alexandria began to face the problem [of evil], influenced by the emphasis on spirit that they found in the Hermetic lore of Egypt.[96]

Runciman concludes that it was the Gnostics of Alexandria and Syria who were responsible – roughly between the first and fourth centuries AD – for finally gathering together all such lines of thought and applying them to Christianity.[97] Thereafter a series of overlapping heresies could be sketchily made out in the historical record. It was these together, Runciman argues, that had preserved the 'constant tradition' from the early Gnostic schools, by way of Manicheism between the third and sixth centuries AD, to reach eventually the Bogomils in the tenth century. They in their turn transmitted it to Western Europe in the form of Catharism in the 12th century.

Hans Soderberg is a second major authority in this field who is satisfied that the religious beliefs and practices of the medieval dualists were connected by 'an uninterrupted traditional chain' to the Gnostic religions that had flourished a thousand years earlier.[98] He believes, moreover, that the Cathars merely gave 'a Christian clothing' to the even more ancient, indeed virtually universal, myth 'of the combat between the two powers.'[99]

But other historians are not at all happy about tracing the origins of medieval dualism so far back.[100] Malcolm Lambert thus speaks for many when he tries to place the whole Cathar/Bogomil phenomenon firmly in the context of its times, seeing it primarily as a reaction to specific economic, political and social circumstances. Even he, however, is prepared to admit that Bulgaria (converted to Orthodox Christianity barely a century before the *pop* Bogomil began teaching) may have provided uncommonly good ground for the heresy because of the possible influence of 'pre-existing dualist beliefs in the country.'[101]

Listening to heretics and heresy hunters

Whatever the personal stance of individual scholars may be on the problem of origins, we've observed a curious phenomenon in reviewing the literature. Very few of the attempts made to trace the history of ideas behind medieval dualism (whether they support or contradict the idea of an ancient tradition) have been willing to pay serious attention to what the dualists themselves – or their opponents in the Church – had to say on the matter.

For example when heresy hunters in Western Europe referred to the Cathars as 'Manichees' it is automatically assumed that they must have been mistaken because Manicheism had been suppressed centuries previously.

In the East, Theophylact, patriarch of Constantinople from AD 933–956, was one of the first to warn of the stirrings of the heresy that soon become known as Bogomilism (although he did not know of Bogomil by name). Writing to Tsar Peter of Bulgaria he was just as quick as his counterparts in the West to link the heresy to Manicheism (and also to the pre-existing dualist religion known as Paulicianism, of which we shall hear more in the next chapter). 'Let the leaders and teachers of this ancient heresy which has newly reappeared be anathema,'[102] he pronounced firmly at the end of his letter. Yet scholars are reluctant to pursue the possibility that the heresy thus anathematised could have been anywhere near as 'ancient' as Theophylact clearly believed.

The same academic scepticism also inhibits research into the implications of the heretics' own statements about their origins – all of which have come down to us through the work of the heresy hunters and thus seethe with hostile comments and interpretations. As early as 1143 or 1144 for example, when Catharism was first beginning to be recognised in Western Europe, the monk Everwin of Steinfeld (near Cologne in Germany) wrote a worried letter to Bernard of Clairvaux appealing for his assistance in the struggle against the heretics:

... who everywhere in almost all churches boil up from the pit of hell as though already their prince were about to be loosed and the day of the Lord were at hand.[103]

Everwin frankly observed that the heresy was gaining ground because of the apparent piety of its missionaries who possessed:

... no house, or lands, or anything of their own, even as Christ had no property nor allowed his disciples the right of possession.[104]

Equally potent, and apparently extremely convincing, was the heretics' insistence that theirs was Christ's original Church – the primitive church itself, reawakened after being forced to lie low 'in Greece and certain other lands ... from the time of the martyrs ...'[105] Though Evil powers had made every effort to destroy the church of the Good God:

We and our fathers of apostolic descent, have continued in the grace of Christ and shall so remain until the end of time.[106]

Martin Lambert's comment is that one of the reasons the Cathar *perfecti* were so convincing was because they:

... honestly thought that they were the only true Christians, that the clergy were the servants of Satan's Church; and that Cathar teaching presented a stream of pure underground Christianity, often persecuted, but always surviving and reaching back to the days of the apostles.[107]

Whether they were right or not is another matter, but we know what the heretics believed. They believed that their faith was meant to guide the world. This was what was destined. This had been the plan of the Good God to fetch the lost souls back to heaven and he had sent Christ to earth to set it in motion.

All had proceeded as it should until the reign of Emperor Constantine in the fourth century. Then, at the very moment when Christianity triumphed over multiple competitors to become the state religion of the Roman Empire, the Devil pulled off his most cunning trick. A clique within the Church that insisted on literal interpretation of the scriptures – rather than the more allegorical approach favoured by Gnostic Christians – seized control and rapidly began to persecute as heretics all those who disagreed with them.

Under interrogation the Bogomil evangelist Basil explicitly mentioned the church father John Chrysostom (AD 347–407), who is indeed known for his 'literalist' views,[108] as a ringleader of this clique of early heresy hunters.[109]

It was such purges between the fourth and sixth centuries AD, said the Cathars and the Bogomils, that had forced their true Church underground. Only now, after the sleep of years, was it was emerging once more from the shadows. In the 10th century it had seemed no more than the rantings of a lone vegetarian in Bulgaria. By the 11th century it had become a cult that had spread throughout the Balkans and to Constantinople. By the mid-12th century it was firmly established in Italy and Occitania and could also claim to have won many followers elsewhere 'scattered throughout the world'.[110]

Though the scholars have paid scant attention, it seemed to us that what the heretics were claiming was dynamite – not only that their forefathers in the dualist Church were the true descendants of the apostles but also that an ancient conspiracy had denied them their rightful role in shaping the destiny of the West. Perhaps even more explosive was the way they clearly saw themselves as part of a long-delayed 'counter-conspiracy' that had begun in the last 50 years of the first millennium and that had grown steadily, one might almost say remorselessly, in the two centuries that followed.

As we continued to explore the strange phenomenon of medieval heresy we could not shake off the feeling that something ancient and hidden, with a profound purpose for mankind, had briefly shown its face a thousand years ago, tried to change the world, and failed.

CHAPTER FOUR

CHAIN OF THE GREAT HERESY

In its Manichean form Gnosticism was once a real worldwide religion, i.e. a worldwide and separate Gnostic community or church (ekklesia) with its many thousands and, later on, even millions of adherents; its own leader, bishops and priests; its own canonical scriptures; and even its own very attractive art. Once Manichaeism spread from southern Mesopotamia as far as the Atlantic in the West and the Pacific in the Far East. It had its adherents in Egypt, in Roman North Africa, in Spain, Gaul, Italy and the Balkans, and in the end even in the regions on the South China Coast. Its history covers the period from the beginning of the third century to modern times. Even in our century [i.e. the 20th century] *Manichaeism was still forbidden by law in Vietnam.*

Johannes Van Oort, Lecturer in the History of Christianity at the Utrecht University[1]

Christianity in the 21st century is enshrined in the law of many lands, and even where it is not practiced it has worked its way both overtly and subliminally into virtually every sphere of life – marriage patterns, child rearing, education, social and political relationships, ethics, philosophy and so on. Subsumed into Western capitalism, it has also had a huge impact, built up over centuries, on our relationship with the material world.

Consider the account of Creation given in the Old Testament book of Genesis (a text that the Church views as inspired and that fundamentalist Christians to this day teach as fact.)[2] The creator is Jehovah, whom the Bogomils and Cathars equated with the Devil. In Chapter One we read how he makes heaven and earth, night and day, the oceans, dry land, grass, herbs, trees, fruit. To fill the oceans: 'God created great whales, and every living creature that moveth, which the waters brought forth abundantly.'

Land animals come next. Then, on the sixth day: 'God created man in his own image, in the image of God created he him; male and female created he them.' Finally Jehovah invites the first couple to 'subdue' the whole earth and gives them:

> ... dominion over the fish of the sea, and over the fowl of the air, and over every living thing that moveth upon the earth.[3]

This is a code of subjugation and domination, even if it includes some common-sense 'replenishing' as well.[4] In the West it set the moral agenda for the Industrial Revolution of the 18th and 19th centuries. And even in the secular modern world it continues, through force of ancient habit and in many subtle ways, to underwrite the environmental irresponsibility of the big economies and the vast multinational corporations they have spawned.

You can see the effects of the Old Testament's righteous sense of dominion everywhere. The fowl of the air are now battery chickens; many species of those great whales that Jehovah made have been hunted to extinction; fish-stocks in the oceans have never been lower; there is a continent-sized hole in the Ozone Layer; and the rainforests of the Amazon – the very lungs of the world – are being logged out or burnt at a terrifying rate to make way for cattle ranches. Of course we do not claim that the Christian Church is solely responsible for all this; but neither should its part in the matter be underestimated. Though fewer and fewer Westerners study the scriptures today, or would claim to be much influenced by them, all the structures, wealth and international power inherited from the Age of Discovery and the Industrial Revolution were built up by people who did.

There are other matters for which the Church and its leaders have been much more completely responsible. In Chapters Six and Seven we will tell the story of the Albigensian Crusades that destroyed the Cathars in the 13th century. No one acquainted with these terrible events could doubt the absolute disregard of the Christian leadership in Europe for the spiritual rights of others or its willingness to use lethal force. The same arrogance and blood-lust also showed themselves in the brutal Crusades between the 11th and the 13th centuries mounted by European Christian armies to recapture the Holy Land.

The faith was therefore only running true to type when it continued to be imposed forcefully by Europeans wherever they went during the Age of Discovery – witness the activities of the Jesuits and other missionaries in Africa, Asia and the Americas, from the 15th century onwards. Indigenous religions and their cultural treasures were systematically demolished and replaced by Christianity – at incalculable cost to the diversity of human ideas. Where this could not be achieved, notably in the disruptive 1,000-year conflict with Islam, massive trauma and lasting damage were inflicted on those societies that would not accept conversion. The suffering, chaos and violence that still continue in the Middle East today result directly from this ancient legacy of pain – and since 11 September 2001 the war has been carried to the West's own front door. In the eyes of Muslim fundamentalists, contemporary Western geopolitics in the Middle East are a continuation of the Crusades by modern means and so must be resisted to the death. The result is a flashpoint, built on a millennium of hatred, that could yet set the whole world in flames.

All in all then it seems reasonable to conclude that established Christianity has been amongst the great determinative forces of history and that the baleful global conditions we confront in the 21st century have much to do with its long-term influence. A moment can be pinpointed when that influence first began to be felt – in the early fourth century AD following the conversion to Christianity of the Roman Emperor Constantine. That was the moment when Christianity first strapped itself to the engine of secular power and (almost immediately, as we shall see) became a persecuting bureaucracy. In its first 300 years, however, it had possessed no unified Church, nor any agreed body of fundamental dogma that it might wish to impose on others, nor the ability to impose it on them. Far from persecuting, Christianity itself had been a despised and persecuted agglomeration of sects with a very wide range of ideas centred around the figure and mission of Christ.

What was smashed?

The heretical churches of the Bogomils and the Cathars that flourished for a few brief centuries in the Middle Ages also centred their ideas around the figure and mission of Christ. How does the impact of their thinking compare with the giant presence and powers of the established Christian Church? The question is asked specifically with reference to their influence on the world stage and their overall importance in the history of mankind.

There are scholars who give what seems to be the obvious answer. They argue that the Bogomil and Cathar movements are best understood as strictly local responses to temporary social and economic circumstances in various parts of Europe between the 10th and the 14th centuries.[5] If their view is correct then to know the whole life story of the heresy we need only examine the immediate conditions surrounding its rise and fall. With no past – and of course no future – its place in history would be small and its impact on the development of Western civilisation negligible or nonexistent.

We've seen that other scholars like Hans Soderberg and Sir Steven Runciman oppose this view, arguing that 'an uninterrupted traditional chain' connects the Cathars and the Bogomils to the religion known as Christian Gnosticism that flourished in Egypt and the Middle East a thousand years earlier. If they are correct then whatever it was that the Church smashed with the Albigensian Crusades in the 13th century can hardly be described as a short-lived social movement. If the links in the chain can be traced back a thousand years, then doesn't the Cathar phenomenon look much more like a bid for power after a millennium of silence by a parallel persecuted religion, secretive, shadowy, and as old as established Christianity itself?

'That most wicked sect of obscene men who are called Paulicians ...'

Working back from the Cathars, for whom there are no unambiguous reports prior to the mid-12th century, we come to the Bogomils. They are first heard of in the 10th century and survived in some isolated communities in Eastern Europe until the 15th century. Not only did they predate and outlive the Cathars, therefore, but also there is consensus amongst the scholars that Catharism in the West did arise as a direct result of Bogomil missionary activity.

The next link in the proposed 'chain of the great heresy' overlaps in time with the Bogomils in a similar way, and again with a significantly earlier origin. The link is formed by a strange and uniquely warlike dualist sect known as the *Paulicians*. They co-existed with the Bogomils and are thought to have played a significant part in shaping the ideas of the *pop* Bogomil himself in the 10th century.[6]

As with most heretical movements, much that we know about them comes from their opponents in the Christian Church. One of these was the monk Peter of Sicily whose *History of the Manicheans who are also called Paulicians* contains valuable contemporary information on the sect. Peter learned about them at first hand in AD 869–70 when Emperor Basil I of Constantinople sent him as an ambassador to the Paulician leader Chrysocheir – who had recently established an independent principality on the Arab-Byzantine frontier.[7]

As we can see from the title of his tract, Peter assumed that the Paulician religion was merely a disguised form of Manicheism. This is understandable. The Paulicians and the followers of Mani were dualists, exactly like the later Bogomils and Cathars. But the Paulicians' account of their own origins, which Peter of Sicily also helpfully preserved for us, makes no claim of descent from Mani. Instead it traces the sect's beliefs back to a certain Constantine of Mananalis who had lived in what is now Armenia during the reign of the Byzantine Emperor Constans I (AD 641–648).[8] Constantine of Mananalis, in his turn, is said to have been influenced by a mysterious 'deacon' who stayed at his home 'after returning from prison in Syria' and gave him a number of books including a 'Gospel book and a book of the Epistles of St. Paul, on which he ... based his teaching.'[9]

So clearly there must have been something 'Christian' about these Paulicians if the teachings of their founder were based on Christian texts. Indeed it turns out that Christ was the central figure in their religion but that just like the Cathars and Bogomils they refused utterly to accept that he had ever been born 'in the flesh' or that Mary was his mother.[10] Since he did not possess a physical body how could he have had a mother? Like the Cathars and the Bogomils they believed him to have been a non-physical emanation of the God of Good, an emissary from the spiritual realms.[11] Like the Cathars and the Bogomils they rejected the cross and all the material sacraments of established Christianity, as well as the cults of saints and of icons.[12] Like the Cathars and the Bogomils they entirely rejected the Old Testament and did not accept every part of the New Testament.[13] And again like the Cathars and the Bogomils they claimed that theirs was the only true Church, descended directly from the first Christian communities, and that the Roman Catholic and Orthodox Churches were imposters.[14]

The supreme leader of the Paulicians, wielding absolute spiritual and secular power, was known as the *didaskalos*. His followers regarded him, says Peter of Sicily as 'the apostle of Christ'.[15] Constantine of Mananalis in the seventh century was revered as the first *didaskalos*, but all his successors held the same title and each was considered 'the authoritative teacher of the Christian revelation in his own generation.'[16]

Although we do not know the exact date that Constantine of Mananalis began his ministry, historians generally set it around AD 655.[17] He acted from the beginning, say historians Janet and Bernard Hamilton, as though he were:

> ... restoring the true Church that had been founded by Saint Paul ... Later *didaskaloi* followed Constantine's example and took the names of Paul's disciples, and also called their churches after places visited by Paul. The implication was that they were restoring the true apostolic Church.[18]

Understandably these heretics referred to themselves simply as 'Christians' (again something they have in common with the Bogomils and the Cathars who likewise called themselves 'Good Christians').[19] The name Paulicians apparently had nothing to do with their attachment to Saint Paul but came into general usage long after the sect was formed and was bestowed on them by others. It is most plausibly explained as a derivation from the *didaskalos* Paul, who led the semi-nomadic sect back to Armenia in the eighth century.[20]

But while the Paulicians thought of themselves as true Christians, the Orthodox Church and the Byzantine Empire thought otherwise. Constantine of Manalis was eventually executed for heresy on the orders of Emperor Constantine IV (AD 668–685). Historians believe it most likely he was burnt at the stake, although the Paulicians themselves put about a story that he was stoned to death. It has been suggested that this was probably 'to draw a parallel between their first martyr and the first Christian martyr Stephen'.[21]

The second Paulician *didaskalos*, who took the name Titus, was also executed for heresy, this time definitely by burning.[22]

During the eighth century the Paulicians enjoyed long periods of official tolerance, although John of Otzun, who became catholicos of Armenia in AD 717, described them as 'that most wicked sect of obscene men who are called Paulicians.'[23] What he objected to most was that they scorned the established clergy as 'idolaters' because of their 'worship of the cross.'[24] But he does not seem to have had the secular support to do anything about this.

It was not until the reign of the Byzantine Emperor Michael I (811–813) that the death penalty was reimposed for followers of the Paulician faith,[25] There then followed a period of massive imperial persecution in which, according to the official chroniclers 100,000 of the heretics were killed[26] – a scale of slaughter fully comparable with the holocaust of the Languedoc Cathars 400 years later. In the 840s, in response to the continuing persecutions, a faction of the Paulicians, including a fighting group 5,000 strong, retreated into Arab territories. By the 850s they had established their own independent mini-state based around the fortress city of Tefrice on the Byzantine frontier. It was to the court of the Paulician leader Chrysocheir at

Tefrice that Peter of Sicily came on his embassy of 869–70. Two years later Chrysocheir was killed in battle with Byzantine forces and Tefrice finally surrendered in 878.[27]

This was a setback, but certainly not the end of the Paulicians. Around 975 they were still causing enough trouble in the Byzantine Empire for the Church to insist that large numbers of them be deported from the Eastern provinces. They were sent to the Balkans, where there was already a long-established Paulician community[28] and where the *pop* Bogomil had begun to spread his own heresy only a few years previously. The Paulicians almost certainly bequeathed to the Bogomils their belief in the state of opposition of the material and spiritual realms – of the God of Evil and the God of Good. Moreover the Paulicians identified this very aspect of their belief-system as the chief factor that distinguished them from the Roman Catholic and Orthodox Churches. They told Peter of Sicily:

> We say the heavenly father is one God who has no power in this world, but who has power in the world to come, and that there is another God who made the world and who has power over the present world. The Romans confess that the heavenly father and the creator of all the world are one and the same God.[29]

This doctrine of the two opposed Gods is precisely the position of the Bogomils and the Cathars. And they also shared with the Paulicians a view of the cosmos as a battleground between good and evil with the fate of humanity as its fulcrum.[30]

In other respects, however, there was much less of a resemblance. Most prominently, although they attributed the creation of the world and all material things to the God of Evil, the Paulicians did not practice any form of asceticism, were not vegetarians, and placed no special value on chastity and abstinence. They were also men of violence who often found themselves in battle and who were widely recognised by others as formidable warriors.[31] In this sense we might regard them as an entire community of that grade of neophytes whom the Cathars called *credentes* ('believers') who were free to fight, marry and make love as they wished, to eat and to drink, and generally to live in the world and to affirm it. Consistent with this it seems that the Paulicians did not make use of any initiation ceremony and thus had no class of initiated adepts or *perfecti* as the Cathars and Bogomils did.[32]

The Praying People and the demon in the soul

Although there can be little doubt that the Paulicians were amongst the important influences on the emergence of the Bogomils, the differences between the two religions make it clear that other factors must also have been in play.

As one of these factors, and the next main link in the chain of transmission, Steven Runciman proposes a sect known as the *Messalians* (literally the 'Praying People').[33] They were Christian Gnostics[34] whose origins can be traced back to the city of Edessa in the mid-fourth century AD and who survived in coherent form until late enough in the seventh century to overlap with Constantine of Mananalis and the first Paulicians.[35] They were said to have been the keepers of a secret tradition and of secret books which Runciman presumes to have been 'heterodox Gnostic legends.'[36] He argues that the riches of this esoteric literary tradition reached the Bogomils directly from communities of Messalians who survived in the Balkans beyond the seventh century and indeed until as late as the 11th century.

Runciman sees Bogomilism as a combination of Paulician and Messalian doctrines – 'a new Christianity ... based on early Christian legend and Eastern Dualism.'[37] Probably the influence of Paulicianism came first:

> ... but as time went on the new faith developed; the heretics came into touch with the Messalians, who gave them access to all the wealth of the Orientalised Gnostic tradition ...[38] The Bogomils ... largely owed their mythology to these books that medieval Byzantium had inherited from the Christians of the first few centuries, when Christian doctrine was still imperfectly circumscribed and Gnostic tendencies were rife.[39]

Naturally in this contentious field, other scholars dispute that the Messalians ever came into contact with the Bogomils at all – on the grounds that the former had ceased to exist before the latter were founded. According to Bernard Hamilton, professor emeritus in crusading history at the University of Nottingham, it is all a matter of mislabelling:

> There is no evidence that organised Messalianism survived beyond the 7th century, even though the label continued to be used by Byzantine heresiologists to describe excesses in Orthodox monastic practice. There can therefore have been no possibility of contact between the Bogomils and a living Messalian tradition.[40]

Let's acknowledge these opposing points of view. Still the fact remains that many Orthodox churchmen of the period, highly skilled in exposing heresy, were convinced, like Runciman, that Messalianism was still alive and well in the Balkans as late as the 11th century – and thus did overlap with Bogomilism. The Bogomils themselves were often mislabelled 'Messalians', not, we would suggest, because of ignorance on the part of the heresiologists but because the Messalian and Bogomil religions were similar in many ways and do strongly suggest some form of influence of the former on the latter.

The Messalians placed great emphasis on a ritual initiation that created a class of *elect* or adepts, called the *pneumatics*, directly comparable to the Cathar *perfecti*.[41] The same term was also used by other sects of Christian Gnostics as early as the first and second centuries AD for their own initiated spiritual elites.[42] So there's a sense of the Bogomils standing at one end of the first millennium, the early Christian Gnostics standing at the other, and the Messalians standing roughly in the middle and somehow connected to both 'ends'.

Other shared characteristics add to this impression. For instance, like the Bogomils (and their offshoot the Cathars), the Messalians rejected the Old Testament and loathed the cross.[43] So too did the early Christian Gnostics.[44] The Bogomils and the Messalians regarded the world as an evil creation. So too did the Gnostics. And as part of this outlook, very similar creation stories were also told by all three groups. Indeed the Messalian version is a classic 'moderate dualist' myth of the kind the Bogomils and the Cathars favoured in their early days before becoming more absolute in their views. As such it does not propose polarised divinities of Good and Evil, one the creator of the spiritual and one of the material realm. Instead the Messalians envisaged the prior existence of a single deity, 'God the first Principle', whose domain was entirely spiritual and good and filled with light. He produced two 'Sons' – emanations – of whom the elder was Satan and the younger Christ. Pride and envy caused Satan to rebel against the Father and led to his expulsion from the good and spiritual heaven:[45]

> The material world was his creation after his Fall and as such was a wicked place.[46]

The Messalians, like the Bogomils after them, and the early Christian Gnostics before them, had a theory to explain how our souls had become trapped in matter. Though similar in general principle and outlook, these theories differ significantly from each other in terms of plot and detail. For the Bogomils, as we've seen in Chapter Three, the idea was that the souls of fallen angels had been encysted in our bodies, or that we carry within us, always seeking a way back to heaven, the spark of divine life breathed by God into the Devil's clumsy 'Adam' and his progeny. The Messalians, on the other hand, believed that every soul was possessed by a demon which bound it by force to the wicked material world. The only way to eject the demon and gain release for the imprisoned soul was through extreme asceticism sustained over a period years[47] – a regime very similar to the extensive apprenticeships and mortification of the flesh that Bogomil and Cathar neophytes underwent before they could receive the *consolamentum* and be elevated to *perfectus* grade.

The Messalians also made use of emotional and dramatic prayer (hence their name 'Praying People') to help drive out the demons.[48] However they had just one prayer in their repertoire – the *Pater Noster* ('Our Father'), also known as the Lord's Prayer.[49] Using prayer to drive out demons is not a custom that we find amongst the Bogomils and the Cathars. Nonetheless, like the Messalians, they too, used no other prayer but the *Pater Noster*. This was because it is the only prayer that the Bible attributes directly to Christ himself.

Described as 'troop of vagabond preachers',[50] the Messalians first appeared in the territory of the Eastern Roman Empire around AD 350. This was less than 40 years after Constantine the Great had extended his official protection to the Christian Church. It was just 20 years after he had forsaken Rome to establish his new capital of Constantinople on the site of the ancient Greek city of Byzantium (modern Istanbul).

With its principal bishoprics in Rome, Alexandria, Antioch and Constantinople, the recently-empowered Catholic Church was by this time flexing its muscles, and in a sense defining itself, by the heresies it persecuted. After winning state sponsorship in AD 312 it had almost immediately taken a strong authoritarian and literalist turn (literalist in the sense of interpreting the scriptures in the most literal manner possible). This, inevitably made the rather free-thinking and creative anarchy of the Christian Gnostics, who had previously been allowed to co-exist with the literalists, a target for heresy hunters. In AD 390 the Messalians were condemned and added to the Church's growing list of banned sects, which, as we will see, already included several other much longer-established Christian Gnostic groups.[51]

Mani, Messenger of Light

The teachings and philosophy of another sect are also an important part of this jigsaw puzzle. Known as *Manicheism* after its founder Mani, it was younger than some of the Christian Gnostic movements but a century older than the Messalians. It too was viciously persecuted by the Church as a 'heresy', rather than as a pagan religion. Yet there is a dispute amongst scholars as to whether Manicheism was Christian in any meaningful sense at all.[52] Certainly it was much *less* 'Christian' than the religion of the Bogomils and the Cathars, and that, as we've seen, cannot accurately be described as 'Christianity'; it was really a completely different faith built up around many of the same New Testament texts and characters.

Perhaps the confusion comes in because Mani sometimes claimed to be the 'Apostle of Christ'[53] (later also one of the titles of the Paulician *didaskaloi*), and because surviving letters sent between communities of Manicheans in North Africa show that they saw themselves as Christians.[54] It is also generally accepted that several of the strong central notions of Christianity, including the idea that there is 'a redemptive meaning to things', are found in Manicheism.[55]

On the other hand there is much in Manicheism that seems to be unmistakably *non*-Christian. For a start, it was an uncompromisingly dualistic religion in exactly the same way as the religion of the Cathars and Bogomils. It saw the human race, endlessly regenerated by the snare of reproduction, as the creation of an Evil God – an idea that we know Christianity rejects. Similarly, Manicheans made little or no use of New Testament texts. They offered worship to the Sun and the Moon as 'vessels of the Light' (in this very unlike the Cathars and the Bogomils). And despite sometimes calling himself the 'Apostle of Christ', it is notable that Mani also frequently used the broader term 'Apostle of God'.[56] He meant that he was an emissary or messenger and he placed himself as the successor to Christ at the end of a line of earlier, non-Christian, apostles.

Obviously the Church saw this as heresy. It involved Christ, but clearly devalued the unique quality of his mission by putting him on a par with the founders of well-known pagan religions. One of Mani's own surviving statements on the matter, in his *Book for King Shapur* (*circa* AD 250) makes this completely clear:

> From age to age the Apostles of God did not cease to bring here the wisdom and works of the spirit. Thus in one age their coming was into the countries of India through the Apostle that was the Buddha; into

another age, into the land of Persia through Zoroaster; into another, into the land of the West through Jesus. After that, in this last age, this revelation came down, and this prophethood arrived through myself, Mani, the Apostle of the true God, into the land of Babel.[57]

In this fragment Buddha, Zoroaster, Jesus and Mani are given as examples, not as a definitive list, of the apostles of God. In another surviving fragment Mani names two more such messengers: the Greek philosopher Plato (427–347 BC), and the Greek deity Hermes.[58] In Mani's time the latter, who we will meet again in Part II, was generally equated with Thoth, the ancient Egyptian god of wisdom.

Meetings with the Twin

Despite the extensive persecution of Manicheism by different regimes in different periods over hundreds of years, some of the details of Mani's biography, and of his claims to a sacred mission, seem to have come down to us fairly reliably.

He was born in or about AD 216 in a village called Mardinu to the south of the city of Ctesiphon near Babylon[59] – a location some 32 kilometers southeast of Baghdad in the modern state of Iraq. In Mani's time Ctesiphon enjoyed great wealth, prominence and political power within Persia as the winter capital of the king. It had served this function for the Parthian Empire that ruled from 247 BC until AD 224 (when Mani was about eight years old), and it continued to do so with renewed grandeur under the Sassanian Empire (AD 224–642) that succeeded the Parthians.

The Sassanians were decidedly national and Persian in character. Their first king, Ardeshir I (AD 224–241) moved rapidly to install the ancient Persian faith of Zoroastrianism as the official religion of the empire and gave enormous powers to its priesthood, the Magi. Living in the neighbourhood of Ctesiphon at this time, therefore, we can be sure that Mani would have been well acquainted with Zoroastrianism – although traditions that he was for some time a Magus himself are unlikely to be true.[60] Since the region was a cultural crossroads of the ancient world, a young man like Mani, deeply interested in spiritual matters, would also have been exposed here to a wide range of other potential influences – amongst them Babylonian astrology, Judaism, Buddhism from India, and the philosophy of Greece.[61]

More directly, it is known that Mani was reared amongst an obscure sect of Jewish Christians called the Elchasaitans[62] (considered to have been

Gnostics,[63] and linked by some scholars with the Essenes of Dead Sea Scrolls fame).[64] They were mystics and visionaries with strict purity laws and repetitive rituals that Mani rebelled against. But through them he was exposed to an additional vital influence on his thinking – the teachings of the Christian Gnostics.[65] Although later to be persecuted as heresy, these teachings were still in free circulation in the first half of the third century and are generally agreed to have had a great impact on the construction of Mani's own distinctively Gnostic religion.[66]

Secret texts passed down within the Elchasaitans, or within his own family, may also have played a role. In this respect it is interesting that some accounts present Mani as the adopted son of an elderly widow. The story goes that on her death she entrusted him with a precious legacy of four books of sacred knowledge – from which, critics alleged, he derived many of the teachings that he later claimed as his own.[67] The content of these books was said to have been gathered in Egypt 'in the time of the apostles' by a certain Scythianus who had learned the 'wisdom of the Egyptians.'[68] Scythianus dictated the books to his disciple Terebinthus. In due course Terebinthus brought the books to Babylonia and on his death they passed to his own disciple – the widow who would adopt Mani in her old age.[69]

Though legends say that he was a sickly child and lame in one leg,[70] it seems that Mani grew up in prosperous circumstances.[71] Later he would claim that throughout his childhood he had received revelations directly from *Ahura Mazda*, the 'Father of the Light' – the God of Goodness in the Zoroastrian faith.[72] He also experienced strange and disturbing visitations of the type normally treated today with powerful anti-psychotic drugs. In one surviving text (the *Cologne Mani-Codex*) he tells us how he was:

> ... guarded by the might of the Light-angels and the exceedingly strong powers. who had a command from Jesus the Splendour for my safekeeping ...[73] They nourished me with visions and signs which they made known to me, slight and quite brief, as far as I was able. For sometimes like a flash of lightening he came ...[74]

The being who sometimes came to Mani like a 'flash of lightening' was an angel – one he regarded as a manifestation of his own higher identity and referred to variously as his 'Light-Self' and as *al-Taum*, 'the Twin'.[75] When Mani was 12 years old the Twin appeared to him in a vision and informed him that he was to be responsible for transmitting a great teaching to mankind. In order to do this, he would have to leave the Elchasaitans at some time in the future. Thereafter the young Mani lived a quiet and studious life, out of the limelight, gathering knowledge in secret, tutored by divine revelations and by his angel:

> With the greatest possible ingenuity and skill I went about in that Law [of the Elchasaitans], preserving my hope in my heart; no one perceived who it was that was with me, and I myself revealed nothing to anyone during that great period of time. But neither did I, like them, keep the fleshly custom ... I revealed nothing of what happened, or of what will happen, nor what it is that I knew, or what it is that I had received ...[76]

It was probably during this same period of learning that Mani honed the skills as a painter, which traditions say he later used to illustrate his teachings, and acquired the knowledge of astronomy and mathematics for which he would also be renowned.[77]

When Mani reached the age of 24, the Twin appeared to him and announced:

> The time has now come for thee to manifest thyself publicly and to proclaim thy doctrine aloud.[78]

Next, says Mani, the Twin:

> ... delivered, separated and pulled me away from the midst of that Law in which I was reared. In this way he called, chose, drew, and severed me from their midst, drawing me to the divine side.[79]

He also initiated Mani into a *gnosis*:

> Concerning me, who I am, and who my inseparable Twin is ... And who my Father on high is; or in what way, severed from him, I was sent out according to his purpose; and what sort of commission and counsel he has given me before I clothed myself in this instrument [the body], and before I was led astray in this detestable flesh ... Moreover, concerning my soul, which exists as the soul of all the worlds, both what it itself is and how it came to be. Beside these he revealed to me the boundless heights and the unfathomable depths;[80] he revealed mysteries hidden to the world which are not permitted for anyone to see or hear ...[81] He showed me all.[82]

THE MASTER GAME

Mani and the Magi

It was at this point, around AD 240, that Mani – a sleeper at last awakened – began his preaching mission.[83] What he was preaching was distinctly *not* Zoroastrianism, and Ardeshir I, champion of the Zoroastrian faith as the official religion of Persia, was still on the throne. Mani seems to have fallen foul of the Magi almost immediately and to have been forced into exile.[84] He travelled to India, by all accounts propagating his teaching with great success there,[85] and returned via the Persian Gulf in 241, the year of Ardeshir's death. Somehow Mani managed to convert Firuz, Ardeshir's youngest son and, through him, obtained a personal audience with the eldest son Shapur – who shortly afterwards succeeded to the throne as King Shapur I.[86] At the coronation Mani was permitted to come forward to proclaim his own spiritual message – an unprecedented honour.[87] And on either 21 March 242 or 9 April 243 (the date is disputed by historians) Shapuhr issued a letter authorising Mani to preach as he wished and protecting him throughout the Persian Empire.[88]

Thereafter, freed of all obstructions, Manicheism won converts at a phenomenal rate causing intense resentment and jealousy amongst the Zoroastrian priesthood. There was a backlash and later in Shapur's reign it seems that the Magi persuaded the king to exile Mani a second time.[89] But in 272, following Shapur's death, Mani returned to Persia and was welcomed by the latest successor to the throne, King Hormuzd, who once again extended royal favour to him.[90]

Hormuzhd's reign lasted barely a year and Bahram I, who succeeded to the throne in 273, was a strong supporter of the old Zoroastrian faith. He reversed the policy of tolerance towards Manicheism and began to persecute its leaders and followers. In 276 his officers arrested Mani at Gundeshapur in southwestern Persia. The self-styled 'Apostle of God' was then subjected to four days of Inquisition-style interrogation by the Magi, and declared to be *zandic* – a 'heretic'. A month of imprisonment in heavy chains followed after which he was flayed alive and then decapitated. His head was impaled on the city gate, from which his skin, stuffed with straw, was also suspended; what remained of his body was thrown to the dogs.[91]

No doubt the level of brutality in his execution was commensurate with the level of the threat that the Magi saw in Mani's new religion which was everywhere overtaking them. And just as was the case with the destruction of Catharism by the Roman Catholic Church a thousand years later, a determined attempt was also made by the Zoroastrians to wipe out Manicheism completely.[92]

They did not succeed. Before his imprisonment and execution Mani had already sent out his 12 disciples, and hosts of followers, to all the corners of the known world.[93] In addition the continuing persecutions by the Zoroastrian state after 276 prompted a large-scale migration of Manichean communities. Some travelled deep into China – where Mani's religion would survive in remote enclaves until as late as the 16th century. Others infiltrated Eastern parts of the Roman Empire, the Roman colonies in North Africa, and eventually all the immense territories under Rome's control as far west as Britain.

Though at times violently opposed by Rome (even before its conversion to Christianity) Manicheism won immense popularity throughout the empire and was particularly well represented in its North African colonies. It was in North Africa that it acquired its most famous acolyte, Augustine – later Saint Augustine of Hippo. Born in AD 354, the son of a pagan father and a Christian mother, he became a Manichean *auditor* or *hearer* in AD 377 – equivalent to joining the Cathar class of *credente*. He held to the Manichean faith for nine years then abandoned it in 386 and was baptized as a Christian in 387. He returned to North Africa where he formed a religious community and was appointed bishop of Hippo in 396. He lived to see the fall of Rome to the Vandals in 410. When he died in 430 Vandal forces had crossed the Mediterranean and were besieging Hippo itself.[94]

Like many converts Augustine zealously detestated his former faith. During his long and influential career as one of the great doctors of the Church he wrote extensively condemning Manicheism and the Manicheans. His anti-Manichean tracts survived the ages and played an important part in shaping the attitudes of medieval Roman Catholics to the Cathar heresy. As we saw in Chapter Two Catharism was frequently identified in the 12th and 13th centuries as a resurgence of the *same* Manicheism that Augustine had censured in the fourth century – a conclusion that modern scholars reject. Nevertheless the Cathar and Manichean religions were, in our view, similar enough in their essentials to make the medieval identification understandable and worth further consideration.

The Cosmos according to Mani

One of the notions upon which Manicheism is founded is that there existed from the beginning of time 'two gods, uncreated and eternal and everlastingly opposed to each other.'[95] One is the God of Evil and Darkness, the other the God of Good and the Light.[96] The realm of Light was the uppermost and was 'without bounds in height and on each side.' The realm of Darkness lay below it similarly boundless in depth and on each side.[97] For untold ages neither was aware of the other's existence, but in the bowels of the Darkness was Satan, with his 'disorderly, anarchical, restless brood' of demonic powers.[98] There was constant agitation, chaos and turmoil, as in the heart of a black thunderstorm, and at some point the Prince of Darkness rose up through the abyss, perceived the Light from the upper world and conceived a hatred for it. Returning to the depths he prepared his forces:

> **Then again springing upwards, he invaded the realms of Light with the intention of there spreading calamity and destruction.[99]**

Like the later Cathars and Bogomils Mani saw the human body as part of the evil creation within which sparks of the Light had been imprisoned. Like the Cathars and the Bogomils he taught that sexual reproduction and reincarnation are the mechanisms by which the cycle of imprisonment is perpetuated. And also like the Cathars and Bogomils he believed that by abstinence and prayer this imprisoned Light could gradually be released, but that we must pass through many incarnations, and much pain, before that would happen.[100]

Such resemblances to the religion of the medieval dualists become all the clearer when we realise, as Yuri Stoyanov confirms, that Light and Darkness in Manichean cosmology are metaphors for spirit and matter.[101] It was the fusion of these two contrary principles, at the beginning of the present cycle of time, which caused the imprisonment and suffering of the soul in the first place.[102] The details of exactly *how* the imprisonment was achieved – how fragments of the Light came to be trapped in Darkness, how Good ended up mixed with Evil, how souls were enwrapped in matter – may have more to do with the inspiration of individual storytellers than anything else. We know that this was a tradition that made broad use of colourful symbols, myths and parables as teaching aids. But the point, in the final analysis, is that the medieval dualists of Europe, exactly like the Manicheans of Persia centuries earlier, envisaged man as a 'mixed' creature who must fight a constant war within himself in order to subdue his baser elements, and to perfect and liberate his soul.

It was to get this point across that the Cathars and Bogomils told stories of angels who had fallen downwards from the pure spiritual realm of heaven to the impure material realm of earth. In the parallel Manichean myth the Prince of Darkness with his demons rushed upwards out of the abyss to attack and destroy the Light. So forceful and impetuous was this onslaught that the Evil One, wielding the 'malign' powers of Smoke, Fire, Wind, Water and Darkness as his weapons, broke through the defences and encroached upon the Light. The Father of Light defended his realm by evoking a proxy – the 'Primal Man' – and arming him with the 'luminous' powers of Air, Wind, Light, Water and Fire. Battle was joined, Satan was victorious, the Primal Man lay in a deathlike trance, and elements of the luminous powers that he had been armed with were now engulfed or 'eaten' by the forces of darkness.[103]

Next the Father of Light created further emanations or proxies – amongst them the 'Living Spirit', identified with the pre-Zoroastrian Iranian god *Mithra*, and a figure called the 'Great Architect'.[104] Together they revived and rescued the Primal Man and began the work of recovering for the Light the luminous powers that had been consumed by the forces of Darkness – a task described as saving the 'Living Soul' from the 'burning house' of matter.[105]

The diabolical counter-attack against the works of the Living Spirit and the Great Architect involved the creation of Adam and Eve 'to fortify', as Stoyanov puts it, 'the imprisonment of the Light elements through the lust and reproduction of the human species.' But the realm of Light sent a saviour to Adam who made him aware of the Light existing within himself – i.e. his immortal soul – and caused him to rebel against the Evil One who had fashioned his body. Ever since the human race has 'remained the principal battleground between the forces of Light and Darkness.'[106]

The saviour sent to Adam is called 'Jesus the Splendour' in the Manichean texts.[107] As time passes other saviours are sent, each of them to renew the *gnosis* needed to awaken man to his true condition. Earlier we listed some of the household names amongst these saviours – Zoroaster, Hermes, Plato, Buddha, Jesus Christ, and last but not least Mani. Other lists echo the spread of Manicheism in Hebraic cultures and feature Seth, Enoch (like Hermes frequently identified with the ancient Egyptian wisdom god Thoth), Noah, Abraham, and again Mani.[108] Similarly the eastwards expansion of Manicheism is reflected in other formulations that refer to Mani as the Buddha of Light or as a reincarnation of Lao-Tsu, the founder of Taoism.[109]

In all cases and in all lists Mani is extolled as the 'Seal of the Prophets'.[110] It is he who brings the final message, the final revelation and the final *gnosis* through which mankind is to complete the great work of freeing the last elements of Light from the prison of Darkness. This work, as described, is almost alchemical in character – an intricate, gradual process of distillation down the ages, incarnation after incarnation, channelling the Light away from the Dark, purifying the soul from its contamination with matter. The denouement is our realisation that the physical earth on which we live was brought into existence as the theatre or laboratory in which this process of endless, painstaking refinement could unfold – *and for no other purpose.*[111] Finally, using all the Light thus reclaimed, the Great Architect and the Living Spirit, assisted by the souls of the Manichean *elect*, are to construct a 'New Paradise' and a spiritual earth to replace the dark, leaden husk of the old material creation that will fall away at the completion of the project.[112]

If it looks like a duck, swims like a duck, and quacks like a duck … then it probably is a duck …

Although the Manicheans, Bogomils and Cathars told different stories about the human predicament, we suggest that closer examination shows that they share a deep and abiding theme. At the heart of it all, for every *credente* and *perfectus*, for every *hearer* and *elect*, was a desire to live in the world in such a way as to minimise spiritual pollution and to improve, strengthen, purify and ultimately (after great struggle) liberate the soul. In all cases this involved accepting and following a system and working within a structure, and these were remarkably the same from the early days of Manicheism in the third century AD to the final crushing of medieval dualism in Europe more than 1,000 years later.

Just like the Bogomil and the Cathar Churches, the Manichean Church was divided into two principal categories. There were the ordinary the rank and file adherents who could marry, have children, own property, eat meat and drink wine. And there was a small highly-committed elite of celibate teetotal vegetarians who lived in personal poverty and renounced all the material pleasures of life.[113] The rank and file were known as the *hearers* and the elite as the *elect* – concepts identical in all respects to the *credentes* and *perfecti* of the medieval dualists. Indeed amongst the Manicheans the term *perfecti* was used interchangeably with *elect*.[114]

Like the Cathar and Bogomil *perfecti* the Manichean *elect* could be men or women and always travelled in adept-disciple pairs. Also like the *perfecti*, the *elect* passed through a strict process of initiation culminating in a ceremony comparable to the *consolamentum*. Following this initiation they were considered to be 'full of the Light' and thenceforward must do nothing to contaminate their inner light with the dark of earthly things.[115]

For the Manichean *elect* that included doing no agricultural work and not even such a simple task as breaking bread. It involved leading a wandering, penniless existence, possessing only 'food for a day and clothes for the year', completely dependent upon the charity of the *hearers* who, by joining the Manichean Church, took on an obligation to care for the *elect*.[116] Although the Cathar and Bogomil *perfecti* did break bread for themselves, they too led wandering, penniless lives and were dependent on the charity of the *credentes* who likewise had a duty to care for them. Moreover even Bernard Hamilton, though not normally a fan of the 'continuing tradition', has to admit that:

> The Manicheans had required their *elect* to observe an ascetic
> rule of life, and their reasons for doing so were identical to those of
> the Bogomils, springing from a conviction that the material creation
> was evil.[117]

Mani taught that messengers like Zoroaster, Buddha, and Jesus – to whose line he also claimed to belong – had been sent to earth out of sympathy for mankind, to remove the clouds of ignorance from our minds, to teach us Truth, and to rescue the Light in us (i.e. our shining souls) from Darkness and Evil.[118] Again these are themes that are entirely familiar from the dualism of the Cathars and the Bogomils.

The reader will recall that the Cathars and Bogomils, believing Jesus to have been a spiritual emanation of the Good God, could not accept that he had ever been born in the flesh and therefore concluded that he must have been an apparition sent down directly from the heavenly realms. The identical idea was voiced by Mani who preached, centuries earlier, that Jesus was not born of woman but came forth from the Father of Light and descended from heaven in the form of a man aged about 30. The body in which he appeared was an illusion and so, accordingly, was his Crucifixion.[119] In one Manichean text he even appears afterwards to his disciple John who is grief-stricken at the supposed death of his master and informs him that the Crucifixion was a spectacle, a phantasmagoria, in short a kind of miracle play performed to impress the masses.[120]

Despite their conviction that material life is evil the Cathars, Bogomils and Manicheans all showed great respect for life and opposed causing pain or suffering of any kind to fellow creatures whether human or animal.[121] All believed in reincarnation.[122] All forbade the use of images and worshipped only through prayers and hymns.[123] We know that the Cathars and the

Bogomils looked with horror on the Old Testament and regarded its God, Jehovah, as the Devil. So too did the Manicheans[124] and Mani himself had declared:

> It is the Prince of Darkness who spoke with Moses, the Jews and their priest. Thus the Christians, the Jews, and the Pagans are involved in the same error when they worship this god. For he led them astray in the lusts that he taught them, since he was not the God of Truth.[125]

Connecting the Cathars to the first century AD

Until the early 20th century scholars were obliged to rely almost exclusively on the works of the persecutors of Manicheism in order to reconstruct the 'lost' Manichean religion that those very persecutors had destroyed. But intact ancient Manichean texts discovered in the Far East in the 1920s and in Egypt in the 1970s have added greatly to our store of knowledge. In consequence it is now generally accepted that Christian Gnosticism, hitherto allocated a relatively minor role in the intellectual parentage of Manicheism, may in fact have been the single most decisive influence on Mani's thinking. H. J. W. Drijvers goes so far as to suggest that even the term 'Christian Gnosticism' is misleading:

> It has usually been assumed that the Christian elements in Manicheism reached Mani through a Gnostic filter ... It is rather more in agreement with the historical situation and development during the third century ... to assume that Mani and Manicheism heavily drew upon the whole of Christian tradition and literature extant in that time without any restriction to a supposedly Gnostic strain.[126]

In other words if Manicheism as it is now understood reveals an overwhelming influence from Gnostic Christianity then this is likely to be because the Christianity of Mani's time was in fact overwhelmingly Gnostic – a controversial conclusion that is nevertheless supported by much recent scholarship. In 1945 a great hoard of hitherto unknown Gnostic texts from the early centuries of the Christian era was found at Nag Hammadi in Upper Egypt. Since the translation and eventual publication of these texts in 1977 it has become apparent that Christianity's relationship with Gnosticism goes back to the very beginnings of the Christian cult in the first century AD. Likewise it is now obvious, and widely accepted, that 'Christian Gnosticism' was not some weird offshoot from the 'mainstream' of Christianity. On the contrary it was part of the mainstream – perhaps even the major part as we will see in the next chapter.

And then something happened. From the beginning of the fourth century AD, as it acquired state power, the Church undertook a radical change of direction. The freethinking and sometimes anarchical approach of the Gnostics began to be frowned upon, their allegorical interpretations of the scriptures were dropped in favour of literal ones, and persecutions for heresy began almost immediately. Could it possibly be true, as the Cathars always claimed, that this was the time when the authentic church of Christianity was forced underground and the imposter Church of Rome was put in its place? And the corollary: could it be true that the authentic church – persecuted, outlawed, oppressed – had nevertheless somehow managed to survive from the fourth century until its doctrines reappeared again 600 years later with the Bogomils?

It seems like a long shot. Nonetheless we've shown that a viable chain of transmission exists connecting the central ideas behind the Cathar and Bogomil religions to the ideas of Mani in the third century. And if the primary influence on Mani was Christian Gnosticism, as the scholars now agree, then it is to the Gnostics we should look for the final links in the chain of the 'Great Heresy'.

CHAPTER FIVE

KNOWLEDGE OF
THE TRUE NATURE
OF THINGS

I shall use the term Gnosticism to indicate the ideas or coherent systems
that are characterised by an absolutely negative view of the visible world
and its creator and the assumption of a divine spark in man, his inner
self, which had become enclosed within the material body as the result
of a tragic event in the precosmic world, from which it can only escape to
its divine origin by means of the saving Gnosis. These ideas are found in
most of the original Gnostic writings that have survived, for the greater
part in the Nag Hammadi Library ...

Professor Roelof van den Broek, editor of

Gnosis and Hermeticism From Antiquity to Modern Times

There is no easy sound-bite description of what Gnosticism was,
or is. As we've already had reason to note several times, the
Gnostic tradition was one in which special emphasis was placed
on individual revelation and self-expression. In consequence, though it is
true that a number of underlying themes, and even certainties, were shared
by all Gnostic sects, there was also a rich and confusing proliferation of
differences amongst them. Sects typically developed around the teachings of
inspired men – the most famous names from the first and second centuries
AD include Simon Magus, Marcion, Basilides and Valentinus. Depending on
the precise nature of the revelation of the founder, each sect then added its
own speculations, metaphors and teaching-myths, sometimes even complete
cosmological systems, to the vast and eclectic body of ideas and behaviour
already loosely categorised as 'Gnosticism'.

This background state of intellectual anarchy, coupled with the luxuriant multiplication of 'systems' within Gnosticism, make the subject a daunting one. But the matter is even further complicated by the determined persecutions inflicted on the Gnostics by the Christian Church between the fourth and the sixth centuries AD.[1] As well as the holocausts of countless individuals, who were prepared to die terrible deaths rather than relinquish their faith, these persecutions resulted in the collection and burning of huge numbers of Gnostic texts. In this way one of the precious 'hard disks', on which was stored a vibrant portion of the intellectual and spiritual heritage of mankind, went up literally in smoke, leaving virtually nothing behind for future generations to ponder over. The thoughts on the human condition of inspired mystics and great philosophers, their journeys into the enigma of death, the liberating *gnosis* that they believed they had discovered of the true nature and purpose of our existence – all this seemed to have been lost. For fifteen centuries those few scholars who still had any interest in learning about this smashed and apparently forgotten religion were obliged to depend for their knowledge almost exclusively on the works of those responsible for smashing it in the first place. The heresy hunters would frequently quote passages from suppressed Gnostic works, or report the content of those works in some detail, in order to preach against and attempt to refute them. But relying on such one-sided material, even – or perhaps especially – in the choice of original texts quoted, was almost bound to produce a very one-sided understanding of Gnosticism. A roughly comparable exercise would be trying to build-up an accurate picture of Judaism from books written by Nazi propagandists.

In the case of the latter we can ignore the Nazi trash because Judaism, unlike Gnosticism, is still a living religion and can speak for itself. But there has been some good fortune too in the case of Gnosticism. The vast majority of its scriptures were destroyed in the pogroms that the Christians unleashed. But towards the end of the fourth century AD an unknown group of heretics in Upper Egypt took the precaution of assembling a 'time-capsule' containing a substantial collection of banned Gnostic texts. Possession of such texts, if detected, was extremely dangerous, so the 'capsule' – actually a large earthenware jar – was buried in the ground, by the side of a great boulder, at the foot of cliffs overlooking the ever-flowing Nile.

Perhaps the owners hoped that things might improve and that they would eventually be able to return to collect their library. But they never did. It's very likely that their heresy was detected and they were killed. During the last two decades of the fourth century the dogmatic faction of Christianity that had converted Emperor Constantine years before was flexing its muscles under the full protection of the Roman state. With tacit support from the local authorities, and sometimes with direct military assistance,[2] hysterical mobs of religious fanatics and unkempt monks were on the loose in Egypt, spreading fear wherever they went.[3] They vandalised temples that had stood for thousands of years in homage to the gods. They defaced ancient inscriptions. They murdered priests and philosophers. It was under their pressure that the sublime religion of ancient Egypt breathed its last. However it was not 'pagans' that the Christian terrorists reserved their worst excesses for. Much higher priority, and the greatest violence, was focussed on fellow Christians – heretics of the numerous Christian Gnostic sects that had been developing and multiplying in Egypt since the first century.[4]

It would have been the members of one such sect who buried the 'time-capsule' beside the boulder at the foot of the cliffs. There it was to remain intact and undisturbed for nearly 1600 years while the life of Egypt, slowly changing, went on around it.

The Nag Hammadi library: time capsule or time bomb?

In December 1945, near the modern town of Nag Hammadi in Upper Egypt, a local farmer named Muhammad Ali was clearing land at the edge of a field owned by his family. By chance he exposed a large intact earthenware jar that had obviously been purposefully buried in an upright position by the side of a boulder. When he broke the jar open out spilled thirteen leather-bound papyrus books and a large number of loose papyrus leaves. He brought the complete haul of priceless knowledge about a long lost religion to his home where his mother put much of the loose-leaf material to use as kindling. But the books – *codices* is the correct term – survived and eventually found their way onto the black market in Egypt. Through good detective work the government's antiquities service succeeded in buying one and confiscating ten and a half of the thirteen codices. A large part of another was smuggled out of Egypt and offered for sale in the US. Professor Gilles Quispel, an expert on Gnosticism at Utrecht University was quickly able to certify to its importance and the codex was rescued.

As Professor Quispel made a provisional translation of the text he found to his astonishment that it seemed to be a Christian gospel but one previously unknown to him that did not appear anywhere in the New Testament. Its title was the *Gospel Of Thomas* and it claimed to contain secret words spoken by Jesus to his 'twin' – one Judas Thomas. The New Testament says nothing about Jesus having a twin.[5]

Despite the pages burnt by Muhammad Ali's mother a total of 52 separate texts survived in the approximately twelve and a half salvaged codices. Direct scientific tests on the papyrus used in their bindings, as well as linguistic analysis of the Coptic script in which they are written, indicates that the codices were manufactured between AD 350 and 400.[6] The age of their content is another matter since the texts themselves are translations into Coptic, the vernacular of Egypt in the early Christian age, of somewhat older source texts originally written in Greek. Scholars are in general agreement that the majority of these were composed or compiled between AD 120 and 150.[7] But it has been persuasively argued that the *Gospel Of Thomas*, at least, is an exception to this rule. Professor Helmut Koester of Harvard University has proposed that this heretical gospel includes some content that may possibly be:

> ... as early as the second half of the first century [AD 50–100] – as early, or earlier than Matthew, Mark, Luke and John.[8]

The date normally ascribed to the four canonical Gospels of the New Testament is in the range of AD 60–110.[9] But in the case of *Thomas* we're dealing with a banned text claiming to be a genuine Christian gospel that may also be genuinely older – i.e. nearer in time to Christ – than any of the canonical Gospels. This has to raise disturbing questions about the canonical Gospels themselves. How canonical are they really? How can we be sure that they contain the truth, the whole truth and nothing but the truth about Christ and the Christic phenomenon? The existence of this 'elder' gospel in the Nag Hammadi collection suggests that Matthew, Mark, Luke and John may have been part of a much wider literature that was at some point 'edited out' of the New Testament. That impression is enhanced by the inclusion of several other heretical gospels amongst the 52 Nag Hammadi texts – the *Gospel of Philip*, the *Gospel of Truth* and the *Gospel to the Egyptians*. Were there others still that Muhammad Ali's mother burnt? Or that didn't make it into the precious Nag Hammadi time capsule and were erased from history by the heresy hunters?

The Organisation (1): hints of a Gnostic secret society

There is much more that is disturbing about the texts of the Nag Hammadi library. Remember that they were composed mainly between the first and third centuries AD, originally in Greek, translated into Coptic some time later, and finally concealed during the late fourth century. We've noted

THE MASTER GAME

that this was a time when the newly Christianised empire of Rome was beginning to turn all its resources against Christian heretics – particularly, and most savagely, against the Gnostics. It is intriguing, therefore, that several of the Nag Hammadi documents make allusions to the existence of something very much like a secret society, usually referred to as the 'Organisation'.[10] Part of its mission, which we will return to in later chapters, is to build monuments 'as a representation of the spiritual places' (i.e. the stars).[11] It is also to use every means possible, including guile and stealth, to protect the sacred knowledge of Gnosticism and to oppose the universal forces of darkness and ignorance that are said to have:

> Steered the people who followed them into great troubles, by leading them astray with many deceptions. They became old without having enjoyment. They died not having found truth and without knowing the God of Truth. And thus the whole creation became enslaved forever from the foundations of the world until now.[12]

The Gnostic religion revealed by the Nag Hammadi texts is unambiguously dualistic. It starkly envisages two potent spiritual forces at work in the fullness of all existence: the God of Light, Love and Goodness, and the God of Darkness, Hate and Evil. As with the Bogomils and the Cathars a millennium later, the Gnostics believed that it was the latter – the God of Evil – who had constructed the material universe and created human bodies. Our souls, however, were from the spiritual realm of the God of Good and yearned to return there. A primary purpose of the God of Evil was to frustrate this desire and keep these lost souls imprisoned forever on the earth – to 'make them drink the water of forgetfulness ... in order that they might not know from whence they came.'[13] The evil powers worked to anaesthetise intelligence and spread the cancer of 'mind blindness'[14] because:

> Ignorance is the mother of all evil ... Ignorance is a slave. Knowledge is freedom.[15]

By contrast the Nag Hammadi texts make it clear that the 'Organisation' serves the spiritual forces of Light. Its sacred purpose is to free human beings from their state of enslavement by initiating them into the cult of knowledge. There could hardly be a more important or more urgent task: in the Gnostic view mankind is the focus, or fulcrum, of a cosmic struggle; individual choices for evil, arising out of ignorance, therefore have ramifications far beyond the merely material and mortal and human plane.[16] For these reasons the Gnostics said 'Our struggle is not against flesh and blood, but against the world rulers of this darkness and the spirits of wickedness.'[17]

The public craftsman

In Alexandria, one of their prime centres, the Gnostics lived in close contact with the last vestiges of the ancient Egyptian religion, and also co-existed with Judaism and early Christianity. They honoured Christ. And in precisely the same way as the later Cathars and Bogomils (as well as the Manicheans and Paulicians) they did not believe him to have been born in the flesh but favoured the apparition or 'phantasm' theory.

Evidence from Alexandria suggests that the Gnostic communities there during the first three centuries after Christ also honoured Osiris, the ancient Egyptian god of rebirth,[18] 'who stands before darkness as a guardian of the Light'.[19] This was not a cult shared by any of the other post-Christian dualist groups.

On the other hand – once again like the Manicheans, Messalians, Paulicians, Cathars and Bogomils – the Gnostics saw Jehovah, the Old Testament God of the Jews and Christians, as a dark force, indeed as one of the 'world rulers of darkness'. He was to them the evil *demiurge* – a Greek term, somewhat derogatory, that means, literally, 'public craftsman'.[20] In other words he was a low-class sub-deity who had created the earth as his personal fief (rather like an odd-job man with a hobby), placed the human race upon it to worship and adore him, and deluded the poor creatures into believing that he was the only God in existence. His sole purpose for us, therefore, was to keep us enchained in spiritual ignorance and darkness for all eternity and enmesh us in acts of evil that would make us truly his forever. For this reason the account given in the Nag Hammadi texts of the 'temptation' of Adam and Eve in the Garden of Eden depicts the serpent not as the villain of the piece, as the Old Testament book of Genesis portrays him, but rather as the hero and true benefactor of mankind:

'What did God say to you?' the Serpent asked Eve. 'Was it "Do not eat from the tree of knowledge" [*gnosis*]'?

She replied: 'He said, "Not only do not eat from it, but do not touch it lest you die".' The serpent reassured her, saying, 'Do not be afraid.

With death you shall not die; for it was out of jealousy that he said this to you. Rather your eyes shall open and you shall come to be like gods, recognising evil and good.'[21]

After Adam and Eve had eaten of the tree of knowledge, the Gnostics taught that they experienced enlightenment, awoke to their own luminous nature and could distinguish good from evil, just as the serpent had promised. Seeing their intellectual and spiritual transformation the demiurge was jealous and roused his demonic companions:

'Behold, Adam! He has come to be like one of us, so that he knows the difference between the light and the darkness. Now perhaps he also will come to the tree of life and eat from it and become immortal. Come let us expel him from Paradise down to the land from which he was taken, so that henceforth he might not be able to recognise anything better.'

And so they expelled Adam from Paradise, along with his wife.[22]

What stands out in this Gnostic Genesis story is the way in which Adam and Eve are expelled from 'Paradise' *down* to the 'land' – where henceforth they are to live in ignorance of their true potential. The underlying concept of a descent from a spiritual paradise into a fleshly and material world is extremely close to the Bogomil and Cathar notion of angels falling from heaven to earth to inhabit human bodies. In both cases the predicament of the soul is the same – trapped in matter, forgetful of its true nature, unmindful of its divine potential, deluded by the wiles of an Evil God, and carried in a frame (the body) that is subject to every whim of that supernatural monster.

The Gnostic texts continue with their version of the book of Genesis telling the story of human history on earth after the 'Fall'. Time passes and we read how the descendants of Adam and Eve achieved a high state of development, manipulating the physical world with clever machines and devices and beginning to engage in profound spiritual inquiries. Out of jealousy the demiurge intervenes again to diminish human potential, calling out to his demonic powers: 'Come, let us cause a deluge with our hands and obliterate all flesh, from man to beast.'[23]

According to the Gnostics, the Flood was not inflicted to punish evil – as the Old Testament falsely informs us – but to punish humanity for having risen so high and 'to take the light' that was growing amongst men.[24] The devastation of the Flood all but achieved this objective. Although there were survivors, they were thrown:

> ... into great distraction and into a life of toil, so that mankind might be occupied by worldly affairs, and might not have the opportunity of being devoted to the holy spirit.[25]

But fortunately there were a few amongst our ancestors who still possessed the old knowledge, and who were determined to pass it down for the benefit of future generations, for as long as necessary, wherever possible, until such a time as a general awakening might occur again.[26]

The 'Organisation' (2): A reawakening in the 10th century?

We could not help wondering how the mysterious 'Organisation' spoken of in the Nag Hammadi texts would have reacted to the persecutions being unleashed on Gnosticism when the texts were sealed away near the end of the fourth century AD. Might its members not have been inclined to see themselves in the same mythical framework as the Flood survivors of the Gnostic creation legends? Of course they were not dealing this time with a literal 'flood' sent by the diabolical God of the Old Testament to steal the light of mankind. But from the Gnostic point of view what they confronted was at least equally dangerous – the investigations of the heresy hunters, the random violence of Christian mobs, the burnings of books and people.

The Nag Hammadi texts invite us to consider the possibility that a secret society, purposefully set up to secure and preserve Gnostic teachings through periods of difficulty, had been in existence at least between the first and third centuries AD (when the texts were composed). If such an 'Organisation' still remained active until the time when the texts were buried then there is every possibility that it could have survived the holocausts of the fourth to the sixth centuries. Even without such obvious shelters and vectors as the Messalians and the Manicheans, it would not have been too difficult for a small and dedicated sect of heretics to have maintained a clandestine existence and to have continued to recruit new members through the Dark Ages between the sixth and the tenth centuries. There is no particular reason, if it was discrete, why it should have attracted much attention or ever been recognised for what it was. There were many remote religious communities of hermits or monks that could have provided it with suitable camouflage until such a time as it chose to step out of the shadows again.

And what better or more auspicious time for Gnosticism to step out of the shadows and make another bid to establish a world religion than the final century of the first millennium? This was precisely the moment – somewhere between AD 920–970 as we saw in Chapter Three – that the heresiarch who called himself Bogomil, 'Beloved of God', began to preach so persuasively in Bulgaria. We know already that the Church he founded had ambitions to achieve a general awakening. We've seen how its influence spread with great rapidity and success, first in territories under the spiritual hegemony of the Eastern Orthodox Church, and later in areas such as northern Italy and Occitania that were under the control of the Roman Catholic Church.

On both fronts the absolute dominance of what was by then thought to be established Christianity was challenged with a doctrine in many respects identical to that of the early Christian Gnostics.

And on both fronts the challenger claimed to be the original church of Christ whose rightful place had been usurped by the incumbent.

Gnostics, Bogomils and Cathars: much in common (1)

Gnosticism is thought by many scholars to have been a late pre-Christian philosophical religion that insinuated itself like a virus into early Christianity and attempted to transform it into a vehicle for propagating its own ideas – hence 'Christian Gnosticism'. On the same evidence that they offer, however, it is equally possible to argue that the Christian cult was Gnostic in origin but was later hijacked by a group of hard-headed scriptural literalists who turned it to their own ends. Either way most authorities point to Palestine in the first century BC as the birthplace of Gnosticism; from there, they say, it spread rapidly to Alexandria which was to become the main centre for its subsequent expansion.[27]

During that epoch, though they had very different backgrounds, Palestine and Alexandria shared the common Hellenistic culture that had prevailed throughout the Mediterranean, Mesopotamia and Iran since the conquests of Alexander the Great in the fourth century BC. This had been – and indeed continued for some time to be – a period of extraordinary vivacity, intellectual endeavour, creativity, rationality and intense spirituality. It brought together in one gigantic Hellenistic melting pot the priests of ancient Egypt, the dualist Magi of Iran, initiates of the mysteries of Mithras, Platonic philosophers from Greece, Jewish mystics, Buddhist missionaries and a host of other influences from near and far. It was somewhere in that 'confused but thrilling encounter,' suggests historian Joscelyn Godwin, that 'Gnosticism was born, the religion of Gnosis – knowledge of the true nature of things.'[28]

There are certain fundamental elements of Gnosticism. Of these the most important is the notion that there exists an entirely spiritual, light-filled realm that is ruled by a benevolent and loving 'Good God', but that the material realm in which we live is the creation of an 'Evil God'. As we've seen, the exploits of Jehovah in the Old Testament served the Gnostics very well as illustrations of this idea during the first and second centuries AD. He had created the world, the Bible said, and his actions were also almost invariably wicked, mean-spirited, jealous, violent and cruel – exactly what one would expect of an Evil God. It cannot be an accident that we find the identical usage of Jehovah in identical contexts for identical purposes by the Cathars and Bogomils between the 10th and 14th centuries.

Another hint that these groups at opposite ends of the first millennium must have been closely linked comes when we remember that all of them believed our souls to have been created by the Good God and to belong in the good realm while our bodies were part of the evil material creation. Gnostics, Cathars and Bogomils all likewise regarded the soul as a *prisoner* in the demonic material world where it was in constant danger of being dragged ever deeper and trapped ever more firmly. All three of them offered it a way of escape (from what would otherwise be eternal confinement) by means of initiation into their system and acquisition of the *gnosis* that they had to teach.

In all three cases this *gnosis* appears to have involved an absolutely convincing and probably instantaneous insight into the miserable situation of the soul, the true nature of matter, and the escape route that Gnosticism offered. In all three cases Christ was seen not as a redeemer (who died to expiate our sins) but as an emanation of the divine who had descended to open men's eyes to their true predicament. Last but not least, although all three groups treated the advent of Christ as a cosmic event of enormous importance, all three also believed that he had never incarnated in the flesh, that his body was an apparition, and that his Crucifixion was therefore an illusion.

Gnostics, Bogomils and Cathars: much in common (2)

The Gnostic religion of the first four centuries of the first millennium, and the Bogomil and Cathar religions of the first four centuries of the second millennium, shared many other intimate details. We've already seen in Chapter Three how the *consolamentum* ritual of the latter, which raised the candidate from the status of *credente* to the status of *perfectus*, was essentially identical to the ritual of adult baptism in the early church which raised the candidate to the status of a fully initiated Christian. The irony, as Steven Runciman points out, is that:

> While polemical churchmen in the Middle Ages denounced the heretics for maintaining a class of the Elect or Perfect they were denouncing an Early Christian practice, and the heretic initiation ceremony [the *consolamentum*] that they viewed with so much horror was almost word for word the ceremony with which Early Christians were admitted to the Church ...[29] Such similarity cannot be fortuitous. Obviously the Cathar Church had preserved, only slightly amended to suit its doctrines of the time, the services extant in the Christian Church during the first four centuries of its life.[30]

What is now clear is that the services used by the early church were, in origin, *almost exclusively the services of early Christian Gnosticism.*[31] They were deleted and replaced as the literalist Christian faction in Rome consolidated its power during the forth and fifth centuries. But it was natural that the banned rituals would continue to be practiced and preserved by surviving Gnostic sects. Some of these have been named in the provisional chain of transmission we sketched out in Chapter Four. But it's likely that many more lived on in secret either in remote communities or by 'veiling' themselves inside the organisations of their religious competitors.

Although all this sounds very cloak-and-dagger it is accepted by historians that many Gnostic and dualist sects were extremely secretive in their behaviour. Understandably, they became adept at concealing themselves from authorities who would burn them. We have cited examples in previous chapters of 'nests of heretics' – Bogomils and Cathars – being exposed within both Eastern Orthodox and Roman Catholic monasteries during the 10th to 14th centuries. It is significant, and even suggestive of a 'standard operating procedure', that veiling of exactly the same sort was also used by the heretics of the fourth and fifth centuries when Gnosticism was being persecuted. Indeed it is most likely that the unknown group of Gnostics who concealed the Nag Hammadi library were themselves Christian monks. At that time two monasteries of the supposedly Orthodox Pachomian order stood within six miles of the spot where the codices were buried.[32]

The initiation ritual of the *consolamentum* served at least two major functions in the religion of the Cathars and Bogomils.

First, through a chain of direct contact, which they claimed stretched unbroken all the way back to the apostles, the laying on of hands transferred the power of the Holy Spirit. As the jolt of sacred energy washed over him, they believed that the candidate's eyes were opened – in an instant – to the full predicament of his soul, separated from its true heavenly home, imprisoned in the realm of an Evil God. What that flash of enlightenment really gave him, in his belief, was the complete knowledge and spiritual power needed to break the bonds of matter and return his soul to heaven.

Professor Roelof van den Broek of Utrecht University has made an argument that the *consolamentum* was not a truly 'Gnostic' initiation because no 'special kind of Gnosis' was transferred by the ritual.[33] The professor is an authority in his field, whose work we highly respect. But this statement requires an overly-restrictive definition of the kind of 'knowledge' that *gnosis* was, and gives no thought as to how it was supposedly acquired. As we've already noted, the Gnostic initiation rituals of the first to the fourth centuries AD, just like the initiations of the Bogomils and Cathars a thousand years later, were simple ceremonies involving the laying on of hands. It is absolutely obvious that what descended on the candidate in all three cases was *not* a specific body of learning to be mastered intellectually either through an oral tradition or from books. It was, instead, *revealed* knowledge, *inspired* knowledge, which passed in an instant like a *charge* of electricity and which he or she had to experience directly and personally. In essence it was not even complicated or difficult knowledge. As Bernard Hamilton maintains, the early Christian Gnostics saw it simply as 'knowledge of the truth about the human condition.'[34] As such you either got it, or you didn't.

Besides, despite his reservations about full Gnostic status for the *consolamentum*, van den Broek himself goes on to affirm:

> Because of their dualism, be it moderate or absolute, the Cathars can be called Gnostics. If the idea that the material world is made by an evil creator and that the soul is locked up in the prison of the body cannot be called Gnostic, then there are no Gnostic ideas at all. In this sense Catharism is a medieval form of Gnosticism.[35]

The second function of the *consolamentum* for the Cathars and the Bogomils was to elevate the candidate from the rank of *credente* to the rank of *perfectus*. In this too they were following a pattern that had been set down by Christian Gnostics in the first four centuries AD. We've already seen that the Manicheans, in exactly the same way as the Cathars and Bogomils, divided themselves into two great classes of *elect* and *hearers*. So too did an earlier Gnostic Church established by Valentinus in the second century AD. He divided his 'good Christians' into two classes – the *pneumatics* ('spirituals', 'full of divinity'[36]) and the *psychics* (those with the potential, through effort, to become spirituals).[37] Marcion, another charismatic heretic of the second century AD, used the same system in the influential and successful Gnostic Church established in his name.[38] As was the case with the Cathar and Bogomil *perfecti*, severe austerities, fasts, vegetarianism and chastity were the domain of the *pneumatics* only. As was the case with the Cathar and Bogomil *credentes*, the *psychics* were free of such obligations but had a duty to care for, worship and protect the *pneumatics*.[39]

Gnostics, Bogomils and Cathars: much in common (3)

Another matter which changed not at all between the 4th century and the 13th century was the peculiarly consistent and cruel manner in which people who held to the Gnostic and dualist perspective were punished by the Church. When you consider what is involved for the victim of a burning at the stake it is obvious that no rational person would choose such a death lightly. So the very fact that so many initiated Gnostics actually chose to die in this awful manner – rather than abjure their beliefs – and that so many Cathar *perfecti* did the same a millennium later, tells us, at the very least, how deeply all these men and women must have been convinced that they were right. Whether they were deluding themselves or not is another matter – and one that is impossible to settle with certainty in this life. But we cannot doubt that *they* were absolutely certain about what would happen to their souls after they had passed through the ordeal of the flames.

As well as having much in common with each other, Gnosticism and the later religion of the Bogomils and Cathars also share one striking characteristic with established Christianity. They are all 'Salvationist' faiths – i.e. they all provide a *system*, and they promise that if it is followed it will 'save' the souls of its adherents. Yet even here, when we look closer, we discover that the Cathars, Bogomils and Gnostics stand together on one side of a line while the guardians of established Christianity stand on the other. This is because the doctrine of Catholicism and of the Eastern Orthodox Church might best be summed up as 'salvation through faith alone' – *blind faith* being all that is required. Whereas what the heretics were all offering was salvation through *knowledge* – revealed knowledge, inspired knowledge, *saving* knowledge – that was experienced directly by the initiate.

Whether a delusion or not, it was on account of this personal *knowledge* of what awaited them after death – and nothing else – that the Gnostic and Cathar heretics endured the flames with such calm certainty.

Pontifex Maximus

The Roman Catholic Church did not invent burning at the stake as a punishment for heresy but took over the idea intact from long centuries of Roman tradition. Since the reign of Augustus Caesar (27 BC–AD 14) all the emperors, in addition to their other responsibilities, had held the office of *Pontifex Maximus* – the title of the ancient high-priest of the state religion of Rome.[40] The religion could (and did) change from emperor to emperor, but the emperor of the day always remained its *Pontifex Maximus*. In order to maintain the mandate of heaven he was required to protect the state religion and punish any attempts to undermine it. This did not concern most creeds, which went about their business peacefully and were tolerated. But it did affect militant evangelistic religious movements like the Christians and the Manicheans which offered a perceptible threat to the dominance of the state cult, and thus to the state itself. Very frequently the offenders were charged with heresy and burnt at the stake.

In 186 BC a mystery cult dedicated to the god Dionysos was banned in Rome and thousands of its initiates executed.[41] On another occasion 'philosophers' were burnt for threatening the proper conduct of religion. Witnesses said they went to the stake 'laughing at the sudden collapse of human destinies' and died 'unmoving in the flames'.[42] A thousand years later when the persecutions began in the Languedoc, Cathar *perfecti* were repeatedly seen to do the same.

The Roman historian Tacitus records a terrible massacre of Christians during the reign of Emperor Nero (AD 54–68). However, this seems to have had less to do with protecting the state cult than with popular hatred of the Christians at that time. Already despised for 'their abominations' they were wrongly blamed for starting the great fire that devastated Rome in AD 64:

> An arrest was first made of all who confessed; then, upon hearing their confessions, an immense multitude was convicted, not so much of arson but of hatred of the human race. Mockery of every sort was added to their deaths. Covered with the skins of beasts they were torn apart by dogs, nailed to crosses, or doomed to the flames. Those who were burned were used to illumine the night-time skies when daylight ended.[43]

It was to be almost 200 years before there were systematic persecutions of Christians by the Roman emperor in his role as *Pontifex Maximus*. Decius was the first of these when he punished Christians who failed to offer animal sacrifices to the pagan gods in AD 250. There were further martyrdoms under Valerian in AD 257–9,[44] and in AD 303–5 Diocletian launched separate pogroms against Christians and Manicheans.[45] Diocletian's *Rescript on the Manichees* ordered the leaders of that sect burnt at the stake together with their most persistent followers. He accused them of committing many crimes, disturbing quiet populations and even working 'the greatest harm to whole cities.' Making clear why to be a Manichean was to be a heretic, he wrote:

It is indeed highly criminal to discuss doctrines once and for all settled and defined by our forefathers, and which have their recognised place and course in our system. Wherefore we are resolutely determined to punish the stubborn depravity of these worthless people.[46]

In other words Dicoletian was burning those poor Manichean *elect* because they disagreed with established religious doctrines and dogmas. The tone of his *Rescript* is eerily similar to papal pronouncements of the 13th century calling down the Albigensian Crusades upon the Cathars of the Languedoc.

As to the Roman persecution of the Christians, authors Timothy Freke and Peter Gandy have made the valid point that 'in its whole history … Christianity was officially persecuted for a total of five years.'[47] This is not the impression given to children brought up in the Western Christian tradition who are led to imagine centuries of sustained persecution. The truth is that there were a few isolated incidents between AD 50 and 250 followed by a few years of – admittedly – awful tortures, again frequently involving burning at the stake, but also scorching in red-hot iron chairs, scourging, 'the frying pan'(!), and consumption by wild beasts.[48]

Such torments ended for the Christians when their champion Constantine the Great defeated his rivals at the Battle of the Milvian Bridge in AD 312 and became the senior ruler of Rome's cruel and violent empire.[49] He immediately extended state tolerance to Christianity. This, however, did not mean that the powers of the *Pontifex Maximus*, which he continued to hold in his hands as emperor, were done away with. It simply meant that in future – with the notable exception of the reign of Emperor Julian the Apostate (AD 332–63) – these powers would no longer be used against Christians. It was not until AD 380 under Emperor Theodosius[50] that Roman Catholic Christianity was adopted as the state religion (while other forms of Christianity were denounced as 'demented and insane').[51] So this technically was the moment when Catholicism formally acquired the right to be protected by the emperor in his capacity as *Pontifex Maximus*. But it had long previously been given carte blanche by Constantine himself to persecute its internal enemies – the heretics.

The first step on the road to the stake

Even by Roman standards Constantine the Great was not a nice man. He had his eldest son Crispus executed (while the latter was *en route* to attend celebrations with him) and his wife Fausta locked in an overheated steam room and poached to death![52] He did not in fact become a baptised Christian until hours before his death, thus allowing himself considerable latitude for cruelty, excess and wickedness along the way. Indeed it is reported that one of the principal reasons for his adoption of Christianity (other than his 'miraculous' success at Milvian Bridge, which is another story) had been that it alone amongst the religions of Rome had promised him expiation of his many sins. Apparently the priests of the pagan temples, horrified even to be asked for expiation by such a brute, had refused him.[53]

So it seems that Constantine, who had good reason to worry about the afterlife destiny of his soul, owed a very large debt to the Christian bishops. By granting them state tolerance in 312–313 he repaid part of it. But he was a politician with an eye to his constituencies. Despite much urging he therefore refused to abolish or interfere in any way with the freedom of religion of the many other popular and powerfully-supported faiths in the empire. Defending the very same policy of tolerance from which Christianity had just benefited, he reminded the bishops:

> It is one thing to undertake the contest for immortality voluntarily, another to compel it with punishment.[54]

This was a matter on which Constantine remained consistent throughout his life – with one exception. That exception was announced in an edict (*circa* 324–326). In it he attacked the 'venomous errors' of Christian heretics, confiscated their properties and initiated other persecutions. The wording of the edict has been preserved for us by Constantine's fawning biographer, the eminent church father Eusebius. It is worth quoting it at some length:

Be it known to you by this present decree, you Novatians,[55] Valentinians, Marcionites [the latter, two well-known Gnostic sects], Paulians and those called Cataphrygians, all in short who constitute the heresies by your private assemblies, how many are the falsehoods in which your idle folly is entangled, and how venomous the poisons with which your teaching is involved, so that the healthy are brought to sickness and the living to everlasting death through you. You opponents of truth, enemies of life and counsellors of ruin! Everything about you is contrary to truth, in harmony with ugly deeds of evil; it serves grotesque charades in which you argue falsehoods, distress the unoffending, deny light to believers ...

The crimes done by you are so great and immense, so hateful and full of harshness, that not even a whole day would suffice to put them into words; and in any case it is proper to shut the ears and avert the eyes, so as not to impair the pure and untarnished commitment of our own faith by recounting the details. Why then should we endure such evils any longer? Protracted neglect allows healthy people to be infected as with an epidemic disease. Why do we not immediately use severe public measures to dig up such a great evil, as you might say, by the roots?

Accordingly, since it is no longer possible to tolerate the pernicious effect of your destructiveness, by this decree we publicly command that none of you henceforward shall dare to assemble. Therefore we have also given order that all your buildings in which you conduct these meetings ... not only in public but also in houses of individuals or any private places ... are to be confiscated ... and handed over incontestably and without delay to the Catholic Church ... and thereafter no opportunity be left for you to meet so that from this day forward your unlawful groups may not dare to assemble in any place either public or private.[56]

It was the first step on the slippery slope of persecution. Within less than a century, in league with emperors like Theodosius, the Catholic Church had begun to burn heretics at the stake ...

When coercion was learnt

H. A. Drake, professor of history at the University of California, thinks that Constantine's out-of-character initiative against the heretics in AD 324–6 was almost certainly the result of pressure from the bishops[57] – i.e.

that the emperor was paying off another instalment of his spiritual debt to them. Besides, looking at his options at the time, it would have seemed like the obvious move to make:

> With heresy, both imperial and episcopal agendas came together. Punishment of improper worship was the one action that Constantine would have been prepared by centuries of imperial procedure to take, and the one that, in his eyes, a new and important constituency had the most right to demand. It had the additional advantage of demonstrating his toughness to militant Christians at very little cost.[58]

Drake has investigated Christianity's rise to power in Rome and its changing relationships with the state between Constantine's initial acceptance of the faith in AD 312, its elevation as the official religion of the empire in AD 380, and the banning of all other faiths in AD 392.[59] This was a period of immense importance for the future of Christianity in which – for good or ill – it set the course that it has followed ever since. It was also the period, as Drake observes, in which 'militant Christians first came to dominate and then to define the Christian movement.'[60] Noting that in the decades after Constantine the Church 'became more militant and more coercive as it became more powerful' he asks: 'What happened to the Christian movement, why was it that the militant wing prevailed?'[61]

During the first three centuries AD we know already that the 'Christian movement' consisted of a diverse mass of sects, all of which defined themselves as followers of Christ despite their wildly varying doctrines and contradictory beliefs.

At one end of the scale there were those like the Gnostics who rejected the Old Testament, interpreted the New Testament allegorically within a dualist framework, did not believe that Christ had been born in the flesh (or crucified), allowed the greatest possible latitude for individual revelation and inspiration, and had no wish to impose dogma on others. Although they claimed to be the original Christians, guarding the true apostolic succession, they were interested not in coercion but in a process of personal enquiry and experience that would lead their initiates to a *saving knowledge* of the truth. They did not believe that there was just one exclusive path to this *gnosis*. As such, blind obedience to any form of dogma, together with intolerance for the beliefs of others, were rejected by all the Gnostic systems.

THE MASTER GAME

At the other end of the scale were Drake's 'militant Christians', the Catholics and their bishops who established their primary power centre in Rome in the early fourth century AD after they had won Constantine's favour. They too claimed to be the original Christians, guarding the true apostolic succession, and it was on the exclusive basis of their doctrines and beliefs that what we now think of as the 'Christian Church' took shape during the decades that followed. They accepted the Old Testament, interpreted the New Testament with adamant literalism, believed in Christ's incarnation, crucifixion and bodily resurrection (and that all humans would experience bodily resurrection too), rejected dualism, allowed no latitude whatsoever for individual revelation and inspiration, and felt it was their duty to impose their beliefs on others. Their interest was in obtaining the complete and *unquestioning faith* of their congregations in the infallibility of the doctrines that they taught. As such, dogma, the enforcement of blind obedience, and violent intolerance for the beliefs of others, were, from the beginning, their stock in trade.

Why did the militant wing prevail? The answer that Drake gives to his own question is in a sense a tautology. The militant wing of the once broad church of Christianity prevailed *because it was militant* and because it was the first to acquire access to the coercive apparatus of the state. As a simple and universal function of human organisation, Drake suggests:

> ... there are persons in every mass movement who are willing to coexist with variant beliefs and others who see such non-believers as outsiders and as a threat that must be neutralised.[62]

If coercive powers are made available to people who cannot tolerate variant beliefs, as they were in Rome in the fourth century, then it is inevitable that they will soon be used to enforce uniformity by destroying or marginalising other religions. But because of Constantine's calculated squeamishness about persecuting pagans, the dogmatic tendencies of the Catholic bishops during their first few decades in imperial favour were channelled exclusively into the fight against heresy. This was a fight that the Church was subsequently to pursue with single-minded ferocity during the 13th and 14th centuries when it destroyed the Cathars and until as late as the 17th century when heretics throughout Europe were still routinely burnt at the stake. Indeed it may well be that it was only through this early process of discriminating against, stigmatising, punishing, terrorising, and physically eliminating internal rivals that the members of the militant faction of Christianity were able to elucidate their own beliefs fully in the first place. 'The existence of heresy cannot be considered apart from the existence of the Church itself,' argues Zoé Oldenbourg:

> The two run *pari passu*. Dogma is always accompanied by heresy; from the very first, the history of the Christian Church was a long catalogue of battles against various heresies.[63]

Thus what had started out as Constantine's 'low-cost' strategy to appease militant Christians, to whom he felt indebted, and to impose uniformity on the more heterodox Christian sects (something that would have appealed to the dictatorial instincts of any red-blooded Roman emperor) was to have unforeseen consequences that rebounded down the ages. Before Constantine there had been an eclectic field of Christians in which no sect held power over any other – because all were persecuted. After Constantine the field was rapidly transformed and polarised. On one side, clustered around a literal interpretation of the scriptures, were the bishops of the Catholic Church – the militants whom the emperor wanted to appease. On the other side was everyone else and every other shade of opinion. The net effect, after AD 324–6, was that all anyone needed to do to become a 'heretic', and to risk losing freedom of assembly, home, property and life, was to disagree publicly with the infallible pronouncements of the bishops – most particularly the supreme bishop of the Church of Rome. It is not an accident that by the 380s the emperors had renounced their age-old responsibility of *Pontifex Maximus* – high-priest of the Roman state religion – leaving it for the popes to pick up.[64]

To this day it remains their official title.[65]

Longing for power long before Constantine

We are not suggesting that militant literalism within the Christian Church was *created* by Constantine's willingness to punish heretics. On the contrary a strong literalist tendency had been present in Christianity long before the fourth century – perhaps as long as any of the Gnostic sects – and simply took advantage of this willingness. The really radical transformation of Constantine's reign was that for the first time it gave literalists the power to impose their views on others.

It's obvious with hindsight that they'd been longing for this for centuries. It's obvious, too, how they consistently made use of rabble-rousing emotional arguments and hateful accusations during their years in waiting simply to stir up trouble for their opponents – sophisticated techniques that modern disinformation specialists would call black propaganda. Everything about their demeanour and rhetoric indicates that these people believed they would one day gain the power of enforcement over others – as they eventually did under Constantine – and that once they had it they would not hesitate to use it.

Consider, for example, the words of Irenaeus, one of the Catholic Church's great scourges of Christian Gnostics during the second century:

> Let those who blaspheme the Creator ... as [do] the Valentinians and all the falsely so-called *Gnostics*, be recognised as agents of Satan by all who worship God. Through their agency Satan even now ... has been seen to speak against God, that God who has prepared eternal fire for every kind of apostacy.[66]

From the first to the fourth centuries there are repeated examples of this sort of rhetoric, often wound up to an even higher pitch and including accusations of cannibalism, sexual promiscuity, infant sacrifice and so on. Another telling detail is that even before Gnosticism was banned, techniques were in use to 'flush out' and identify its initiates for possible future persecution. Because the Gnostic *perfecti* were generally vegetarian, one well-tried method of identifying their presence amongst the orthodox clergy and monks of Egypt was to make meat-eating compulsory for all once a week.[67]

It is the victors who write history, not the losers; so we don't know whether such witch-hunts and hate campaigns had begun to spark off physical violence against the Gnostics as early as the second century. But the Gnostics' side of the story may have survived in one of the Nag Hammadi texts, the *Second Treatise of the Great Seth*, which says in part:

> After we went forth from our home, and came down to this world, and came into being in the world in bodies, we were hated and persecuted, not only by those who are ignorant [pagans], but also by those who think they are advancing the name of Christ, since they were unknowingly empty, not knowing who they are, like dumb animals.[68]

Massacre of the Innocents

Constantine's edict of AD 324–6, cited at length earlier, handed the militant Christians the one thing they'd obviously wanted all along – the power of the state to persecute their old opponents, the Gnostics. It is notable that the edict is expressed in the peculiarly violent rhetoric favoured by the militants. As Drake points out it was a very deliberate choice of words when the emperor characterised the beliefs of Gnostics as 'venomous' – a term comparing those who held them to snakes. Similarly:

> ... he likens heresy to a disease, something capable of infecting healthy souls. Such images are important as labels that serve both to identify and stigmatise a group, making it easier to single out its members and deny them humane treatment ... This step, however limited in scope and duration, opened the door for the more massive coercion campaigns that would occur at the end of the century.[69]

During the last decade of Constantine's rule the evidence shows, as expected, that militants began to use the new powers he had given them;[70] but they did so quite tentatively at first – as though feeling out the opposition. Under the reigns of his sons they became significantly more persecuting.[71] During the 15 years that Emperor Theodosius was on the throne (AD 379–395) he outdid all his predecessors by passing more than 100 new laws aimed at the Gnostics – laws that deprived them of their property, their liberty and frequently their lives, confiscated their places of assembly and commanded the destruction of their books.[72] It is unlikely to be a coincidence that this was the precise period in which the codices of the Nag Hammadi library were hidden away in Upper Egypt to escape detection and destruction. And though records are incomplete, we know that there was also state sponsorship of anti-heretical terrorism during the same period in Lower Egypt.

Maternus Cynegius, Theodosius's governor in Alexandria from AD 384–388 was renowned for his relentless harrassment and persecution of heretics and pagans.[73] In that great cosmopolitan city, one of the first strongholds of Gnosticism, a local syncretistic and universalising cult dedicated to the composite deity *Serapis* (a fusion of two ancient Egyptian gods, *Osiris* and *Apis*) had long enjoyed the patronage of people from many different social and religious backgrounds. Scholars believe that Christian Gnostics may have participated in the mysteries of Osiris in his Serapis incarnation 'while professing to place upon what they saw there a Christian interpretation.'[74] It is also notable that several of the Alexandrian Gnostic sects made direct use of figures of Serapis – generally depicted as robed and bearded in the Greek rather than Egyptian style – as a symbol of the God of Goodness.[75]

Such flexibility and open-mindedness in the search for spiritual truths had been characteristic of Alexandria since its foundation some seven centuries previously. But precisely because of this venerable tradition of tolerance and fusion many of its citizens were shocked, and then outraged, when Cynegius began to put the military forces he commanded as governor – supposedly for the protection of all sections of the community – at the disposal of the Catholic campaign to abolish other religions.[76]

In 391, three years after Cynegius's death, state-sponsored persecution was still on the increase. In parallel Theophilus, the Catholic archbishop of Alexandria, had been rousing the Christian masses against Gnostics and pagans. Riots were engineered and many members of the oppressed sects fled to the shelter of the Serapeum. This was the great temple dedicated to Serapis that had been built by Ptolemy I Soter (323–284 BC), the former general of Alexander the Great who established the dynasty that ruled Egypt until the time of Cleopatra (51–30 BC). The refugees felt sure that they would be safe there, on ground for so long deemed sacred. But they were wrong. Again at the instigation of Theophilus a huge Christian mob, including large numbers of monks, besieged and then attacked the Serapeum.[77] The temple's irreplaceable library of ancient books and scrolls, arranged in the cloisters around the central building,[78] was ransacked and burnt. Then with imperial troops openly supporting the Christian assault, the defenders were massacred and the temple itself was raised to the ground.[79]

Reviewing the affair some time later the emperor held the victims responsible for their own destruction and did not punish the attackers.[80] Nor was the loss of the temple library to be lamented. Theodosius's well-known view was that all books contradicting the Christian message should be burnt 'lest they cause God anger and scandalise the pious.'[81]

The first Inquisition and the ancient enemy

In the early fifth century, though their numbers had drastically declined after the persecutions of Theophilus, church and state still kept the pressure on the remaining Gnostics in Egypt. We know, for example, that Cyril, who succeeded Theophilus as archbishop of Alexandria, enforced the persecution of a group that believed the material world to be the creation of the demiurge[82] – a classic Gnostic view – and that refused to accept Cyril as their *illuminator* (a classic Gnostic concept).[83] His emissary Abbot Shenoute seized their 'books full of abomination' and 'of every kind of magic' and warned:

> I shall make you acknowledge Archbishop Cyril, or else the sword will
> wipe out most of you, and moreover those of you who are spared will go
> into exile.[84]

Cyril was a man to take seriously. In AD 415 he provoked the gruesome murder of an extraordinary woman of Alexandria, Hypatia, a pagan philosopher said to have been of 'the school of Plato and Plotinus.'[85] She was famous and much loved in the city for her 'attainments in literature and science, as to far surpass all the philosophers of her own time.'[86] Some reports suggest that it was out of jealousy at her obvious popularity that the archbishop had her killed. Whatever the reason she was dragged from her house on Cyril's orders by a Christian mob, carried into a church and hacked limb from limb with broken tiles (*ostrakois*, literally 'oyster shells', but the word was also used for brick tiles on the roofs of houses).[87] Finally, reports one pro-Christian commentator of the time:

> ... they carried her to a place named Cinaron, and they burned her body
> with fire. And all the people surrounded Archbishop Cyril and named him
> 'the new Theophilus', for he had destroyed the last remains of idolatry in
> the city.[88]

With such an atmosphere of Christian fanaticism prevalent throughout the Roman world it is not surprising that the numerous Christian Gnostic sects of the second and third centuries had soon all but disappeared. In AD 447 Pope Leo the Great still felt it necessary to condemn Gnostic writings as a 'hotbed of manifold perversity' which 'should not only be forbidden, but entirely destroyed and burnt with fire.'[89] But by the end of the fifth century it seemed that organised Gnosticism was a thing of the past.

Some of those prepared to risk their lives for their Gnostic beliefs certainly joined the ragged group of charismatic preachers known as the Messalians. Established at Edessa in the mid-fourth century, they were still going strong in the sixth century. We saw in the last chapter how they might have formed part of the chain of transmission that would ultimately bring Gnostic texts and teachings to the Bogomils and thence to the Cathars of medieval Europe.

But it was Manicheism, also a Gnostic religion with strong Christian elements, that would have provided the most obvious haven for survivors of the disbanded sects.[90] Perhaps because of this, and because Manicheism was an evangelistic faith that still posed a real threat to the Church, it became the primary target of persecution during the fifth century. So violent and thorough was this persecution that by the end of the sixth century, though it was to survive for another thousand years in the Far East, Manicheism was a dead force in the Roman world.[91]

The final measures were the work of Justinian (AD 527–565) who ruled the Eastern Roman Empire from Constantinople. Mass burnings of Manicheans soon followed when he equated heresy with treason and subjected both offences automatically to the death penalty.[92] The Manicheans had begun to act like a secret society, disguising their identity and pretending to be good Christians.[93] Justinian's response was not only to burn them at the stake but to burn any of their acquaintances, Manichean or not, who had failed to denounce them.[94] Significantly, in our view, he also created an official investigative agency, the *Quaestiones*, which was specifically tasked to root out and destroy the Manichean heresy.[95]

Seven centuries later did Pope Innocent III have Justinian's initiative in mind when he created a very similar instrument of terror and oppression called the Inquisition?[96] It was to become greatly feared and would ultimately take on a global role as Catholicism advanced into the New World and Asia. It's easy to forget that when Innocent established it in 1233 he did so with the specific purpose of rooting out and destroying the Cathar heresy – which we know he believed to be a resurgence of the more ancient heresy of Manicheism.

So by unleashing the Inquisition in the 13th century, it is almost as though Innocent was trying to pick up where his predecessor had left off in the 6th century. This would have been perfectly in character because together with many other European churchmen of the period he appears to have had a genuine sense of continuity about what the Bogomils and Cathars represented and how they were to be handled. The heretics, too, felt themselves to be part of a continuum and dealt with the Church like an old enemy who they already knew very well.

What was odd was that so few of the participants on either side seemed surprised, after such a long silence, that a fully-fledged Gnostic 'anti-Church' was now straddling Europe like a colossus, confronting both Rome and Constantinople, and threatening to turn the tables of the world.

CHAPTER SIX

THE RIVALS

A monstrous breed ... You must eliminate such filth.

Pope Innocent III (1198–1216), speaking of the Cathars [1]

The *Second Treatise of the Great Seth*, one of the Nag Hammadi texts, speaks of the Gnostics' experience of persecution at the hands of people who believed themselves to be Christians. The setting could be anytime in the first four centuries AD before the texts were concealed. The *Treatise* then goes on to make a further allegation – one that the Cathars and Bogomils were to repeat a thousand years later. This is that the established Church is an impostor – an 'imitation' of the true Church that it has displaced.[2]

So we're now better able to understand the references in the *Treatise*, cited in the previous chapter, to 'empty people' who 'think that they are advancing the name of Christ' when they persecute others. The writer is either speaking of the Catholic Church itself, or of the militant, literalist faction always in favour of persecuting its opponents, that would ultimately dominate the Church during the reign of Emperor Constantine – and that would impose its agenda on the future. Set against it, and persecuted by it, are the Gnostic adepts, 'Sons of Light', founders of the true Church, described as 'an ineffable union of undefiled truth'.[3] The impostor Church has 'made an imitation' of their 'perfect assembly' and 'having proclaimed a doctrine of a dead man'[4] (the crucified Jesus Christ), it has tricked its followers into lifetimes of:

... fear and slavery, worldly cares, and abandoned worship ... For they did not know the Knowledge of the Greatness, that is from above, and from a fountain of truth, and that it is not from slavery and jealousy, fear and love of worldly matter.[5]

It should be obvious to the reader by now that this simple statement of Gnostic dualism, which lay at Nag Hammadi for 1600 years after being buried there in the late fourth century, could equally well have been written by a Cathar or Bogomil *perfectus* of the 12th or 13th centuries. There is the same horror of worldly matter and the same sense that it entraps and enslaves the soul. There is the same belief that while ignorance can extend the soul's imprisonment, knowledge can set it free. And there is the same concept of what this knowledge is – i.e. that it concerns the existence of a spiritual realm of greatness 'above' which is the domain of the God of Good, the source of truth, and the long-lost home of the soul.

The reader will recall that according to Cathar and Bogomil doctrine, Christ was not a physical human being 'in the flesh' but an immensely convincing apparition.[6] The *Second Treatise of the Great Seth* clearly has the same thing in mind when it puts these words into Christ's mouth after the Crucifixion:

> I did not succumb to them as they had planned ... I was not afflicted at all. Those who were there punished me, and I did not die in reality but in appearance ...[7]

Many other religious ideas that we have come to associate with the Cathars and Bogomils also appear a millennium earlier in the *Second Treatise of the Great Seth* – for example that the god of this world is evil and ignorant and can be identified with the God of the Old Testament, and that his minions, the Catholic bishops are 'mere counterfeits and laughingstocks.'[8] The passages we've quoted here are just fragments of the *Treatise* – itself only a small part of the overall collection of 52 Gnostic texts preserved in the Nag Hammadi library. Virtually any of them could serve, without alteration, as a manifesto of Cathar and Bogomil beliefs. It therefore seems to us inconceivable, as many scholars continue to argue, that there is no link between the religion of the early Christian Gnostics and the later religion of the Cathars and the Bogomils.

There is in our view more than a link. Despite some superficial differences – and their significant separation in time – these two religions have so much in common at the level of their vital concepts, cosmology, doctrine and beliefs that they're almost impossible to tell apart. When we consider that essential elements of ritual, symbolism, initiation, structure and organisation were also the same, and that both the Gnostics and the medieval dualists were persecuted with the same spirit of savage repression by the same opponent and for the same reasons, it is increasingly difficult to resist the conclusion that they must, indeed, have been one and the same thing.

Seizing control of the tradition

Because the Catholic Church won the power-struggle against the Gnostics it gained victor's privileges over the way history would be told. It's not surprising, therefore, while all other beliefs and doctrines are regarded as aberrations, that Catholic beliefs and doctrines tend to be treated as orthodox (literally 'straight-teaching') and also as 'authentic', 'of true apostolic descent', etc, in most historical accounts.[9] However, a dispassionate look at what is now known about the broad and eclectic character of Christian beliefs in the first three centuries does not support the Catholic claim to primacy. There is no doubt that the evidence shows us the nucleus of the faction that became the Catholic Church forming around dogmatic militants like Irenaeus and Tertullian. But after the discovery of the Nag Hammadi texts, and the gradual revelation of their contents that has followed, it has been impossible to ignore the presence, and equal weight, of the Gnostic Churches in the same period. Since Catholics and Gnostics alike claimed that the teachings in their possession were the earliest and the most 'authentic', why has the Catholic version for so long been accepted as gospel (literally!), and left unchallenged, while the Gnostic version was hunted down and persecuted out of existence? Isn't it equally possible, as the Nag Hammadi texts themselves invite us to believe, that the tradition of the Gnostics was all along the 'authentic' one?

Scholars have known for many years, for example, that the Valentinian Gnostics of the second century AD accepted not only the four Gospels of the New Testament that have come down to us today (Matthew, Mark, Luke and John), 'but many additional documents professing to contain traditions of the secret teachings of Jesus.'[10] Writing in 1967 Henry Chadwick, the great historian of Christianity was happy to accept that such 'secret teachings' did in fact once exist and suggested that they would have been similar to 'the *Gospel of Thomas* [one of the Nag Hammadi texts] recently recovered from the sands of Egypt.'[11] But he was not interested in questions concerning the *authenticity* of these Gnostic traditions. He simply took it for granted that whatever 'secret teachings' the Gnostics possessed must self-evidently have been false. Chadwick even seemed happy to gloss over the pseudoscientific claptrap of the heresy-hater Irenaeus who, he observed approvingly:

> ... ingeniously vindicated the fourfold gospel on numerological principles. Four, he urged, was a sacred number corresponding to the four winds, or the four faces of the cherubim in Ezekiel ...[12]

Chadwick accepts that even as late as the last two decades of the second century AD a substantial oral tradition was still in circulation, purporting to transmit the true words of Christ. This tradition, he notes, was 'regarded as an authority which had not yet been wholly merged with the written gospels.'[13] In other words the canonical New Testament was still incomplete by the end of the second century,[14] and the eventual course of Christian doctrine was not yet set in stone.

Chadwick suggests that *circa* AD 185–190, with many different ideas (both written and oral) in circulation, Irenaeus, together with others from the proto-Catholic group, saw the advantage 'which a written document possessed and which oral transmission did not.'[15] Although the Gnostic leader Marcion had prepared his own canon some time before – much to the consternation of the Catholics – few of the other proliferating Gnostic sects of the period accepted it and the possibility that they would ever be able to agree amongst themselves for sufficiently long to put a representative Gnostic canon together seemed remote.

Amongst the proto-Catholic group there was no such hesitation. Knowing that those who controlled the written document would effectively have 'the control of authentic tradition',[16] they launched their own initiative to compile and create a canonical New Testament. Since this group was dominated by men like Irenaeus who regarded their own views as infallible and were intolerant of the views of others, they were naturally inclined to label whichever texts or traditions supported their views as belonging to the authentic apostolic line and to cast into the outer darkness as inauthentic any that contradicted them.

What justified this, notes Chadwick, was that 'the teaching given by the contemporary bishop of, say, Rome or Antioch' was held by the Catholics to be 'in all respects identical with that of the apostles.'[17] As Irenaeus himself put it in the second century with reference to the so-called *Rule of Faith* (a short summary of the main points of Catholic belief that he and other heresy hunters favoured):

> This rule is what the bishops teach now and therefore comes down from the apostles.[18]

Thus, irrespective of its actual origins and authenticity, *any* teaching given by the Catholic bishops was automatically deemed authentic and to have come down from the apostles. *Vice versa*, any teaching of which they did not approve was automatically deemed inauthentic and not descended through the proper apostolic line – in other words, heretical.

In an era when oral traditions were still dominant, and the bestowal of canonical status upon texts was in the hands of a militant faction, such circular arguments could only have one outcome. There is little doubt that the proto-Catholics deliberately manipulated the gradual formation of the New Testament so that it could serve them in their early battles against the Gnostics and reinforce their own claims to authenticity and exclusivity as the sole mediators of Christ's message.

No eyewitnesses we can trust

Can we be sure of anything that the New Testament has to tell us?

No matter how dense the smokescreen surrounding the vexed issues of authenticity, few would dispute that somewhere in the century between 50 BC and AD 50, mysterious and powerful events occurred in Palestine that set in motion the Christian phenomenon. But it is not at all certain what sparked the phenomenon off. Was Christ really the Son of God, born as a flesh-and-blood human being and murdered on the cross – thus somehow redeeming our sins? That's the Catholic position. Was he a projection or emanation from the divine – an 'appearance' only, not really flesh-and-blood? That's the Gnostic and Cathar position. Or could he simply have been an urban legend blown out of all proportion, or perhaps even an artificially constructed myth designed to serve the purposes of a particular religious cult?

The first two possibilities, Catholic and Gnostic/Cathar, are both based on unprovable articles of faith and therefore are equally likely – or unlikely – to be true.

Though its defenders claim otherwise, there is no superior logic whatsoever in the Catholic position. It is, after all, no more logical or inherently more probable to insist that Christ was the Son of God in human flesh born of a virgin than to insist that he took form only as a very convincing apparition.

The third possibility – that the whole story was made up – has much to recommend it. The prime issue is the remarkable absence of solid and convincing historical evidence to confirm that the figure known to the world as Jesus Christ ever actually existed. He might have; it can't be ruled out. But it's equally possible that there never was any such being – whether man or apparition. His obvious resemblance to several other much older 'dying and resurrecting god-men' – notably Osiris in Egypt and Dionysos in Greece – has not gone unnoticed by scholars, and the possibility must be confronted that 'Jesus Christ' was a myth, not a man. Since no part of the canonical Gospels is thought to date earlier than about AD 60, and some parts may be as late as AD 110, it is within the bounds of reason that everything we know about Christ's person, words and deeds was simply invented some time during the first century AD and then passed into the oral tradition in the form of 'eyewitness accounts' of events that had supposedly taken place a couple of generations previously. Extensive editing in the late second century AD began to standardise the oral traditions into the beginnings of the canonical New Testament. By then, needless to say, there was no one left alive who could claim to have witnessed, or to have known anyone who had witnessed, or even to have known anyone who had known anyone who had witnessed, the events surrounding Christ's life and death.

Somehow this secret religion went on

In the early years, along with many smaller factions, we've seen that two main competing forms of Christianity evolved, approximately in parallel, and that there is no clear evidence of which came first. Both claimed primacy and sought to reinforce their position with their own selections from the whole stock of oral and written traditions available in that period. The literalist form, which was to become Catholicism, gained the upper hand – and the ear of Constantine. Gnosticism, the interpretive and revelatory form of Christianity, lost out, was declared a heresy and persecuted.

We make no claim ourselves as to which form was the oldest or most 'authentic.' The issue is strictly-speaking irrelevant to the hypothesis we're developing here. Our point is simply that until literalist Catholicism began its sustained campaign to wipe out interpretive Gnosticism, Christianity had been diverse enough to accommodate both simultaneously. The persecutions of the Gnostics were so successful that by the end of the sixth century it seemed that only the literalist form had survived. However the fact that a strong Christian Gnostic religion emerged again in the 10th century in the form of Bogomilism makes it impossible for us to accept that the destruction of Christian Gnosticism in the sixth century was as final as it looked. Somehow this secret religion went on – either through the Manicheans, the Messalians and the Paulicians – or by another less obvious route.

This is why the 'Organisation' spoken of so cryptically in the Nag Hammadi scriptures continues to intrigue us. In Chapter Five we saw that the references made to it seem to hint at the existence of a secret society charged with a mission to protect, restore and repromulgate Gnosticism after times of trouble.

It would all sound like so much ancient wishful thinking were it not for the fact that this was more or less what happened at the end of the first millennium. The sudden appearance of Bogomilism in Bulgaria during the last decades of the 10th century was not some isolated heresy. It marked the first step in the repromulgation and resurgence of a fully-fledged Christian-Gnostic religion after 400 years absent from the scene. The next step was its rapid westwards expansion as Catharism during the 12th century. By the beginning of the 13th century it had become a genuinely pan-European faith and the only serious rival that the established Church had faced for a thousand years.

We know that the Church did not identify it as a new rival, but as an old and dangerous one seemingly returned from the dead. Perhaps this sense on the Church's part, of being drawn back into an ancient conflict, one that struck at the very heart of all its shaky claims to legitimacy and authenticity as the true faith, explains the terrible events that followed.

Christ and Antichrist

All wars are terrible – no matter in what epoch they are fought, or with what weapons. Medieval wars were particularly ghastly. But the wars of the Catholic Church against the heresy of Catharism in the 13th century, the so-called *Albigensian Crusades*, must rank high on the list of the most repulsive, brutal and merciless conflicts that human beings have ever had the misfortune to be involved in.

The Cathars are innocent in these matters, by any sane standards of justice. All they did was reject the authority of the pope and give their loyalty to another religion that sought to correct what it saw as the false doctrines of Catholicism. The rational modern mind cannot blame them for acting independently in this way, let alone detect any reason why their beliefs and behaviour should have merited so gruesome a punishment as burning at the stake. We know that the past is another country – where people do things differently. We understand that the medieval world, full of superstition and the fear of damnation (a fear fostered by the Catholic Church and used as a weapon of mind-control) was not governed by the same codes of interpersonal decency that we try to live by today. Yet the savage persecution of the Cathars, carried out in the name of the Church, and frequently on the direct orders of its bishops, went so far beyond what was normal – even for that bloodstained period – that it has to raise disturbing questions about the beliefs of the perpetrators.

Because our primary focus in this book is on the long-term survival of a secret religion, irrespective of its 'authenticity', we will not pursue such questions further here – notably the vexed issue of whether Catholic or Cathar teachings represent 'authentic' Christianity. Nonetheless it seems patently obvious to us that the spirit of the gentle and loving Jesus who pervades the New Testament did *not* ride with the Catholic clergy and knights who ravaged the once free land of Occitania in the first half of the 13th century. A chronicler of the time, one of the two authors of the epic *Chanson de la Croisade albigeoise* ('Song of the Albigensian Crusade'), summed the problem up in an ironic unofficial epitaph for Simon de Montfort, the fearsome general who led the Catholic armies in Occitania for almost a decade of unremitting slaughter before being killed in battle in 1218. He was buried with much pomp and ceremony at Carcassonne where, the *Chanson* reports:

> Those who can read may learn from his epitaph that he is a saint and a martyr; that he is bound to rise again to share the heritage, to flourish in that state of unparalleled felicity, to wear a crown and have his place in the Kingdom. But for my part I have heard tell that the matter must stand thus: if one may seek Christ Jesus in this world by killing men and shedding blood; by the destruction of human souls; by compounding murder and hearkening to perverse council; by setting the torch to great fires; by winning lands through violence, and working for the triumphs of vain pride; by fostering evil and snuffing out good; by slaughtering women and slitting children's throats – why, then, he must needs wear a crown, and shine resplendent in Heaven.[19]

In other words, unless the lessons of humility, nonviolence, forgiveness and unconditional love so plain to read in the New Testament have somehow been turned upside down, inside out and back to front, there is *no way* that anyone seeking Christ in this world is going to find him by following Simon de Montfort's route. And if that is the case, since we're in a position today to stand back from the propaganda and prejudices of the time, doesn't it suggest that the entire Catholic onslaught against the Cathars was fundamentally unchristian?

Or even, as the Cathars themselves suggested, 'anti-Christian'?

'More evil than Saracens …'

We've already filled in the background to the Albigensian Crusades in earlier chapters. The tremendous success of the Cathar heresy in Occitania and other parts of Europe during the 12th century had for many years been watched with envy and growing alarm by the Catholic hierarchy in Rome. By the early 13th century it is estimated that more than half the Occitanian population had abandoned the Church and that growing numbers were looking exclusively to Catharism to meet their spiritual needs. Worse still, as we saw in Chapter Two, the local nobility gave tacit and sometimes even overt support to the Cathars, frequently had relatives amongst them, sided with them in disputes with the bishops, and were closely linked to some of the leading *perfecti*. Once it had become clear that the Cathar religion was not a flash in the pan, but quite possibly formed part of a great coordinated plot against the Church, it was obvious that sooner or later one pope or another was going to have to do something about it. The only question was what exactly, and when?

That the 'what' should be the terror weapon of a crusade had probably been decided by Pope Innocent III some years before the perfect excuse to use such a weapon of terror presented itself.[20] But when that happened he acted immediately.

The precipitating incident was the assassination of the papal legate to Occitania, one Peter de Castelnau, in January 1208. A former monk of the Cistercian Abbey of Fontfroide, de Castelnau was in Occitania on Innocent's orders accompanied by another leading Cistercian, Arnaud Amalric, the abbot of Cîteaux.[21] In 1207 they stirred up deep-seated resentments when they tried to form a league of southern barons to hunt down the Cathars. Raymond VI, the powerful Count of Toulouse refused to join and was excommunicated by de Castelnau. The excommunication was withdrawn in January 1208 after Raymond had been forced to apologise personally to the papal legate – a shameful climb-down for such a highly-placed nobleman. The very next morning one of Raymond's knights, perhaps seeking to avenge the humiliation of his master, rode up to de Castelnau as he prepared to ford the River Rhone and ran him through with a spear. He died on the spot.[22]

Two months later, on 10 March 1208, Innocent declared the Crusade – the first time ever that the term 'crusade' was used for a war against fellow Christians. Like the Christian emperors of Rome long before, he clearly gave the highest priority to the extirpation of heresy – higher even than to the wars to regain the Holy Land. He wrote:

> Attack the followers of heresy more fearlessly even than the Saracens – since they are more evil – with a strong hand and an outstretched arm. Forward then soldiers of Christ! Forward brave recruits to the Christian army! Let pious zeal inspire you to avenge this monstrous crime against your God.[23]

Meanwhile Arnaud Amalric, abbot of Cîteaux, had been sent to northern France to rally support amongst the nobles there. 'May the man who abstains from this Crusade,' he is quoted as saying, 'never drink wine again; may he never eat, morning or evening, off a good linen cloth, or dress in fine stuff again to the end of his days; and at his death may he be buried like a dog.'[24]

But such browbeating was hardly needed to mobilise the rednecks at the court of the king of France. They were raring to go anyway. Here was an opportunity to acquire wealth and status with an adventure relatively near to home and to earn papal indulgences and forgiveness of sins that would normally have required much harder work in the Holy Land. Along with dozens of B-list aristocrats like Simon de Montfort who were looking to get rich quick, thousands of volunteers at the foot-soldier level also poured in from all walks of life. The lowliest man could benefit since crusading meant the automatic postponement of all his debts and the release of his property from the hold of creditors for the duration of his service.[25]

Still the preparations took more than a year. By February 1209 military detachments for the Crusade were reported to be massing all over northern France.[26] But it was not until St. John's Day, 24 June 1209, that the full force, estimated to number 20,000 men, had assembled at the French city of Lyons ready for the march south. Simon de Montfort was with it but not yet its general. For this first campaign the terrifying Christian horde was headed by Arnaud Amalric himself.[27] It need not be imagined that being a Cistercian abbot, supposedly dedicated to a lifetime of Christian peace and charity, would inhibit him in any way on the battlefield. Far from it. At Béziers, the first Cathar city that he attacked, Arnaud Amalric was about to order an infamous atrocity …

Hell's Army

Conditioned by television images of modern warfare with smart bombs and other high-tech weaponry it is difficult to imagine the atmosphere of primal harm and menace that must have radiated like heat off the big medieval army that marched out of Lyons on 24 June 1209.

Its iron fist, mounted, armoured from head to foot and heavily-armed, was an elite fighting force of trained killers. These were the knights – the samurai class of old Europe. Gathered from the aristocracy, they were men who had been groomed for warfare since childhood. They probably totalled no more than 1,000 individuals, but each of them, depending on his resources, was supported in battle by anything from four to thirty hand-picked cavalry and infantry who fought at his side as a skilled and disciplined unit.[28]

Lower down the social ladder the theme of discipline in the crusading army was continued amongst divisions of professional soldiers specialised in particular military arts. They included the gunners who operated the great war-catapults and stone-guns – the trebuchets and mangonels that had a range of almost half a kilometer and could hurl projectiles weighing 40 kilograms. There were teams of battering-ram specialists who would breach the city-gates, while other teams assembled and operated huge siege towers from which archers could fire down on the defendants inside the walls. Sappers and siege engineers were also needed for the business of filling in moats and undermining foundations.[29]

Less disciplined but equally deadly, and in a way far more frightening, were the mercenaries, known as *routiers*, who had been hired for their unprincipled ferocity. These were times of widespread poverty and frequent famines in Europe, and droves of the landless, the unemployed and the dispossessed wandered the countryside. The most efficient and ruthless amongst them formed up into lawless bands, looting and killing to support themselves, and were hired *en masse* by the Christian army that the pope had unleashed on Occitania.[30] 'They were,' notes Zoé Oldenbourg:

> ... desperate fellows with nothing to lose, and therefore would plunge on through thick and thin regardless ... They formed a series of shock battalions, all the easier to utilise since no one had the slightest qualms about sacrificing them. The most important thing ... was the terror they inspired in the civilian population ... Not content with mere pillage and rape they indulged in massacre and torture for the sheer fun of the thing, roasting children over slow fires and chopping men into small pieces.[31]

Even lower down the pecking-order than the feared routiers were the

THE MASTER GAME

ribauds, the unpaid camp followers, numbering several thousands in their own right, who had attached themselves unofficially to the Crusade. They too were desperate people – a ragged bunch of bare-arsed muggers, rapists and corpse looters. But weirdly they elected their own 'king' on the campaign who divided the chores and the spoils of war amongst the rest.[32]

Last but not least there were the *holy rollers* – wild, itinerant Christian preachers and groups of their fanatical followers armed with crude weapons like scythes and clubs who hoped to gain a special dispensation in heaven by murdering any Cathars that the main army missed.[33]

It seems richly ironic that the self-proclaimed Catholic Church of so peaceful and loving a figure as Jesus Christ was not only prepared to raise an army to massacre those who disagreed with it, but also to pack its ranks with the most notorious murderers and brigands of the age. But if we look at the whole affair from the Cathar perspective the sense of disconnect goes away. It is *not*, as its later apologists would claim, that the church of a good and loving God was somehow (aberrantly, temporarily) provoked into extreme violence by extreme circumstances. In the Cathar take on this, the Catholic Church served the God of Evil; accordingly it was behaving entirely in character when it recruited an army of demons.

Now formed up behind Arnaud Amalric into a vast column of men and supplies more than 4 miles in length, this demonic force – or army of valiant crusaders depending on one's point of view – bristled with axes and pikes and seethed with the intent to do violence.

'Kill them all': the Feast of Saint Mary Magdalene and the workings of divine vengeance ...

After taking a meandering course through Occitania, pausing only to accept the surrender of settlements unable to defend themselves and to burn small groups of Cathars along the way, Arnaud Amalric and his 20,000 hooligans fetched up in front of the prosperous city of Béziers on 21 July 1209. Its walls were very thick, very high and very well defended and everyone assumed that this was going to be a long siege.

Some curiosities now coincide.

It is our hypothesis that the Cathars were the descendants, through an underground stream of secret religion, of the Christian Gnostics of the first few centuries. Scholars agree that the Christian Gnostics of that period had a special reverence for Mary Magdalene, who plays a small but highly significant role in the New Testament. By comparison her status in the Nag Hammadi texts is elevated to that of Christ's first apostle, his closest confidante, and perhaps even his lover.[34] We were therefore naturally interested to learn that the area around Béziers had been known for centuries before the Crusade for its special and fervent dedication to Mary Magdalene.[35] A local tradition had it that she had fled here by ship from Palestine in the mid-first century, landed at Marseilles, and become the first Christian missionary in what was then the Roman Empire's *Provincia Gallia Narbonensis*.[36] Odder still, 21 July, the date that the pope's army pitched camp before Béziers, was the eve of the annual Feast of Mary Magdalene, held on 22 July.[37] Oddest of all, however, was what would happen on the feast day itself.

Béziers was by no means entirely a Cathar city. There may have been as many as several thousand Cathar *credentes* living there, but Catholics are likely to have been in the majority. We know that there were 222 Cathar *perfecti* present on the day the siege began because a list of their names, prepared by Renaud de Montpeyroux, the Catholic bishop of Béziers, has survived.[38] The bishop (whose predecessor had been assassinated in 1205) scuttled through the gates with the list soon after the crusaders began to arrive and returned from their camp a few hours later with an offer. If the townsfolk would hand over the 222 named Cathar notables for immediate burning then the city and everyone else living in it would be spared.[39]

It was in fact a pretty good offer but, to their lasting moral credit, the Catholic burghers of Béziers rejected it, stating that they 'would rather be drowned in the salt sea's brine' than betray their fellow citizens.[40]

What was to follow was a good deal worse than drowning.

It started on the early morning of the 22 July with a minor and wholly unnecessary skirmish. Separated by some distance from the main force of the crusader army, the ribauds – camp followers – had gathered by the banks of the River Orb which flowed a little to the south of the city walls. A bridge leading to one of the city gates spanned the Orb at this point and now one of the ribauds strolled onto it, shouting insults and challenges to the defenders. Angered by his temerity some inside rushed spontaneously out through the gate and down onto the bridge where they caught and killed him and threw his body into the water. Probably they expected to retreat to the safety of the city at once but before they could do so a gang of camp followers swarmed onto the bridge and locked them in combat. At the same moment, with what was obviously an experienced eye for the main chance, the elected 'king' of the ribauds 'called all his lads together and shouted 'Come on, let's attack'.[41]

Within minutes, driven on by an ugly cocktail of crowd-psychology, bloodlust and greed, a howling mob bore down on the scrum at the bridge.

According to the chronicler of the *Chanson de la Croisade albigeoise*:

> There were more than 15,000 of them, all barefooted, dressed only in
> shirts and breeches, and unarmed save for a variety of hand weapons.[42]

Hatchets? Butchers' knives? Cudgels? The mind boggles at the thought
of what primitive bludgeons and rusty blades these dregs of the Crusade
wielded as they forced the bridge and pursued the foolish skirmishers
back up the slope towards the city walls. No one is quite sure exactly
what happened next but by now the whole crusader camp was roused
and bands of mercenaries and regular soldiers were charging into the fray.
Most probably the ribauds succeeded in seizing control of the gate as the
skirmishers tried to slip back inside, and were able to hold it open whilst
crusader reinforcements poured through. But whatever the mechanism,
the result was the same. With their defences hopelessly breached the proud
citizens of Béziers were now doomed beyond any redemption:

> No cross or altar or crucifix could save them. And these raving beggarly
> lads, they killed the clergy too, and the women and the children. I doubt
> one person came out alive.[43]

The leaders of the Crusade made no attempt to stop or even limit the
massacres. Quite the contrary, as the knights rushed to arm and mount,
eager not to miss the action, a group of them reportedly asked Arnaud
Amalric how they were to distinguish the many Catholics in the town
from the heretics they had come to kill. The abbot is notorious for replying
in Latin: '*Caedite eos. Novit enim Dominus qui sunt eius.*'
Which means:

> 'Kill them all; God will look after his own.'[44]

Though most of the killing was done by the lower orders, a particularly
awful bloodbath was unleashed inside the Church of Mary Magdalene
by the knights themselves. Here a multitude of Cathars and Catholics –
old and young, men, women and children – were cowering in fear. Their
numbers were estimated by chroniclers at the time as between 1,000 and
7,000. Just like the Gnostic and pagan refugees who had taken shelter inside
the Serapeum in Alexandria nine centuries previously when it was attacked
by Christian forces, they probably hoped that the hallowed ground would

save them. And just as in Alexandria, it didn't. The knights burst in and slaughtered them all.[45]

By noon, a few hours after the fighting had started at the bridge, the entire population of the city had been murdered. Working with all the contemporary estimates, and allowing for exaggeration in some cases, modern scholars generally concur on a figure of between 15,000 and 20,000 for the total number of the dead of Béziers.[46] Guiraraut Riquier of Narbonne, one of the last of the Occitanian troubadours, expressed the scale of the tragedy in a song:

> Béziers has fallen. They're dead. Clerks, women, children. No quarter.
> They killed Christians too.
>
> I rode out. I couldn't see or hear, a living creature ... They killed seven
> thousand people, Seven thousand souls who sought sanctuary in Saint
> Madeleine.
>
> The steps of the altar, were wet with blood. The church echoed with the
> cries. Afterwards they slaughtered the monks who tolled the bells.
> They used the silver cross, as a chopping block to behead them.[47]

Clearly Riquier's sympathies were not with the crusaders and he had no interest in making them look good. We might think that the whole scene was just something he'd invented as anti-Catholic propaganda were it not that all other accounts of the sack of the city, supported by archaeological evidence, also speak of a fearful massacre taking place inside the Church of Mary Magdalene.[48] Indeed the Catholic forces felt they had nothing to hide or be ashamed of in the killing of so many heretics in so holy a place.

The Cistercian chronicler Pierre des Vaux-de-Cernay proclaimed:

> It was right that these shameless dogs should be captured and
> destroyed on the feast day of the woman [i.e. Mary Magdalene] they
> had insulted and whose church they had defiled ...[49]

Arnaud Amalric, abbot of Cîteaux and leader of the Crusade, was thrilled too – and not just with the slaughter in the church but with the overall tally of the day. In a breathless letter to his master Pope Innocent III, the man at the source of all this carnage, he wrote proudly:

Nearly 20,000 of the citizens were put to the sword, regardless of age or sex. The workings of divine vengeance have been wondrous.[50]

Truth in extremes

Our purpose thus far has been to track the secret tradition that lay behind Catharism, that kept a complex system of Gnostic spirituality alive in the West through a thousand years of persecution, and that the Albigensian Crusades were designed to obliterate forever. We will not offer a detailed history of the Crusades themselves since several excellent books already exist that provide a thorough record of the main sieges and battles. Nevertheless, the best chance to study human behaviour always comes in the starkest, most dangerous and most extreme circumstances. For this reason, as we will see in the next chapter, the Crusades provide a unique opportunity to get closer to the truth about the two sides.

The truth is that upon the citizens of Béziers, who had threatened no one, aggressed no one, gone out to make war on no one, and merely followed their own harmless beliefs, the Catholic side unleashed an army from hell to inflict a hellish atrocity of rare and terrible evil. Zoé Oldenbourg suggests that we should reflect on what this tells us:

> Massacres such as that at Béziers are extremely rare; we are forced to accept the proposition that even human cruelty has its limits. Even amongst the worst atrocities which history has to show us through the centuries, massacres of this sort stand out as exceptions; and yet it is the head of one of the leading monastic orders in Catholic Christendom who has the honour of being responsible (while conducting a 'Holy War' to boot) for one such monstrous exception to the rules of war. We should be on our guard against underrating the significance of this fact.[51]

Nor did the atrocities stop with Béziers. They went on and on, seemingly endlessly, each with some mad demonic quality of its own. But soon after Béziers, having bathed in sufficient blood to satisfy his appetite, Arnaud Amalric opted for a less 'front-line' role. His successor, chosen to prosecute the Crusade with the utmost vigour, was Simon de Montfort, described as a man who 'prayed, took Communion and killed as easily as drawing breath.'[52]

CHAPTER SEVEN

THE SWORD
AND THE FIRE

*It was not until the formation of the Holy Office [of the Inquisition] that
the world was presented with the spectacle of an organisation prepared
to kill, starve, and dispossess those who had deviated a hair's breadth
from its own theological preoccupations. No other major religion has ever
produced such an organisation. There are secular organisations which
have acted with equal ferocity and efficiency, but, unlike the Inquisition,
they did not last for seven centuries.*

Arthur Guirdham, The Great Heresy

The crusading army rested three days in the meadows around the
reeking corpse of Béziers, then marched off to besiege the great city
of Carcassonne – which surrendered two weeks later without putting
up a fight. A condition of the surrender was that this time the inhabitants
would not be slaughtered; instead all their property was confiscated and they
were expelled from Carcassonne, penniless and homeless, never to return.

In August 1209 Simon de Montfort officially took command of the
army, and of a new title, Viscount of Béziers and Carcassonne.[1] But by mid-
September the vast majority of the forces at his disposal had packed their
bags and gone home. This was a routine and predictable desertion since
the indulgences and remission of sins that the pope bestowed on crusaders
required them to put in a minimum of 40 days on campaign. The surrender
of Carcassonne was accomplished just within the 40 days but after that, in
the minds of most of the volunteers, the campaign was over.

With a small band of dedicated knights de Montfort hung on in what
was now the heart of very hostile territory over the winter. Then in 1210 –
and yearly thereafter – the pope preached another crusade and the ranks of
the army swelled once more.[2]

A macabre highlight of the 1210 campaign was the capture of the fortress of Bram after three days of stiff resistance. Because they had put up a fight the surviving members of the garrison, numbering over 100, suffered a terrible punishment. On de Montfort's orders their eyes were put out. Then their noses and upper lips were crudely hacked off. One man was left one eye, not out of charity but so that he could lead the stumbling, blinded, mutilated soldiers to Caberet, the crusaders' next target, as a very particular message for the defenders there.[3]

At Béziers, because the city's entire population, heretic and Catholic alike, had been indiscriminately massacred, there could be no mass burning of heretics. Although de Montfort had personally supervised the immolation of a small group of Cathar *perfecti* at Castres in 1209,[4] it was therefore not until the 1210 campaign that the opportunity came his way to burn a large number of heretics at once – a sight, according to the pro-Catholic chronicler Pierre des Vaux-de-Cernay, that all the crusaders experienced with feelings of 'intense joy'.[5]

The opportunity was provided by the fortress city of Minerve where it was known that many Cathar *perfecti* – both men and women – had taken refuge. De Montfort laid siege to the stronghold in June 1210 and forced its surrender some weeks later after cutting off its water supply and deploying his war-catapults and stone-guns to bombard it mercilessly. As had been the case at the surrender of Carcassonne there was no massacre; but this time the Cathar *perfecti* sheltering in Minerve were identified and singled out. Their choice was either to recant or die. Initially none recanted, and one of the *perfecti* explained to a Catholic priest: 'Neither death nor life can tear us from the faith to which we are joined.'[6] On 22 July 1210, the exact anniversary of the sack of Béziers (and again, significantly, the feast day of Saint Mary Magdalene)[7] Vaux-de-Cernay reports that a huge fire was prepared. While it blazed and roared the prisoners were brought out before it and:

> ... more than one hundred and forty of these heretical *perfecti* were flung thereon at one time. To tell the truth, there was no need for our men to drag them thither; for they remained obdurate in their wickedness, and with great gaiety of heart cast themselves into the fire. Three women, however, were spared; being brought down from the stake ... and reconciled with the Holy Roman Church.[8]

What stands out from the next year's campaign – 1211 – is the fate of an even larger group of *perfecti*. On 3 May 1211, after a lengthy siege, the crusaders breached the walls of Lavaur and poured through, seizing the city. Amongst the captives were more than 400 *perfecti*, both men and women, who were burnt on a gigantic bonfire.[9] Though not Cathars, the 80 knights who had commanded the garrison were hanged for protecting them. Guiraude, the Lady of Lavaur, was also brutalised then murdered. This high-ranking Occitan noblewoman was a Cathar *credente*, much loved in the city, of whom it was said: 'Never did a living soul leave her roof without having eaten well first.'[10] De Montfort handed her over to a band of mercenaries who dragged her through the streets heaping indignities upon her, before throwing her down a well and killing her with stones.[11]

A month later de Montfort burnt 60 more Cathar *perfecti* at Cassis.[12]

In 1213 King Peter II of Aragon, famous for having recently won a great victory against the Moors in Spain, intervened against the crusaders. Some of the hard-pressed Occitan noblemen who were protecting the Cathars were his relatives, and there was a large population of Cathars in Aragon itself. Peter brought hope, a splendid force of 2,000 battle-hardened knights and 50,000 infantry into the equation – more than enough to change the course of the war. But it was not to be. Though he was heavily outnumbered, de Montfort attacked Peter at Muret and, through brilliant, ruthless generalship, succeeded in killing him in battle.[13] At the sight of this terrible and totally unexpected catastrophe the Aragonese and Occitan forces hesitated, then began to retreat. The retreat turned to panic and then to a rout with De Montfort's knights in hot pursuit. Thousands were cut down, drowned in a nearby river, or crushed as they fled.[14]

It took the Occitan nobles three years to lick their wounds and gather their strength before they were ready to take on de Montfort again. Nonetheless by 1216 the Count of Toulouse had succeeded in raising an army and, for the first time, began to inflict serious reverses on the crusaders. Using his favoured strategy – if in doubt attack – de Montfort tried to take the initiative by besieging Toulouse. The city fought back ferociously and – refusing to be put on the psychological defensive – routinely sent out armed sorties to attack de Montfort in his own camp.

The siege dragged on for many months and the defenders' sorties grew ever more daring. On the morning of 25 June 1218, while repelling one of these raids, de Montfort was killed outright by a projectile from a stone-gun mounted on the walls of Toulouse and said to have been fired by a crew of women and young girls.[15] The *Chanson de la Croisade albigeoise* describes his death:

A stone flew straight to its proper mark, and smote Count Simon upon his helm of steel, in such wise that his eyeballs, brains, teeth, skull and jawbone all flew into pieces, and he fell down upon the ground stark dead, blackened and bloody.[16]

The darkest hour before the falsest dawn

With de Montfort thus felled like a pole-axed ox his son Amaury took charge and abandoned the failed siege within a month. In 1219, however, he was back in action leading yet another crusade. This time he was joined by Prince Louis of France, out to do his crusading duty and bringing with him '20 bishops, 30 counts, 600 knights and 10,000 archers.'[17] The two armies met in front of the unfortunate city of Marmande, which Amaury had already besieged, and launched a joint attack, overwhelming its defences.

Then another of those demonic interludes of the Crusades took place – when the Catholic troops, urged on by their bishops, fell upon the fleeing citizens in the narrow streets of the city. From the *Chanson* comes this harrowing description of what they did at Marmande:

> They hurried into the town, waving sharp swords, and it was now that the massacre and fearful butchery began. Men and women, barons, ladies, babes in arms, were all stripped and despoiled and put to the sword. The ground was littered with blood, brains, fragments of flesh, limbless trunks, hacked-off arms and legs, bodies ripped up or stove in, livers and hearts that had been chopped to pieces or ground into mash. It was as though they had rained down from the sky. The whole place ran with blood – streets, fields, river bank. Neither man, nor woman, young or old survived; not a single person escaped ...[18]

Did the Catholic forces serve the God of Evil, as the Cathars claimed?

We cannot say whether a 'God' of any sort was behind the butchery at Béziers and Marmande, the mass burnings and martyrdom of the *perfecti* and the ruin of Occitania. But since the Albigensian Crusades were launched and maintained exclusively on the pope's initiative, we can say, without equivocation, that the Catholic Church was directly responsible for all these evil things, and that it was acting in the name of its God.

Soon after Marmande, their 40 days of crusading up, their sins forgiven and their indulgences earned, Prince Louis and his French soldiers went home. Amaury de Montfort and his much diminished army were left to continue the campaign but it soon became obvious that they were not capable of winning it alone. Part of the problem was generalship: although a competent soldier, Amaury was a man of greatly inferior calibre to his warrior father. But equally important was a renewed spirit of national resistance in Occitania, where the people and nobles now began a determined fightback against the occupying forces. Under the leadership of the Count of Toulouse, huge territories were recaptured and by the time of his death in August 1222 the war of liberation seemed unstoppable. The advances continued under his son and in January 1224 the young Count of Toulouse and the Count of Foix – the other main leader of the Occitanian resistance – signed a peace treaty with Amaury de Montfort that secured the withdrawal of the bulk of crusading forces.[19]

But doom still overshadowed Occitania and its citizens of all religious persuasions who had protected the Cathars so bravely, and died so uncomplainingly on their behalf, through the 15 years of horror from 1209 to 1224. It is a quite remarkable fact of these dreadful wars that the Cathars never once seem to have been blamed by their non-Cathar countrymen for the catastrophe that all were now plunged in together. And it is remarkable too, although Cathar *credentes* did join the resistance, that there is not a single example in all the extensive records of the Albigensian Crusades of Cathar *perfecti* ever participating in any way in violence. Despite enormous provocation – literally to the death – they seem to have adhered with almost superhuman consistency to their principles of absolute pacifism and non-resistance.[20]

Nor is it that they were simply suicidal and wanted to die – something that they have frequently and quite wrongly been accused of. Despite their negative view of material life the Cathars were utterly opposed to suicide and believed that each of us, so far as possible, should live out the natural term of our soul's imprisonment. Accordingly the *perfecti* disguised themselves, abandoned the wearing of their characteristic black robes, went on the run, sheltered where they could in safe-houses, caves, or forests, and used any and every form of evasion short of actually fighting back. As Zoé Oldenbourg observes:

> It is easy to see how, to that hard-pressed society, such hunted, indomitable pacifists must have appeared as the only true fathers in religion and sources of spiritual consolation, the one genuine moral authority which men could obey.[21]

The Pope hires the French to finish the job

The treaty of January 1224 was the falsest of dawns. Only a month after he had signed it Amaury de Montfort divested himself of his inherited title to the vast swathe of Occitania that his father had won during his glory years. All these lands that the de Montforts had stolen from their rightful Occitanian owners were now officially handed over by Amaury to a man much better equipped to consolidate the spectacular land-grab forever – the king of France.[22]

Previously, under King Philip Augustus, the French monarchy had resisted direct involvement in the Albigensian Crusades – despite many strident demands from the papacy for French intervention. Although Philip had not objected to the participation of his son Louis, as well as some of his barons and lesser nobles, he had made a clear policy decision to stay out of it himself. But when the old king died on 14 July 1223, it was Louis who succeeded to the throne[23] – the same Prince Louis who had ordered the despicable massacre at Marmande in 1219.

Now crowned Louis VIII, and with legal title to much of Occitania handed to him on a plate by Amaury de Montfort, he was ready for a return visit. This time what he had in mind was full-scale annexation under the disguise of a crusade. Even so he drove a hard bargain with Pope Honorius III (Innocent III's successor) who, conveniently, had begun to urge him to mount a new crusade into Occitania from the moment he had ascended to the throne. So desperate was Honorius to smash the Cathars once and for all that he made an unprecedented agreement with Louis. In return for subduing Occitania, the crown would be rewarded to the measure of one tenth of all French Church revenues for five years.[24]

In the spring of 1226, almost two years after he had received the title-deeds to Occitania from Amaury de Montfort, Louis VIII set out on his bogus 'crusade' of annexation. So overwhelming was the force he led that he received the surrender of several great cities, including Carcassonne and Narbonne, without even having to fight. His first and last major setback occurred on 8 November 1226 when he was suddenly taken ill and died.[25]

But still the campaign went on. Louis had been married to Blanche of Castile, a hard-hearted and determined women with vast ambitions for their 12-year-old son (also Louis – the future 'Saint King' Louis IX) to whom she was now regent. On her orders the French army remained in Occitania, gradually wearing down the resistance – once again represented mainly by the Counts of Toulouse and Foix. In 1228 and 1229 the French adopted a scorched earth policy, unleashing a terror campaign on the countryside, burning farms and villages throughout Occitania, destroying crops, driving the inhabitants out as refugees. By 1229 the will of the people to resist further after years of exhausting conflict had been utterly destroyed and the counts sued for peace.[26]

It was a crushing peace that included a public scourging in Notre Dame Cathedral in Paris of the Count of Toulouse on 12 April 1229.[27] And although it marked the official end of the Albigensian Crusades, it robbed Occitania of its independence forever, putting a huge area of this once free land under French control – effectively as an occupied state – and leading to its full annexation into the kingdom of France within half a century.

One of the provisions of the treaty allowed the count to retain nominal title to some of his hereditary domains around Toulouse but also obliged him to go into exile for five years, this exile to start no later than June 1230. In order to reduce even further his time amongst his own subjects, and thus his potential as a focus of rebellion, he was detained in Paris as a house prisoner in the Louvre Palace for six months after signing the treaty. By the time he reached Toulouse in November 1229 he found that the city's massive defensive walls had been pulled down to ensure that it would never again become a centre of pro-Cathar and anti-French resistance.[28]

Pieces of silver

Despite the mass holocausts of *perfecti*, and increasingly focussed persecution, Catharism continued throughout the 1220s to be a vibrant religion that had an important place in the life of Occitania and that still attracted large numbers of *credentes*. There is evidence from the first half of the decade, when it seemed that the curse of the Crusades had been lifted, of fairly active reorganisation and restructuring of the Cathar Church. The jurisdictional boundaries of bishoprics were re-established and in 1225 the Cathars even felt confident enough to establish a new bishopric – that of Razes.[29] Although many *perfecti* had been lost to the stake it has been calculated that several hundred, both male and female, were still active in Occitania in 1225.[30] So clearly, while the Albigensian Crusades had done much damage and taken many lives, they had not yet succeeded in their primary goal of eradicating the heresy of Catharism.

Military activities had of course occupied centre stage during the Crusades, but an element of heresy hunting had followed every campaign since 1209. In July 1214, for example, at the height of Simon de Montfort's successes, we find Foulques, the hated Catholic bishop of Toulouse, appointing a certain:

> Brother Dominic and his companions ... to extirpate heresy and
> eliminate vice, and promote the teachings of the Faith ... as preachers
> in our diocese.[31]

This 'Brother Dominic' was Father Dominic de Guzmán, the Spanish monk who was to establish the famous Dominican monastic order in the Toulouse area on 11 February 1218.[32] Early on in the Albigensian Crusades, when Arnaud Amalric was still papal legate, Dominic had been invested with inquisitorial powers. Until his death in 1221 he deployed these powers mercilessly and his systematic programme of persecutions and investigations in Occitania laid the groundwork that would lead to the formal establishment of the much-feared papal Inquisition in 1233.[33]

The reverses suffered by the crusaders after Simon de Montfort's death in 1218 had been a set-back to the heresy hunters too. But all this changed when the French renewed the Crusades in 1226 and, under the devout guidance of Blanche of Castile, made it clear that they supported the strongest action against heretics. Soon afterwards Peter Isarn, the Cathar bishop of Carcassonne, and Gérard de la Mothe, a Cathar deacon from La Bessède, were burned at the stake.[34]

The peace treaty that Count Raymond VI of Toulouse went to France to sign, and endured a public scourging for on 12 April 1229, introduced draconian procedures for the hunting down of heresy.[35] In the following years the gradual expansion of the use of these procedures, always backed up by 'the secular arm' – i.e. the French occupation forces – meant that the Church came to exercise unlimited power over the life and liberty of the people of Occitania. As a signatory to the treaty Count Raymond was even obliged to persecute heretics himself – the same heretics who he and his father had fought so hard to protect for the past 20 years. He was to order his own bailiffs to hunt them down on the much reduced lands that the treaty had left nominally under his control, and he was to assist in hunting them down on the far larger lands that had been ceded to the French crown:

> We will purge these lands of heretics and of the stench of heresy and
> we will also aid the purgation of the lands which the Lord King shall
> hold ... In order better and more easily to unmask them [the heretics],
> we promise to pay two marks of silver for the next two years and, after
> that, one mark to every person who causes a heretic to be arrested, on

condition that the heretic is condemned as such by the bishop of the place, or by a competent authority.[36]

As well as paying blood money to informers, Raymond was also required to pay large sums directly to the Church – 10,000 marks, supposedly to repair damage done to its property by heretics, 4,000 marks to the monasteries, and a further 4,000 marks to support 14 masters of Catholic theology at the University of Toulouse.[37] The idea, comments medieval historian Martin Barber, was to fill the land 'with bastions of orthodoxy where heretics could find no comfort or protection.'[38]

Informer culture

At the same time the heat was turned up on individual Cathars at all levels with a whole raft of new statutes. These 45 cold-hearted, methodical, pettifogging, bureaucratic decrees made the suppression of heresy obligatory under common law. A few examples will give us a glimpse of just how far the Church was prepared to go in invading and taking control of people's everyday lives and drawing them into inhumanities:

- In every parish throughout the land the Catholic bishops were to nominate a priest and two or three trusted laypersons 'of unblemished reputation, who shall take an oath to search out, loyally and assiduously, such heretics as may be resident in the said parish.' The job of these state-sponsored vigilantes required them to 'make a close inspection of all suspect houses, their chambers and cellarage, and likewise all concealed hiding places, the which to be demolished.' They were to arrest not only heretics but also anyone who had helped heretics in any way.

- A person who had permitted a heretic to stay on his land was to confess to this crime forthwith: 'else on conviction he will forfeit his lands in perpetuity, and be liable to personal punishment.'

- Persons whose lands were used by heretics without their knowledge or agreement were subject to the same penalties.

- 'The house in which a heretic is discovered shall be razed to the ground, and the land on which it stands confiscated.'

1. The *Benben* stone of the pyramid of Amenemhet III displayed at the Egyptian Antiquities Museum in Cairo. Note the 'eyes' at the centre of the pyramidion, the latter said to have been originally covered with gold leaf.

3. Statue of Giordano Bruno at Campo dei Fiori in Rome.

2. François-Édouard Picot's 1827 painting on the ceiling of Room 30 of the Louvre: *L'Etude et le Génie dévoilent à Athènes l'Antique Egypte*. The 'unveiled' Isis on a throne flanked by lions is contemplating a landscape of pyramids and an obelisk.

4. View of the 'octagonal ellipse' in the Piazza San Pietro from the roof of the Basilica.

6. A Knight Templar, showing the *croix pattée* that characterized order, and th octagonal frame within which it can be imposed.

5. Sully Wing Room 26: this is the room that most symbolized the 'sacred' union of Anne of Austria and Louis XIII. The wood paneling of the room is from her apartments form Château Vincennes, and on the east wall hangs a portrait of the queen depicted as 'Minerva'. Facing the queen is a portrait of Louis XIII. Between them has recently been placed a statue of the Egyptian God Amun of

7. 'Here is seen the very ancient goddess and queen of the Egyptians', etching from the fifteenth century. Note the boat and the 'dog' on the standard

8. Coat-of-arms of Paris, fifteenth century.

9. The coat-of-arms of Paris commissioned by Napoleon in 1811, showing Isis on the prow of the boat and her star, Sirius, leading the way. Note the three bees of 'Charlemagne' to symbolize imperial solar royalty. Also note the Hermetic caduceus piercing the crown supporting the imperial eagle.

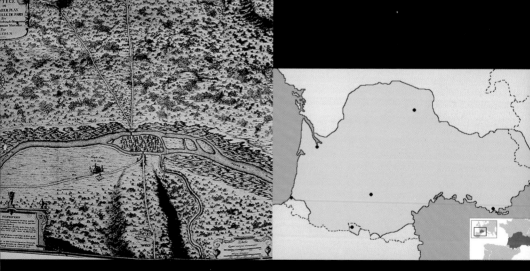

10. A reconstruction map of the region of Paris before the city was built, showing the location of the Temple of Isis (where the Abbey of Saint-Germain-des-Prés now stands). The region, some sixteenth-century historians claimed, was thus known as 'near the Temple of Isis', hence the 'Isi' in 'Parisi'.

11. Occitania. Inset shows relevant portion of modern France.

12. Aerial view of the Louvre looking east. Note the Historical Axis passing through the equestrian statue of Louis XIV (as 'Alexander the Great'), then through the south flank of the Cour Carrée and extending towards the horizon where the rising of Sirius took place. Note the 'boat' shape of the Île de la Cité on the right.

13. Aerial view of the Historical Axis of Paris looking west from the Louvre towards La Défense on the distant horizon. Note the deviation of the axis.

15. Winter solstice sunrise at Karnak-Thebes along main axis. Compare to sunset in Paris along the Champs-Élysées on 6 August (see left). The orientation is 26.5 degrees from the latitude at both locations.

14. Sunset on 6 August along the Historical Axis (Champs-Élysées). This date is the feast of the Transfiguration of Christ, here clearly evoking solar symbolism also linked to Louis XIV, the Sun King, under whose reign the Historical Axis was first defined.

16. Sunset on 6 August along the Historical Axis (Avenue de la Grande Armée). The Grande Arche is, however, turned 32 degrees from due west such that the sun will be in the centre of the arch on 24 June, St. John's Day, celebrated by the Freemasons as the 'New Year' (see right).

17. View of the Grande Arche looking east. The 6 degrees deviation of the Grande Arche's axis from that of the Historical Axis is obvious. This produces an orientation of 32 degrees north-of-west towards the sunset horizon, matching the sunset on 24 June (see left).

18. The equestrian statue of Louis XIV as 'Alexander the Great'. The legend that Alexander was the son of Amun, the supreme sun-god of Egypt at Thebes (modern Luxor), was well known to classical scholars in the seventeenth century, and it is no surprise that Louis XIV, who insisted on being seen as the 'Sun King', was often depicted in art as Alexander the Great or Apollo.

19. Revolutionary etching showing Voltaire (left) and Rousseau (right) introducing the Supreme Being to the French people, the deity here shown as an eye within a blazing sun (known also as a 'glory') instead of a triangle or pyramid.

20. The 'eye in the pyramid' on the frontispiece of the Declaration of the Rights of Man and the Citizen, drafted in August 1789.

21. The reverse motif of the Great Seal of the United States. This same motif also can be seen on the US one-dollar bill.

22. August 1793. The so-called 'Fountain of Regeneration' (also known as 'Isis of the Bastille'). This was a statue of the Egyptian goddess Isis with water sprouting from her nipples. The president of the National Convention is filling his cup with the 'regenerative' liquid symbolizing the new order, social and religious, for the French Republic, while the revolutionary crowds cheer.

23. August 1793: a 'pyramid' outside the Hôtel de Ville in Paris in honour of the Supreme Being.

JOSÉPHINE.

« Mes freres et mes sœurs,—dit l'aimable compagne
Du grand Napoléon, cet autre Charlemagne.—
Mon epoux a dit vrai, l'exemple, les leçons
Des vertus, de l'honneur, viennent des Francs-Maçons.

(Paroles de l'Impératrice Joséphine à la fête d'adoption des Francs-Chevaliers à Strasbourg en 1803.)

DECHEVAUX-DUMESNIL,
Rédacteur en chef du Journal le FRANC-MAÇON.

24. An etching in the journal *Le Franc-Maçon* showing the Empress Joséphine in her Masonic regalia at the ceremony of 'Adoption des Francs-Chevaliers' at a lodge in Strasbourg in 1803. The ditty translates as: 'My Brothers and Sisters,' says the lovely companion of the great Napoleon, this other Charlemagne, 'my husband spoke true when he said that the examples and lessons of virtue and honour come from Freemasons.'

25. Head of Cybele/Isis found in Paris in 1675 in the St. Eustache gardens. It probably dates from the Antonine period and was brought from Italy. Compare the tourelle on the head of the goddess to that on the Arc de Triomphe, Place de l'Étoile.

26. A goddess placing the imperial laurels on Napoleon, and at his feet another goddess wearing the tourelle of Cybele/Isis.

27. The goddess Isis on the façade of the Louvre looking east at the rising sun in the Cour Napoléon.

28. The *Loge Bonaparte* (1853), one of many Masonic lodges bearing the name of Napoleon, showing Napoleon and Joachim Murat in Masonic regalia. The caption at the top reads 'Where the laws of Freemasonry rule, also rules Happiness'.

29. Revolutionary etching showing Napoleon introducing the Supreme Being to all religious groups. Note the Giza pyramids on the top register.

30. The 'missing' obelisk at the temple of Luxor.

31. The obelisk of the Concorde that once stood outside the

- 'If the resident bailiff of a locality suspected to be a haunt of heretics does not hunt the said heretics down zealously, he shall lose his position without compensation.'

- 'All persons may search out heretics on their neighbours' land.'

- Heretics who had abjured Catharism and returned to the Church were to wear 'two crosses on their outer garment, one on the right and other on the left side, and of a different colour from the garment itself …'

- In every parish all males over 14 years of age and all females over 12 were required to swear an oath before their bishop, renewable every two years thereafter, that they would be loyal Catholics, abjure heresy, help to hunt down heretics, and inform on any heretics known to them. In the process the name of every person dwelling in every parish was to be recorded and those who failed to take the oath were to be treated as suspected heretics.

- Every person of either sex on the parish lists (again aged over 14 in the case of males and over 12 in the case of females) was to be compelled to confess to their parish priest at least three times a year and to take Communion at Christmas, Easter and Pentecost. 'Priests are to seek out any who fail to attend Holy Communion, and who thereby incur suspicion of heretical beliefs.'

- Lay persons were forbidden to possess any of the books of the Old and New Testament 'with the exception of the Psalter, the Breviary, and the Book of Hours of the Blessed Virgin; and it is rigorously forbidden to possess even these in the vernacular tongue.'

- 'Any person denounced by public opinion, and whose ill reputation is known to the bishop, shall properly be called a heretic.'[39]

And so the statutes droned on, releasing into the free air of Occitania the horrible odour of a Nazi-style informer culture and, as Zoé Oldenbourg observes, setting up 'a system of virtual police control over the entire population.'[40] We use the word Nazi advisedly here. A decade and a half earlier, in 1215 at its Fourth Lateran Council, the Catholic Church had already anticipated the Warsaw Ghetto by more than 700 years when it compelled the Jews of Europe to stitch a prominent yellow circle onto their clothing.[41] Now, following the 1229 treaty, we see the same treatment – albeit with the different symbol of the two crosses – applied to reconciled heretics. Considered a 'symbol of shame' the two crosses came routinely to be coloured yellow as specified in a later statute which also gave the exact dimensions of the crosses and more information on how they were to be worn. All reconciled heretics, states the relevant law:

> ... shall carry from now on and forever two yellow crosses on all their clothes except their shirts, and one arm shall be two palms [8 inches] long while the other transversal arm shall be a palm and a half [6 inches] long, and each shall be 3 digits [2.25 inches] wide, with one to be worn in front of the chest, and the other between the shoulders.[42]

Required under severe and possibly fatal penalty not to 'move about either inside or outside' their homes without wearing the crosses, reconciled heretics were moreover obliged to 'redo or renew the crosses if they are torn or destroyed by age.'[43]

The Dominican flying squad

One gets a sense of the kind of cold, calculating, minds that must have been at work behind the dreaming-up and enforcement of such regulations – regulations that were designed to sever the bonds of warmth and trust that link human beings one to another. The clear objective was to create an atmosphere of suspicion, blame and jeopardy, and to whip up a frenzy of denouncements by capitalising on people's fears of loss of property – and far worse.

The following years saw many heretics seized and killed. On one occasion, for example, shortly after he had taken office as bishop of Toulouse in 1231, Raymond de Fauga was able to gloat over the mass-burning of 19 high-ranking Cathar *perfecti* who had been betrayed, ambushed and captured at one of their meetings.[44] De Fauga was a Dominican, the monastic order established by the late Saint Dominic with the explicit purpose of attacking heresy. Since 1215 these austere and zealous monks had occupied three houses near Toulouse's Narbonne Gate. In 1230, in recognition of their growing importance, they moved to a new site beside the Saracen Wall.[45] By 1234 there were more than 40 of them in Toulouse alone and they had established missions in many other parts of Europe as well.[46]

Tremendous recognition, prestige and power had begun to come their way when Pope Gregory IX had succeeded Honorius III in 1227. Gregory was unhappy with the system so far established in Europe for the suppression of heresy. Though primarily under the control of the bishops, other figures with overlapping responsibilities were also frequently involved. The result was chaos and inefficiency at a time when attention was beginning to be focussed on the supposed 'danger' posed by Cathar communities in Germany, France and northern Italy, as well as the continuing survival of Catharism in Occitania. With the linked Bogomil heresy still looking very strong further East, the paranoid tendencies of the Catholic Church went into overdrive and there was a widespread conviction that enemies were hiding themselves everywhere.

The benefit in this for the Dominicans was that in 1231 Pope Gregory appointed them as his own personal 'flying inquisition', superior to the bishops and independent of them, to discover, arrest, interrogate and condemn German Cathars. In 1233, seeing the success of their work in Germany, Gregory also asked them to do the same job in France and in Occitania.[47] Success bred success, triumph followed triumph, and soon the Dominicans, aided to some extent by Franciscans and local prelates, had been appointed as the official papal Inquisition, overriding all other authorities in any matter concerning heresy.[48]

The term 'inquisition' had long been used for the process of extracting confessions from heretics, and 'inquisitions' – interrogations and mass trials of suspected heretics – were periodically held by the bishops. But this was the first time in the history of the Church that officials had been appointed whose only function was to conduct inquisitions, who were officially titled 'inquisitors', and who were responsible directly and exclusively to the pope.[49]

You never expect the Spanish Inquisition

When we began this research we did not know ourselves that the famed (but misnamed) 'Spanish Inquisition' (subject of a memorable Monty Python sketch) had first been established in April 1233 by Pope Gregory IX. Nor did we know that the original and explicit purpose of the Inquisition was to root out and destroy the Cathar heresy. Building on the repressive structures that had already been firmly laid down in Occitania, the Dominican inquisitors were empowered after 1233 to use virtually any measure they wished to extract confessions and to crush the Cathar faith. They began at once to institute a reign of terror – true and awful terror from which no one was safe.

A chilling example is provided by the behaviour of Raymond de Fauga, the Dominican prior who Pope Gregory IX had appointed as bishop of Toulouse in 1231. A few years later, on 4 August 1235 (by chance the first official feast day for the recently canonised Saint Dominic) de Fauga held Mass at the order's convent in Toulouse and then made his way to the refectory to take dinner with the other monks. While he was washing his hands an informer was admitted bringing him a titbit of hot news from his spy-network. In a nearby house an elderly Cathar lady lay in a fever and close to death. She was a *grande dame* of a good family and had been visited shortly before by a fugitive *perfectus* who had given her the *consolamentum* and then slipped away.[50]

Annoyingly, it was too late to catch the *perfectus*. But the old woman wasn't going anywhere! Joyfully seizing the opportunity to bring another sinner to justice de Fauga and his fellow Dominicans, dressed only in monks' habits, left their dinner and hurried at once to the house pinpointed by the informer. It was very close, in the Rue de l'Olmet sec, and turned out to belong to a certain Peitivin Brosier who had long been suspected as a Cathar sympathiser.[51] The dying woman was his mother-in-law, and as the Dominicans brushed past Brosier into her sick room it seems he only had time to warn her that the 'lord bishop' was coming. In her fevered state she unfortunately did not understand that he meant the Catholic bishop of Toulouse and mistook de Fauga for a Cathar bishop.[52]

A horrifying scene then unfolded as the Dominican took advantage of the frail old lady's confusion, spoke to her in familiar dualistic terms 'about contempt for the world and earthly things'[53] and began to question her concerning her faith. Having no reason to suspect that she had fallen into the hands of a skilled and unscrupulous impostor, she innocently revealed all her Cathar beliefs and confirmed the extent of her attachment to them. De Fauga, whose cynicism was bottomless, even carried the charade so far as to urge her to remain steadfast in these beliefs, admonishing her firmly:

... the fear of death should not make you confess aught else than that which you hold firmly in your whole heart.[54]

The old woman's honest reply, as one would expect from a dying *credente* who had been recently consoled, was that she would certainly not lie about her beliefs, and thus obliterate the benefits of the *consolamentum* she had received, when there was so little of her life left to her.[55] For de Fauga, who had everything he needed, this was the perfect moment to reveal his true identity. Looming over her bed he pronounced her a heretic and ordered her to recant and embrace the Catholic faith.

The old lady was by now fully awake to her predicament and, like many a brave Cathar before her, refused to recant. De Fauga and the other Dominicans insisted that she must. The badgering went on for some time in front of a growing number of witnesses who had crowded in from the neighbourhood, all keen to see how this was going to end. Finally, since his victim 'persevered with increasing stubbornness in her heretical alliance',[56] de Fauga decided to 'relax her to the secular arm' – the Church's usual euphemism for having local civil authorities do the dirty work of executing a heretic.[57] In this case, to speed things up, a magistrate had already been called and now legally sentenced the dying woman to death![58]

Runners were despatched to prepare a huge fire at the public execution ground, a place called *Pre du Comte* (the count's meadow), and word of the spectacle was sent out all over Toulouse attracting a large crowd. For the old woman it must have seemed a vision straight from hell, exactly what her beloved Cathar Church had always told her this world was anyway. Since she was quite unable to walk, the Dominicans had ordered her to be tied to her bed. She had then been carried out of her son-in-law's house, bed and all, and brought to this place. Now, after refusing one more chance to recant, she was thrown into the raging flames and burnt alive.

'This done', concludes William Pelisson, one of the witnesses to these events and himself a Dominican inquisitor who entirely approved of de Fauga's actions:[59]

> The Bishop, together with the monks and their attendants, returned to the refectory and giving thanks to God and the Blessed Dominic, ate with rejoicing what had been prepared for them.[60]

One wonders what happened to the old woman's son-in-law, Peitivin Brosier. All we know from Pelisson's cheerful account is that he was arrested.[61] Under the rules of the Inquisition in force at the time it is unlikely that he would have survived his subsequent – inevitable – interrogation without recanting the Cathar faith, accepting Catholicism fully and informing on his friends. Even then he would have remained a prisoner in close confinement for the rest of his life. All other members of his family, as well as all his known associates and all members of his wife's family and all their known associates would have been interrogated and their statements cross-referred to detect any inconsistencies that might expose other heretics amongst them.

And of course, since he'd sheltered his mother-in-law – a proven heretic – it goes without saying that his house in the Rue de l'Olmet sec would have been razed to the ground.

That was just the way the Inquisition worked.

Paradox

When William Pelisson concluded his congratulatory report of the trapping and brutal murder of a helpless old lady, he modestly expressed the view that such a great achievement should not be credited to the Dominicans alone:

> God performed these works ... to the glory and praise of His name ... to the exaltation of the faith and to the discomfiture of the heretics.[62]

Reading these sentiments, we find ourselves – not for the first time – overtaken by the sense of a really weird 'disconnect' between the words and the deeds of Catholic holy men like Pelisson. He was part of a Christian gang that had just done the most awful thing – something really psychotic and unbelievably cruel – to a fellow human being. But instead of being ashamed of such wickedness, he was proud of it and felt that it glorified his God! Nowhere in the New Testament is it possible to find justification for such behaviour, so which God did he think he was talking about?

Once again the sense of disconnect goes away if we look at the whole scene from a Cathar perspective. Then the vile deeds of the Dominicans make perfect sense. Of course they acted as they did. Of course they took delight in the pain and suffering of the old lady. Theirs was the church of the God of Evil. What else would you expect of them?

We're only half serious ... Who's to say that there's even such an entity as 'God' at all, let alone Good and Evil Gods? Since there will never be any certainty on such matters this side of the grave, all we can do is weigh up the competing theories and compare them with the behaviour of the participants. When we do that it is clear that Cathar theology provides an internally consistent explanation for why the Catholic Church burnt people at the stake and butchered the populations of whole cities. No such internally consistent explanation is forthcoming from Catholic theology; on the contrary the massacres and the many acts of prolonged, deliberate cruelty that the Catholic Church was responsible for represent a profound and inexplicable paradox when set against the teachings of Christ.

Making hell on earth

Every year from 1233 onwards, this impossible paradox of gentle Christ and brutal Church was repeatedly reinforced by the Inquisition. The first two official inquisitors in Occitania, Peter Seila and William Arnold, both of whom were recruited from amongst the Dominicans of Toulouse, were appointed by Pope Gregory IX in late 1233.[63] Like all natural bureaucracies with high-level backing the Inquisition grew unrestrainedly. By the end of the decade numerous different teams of inquisitors like Seila and Arnold were at work throughout Occitania interrogating, cross-referencing, condemning and burning. From the beginning they were a law unto themselves, independent both of the bishops and the civil authorities, with unlimited authority to act against heretics.

Their standard methodology was deliberately intimidating, designed to spread terror in any community they descended upon and to 'drive a wedge into the façade of community solidarity, so that the loyalties and fears which had held it together could be undermined.'[64] Task forces, typically led by one or two inquisitors supported by an attendant band of soldiers, clerks and magistrates, roamed the land going from village to village, town to town, city to city. The idea, was that each unit should be self-sufficient as detective, gaoler, judge, jury and executioner, identifying suspected heretics and 'processing' them from freedom either to repentance or the stake in as short a time as possible.

Methods of operation were constantly refined in response to the latest evasions and escape plans of the heretics, although by the 1240s large parts of the procedure had been standardised and written up by the Dominicans in a series of detailed technical manuals. From these we learn that in each parish the Inquisition would begin with a public meeting which the entire local community would be required to attend. Once everyone was assembled the inquisitor would appear and address them with a general sermon condemning the Cathar heresy. Then notice was served on all males over 14 and all females over 12 ('or younger if perchance they shall have been guilty of an offence')[65] to appear individually before the inquisitor over the coming days. If no previous inquisition had visited the parish an announcement would be made granting:

> ... indulgence from imprisonment to all from that place who have not been cited by name or who have not yet earned the indulgence, if within a specified time, they come voluntarily as penitents to tell the exact and full truth about themselves and about others.[66]

In other words, those who pre-emptively informed on themselves or others, and were willing to recant their heresy, would earn exemption from punishment, perhaps even escape punishment altogether. By contrast those who knew something – anything – and decided to keep quiet about it were taking an immense risk that their neighbours or friends might inform on them. If that were to happen they would be judged to have misled the Inquisition – an offence for which extreme penalties applied.[67] In such circumstances, notes the historian Martin Barber:

> The temptation to denounce others was almost overwhelming, if only for defensive reasons ... In a community that had had frequent contact with heretics ... nobody was likely to be innocent in the eyes of the Church, and therefore anybody could have been written into the Inquisitors' copious records.[68]

The atmosphere of mutual suspicion was increased – together with the likelihood of denunciations – by the way that all the parishioners were then interrogated, one by one, with no opportunity for the others waiting in line to hear what was being said by their neighbours. Again and again these *in camera* interviews proved to have an unnerving effect, demoralising communities all across Occitania, turning their attention inwards on themselves in a most negative manner, and weakening their will to cooperate in a fightback.[69]

Indeed the Inquisition's sweeping powers had set aside at a stroke all the ancient legal safeguards that had formerly protected individual rights in medieval society. An example was the right for the accused to be represented whilst undergoing interrogation. Theoretically even the Inquisition had to abide by this. In practice, however, no accused heretic was ever represented as he stood before the inquisitors. This was because any lawyer foolish enough to defend an accused heretic would immediately have been suspected and accused of heresy himself. Once that happened (accusation was enough; he didn't have to be found guilty) his arguments would have become inadmissible and he would have stood in immediate jeopardy of his own life.[70]

The idea of undergoing the full process of interrogation by the Inquisition would have been a terrifying prospect whether one were a heretic or not. Questioning was inexorable and, on top of an array of psychological techniques, it's known that the inquisitors routinely used torture to extract confessions long before the pope gave his official blessing for them to do so in 1252.[71] Between the torture and interrogation sessions, the accused would be confined in deeply uncomfortable conditions intended to undermine his will further. Cells of the 'little-ease' variety – in which the prisoner had room neither to sit, stand up or lie down – are reported to have been particularly favoured by the inquisitors. Other devices included keeping cells knee-deep in water, or permanently dark, starving prisoners, and shackling them hand and foot in heavy chains.

In the most recalcitrant cases such interrogations could continue over periods of months or even years.[72] However, once a confession had been extracted and a judgement made, the chances in law of reversing it were about zero – even if the judgement were manifestly faulty. Since appeals were not allowed the inquisitors literally held the powers of life and death in their hands, without any checks or balances.[73] They were amongst their enemies and could do what they liked to them. The consequence was that many Cathars were burnt at the stake, many who recanted on pain of death nevertheless remained imprisoned for life, and countless numbers of those who may not even have been Cathars themselves but who had at one time or another spoken to a Cathar, or had some other such trivial contact with the heresy, were exiled from their homeland for years fulfilling arduous pilgrimages imposed on them by the Inquisition.[74]

Burning the living and the dead

Seila and Arnold, the first two inquisitors, were the prototypes of a ruthless breed who would continue to rend the enemies of Catholicism for another six centuries. Soon after taking office they were able to arrange a spectacular demonstration of the efficient spy-network already at their disposal when they succeeded in trapping and arresting Vigoros de Baconia one of the leading Cathar *perfecti* in Toulouse. He was summarily tried, condemned and burnt alive.[75]

During the two years from 1233 to 1235 the two inquisitors initiated what has been described as a 'veritable reign of terror', first in Toulouse and then far and wide throughout Occitania.[76] Burnings of individuals and small groups became commonplace and on a number of occasions there were larger catches to be had. In 1234 for example, on their very first visit to Moissac, Seila and Arnold presided over the mass burning of 210 Cathar *perfecti* who they had condemned as 'contumacious heretics'.[77]

Keeping a record as ever, the faithful Dominican commentator William Pelisson tells us that with this splendid *auto-da-fé*:

... great fear was aroused among the heretics and their believers in that land.[78]

More fear was on the way the following year, 1235, when a general inquisition was held in Toulouse on Good Friday. Voluntary mass confessions occurred as people rushed to implicate themselves and others before someone else did. Threatened with execution one Cathar sympathiser avoided the stake by taking the city magistrate and the inquisitors to a place where 10 *perfecti* were in hiding: three managed to escape; the other seven were burnt.[79]

During 1234 and 1235 large numbers of new inquisitors had been appointed from amongst the Dominicans but even so had proved insufficient to the task of interrogation, filing and cross-referencing that the cult of mass confessions had now generated. Franciscans and parish priests were therefore conscripted to help.[80] Adding to the overall burden was the matter of the paperwork from earlier investigations of heresy by the episcopal and other authorities. Undertaken before the Inquisition had been formed, and going back as far as 1209, these investigations had produced information, tip-offs and denunciations which the years of war had made it hard to follow up. Now the Inquisition was determined to make good the deficit.

On examination of the older records, and the full cross-referencing of all statements, it became clear that many who had formerly been exonerated as good Catholics had in fact been heretics all along. Those still living were arrested and burnt alive. But the remains of those who had already died during the intervening years were not forgotten! Wherever they had been buried they would be assiduously sought out and exhumed so that they too could be burnt.[81] Sometimes whole piles of mouldering disarticulated skeletons would be brought in at once, paraded through the streets and then burnt in a heap.[82]

Such severely demented behaviour (shall we call it *necropyria*?) would require urgent psychiatric restraint today. In Occitania in the 1230s and the 1240s it was lauded by the Church but naturally caused much anger amongst the relatives of the deceased who were publicly shamed in this way. A particular source of resentment was that the property of posthumously-condemned heretics was subject to confiscation, just as it would be if the heretic were still alive, which had the effect of impoverishing his descendants.[83] Inevitably the civilian population began to hate the inquisitors. In one case, in the city of Albi, an inquisitor named Arnald Cathala was beaten up and nearly killed by an angry mob after he went personally to exhume the corpse of an old women, recently revealed as a heretic, who had passed away some years before.[84]

Even by the late 1230s and early 1240s, despite being the focus of a concerted, well-funded, well-staffed Church operation to wipe them out to the last man, there were still sufficient numbers of Cathar *perfecti* in circulation – and able with local support to evade the inquisitors – to keep the heresy alive. Evidence of this astonishing persistence in the face of extreme adversity comes from the sheer number of penances still being imposed on convicted heretics. Over just two and a half months in 1241–42 Peter Seila, (the reader will recall him as the first inquisitor to be appointed in 1233) imposed penances on 732 heretics in nine different locations.[85]

The fall of Montségur

One amongst several reasons for the longevity of Catharism in Occitania was that the heretics were able to hold onto their major fortress of Montségur for many years after the French occupation of 1229. It provided a place of refuge to which *perfecti* could flee to rest and recuperate after risky missions in the occupied territories and its symbolic importance as a symbol of hope and resistance was vast. Its walls were high, believed impregnable, and it stood on top of a remote and inaccessible rocky crag.

In May 1242 two of the most loathed inquisitors, the Dominican William Arnold (again one of the original appointees back in 1233) and the Franciscan Stephen of Saint-Thibery, arrived in the little town of Avignonet with their hit-squad of enforcers. They had been on the road for seven months conducting general inquisitions across most of the region from Lavaur in the north to Fanjeaux in the south and spreading the usual tidal wave of terror wherever they went. Now it was Avignonet's turn.[86]

Except on this occasion it wasn't. The local bailiff, Raymond of Alfaro, was a Cathar sympathiser and immediately sent word by fast teams of riders to Montségur, 70 kilometers to the south. There the lord of the castle, one Peter Roger of Mirepoix, decided, to take action. On the night of 28 May 1242 he arrived at Avignonet with a group of heavily-armed knights who massacred the entire inquisitorial team of 10. Later one of the assassins, William Golarian, explained that they had mounted the attack so that 'the affair of the Inquisition could be extinguished and the whole land would be free, and there would not be another Inquisition.'[87]

Talk about wishful thinking! Far from extinguish the Inquisition, Avignonet proved to be the catalyst that led to Montségur being placed under siege by the forces of the French king – now the young Louis IX (who, as one might expect of a future Catholic saint, prosecuted heretics mercilessly). The siege began in May 1243 and ended, after 10 months of violent assaults and bombardments, with the surrender of Montségur, in March 1244.

Rather more than 200 Cathar *perfecti* had taken refuge there, including Bertrand Marty who had the rank of bishop. Eyewitness reports tell us that on 17 March 1244 they were all 'brutally dragged forth from the fortress of Montségur.'[88] Further down the slope, on a level area, a large rectangular enclosure defined by a wooden palisade had been filled up with firewood, straw and pitch. Now, without ceremony, soldiers set light to the piled firewood and the wretched heretics were thrown in a mass inside the palisade. 'There,' as one commentator of the period assures us, 'they experienced the fire of Hell.'[89]

The last Cathars

Montségur was a catastrophe, but still it did not mark the end of Catharism. Through the remainder of the 1240s the struggle between Inquisition and heretics went on and there were many more executions. In 1245–46, for example, the Inquistion of Toulouse had to deal with cases involving more than 600 villages and towns.[90] In one of these villages for which more detailed records are available, Mas-Saintes-Puelles (to the west of Castelnaudry), we know that a staggering total of 420 suspected heretics, roughly two-thirds of the population, were interrogated by Inquisitors Bernard of Caux and John of St. Pierre. This information has come down to us in two of the Inquisition's original registers detailing the interrogations of more than 5,500 different people from 104 different places. It is known that there were originally 10 registers.[91]

Gripped in the cold, dead hand of such a powerful, vindictive, and impressively well-organised bureaucracy, the Cathar heresy began to falter and then slowly to die. By the 1250s the Inquisitor Rainer Sacconi was able to estimate with satisfaction that there were not more than 200 *perfecti* left in all of Occitania[92] – too small a number, reckons historian Joseph Strayer, 'to preserve the structure of the Cathar Church.'[93] As a result, though the heresy was to persist into the next century, it had been so reduced by the Inquisition that it no longer represented a danger to Catholicism.[94]

The last upsurge was focussed around the highlands of the county of Foix – an old centre of the resistance. Here in 1299 a *perfectus* named Pierre Autier, together with a small group of followers began to evangelise amongst the rugged farmers and shepherds of the region. For a few brief years he enjoyed great success and even set in motion something of a revival, but he never really stood a chance. Soon the inquisitors were after him – big names like Bernard Gui, Geoffrey d'Ablis and Jacques Fournier. In 1309, with utter inevitability, Autier was caught. We know that he then underwent 10 months of interrogation by the inquisitors who finally burnt him alive in 1310.

One more prominent *perfectus* remained to be executed, a certain William Belibaste. Finding the going too hot in Occitania he had become a refugee in a small Cathar community across the border in Spain. There he was reached by an *agent provocateur* from the Inquisition who worked himself into his confidence and eventually tricked him into making a short return visit to Occitania. When he did so in the spring of 1321 he was captured, thrown into irons, tried and condemned. In the autumn of 1321 he was burnt at the stake.[95]

He was the last of the estimated 5,000 Cathar *perfecti* who were formally burnt alive in the name of the Christian God during the 112 years following the start of the Albigensian Crusades in 1209.[96] He was also the last Cathar known to history.

A quiet natural death?

Probably the heresy did survive for a few more years in some remote pockets of Occitania to be rooted out by inquisitions too small to have been reported by anyone. But the apocalypse at Montségur in 1244, the long downhill journey thereafter, and the demise of Autier and Belibaste in 1310 and 1321, really did mark the end of it.

Numerous Cathars fled Occitania. As well as nearby parts of Spain, where Belibaste would have done well to stay, another favoured refuge close to home was amongst their co-religionists in northern Italy. But the inquisitors were at work there too. In November 1276 all members of the Cathar community of Sirmione were arrested. And in February 1278 'about 200' were rounded up and burnt in Verona – the headquarters in exile of the Toulousan Cathar Church.[97]

Longer-term it seemed like the only secure refuge was in the ancient Byzantine Empire where the Bogomils, the mother church of Catharism, remained relatively strong during much of the 14th century. As late as 1325, four years after Belibaste had perished at the stake, we find Pope John XXI complaining to the leader of Bosnia about the heretics who are fleeing to his country and taking shelter there.[98]

Indeed although lands in the Byzantine Empire did not strictly-speaking come under the jurisdiction of the pope in Rome, but of the patriarchate in Constantinople, there had been constant papal interference in this part of the world since the early 13th century – round about the same time that the Albigensian Crusades began in the west.[99] For example Pope Gregory IX, who created the Inquisition in 1233 to smash the Cathars, deposed the Catholic bishop to Bosnia at around the same time for failing to take action against the Bogomils and replaced him, significantly, with a Dominican. Gregory also declared a crusade against Bosnia to root out heresy there. The crusade, which continued until 1240, was willingly led by the Duke of Croatia. 'In practice,' notes Bernard Hamilton, 'this was a Hungarian war against Bosnia that was given Crusade status …'[100] On another occasion, in 1238, the pope incited his ally King Bela IV of Hungary to mount a crusade against Bulgaria as well. Any possibility that this might go ahead, however, was stopped by the Mongol invasion of Hungary in 1241–42.[101]

By the 14th century the Ottoman Turks were on the move, eating up and incorporating into their Islamic state many areas of the former Byzantine Empire. They conquered Bulgaria in 1393 and thereafter Bogomilism was never heard of again in that land; indeed the last surviving report of Bulgarian Bogomilism comes to us from no later than 1370.[102] It lasted longer in Bosnia but was finally wiped out there after the invasion of Sultan Mehmed II (called the 'Conqueror') in 1463.[103] By the end of the 15th century the population of Bosnia was almost entirely Muslim.[104] As the historian Malcolm Lambert has researched:

> After a major expenditure of effort on refutation and, above all, police work, the Cathars were finally put down by the Western Church; by contrast Byzantine Bogomilism died a quiet natural death …[105]

Though the Inquisition never reached the wild lands of Bulgaria and Bosnia, its brutal success in Occitania, and the growing numbers of Cathars fleeing east to tell of horrors they had witnessed, must have been profoundly discouraging for the whole Bogomil movement. This perhaps explains the loss in energy that becomes apparent in Bogomilism from the early 14th century onwards – after which, though still thriving in the East, it seems to have abandoned all sense of its world mission. The Muslims brought about its final demise but even without their role the Catholic and Orthodox Churches had by then become so vigilant concerning heresy that there would have been no second chance for the Bogomil faith to evangelise and gain converts in the Christian world.

After Occitania was lost, all was lost. The millennial opportunity had come, and been seized, and then snatched away. An ancient Gnostic religion offering a stark alternative vision of Christianity had mysteriously reappeared after centuries in darkness, flourished mightily at first and made a bid for universality, only to fail utterly in the end …

Or had it?

Renaissance

In the summer of 1460, shortly before the last embers of the Bogomil faith were stamped out by Sultan Mehmed II's invasion of Bosnia, a Tuscan monk named Leonardo da Pistoia rode unobtrusively into the Florence on a donkey. Attached to his side was a bundle of cloth in which a small collection of books had been packed.

Leonardo, who had travelled a long way, took his precious cargo directly to the Doge of Florence, Cosimo de'Medici.

An intellectual nuclear bomb was about to explode.

Part II:
The Sacred Cities

[As] *the embodiment of the Italian Renaissance, the Medici were enormously rich and through their wealth and character ruled Florence, controlled the Papacy, and influenced the policies of an entire continent.*
Christopher Hibbert, *The House of Medici: Its Rise and Fall*

For want of a better term, I shall call it 'astral magic' ...
Frances Yates, *Giordano Bruno and the Hermetic Tradition*

CHAPTER EIGHT

THE OTHER
SECRET RELIGION

In the summer of 1460, shortly before the last embers of the Bogomil faith were stamped out by Sultan Mehmed II's invasion of Bosnia, a Tuscan monk named Leonardo da Pistoia rode into the Florence on a donkey. He had been away for several months on a dangerous mission to Macedonia for his learned and immensely wealthy master, Cosimo de'Medici, the Doge of Florence, who employed him to procure rare and ancient writings. Already a vast library of extraordinary scrolls, codices and books had been built up. Yet Leonardo knew that Cosimo would remain dissatisfied until he had in his hands certain very specific and once widely-circulated books suppressed by the Church and lost to the world for close to a thousand years. Cosimo was convinced that these books must still exist somewhere – and had ordered Leonardo to seek them out and buy them no matter what the cost.

Now at last, after returning many times to Florence with lesser prizes, Leonardo took great pride in the fact that he had found the ancient books that his master sought. They were books of knowledge, purported to have come down from Thoth, the wisdom god of the Egyptians, who had been known to the Greeks as Hermes Trismegistus. And though neither Leonardo nor Cosimo were aware of this, these highly mysterious *Hermetic* texts had been compiled in Alexandria during the first three centuries of the Christian era, i.e. at the same time and in the same place as the Nag Hammadi Gnostic texts. The link between the two collections becomes even stronger when we realise that a fragment of one of the Hermetic texts that Leonardo had purchased – a document known as the *Asclepius* – was also reproduced amongst the Gnostic codices buried at Nag Hammadi in the late fourth century and not recovered until 1945.[1]

The body is a tomb

No one can dispute that the Roman Catholic Church has a long track-record of vigorous opposition to all forms of knowledge, scripture, enquiry, wisdom and religious self-expression that do not accord with its own views. The reader will recall that it was mobs of Christians, aroused by Theophilus, the Catholic archbishop of Alexandria, who sacked the Serapeum in Alexandria in AD 391. They killed all the 'pagans' and Gnostics who had taken shelter inside it and razed to the ground the wonderful library that had been arranged around its cloisters together with its entire irreplaceable collection of ancient books and scrolls. We saw in Chapter Five that this atrocity was just one amongst many in the ruthless suppression of Gnosticism and paganism by the Catholic Church, and its generally very efficient destruction of their texts and traditions.

A different expression of this same antagonism to knowledge outside the narrow band accepted by orthodoxy was the closure in AD 529 by the Christian Emperor Justinian of Plato's revered Academy in Athens.[2] Originally established by Plato himself in the 380s BC on a site a mile outside Athens that was already held sacred, the Academy enjoyed more than 900 years of continuous existence until Justinian and Christian bigotry shut it down for spreading 'pagan' ideas.

Today we do not know exactly what was taught at the Academy. However, Plato's own copious surviving writings have led the majority of scholars to infer that the original syllabus was designed to produce a select few wise philosophers, deeply knowledgeable in mathematics (including the theory of harmonics and astronomy), dialectics, natural science, and political theory[3] who would:

> ... leave the Academy for politics, not as power seekers themselves but to legislate or advise those in power.[4]

It is known that the great Christian Gnostic teacher Valentinus, an Egyptian, studied Platonic philosophy at Alexandria in the early second century AD,[5] so it is perhaps not surprising to find the Catholic apologist Hippolytus (AD 170–236) accusing the Gnostics of being 'disciples of Plato' and following the Platonic system in making 'arithmetical science the fundamental principle of their doctrine.'[6] For our purposes it is also interesting that Plato seems to have been the first to use the term *demiurge* – Greek for 'public craftsman' – to describe the creator of the material world. In exactly the manner later copied by the Gnostics he meant to imply that the creator was a subordinate power, not the true God,[7] and that the material world was a corrupt, imperfect copy of the ideal world.[8] Tim Freke and Peter Gandy point out that Plato also frequently liked to quote a common phrase of the pagan mystery religions of his period – that phrase being *soma sema*, 'the body is a tomb':

> Gnostic initiates also understood that those who identified with the incarnate physical self were spiritually dead and needed to be reborn into eternal Life ...[9]

It is beyond the scope of this book to present a full exposition of the similarities – and the differences – between Platonism and Gnosticism. The point we wish to make is simply that the suppression of Plato's Academy in AD 529 was part of a much wider attack on the pursuit of knowledge that also included the virtual destruction of Christian Gnosticism – until, we propose, it resurfaced in Bulgaria in the 10th century as Bogomilism. During the intervening centuries book burning was deemed an act of piety by the Church and the persecution of scholars who ventured outside strict ecclesiastical boundaries was deemed an act of righteousness and a service to God.

The enraged enforcement of an unearned spiritual monopoly

It is with good reason that historians refer to the period between the 5th and the 10th centuries AD as the Dark Ages. But things were to get much darker before European culture was to see any lasting glimmers of light. We've documented aspects of the astonishing 'mini-Renaissance' that accompanied the sudden upsurge of Catharism in Occitania in the 12th century. And we've documented the reaction of the Church – the Albigensian Crusades that laid waste the cultural development of the region, a century of terrorism and mayhem, the holocaust of 5,000 Cathar *perfecti*, and, last but not least, the Inquisition.

It should be obvious to the reader by now that Cathars and Catholics had very different attitudes to the uses and control of knowledge, and that these attitudes were rooted in their very different underlying philosophies.

For the Cathars, inheritors of the Gnostic tradition, the predicament of humanity was ignorance; it was knowledge, therefore, that would provide the only sure route of escape. And since they believed that the greatest store of relevant knowledge was contained in the New Testament – the fundamental document of Christianity – they felt strongly that every Cathar should be able to read it in his or her own language.

Accordingly the Cathars of Occitania had the New Testament translated from Latin, in which it had hitherto been locked away from the masses, into the vernacular *langue d'oc*, and large numbers of copies, laboriously prepared by hand, were put into circulation. The demand for a cheap convenient material on which such copies could be made led them to become the pioneers of paper-making in Europe, establishing numerous apprenticeships in the new trade[10] and contributing greatly to the subsequent spread of this liberating technology.

In parallel, Cathar children were taught to read and study the New Testament from an early age, thus gaining the gift of literacy that was so rare in general in Europe in that period. Rare too was the fact that both sexes were taught equally, not just the males as was often the norm elsewhere.[11] The result was that educated, literate, free-thinking women became a feature of Cathar communities during the short period that the heresy flourished.

In this, as in many other respects, the behaviour of the Cathars can only be described as enlightened – no other word will do – while their campaign to provide accessible vernacular editions of the New Testament was clearly an initiative far ahead of its time. By contrast the reader will recall from Chapter Seven that the Catholic Church and the Inquisition strictly forbade lay persons to possess the New Testament 'with the exception of the Psalter, the Breviary, and the Book of Hours of the Blessed Virgin'. Moreover even these limited selections were permitted only in Latin whilst translations into the 'vernacular tongue' were 'rigorously forbidden'.[12]

It seems ironic that the so-called *heretics* were the ones doing everything they could to spread knowledge of the New Testament while the 'true Church' was doing everything it could to limit and control such knowledge. But to understand this behaviour we need only remind ourselves of the basic philosophy of Catholicism – which utterly opposes any personal quest for knowledge and instead teaches blind faith and absolute mindless trust in the infallibility of papal dogma. It was this doctrine that snuffed out the brilliant light of scientific and spiritual enquiry that had flourished around the great libraries of Alexandria during the last three centuries BC and the first three centuries AD. It was this doctrine that plunged the world into the Dark Ages by suppressing not only Gnostic enquiry but also the vast bulk of 'pagan' classical knowledge. And it was this same doctrine of blind faith and unquestioning obedience – still top of the Catholic agenda a thousand years later – that led directly to the gross moral errors of the Albigensian Crusades and the Inquisition in the 13th and 14th centuries, and to yet more suppression of books and knowledge, more burning of heretics, more terror and stupidity.

By the 15th century, though the persecution of individual heretics was far from over, European society was exhausted and sickened by all this mad violence, censorship and bigotry. By then, too, with the complete destruction of the Cathar threat well behind it, the vigilance of the Church itself had inevitably begun to slacken. Not quite certain what sort of backlash they might ultimately incur – but willing to take the risk – certain open-minded scholars took advantage of the lull to begin a quest for ancient manuscripts. Their frank hope was that by rediscovering the lost wisdom of the past they might better guide the world towards its unknown future.

One such scholar was Cosimo de'Medici who employed the monk Leonardo de Pistoia as his bookfinder. Now riding into Florence on the back of the little donkey that had carried him all the way from Macedonia, Leonardo anxiously fumbled in the bundle strapped at his side and felt once again the reassuring outline and weight of the miraculous, wonderful books that he was bringing to his master.

A philosopher with fire-power

The origin of the House of Medici is obscure, but 'Medici' means literally 'medical doctors' so a background amongst physicians and apothecaries is thought likely. Further back the family's ancestry may have included a humble charcoal burner who had moved into Florence from the nearby district of Mugello. But an apocryphal origin added much colour to their name. Legend had it that the family had been founded in the fifth century by a brave knight who came to Mugello and helpfully killed a fearsome giant who had been plaguing the local population. As a reward he was allowed to add to his shield eight red balls, one for each of the dents from the giant's attack. These red balls, others have suggested, either represented apothecaries' pills or coins of the famous banking family that the Medici would later become.

Since 1239 the Medici had been official *gonfaloniere* of Florence (standard bearers and custodians of the city banner). By 1389, the year Cosimo was born, the family was already prominent and rich due to the banking activities of Cosimo's father, Giovanni. He had apparently benefited greatly from his personal friendship with Pope John XXIII, Baldassare Cossa, who later, in 1414, was to be accused of heresy, simony, tyranny, the murder of his predecessor Pope Alexander V, and the seduction of no less than 200 girls and ladies of Bologna![13]

Named after Saint Cosmas, on whose feast day – 27 September – he had been born, Cosimo was educated at the Camaldolese monastery of Santa Maria degli Angeli, where he learnt French, German and Latin and a spatter of Hebrew, Greek and Arabic. In his teens he attended the lectures and lessons of one of the most prominent scholars in Florence, Roberto de'Rossi, also a member of an old and rich Florentine family. Through the influence of de'Rossi the young Cosimo acquired and developed a lasting respect and love for classical works, particularly Plato, and an insatiable interest in man's role and purpose on earth. In short, he was a philosopher in the ancient mould who, as it would turn out, would acquire the sort of fire-power that few lovers of wisdom ever enjoy.

Through political machinations and more especially through his influence on the papacy (he had befriended the popes and practically ran the finances of the Vatican), Cosimo was able to add greatly to the already enormous wealth of the House of Medici. His influence grew accordingly and he was soon the *de facto* ruler of Florence, a position that he was to maintain for the rest of his life. In 1458, just two years before the lost texts of the Hermetica were delivered to him, Cosimo was described as 'master of the country' by Pope Pious II:

> Political questions are settled in his house. The man he chooses holds office ... He it is who decides peace and war and controls the laws ... He is king in everything but name.[14]

The Florentine historian, Francesco Guicciardini, went even further when he said that Cosimo 'had a reputation such as probably no private citizen has ever enjoyed from the fall of Rome to our own day.'[15]

All the learning of Constantinople and a new Platonic Academy

In 1438 Cosimo came up with a brilliant idea that, in a curious and indirect way, was to change the course of Western scholarship. For centuries, as the reader will recall, the Catholic Church, headed by the pope in Rome, had been in conflict over doctrinal issues with the Eastern Orthodox Church, headed by the patriarch in Constantinople. This great religious 'West versus East' schism reached a crisis point in the 1430s when Constantinople was beginning to be seriously threatened by the Muslim Ottoman Turks. Since

THE MASTER GAME

the dramatic fall of Egypt and Alexandria to the Muslims in AD 642, the 'Eastern' empire of Rome, which extended from Turkey through to Egypt, had been slowly gnawed away by the Muslim forces. By 1438, all that remained in Christian hands was its capital, Constantinople, called the 'Second Rome'. In the famous words of Mehmed II, the Ottoman sultan who would eventually capture the city in 1452 after a siege of six weeks, it was just 'a monstrous head without a body'.

In 1438 John Paleologus, the Eastern Roman emperor whose seat was Constantinople, appealed to the pope in the name of all Christianity for military help to save the last bastion of Christendom in the East from falling into the hands of the Muslims. In response, Pope Eugenius IV decided to call for a great council to meet somewhere in Italy. Cosimo de'Medici, seeing the enormous prestige such a council would bring, especially if it achieved a reconciliation between the Eastern and Western churches, was determined that the venue should be his own city. Through his friendship with the pope, and by offering to cover all expenses plus a generous loan to the Vatican, Cosimo had his way, and in the winter of 1439, after a night of storms and torrential rains, the Eastern emperor, the Greek Orthodox patriarch and the pope all made their triumphal entries into Florence.

Months of deliberations and ecumenical debates followed until at last, in July 1439, the Council of Florence reached a compromise that brought the two churches together again. Predictably their reunification was short-lived; indeed the Eastern delegates barely had time to return to Constantinople before repudiating the feeble agreement. But there was an unexpected upside. Florence, all of Italy, and in due course the rest of Western Europe as well, were to benefit incalculably from the exciting intellectual stimulant provided by the large retinue of Byzantine-Greek scholars who had accompanied the Eastern emperor to the council. These scholars were amongst the prime catalysts in the remarkable Renaissance of classical history, art and philosophy that was soon to follow and they added new force to the already keen and burning interest of Cosimo de'Medici in Plato's works. The great Byzantine scholar, Bessarion, who had accompanied the Eastern emperor to Italy, was persuaded to remain behind, as well as his colleague Plethon, a leading authority on Plato.[16]

After attending lectures by Plethon, Cosimo had another inspiration. He would use some of his immense wealth to establish a Platonic Academy in Florence, modelled on Plato's original. Plethon's departure, and Cosimo's involvement with other issues, delayed the project for several years. Nonetheless the idea of the Academy did finally come to maturity. Its first home was the

Villa Montevecchio in Florence and Cosimo appointed his adopted son, the brilliant scholar Marsilio Ficino, as its first director. Ficino had, in fact, been groomed for such a task by Cosimo over the years after noting the young man's keen enthusiasm for Plato's works, and it was Cosimo who had generously paid for Ficino's education and for his special studies in Greek and Latin.

Cosimo had for many years been an avid collector of rare and important books and made some valuable additional acquisitions from the Byzantine-Greek scholars who had attended the 1439 Council of Florence. His library, regarded as the most extensive collection of classical and religious works in Europe, formed the nucleus of the Medici Academy and was to serve eventually as a model for the Vatican's own library. Until 1460, however, the ultimate prize – the fabled works of Hermes Trismegistus – had eluded him as well as all other collectors in Europe.

Travel-stained and weary, the monk Leonardo da Pistoia now calmly directed his little donkey into the Villa Careggi, the sumptuous residence of Cosimo de'Medici in Florence. He was admitted at once and delivered the bundle that he had carried so far directly to Cosimo himself.

Older than Moses, greater than Plato

It was well known to European scholars of the Renaissance that the great Greek philosopher Plato, and before him Solon and Pythagoras, had visited the land of Egypt and there had allegedly learnt the wisdom of the Egyptian sages. Plato, it was said, had special respect for the Egyptians – who he referred to as a 'race of philosophers'.[17] In his *Timeus*, famous for containing the earliest-surviving direct references to Atlantis, he recounted a story that had supposedly been told by Solon, the celebrated Athenian statesman and poet, after the latter had visited Egypt *circa* 600 BC. There, at Sais in the Delta area, Egyptian priests at the Temple of Neith apparently recognised Solon's wisdom and agreed to discuss with him issues related to the origin of the world. After listening to Solon expounding some of the Greek myths, however, one of the priests interrupted him and exclaimed:

> O Solon, Solon, you Greeks are all like children, and there is no such thing as an old [wise] Greek … You are all young in mind … you have no belief rooted in ancient tradition and no knowledge hoary with age …[18]

Solon apparently was told by the Egyptian priests that deluges and fire had periodically ravaged the earth, causing civilisations to collapse and disappear. However, because of the disposition of the Nile Valley, Egypt had

THE MASTER GAME

miraculously been spared and all her ancient temples and sanctuaries had survived. In them and them alone was preserved a complete memory of the great events of the distant past and of deeds previously accomplished by mankind. They even contained a record of the origins of the world and knowledge of that golden age when mortals had fraternised with the gods.

Classical writers who had visited or lived in Egypt, such as Herodotus, Diodorus Siculus and Proclus Diadochus, likewise extolled the immensely old wisdom of the Egyptian priests, and especially their revered knowledge of the heavens and the motion of the stars. Many deemed Egypt a sacred land, a land in which the gods had once dwelt and taught men the divine and sacred science, and where the secrets of immortality had been revealed to those who were fully worthy.[19] However, this wonderful and pristine Egyptian science had thus far remained out of the reach of Renaissance scholars such as Cosimo de'Medici because it was written in the mysterious and impenetrable hieroglyphic language which no one anymore could understand. Ancient and holy Egypt had fallen into a deep coma from which, it seemed, it might never again awake.

One can therefore imagine the intellectual shockwave that passed through the learned circles of Florence in 1460 when Cosimo de'Medici excitedly announced that he had in his possession a collection, translated by some unknown hand into Greek, of the fabled lost books of Hermes Trismegistus. The late Dame Frances Yates, a world authority on the Renaissance, puts the scale of the discovery into context:

> From ... early Christian writers, more about Hermes Trismegistus could be learned, particularly from Clement of Alexandria, who, in his striking description of the procession of the Egyptian priests, says that the singer at the head of the procession carried two books of music and hymns by Hermes; the *horoscopus* carried four books by Hermes on the stars. In the course of this description Clement states that there are forty-two books by Hermes Trismegistus, thirty-six of which contained the whole of the philosophy of the Egyptians, the other six being on medicine. It is very improbable that Clement knew any of the Hermetica which have come down to us, but the Renaissance reader believed that he had in the *Corpus Hermeticum* and the *Asclepius* precious survivors of that great sacred library of which Clement speaks.[20]

Cosimo and his contemporaries believed that the 'divine' Plato had himself been taught philosophy by the priests of Egypt. It was the desire to regain contact with the source of that philosophy that mostly fired the imagination of Cosimo de'Medici and led him to action.

Drop Plato, translate Hermes instead

When the Hermetic texts reached Cosimo, it so happened that his adopted son, Marsilio Ficino, was busy translating the works of Plato from Greek into more accessible Latin. Cosimo ordered the young man to drop Plato at once and to concentrate all his efforts full-time on the translation of the Hermetica.

Ficino, then 27 years old, had already acquired a reputation as a fine scholar, theologian and linguist – especially in Greek and Latin. Born in 1433, he was the natural son of a Florentine physician, the latter a close friend of Cosimo de'Medici. Cosimo adopted Ficino after the death of his father, and encouraged him to pursue his passion for Plato's works.

Roman Catholicism had a long history of disapproval of Platonic philosophy going back before the closure of the original Academy in 529. By the 1400s, however, Plato was beginning to find supporters again within the Church – and Ficino was one of these. He therefore set out very deliberately to apply his intellect to an integration of Plato's philosophy with Roman Catholic teachings. He would also try to do the same, as we shall see, with the philosophy found in the books of the 'Egyptian sage' Hermes Trismegistus. But what was amazing was that the man who was to be the head of Cosimo de'Medici's Platonic Academy should have been ordered to put aside Plato and to focus instead on the translation of the books of Hermes. As Frances Yates comments:

> It is an extraordinary situation. There are the complete works of Plato, waiting, and they must wait whilst Ficino quickly translates Hermes, probably because Cosimo wants to read him before he dies. What a testimony this is to the mysterious reputation of [Hermes] the Thrice Great One! ...[21]

Within a year Ficino managed to complete a Latin translation of the 14 books or 'tracts' of the Hermetica (as the collection that Leonardo da Pistoia had brought back from Macedonia is now known). In 1473, ten years after finishing this work, Ficino was ordained a priest of the Roman Catholic Church and eventually became a high official at the Cathedral of Florence. It is widely accepted by scholars that his translations of the Greek classics and, especially, the works of Plato, were part of the impetus behind the Italian

Renaissance. But what is less appreciated is the huge, indeed revolutionary, effect that Ficino's translation of the Hermetica was also to have on Western culture and on the Catholic Church itself.

The full corpus

Ficino had given his translation the title of *Pimader*, the name of the mysterious 'universal mind' that supposedly had revealed to Hermes Trismegistus the divine wisdom imparted in the Hermetica.

Although the printing press had just been invented 15 years before,[22] the publication of *Pimander* was a huge success. It had first circulated in handwritten copies but eventually was printed in 1471 in Treviso (apparently without permission from Ficino) under the title *Pimander or the Power and Wisdom of God*. This was somewhat misleading since the term *Pimander*, which is derived from the original Greek *Poimadres* – itself derived from *Peime-n-Ré*, meaning the 'knowledge of Ré', the Egyptian sun-god – only appears briefly in the opening part of the book. None of the other tracts in the Hermetica mention *Pimander* at all.

Be that as it may the Treviso edition was so successful that it prompted another publisher at Ferrera to bring out a rival edition in 1472, again without Ficino's permission. By 1543, the same year that Copernicus's famous *De revolutionibus orbium coelestium* ('*On the Revolutions of the Heavenly Spheres*') was first published in Nuremberg, there were over 50 separate editions of the Hermetica circulating in Europe!

When Ficino had translated the texts back in 1463, he had not included a tract called the *Logos Teleios*, *the Perfect Discourse*, better known as the *Asclepius*. This was because the latter (a fragment of which, the reader will recall, was also found amongst the Nag Hammadi Gnostic texts) had already been translated into Latin from a Greek original sometime in late antiquity and had been circulating among European scholars since medieval times. We shall come back to the *Asclepius* in due course but, in brief for now, this book purports to explain the magical religion of the Egyptians and, more importantly, the mysterious talismanic skills that they supposedly deployed to draw down the powers of the stars into statues and other objects.[23] It was this type of magic that was to impress Ficino deeply and to influence his many followers.

The *Asclepius* was printed for the first time in 1469 with the complete works of Apuleius, only two years before the first printed edition of Ficino's *Pimander*. It thus quickly became customary to attach the *Asclepius* to the Hermetica, the whole forming one major corpus generally known as the 'philosophical' Hermetica or *Corpus Hermeticum*. There is also a further booklet known as the *Definitions of Asclepius* that is sometimes added to this corpus.

According to French scholar Jean-Pierre Mahé, professor of humanities at the Sorbonne in Paris, the *Definitions of Asclepius* was rediscovered in 1484, that is two decades after the rediscovery of the Hermetica, in a far more dramatic and flamboyant manner than the Ruritanian spectacle of a monk riding his little donkey into Florence. Apparently a certain Senore Ludovico Lazzarelli, in an obscure tract titled *The Letter of Enoch*, narrated how his master, Don Giovanni Mercurio da Correggio, had helped him to find these lost *writings of Hermes Trismegistus* (called also *Mercurio* by the Italians). On Palm Sunday in April of the year 1484, Giovanni Mercurio, then exactly 33 years old, that is the supposed age of Christ at his Crucifixion, rode into Rome on a black stallion guided by two servants, and made his way towards the Vatican. Dressed in black and wearing a golden belt and purple shoes, Giovanni Mercurio had placed on his head a crown of thorns, and upon his brow was fixed a silver plaque in the form of a lunar crescent on which were written these words:

> This is my son Pimander, whom I personally chose. From early childhood he has grown to sublime heights, and I have empowered him with all my compliance to cast away demons and to install my truth and my justice upon all nations. Be warned not to oppose him! Heed his words and obey him with fear and reverence. These are the words of the Lord of all the sanctuaries of the world, Jesus Christ.[24]

Giovanni Mercurio then pulled a heap of leaflets out his saddlebag and threw them all around. The crowds gathered; some thought him mad, others thought that he was making some strange vow, but the majority hailed him as a prophet. At the Vatican, the Swiss Guard baffled by this strange scene, stood aside and let him pass. In the cathedral Giovanni Mercurio announced that he was the reincarnated Pimander. He spent the next few days talking to the crowds then returned to his hometown in Bologna, where he was widely acclaimed by women and children. Not surprisingly, he was soon arrested by the Inquisition for blasphemy and threatened with the stake. In 1486, however, he was released under the protection of the then king of France, Charles VIII.

Almost every aspect of this whole strange episode underlines the incredible religious impact that the Hermetica had on the collective mind of the Renaissance and, even more curious, the way that Hermes/Mercurio Trismegistus was being attached to the Christian faith.

A repercussion of Giovanni Mercurio's strange but short career as a 'prophet' of Hermes Trismegistus, was that the poet and astrologer Lodovico Lazzarelli, who had been an eyewitness to Giovanni's cavalcade into Rome on that Palm Sunday back in 1484, also succumbed to the Hermetic spell, and adopted the mystical name of 'Enoch' (another alleged incarnation of Hermes).[25] Lazzarelli became Giovanni's most ardent disciple and, according to him, here is how the *Definitions of Asclepius* were found:

> It was by chance, while scrutinising relentlessly the old books of those who inspired me, and while over a cup full of the most suave nectar which, I do not doubt, had flowed from the huge *crater* [bowl] of *Hermes Trismegistus*, by which I mean a small book in Greek having the title of the *Definitions of Asclepius*. As soon as I read it, its conciseness and the mysterious authenticity of its wisdom enchanted me and filled me with admiration.[26]

Lazzarelli made it his task to translate the *Definitions of Asclepius* immediately into Latin, but it was only after his death in 1507 that this book was eventually printed – alongside the work of the French Neoplatonist and occultist Symphorien Champier, in his *Book of the Quadruple Life*. Now, at last, the full works attributed to Hermes Trismegistus were in the hands of Western scholars, and something quite extraordinary was about to happen …

Veiling Hermes in the Church (1)

In the mind of Marsilio Ficino, Hermes Trismegistus was a historical person who had lived in ancient Egypt and had actually been the author of the Hermetica. This view was shared by all the Renaissance humanists and philosophers – notably the great Christian Hermetic-Cabalist Giovanni Pico della Mirandola – who, like Ficino, were totally seduced by the Hermetica. As professor Jean-Pierre Mahé explains:

> According to Marsilio Ficino, [Hermes] Trismegistus [Hermes Thrice-Great] had merited his surname by becoming at the same time the greatest of philosophers, the greatest of priests and the greatest of kings … And his successors were Orpheus, Aglaophemus, Pythagoras and Philolaus, the teacher of Plato … Thus, the works of Trismegistus were the true source of ancient wisdom. Not only the divine Plato, but also the legendary Pythagoras and even the inspired poets such as Orpheus, perpetuated

the same Egyptian doctrine: all bouncing the echo, as it were, of a single and same ancient theology, the *prisca theologia* ...[27]

Concerned, however, not to undermine the authority of the Bible and awake the Inquisition, the early Hermetic scholars accepted that Hermes Trismegistus came after Moses. This play-it-safe idea had originated with Saint Augustine, the Manichean *hearer* who converted to Catholicism and became one of the great doctors of the Church (see Chapter Five). Augustine accepted that Hermes Trismegistus lived long before the Greek philosophers, but insisted that he,

> ... came after Abraham, Isaac, Jacob, Joseph and even Moses. Because Moses was born in the time of Atlas, brother of Prometheus, who was a great astronomer ... he was the grandfather of the older Mercury [Hermes], himself the grandfather of [Hermes] Trismegistus.[28]

But some did not agree with this chronology. Lazzarelli, who had translated the *Definitions of Asclepius* and utterly believed in Hermes Trismegistus's older origin, argued:

> ... It was not at the times of Moses that Trismegistus had lived, but long before, as one can easily ascertain from the works of Diodorus of Sicily. The latter reported, in his chronology of the kings of Egypt, it was first gods that ruled then human brings. Hence it is evident that Mercury (Hermes) Trismegistus lived in the times of the gods ... whereas Moses lived at an epoch where the Bible and many other ancient writings known in Egypt clearly state when ruled pharaohs ...[29]

If you visit the famous Cathedral of Siena located between Rome and Florence, you will find that the entire floor, which dates back to 1488, is paved with exquisite marble designs depicting religious and mythological scenes. One of these scenes shows the Egyptian sage Hermes Trismegistus handing a book to an oriental figure standing in a respectful manner bowing slightly. Written upon the book in Latin are the words '*Suscipite O Licteras Et Lege Egiptii*', meaning 'Take up thy letters and laws O Egyptians', and the bowing figure, according to Frances Yates, was 'perhaps intended to be Moses.'[30] What seems to support this amazing identification is the plaque under the feet of the figures which states: 'Hermes Mercurius contemporaneous of Moses', implying, says Yates:

... a *supplication* from the lawgiver of the Hebrews (if the suppliant figure is Moses) to the lawgiver of the Egyptians to revive Egyptian piety and morality ... The representation of Hermes Trismegistus in this Christian edifice, so prominently displayed near its entrance and giving him so lofty a spiritual position, is not an isolated phenomenon but a symbol of how the Italian Renaissance regarded him and a prophecy of what was to be his extraordinary career throughout Europe in the sixteenth century and well on into the seventeenth century ...[31]

Veiling Hermes in the Church (2)

The ancient Egyptian sage Hermes Trismegistus, and by extension the writings attributed to him, were indeed due for a glittering Renaissance career. In 1544, for example, when the French humanist Adrien Turnèbe (better known simply as Turnebus) published in Paris the first edition of the original Greek text of the Hermetica accompanied by Ficino's translation in Latin, the theologian Petrus Paulus Vergerius had this to say in the preface:

Hermes Trismegistus was an Egyptian by race ... He flourished before the time of pharaoh, as many of the *chronographi* think. Some, among whom is Cicero, suppose that he is the person whom the Egyptians call Thoth ... He must have lived, therefore, before pharaoh, and consequently, before Moses also ... He wrote at the time many books of mystical philosophy and theology. Among these writings, there are two of special importance: the one is called *Asclepius*, and the other, *Poimandres* [i.e. the *Pimander*].[32]

After Turnebus's publication came the work of the bishop of Aire, François Foix de Candale, better known as 'Flussas', who published a new edition of the Hermetica. Flussas was even more enthusiastic than his predecessors, and dedicated the work to the Holy Roman Emperor Maximilian II, informing him that Hermes Trismegistus had attained to a knowledge of divine things which he first wrote in Egyptian, then in Greek, surpassing that 'which was revealed to the Hebrew prophets, and equalling that of the Apostles and Evangelists':

What more is made known to us by those who were instructed by our Saviour himself? And yet this man [Hermes] was anterior in time not only to the disciples of our Lord, but also to all the prophets and teachers of our law, and, as the ancients say, to Moses himself.[33]

In 1591 came the Italian Neoplatonist scholar Francesco Patrizi da Cherso, also known as Franciscus Patricius, who was also to publish an edition of the Hermetica in his work *Nova de universis philosophia* ('*New Philosophy of Universes*'). Patrizi not only saw Hermes Trismegistus as the source of all wisdom, but in the preface of his book, which is addressed to Pope Gregory XIV, Patrizi actually urged the pope to order that the Hermetica should be taught to everyone, even to the Jesuits, because it could somehow serve as a 'conversion' tool for the Catholic Church:

> I hope that you and your successors will adopt this new restored religious philosophy and cause it to be studied everywhere ... I would have you then, Holy Father, and all future Popes, give orders that some of the books which I have named shall be continually taught everywhere, as I have taught them in the last fourteen years at Ferrara. You will thus make all able men in Italy, Spain and France friendly to the Church; and perhaps even the German Protestants will follow their example, and return to the Catholic faith. It is much easier to win them back in this way than to compel them by ecclesiastical censures or by secular arms. You should cause this doctrine to be taught in the schools of the Jesuits, who are doing such good work. If you do this, great glory will await you among men of future times. And I beg you to accept me as a helper in this undertaking.[34]

The 'doctrine' that Patrizi was referring to is the same that Plato had once taught and which, at least according to Patrizi, had been originally developed and transmitted to man in ancient Egypt by Hermes Trismegistus. Patrizi believed that it was passed on to Plato during his stay in Egypt and then passed by Plato himself to his pupil Aristotle, the tutor of Alexander the Great.[35] Amazingly, Patrizi seems to be asking the pope to *canonise* the Hermetica and other related writings which, he believed, contained a pristine doctrine, a *prisca theologia*, rooted in ancient Egypt. Yet, seen in the context of his times, Patrizi's seemingly heretical request to the pope is not as far-fetched as it at first appears. In fact there had been one pope at least who took such ideas very seriously indeed ...

Pico della Mirandola, Hermetic magic and the Cabala
One of the most brilliant minds of the Renaissance belonged to a young Florentine scholar named Giovanni Pico della Mirandola. The scion of a noble family of Modena, Pico was much influenced by the ideas of Marsilio

Ficino on Hermeticism and, more especially, Hermetic magic which Pico not only completely accepted, by would propagate with even more fervour and enthusiasm.

Whilst wholeheartedly sharing Ficino's view that Hermes Trismegistus was a 'gentile' prophet of Christianity, Pico della Mirandola went further. What he saw in the Hermetica was a form of mystical teaching and 'natural magic' which he also associated with the Jewish Cabala. The reader will recall from Chapter Two that this was a system of mysticism rooted in esoteric Judaic traditions, that had received its most extensive elaboration and development amongst the Jewish communities of coastal Occitania during the 12th century. Now, more than 300 years later, Pico felt with all his heart that these two types of Cabalistic magic, Jewish and 'Egyptian', needed to be merged and used for the benefit of the Christian Church.

According to Frances Yates, 'the marrying together of Hermeticism and Cabalism' was an invention of Pico della Mirandola, who also 'united the Hermetic and Cabalistic type of magic' to create a powerful intellectual brew loosely termed the Christian Hermetic-Cabala which was to have far-reaching consequences amongst Renaissance theologians, reaching even as far as the Vatican itself.[36] And although magic, in the medieval sense, was abhorred and virtually outlawed by the Church, Pico successfully argued that what the Church had in mind concerned the diabolical 'modern' type of magic which, he agreed was detestable. What he was advocating, he explained, was something quite other – the beautiful, ancient and innocent *magia naturalis*, i.e. the 'natural magic' of the wise Egyptian sage Hermes Trismegistus. This was seen by many, not just Pico, as a form of 'sympathetic magic', which could establish a benevolent link between heaven and earth. In short, what Pico had in mind was that 'Egyptian' form of talismanic magic as found in the Hermetica and, more especially, in the *Asclepius*.[37] But unlike Ficino, Pico believed that this 'Egyptian' magic must be 'supplemented' by 'practical Cabala', i.e. Cabalistic magic. And precisely this, says Yates, is the intellectual contribution to Renaissance magic that Pico was to develop with amazing success.[38]

Cabala in fact, literally means 'tradition', namely that special Jewish mystical tradition that was supposedly handed by God to Moses in the sacred Hebrew language and which, according to Cabalists, conveys mystical and magical meaning encoded in the 22 letters of the Hebrew alphabet. Hebrew letters and the words they form are viewed by Cabalists in very much in the same way as the statues and objects of the Egyptians were most likely viewed by their devotees – that is to say as *talismans charged* with magical and mystical meaning that can be released through a form of 'magic'. Thus, according to Pico, both the Hermetic-Egyptian and Cabalistic-Hebrew magical systems – which supposedly had emanated, respectively, from the Egyptian lawgiver Hermes Trismegistus and the Jewish lawgiver Moses – complement one another. The next step, surely, was to merge them? And since both these ancient sages received their wisdom from God and were thus 'prophets' of Christianity, then, in Pico's logic, the now merged Hermetic-Cabalistic magic rightfully belonged to the Christian Church!

It is not within the scope of this book to review and elaborate on the complex 'science' of Cabala, nor is it possible to enlarge and give details on how Pico proposed to merge this system with the Hermetic magic of the *Asclepius* or, indeed, incorporate it within the Catholic religion. Briefly, however, Pico essentially saw his Christian Hermetic-Cabala as the means through which the 'truth' of the Trinity could be proved and confirmed to the people. Or as Pico himself was to put it, his Christian Hermetic-Cabala was the means of 'confirming the Christian religion from the foundations of Hebrew wisdom.'[39]

It also did not take much imagination for the Church to see that Pico's clever variant of the ancient Jewish mystical tradition could serve as a 'conversion tool' to bring Jews into the Catholic faith. One example of such a simple but devastatingly effective 'tool' was Pico's very forceful argument that the name of Jesus, *Iesu* in Hebrew, if interpreted through Cabalistic principles and methodologies, could be proved to mean 'God', the 'Son of God', and also the spirit or 'wisdom of God', i.e. the Christian Trinity of Father, Son and Holy Spirit.[40] In short, Pico proposed to win the Jews over using their own mystical game. And indeed with such seemingly simple but convincing manipulation of Hebrew words using 'Christian Hermetic-Cabala', it seems that many Jews living in Italy were persuaded that 'Christian truths' were locked within their own religious scriptures and thus felt compelled to convert to the Catholic faith.[41]

Not surprisingly, Pico's bold but unwise claim 'that there is no science that gives us more assurance of Christ's divinity than magic and the Cabala' was bound to attract the somber attention of the papal Inquisition whose henchmen missed the point of Pico's 'good intention' and promptly accused him of heresy.[42] Matters got progressively worse between Pico and the Church, and he had to take refuge in France and seek the protection of Charles VIII. He eventually returned to Italy bearing letters from the king of France, and soon found himself under the protection of Lorenzo the Magnificent, the powerful Medici ruler of Florence from 1469–92. In the tradition of his grandfather Cosimo, Lorenzo gave the fugitive political support and interceded on his behalf with the pope.[43] Pico spent his last years in Florence where he died in 1494, at the youthful age of 31.

Perhaps it should be mentioned that, coincidently, Pico had been born in the same year that Marsilio Ficino had completed the first Latin translation of the Hermetica. These propitious coincidences seem to have been part of Pico's life. The year before his death, Pope Innocent VIII, who had condemned Pico for heresy, was succeeded by the infamous Pope Alexander VI who, unlike his predecessor, was rather open, indeed even sympathetic, towards magic, Cabala and Hermeticism. In June 1493 Alexander VI gave his absolution to Pico della Mirandola, revoked the charges against him, and even wrote him a personal letter in which he describes Pico as a 'faithful son of the Church' inspired by a '*divina largitas*' ('divine bounty').[44]

Suddenly and, for a brief moment, there was a crack in the doors of the Vatican. Through it, quietly but surely like a thief in the night, the wisdom and magic of the 'Egyptian sage', Hermes Trismegistus, slipped quickly inside ...

The Borgias, orgies in the Vatican, Isis and Osiris on the ceiling

Pope Alexander VI's family name was Rodrigo Borgia. Born in the former Cathar stronghold of Aragon in northeastern Spain, he came from an immensely wealthy, powerful and ultimately notorious family. His uncle the bishop of Valencia (later to become Pope Calixtus III), had supervised his education in Bologna in Italy and later made him a cardinal of the Roman Church. Through bribery and intrigue he thereafter succeeded in amassing a huge personal fortune. Father of an unknown number of illegitimate children, he also had four legitimised children from a Roman noblewoman, Vanozza de'Cattanei. These included the twisted Cesare Borgia and the beautiful Lucrezia Borgia, whose names would come to epitomise intrigue and foul play.

In spite of his licentious reputation – and somewhat amazingly, all things considered – Rodrigo was elected pope in 1492 and adopted the name of Alexander VI. He immediately began to manipulate and control the Vatican through bribery and by appointing members of his own family in key positions. Cesare Borgia, his celebrated evil son, was promoted to cardinal while still in his teens, along with another young man of the Borgia clan, Alessandro Farnese, the future Pope Paul III. The latter was the brother of the pope's favourite mistress, Giulia Farnese, known as '*Giulia la bella*', (from whom the pope had at least one illegitimate child). There are contemporary accounts of wild orgies at the Vatican, and historians have even traced at least two assassinations by poisoning directly related to Pope Alexander VI. Indeed, so corrupt and evil was the papacy of Alexander VI that after his death, even the Vatican itself could not avoid condemning him as the worst of the so-called *bad popes* – a polite understatement to describe the huge damage to the reputation of the Catholic Church done by the Borgias.

There is another, yet more bizarre story about Alexander VI which, we think, might explain his interest and even sympathy for Christian Hermetic-Cabala and the 'Egyptian' *magia naturalis* of Hermes Trismegistus which Pico had so fervently expounded ...

A Dominican abbot called Giovanni Nanni – also known as Annius of Viterbo – was a renowned historian who also acted as the personal secretary to Alexander VI.[45] In his better known work concerning the chronology of man from the Flood to the fall of Troy, Nanni advanced an extraordinary theory that the Borgia family of Pope Alexander VI were *descendants* of the Egyptian god Osiris, also known in Nanni's days as the 'father of the Egyptian Hercules'.[46] Using such classical authorities as Herodotus, Diodorus Siculus and others – as well as the 'authority' of certain ancient texts which Nanni himself had forged – Nanni presented an astoundingly convincing theory that the 'wisdom of the Egyptians', that is the Hermetic wisdom, had been transferred directly to the Italian people by Osiris when he had roamed the world in ancient times on a great civilising-mission.[47] According to the Danish scholar, Erik Iversen, Nanni then 'provided a heroic genealogy for his papal patron by demonstrating that the Borgia family descended directly from the Egyptian Hercules, the son of Osiris, and that the bull on the family crest was, in fact, the Osirian *Apis*.'[48]

The pope must have taken such ideas very seriously indeed, for he promptly commissioned the renowned Renaissance painter Pinturicchio to decorate the ceiling of the Borgia apartments at the Vatican with scenes of Hermes Trismegistus along with the Egyptian goddess Isis and the Osirian Apis bull – i.e. Serapis, the composite Graeco-Egyptian deity of ancient Alexandria. One such scene is clearly an allegory of the Hermetic 'natural' or 'astral' magic found in the *Asclepius*, where Hermes Trismegistus stands under a huge sky-globe with a large star dangling over his head, and is surrounded by various wise-looking men or sages, probably representing the classical philosophers, who are standing in reverence around him as if receiving his teachings.[49]

This strange episode of Nanni and the Borgia Pope is, of course, somewhat farcical and has nothing or little to do with the erudite and scholarly approach that Ficino, Pico della Mirandola and other savants applied to the Hermetic writings. Nonetheless, it stands as evidence of how deep the Hermetic influence had penetrated in those Renaissance days in Italy and the rest of Europe. More importantly, it testifies to the strange lure that its mysterious Hermetic-Cabalistic talismanic 'magic' had on those seeking the divine secrets through the rediscovered ancient wisdom believed to be incorporated in the writings of the 'Egyptian' Hermes Trismegistus.

The mystery of the *Picatrix* and the star-people

Although it can be said with absolute certainty that Ficino developed his own brand of talismanic and 'natural magic' from his readings of the *Asclepius*, some scholars, such as Frances Yates for example, also think that he was much influenced by another Hermetic book on magic entitled *Picatrix*[50] – a book that is not normally associated with the canon of the Corpus Hermeticum although versions of it had been circulating in Europe since at least the 13th century. Indeed, a copy of the *Picatrix* was found in Pico della Mirandola's private library, and it is also almost certain that Ficino and others of his group possessed copies or, at the very least, knew where to find such copies.[51]

The *Picatrix* was first translated into Latin from an Arabic version, now lost, which is believed to have been written in the 12th century in Spain, although some scholars think that it might have been originally composed in Egypt in the mid-11th century. In the Arabic version this book bore the title *Ghayat Al Hakim*, which means the 'The Aim of the Sage' (also sometimes translated as 'The Goal of the Wise') and no one really knows why Italian Renaissance scholars named it *Picatrix*.[52]

With its source said to be 224 ancient manuscripts on Hermeticism, astrology, magic, Cabala and alchemy, the *Picatrix* is considered one of the most complete works on ancient talismanic magic in existence. There are, today, various European translations available: in German by Helmut Ritter in 1933; in Spanish by Marcelino Villegas in 1982; in Latin by David Pingree in 1986; and in Italian by Davide Arecco and Stefano Zuffi, also in 1986. A partial English translation was published in 2002 by Hashem Attallah, and we understand that, David Pingree, has been working on an English translation in recent years.[53] Pingree published an extensive article on the *Picatrix* in the *Journal of the Warburg Institute* in 1981, and there are some very useful commentaries on it, supported by extensive quotations, in Frances Yates's book *Giordano Bruno and The Hermetic Tradition* published in 1964, on which we have mostly based our investigation. Yates, who studied the German and Latin versions of the *Picatrix*, concluded that this work must be associated with the Hermetic tradition, since not only is much reference to Hermes Trismegistus made in it but also it almost certainly draws from the ideologies of the *Sabaeans* – Arabs of Harran (a location in the southeast of modern Turkey) who had adopted the Hermetica as their own 'religion' in the ninth century AD and who also practiced the talismanic magic of the *Asclepius*.[54]

The Sabaeans' venerated the moon-god *Sin*, and they are known to have been avid stargazers and astrologers. An interesting theory of how they got their name has been put forward by Selim Hassan, an Egyptologist who worked at the Giza pyramids in Egypt in the 1930s.[55] Hassan proposed that the name Sabaeans, which is *Saba'ia* in Arabic, may have come from the ancient Egyptian word *saba'a* which means 'star'. Apparently the Sabaeans of Harran had performed yearly pilgrimages to the Giza pyramids from time immemorial until at least as late as the 11th century AD. At the pyramids they are known to have conducted astronomical observations and rituals which may have been remnants from the old astral religion of ancient Egypt. Hassan believed that the Sabaeans had recognised the Giza pyramids as monuments dedicated to the stars, which probably inspired them to take the name *Saba'ia* i.e. the 'star-people'.[56]

There is, however, another possible explanation. When the Hermetic and Gnostic sects were persecuted in Egypt by the Roman Church, some initiates may have fled to Harran carrying with them copies of the Hermetic and Gnostic writings. Harran, with its moon-worship cult – note in Egypt that Thoth-Hermes was also a moon-god – and its star-worship and astral magic, would have been an obvious place for the Hermetists and Gnostics seeking refuge and protection from the Roman and Christian persecutions. At any rate, whatever the true origins of the Sabaeans, it seems clear that their astral and talismanic magic was passed on to Arab scholars in Spain and Occitania, and that much of it survived in books such as the *Picatrix*. It is not within the scope of this investigation to pass into review the whole content of the *Picatrix*, but suffice to say here that it served as a sort of practical manual for talismanic magic or, to be more specific, it provided a step-by-step explanation of how to make talismans by pulling into them the power of the spiritual and astral world.

Perhaps an example may be useful here. Imagine two identical AA batteries, the sort we use everyday to power electronic equipment such as CD players, penlights, cameras and the like. One of the batteries, however, is fully charged while the other is empty. The charged battery has the potential to release energy to power music, light and so forth; the other is simply an inert object that produces nothing. In a similar way any object can be charged with *intellectual, spiritual or emotional* energy, just like the battery can be charged with electrical energy. In short, a talisman can be created. Imagine a young man who takes his lover to a restaurant dinner by candlelight and, at the appropriate moment, after having made a full declaration of love, pulls out a small box with a diamond ring in it and offers it as a token of his love. Whatever the reaction, that ring is henceforth not just a ring; it is a talisman.

Today we use the words 'sentimental value', but an ancient Egyptian or Sabaean or, if you prefer, a Hermetic thinker, would use the words 'talismanic value'. We all have our talismans: rings, necklaces, bracelets, amulets, crystals and so forth. And we generally would be quite disturbed and unhinged should they get lost or stolen. Many cutting-edge researchers have long accepted that ancient Egyptian art, statuary, obelisks, pyramids and even whole cities were meant to act as powerful talismans. It is also recognised that the subliminal effect of such talismans can be increased manifold by adding a variety of sensual stimuli other than mere visuals. Carefully chosen music, for example, will almost certainly enhance the experience, as well as perfumes, incense and lighting conditions. We all know how vastly different it is to visit a cathedral with a noisy group of tourists and again alone when a choir is singing hymns in soft candlelight with the smoke of incense filling the air.

It should be noted also that such talismanic environments do not necessarily have to be artificial. The natural environment can, and often does, act as a 'temple'. Just think of a Scotsman after years of absence returning to his beloved Highlands, or a Berber returning to the desert after a long spree in a city, and you will get the idea. This, in part, is what Ficino and Pico called *natural magic*.

But it is the perfect *combination* of an artificial 'temple' with a natural 'temple' that can act as the most inspiring and effective 'temple-talisman' of all. Think of the Palace of Versailles in France, the Taj Mahal in India, Angkor Wat in Cambodia. Think of a city like Paris in the spring, or Rome in the summer, or Washington, DC in the fall and you begin to understand the principle here.

All this may sound like some hocus-pocus pseudoscience in our present climate of intense empirical, rational and analytical thinking. But irrespective of what we may think of talismanic magic or so-called *sacred science*, the fact remains that we are complex creatures and we have evolved over billions of years under the subtle influence of nature. Our senses act as finely tuned receivers that enable us to understand nature and the cosmos around us intuitively. Such abilities are quite simply, *natural magic* and in ancient times were skillfully amplified by enhancing and capturing the multiple aspects of nature within well-defined symbols and talismans. We would go so far as to say that the ancient Egyptian priests were the true masters of this arcane magic and that an Egyptian temple was not really a temple at all so much as a powerful talisman meant to influence events in the macrocosm. Enter an Egyptian temple and you enter a model of the universe as perceived by the inner human mind. A temple was not merely a place of worship, but an environment that you had to integrate with – its ambiance, its harmonic proportions, its carefully chosen images, its symbols, it magical texts and its talismanic statuary, all of which were charged with archetypal values, cosmic principles and natural ideals. And yet in the *Picatrix* we are presented with something far more ambitious than a sacred talismanic temple. We are presented with no less than an esoteric manual for the transformation of great cities, and even perhaps the whole *world*, into talismans ...

Temple of the world

In the Hermetic text known as the *Asclepius* there is a call sent to a future generation of 'wise men' to bring about the full *restoration* and *restitution* of the true religion of the world[57] – that is the magical talismanic religion which was once practiced in the sacred land of Egypt. This call is highly reminiscent of the mysterious 'Organisation' spoken of in the Nag Hammadi Gnostic texts which date from approximately the same period and which even include a fragment of the *Asclepius*. As the reader will recall from Chapter Five the texts leave us with the impression that this 'Organisation' was some sort of Gnostic secret society and that its objective was also the restoration of a 'true religion' – in its case, Gnosis.

Let's look at the relevant passages of soaring prose in the *Asclepius*, in which Hermes Trismegistus laments and prophecies to his favourite pupil *Asclepius* the forthcoming and inevitable destruction of Egypt and its ancient and most revered religion:

> Do you not know, Asclepius, that Egypt is an image of heaven or, to be more precise, that everything governed and moved in heaven came down to Egypt and was transferred there? If truth were told, our land is the temple of the whole world. And yet, since it befits the wise to know all things in advance, of this you must not remain ignorant: a time will

THE MASTER GAME

come when it will appear that the Egyptians paid respect to divinity with faithful mind and painstaking reverence – to no purpose. All their holy worship will be disappointed and perish without effect, for divinity will return from earth to heaven, and Egypt will be abandoned. The land that was the seat of reverence will be widowed by the powers and left destitute of their presence. When foreigners occupy the land and territory, not only reverence will fall into neglect but, even harder, a prohibition under penalty prescribed by law – so-called – will be enacted against reverence, fidelity and divine worship. Then this most holy land, seat of shrines and temples, will be filled completely with tombs and corpses.

O Egypt, Egypt, of your reverent deeds only stories will survive, and they will be incredible to your children! Only words cut in stone will survive to tell your faithful works, and the Scythian or Indian or some such neighbour barbarian will dwell in Egypt. For divinity goes back to heaven, and all the people will die, deserted, as Egypt will be widowed and deserted by god and human. I call to you, most holy river, and I tell your future: a torrent of blood will fill you to the banks, and you will burst over them; not only blood will pollute your divine waters, it will also make them break out everywhere, and the number of the entombed will be much greater than the living. Whoever survives will be recognised as Egyptian only by his language; in his actions he will seem a foreigner.

Asclepius, why do you weep? Egypt herself will be persuaded to deeds much wickeder than these, and she will be steeped in evils far worse. A land once holy, most loving of divinity, by reason of her reverence the only land on earth where the gods settled, she who taught holiness and fidelity, will be an example of utter unbelief. In their weariness the people of that time will find the world nothing to wonder at or worship. This all – a good thing that never had nor has nor will have its better – will be endangered. People will find it oppressive and scorn it. They will not cherish this entire world, a work of God beyond compare, a glorious construction, a bounty composed of images in multiform variety, a mechanism for God's will ungrudgingly supporting his work, a unity of everything that can be honoured, praised and finally loved by those who see it, a multiform taken as a single thing. They will prefer shadow to light, and they will find death more expedient than life. No one will look up to heaven. The reverent will be thought mad, the irreverent wise; the lunatic will be thought brave, and the scoundrel will be taken for a decent person. Soul and teachings about soul (that the soul began immortal or else expected to attain immortality) as I revealed them to you will be considered not simply laughable but even illusory. But – believe me – whoever dedicates himself to reverence of mind will find himself facing a capital penalty. They will establish new laws, new justice. Nothing holy, nothing reverent nor worthy of heaven or heavenly beings will be heard or believed in the mind. How mournful when the gods withdraw from mankind! Only the baleful angels remain to mingle with humans, seizing wretches and driving them to every outrageous crime – war, looting, trickery and all that is contrary to the soul ...[58]

This superb piece of early Hermetic writing very much appears to anticipate the plight of the Egyptians under the Roman occupation of Egypt and, most intriguingly, it also seems to foretell the collapse of the Egyptian religion that was engineered after Christianity became the state religion of the Roman Empire. Since the *Asclepius* is dated to no later than the third century AD and, more intriguing, since the decree of the very Christian Emperor Theodosius outlawing 'paganism' was not to be issued until AD 391, then the eerie premonitions of the unknown author of this ominous tract are, to say the least, extraordinary. Yet this is not all. For the *Lament* goes on to promise hope for the future in words that resonate like a temple bell:

When all this comes to pass, Asclepius, then the master and father, the god whose power is primary, governor of the first good, will look on this conduct ... and in an act of will – which is god's benevolence – he will take his stand against vices and the perversion in everything, righting wrong, washing away malice ... then he will restore to the world to its beauty of old so that the world itself will again seem deserving of worship and wonder, and with constant benedictions and proclamations of praise the people of that time will honour the god who makes and *restores* so great a work. And this will be the geniture of the world: a *reformation* of all good things, and a *restitution* most holy and most reverent of nature itself ...[59]

Restoration, reformation and restitution to the ways and beauty of old ... But a 'restoration, reformation and restitution' by whom? How ... and when?

As the text continues it becomes clear that part of the plan – if it is a plan – includes the building or rebuilding of a magical talismanic city along certain well-defined astronomical and symbolic principles:

THE MASTER GAME

The gods who exercised their dominion over the earth will be restored one day and installed in a city at the extreme limit of Egypt, a city which will be founded towards the setting sun, and into which will hasten, by land and sea, the whole race of mortal men ...[60]

According to Frances Yates, the above passage presents us with the image of an enchanted utopia, a sort of ancient Egyptian version of Camelot, created by the manipulation of astral magic by adept priests who, as she says, were conversant in 'astronomy, mathematics, music, metaphysics, and indeed practically everything for the introduction of the *spiritus* [astral power] into talismans.' And all this was achieved, notes Yates by making 'images of stars inscribed on the correct materials, at the right times, in the right frame of mind and so on.'[61] As for the magical city itself, Yates thinks that it 'might thus be seen both as the ideal Egyptian society before its fall and as the ideal pattern of its future and universal restoration.'[62]

There is, too, another eerie passage in the *Asclepius*, where Hermes Trismegistus again addresses his pupil and gives us a tantalising glimpse of how the ancient Egyptians saw their sacred land as a model or 'image' of the heavenly landscape and a parallel world of the gods:

Do you not know, Asclepius, that Egypt is an image of heaven? Or, to be more precise, that everything governed and moved in heaven came down to Egypt and was transferred there? If truth were told, our land is the temple of the whole world ...[63]

In a Hermetic tract known as the *Kore Kosmou*, the 'Virgin of the World' – i.e. Isis, the Egyptian goddess, the consort of Osiris – makes the following revelation to their son Horus:

The earth lies in the middle of the universe, stretched on her back as a human might lie facing towards heaven ... Her head lies toward the south ... her right shoulder toward the east, and her left shoulder towards the west; her feet lie beneath the Great Bear [north] ... But the right holy land of our ancestors [i.e. Egypt] lies in the middle of the earth; and the middle of the human body is the sanctuary of the heart, and the heart is the headquarters of the soul; and that, my son, is the reason why men of this land ... are more intelligent [wise]. It could not be otherwise, seeing they are born and bred upon Earth's heart.[64]

In the above we have an actual geographical scheme which is based on some form of astral magic, where Egypt is said to be at the very centre of the world, right at the crossing of some prime meridian. It is interesting to note that the Great Bear constellation is mentioned in this scheme, for it is well known that ancient Egyptian temples were ritualistically aligned to the Great Bear constellation i.e. Ursa Major, in a ceremony known as the 'stretching of the cord'. It can now be better understood why in the *Asclepius* the whole of Egypt is said to be a 'temple' or, more specifically, that Egypt is the 'temple of the world'. Was this what the ancients meant when they called Egypt the 'land of the gods'? Was it, quite literally, a *sacred land* fashioned in the image of the cosmos?

The city of Adocentyn

Part IV of the *Picatrix* seems to elaborate on this theme. Here Hermes Trismegistus is presented as the founder of a magical solar city that, we are told, was designed around astrological ideas and that contained fantastic talismanic statues and other such wonders. The secret knowledge of this magical city of Hermes, claims the unknown author of *Picatrix*, was passed down the ages by the Chaldean Magi who were adepts in the science of talismanic magic:

> There are among the Chaldeans very perfect masters of this art and they affirm that Hermes was the first who constructed images by means of which he knew how to regulate the Nile against the motion of the moon. This man also built a temple to the sun, and he knew how to hide himself from all so that no one could see him, although he was within it. It was he, too, who in the east of Egypt constructed a city 12 miles long within which he constructed a castle which had four gates in each of its four parts. On the eastern gate he placed the form of an eagle [Horus?]; on the western gate, the form of a bull [Apis?]; on the southern gate the form of a lion [Sphinx?], and on the northern gate he constructed the form of a dog [Anubis?]. Into these images he introduced spirits which spoke with voices, nor could anyone enter the gates of the city without permission. There he planted trees, in the midst of which was a great tree which bore the fruits of all generation [immortality?]. On the summit of the castle he caused to be raised a tower thirty cubits high on the top of which he ordered to be placed a light-house, the colours of which changed every day until the seventh day after which it returned to the first colour, and so the city was illuminated with these colours. Near the city there was

THE MASTER GAME

abundance of waters in which dwelt many kinds of fish. Around the circumference of the city he placed engraved images and ordered them in such manner that by their virtue the inhabitants were made virtuous and withdrawn from all wickedness and harm. The name of the city was Adocentyn ...[65]

Dame Frances Yates' commentary is most helpful:

Passed through the vivid imagination of the Arabs of Harran, we seem to have here something that reminds us of the hieratic religious magic described in the *Asclepius*. Here are the man-made gods, statues of the animal- and bird-shaped gods of Egypt, which Hermes Trismegistus has animated by introducing spirits into them so that they speak with voices and guard the gates of this magical utopia. The colours of the planets flash from the central tower, and these images around the circumference of the City, are they perhaps images of the signs of the zodiac and the decans [constellations] which Hermes has known how to arrange so that only good celestial influences are allowed into the City? The law-giver of the Egyptians [Hermes] is giving laws which must perforce be obeyed, for he constrains the inhabitants of the City to be virtuous, and keeps them healthy and wise, by his powerful manipulation of astral magic ... One might say that this City shows us Hermes Mercurius [Trismegistus] in his triple role of Egyptian priest and god-maker, of philosopher-magician, and of king and lawgiver ... The pious admirer of those two 'divine' books by the most ancient Hermes – the *Pimander* and the *Asclepius* – must surely have been struck by this vivid description of a City in which, as in Plato's ideal *Republic*, the wise is the ruler, and rules most forcibly by means of the priestly Egyptian magic such as described in the *Asclepius* ...[66]

In the original Arabic version of the *Picatrix* the name of the magical Hermetic city is not given exactly as Adocentyn but as *Al Ashmunain*. This turns out to be a real location in Middle Egypt. It stands on the banks of the Nile where there is an abundance of vegetation, fish and fauna, and would indeed have been a paradisiacal spot in antiquity. It was the main cult centre of Thoth/Hermes in Greek and Roman times[67] and a famous temple dedicated to Thoth once stood here.[68] For this reason the Greeks called it *Hermopolis* i.e. the city of Hermes. Its original Egyptian name was *Kmun*, meaning 'eight', apparently in honour of a group of eight gods, the *Ogdoad*, who represented the world before creation.[69]

We cannot be sure that it was *Kmun*/Hermopolis/*Al Ashmunain* that was envisaged by the writers of the *Picatrix* when they summoned up their vision of the magical, talismanic city of Hermes Trismegistus. The problem is that Adocentyn, as they described it, bears no resemblance to any real region in Egypt – although certainly this was a land in which many 'temples to the Sun' existed, the most famous being Heliopolis in the north and Karnak-Luxor in the south. The term *Ashmunain* in the original text of the *Picatrix* could also be a corruption of *Ain Shams*, meaning the 'Eye of the Sun', a name still used by Egyptians today to denote the region of Heliopolis.

But what really interests us about the talismanic city of the *Picatrix* is not so much its very plausible connection to real sacred cities of ancient Egypt. Far more important, in our view, has been its role as an archetype or template for cities to be built or rebuilt *in the future*, including the capitals of Britain, Italy, France and the United States. We will demonstrate in later chapters that in each of these cases prominent monuments, works of architecture, and sometimes the street plans of whole districts, appear have been harnessed to a secret Hermetic scheme.

If we are right then we have come across the traces of an organisation that has hitherto sustained its existence and purpose undetected for hundreds of years while carrying out immense projects of occult urban planning – all of them 'hidden' in full public view. To understand why anyone might have been motivated to do such an audacious thing we must first explore the Hermetic religion that lies behind the cosmic city of Adocentyn.

CHAPTER NINE

TWO PHOENIXES

A divine city hath been built for me, I know it and I know the name
thereof ...   Ancient Egyptian *Book of the Dead*[1]

I have come into the city of god – the region which existed in primeval
time.   Ancient Egyptian *Book of the Dead*[2]

The opening into the city is fire ... and the god hath made it for those who
follow willingly in his train ... He hath made the city so that he may dwell
therein at will, and none can enter therein except on the day of the great
transformations ...

Ancient Egyptian *Book of the Dead*[3]

Specialised scholars who study ancient literature often argue that there is no strong genetic link between the known religious texts of ancient Egypt (which span the period from roughly 2300 BC to 0 BC) and the Hermetic texts composed in Alexandria in Egypt between approximately AD 1 and AD 300. 'There is a want of technical Egyptian mythological, liturgical and sacerdotal knowledge in the [Hermetic] texts,' explains Tobias Churton:

We really learn nothing about Egyptian religion, except in the most general terms, terms which would not stretch the vocabulary gained by the average reader of a tourist guide to ancient Egypt today.[4]

The scholarly dissection of the Hermetica began with Isaac Casaubon (1559–1614) who late in his life argued, successfully, that none of the texts could possibly have been written by an ancient Egyptian named Hermes Trismegistus – as had been widely believed since their rediscovery in 1460. By skilful textual analysis he rightly attributed them to the early Christian period in the first three centuries AD and thus, it seemed, 'debunked' the notion that they were as old or older than Moses. Casaubon's findings took many years to be fully accepted, but wherever they were accepted they removed from the texts the aura of prestige that their false antiquity had given them. The inevitable result, over the next century and a half, was that:

> ... the Hermetic writings lost their hold on men's interest, and sank into comparative neglect.[5]

A renewal of academic interest in the Hermetica was brought about almost single-handedly in the 1960s by Dame Frances Yates, whose works we cite frequently in this book. By 'making Hermes a major figure in the preliminaries to the scientific revolution' and a vital catalyst of the Renaissance she has ensured that the Hermetic writings are now once again 'required reading for many students of early modern thought and letters.'[6]

In Yates' view Casaubon's debunking exercise in the 17th century had thrown out the baby with the bathwater. To be sure, the texts were *not* ancient Egyptian in origin – Casaubon was right about that. Nevertheless the 'Egyptian illusion', which misled the scholars of the Medici Academy and their successors all over Europe for the best part of two centuries, gave the Hermetic texts the power and leverage – and enough time – to effect profound changes in the way that people thought about the world and understood the human predicament.[7]

Preserving the essence

This argument for pragmatic study of the *effects* of the Hermetic writings, regardless of any debate about their antiquity, has made the subject academically respectable again but has done nothing to advance our understanding of their origins. We are left to believe that these astoundingly sophisticated texts arose fully-formed out of nowhere in the first three centuries AD, with no background or evolution, and are asked to accept that:

> The precise provenance of the philosophical Hermetica remains to a large extent a mystery.[8]

The one certainty, all the experts agree, is that there must have been a close connection between the philosophers and religious thinkers who composed the Hermetica in Alexandria in the first three centuries AD and the philosophers and religious thinkers who composed the Gnostic texts in Alexandria in exactly the same period. It is not simply that certain texts of the Hermetica (including the *Asclepius*) were part of the Nag Hammadi Gnostic library[9] – although this is strongly indicative of overlapping interests in the Hermetic and Gnostic communities of that period. Much more significant are the deep structural connections at the level of ideas that can be demonstrated between the two collections of texts.

The painstaking work that has revealed these connections, and begun to get to grips with the amazing philosophical and religious undercurrents of late antiquity, has all been done by orthodox, 'mainstream' scholars. Since Casaubon, however, (with a few remarkable exceptions who we'll meet in later chapters) it has been tantamount to academic suicide to reinvestigate the supposedly settled question of any possible ancient Egyptian origin for the Hermetic texts.

Our primary objective in this book is to follow the traces of what we suspect may be a 'conspiracy', or something very like one, based on Hermetic and Gnostic ideas and originally formulated about 2,000 years ago. In complete contradiction to the scholarly consensus it is our proposal that the Hermetic texts *are* closely connected to the much older ancient Egyptian religion. They may have been deliberately designed to preserve its *essence* while dispensing with its substance. To take a metaphor from Gnostic and Hermetic teachings of reincarnation, the intention may have been to transfer the *soul* of the Egyptian system, at the point of its death under the Roman Empire, into an entirely new and different 'body' better adapted to the times.

Building the City of the God

There is a consistent emphasis on cities throughout the Hermetic literature.

At the end of Chapter Eight we drew particular attention to the magical 'cosmic city' of Adocentyn, said in the *Picatrix* to have been built in the remote past by Hermes Trismegistus and so designed that it brought benevolent celestial influences streaming down on its inhabitants. We also pointed out that a similar magical city built by the gods is described in the *Asclepius*, probably the best-known of all the Hermetic texts. There it is intriguingly portrayed not as a city of the past but as a prophesied city – a city of the future:

> ... which will be founded towards the setting sun, and into which will hasten, by land and sea, the whole race of mortal men ...[10]

If there is no genetic connection between the ancient Egyptian and the Hermetic texts, as scholars tell us, then it is presumably a coincidence that Chapter 183 of the ancient Egyptian *Book of the Dead* dated to about 1200 BC, contains this curious passage:

> I come from the city of the god, the primeval region; soul, *ka* and spirit are what is in this land. Such is its god, namely the Lord of Truth possessor of provisions, he to whom every land is drawn ...[11]

Soul, *ka* and spirit are the names given to different elements of the person all believed by the ancient Egyptians to survive death, while 'Lord of Truth' is a frequently used epithet for the wisdom god Thoth-Hermes. So here in the *Book of the Dead* we have a 'city of the god' (indeed a city of the god who would become Hermes) towards which 'every land is drawn'. Isn't that essentially the same concept that crops up more than 1400 years later in the supposedly unconnected *Asclepius* (*circa* AD 268–273) where 'the whole race of mortal men' hasten towards a city built by the gods?

Going further back in time we come to the ancient Egyptian *Pyramid Texts*, the world's oldest scriptures, dated to around 2300 BC. Here too we find references to the sacred functions of cities that are echoed in the much later and supposedly unconnected Hermetica. Of particular interest is Utterance 319 in which we learn that it is the responsibility of the king, during his reign, to *build the city of the god*:

> The King has united the heavens, the King has power over the southern and northern lands, and the gods who were aforetime, the King has built the city of the god in accordance with its proper due.[12]

This idea that it is the sacred duty of the king to build a city that will harmoniously unite earth and heaven for the benefit of its inhabitants would be taken up some 4,000 years later by the great Hermetic philosopher Tommaso Campanella. Based entirely on his studies of the Hermetica, Campanella claimed in the early 17th century that he could 'make a city in such a wonderful way that only by looking at it all the sciences may be learned.'[13] He would go on, as we will see in Chapter Twelve, to prophesy that King Louis XIV of France would be the one who would actually build this magical 'City of the Sun.'

We recall the words of Frances Yates, reported in Chapter Eight, to the effect that Adocentyn, the magical city of the *Picatrix*, kept its citizens healthy and wise through the 'powerful manipulation of astral magic' which ensured that only 'good celestial influences' could reach them. How different is this from Campanella's claim to be able to make a city from which its inhabitants could learn and benefit merely by looking at it? Or from this passage in the ancient Egyptian *Pyramid Texts* where the king says:

> I build you, O city of mine; You shall do for me every good thing which I desire; You shall act on my behalf wherever I go ...[14]

Sky and ground

We suggest that key shared concepts underlie this shared interest in the cosmic 'City of the God' and/or 'City of the Sun' that is found in both the ancient Egyptian and the Hermetic texts. The most important of these concepts is, indeed, the unifying theme of the entire corpus of Hermetic writings:

> That which is below corresponds with that which is above, and that which is above corresponds with that which is below, in the accomplishment of the miracle of the one thing ...[15]

The passage quoted is from *The Emerald Tablet of Hermes Trismegistus*, not part of the so-called *philosophical* Hermetica but one of a large number of *alchemical* Hermetic tracts from various periods that fall largely outside the scope of this discussion. Nonetheless in both the alchemical and the philosophical Hermetica, as throughout the much older ancient Egyptian texts, we encounter the consistent deployment of a distinctive metaphor in which 'sky', 'heaven', 'above' and other related terms represent the spiritual, immaterial realms to which the soul properly aspires, while 'ground', 'earth' and 'below' represent the world of gross matter in which the soul is imprisoned. Implicit – and often explicit – in the relevant texts is the understanding that perfection belongs exclusively to the 'above' world, while the world of 'earth' and 'below' is corrupt and eternally imperfect.

Let's look first at a few examples from the ancient Egyptian texts, all of which in different ways explore, describe and prepare the initiate for life after death as it was conceived in the religion of the pharaohs:

> Your soul is bound for the sky, your corpse is beneath the ground ... You shall go up to the sky ... You shall ascend to those who are above the earth ...[16] (*Book of the Dead*)

You shall ascend to the sky, you shall traverse the firmament, you shall associate with the stars ...[17] (*Book of the Dead*)

This King is Osiris in a dust-devil; earth is this King's detestation ... This King is bound for the sky ...[18] (*Pyramid Texts*)

Arise, remove your earth, shake off your dust, raise yourself, that you may travel in company with the spirits, for your wings are those of a falcon, your gleam is that of a star ...[19] (*Pyramid Texts*)

'How lovely to see you, how pleasing to behold!' says Isis, 'when you ascend to the sky, your power about you, your terror about you, your magic at your feet ... The doors of the sky are opened for you, the doors of the starry firmament are thrown open for you ...'[20] (*Pyramid Texts*)

A particularly clear example of what we might call ancient Egyptian 'matter-spirit dualism,' is found in the *Coffin Texts*, *circa* 1900 BC:

The King is pure on that great tomb-plateau; the King has got rid of his evil; the King has discarded his wrongdoing; the King has cast down to earth the evils which were on his flesh ...[21]

This passage contains the by now familiar equivalences (matter = evil; spirit = good) that we've encountered repeatedly in Part I of this book amongst the Gnostics of the early Christian era and their dualist successors the Bogomils and the Cathars. Yet it was composed 2,000 years before any of the surviving Gnostic texts and 3,000 years before the upsurge of the Cathar phenomenon in Western Europe in the 12th century AD.

In our view it is not a coincidence that the Hermetic texts are redolent of exactly the same system of ideas. A few extracts are sufficient to make the point:

Evil, as I have told you before, must needs dwell here on earth, where it is at home; for the home of evil is the earth.[22] (Hermetica, *Libellus IX*)

It came to pass that evils inherent in matter were intermingled with the human body.[23] (Hermetica, *Asclepius III*)

The soul of a child ... is still hardly detached from the soul of the Kosmos. But when the body has increased in bulk, and has drawn the soul down into its material mass, it generates oblivion; and so the soul separates itself from the Beautiful and Good, and no longer partakes of that; and through this oblivion the soul becomes evil.[24] (Hermetica, *Libellus X*)

I see that by god's mercy there has come to be in me a form which is not fashioned out of matter, and I have passed forth out of myself and entered into an immortal body.[25] (Hermetica, *Libellus XIII*)

You are purified, now that you have put away the earthly tabernacle.[26] (Hermetica, *Libellus XIII*)

The last quoted remark, although from the Hermetica, could equally well sum up the state of the Cathar *perfectus* in receipt of the *consolamentum* – who thereafter severed all connections with the world of matter. Meanwhile in the *Pyramid Texts* of the ancient Egyptians the formula 'remove your earth, shake off your dust'[27] was used in exactly the same way and to exactly the same purpose.

The divided creature

Scholars do not dispute the existence of a strong genetic link between Gnostic and Hermetic beliefs. On the contrary such a link is fully accepted. As we've seen, however, the notion of a similarly close link between the Hermetic religion and the ancient Egyptian religion is outright rejected. It's provocative then that all three systems appear to be in complete agreement in their analysis of the fundamental dilemma of the human being as an ambiguous or 'dual' creature composed both of matter and of spirit.

The doctrine of the Gnostics, Bogomils and Cathars on this subject has been explored extensively in Part I. The reader will recall the vivid picture painted in their teachings and myths of the souls of fallen angels trapped in the 'alien' material world within the gross physical bodies of men and women. The view that emerges of the human condition is undeniably that of a creature made of 'mud' and corruption that is paradoxically illuminated by a divine and deathless spark – a creature in large part of 'earth' that also contains a fragment of 'heaven'.

Could this permanent state of duality be what the composers of the ancient Egyptian *Book of the Dead* were hinting at with an enigmatic formula found in Chapter 156 that reads 'His one arm is toward the sky, his other arm is toward the earth'?[28] It is certainly what the Hermetic sages had in mind in the *Pimander* when they wrote:

Man, unlike all other living creatures upon earth, is twofold. He is mortal by reason of his body; he is immortal by reason of the man of eternal substance ... He is exalted above the structure of the heavens ... yet he is mastered by carnal desire and by oblivion.[29]

In the Hermetic text that bears his name, the student Asclepius asks Hermes the obvious question about this arrangement:

But what need was there, Trismegistus, that man should be placed in the material world? Why might he not have dwelt in the region where God is, and there enjoyed perfect happiness?[30]

In reply Hermes explains that God first created man as an 'incorporeal and eternal being' – the reference here is to the spiritual man, the immortal soul, the 'divine spark'. Then, however:

Perceiving that the man whom he had made could not tend all things on earth unless he enclosed him in a material envelope, God gave him the shelter of a body to dwell in, and ordained that all men should be formed in like manner.[31]

While we recognise that the Hermetic script at this point diverges sharply from the Gnostic/Cathar script (in which the soul of man is made by the God of Good and the body of man is made by the God of Evil) the general scenario of incorporeal souls immersed in matter nevertheless remains almost identical in the two religions. One profound difference must however be acknowledged concerning their attitudes towards matter – for while the Gnostics and Cathars deduced from their beliefs that matter should be hated, the Hermeticists reached a much more positive conclusion about the creation and about man's place in the scheme of things:

Thus he [God] fashioned man of the substance of the mind, and the substance of body – of that which is eternal and that which is mortal – blending and mingling together portions of either substance in adequate measure, to the end that the creature so fashioned might be able to fulfil the demands of both sources of his being, that is to say, to venerate and worship the things of heaven, and at the same time to tend and administer the things of earth.[32]

THE MASTER GAME

Knowledge, reason, intelligence …

Later in the same Hermetic text – the *Asclepius* – the argument verges back into close proximity to Gnostic ideas when it reminds us that it is the ultimate destiny of the human soul to end its sojourn on earth and return to the heavens where it belongs:

> God saw that of all living creatures men alone had need of reason and knowledge, whereby they might repel and put away from them the evil passions inherent in their bodies; and for this cause he imparted to them the gift of reason; and at the same time … he held out to them the hope of immortality, and gave them power to strive toward it.[33]

In the case of the Gnostic religion the reader will recall from Part I that the return to the heavenly realm could not be achieved by blind faith but was to be striven for through *gnosis* – 'revealed knowledge of the reality of things'. In the case of the Hermetic religion we see this same emphasis on knowledge, now also combined with the 'gift of reason'. Indeed the *Asclepius* goes so far as to state that the 'divine part' of man consists of 'mind, intellect, spirit, and reason,' and to assert that it is on account of these 'higher elements' that he is 'found capable of rising to heaven'.[34]

This goal of the return to heaven, the *Pimander* asserts explicitly, is the 'consummation for those who have got *gnosis*.'[35] And in one of the *Discourses of Hermes* a helpful definition is even offered of the precise kind of knowledge involved in *gnosis*. It seems that it 'cannot be taught by speech, nor learnt by hearing':

> Knowledge differs greatly from sense-perception … Knowledge is incorporeal; the organ which it uses is the mind itself; and the mind is contrary to the body.[36]

The individual's quest for *gnosis*, in both its Hermetic and purely Gnostic forms, involved putting off the material world and its illusions. The reader will recall from Part I the asceticism of the Gnostic sages of Alexandria and of their successors the Cathar and Bogomil *perfecti*. The writers of the Hermetic texts would have approved: 'If a man understands the design of god,' says the *Asclepius*, 'he will despise all material things.'[37]

On the other hand, for those who persist in willful ignorance, all the vices and evils that are inherent in the material realm:

... grow in strength, and lacerate the soul with incurable sores; and infected and corrupted by the poison, the soul breaks out in tumours, so to speak, save in the case of those whose souls are cured by the sovereign remedy of knowledge and intelligence.[38]

Like so much else in the Hermetica, this constant emphasis on the role of knowledge and intelligence in the soul's struggle to win immortality seems to have strong precursors in the ancient Egyptian funerary texts. There we encounter a bearded god called *Sia* who attends Ra in the solar barque. Sia's special quality is that he is the personification of intelligence[39] so it is interesting that his role in bringing the soul of the deceased safely through the Netherworld is repeatedly emphasised. In Spell 237 of the *Coffin Texts*, for example, the deceased embarks on his afterlife journey with confidence stating: 'I know what Sia knows, and a path is opened for me ...'[40] Earlier in Spell 38 we read: 'I have seen the chest [i.e strongbox] of Sia and I know what is in it ...'[41] Another metaphor for the crucial importance of intelligence is employed in Spell 689 which states: 'This King has swallowed Sia, he has eaten magic from the magician.'[42] In the *Book of What is in the Duat* we find Sia accompanying the deceased on his journey through the Netherworld and opening gates of fire that would otherwise remain closed to him.[43]

Stars and angels falling to earth

In the ancient Egyptian system the afterlife journey through the Netherworld – the *Duat* – was the opportunity for the 'perfected spirit' (i.e. one that had acquired the necessary knowledge during incarnation on earth) to throw off forever the entrapments of matter, ascend to the spiritual realms and become, metaphorically, a star in heaven. In the case of initiates in the Gnostic system, whether in its early Christian or later Cathar forms, we know that this sought-after 'ascent to heaven' was in fact understood as a *re-ascent* of our angelic souls to the heavenly realms from which they had fallen long ago.

The reader will recall from Chapter Three vivid descriptions of angels falling 'like rain upon the earth' through a hole in heaven, having been tempted downwards by Satan who then trapped them in human bodies and the cycle of reincarnation. There are some striking but neglected passages in the ancient Egyptian texts which seem to us to be expressions of essentially the same idea and once again provide support for a mysterious connection between the religion of ancient Egypt and the Hermetic and Gnostic religions. For example in Chapter 99 of the *Book of the Dead* we read:

This land is baleful and the stars have overbalanced themselves and have fallen on their faces therein, and they have not found anything which will help them to ascend again ...[44]

Routine use is made in the ancient Egyptian texts of the star as a metaphor for the beatified and 'perfected' soul. We therefore see little difference in intent between this image of fallen stars unable to get back to the sky and the Gnostic image of fallen angels unable to return to heaven. Of course the purest and most spiritual angels in the Gnostic/Cathar system were those who resisted temptation and never fell to earth at all. So it was too amongst the ancient Egyptians as far back as the *Pyramid Texts* in 2300 BC:

The King is one of those ... beings ... who will never fall to the earth from the sky ...[45]

Reproducing eternity in a copy

At the heart of all such imagery, whether ancient Egyptian, Gnostic or Hermetic, is the sense of a radical rupture between matter and spirit, sky and earth. We've seen how all three of these religions taught the need for some sort of special knowledge – *gnosis* – as a way of escape for souls trapped 'below'. In the case of the Cathars the saving knowledge was acquired through asceticism, study, and the initiation ritual known as the *consolamentum*. In the case of the Hermeticists and the ancient Egyptians, as we saw earlier and in Chapter Eight, there was a curious interest in cities which were to be made, so far as possible, in 'the image of heaven'. By somehow replicating or 'copying' celestial perfection on earth, the clear implication of the Hermetic texts is that such cities would provide untold benefits to their inhabitants, constrain them 'to be virtuous' and keep them 'healthy and wise'.[46]

In the *Pimander*, the first book of the Hermetic collection, we even find this idea of replication of the above by the below employed in describing the process of creation. We are led to understand that there exists an 'archetypal form', perceptible only to the mind and not at all to the senses, 'which is prior to the beginning of things and is limitless.' The material world:

... issued from God's Purpose, which beheld that beauteous world [i.e. the archetypal form] and copied it.[47]

The *Asclepius* likewise speaks of a 'higher' archetypal *Kosmos* that is imperceptible to the senses but that nevertheless influences and shapes the lower 'sensible' *Kosmos* that we inhabit as beings of matter:

> If you consider the whole, you will learn that in truth the sensible Kosmos itself, with all things that are therein, is woven like a garment by that higher Kosmos.[48]

A little later the same text adds:

> God ... stands unmoved; and eternity likewise is ever changeless, containing in itself a Kosmos which is without beginning, even that Kosmos which we rightly call 'imperceptible to sense'. This sensible Kosmos [i.e. the universe of matter and space that we see all around us] has been made in the image of that other Kosmos, and reproduces eternity in a copy.[49]

In the *Discourses of Hermes to Tat* we learn more about the mechanisms of the 'copying' process:

> The forces do not work upward from below, but downward from above. The things in heaven receive no benefits from the things on earth; but the things on earth receive all benefits from the things in heaven.[50]

In the beautiful and mysterious *Kore Kosmou* the point is re-emphasised with more detail:

> All the world which lies below has been set in order and filled with contents by the things which are placed above; for the things below have not the power to set in order the world above. The weaker mysteries, then, must yield to the stronger; and the system of things on high is stronger than the things below.[51]

Hermetic landscapes

We are now better equipped to understand the central Hermetic notion, introduced in Chapter Eight, of ancient Egypt as an 'image of heaven':

> Do you not know, Asclepius, that Egypt is an image of heaven? Or, to be more precise, that everything governed and moved in heaven came down to Egypt and was transferred there? If truth were told, our land is the temple of the whole world ...[52]

If the land of Egypt is 'an image of heaven', and for that reason 'the temple of the whole world', then it's easy to understand how those who believed this might have wanted to build temples that were also – in their own smaller-scale way – 'images of heaven'. The same logic would also apply to the creation and positioning of great monuments. And of course to the planning and building – or rebuilding – of cities. In other words if we know that a person is a committed initiate of the Hermetic system then we can predict that he or she will take an interest in temples, monuments and cities that in some way 'imitate' or 'copy' heaven. If it so happens that the initiate is a great king or a person otherwise in a position to have a major influence on decisions about the built environment, we might expect to see that interest turned to action.

It is understood that the earthly 'copy' is and always will be inferior to the heavenly archetype on which it is modelled because 'there is nothing good on earth; there is nothing bad in heaven,' and because while 'nothing in heaven is in bondage, nothing on earth is free.'[53] Nevertheless, the clear logic of the Hermetic texts is that it is better to copy the perfection of heaven on earth – however inferior the results – than to do nothing at all. In the *Discourses of Hermes to Tat* we read:

> All things on earth ... are unreal; but some of them – not all, but some few only – are copies of reality ... When the appearance flows in from above, it becomes an imitation of reality. But apart from the working of power from above, it remains an illusion; just as a painted portrait presents to us in appearance the body of the man we see in it, but is not in itself a human body.[54]

It seems perfectly obvious from this that a Hermetic king would prefer to dispose his monuments, temples and cities so that 'power from above' would be able to work in them. And the way to do that, as the texts themselves suggest, would be to fashion the built environment as an 'imitation of reality', 'an image of heaven', 'a reproduction of eternity in a copy'...

The beauty of the archetype

Practiced in Europe between the 10th and the 14th centuries, the Gnostic religion of the Bogomils and the Cathars taught an intense 'matter-spirit dualism'. As we would expect in such closely interconnected systems, it also made use of 'sky-ground' metaphors of the specifically Hermetic and ancient Egyptian type. In Chapter Three we cite several examples of such Bogomil and Cathar teachings, including the notion that a number of their sacred books had been 'written in heaven and brought down to earth' and the following classically 'Hermetic' doctrine:

> For just as it is on earth, so also it is in the firmament, because replicas of what are in the firmament are on earth.[55]

Once again we find striking precedents in the supposedly unrelated funerary texts of ancient Egypt. There are, for example, numerous exhortations calling upon initiates to make copies on the earth of a region of the sky called the *Duat* incorporating the constellation of Orion – associated with the god Osiris – and the star Sirius, associated with the goddess Isis.[56] This was the sky-region believed to be the location of the ancient Egyptian Netherworld, where souls journeyed and were judged after death. It was therefore thought to be vitally important to gain foreknowledge of it and of the trials that awaited the soul there. We learn from the *Book of What is in the Duat* (*circa* 1400 BC), that one way to attain this *gnosis* was to build copies on the ground 'of the hidden circle of the *Duat* in the body of *Nut* [the sky]'[57]:

> Whosoever shall make an exact copy of these forms, and shall know it, shall be a spirit well-equipped both in heaven and in earth, unfailingly, and regularly and eternally.[58]

> Whosoever shall make a copy thereof, and shall know it upon earth, it shall act as a magical protector for him both in heaven and in earth, unfailingly and regularly and eternally.[59]

For a supposedly unrelated text, it is odd that the *Book of What is in the Duat* seems to draw the same distinction as the Hermetica between the heavenly archetype, that is perceptible only to the mind, and the earthly copy that is perceptible to the senses. Both traditions therefore necessarily imply a group of initiates who were trained to 'see' – i.e. attain *gnosis* of – what otherwise only the gods could see:

> The secret representation of the *Duat* is not known to men and women.[60]

> Whosoever shall make a copy of these representations according to this copy of what is in the *Lament* of the *Duat*, *which cannot be looked at or seen*, and whosoever shall know these secret images, shall be in the condition of a spirit who is equipped for journeying ...[61] [Emphasis added]

To become 'a spirit equipped for journeying' was, of course, the goal of the entire ancient Egyptian religious system in the sense that it sought to equip its initiates for spiritual immortality and freedom from the fetters of matter. But it was possible to fail in this quest and for the soul to be destroyed utterly. Consistent and repeated evil acts were inevitably fatal to the soul of the perpetrator. Willful ignorance – always detested by the Hermetic sages – was also believed to be extremely dangerous to one's prospects of eternity. Thus:

> He who hath no knowledge of the whole or part of the secret representations of the *Duat*, shall be condemned to destruction.[62]

We reiterate that the *Duat*, for the ancient Egyptians, was understood to be a region of the starry sky and that those who aspired to immortality rather than extinction in the afterlife were more or less obliged to attain knowledge of it. Is it a coincidence that an almost identical scenario is painted in the Hermetic texts where, after a lengthy exposition on the sky and stars, we are abruptly told:

> He who has not failed to get knowledge of these things is able to form an exact conception of god ... But it is impossible, my son, for one who is yet in the body to attain to this happiness. A man must train his soul in this life, in order that, when it has entered the other world, where it is permitted to see God, it may not miss the way which leads to him. But men who love the body will never see the vision of the Beautiful and Good. How glorious, my son, is the beauty of that which has neither shape nor colour.[63]

In other words the beauty of the archetype, which 'cannot be looked at or seen' by uninitiated men and women because it is perceptible only to the mind and not at all to the senses.

Transforming the world

The recurrent emphasis on intelligence, reason and the use of the mind to 'train the soul' that characterises the Hermetic texts was also the wellspring of their immense influence on science and scientific thinking following their rediscovery in the mid-15th century. By promoting the individual's quest for knowledge and illumination they would prove as powerful an antidote to the dogmas and received wisdoms of the Church during the Renaissance and the Enlightenment as the Gnostic teachings of the Cathars had done in the Middle Ages. Nor in our view is it an accident, but an almost inevitable by-product of these closely-related systems of thought – wherever and whenever they may be applied – that Cathar Gnosticism stimulated its own 'mini-Renaissance' across southern Europe in the 12th century.

We speculated in Chapter Two that this Cathar revolution in religious and philosophical ideas, music and poetry, culture and social order, might have transformed the world if the Church had not crushed it – utterly – in the 13th century. It's true that in the Balkans a few scattered Bogomils lingered on as late as the 15th century. To all extents and purposes, however, we accept that the hitherto unbroken chain of Gnostic heresy stretching back to the dawn of the Christian era was snapped when the very last Cathar *perfectus*, William Belibaste, was burnt at the stake in 1321.

We find it rather remarkable, therefore, that *another embodiment* of essentially the same ideas should have slipped through the gates of Western culture less than 120 years later. We mean, of course, the Hermetic texts, their emergence from the wilderness after a millennium of silence, and their transferral to the Medici Academy in Florence in 1460.

Either by accident or by some hidden design, they arrived at exactly the right place and time to bring alive again the ancient religion of 'salvation through knowledge' that the Church thought it had just killed. In this latest incarnation, however, it would wear a much more overtly 'ancient Egyptian' and much less 'Christian' face. Perhaps for that very reason it would also set out a more positive and life-giving route towards the goal of world transformation than Gnosticism, with its world-hatred, could ever have achieved.

The Hermeticists shared the Gnostic view that evil is inherent in matter, and thus – through the body – in mankind. Yet they did not allow this recognition to seduce them into the mood of hopeless nihilism and species suicide that one sometimes senses could have led Cathar dualism down a very dark road. Far from that, the Hermetic 'way' accepted the human condition, sought our transformation through the elevation of the spiritual element within us, and handed the responsibility directly to the individual and to his own conscience:

> It is man's duty not to acquiesce in his merely human state, but rather, in the strength of his contemplation of things divine, to scorn and despise that mortal part which has been attached to him because it was needful that he should keep and tend this lower world.[64]
> (Hermetica, *Asclepius*)

THE MASTER GAME

Moreover 'keeping and tending the lower world' in the Hermetic scenario is not a repulsive and humiliating imprisonment in matter but a sacred responsibility with a vital role in the cosmic scheme of things that can only be fulfilled by man. The texts speak eloquently for themselves:

Man is a being partly divine and partly mortal; not that he is to be thought the lower because he is mortal in part; we ought rather to regard him as exalted by his mortality in that he is by such a lot more fitly and effectively constituted for a purpose preordained. For since he could not have met the demands of both his functions if he had not been made of both kinds of substance, he was fashioned out of both, to the end that he might be able both to tend the earth and to do service to the Deity.[65]

Man is a marvel, then, Asclepius; honour and reverence to such a being! ... Strong in the assurance of that in him which is divine, he scorns the merely human part of his own nature ... He raises reverent eyes to heaven above; he tends the earth below ... He has access to all; he descends to the depths of the sea by the keenness of his thought; and heaven is not found too high for him, for he measures it by his sagacity, as though it were within his reach.[66]

To man is given charge of that part of the universe which consists of earth and water; and this earthly part of the universe is kept in order by means of man's knowledge and application of the arts and sciences. For God willed that the universe should not be complete until man had done his part.[67]

If man takes upon him in all its fullness the function assigned to him, that is, the tendence which is his special task, he becomes the means of right order to the Kosmos, and the Kosmos to him.[68]

Despite the protests of scholars that there is no clear link between the Hermetica and the religion of ancient Egypt, the pharaohs too believed that it was their function, and the function of their divine land, to interact in the correct manner with heaven and thus to serve as a force for the maintenance of right order (*Ma'at*) in the universe.[69] Indeed the pharaoh was a Hermetic king *par excellence* and we've suggested that one of the ways that he could fulfil his responsibility to cosmic 'right order' would have been to build a temple, or even a city, 'in the image of heaven'. We've shown specific textual authority for such a course of action in the *Book of What is in the Duat* of the 14th century BC. Likewise in the highly enigmatic *Building Texts* inscribed at the Temple of Edfu in Upper Egypt in the third century BC the following words are put into the mouth of the god Thoth-Hermes himself:

> I will cause its [i.e. the temple's] long dimension to be good, its breadth to be exact, all its measurements to be according to the norm, all its sanctuaries to be in the place where they should be, *and its halls to resemble the sky.*[70]

Dedicated to Horus, the golden son of Isis and Osiris, the Edfu temple was built in several stages between 246 BC and 51 BC by pharaohs of the Graeco-Egyptian Ptolemaic dynasty on a site that had been sacred since before 3000 BC. Although there is no doubt that they took their conversion to the ancient Egyptian religion extremely seriously, the Ptolemies were newcomers, having ruled Egypt only from the late fourth century BC following the conquests of the god-king Alexander the Great.

Before his premature death in 323 BC Alexander founded a great city on Egypt's Mediterranean coast that would ever afterwards bear his name – Alexandria. A few centuries later it was here that Christian Gnosticism and its pagan Hermetic twin would emerge phoenix-like from the ashes of the ancient Egyptian religion and begin to wing their way silently towards the modern world.

CHAPTER TEN

CITY OF THE GOD-KING

The city still shall follow you ...
> Constantine P. Cavafy, Alexandrian poet (1863–1933), 'The City'

Alexandria, the capital of memory!
> Lawrence Durrell, *The Alexandria Quartet*

When alive, Alexander had founded a city; when dead? He gave birth to the universal metropolis ...
> François de Polignac, *L'Hombre d'Alexandre*

In the autumn of 332 BC, Alexander the Great marched triumphant into Egypt at the head of his Macedonian army after it had crushed the Persians at the Battle of Issus in Syria. The Egyptians had been under much-detested Persian occupation for nearly two centuries, and Alexander was now hailed as their liberator. He entered the Nile Valley at Memphis and was immediately crowned pharaoh and legitimate successor of the pharaohs – the divine solar kings who had ruled this ancient land since time immemorial.

Alexander's behaviour at this point tells us much about his state of mind. His very first act as pharaoh was to order the complete restoration and restitution of the famous twinned temples of Karnak and Luxor in Upper Egypt (about 500 miles south of Memphis) which had suffered damage and degradation under the Persians. Why did Alexander give this matter such priority? The answer is to be found in the strange circumstances of his birth in 356 BC.

Alexander's mother, Olympias, was the daughter of the king of Ipirus (today part of northwestern Greece), and a high-priestess of the Temple-Oracle of Zeus-Amun at Dodona located southwest of the modern city of Ioannina. This oracle was one of the most revered in the ancient world and the story of its foundation was linked to the Temple of Amun at Karnak-

Luxor in Egypt; it was also considered to be 'twinned' to the Temple-Oracle at the Oasis of Siwa in Egypt – which was likewise dedicated to Zeus-Amun. The Hellenic scholar Joan Wynne-Thomas, presents us with a concise overview of these connections:

> During the fourth century BC there were public sacrifices in Athens to Zeus-Ammon, whose original cult was at the Siwa Oasis in Egypt. The cult was, of course, Egypto-Greek, as Ammon or Amun, also in Egyptian Amun-Ra, was the all powerful god of the Egyptian pantheon, whom the Greeks equated with their own great god, Zeus.[1]

Any attempt to explore in detail how and why the Egyptian solar cult of Amun (Zeus-Amun) came to mainland Greece is outside the scope of this book. But the legendary background is given by the ancient Greek historian, Herodotus, who visited Egypt around 450 BC, a century or so before the birth of Alexander the Great. This is the story as he reported it:

> About the oracles – that of Dodona in Greece and of Ammon in Libya [Western Egypt or Siwa] – the Egyptians have the following legend: According to the priests of the Theban Zeus [priests of Amun-Ra at Karnak-Luxor], two women connected with the service of the temple [Karnak-Luxor] were carried off by the Phoenecians and sold, one in Libya [Siwa] and one in Greece, and it was these women who founded the oracles of these two countries. I asked the priests at Thebes what grounds they had for being so sure, and they told me that careful search had been made for the women at the time, and that though it was unsuccessful, they had afterwards learned that the facts were just as they had reported them.

> At Dodona, however, the priestesses who delivered the oracle had a different version of the story: two black doves flew away from Thebes [the district of Karnak-Luxor] in Egypt, and one of them alighted in Dodona, the other in Libya [Siwa]. The former perched on an oak, and speaking with a human voice, told them that there, on the very spot, there should be an oracle of Zeus. Those who heard understood this to be a command from heaven, and at once obeyed. Similarly, the other dove which flew to Libya [Siwa] told the Libyans to found the oracle of Ammon – which is also an oracle of Zeus. The people who gave me this information were the three priestesses Dodona ...[2]

Also according to Herodotus, it was the Egyptians who originated and eventually taught the Greeks to use 'ceremonial meetings, processions and liturgies'. He said that the Greeks had even modelled their gods on those of the Egyptians.

Dodona, Olympias, Egypt and the Persians

Nowadays such views are scoffed at by Hellenistic scholars and Egyptologists alike. Despite the well-known tendency of the Greeks to 'identify' their gods with specific ancient Egyptian deities – e.g. Zeus-Amun or Hermes-Thoth – the academic concensus is that the two pantheons as structurally unrelated. Yet it seems beyond doubt that the cult of Amun-Ra did find its way into Greece at least as early as the fifth century BC, perhaps even much earlier, and was somehow involved with the Temple-Oracle at Dodona.

Dodona itself is located in the lovely pastoral and mountainous region of Ipirus adjacent to the ancient kingdom of Macedon where Alexander the Great was born. No one really knows the truth about exactly when or why it was consecrated, but according to consensus:

> The original shrine of the oracle probably existed before 2000 BC, and was dedicated to the 'Earth-mother' or goddess. This was a cult of southern Greece which had, like the cult of Zeus, originated in the East. Archaeological finds date from the Early Bronze Age, approximately 2500 BC, and are in the Museum of Ioannina. There is a mention of the shrine by Homer, in the *Iliad*, which is the earliest reference known ...[3]

The priests of Dodona were known as the *helli* or *selli*, and it was they who interpreted the proclamations and prophecies made at the oracle. This they did by listening to the rustling of leaves from an oak grove within the sanctuary. Legend had it that it was from the wood of this sacred grove that a figurehead was fashioned to the prow of Jason's ship carrying the Argonauts (hence the *Argo*'s gift of speech and prophecy).

The Dodona temple-oracle was held in particular reverence by Philip II of Macedon, the father of Alexander the Great, who had consulted it on numerous occasions. But Philip's links with the oracle were to go much deeper when he married Olympias. The latter, as we have said, had been a priestess at Dodona and is known to have been a zealous devotee of the god Amun of Egypt.

Philip met Olympias when he was 26 years old and she 16. The fateful encounter took place on the island of Samothrace, off the Thracian coastline of Greece. Philip and Olympias had both come independently to the island in order to attend the religious celebration of the *Cabeiri*, a curious festival where violent fertility and sexual rituals were performed in various mythical settings. It was during one of these events that Philip and Olympias fell in love, and thus began that potent union that was to change the course of world history.

Endowed with a deep and mystical nature, the young and lovely Olympias was obsessed with the idea that she was destined to bear a divine child in the likeness of the god Dionysos – in Greek mythology the handsome and heroic son of Zeus, who had been born from the womb of the mortal Semele. Dionysos literally means 'Son of God', and Olympias would certainly have been acquainted with the works of the Greek historian Herodotus who, a century earlier, had identified Dionysos with the Egyptian god Osiris.[4]

When Olympias became Philip's queen in 357 BC, Egypt was under assault by the Persians, the most bitter enemies of the Greeks and Macedonians. In 525 BC Cambyses, the son of the legendary Cyrus I, had occupied Egypt and thus widened his already vast empire. His successor, Darius I, consolidated Persian rule in the Nile Valley after suppressing a major Egyptian revolt there. Then he took his army north across the Mediterranean and occupied Thrace and Macedon before being decisively defeated at the Battle of Marathon in 490 BC. A decade later the Persian king, Xerxes, invaded Greece and brought terrible destruction on Athens, but he too was eventually defeated in 479 BC.

Even though Darius and Xerxes had failed in Greece, the fear that a new Persian invasion would be attempted at some point was a very real one. Neighbouring countries were also targets. By 356 BC, when Alexander was born, Egypt had freed herself from Persian rule but was under attack again and was finally reoccupied in 350 BC. Humiliated and defeated, Egypt suffered heavily under the new 'King of Kings' of Persia, Artaxerxes III, who was a brutal and merciless oppressor – as was his equally vicious son, Oarses. So despised was their rule that they were eventually poisoned by one of their eunuchs called Bogoas, who offered the throne of the King of Kings of Persia to Darius III. Bogoas was duly 'rewarded' by being forced to swallow his own poison.

Nectanebo, Osiris, and the ancestry of Alexander

For a brief period Egypt managed to oust the Persians yet again, and the last native pharaoh to rule there was Nectanebo II, who had usurped the throne from his brother Teos in 358 BC – two years before the birth of Alexander. There is a tale told of Nectanebo II that seems worth recounting, even though it is almost certainly fictional, in view of its association with the strange circumstances surrounding Alexander's birth. But first we should place Nectanebo II in the correct historical setting.

After initial successes in resisting the Persians, Nectanebo II was hailed by his people as a great hero and liberator. Much loved for his military deeds and for his devotion to the supreme god Amun (whose 'son' he deemed himself to be) he was also renowned as a powerful magician[5] – a reputation that was taken very seriously in ancient Egypt. As Alexander was to do some years later, Nectanebo marked his coronation by ordering a massive restoration programme for the many sanctuaries of Amun that had been destroyed or desecrated by the Persians. He paid special attention to the restoration of the temple complex of Karnak-Luxor. It had been Nectanebo's own father who had been partly responsible for the magnificent Avenue of Sphinxes (a segment of which survives to this day) that joined Karnak with Luxor. Nectanebo also restored the existing temples of Amun at the Oasis at Siwa, and built a magnificent new one there, the remains of which still stand at the Umm Ubaydah area of the modern oasis.[6]

Married to Philip or not, we may imagine that the association of Nectanebo II with the Temple-Oracle of Amun at Siwa must have impressed the young Olympias who, as we recall, harboured dreams of giving birth to a 'son of Amun'. Surely the idea of being seeded by a pharaoh in whose veins flowed the blood of the god Amun, and who had such close links with the oracular centre of Amun at Siwa as well as Luxor, would have been one of the wild fantasies of this very impressionable and very young queen? In this respect, the strange stories reported by some of Alexander's biographers might contain an element of truth in them. According to one such account found in Pseudo-Callisthenes, Nectanebo fled Egypt after the Persian invasion that ultimately dethroned him, and made his way to Macedon in Greece. There he was received at the court of Philip II to whom Nectanebo presented himself as a magician and astrologer. At night, however, the exiled pharaoh turned into a huge snake, a symbol of Amun, and in this form seduced and impregnated Olympias.[7]

Another legend, this time associating the royal ancestry of Alexander the Great with the god Osiris of Egypt, is told by the Greek chronicler

Diodorus Siculus who lived in the first century BC. In Book I of his famous *Bilbiotheca Historica*, Diodorus recounts the mythical origins of the non-Hellenic and Hellenic people of Greece up to the destruction of Troy. It is in this first book, that the story of Macedon, a mysterious 'son' of Osiris, is narrated.[8]

According to Diodorus, Osiris left Egypt with his brother Apollo on a universal mission to teach men to plant the vine and sow crops of wheat and barley:

> ... two sons of Osiris, Anubis and Macedon, ... took the field with him ... Osiris also brought Pan [the Egyptian Min] on this expedition.

> [After visiting the countries of Africa and Asia] Osiris ... crossed over into Europe at the Hellespont. In Thrace he slew Lycurgos, a barbarian king who opposed his plans ... And he left his son Macedon behind as king of Macedonia, which was named after him ...

Diodorus does not give us his sources. It is generally thought that for the part of his *Bibliotheca* dealing with Greek history, he drew from the works of earlier writers such as Ephorus and Hieronymus of Cardia. For his Egyptian material the evidence suggests that Diodorus relied heavily on Hecataeus of Abdera.

Hecataeus (365–270 BC) lived in Alexandria – the prototypical city of the classical world founded in Egypt by Alexander the Great. There Hecataeus benefited from the liberal protection of Ptolemy I Soter, the general in Alexander's army who set himself up as pharaoh of Egypt in 305 BC after Alexander's premature death. As a foreign traveller who reached as far south as the temples of Karnak and Luxor, Hecataeus was an eyewitness to the early stage of Greek and Egyptian fusion in Egypt. He produced a rather idealised account, the *Aegyptiaca*, aimed at Greek readers, and it was this text that was to serve as Diodorus's source when he came to write his own history of Egypt 200 years later.

Let us look at the context when Hecataeus was in Egypt. First, it is well known that Ptolemy I Soter was extremely keen to promote any idea that would integrate his newly founded 'pharaonic' Macedonian dynasty with that of the true Egyptian solar pharaohs whose divine lineage was believed to extend back to the god Osiris. It is, therefore, quite possible that Hecataeus made up the story of Osiris's journey to Greece and the founding of Macedon by one of his 'sons' – Macedon – in order to create a link between the Macedonian 'pharaoh' of Alexandria and the mythical ancestry of Egyptian pharaohs.

In Egyptian mythology Osiris had only one son, Horus, whose sacred animal was not the wolf, as Diodorus says, but the *hawk* or falcon. It is easy to see how such a mythological association between Osiris and the origin of the Macedonian royal family, when it is also coupled with the strange tales told by Pseudo-Callisthenes about the pregnancy of Olympias, would create a belief that Alexander was somehow linked by birth to the gods of Egypt and, by extension, would add legitimacy to the Macedonian claim to pharaonic kingship in Alexandria. This strange belief and, especially, as we shall see, the persistent theme of a symbolic sexual union between the god Amun and Olympias, would have untold repercussions on the future history of Egypt and, by cultural osmosis, the rest of the Hellenistic world.

Lightning seed and the star Sirius

Legend has it that when Olympias gave birth to Alexander the two stone eagles that decorated the roof of her apartments were struck by lightning. Other accounts speak of living eagles that came to perch there. Others say that at that very same moment the Temple of Diana-Artemis at Ephesus was destroyed by fire while the goddess herself was in Macedon attending Alexander's birth. This link involving Diana-Artemis, eagles and the lightning bolt is most interesting. For Diana-Artemis was worshipped at Ephesus in the form of a sacred *omphalos* – a conical or pyramid-shaped stone which had supposedly 'fallen from the sky' as though ejected from a lightning bolt It was also said that the foundation of the Oracle of Apollo in Delphi occurred when two eagles sent from Zeus alighted near the *omphalos* there. Meanwhile in Egypt a pyramid-shaped 'stone from heaven' called the *Benben* had formed the central symbol of religious worship at the sacred city of Heliopolis since before history began.[9] Indeed such *baetyls* and *omphali* played a significant role in many ancient religions, and were typically associated with fertility and the birth of divinities.

According to Plutarch, Olympias claimed that she had become pregnant when lightning had struck her womb and fertilised her with the seed of Zeus-Amun – thus siring Alexander.[10] Elsewhere Plutarch narrates how the womb of the sacred cow-goddess of Egypt (a form of Isis) was also seeded by the god's lightning in order to create the new Apis calf, symbol of the ruling solar pharaohs, i.e. the Horus-king.[11] In Egyptian religious iconography, the goddess Isis was often represented by a cow with a five-pointed star above her head, the latter being the star Sirius, called *Sothis* by the Greeks. Traditionally the heliacal (dawn) rising of this star denoted the moment of the divine birth of the solar kings of Egypt. It is therefore notable that many classical authors fix the birth of Alexander at 20 July in the Julian calendar, a date that would have been on or near the heliacal rising of Sirius in that epoch. The implication is that this star must have played an important role in his birth-myth. As French author Jean-Michel Angebert points out, it even led Alexander to abandon the old Greek calendar and replace it with one like that of the Egyptians that was based on the heliacal rising of Sirius. He did this some time before his armies reached Egypt:

> The doors of Egypt now lay open for him. But Alexander met up with further resistance at the port of Tyre, the siege of which lasted for six months, from January to July 332 BC, which Alexander did not want to leave behind. There occurred, then, an extraordinary event: the taking of the city corresponded to the astronomical date of the heliacal rising of Sirius, the Dog-star, which meant that the star, after having been absent in the sky for a part of the year [70 days], reappeared in the east horizon to mark the victory of Alexander and to announce that he would soon be wearing the crown of pharaoh ... [thus] Alexander the Great, pious son of Amun, modified the Greek calendar such that henceforth the rising of Sirius would mark the New Year, as it was done in Egypt ...[12]

Further strengthening the sense of a definite association between Alexander and the star Sirius, Jean-Michel Angebert also draws attention the so-called *ascent to the sky of Alexander*. This was an illustrative theme popularised in medieval times which showed the deified Alexander rising to heaven and the Sun on a carriage towed by griffins with a five-pointed star – identified as Sirius by Angebert – leading the way:

> Many scenes, sculptures, paintings and even jewellery represent this apotheosis ... Concerning the 'ascension' of the hero, we often see Alexander standing in the chariot of Helios (the sun) pulled by griffins or lions; another type of representation shows him being carried on his throne; a third type shows Alexander being carried by eagles towards the sun. On all these representations, a star is seen shining over the head of the figure, an obvious symbol of Sirius, the celestial body which presides over the destiny of kings according to the Egyptians ...[13]

This association with the 'birth star' Sirius is also found with Alexander's successors and in the city of Alexandria itself. For according to French Egyptologist Sydney H. Aufrère, a specialist in Ptolemaic studies,[14] the Ptolemaic queens were portrayed wearing the headgear of the goddess Sothis i.e. Sirius. Aufrère also shows that the goddess of the *Pharos*, the famous Lighthouse of Alexandria, one of the Seven Wonders of the Ancient World, was once again none other than Sothis-Sirius. This strongly suggests that the spot of bright light that mariners would see when approaching the coastline of Egypt was likened to the spot of light from the star Sirius when *rising in the east* to guide the mariners back to Alexandria.

Son of Amun

Plutarch also reported another version of the birth-myth of Alexander which seems to be related to the Nectanebo story told by Pseudo-Callisthenes, but this time without the presence of Nectanebo. In the Plutarch version Philip II peeped through the keyhole of Olympias's chamber on the night of their nuptials, and was aghast to see his virgin-wife in their bed copulating vigorously with a huge snake. Deeply shocked Philip went to consult the Oracle of Apollo at Delphi where he was told that he must henceforth make special sacrifice to Zeus-Amun, for the snake was a well-known symbol of Zeus-Amun.

Another incident that also seems to reflect this link between Alexander and Zeus-Amun concerns the city of Aphitis which surrendered to the forces of Phillip II without a struggle on the day of Alexander's birth. The people of Aphitis were worshippers of Zeus-Amun on account of which, 150 years earlier, Aphitis had been spared by the great Spartan general, Lysander. This was because Lysander himself was a devotee of Zeus-Amun and had actually performed a pilgrimage to Siwa to consult the oracle there.[15]

After Alexander was crowned pharaoh of Egypt at Memphis and recognised as the legitimate heir to Nectanebo II, he too set out with a small party of friends to the Oasis of Siwa. His companions included his childhood friend, Ptolemy (future 'pharaoh' of Egypt), and Callisthenes, the great nephew of Aristotle. They followed the desert route west from Rhakotis (the site of the future Alexandria) towards Mersa Matruh some 320 kilometers away. Today the journey from Alexandria to Mersa Matruh is covered in four hours by car, but Alexander and his group took at least week on horseback.

From there the royal party turned due south and inland and began their slow march towards Siwa, which required a further eight days. Now, as it would have been in Alexander's time, the whole route is arid flat desert with only the occasional mound or hill to change the monotony of the quasi-lunar landscape. After hours of this, however, the vista suddenly changes into a sort of mini-Grand Canyon, and in the distance, like some desert Shangri La, spreads the lush oasis flanked by two lakes in the east and west.

Upon entering Siwa, Alexander was hailed with the cries 'son of Amun'. With great ceremony he was then escorted to the Temple-Oracle of Zeus-Amun where he was taken by the high-priest into the inner sanctuary. No one knows what happened to Alexander there, or what he saw, but it is probable, amongst other things, that he was shown an *omphalos* sacred to Amun as evidence of his own divinity.[16]

The intellectual parenthood of Alexandria

Far to the south of Siwa the city of Thebes, our modern Luxor, with its vast temple complex dedicated to the supreme god, Amun, was the sacred city *par excellence* of the ancient world even at the height of Greek civilisation. And although Heliopolis – in the north of Egypt near the Great Pyramids – had been pre-eminent in earlier times, it was now at Thebes that the solar kings of Egypt were deemed to be legitimised and divinised. So it was perfectly natural, and indeed predictable, that Alexander the Great, in his capacity as the 'son of Amun' would have wanted to link his own person to Thebes.

This was why he acted so swiftly to restore the temple complex there, the most important centre of Amun worship in Egypt. When we consider that he also had the temple's inner sanctuary converted into a chapel bearing his own name it is clear that he soon intended to perform a pilgrimage to Luxor – there to be consecrated, like all solar kings before him, as the 'son of Amun'. Fate intervened, however, and Alexander died on campaign in Babylon. His troops decided that he should be buried in Egypt, in the land of his 'father' Zeus-Amun.[17] Ptolemy, now in control of Egypt, and soon to become pharaoh, intercepted the funerary cortege and took command of the body of Alexander which, some years later, he would finally bring to Alexandria.

Alexandria had been Alexander's dream. He had wanted to create a new city dedicated to wisdom and learning – a sort of intellectual bridge on the shore of the Mediterranean Sea that would unite East and West. It was to be a city that would enlighten the world.

When Alexander was a boy, his father, Philip II, selected for him a special tutor. The choice fell on Aristotle, the greatest and most imaginative and influential philosopher of the epoch.

Aristotle was born in the year 384 BC at the city of Stagira in Macedon. His father, Nicomachus, was the personal physician and friend of the king of Macedon, Amyntas III, the grandfather of Alexander the Great. At 17 Aristotle travelled to Athens and entered Plato's Academy, and soon became its most noted pupil, so much so that his master, Plato, called him the 'intelligence of the school'. When Plato died in 347 BC, Aristotle left the Academy and embarked on a journey that took him to all parts of Greece and Asia Minor. Then in the year 342 BC Philip II of Macedon summoned him to his court at Pella, and appointed him tutor to his 14-year-old son, Alexander. Aristotle, who was now 42, brought along his brilliant nephew Callisthenes and also the scientist Theophrastus. The team of learned men were provided with a country residence at Mieza near Pella where, for the next three years, Alexander was tutored and groomed.

When Alexander became king at the age of 21, Aristotle left Macedon and returned to Athens, where he founded his famous Lyceum. It was there that he created the first prototype of a university library; it would eventually be transferred after his death to the Great Library of Alexandria in Egypt. Aristotle died at the age of 62, a year after Alexander's death in Babylon. His lectures were collated in 150 volumes devoted to philosophy, ethics, politics and, his great love, the natural sciences. Until the middle ages Aristotle was regarded as the supreme authority on all matters concerning science. He was to write, probably with Alexander in mind, that:

> If there is one man superior in goodness and political capacity to all others, such a person may be like a god among men ... and should be gladly obeyed, for they are permanent kings.[18]

There is much speculation and debate as to what extent Alexander's sense of mission might have been influenced by Aristotle. Apart from teaching the sciences to Alexander, the philosopher's main objective was to install in his pupil his concept of 'virtues', the most important of which, according to Aristotle, was *reason*. A few years before Aristotle became tutor to Alexander, he had completed his famous work, the *Politics*, in which he examines various systems of *constitutions* and expounds on the idea of the *ideal state*. And it would seem almost certain that Aristotle discussed his concept of the 'ideal state' with the young Alexander and imbued the future hero-king with those high virtues and ideals that were eventually to be put into practice at Alexandria in Egypt.[19] Alexander also received from Aristotle copies of Herodotus's *Histories* as well as Homer's *Iliad* and *Odyssey*, which became the future world-conqueror's most precious possessions.

In the *Odyssey* Homer speaks of the fabled island of Pharos off the coast of Egypt in connection with the Argonauts, while Herodotus recounts how Helen of Troy and Paris took refuge at Heracleion, a few miles east of the future Alexandria. So enthralled and influenced was Alexander by these epics that apparently he once angrily slapped Callisthenes, the great nephew of Aristotle, for openly criticising Homer. It was such literary influences, and the influence of his mother Olympias, that must have fired Alexander in his quest to weld the Eastern and Western worlds into one great empire ruled from a capital 'City of Light' modelled on the ideal state: Alexandria.

The founding of the universal city

It is often said that sound military principles are sufficient to explain why the peninsula of Rhakotis on the Mediterranean Sea was chosen as the site of Alexandria. The assumption is that Alexander saw in the natural harbour formed between the small island of Pharos and the peninsula the ideal place to build a port. Tradition has it that although Alexander had selected the site, it was the architect Dinocrates of Rhodes who actually designed the city. In opposition to this view, we shall attempt to show that a strong Egyptian influence also cast its spell over the whole enterprise from the very beginning.

There was a kind of enchantment and magic about this place that was unlikely to have been ignored by Alexander and his other educated companions such as Ptolemy and Callisthenes, especially in the high spirits and frame of mind they were in. They all were keen readers of Homer's works and surely were now acutely aware that in the *Odyssey* Homer wrote:

> There is an island in the surging sea which they call Pharos, lying off the coast of Egypt ... It has a harbour with good anchorage and hence they [the Argonauts] put out to sea after drawing water.[20]

To Alexander and his loyal companions, Homer's *Iliad* and *Odyssey* had the same forceful effect as the Bible had on the crusading Christian knights in medieval times. Most educated Greeks could quite easily recite long sections from Homer, and often quoted Homer, as we do the Bible today, as the source of moral and practical examples for daily life. Leaders such as Alexander – perhaps especially Alexander – used the *Iliad* and the *Odyssey* not only for spiritual and moral guidance, but also as a practical guidebook for their own lives. And there is much to suppose that Alexander saw himself as a Homerian hero of boundless courage and dash.

It must be realised that such heroes were not viewed by the Greeks as mythological and legendary characters but rather as real historical men and women who had lived in a golden age among the gods. When Alexander and his companions came upon the island that Homer had described in such warm terms we may therefore safely imagine that they took it as a favourable omen from the gods. It was recalled by Alexander and his engineers and architects that Pythagoras, the 'father of geometry', and likewise the noble Plato after him, had also sojourned in Lower Egypt as guests or 'students' of the Heliopolitan priests and had learnt from them the wisdom that had made Greek culture great. Such evocative visions of Homer, Pythagoras and particularly Plato, the tutor of Aristotle himself, surely inspired the young conqueror, then barely 24 years old, to raise, near this magical Homerian island of Pharos, a great and wonderful city. What he had in mind was a metropolis that would rival Athens and in which the teachings of Pythagoras, Plato and Aristotle could mingle with the ancient wisdom of Egypt.

So, using Pythagorean geometry, Alexander's architect, Dinocrates, began to draw the plan of the future Alexandria, with Alexander himself supervising every small detail. The city, oblong in shape, would be developed on a system of parallel grids. The main east-west artery, to be known as the *Canopus Way*, would bear the name of the Homerian hero Canopus, the legendary navigator who steered the ship bearing Helen of Troy. According to a legend, Helen and her lover, Paris, had taken refuge at the city of Canopus (modern Abu Qir) at the eastern end of the Alexandrian shoreline on their way to Troy. Helen was the daughter of the god Zeus from his union with Leda, as well as the sister of the famous immortals the *Dioscuri*, i.e. the twins Castor and Pollux, who became stars in the zodiacal constellation of Gemini.

Helen of Troy, the Egyptian Aphrodite and Isis-Pharia

There is curious story told of Helen which is of relevance to the connection Alexander the Great felt with Egypt, and gives us more background to his mystical claims to descend from the divine lineage of the pharaohs. This story is found in a poem of Stesichorus (632–553 BC) which has it that after escaping from her husband, King Menelaus, Helen and Paris attempted to sail to Troy. On the way their ship was driven by a storm to the shores of Egypt near

Canopus. Here the 'real' Helen was detained by the Pharaoh Proteus, whilst a 'phantom' Helen – a very similar idea to the 'phantom' or 'apparitional' Christ of the later Gnostic gospels – went on to Troy with Paris.

Stesichorus's version of the story was later made into a play by Euripides around 412 BC, but underwent further mutation, placing the 'real' Helen in the custody not of the legendary Proteus but of his equally legendary son Theoclymenus. Herodotus, too, reports a somewhat similar story which he tells us he obtained from an Egyptian priest.[21] He also speaks of a temple dedicated to 'Aphrodite the Stranger' in honour of Helen, within the royal city of Memphis:

> Within the enclosure there is a temple dedicated to Aphrodite the Stranger. I should guess, myself, that it was built in honour of Helen, daughter of Tyndraeus, not only because I have heard it said that she passed some time at the court of Proteus, but also, more particularly, because of the description of Aphrodite as 'the Stranger', a title never given to this goddess in any of her other temples (in Egypt).[22]

To the Greeks the 'Egyptian Aphrodite' was the goddess whom the ancient Egyptians called *Hathor*.[23] But the Greeks also associated the goddess Isis, in her loving aspect, with Aphrodite. This suggests that they appreciated the very close connection that does in fact exist between Hathor and Isis in the ancient Egyptian pantheon and, presumably, the association that Hathor and Isis share with the star Sirius. In Ptolemaic Alexandria Isis also became the protecting deity of the port and of its famous lighthouse, the *Pharos* (named after the island of Pharos on which it stood). In this capacity, Isis was known as *Isis-Pharia*, the protector of mariners, suggesting another connection with Helen of Troy who – presumably on account of her many nautical adventures – was similarly called the 'patron goddess of sailors'.

There was a temple dedicated to Isis-Pharia near the *Pharos*. Apparently also her colossal statue once stood directly outside the *Pharos*, and is likely to have been perceived as part of the lighthouse complex. In Roman times Isis was frequently known as *Stella Maris*, i.e. 'Star of the Sea',[24] and the same epithet has, for a very long while, been applied by Christians to the Virgin Mary. Sir James George Fraser, the great British mythologist of the 1920s goes so far as to suggest a causal link:

> To Isis in her later character of patroness of mariners the Virgin Mary perhaps owes her beautiful epithet of *Stella Maris*, 'Star of the Sea',

under which she is adored by tempest-tossed sailors. The attributes of a marine deity may have been bestowed on Isis by the seafaring Greeks of Alexandria. They are quite foreign to her original character and to the habits of the Egyptians, who had no love of the sea. On this hypothesis Sirius, the bright star of Isis, which on July mornings rises from the glassy waves of the eastern Mediterranean, a harbinger of halcyon weather to mariners, was the true Stella Maris, 'the Star of the Sea'.[25]

Let us also note that many of the Ptolemaic queens of Alexandria, and especially the celebrated Cleopatra, identified themselves with Isis-Pharia or *Isis-Sothis* (Sirius) and, to emphasis their beauty and art of love-making, with *Isis-Aphrodite* as well. Glamorous Cleopatra posed as the goddess *Isis-Aphrodite* when she presented herself to Mark Antony in Tarsus. According to Egyptologist Julia Samson:

The dramatic couple quickly became linked in people's minds with the gods: Antony with Bachus (Dionysos) whom the Greeks associated with Osiris; and Cleopatra with Venus (Aphrodite) and long associated with Isis ...[26]

The connection between Sothis-Sirius and Isis-Pharia of the *Pharos* is probably due to the beacon of light from the lighthouse as it was seen from afar by sailors approaching the harbour, and may explain why the *Pharos* lighthouse was sometimes called 'the second Sun'[27] – a term used by the ancient Egyptians for the star Sirius.[28] At the Temple of Isis on the island of Pharos, the statue of the goddess wore a crown made up of a sun/moon disc surmounted by two gazelle horns.[29] These horns, according to French Egyptologist Sydney H. Aufrère, are similar to those of the goddess *Satis*, the divine gazelle who watches over the Nile's flood.[30] The same headdress is seen on representations of the Ptolemaic queens at temples in Upper Egypt such as Dendera, Philae, Edfu and others. Dr. Aufrère also points out that Ptolemy III, in the Decree of Canopus of 238 BC, states how he had adjusted the religious and civic calendars (which had become desynchronised with the passage of time) so that the start of the new year would once again coincide with the heliacal rising of Sirius – an event which itself coincided closely with the beginning of the Nile's flood in mid-summer. Aufrère also offers this account of why one of the many names of Sirius was the 'Eye of Ra':

In order to explain the mechanism of the Flood on the religious level, there was witnessed at the opening of the new year a fusion or 'coalescence' of the solar and lunar myths, such that the 'Distant One' was considered both as the 'Eye of Ra' and the 'Eye of Horus' – in other words Sirius and the full Moon. The two – the star and the Moon – unite the magical effects of their manifestations which result in the Nile's Flood. Sirius by its rising announced the New Year and the Flood, and the full Moon symbolising the fullness of the latter.[31]

Brief excursion to Paris

According to the French Egyptologist Bernard Mathieu:

> ... Isis was named *Pelagia* ('of the sea'), or *Euploia* ('of safe navigation') and *Pharia* ('of Pharos'), and was said to have invented the sail and had a temple on the island of Pharos. She was so famous in the whole Mediterranean world that we find her even in 17th century manuscripts, and comfortably installed on the prow of the boat on the coat-of-arms of Paris which Napoleon commissioned in 1811 ...[32]

The reader will recall from Chapter One the bizarre religious rituals and symbolism of the French Revolution that frequently seemed to link the city of Paris explicitly to the goddess Isis. The comments made by Dr. Mathieu suggest that such a link may have some basis in historical truth. It is also notable that the 17th century writer, Jean Tristan, claimed that the name Paris was actually derived from Isis-Pharia or, more precisely, was from *Pharia-Isis* abbreviated to *Paria-Isis* and, finally, to *Paris*.

Tristan based his hypothesis on ancient coins dating from the time of the Roman Emperor Julian which depict his empress, Helen, as Isis-Pharia or *Faria*.[33] Julian, who reigned some decades after Constantine, brought a very temporary halt to the onward march of Christianity and was commonly known as 'Julian the Apostate' for having re-adopted the ancient pagan cults and declared himself a 'follower of Helios', the sun-god. Helios in turn was a divinity whom the Romans closely associated with Alexander the Great.

Julian had governed Gaul – ancient France – for five years and had resided in Lutecia, ancient Paris, for three years between AD 358 and AD 360. Julian and his wife Helen were also devotees of the Alexandrian god Serapis and the goddess Isis-Pharia, and may have imposed, or at the very least encouraged, her cult on the inhabitants of Lutecia. At any rate, Jean Tristan was to write:

> The Parisians received their name of *Paria-Isis*, because of the cult of this
> goddess which had been introduced in Illyria and in Gaul, in the region
> next to the River Seine and in Lutecia, called 'Lutecia of the Parisians' or
> Farisians because of this.[34]

As further support to this hypothesis, the French classicist Jurgis
Baltrušaitis points out that in a fragment of a manuscript from Saint-Hilaire
concerning the Council of Rimini, the city of Paris is actually referred by
him as *Farisea Civitas*, i.e. the 'city of the Farisians' or, as Jean Tristan has
suggested, the city of those who worship Isis-Pharia *or Faria-Isis* (Pharia-
Isis).[35] We shall return to this in a later chapter.

The Canopus Way

The Roman writer Arrian tells us that when Alexander came to the site
on the coast where his future city, Alexandria, would rise:

> ... he was taken by a strong desire to carry out his project, and setting
> out himself the plan of the city, he fixed the place where the Agora
> should go, the number of sanctuaries and to which deities [they were
> dedicated]: the Greek gods but also to Isis, goddess of Egypt ...[36]

The *Agora* was the equivalent of a town hall or square where public
meetings were held in Greek cities. In the case of Alexandria the Agora
was located at the intersection of two main arteries, the north-south artery
known as the *Soma* and the east-west artery known as the *Canopus Way*.
This arrangement formed a huge cross and it was at the intersection of its
two arms, according to most accounts, that was eventually raised a small
Doric temple to serve as the mausoleum for the golden sarcophagus of
Alexander the Great.

At both ends of the Canopus Way were gates. The west gate was called
the 'Gate of the Moon' (*Selene*) while the east gate was the 'Gate of the
Sun' (*Helios*).

It has always been assumed that the physical layout of Alexandria was
designed in accordance with the principles of Greek city planning based on
a rigid grid system with sets of parallel roads crisscrossing each other at
right angles. In fact such grid plans were also known in Egypt long before
the Greeks. The French Egyptologist, André Bernand, rightly observes
that the Giza necropolis in the area of the Great Pyramids is effectively
a mortuary city gridded with roads running east-west and north-south. A

similar scheme can be seen at Saqqara and, much further south, at Akhetaten (modern el-Amarna), the city of Pharaoh Akhenaten.[37]

This notwithstanding, what is often not considered as a direct influence on the design of Alexandria is the state of mind of the 24-year-old Alexander the Great at the time of the foundation of the city. He had just conquered the hitherto invincible solar Persian King of Kings, Darius III, and was now the undisputed ruler of the known world. He had been hailed as hero and liberator by the Egyptians, and recognised as the legitimate successor of Pharaoh Nectanebo II. He had been proclaimed the 'son of Amun' and 'son of Isis' plus all the other titles attributed to a legitimate pharaoh of Egypt. And all this had happened almost certainly immediately *before* the foundation of the city of Alexandria.

Another factor to note is Alexander's deep psychological identification with the temple complex of Karnak-Luxor at Thebes as an expression of his identification with the god Amun. The French scholar François de Polignac has pointed out that Alexander demonstrated an unusual knowledge and sensitivity to Egyptian religious customs by paying so much attention to the restoration of this temple and, more particularly, by grafting his own name onto the inner sanctuary near the temple's sacred 'birth room' or *mammisi*. These acts suggest that Alexander must have been closely advised by a native Egyptian high-priest, probably much in the same way that the high-priest Oud-ja-Hor-esne of Sais had acted as advisor to the Persian king, Cambyses, and the high-priest Manetho of Heliopolis was to become senior advisor to Ptolemy I Soter, the successor of Alexander the Great in Egypt.[38]

We have seen how Alexander had developed a connection with the star Sirius, the star of Isis and divine birth, when he changed the Greek calendar at Tyre. We have seen, too, how the rising of this star was the 'calibrator' of the Nile's flood and we will show in a later chapter how its position on the eastern horizon often served to align the axis of ancient Egyptian temples dedicated to the birth of Horus, the 'son' of *Isis-Hathor*. Finally, we have also noted that the heliacal rising of Sirius during Alexander's lifetime fell on the 'official' date of his birth, i.e. 20–21 July (Julian).

It would be odd, indeed improbable, if such a rich network of symbols, ideologies and mythical associations had *not* influenced Alexander when he was about to supervise the design of a city on the Mediterranean shore of Egypt opposite the enchanted island of Pharos ...

Brief excursion on Napoleon and Sirius

Before Napoleon invaded Egypt and occupied Cairo at the end of the 18th century he commissioned the famous mathematician Gaspard Monge to round up a group of the finest scholars – called the *lumières* or 'lights' in those days – to accompany the expedition. Comprising a total of 167 men, the group of savants included the mathematician Jean Baptiste Joseph Fourier, the chemist Claude Louis Berthollet, the naturalist Étienne Geoffroy Saint-Hilaire, the geologist Déodat de Dolomieu, the geographer Edme François Jomard and the engineer Nicolas-Jacques Conté. Such men were to form the basis of Napoleon's *Institut d'Égypte*, a sort of academy of science – the first of its kind ever to study ancient Egyptian monuments – founded on 22 August 1798, very soon after the invasion. Dominique Vivant-Denon, a painter and a favourite of the future empress, Joséphine, became the *Institute*'s first director while Monge was made its first president.

The reader may recall from Chapter One that Monge was a Freemason and a prominent member of the *Nine Sisters* lodge in Paris. He was instrumental in creating the so-called *Republican calendar* which, we also saw in Chapter One, was almost certainly modelled on the ancient Egyptian civic calendar 'calibrated' by the heliacal rising of Sirius. On 22 September 1798 the first volume of the *Institut d'Égypte*'s journal was published. Its title was the *Décade égyptienne,* a name selected by Monge to evoke this new Republican calendar.

It was on 5 March 1798 that Napoleon left Paris for Toulon to meet up with the fleet that he had readied to sail for Egypt. And it was on 21 July 1798 that Napoleon engaged the Egyptian Mameluk army at the Battle of the Pyramids. Whether by design or by chance is yet to be decided but it is a fact that both these dates have a direct association with Isis, her 'boat' and her 'star'. In ancient Rome 5 March had marked the well-known *Feast of Navigium Isidis* or *Isis-Pharia*, when an effigy of the goddess seated in her boat was carried in procession around the city. And 21 July (Julian) was the date of the heliacal rising of Sirius. Coincidence? Perhaps. But we shall return to such issues in later chapters.

Mapping ancient Alexandria

After Napoleon, the fine example set by the *Institut d'Égypte* later prompted the new ruler of Egypt, Muhammad Ali Pasha, to fund the education and training of Egyptian scholars in France. His most prominent scholar was the astronomer Mahmoud El Falaki, better known as Mahmoud Bey, who was to found the first modern astronomical observatory in

Egypt. Mahmoud Bey was also trained as an engineer and geographer, a combination that was to serve him well in his 'Alexandria mapping project' that was to come later under Khedive Isma'il in 1865. Perhaps it should be also noted that Mahmoud Bey's numerous other contributions in science, such as the charting of geomagnetic and meteorological phenomena around the globe, earned him the respect and official praise of the Belgian as well as the French *Académie des Sciences*.

During his Alexandria mapping project, Mahmoud Bey carried out excavations and through them was able to determine that there had been eleven main streets running parallel along the width of the ancient city, and seven main streets also running parallel but at right angles to the other eleven. The two principal arteries were confirmed as the Canopus Way running the length of the city and the Soma running the width of the city, thus, as we've observed, forming a huge 'cross' by their intersection.

Some European archaeologists were quick to criticise Mahmoud Bey's 'reborn' plan of ancient Alexandria, but according to Dr. Jean-Yves Empereur, director of the Centre of Alexandrian Studies in Egypt:

> ... In spite of the criticisms levelled at it in the later 19th century, this plan is still used by archaeologists today ... Mahmoud El Falaki decided to publish his plan in Copenhagen in 1872, six years after he had completed it. It is an outstanding work, reflecting the considerable resources employed in its production, rendered even more effective by the support of the Khedive and the solid training of its maker. Almost a century and a half after its publication it is still used as a reference work by archaeologists working in Alexandria.[39]

The Gate of the Sun and the Gate of the Moon

After digging several trial pits and trenches, Mahmoud Bey was able to establish that the Canopus Way was approximately 2300 meters long and that its axis was oriented to a point on the horizon about 24° north-of-east.[40] Two factors indicate that this alignment was not accidental but was interwoven in the astronomical ideologies prevailing at the time. The first, of course, is the conspicuous angle of 24° north-of-east which immediately brings to attention a possible solar alignment close to the summer solstice. The other factor, perhaps even more obvious, is that the gate on the eastern side of the Canopus Way was called the *Gate of Helios*, i.e. the 'Gate of the Sun', again strongly suggestive of a solar alignment. The sun's rising points on the eastern horizon as observed from Alexandria fluctuate between 28° south-of-east (winter solstice) and 28° north-of-east (summer solstice), with the mid-point, due east, falling on the spring and autumn equinoxes.

In his *Life of Alexander* the famous first century author Plutarch tells us:

> Alexander was born the 6th of *Hecatombaeon,* which month the Macedonians call *Lous,* the same day that the Temple of Diana at Ephesus was burnt ...[41]

Hecatombaeon, or *Hekatombaion,* the first month in the ancient Greek year, began on the first new moon immediately following the summer solstice. From this, many chronologists have calculated that Alexander must have been born on 20 July (in the Julian calendar) or very near to that date. Since this was also the time of year when the Sun rose in the zodiac sign of Leo, it may explain the powerful leonine symbolism that ancient writers associated with Alexander's birth and character.[42]

The persistent mythological connections between Alexander and Diana, which we explored earlier, are also of interest. Diana, the Artemis of the Greeks, was often identified with the Egyptian goddess Isis, the mother of Horus, the mythical prototype of the solar pharaoh-kings of Egypt with whom Alexander was keen to identify. These 'Horus-kings' were traditionally believed to be born under the protection of the star Sirius, the heliacal rising of which was the celestial sign that divinised and legitimised the reign of each and every future king of Egypt. It is a verifiable astronomical fact, and in our view most unlikely to be a coincidence, that the helical rising of Sirius in Alexander's epoch occurred on 20 July as seen from the latitude of Egypt's ancient capital Memphis. Tradition has it that it was Alexander himself who fixed the central axis of the future city of Alexandria, later to be known as the *Canopus Way.* It is thus also unlikely to be coincidental that this axis turns out to have been aligned approximately 24° north-of-east, targeting the point of sunrise on the day of the heliacal rising of Sirius through the appropriately named 'Gate of the Sun'.

Alexander, admittedly promiscuous in his choice of divine ancestors, is known to have claimed descent from Dionysos and Heracles – both of whom were associated with the Egyptian god Osiris by Herodotus, one of Alexander's favourite authors. Bearing this in mind, let us note that if we extend the axis of the Canopus Way further in the direction of the horizon we find it passing the ancient city of Herakleion (later submerged by an earthquake and recently relocated by marine archaeologists in Abu Qir Bay).

At least since the time of Herodotus it was known that a temple dedicated to Heracles-Osiris had stood at Herakleion.

The Gate of the Moon at the other (western) extremity of the Canopus Way may also have had astronomical connotations linked to the myth of Isis and Osiris. We've seen that Isis, and the many Ptolemaic queens who emulated her, were commonly depicted with the full-moon disc and/or lunar crescent above their heads – a motif that continued to be used for the goddess-queens of Alexandria in Graeco-Roman times. Cleopatra is well known to have identified herself with 'Isis and the Moon', and when she bore twins – a boy and girl – by Mark Antony, she called them Selene (Moon) and Alexander-Helios (Sun), clearly an allusion to Isis and Osiris/ Dionysos as well as to the city of Alexandria itself with its Moon and Sun gates. In order for a full moon to occur, it must be in almost direct opposition to the Sun. This seems to explain why the west end of the Canopus Way was named 'Gate of the Moon' and the eastern extremity named 'Gate of the Sun'.

With all such possible symbolic alignments it would seem likely, if not certain, that the city of Alexandria was sacred to Isis or, more specifically, to *Isis-Pharia* who dovetailed perfectly with the Alexander-Dionysos-Helios myth. Indeed, so important was Isis to Alexandria that she became effectively its co-tutelary deity being held in equal reverence to its very own specially-invented supreme god Serapis. The reader will recall from Chapter Five that it was within the compound of the great Temple of Serapis in Alexandria – the *Sarapeum* – that a great number of Gnostics and so-called *pagans* were massacred by Christian mobs in the late fourth century AD.

The making of a universal god

When Alexander the Great died on campaign in Babylon in 323 BC, his vast empire was split into smaller dominions to be shared among his generals. His closest friend, Ptolemy, son of Lagos, inherited the kingdom of Egypt and was crowned pharaoh in 305 BC after the death of Alexander IV (the son of Alexander the Great by the Persian Princess Roxanne). Ptolemy adopted the name *Soter*, meaning the 'Saviour', and thus is best known to historians as Ptolemy I Soter.

A very wise and enlightened man, Ptolemy set out to fulfil Alexander's dream to make his city, Alexandria, a universal centre of wisdom and learning. He recruited as his principal advisor an Egyptian high-priest from Heliopolis called Manetho, and consulted him on all matters related to religion, history and protocol. Manetho, who came from the Delta city of Sebennytos, is best known to Egyptologists for having compiled a chronology of all the dynastic and predynastic pharaohs which, to a great extent, is still used as reference today. It is almost certain, too, that Manetho was the principal contributor to the creation of the 'new' god Serapis for the city of Alexandria.

It seems that Ptolemy I Soter wanted to find an ideal deity for the cosmopolitan citizens of the universal city of Alexandria – the latter now perceived as the symbol of a regenerated Egypt that he, Ptolemy, was destined to govern. The choice quite naturally went towards the most revered of Egyptian gods, Osiris, or, to be more specific, as we saw in Chapter Five, to a special form of Osiris known as *Osiris-Apis*, the *Wesir-Hapi* of the ancient Egyptians. This linked Osiris to the worship of the bull-god Apis, a very ancient cult with its main centre at Memphis in Lower Egypt.[43] According to Herodotus, who visited Egypt when this cult still flourished, the sacred Apis bull was:

> The calf of a cow which is incapable of conceiving another offspring; and the Egyptians say that lighting descends upon the cow from heaven, and that from thence it brings forth the Apis. This calf, which is called Apis, has the following marks: it is black, and has a square spot of white on the forehead; and on the back the figure of an eagle ...[44]

Indeed, the Apis bull was said to be born from the womb of a sacred cow known as 'Isis', and when the Apis bull died he was considered to have become Osiris. As Egyptologist George Hart states:

> Following concepts about the dead pharaoh in the Underworld, Apis, upon dying, became the god Osiris. It is the sacred bull of Memphis in his form of Osiris-Apis that provides the Egyptian nature of the hybrid god created under early Ptolemaic rulers known as *Serapis*.[45]

The close similarity between the Apis bull cult and the Isis and Osiris cult is obvious. And the close identification between the Apis *calf* and the Horus *child* said in Egyptian mythology to have been born from the womb of Isis is thus inescapable: (1) The Apis bull was associated with the Horus-king or living pharaoh; (2) the sacred 'Isis' cow became pregnant by divine intervention in the same manner that the goddess Isis had become pregnant; (3) the sacred 'Isis' cow bore only one calf in the same way Isis had born only one son; (4) the Apis became 'Osiris' after death in the same way that the

Horus-king – the pharaoh – was also devoutly believed to became 'Osiris' after death. As Hart further explains:

> The pharaoh identifies closely with Apis-bull imagery (with its inherent notion of strength and fertility) being an ancient characteristic in the propaganda of the god-king, as can be seen from carved slate palettes and in one of the names used in the royal protocol 'victorious bull'. Celebrating his jubilee festival, a ceremony concerned with the rejuvenation of the monarch's power, the pharaoh strides briskly alongside the galloping Apis bull. The ritual which took place at Memphis is vividly portrayed in a relief on a block from a dismantled chapel in the Temple of Karnak at Thebes ...[46]

A contemporary account of the Apis cult is given by Diodorus Siculus, who visited Egypt in the first century BC. Diodorus describes the funeral of the Apis bull in much the same terms as that of a pharaoh:

> After the splendid funeral of Apis is over those priests who have charge of the business seek out another calf as like the former as they can possibly find, and when they have found one an end is put to all the mourning and lamentation, and such priests as are appointed for that purpose lead the young bull through the city of Nile and feed him forty days. Then they put him into a barge wherein is a golden cabin and so transport him as a god to Memphis ... For the adoration of the bull they give this reason: they say that the soul of Osiris passes into a bull and therefore whenever the bull is dedicated, to this very day the spirit of Osiris is infused into one bull after another for posterity.[47]

The most crucial aspect of the ancient Egyptian mystery religion is that the 'son of Osiris' i.e. Horus, was perpetually reincarnated in the person of the pharaoh, and after each pharaoh died he became 'Osiris' while his eldest son became the new living 'Horus'. Or to put it another way, each successive pharaoh was the living embodiment of Horus while, at the same time – as was the case with the Apis bull – it was held that his soul would become 'Osiris' after his death. It can be seen, therefore, that the idea of the combined name 'Osiris-Apis' – which transmutated to Serapis – was modelled on the idea of 'Osiris-Horus' and, consequently, must be understood to be the ultimate name that symbolises the legitimacy and divinity of the ruling pharaoh.

This is precisely how Alexander the Great wanted to be perceived by the world, and this was also in the mind of Ptolemy when he was crowned the successor of Alexander in Egypt. When, in the summer of 323 BC, Alexander lay dying in Babylon from malaria (made worse by drinking excessive quantities of wine as a 'cure'), his priests prepared a makeshift Temple of Osiris-Apis, i.e. Serapis, in his encampment, leaving us with no choice but to conclude that Alexander had embraced this god as his own. According to the official royal journal kept by the scribe Eumenes,[48] Alexander was seized by a violent fever on 4 June which persisted for several days and, by 8 June, it was becoming clear to all that he was dying:

> 8 June: The fever continues. The Macedonians, thinking that he was dead, came screaming to the gates of his palace and insisted to see him. The doors were opened. They all passed in procession in front of the bed. In silence he [Alexander] greeted each of them by nodding his head or by making a sign with his eyes. In the Temple of Serapis, Peithon, Attalos and Demophon [Alexander's close companions] slept in turn waiting for an oracle from the god to tell them if they should transport Alexander to his sanctuary for him to be cured. The fever continued all night.

> 9 June: Same condition [the king is now in a coma]. New consultation of the god ['father' of Alexander] by Kleomenes, Menidas and Seleukos who relayed in the Temple of Serapis to sleep and to consult the god.

> 10 June: The god gave his reply, which was not to bring Alexander to the temple as he was better off where he lay resting. The companions reported this to the soldiers. A short while later, towards evening, Alexander died.[49]

The above text make it clear that a temple or shrine of Serapis had been raised somewhere near Alexander's palace in Babylon, and that this god was consulted over a matter of great importance – i.e. whether or not Alexander's body should be transported to the principal 'sanctuary' of Serapis, i.e. Osiris-Apis, in Egypt. There is an apparent anomaly in the text which refers to Serapis as the 'father of Alexander' when we know that Amun of Siwa already filled that role. But perhaps in the minds of the Macedonians at least, no clear distinction was made between Serapis and Amun, since both in the Egyptian tradition were 'fathers' to the pharaohs. Herodotus clearly equates Amun of Siwa with Zeus,[50] and we know that Serapis was also equated with Zeus by the Alexandrians.

The labyrinth of Serapis

The main sanctuary of the Osiris-Apis bull (Serapis) was near Memphis in Lower Egypt, not far from the complex of the Pyramid of Djoser at Saqqara. Here, from at least 1400 BC, successive generations of Apis bulls were buried, in huge stone sarcophagi, in a subterranean labyrinth known today as the Serapeum (the same name applied to the Temple of Serapis at Alexandria). Herodotus, who wrote his *Histories* a century before Alexander's arrival in Egypt, is the first foreigner to mention the 'Temple of Apis'. It probably was still operational well into Christian times, but by the middle ages the Serapeum had been completely buried in sand and its location forgotten. It was not until 1850 that it was re-discovered by the French archaeologist, Auguste Mariette. The story goes that Mariette, while trekking in the desert near Saqqara, stumbled on one of the many small sphinxes mentioned by the ancient geographer, Strabo, that had once had flanked the processional road leading to the Serapeum. He was to later write:

> 'One finds,' said the geographer Strabo [first century AD], 'a temple to Serapis in such a sandy place that the wind heaps up the sand dunes beneath which we saw sphinxes, some half buried, some buried up to the head, from which one can suppose that the way to this temple could not be without danger if one were caught in a sudden wind storm.' Did it not seem that Strabo had written this sentence to help us rediscover, after over eighteen centuries, the famous temple dedicated to Serapis? It was impossible to doubt it. This buried Sphinx, the companion of fifteen others I had encountered in Alexandria and Cairo, formed with them, according to the evidence, part of the avenue that led to the Memphis Serapeum ...[51]

Inspired by his find, Mariette organised a workforce and, within a few weeks, had uncovered the entrance to the Serapeum which, even today, remains a hugely impressive and awe-inspiring place. It is located about a kilometer to the northwest of the stepped Pyramid of Djoser, and is approached from the east through a sloped alley going downwards into the bowels of the sand-rock desert. The vastness of this underground maze is what first hits you, with its dark and sprawling corridors running in several directions like a hellish labyrinth built for giants. Today there is low-wattage electric lighting but even so, if left wandering alone in this strange Hades, one is gripped by a curious sense of uneasiness, a sort of slow panic that mingles with the eerie and deathly stillness. There is something almost unnatural and something almost superhuman here. For what is seen all along the huge tunnels and corridors are dozens and dozens of enormous sunken niches, the size of large living rooms, in which were inserted massive granite sarcophagi that once contained the mummified corpses of the Apis bulls. The size and weight of these sarcophagi – some over 60 tons and cut from a single block of granite – fires the imagination for, at least on face value, it is very difficult to see how they were brought down here in the first place let alone manoeuvred into the niches. One has the sense that deep and dark mysteries were performed here. Their atmosphere still lingers – the charged residue of place where, in the words of the ancient Greeks, men were transformed into gods.

Alexander's return

Nectanebo II (the 'father' of Alexander in some legendary accounts) had his tomb built not far from the Serapeum at Saqqara.[52] Could this have played a part in the strange events that took place after Alexander's death and the dilemma confronting his generals and officers as to where the remains of their heroic demi-god should be taken? For while still in Babylon, the body of Alexander was prepared in the ancient Egyptian manner by embalmers brought specially for this task. Alexander's body was then placed within a golden sarcophagus and a huge catafalque was built – the size of a house on wheels according to some eye witnesses – in order to transport the dead hero-god back to Egypt.

The journey took almost two years. Finally when it arrived at the borders of Egypt the catafalque was met by Ptolemy and the golden sarcophagus taken to Memphis. There it was buried near the Serapeum in a sumptuous tomb befitting the hero-god. So entrenched is the idea that Alexander's 'lost tomb' lay hidden in Alexandria that it generally comes as a surprise for some to know that his coffin remained at Memphis for at least *ten years*, and perhaps even longer, before finally being taken to Alexandria. At that time the city of Memphis was still the capital of Egypt, and the Temple of Heliopolis was still functioning as the priestly school for the state. As for Ptolemy himself, he was still *satrape*, i.e. governor of Egypt, under the authority of Alexander IV, the son of Alexander the Great by his Persian wife, Roxanne. In 310 BC, however, when the Alexander IV was 13, he was assassinated, and the succession not settled. Against this background, five years later, Ptolemy seized his chance and declared himself pharaoh of Egypt in 305 BC.

We may guess that it was to strengthen and symbolise his own legitimacy as the true successor of Alexander the Great that Ptolemy transferred Alexander's golden sarcophagus, and along with it the cult of Serapis-Osiris-Apis, to the newly built city of Alexandria. It is also likely that the kernel of the future Great Library of Alexandria was brought at this time from the great temple-library at Heliopolis.

This then was the manner in which Alexandria was turned into the new 'capital' of Egypt and created the great spark of enlightenment that was to illuminate the Western world at the time of the Renaissance.

A special gnosis

It has long been recognised that the ancient Egyptians did not have a 'religion' – at least not in the sense that we understand the meaning of this word today. And although the term Egyptian 'religion' has been extensively used in Egyptology, and we ourselves use it in this book, the fact remains that it cannot be found in the vocabulary of the ancient Egyptians. It simply does not exist. As the eminent Egyptologist and philologist Alan H. Gardiner explains:

> From the Egyptian point of view we may say that there is no such thing as 'religion'; there was only *heka*, the nearest English equivalent of which is 'magical power' ...[53]

Everything about the ancient Egyptian monuments and texts leads us to suppose that *heka*, i.e. magical powers, were believed to be acquired through a very intense spiritual and intellectual learning process involving elaborate and secret initiations. *Heka* was a sort of *sacred science* or, as we prefer to call it, a *special gnosis*, and it was thought to be the gift of Thoth, the ancient Egyptian god of wisdom (the Hermes Trismegistus of the Greeks). According to British Egyptologist Patrick Boylan, professor of Eastern languages at University College Dublin:

> Thoth ... is god of wisdom and orderer of the cosmos. His word has to call things into being ... [and is] endowed with magical powers. Magic presupposes always a special Gnosis. The magician claims to possess a higher and deeper knowledge of the secret nature of things, and the hidden connection which holds things together. He is the wise one whose words have power to control mysterious forces, and to ward off invisible perils. And the magician does all this by the power of his special gnosis ...[54]

THE MASTER GAME

This *special gnosis* or magical knowledge was said to have been gathered by Thoth and written in sacred books which, according to a legend found in the Egyptian *Book of the Dead*, were taken to the Temple of Heliopolis by the goddess Hathor, whose star, the reader will recall, was Sirius.[55] A rather similar legend that associates Thoth and his sacred books to the city of Heliopolis is found in the *Westcar Papyrus*. In this 3500-year-old text a story is told about a magician brought to the court of Pharaoh Khufu, the legendary builder of the Great Pyramid at Giza. Khufu is keen to find the secret chamber of Thoth (presumably where the magical 'books' were kept) in order to design his pyramid, and he is told by the magician that it will be found at Heliopolis in some sort of 'inventory room' or library or hall of scriptures and records.[56] This story therefore associates the idea of the pyramid with the magical knowledge of Thoth – knowledge, as we shall see, that was specifically connected to the *stars*. As the French Egyptologist and author Christian Jacq asserts:

> The greatest centre of magic in Egypt was probably the holy city
> of Heliopolis, the city of the sun, where the most ancient theology
> developed. Here were preserved numerous papyri, 'magic'
> in the widest sense of the word, including medical, botanical,
> zoological and mathematical texts. Most Greek philosophers
> and savants travelled to Heliopolis to study some of that
> knowledge ...[57]

Jacq then goes on to say that at Heliopolis and other similar learning centres was practiced the most 'sacred science that requires specialists trained for many years to grasp the most secret forces of the universe.'[58] Everything points to the fact that the most important aspect of this 'sacred science' or special *gnosis*, rested on the belief that the influences and powers of the stars could be somehow drawn down to earth. As Christian Jacq and others have pointed out, the edifices of the ancient Egyptian sacred science rested on the fervent conviction that innate objects such as amulets, statues, shrines, monuments, temples and even whole cities could be imbued with the divine essence of the star-gods which was harnessed with the application of *heka* i.e. magic.

Western civilisation in the 21st century does not, by and large, believe in magic. Earlier civilisations did and the ancient Egyptians were emphatically amongst them. What they understood by *heka* however, does not necessarily accord with modern ideas of magic at all and therefore needs to be clearly defined. According to Dame Frances Yates of the University of London, who made a lifetime study of these matters:

> The type of magic with which we are to be concerned differs profoundly from astrology which is not necessarily magic at all but a mathematical science based on the belief that human destiny is irrevocably governed by the stars, and that therefore from the study of a person's horoscope, the position of the stars at the time of his birth, one can foretell his irrevocably foreordained future. This magic is astrological only in the sense that it too bases itself upon the stars, their images and influences, but it is a way of escaping from astrological determinism by gaining power over the stars, guiding their influences in the direction which the operator desires. Or, in the religious sense, it is a way of salvation, of escape from material fortune and destiny, or of obtaining insight into the divine. Hence 'astrological magic' is not a correct description of it, and hereafter, for want of a better term, I shall call it 'astral magic' ...[59]

Frances Yates, as we shall see in the next chapter, was speaking here not of ancient Egyptian 'astral magic' but, more specifically, of the *revival* of the Egyptian magical religion during the Italian Renaissance. But she might as well also have referred to ancient Egypt itself, for the definition she gives covers precisely the sort of 'astral magic' that seems to have existed in Egypt since time immemorial.

A time of change

In the years after the coronation of Ptolemy I Soter as the successor of Alexander the Great, the city of Alexandria began to flourish. First a magnificent tomb was built to house Alexander's coffin and then various monumental and religious projects were planned. Most notable among these were the *Pharos*, one of the Seven Wonders of the Ancient World, the great temple and library complex of Serapis – the Alexandrian Serapeum – and, of course, the legendary Library of Alexandria.

It was at the Alexandrian Serapeum that the Ptolemies regenerated the cult of Serapis, the supreme universal god, and where a huge statue of the Serapis was erected. And at the *Pharos*, as we have already seen, was raised a great temple dedicated to Isis, 'consort' of Serapis, but now specially designated in this new maritime city as Isis-Pharia.

As for the famous library, this was dedicated to the seven muses or sisters, patrons of music and the arts. It is most likely that much of the library's original collection was derived from stocks brought from other parts of Egypt, especially Heliopolis and Memphis, which had been preserved since time immemorial in the temple-libraries of the ancient Egyptians. Also literary works of philosophy, religion, science and the arts were imported from other parts of the world, especially Greece. Ptolemy I Soter, moreover, took a great personal interest in having brought to him a copy of the Old Testament of the Hebrews and, for the first time ever, had the latter translated into Greek, making it available to the non-Jewish world. Thus an incredible intellectual and spiritual vortex began to swirl in Alexandria, and the result would be the creation of an even more powerful magical religious philosophy which was to be attributed to Hermes Trismegistus, the name given to the Egyptian wisdom god, Thoth, by the Graeco-Egyptian population of Alexandria.

Over the coming centuries, as we shall see, the ancient Egyptian magical tradition was to dress itself in Greek garb and subliminally inject itself into Western Europe.

Metamorphosis

In 586 BC, the Babylonian king, Nebuchadnezzar II, captured Jerusalem causing a mass expulsion of Jews, many of whom found their way into Egypt. Evidence of a Jewish presence in Egypt in those times is widespread from the Nile Delta area in the north to the distant south at Elephantine near Aswan. Also two centuries later, when Ptolemy I Soter took control of Palestine and Jerusalem, he brought back Jewish mercenaries and encouraged Jews to settle in his newly founded city of Alexandria. By the first century BC and the reign of the fabled Cleopatra, last of the Ptolemaic rulers, a large segment of the population of Alexandria was made up of Jews who had adopted Greek language and customs. And there can be no doubt that it was with the Jews of Egypt that a patriarchal monotheistic religion that abhorred idols and graven images began to take hold in the ancient land of the pharaohs.

In 30 BC the Roman legions of Octavian (the future Emperor Augustus) reached the gates of Alexandria to challenge his arch-rival, Mark Antony. Inside the virtually defenceless city there was panic and pandemonium. The armed forces commanded by Antony and Cleopatra had been decisively defeated at the naval Battle of Actium and now any resistance to Octavian would simply be foolish bravado. Indeed, earlier Mark Antony, in a moment of heroic folly, had attempted a valiant charge against Octavian's Roman legions only to find himself deserted by his own men who hailed Octavian as their true leader. Thus abandoned but still unable to face defeat, Mark Antony committed suicide, begging the last of his loyal soldiers to finish him off. When the news reached Cleopatra, she became determined not to be captured alive by Octavian, and committed the most famous suicide in history by being bitten by a deadly asp.

Thus 3,000 years of pharaonic civilisation came abruptly to an end. Octavian immediately declared Egypt to be a province of Rome, and the might of the Caesars fell on this ancient and sacred land like a gigantic sledgehammer. Within years Egypt was reduced to nothing more than a granary to feed Rome's legions.

Alarmed at changes they saw being introduced all around them, what the Egyptian priests undoubtedly feared most was the extinction of their magical religion. Throughout the three centuries of Ptolemaic rule, the ancient Egyptian temple-cult had not only survived but had received active state sponsorship and had boomed everywhere. This was because its time-honoured antiquity had a powerful, almost enchanting appeal for the Ptolemies who found that it meshed perfectly with their own mythologies and ideas of the divine. Indeed, the ancient Egyptian magical religion was seen as a boon for the universal dream of the Ptolemies and, like many other things, fitted the city of Alexandria like Cinderella's slipper. The Romans, on the other hand, saw the connection simply as another source of political power to run Egypt and its resources efficiently. It is true, of course, that Roman emperors appointed themselves as 'pharaohs' and even adopted the religion of Serapis and Isis. They also restored temples and built new ones in honour of the Egyptian deities – the famous Temple of Dendera was restored to its present-day appearance by Emperor Tiberius.[60] None of this, however won over the Egyptians let alone the Egyptian priests. They knew that under the Romans, things would inevitably be very different. The enlightened Ptolemies saw themselves as successors to the Egyptian pharaonic tradition, whereas the Romans had come as conquerors and masters. As the Coptic scholar Dr. Jill Kamil points out:

> The institution of sacrosanct monarchy, a cardinal feature of Egyptian life in pharaonic times which had been maintained by various later dynasties (the Ptolemies, for example), was lost in Roman times. The emperors may have claimed to be divine but it was their prefects who ruled Egypt, reduced the prestige of the priests, and exerted pressure on the people. They siphoned off the wealth of the land to Rome and recruited Egyptians to fight Roman wars in other countries. The Egyptians, who had accepted

Ptolemaic rule, resisted Roman. It is not difficult to see the difference between them. Under the Ptolemies, Egypt had retained its integrity and had a stable economy. Under the Romans the country was shorn of identity and impoverished. It was no more than a private estate for the emperor and a pleasure-ground for the Roman upper classes.[61]

There was at first some semblance of prosperity and even a sense of protection under the Romans,[62] but on the whole it did not benefit the Egyptians themselves. The wealth extracted from agriculture fed the Roman garrisons and filled the treasury of Rome; and if any new temple or hydraulic project was built by the Romans it was done for strategic reasons and to strengthen their political and military hold on Egypt. Soon the Egyptians – now a people mixed with 'Egyptian' Greeks and Jews – began to revolt. In AD 115 a huge revolt, apparently led by the Jews, was brutally crushed by the Romans. Another massacre was to take place in Alexandria during the visit of the mad Emperor Caracalla in AD 215, after he was accused by the rash Alexandrians of his brother's assassination. And an even more serious revolt took place in AD 297, this time firmly put down by Emperor Diocletian who recaptured Alexandria after a siege of eight months.

But not all imperial visits were aggressive. There was the time when Emperor Vespasian had come to Alexandria and, like Alexander the Great before him, was proclaimed 'son of Amun' and even the 'reincarnation' of Serapis. So seriously did Vespasian take this that he apparently went through the streets of Alexandria performing 'miracles', and on one occasion restored the sight to a blind man.[63]

Then there had been the relatively peaceful visit of Emperor Hadrian to Alexandria and to Thebes in Upper Egypt in AD 130. Whilst in Egypt Hadrian's favourite companion and lover, a youth called Antinous, drowned in the Nile whereupon Hadrian promptly ordered that a city be founded near the tragic spot to be called Antinoupolis. Hadrian also left us an observation of very great value concerning the worship of Christ and of Serapis in Alexandria when he wrote as follows to Servianus, the governor of the city:

So you praise Egypt, my very dear Servianus! I know the land from top to bottom … In it the worshippers of Serapis are Christians, and those who call themselves Bishops of Christ pay their vows to Serapis … Whenever the patriarch himself comes to Egypt he is made to worship Serapis by some and Christ by others.[64]

Amid such alarming religious syncretism, and constantly threatened by the temperamental debaucheries and cruelty of the Roman emperors, the Egyptian priesthood must have paused to reflect. So far they had succeeded, beyond their wildest dreams, in ensuring the survival of their age-old magical religion by accommodating and converting the Ptolemies. Now, however, they saw the Romans as a much more serious and perhaps even insurmountable danger. When the Romans had arrived in Egypt in AD 30 an intellectual and literary osmosis had long taken place between the Greeks and the educated Egyptians, many of whom were priests, scribes and functionaries associated with the temple-cult. As Dr. Kamil explains:

> The languages in official use in Egypt were Greek and Egyptian, Greek being the more widely used. Egyptian literates had learned Greek long before the conquest of Alexander. They also realised that if they transcribed their own language in the Greek alphabet, which was well known among the middle classes and was simpler to read than demotic (the cursive form of hieroglyphic writing in its latest development), communication would be easier. Scribes started translating Egyptian sounds in Greek, adding seven extra letters from the demotic alphabet to accommodate the sounds from which there were no Greek letters. The emergence of this new script, [is] now known as Coptic ...[65]

There had been much encouragement in the exchange of ideas and written works, and the first Ptolemies, such as Soter and Philadelphus, would actually issue decrees that important Egyptian writings from the temple libraries should be translated into Greek, the *lingua franca* of Egypt and its neighbours.[66] As noted above, tradition has it that Ptolemy I Soter also commissioned 72 erudite Jewish scholars to translate the Old Testament into Greek, a version now known as the *Septuagint* which was to serve as the basis for future Latin translations.

Not surprisingly a very powerful spiritual and intellectual mutation began to occur in Alexandria which ended up producing a 'neo-Egyptian' wisdom philosophy that was readily embraced by the cosmopolitan inhabitants. One element of this was Christian Gnosticism, which we have examined at length in Part I, and which is represented most strongly today in the surviving Nag Hammadi texts. Another, closely linked but with its own distinct character, was the 'pagan' Hermetic literature we've explored in Chapters Eight and Nine. Also compiled in Alexandria in the first three centuries AD, it is these Hermetic texts, claims Jill Kamil, that most perfectly sum up the intellectual and spiritual yearnings of the period:

> Although, therefore, Egypt was ruled by a Greek speaking elite, and the bulk of the population was largely illiterate, there was a bilingual community that was multinational. This is nowhere more clearly demonstrated than in a collection of syncretistic treatises known as the *Corpus Hermeticum*. The corpus was purportedly written by Thoth, the ancient Egyptian god of wisdom who, under his Greek name Hermes Trismegistus, gave the compilation its name. The Hermetic texts, some composed in Greek, some translated from Egyptian into Greek, were a blend of semi-philosophical treatises on the divine, ancient Egyptian wisdom and literature, and esoteric teachings including cosmological conceptions and mysticism. Through such literature, one can best appreciate the varied and subtle ways in which the consciousness of the divine manifested itself among the whole cultural amalgam in Egypt.[67]

In the Chapter Eight we saw the effects of this strange and mysterious Hermetic literature after it burst upon the European scene in 1460. Let us now place it at its origins into is proper intellectual and cultural setting alongside the emergent force of Christianity in both its Gnostic and its 'literalist' forms.

The three major players

Around the year AD 30, some sixty years after Octavian invaded Egypt, it is claimed that a man called Jesus from the town of Nazareth was crucified in Jerusalem. This claim – that Christ was indeed man as well as god – is central to the doctrine of Roman Catholicism. On the other hand the reader will recall from Part I that the Gnostics held an entirely different view which did not admit the physical incarnation of Christ. Who is to say, at this remove of 2,000 years, which side was right and which was wrong, whether or not Christ was a man, or an apparition, or ever existed at all? Christianity exists, of that there is no doubt. It has shaped the world we live in. But Christ himself still proves elusive and nothing about the story of his life and death, or even about what happened to his followers during the first 30 or so years after his death, can honestly be said be to confirmed as solid historical fact.

Tradition has it Saint Mark went to Rome and in that city wrote his famous 'Gospel'. Then, during the reign of Emperor Nero at about AD

60, he left Rome and travelled to Alexandria on his apostolic mission to convert the Egyptians. The great persecution of the Christians had already begun in Rome under Nero, and thus Egypt was not only a safer place to be but, and perhaps more important, was ripe for such a mission to succeed. And succeed it did, well beyond the wildest of Saint Mark's expectations.

According to Egyptian-Coptic tradition the first person in Egypt to be converted to Christianity by Saint Mark was a Jewish shoemaker from Alexandria. Whether this is historically true or not is unimportant, but it does emphasise the fact that the large Jewish population of Alexandria would have been an obvious target for such conversion to a new Judeo-Messianic cult. It is possible, indeed very probable, that some of the early followers of Jesus – whoever this mysterious figure really was! – found refuge in Egypt and formed the first nucleus of proto-Christian adepts in Egypt. Conversion thus naturally began within the existing Jewish population and then gradually spread to the indigenous as well as to the Graeco-Roman populations.

This process, almost organic in its progress, had the inevitable effect of producing a variety of religious factions in Alexandria. Right from the outset two key players were the Christian Gnostics on the one hand, who frequently interpreted the scriptures symbolically and allegorically, and 'literalist' Christians on the other who interpreted the scriptures literally. We have considered both at length in Part I.

A third major player resisted the Christian tide and remained 'pagan', retaining many original ancient Egyptian beliefs but now expressed in Greek, with rituals structured for Greek-speaking adepts. These were the Hermetists – so called, as we know, because they followed the teachings of Hermes Trismegistus, the *alter ego* of the ancient Egyptian wisdom god Thoth. Vilified and hated by the Catholic Church, the Gnostics and Hermetists found in each other a common bond – this being the search for salvation and spiritual illumination through divine knowledge, that is to say through *gnosis*. And although the Gnostics were labelled 'heretics' by the Church and the Hermetists were branded as 'pagans', both were perceived as equally dangerous enemies and were, accordingly, persecuted with equal ferocity.

We've seen in Chapter Five how the persecution reached a point in the late fourth century AD when the Christian Emperor Theodosius closed all the 'pagan' temples in Egypt. Gnostics and pagans alike were hounded into the desert and their places of worship either destroyed or 'converted' into Catholic churches, while their books were seized and burnt. It seems, however, that both groups had previously taken precautions to ensure that their sacred texts and ancient traditions would not be completely erased.

We followed the story of Gnosticism in Part I and how it survived as a living tradition until the destruction of the Cathars and the Bogomils in the 13th and 14th centuries. We also reported the story of the Nag Hammadi Gnostic texts in Part I, their loss to the world for sixteen centuries, their miraculous recovery in 1945, and their implications for our understanding of Christianity.

The Hermetic texts, the so-called *writings of Hermes Trismegistus*, came to light rather sooner. Copies had been smuggled out of Egypt, probably during the fifth or sixth century AD, with some reaching Byzanthium and Macedonia. One complete collection would pass from hand to hand, albeit recopied several times but nonetheless remaining essentially the same for a thousand years until, as we described in Chapter Eight, an aging Italian monk found it, recognised it for what it was, and brought it to Cosimo de'Medici.

The man of his epoch best suited to respond to such a discovery, Cosimo's early sponsorship launched the Hermetic message on a glittering Renaissance career that saw it infiltrate its symbolism into the very apartments of the pope before the end of the 15th century. Where Christian Gnosticism had been utterly crushed in Occitania after its re-emergence as Catharism, is it possible that the 'pagan' branch of the Alexandrian *gnosis* – i.e. Hermeticism – was about to succeed in overthrowing the hated tyranny of the Catholic Church?

In the later part of the 16th century, in a Europe devastated by the awful wars and persecutions arising from the conflict between Reformation and Catholic reaction ... men turned to the Hermetic religion of the world to take them above these conflicts ...

Frances Yates, *Giordano Bruno and the Hermetic Tradition*

Perchance your fear in passing judgement on me is greater than mine in receiving it ...

Response of Giordano Bruno to the cardinals of the Inquisition after they sentenced him to be burnt at the stake. Reported in January 1600 by Gaspar Schopp, an eyewitness of his trial.

Some say the Renaissance ended with his death.

About Giordano Bruno, in Kenneth J. Atchity's *The Renaissance Reader*

CHAPTER ELEVEN

THE PROPHET
OF HERMES

uring the Cathar crisis of the 12th and 13th centuries the Roman
Catholic Church was obliged to compete with the high standards
of behaviour and morality set by the Cathar *perfecti*. But after the
heretics had been crushed the pressure was off and by the 16th century the
reputation of the Vatican had once again become severely tarnished. Not only
were there the ongoing excesses and horrors of the Inquisition – which was
passing through a phase of renewed frenzy. Also there had been the numerous
scandals of the 'bad popes'. Amongst these, as we saw in Chapter Eight, the
Borgia Pope Alexander VI stands out for his bizarre behaviour, not to mention
the intrigue and homicidal cruelty of his two children, Cesare and Lucretia
Borgia, and the wild parties and orgies that took place at the Vatican.

All this debauchery began to cause many in Europe to doubt the papacy.
Such doubt first led to derision, then cautious protestation and finally to open
revolt by 'Protestant' groups outside Italy. The main thrust of the movement
was spearheaded in Germany by a country pastor, Martin Luther, in a bold
bid to wrangle Christianity away from the clutches of the papacy in Rome.

Awful carnage ensued where Catholic and Protestant armies battled for
decades. By the second half of the 16th century many were utterly sickened
by the terrible bloodshed and destruction and had began to hope for a
saviour or champion who could unite Europe again in peace and prosperity.
In the year 1569 all eyes fell on the Bourbon family in the kingdom of
Navarre, and on France where the religious crisis between Catholics and
Protestants (known as *Huguenots*) was reaching a turning point.

The rise and rise of Catherine de'Medici

At the head of the military Catholic League in 1569 was the French
king, Charles IX, but in reality much of the power of this rather sickly

and weak monarch was vested in his ambitious and domineering mother, Catherine de'Medici. Born into the powerful and influential Florentine family in 1519, Catherine's parents were Lorenzo de'Medici, the Duke of Urbino, and Madeleine de la Tour d'Auvergne, the latter linked to the French royal family. Orphaned at a very young age, Catherine was once kept as hostage when the Medici Palace was attacked and occupied by an angry mob of Florentines who revolted against the papacy. Finely educated in convents around the city during the siege of Florence, she was at last set free and taken to Rome after her warring uncle, Pope Clement VII (Giulio de'Medici), crushed the rebellion in Florence. The pope then negotiated with King Francis I of France for Catherine – at that time just 14-years-old – to marry the king's second eldest son, Henry of Orléans.

Wanting to make a suitable impression on the French court to counter her rather short stature and not-too-pretty countenance, the youthful Catherine de'Medici consulted a Florentine artisan who presented her with the very first example of a pair of modern high-heeled shoes, which caused quite a stir when she arrived. Immediately disliked by the French, she nonetheless became their queen when the eldest son of Francis I died, leaving the throne to her husband, Henry of Orléans, who was crowned as Henry II. Henry, meanwhile, had been having a passionate affair with Diane de Poitiers, a ravishingly beautiful courtesan 20 years his senior. But in spite of this, Catherine de'Medici bore him no less than ten children; three died at birth; three others were destined to become kings of France: Francis II, Charles IX and Henry III.

Henry II's hatred for the Protestant Huguenots of France and the violent repression that he imposed on them, finally led to an all out civil war. He was to die from a horrible jousting accident in 1559. It was then that Catherine de'Medici started a long reign of co-regency with her sons; first with Francis II, who died a year later in 1560, then with her second son Charles IX, who died in 1574, and finally with Henry III who died in August 1589, just a few months after Catherine's own death in January of that same year.

At first Catherine had oscillated between Huguenots and Catholics in an attempt to bring peace to France, and she even went as far as to arrange a marriage between her daughter, Marguerite, and Henry of Navarre, the dashing Protestant Bourbon prince, the future Henry IV of France. The kingdom of Navarre, which was situated in northern Spain, was ruled by a rogue French dynasty, the Bourbons, who bitterly opposed the Catholic League. Henry's mother, Jeanne d'Albret, the queen of Navarre, was a staunch Protestant and saw to it that her son also followed suit. Trained in military skills by Gaspard de Coligny, an able Protestant general of Navarre, Henry of Navarre proved to be a natural military strategist who excelled at hand-to-hand combat, starting at the young age of 16 when he personally led the first cavalry charge of the Huguenots against the Catholics at the Battle of Arnay-le-duc. Finally, in 1570, a precarious peace treaty was signed by Catherine de'Medici, queen of France, and Jeanne d'Albret, queen of Navarre, and a marriage was proposed between Catherine's daughter, Marguerite de'Medici, and Jeanne's heroic son, Henry of Navarre. After lengthy negotiations between the two rival queens, an agreement was reached in 1572 and the marriage ceremony was planned to take place in Paris. Upon arrival in Paris in June, however, the queen of Navarre suddenly died of a lung infection and, in consequence, her son Henry became the new king of Navarre. He and Marguerite de'Medici married on 18 August 1572 but Henry refused to attend Catholic Mass after the wedding with the French royal family. And barely a few days later, one of history's most gruesome 'days of infamy' was to crush all hopes of peace between the Protestant Huguenots and the Catholics in France.

The St. Bartholomew's Day Massacre

During the royal wedding of Henry and Marguerite, thousands of Huguenots, including Henry's famous cousin, the Prince of Condé, had poured into Paris for the celebrations. Rumours began to spread of a plot against Catherine de'Medici, who urged her frail and weak-minded son, Charles IX, to act swiftly and harshly against the Huguenots. There followed an attempt to assassinate the Prince of Condé which sparked a huge riot against Catherine; in return the royal guards were ordered to attack the unprepared Huguenots. A terrible massacre ensued, and the streets of Paris, it was later said, were knee-deep in blood. This gruesome genocide has gone down in history as the 'St. Bartholomew's Day Massacre' because it took place on 24 August, the festival of that saint.

Against the background of such charged events, Henry of Navarre found himself effectively a prisoner of the most Catholic French royal family into which he had married. In a bid to save his own life as well as the Protestant cause, he pretended to abandon Protestantism. After convincing the crafty Catherine de'Medici that he had sincerely converted to Catholicism, Henry finally escaped three years later to his kingdom in Navarre to raise an army against the Catholics.

Meanwhile Charles IX died and was succeeded by Henry III, Catherine's last and favourite son. Aloof and apparently fond of young men known as the *mignons*, a quaint French word for homosexuals, Henry III spent much of his time in questionable pastimes which included dressing up as a woman, taking part in macabre processions around Paris wearing a sinister monk's cloak and cagoul, and joining a group of Capuchin friars who impersonated the 'Virgin Mary' and 'Maria Magdalena' while a third, perhaps the king himself, impersonated 'Jesus'.[1] Additionally Henry was the patron of two religious military orders – the 'Knights of the Holy Spirit' and 'Knights of the Phoenix' – which were reported to have conducted unusual rituals involving the king.[2]

With no marriage or heirs in sight, Henry III seemed destined to be the last of the powerful Orléans-Medici dynasty to rule France. Attention fell on his dashing renegade brother-in-law, Henry of Navarre who was the next in line to the throne of France. And many began to see in him the god-sent king who would unite Protestants and Catholics once again.

A Mass for Paris

In 1586 Henry of Navarre set up his military headquarters at La Rochelle, traditionally a strong fortress city and symbol of Protestant resistance. From there he would oppose the powerful Catholic League formed by an unholy alliance of Spain, France, the Vatican and the Hapsburgs in Germany, the latter the traditional seat of the Holy Roman Empire. In the fall of 1587, Henry of Navarre confronted the Catholic army of Henry III of France at Coutras, near Bordeaux. Henry III's army was led by one of Henry III's *mignons*, the Duke of Joyeuse, who was no match for Henry of Navarre. The Catholics were crushed and the Duke of Joyeuse was killed in action.

Not unexpectedly, Henry of Navarre was immediately condemned as a heretic by the pope and declared unfit to succeed to the throne of France. Philip II of Spain, unquestionably the real power behind the Catholic League, then proposed that his daughter, Isabella, should become queen of France. Bullied by the immensely powerful Count of Guise, a staunch Catholic, Henry III fled Paris, and the Catholic League took over.

Henry III struck a secret deal with Henry of Navarre and promised him the succession to the throne if he would help him recapture Paris. The next move was the assassination of the Count of Guise by Henry III's *mignons* on 23 December 1588. He and Henry of Navarre then laid siege to Paris in early 1589. In the midst of this crisis, however, Henry III was himself knifed by a fanatical Jesuit monk, Jacques Clément. On his deathbed, coughing blood from his lung wounds, Henry apparently managed to master enough strength to proclaim Henry of Navarre his legitimate successor.

The Catholic League refused Henry of Navarre entry into Paris and the crown of France unless he would attend a Catholic Mass. It was then that Henry immortalised the phrase, 'Paris is well worth a Mass!' and once again abjured Protestantism in the name of expediency. Henry of Navarre was crowned King Henry IV of France at Chartres Cathedral in 1594 and, on 22 March, the spring equinox, rode into Paris on his celebrated white steed amid huge cheers and jubilations.

The Hermetic mission of Giordano Bruno

It will be clear from the brief sketch given above that the religious struggle which most concerned the Catholic Church during the 16th century was its fight against Protestantism. The Cathar wars were a thing of the past, dualist heresy was dead and buried, and although the Protestants were 'heretics' they were nothing like as heretical as the Cathars had been 400 years before. Indeed, apart from a shared anti-materialism, the Cathar religion had no more in common with Protestantism than it did with Catholicism and belonged, as we have seen, to the tradition of Gnostic Christianity that took shape in Alexandria in the first three centuries AD.

Out of the same Alexandrian melting-pot, in the same period, emerged a second tradition that also claimed to pass on a sacred soul-freeing *gnosis*. We've seen in previous chapters that the name of this second tradition was Hermeticism – after Hermes Trismegistus – and that the Church regarded it as 'pagan' rather than Christian. Unlike the Gnostic tradition, which we suggest survived in a virtually unbroken chain of heresy from the early Christian period until the crushing of the Cathars, the continued survival of Hermeticism from the 5th to the 15th centuries is much harder to attest.[3] What brings this ancient tradition to life again, at least in the West, seems purely and simply to be the recovery of its primary texts, their translation at the Medici Academy in the 1460s, and the subsequent international 'movement' that the texts inspired. It may be the case, however, that there was more than immediately meets the eye to the phenomenal success of this revived Hermeticism. The sheer speed with which it took off and the way in which it so rapidly managed to work its way into the heart of the Vatican, as we reported in Chapter Eight, are hard to explain. It is almost as though some sort of system or 'organisation' was *already in place* when the texts resurfaced that had both the will and the capacity to exploit their full potential for undermining the established Church.

If so Giordano Bruno, perhaps the greatest Hermetic magus of the 16th century, is likely to have been part of the plot (though he may have possibly have been too stubborn and independent a thinker to have plotted efficiently!). Born in 1548 at the little town of Nola near Naples he was burnt agonisingly to death over a slow fire by the Inquisition in 1600 for having spent the previous 21 years trying to destroy Catholic Christianity …

The reader will recall that the majority of papal inquisitors were Dominicans. Ironically, as a young man, Bruno himself had been a Dominican monk, at their monastery in Naples. It was a foretaste of what was to come that even at this early stage he was accused of heresy by his fellow monks. His crime was to have been caught reading the banned works of Erasmus and those of Marcilio Ficino and Giovanni Pico della Mirandola expounding the Hermetic tradition.

Bruno's stubborn attitude and fierce free will were not assets for the controlled life at the monastery. In 1576, when he was 28 years old, he finally ended up repudiating this oppressive religious order and emotionally defrocked himself in public. Learning that the Inquisition was preparing an indictment against him (which consisted of no less than 130 separate charges of heresy!) he then wisely went on the run.[4]

Impulsive, argumentative, brilliant – indeed a genius – Bruno was an all-out Hermetist who harboured wild dreams of the full restoration of the 'Egyptian' religion of Hermes Trismegistus. But unlike Pico della Mirandola's rather feeble attempt to integrate Hermeticism with Christianity through the Cabala (see Chapter Eight) Bruno had something much more radical in mind: the actual *replacement* of Christianity by the Hermetic magical religion of Egypt.

Bruno's travels

After fleeing the Inquisition in 1576 Bruno turned up in quick succession in Genoa, Turin, Savona and Noli. In 1577 he spent a few weeks in Venice where he published his first book, unfortunately now lost, under the title *Dei segni dei tempi* ('*Signs of the Times*'). His next stop was Padua and after that Milan where he first heard of an English nobleman, Sir Philip Sydney, who would later come to play an important role in his life.[5]

In 1578 Bruno travelled to Geneva, where he hoped to win the protection of the Marquis of Vico, a wealthy and influential Italian Protestant living in exile. Bruno made it clear that he did not want to adopt Protestantism himself, only to live and work quietly, but the authorities would not permit him to do so. He fell into a slanging-match with an eminent professor of Geneva, was arrested for his temerity and forced to apologise. Soon afterwards he left the city in disgust.[6]

From 1579–1581 Bruno lived in Toulouse, capital of the former Cathar domain of Occitania and now fully integrated into France. He took his doctorate in theology at the University of Toulouse and was subsequently appointed to a chair in philosophy there. Once again, however, his instinctive nonconformism and outspokenness led him into conflicts with other scholars and with his students.[7]

In 1581 Bruno sought refuge in Paris where he delivered a series of 30 lectures that were reportedly widely admired. He quickly began to acquire a reputation for his 'enormous erudition, prodigious memory, and eloquence.'[8]

Bruno at the French court

In 1582 Bruno was summoned to the French court by the slightly unhinged Henry III who was then at the apogee of his doomed reign. Bruno, it seems, was at first very well received by the king, and in due course was given a position at the *Collège de France* to teach the art of memory and mnemonics.[9] In Bruno's own words:

> I gained such a name that King Henry III summoned me one day and asked me whether the memory which I had and which I taught was a natural memory or obtained by magic art; I proved to him that it was not obtained by magic art but by science. After that I printed a book on memory entitled *De Umbris Idearum* ['*The Shadow of Ideas*'] which I dedicated to his majesty, whereupon he made me an endowed reader.[10]

That the art of memory had nothing to do with magic is, strictly speaking, not true; and Bruno knew this.[11] But he made the statement quoted above during his trial by the Inquisition in 1600, and thus would have been most reluctant to admit to using pagan magic in his teachings. Nevertheless the cultivation of a powerful memory, and more specifically the kind of super-memory that Bruno had mastered through the art of mnemonics, was indeed very much part of the system of magic that was once practiced by the ancient Egyptians and divulged in the Hermetic writings. As Frances Yates comments:

> Bruno's relations with Henry III are only documented from what Bruno himself told the Inquisitors ... If Henry looked at the *De Umbris Idearum* [the book Bruno dedicated to him] he would certainly have recognised its magic images ... at one time the king sent to Spain for magic books ... one of which was the *Picatrix*. It is also incredible in view of his mother's

addiction to magicians and astrologers [Catherine had, after all, been a member of the Medici elite in Florence], that Henry should not have known a good deal about magic. The more probable version of the story would be that Henry was attracted by the rumour about magic in connection with Bruno, and this was why he sent for him.[12]

Images, especially images of stars and other celestial objects such as the Sun, planets and the zodiac, in short all the symbols of *astral magic* found in the Hermetica's *Asclepius* and in the *Picatrix* (see discussion in Chapter Eight), were indeed used by Bruno as powerful memory devices. To speak more technically, they served for him as 'talismans' by means of which memories could be permanently imprinted on the mind.[13] Also incorporated into Bruno's magical art of memory was to be found the new and still very controversial theory of the great astronomer Nicolaus Copernicus with its Sun-centred/heliocentric dynamics so abhorred by the Catholic Church at the time. Bruno, in fact, saw himself as a disciple of Copernicus; but being Bruno, he wanted to go even further than the shy Polish man by boldly proclaiming that the universe was infinite and made up of infinite number of suns, i.e. the stars, each having planetary systems populated by living creatures just like our own planet. And thus Bruno, through his remarkable intuition, can be said to have anticipated by nearly four centuries our modern ideas of the cosmos.[14]

Copernicus's theory, by correctly placing the Sun rather than the Earth at the centre of our own planetary system was understood by Bruno as evidence of divine harmony and universal unity, in which all the planets were governed by a central authority. Seen through the complex and symbolically-inclined mind of Bruno, the heliocentric system, brought down to earth by the power of astral magic, provided the model for the ideal society. Such a society would of course be ruled by a great 'solar monarch', advised by philosopher-priests, whose reign would usher in the magical Hermetic religion around which all the nations of the world would unite. To Bruno's way of thinking the French, or perhaps even the English in the person of their illustrious Queen Elizabeth I, might prove to be the source of such a benign and charismatic ruler.

Thus it was, after sojourning a year at the French court, that Bruno travelled to England in March 1583. His purpose, as discerned by the Baron Cobham, English ambassador to Paris at the time, was to promote a 'religion I cannot commend'.[15] Or as Frances Yates puts it:

Giordano Bruno, Hermetic magician of a most extreme type, [was] now about to pass into England to expound his 'new philosophy'.[16]

Bruno in London and Oxford

Bruno was to spend two very active years in England during which he converted his life 'from that of a wandering magician into that of a very strange kind of missionary indeed.'[17] He took up residence in London at the house of the French ambassador, Michel de Castelnau, Sieur de la Mauvissière, having earlier been introduced to him by the king of France, Henry III.

No sooner had Bruno settled in his new home than he began to write in earnest. His first publication was a book on the art of memory dedicated to his host, the French ambassador. Bruno was hoping that, as in France, his special knowledge of this 'magical art' would attract the attention of scholars, perhaps even the favour of the court, and obtain for him a scholarship at Oxford.

He was, however, soon to be disappointed. In June 1583, just a few months after his arrival in England, Bruno somehow found his way into a debate with a group of Oxford scholars during an evening organised for the entertainment of Prince Albert Laski of Poland. Bruno delivered a lecture on 'the immortality of the soul' and on his personal vision of the Copernican theory but was heckled and interrupted by an elderly Oxford gentleman. 'Learn how roughly and rudely that pig behaved,' Bruno commented later:

> ... and with what patience and humanity the Nolan [Bruno] replied, showing himself to be indeed a Neapolitan, born and bred beneath a kindlier sky. Hear how they [the Oxford dons] made him leave off his public lectures on the immortality of the soul and on the quintuple sphere.[18]

Bruno (who liked to be known as 'the Nolan' after Nola, his place of birth) had a deep aversion for narrow-minded scholars like those he encountered at Oxford. He called them 'Grammarians', 'Aristotelians' (Aristotle, unlike his master Plato, had long been a favoured philosopher of the Catholic Church) and 'pedants'. Rather than seeking divine truth, he complained, they quibbled and endlessly debated with each other over trivialities. Worse, there was many a scholar of this type who 'understood but did not dare to say what he understood [and] ... saw but did not believe what he saw'.[19] In Bruno's view, all such were to be pitied for their inability to develop deeper insight or to grasp the importance of the intuitive faculty that the ancients had once harnessed with their 'profound magic'.

At the heart of Bruno's attack on his fellow scholars was the view that their titles and positions merely served to disguise their fundamental emptiness. They were quite the opposite of the Gnostic and Hermetic sages of antiquity whose search for knowledge and truth had *not* depended solely upon the analysis and observation of nature. Those remote figures, Bruno knew, had relied additionally, and especially, on deeper insights that could be reached only by intuition harnessed through *natural magic* – in the manner of the high initiates of ancient Egypt.

None of this means that Bruno condemned analytical or mathematical science; quite the contrary, as his support for Copernicus proves. Indeed, Bruno was among the very first to speak openly at Oxford on the heliocentric theory of Copernicus. But with a major difference. Unlike others scholars, the Nolan insisted on placing the theory within 'the context of the astral magic and sun-worship' that was evident in the Hermetic texts, as well as extending it to support his own cosmological vision of an infinite universe with numberless inhabited worlds.[20] It was because the stiff Oxonians of the 16th century were not ready for such cutting-edge ways of thinking that they treated Bruno insultingly and forced him to abandon in midstream his lecture on the immortality of the soul.

Sidney and Dee

Present that day was the young and influential English statesman, Sir Philip Sidney, who had come on the command of Queen Elizabeth I to escort the Polish nobleman, Prince Albert Laski, to the debate. The queen had high regard for Sidney, and it was no secret that his uncle, the debonair Earl of Leicester, Sir Robert Dudley, had once been Elizabeth's favourite and, according to some, even her secret lover.

Philip Sidney was a refined scholar and poet and would, almost certainly, have been familiar with the Hermetic texts, which by this time had been circulating in Europe for more than a century. A great patron of scholars and artists Sidney is credited with ushering in the age of Elizabethan poetry with his acclaimed sonnet sequence 'Astrophel and Stella'. This he composed as the result of his passionate love for Penelope Devereux, the beautiful young wife of Lord Rich. Sidney was also well acquainted with the famous court astrologer and 'magician', Dr. John Dee – although the extent and depth of this connection is unclear.

Dee was a genuine mathematician, but had also previously served as astrologer to Mary Tudor. She had ended up accusing him of practicing evil magic on her and had imprisoned him at Hampton Court. Dee was released in 1555 and later resumed his work as official astrologer and magician at the court of Elizabeth I – from whose royal support, favour and protection he was fortunate to benefit. It was John Dee in his role as astrologer who advised the court on the most favourable date for Elizabeth's coronation.

Dee seems to have been an alchemist, cabalist, astronomer, astrologer and mathematician all rolled into one, but is remembered mostly as a 'conjuror' and 'magician'. He believed, with utter conviction, that he could communicate with the spiritual world and 'angels' through crystals. To further his work in this area he employed a certain Edward Kelly, a clairvoyant with a rather dubious past, to assist him.

At the time Bruno arrived in England, Dee was preparing to travel to Poland and Bohemia to give séances and exhibitions of his conjuring at the courts of various princes. We shall see in a later chapter how this magical mystery tour of Dee's was to be among the catalysts that led to the formation a secretive movement known as Rosicrucianism. Not unlike Bruno, the Rosicrucians made use of Hermetic magic and the Cabala as tools for religious reform.

The Expulsion of the Triumphant Beast

Although Bruno did not meet Dee, he did know Philip Sidney, a fact which is attested by Bruno himself in the dedication of his most important book, *Spaccio della Bestia Trionfante* ('*The Expulsion of the Triumphant Beast*'), published in 1584.

The peculiar and striking title of this work is to be understood on at least two levels. First, as Bruno also states in his dedication to Sidney, 'driving out of the triumphant beast' is a metaphor for driving out 'the vices which predominate, and oppose the divine part of the soul.'[21] What this calls to mind is something closely akin to the Gnostic/Cathar/Manichean vision of the soul imprisoned in the world of matter and ever more deeply entrapped by surrender to the fleshly vices. But at the second level of meaning the 'triumphant beast' is unquestionably the pope, and with him the entire established structure of Catholic Christianity. At this level the 'expulsion' envisaged by Bruno is to make way for his 'Egyptianism as a religion'[22] based on the teachings of Hermes Trismegistus:

It is the good religion which was overwhelmed in darkness when the Christians destroyed it, forbade it by statutes, substituted worship of dead things, foolish rites, bad moral behaviour and constant wars.[23]

One of the very peculiar and distinctive aspects of the religious revolution proposed in the *Spaccio,* notes Frances Yates, and one clearly attributable to the influence on Bruno of the Hermetic texts:

> Is that it begins in the heavens; it is the images of the constellations of the zodiac and of the northern and southern constellations which are reformed or cleansed through a council of the planetary gods ...[24]

The *Spaccio,* in short, is a treatise on Hermetic astral magic, filled with references to the stars, the zodiac and the constellations, that goes to great lengths to explain how their powers can be brought down and vested in earthly things through 'the magic and divine cult of the Egyptians.'[25] Bruno's intention was clear enough. He wanted to show that Egyptian wisdom came earlier than that of the Greeks, and certainly much earlier than that of the Christians and, therefore, must be regarded as 'the best religion and the best magic and the best laws of them all'.[26]

Bruno reproduces a passage in the *Spaccio* from the famous *Lament of Hermes*. In this text, the reader will recall from Chapter Eight, Hermes Trismegistus tells his pupil Asclepius that the religion of Egypt will fall, and be lost under the hands of invading barbarians, and vanish from the world. But Hermes also says that a time will come when it will be restored and accorded a place of honour once again – and so too does Bruno:

> The marvellous magical religion of the Egyptians will return, their moral laws will replace the chaos of the present age, the prophesy of the *Lament* will be fulfilled ...[27]

In Bruno's eyes, 'the sign in heaven proclaiming the return of Egyptian light to dispel the present darkness was ... the Copernican sun.'[28] Accordingly he looked on the Copernican diagram of the concentric orbits of the planets encircling the Sun as a sort of hieroglyph or talisman. It functioned as a magical Hermetic seal that he, Bruno, thought he understood at its deepest level. He became in consequence acutely aware of the huge 'revolution' which it was about to unleash and of its potential for inflicting a total upheaval on the dogmas of the Church. Bruno's strategy – simple really – was to integrate this inevitable Copernican truth that was about to revolutionise science and religion into his own Hermetic revolution. He believed that Copernicus had vindicated the Sun-centred system of the ancient Egyptians, and that it was now up to the Nolan to revive and restore that lost faith it in order to reform the world.

As above so below

We said above that the great religious reformation envisaged by Bruno, which he expounded in the *Spaccio della Bestia Trionfante*, is supposed to begin in the heavens among the stars. Here, a great council of 'magicians', including the Egyptian goddess Isis, is convened by Jupiter (Zeus-Amun) in order to reform the images of the constellations and thus, at the same time, through astral magic, also reform the earthly world below. Such ideas, notes Yates, are clearly pulled from the *Kore Kosmou* (the 'Virgin of the World'), a well-known Hermetic tract in which Isis addresses Horus and another pupil called Momus, and explains to them how things below on earth must be kept in 'sympathy' with things above in heaven in order to avoid chaos and destruction.[29] There is a strange and telling passage where Hermes reveals to Momus that he, Hermes, plans to invent a 'secret engine', or celestial mechanism, a sort of cosmic clockwork regulated by the cogwheels of the planetary orbits, the constellations, the zodiac, the Moon and the Sun, in order to control events on Earth as well as the lives of men:

> 'Momus', said he [Hermes], 'I will devise a secret engine linked to unerring and inevitable fate, by which all things in men's lives, from their birth to their final destruction, shall by necessity be brought into subjection; and all things on earth likewise shall be controlled by the working of this engine' ...[30]

It seems clear that Bruno believed that the great religious reform that many were dreaming of could, as in the *Kore Kosmou*, be brought about by Egyptian astral magic or, as Yates was to put it:

> ... [by] manipulating the celestial images on which all things below depend in order to make the reform come. For in the *Spaccio* Bruno has Jupiter proclaiming: 'If we thus renew our heaven, the constellations and influences shall be new, the impressions and fortunes shall be new for all things depending on this upper world.'[31]

'And what', asks Yates, 'does this remind us of?'

> Surely of the magical city of Adocentyn in *Picatrix*, built by Hermes Trismegistus, who placed around the circumference of the city 'engraved images and ordered them in such a manner that by their virtue the inhabitants were made virtuous and withdrawn from all wickedness

and harm.' This ... provides the connection between Hermes Trismegistus as magician and Hermes Trismegistus as law-giver of the Egyptians, who gave them their good moral laws and kept them in it. And this, I believe, may be also the connection in the *Spaccio* between the manipulation or reform of the celestial images and the universal religious and moral reform.[32]

In the *Picatrix* we learn that Hermes built a temple dedicated to the Sun, a sort of Hermetic solar temple if you will. The reader will recall that this solar temple, as well as the magical city of *Adocentyn*, much resembled another Hermetic metropolis described in the *Asclepius* in which:

... the gods who exercise their dominion over the earth will be restored one day and installed in a city at the extreme limit of Egypt, a city which will be founded towards the setting sun, and into which will hasten, by land and sea, the whole race of mortal men ...[33]

It may be worth noting at this stage that there did once exist two great solar temple-cities at both extreme limits of Egypt, one in the north, which was the 'City of the Sun' at Heliopolis, and another in the south, the solar city of Karnak-Luxor at Thebes – which is indeed oriented towards the setting sun. So could the Hermetic city of the *Picatrix* somehow have been modelled on ancient Thebes? And, more importantly, what effect are such statements in the *Picatrix* and the *Asclepius* likely to have had on the prepared minds of Bruno and other Renaissance Hermetic reformers? Might they not have been inspired to accelerate the great religious changes they sought by building a magical solar city somewhere in Western Europe?

The high possibility that Bruno would have associated his own Hermetic reformation of Europe with the founding of magical 'solar' cities is confirmed by one Guillaume Cotin with whom Bruno spent some time after he returned to France from England in 1585. Cotin, the librarian at the Abbey of St. Victor in Paris, reports that Bruno had:

... heard it said that the Duke of Florence [a Medici] wished to build a *Civitas Solis* [literally a 'City of the Sun'] in which the sun would shine every day of the year ...[34]

Just the mention of the words *Civitas Solis* should immediately bring to the mind of any student of Renaissance magic and the Hermetic tradition the strange mission to Paris of yet another Hermetic thinker. The man in question was Bruno's contemporary and, like him, was also a 'defrocked' Dominican monk hounded out of Italy by the Inquisition. Like Bruno, too, he was inspired by the Hermetic vision of religious revolution. The greatest similarity of all, however, is that this Bruno clone is famous for having written a book entitled *Civitas Solis* – '*The City of the Sun*' – and for seeking out an enlightened monarch of 'solar' pedigree to install such a utopian city somewhere in the heart of Europe.

Bruno's fatal decision

We'll meet the author of the *Civitas Solis* later in this chapter.

Meanwhile Bruno left England in 1585 and sailed back to France, only to find Paris in turmoil and a far less hospitable place for him than it once had been. King Henry III, whose favour Bruno had formerly enjoyed, was totally preoccupied with the religious war within his realm that was by this point reaching a crescendo.

The situation, which we sketched out earlier, was explosive. The Catholic forces, assisted by the Spanish and led by the Count of Guise, were mobilised outside Paris. Pope Sixtus V had declared the Protestant leaders Henry of Navarre and the Prince of Condé to be heretics, thus supposedly debarring Henry from the throne of France – a move which, by its provocative implications, was virtually a declaration of war against Navarre and the Huguenots. The Catholic clergy in Paris, especially the Jesuits, were inciting the populace with inflammatory sermons against the 'heretics' and Huguenots, forcing the meek Henry III to retreat into his convoluted acts of piety, scarcely to be seen in public except during those bizarre and morbid religious processions in which he participated doing 'penance'. It was obvious to Bruno that he could no longer rely on royal support.

After quarrelling with the scholars at the college at Cambrai, who were incensed over a public attack Bruno had made on Aristotle, the Nolan left France in September 1586 and went to Germany, then Poland, then back to Germany where he stayed until the summer of 1591. At this time that he was seized by a deep – and for him fatal – nostalgia for Italy and a naïve hope that the newly elected Pope Clement VIII could somehow be persuaded to adopt his plans for a universal Hermetic reform.

Events in France may have encouraged Bruno: Henry of Navarre had been crowned King Henry IV, and there was already much hopeful talk that this once staunch Protestant prince would soon convert to Catholicism. This was probably seen by Bruno as a sign of the impeding great reformation –

albeit here within a Catholic framework – that he, Bruno, had been divinely commissioned to bring about.

Fired by such misplaced ideas about himself and his mission, Bruno was probably in an unusually susceptible state of mind when he received an invitation to become the private tutor to a certain Señor Zuane Mocenigo, a Venetian nobleman who claimed to be a great admirer of the Nolan's works. Mocenigo was put into contact with Bruno through the Venetian bookseller, Giovanni Battista Ciotto, who knew of the heretic's whereabouts in Germany. Oblivious to the grave danger of returning to Italy, Bruno impulsively accepted Mocenigo's offer and left for Venice in late 1591.

At first the Nolan did not stay with Mocenigo, but took up residence independently in Venice. He also travelled to Padua where he stayed from January to March 1592. Ironically, had he stayed a little longer he would probably have met the author of the *Civitas Solis*, who was not to arrive in Padua until October that same year. Had they met, the author of *Civitas Solis* would certainly have warned Bruno of the terrible risks he was taking by staying in Italy, and might have even convinced him to return to Germany where he could live in relative safety.

But as it turned out, history had reserved for Bruno a far more sinister fate in Rome …

The Field of Flowers

In March 1592, Bruno finally went to reside at the home of Mocenigo. The latter was not the gentle student that Bruno was led to believe, but turned out to be a very possessive and vindictive man. It seems Mocenigo wanted Bruno to teach him the 'art of memory and invention' so that he could acquire the Nolan's intellectual powers for himself. Bruno, however, seems to have been more concerned with a book that he had just completed which he intended to dedicate to the Pope Clement VIII in order to win his attention and, hopefully, his support and sponsorship. When Bruno announced his intentions to Mocenigo and furthermore informed him that he was going to Frankfort to have the book printed, Mocenigo flew into a fit of rage, locked Bruno in his room, and called in the Venetian Inquisition.

Bruno was arrested and accused of heresy on several counts, being ordered to renounce his beliefs or face trial. Apparently Bruno did renounce but the Venetian inquisitors were unconvinced of his honesty and sent him to Rome for further questioning.

Thus began an eight-year ordeal at the hands of the Roman Inquisition. Tortured and tormented in the Vatican dungeons, Bruno stood accused of heresy on several counts, including his claims of an infinite populated universe (in line with modern science), that the Earth itself is a planet (it is), and that the symbol of the cross was known to the ancient Egyptians (it was, in the form of the *ankh*, or *crux ansata*, symbolising the 'life-force').

Ordered to retract these and his other 'heresies' or else face death by burning, Bruno courageously stood firm. He not only refused to retract but also withdrew the retractions he had made earlier in Venice. Fired by his convictions, he defiantly told his accusers that he had neither said nor written anything that was heretical, but only what was true. When his sentence was passed, Bruno bravely stared at the cardinals lined up in front of him and calmly told them: 'Perchance your fear in passing judgement on me is greater than mine in receiving it.'

On the morning of 17 February 1600, Bruno, garbed with a white shirt, was taken to the Campo dei Fiori, the 'Field of Flowers', a small piazza not far from the Roman Pantheon. There, the Nolan was securely tied to a wooden pole around which were stacked planks of wood and bundles of sticks. 'I die a willing martyr', he is said to have declared as the fire was being lit all around him, 'and my soul will rise with the smoke to paradise.' A young Protestant, Gaspar Schopp of Breslau (Wrocław), who had recently converted to Catholicism and thus enjoyed the favours of the pope, was an eyewitness to the burning, and reported that 'when the image of our Saviour was shown to him before his death he [Bruno] angrily rejected it with averted face'.[35] The truth is that a Dominican monk had tried to brandish a crucifix in Bruno's face while he suffered in the flames. In an act reminiscent of the courage of the Cathar *perfecti*, and of their detestation for the cross, poor Bruno, his legs now charred to the bone, mustered enough strength to turn his head away in disgust.

A few days earlier Bruno had written his own epitaph:

> I have fought ... It is much ... Victory lies in the hands of Fate. Be that with me as it may, whoever shall prove conqueror, future ages will not deny that I did not fear to die, was second to none in constancy, and preferred a spirited death to a craven life.[36]

The 'Organisation' at work again?

By burning Giordano Bruno the Inquisition sent a clear and unmistakable message of intolerance to all who dared think like him: such ancient heresies would be crushed, whenever and wherever they emerged. Bruno's dreams of a great universal Hermetic reform or revival – whether within the Christian framework or outside it – nosedived and burrowed deep underground. From now on any person or group thinking of religious change of any kind, or even proposing scientific theories deemed contrary to Christian teachings and dogmas, knew very clearly what awaited them.

Not surprisingly perhaps, it was after the death of Giordano Bruno that Europe was to see the resurgence of secret societies and fraternities. It was as if from the ashes of Bruno's funeral pyre arose an invisible phoenix that flew out to nurture universal reform elsewhere in Europe. Frances Yates buries in her excellent book on Bruno and Hermeticism devastating hint as to the identity of this invisible, nurturing and revolutionary 'phoenix':

> ... one of the most significant aspects of Giordano Bruno [is that] he came at the end of that sixteenth century with its terrible exhibitions of religious intolerance, in which men were seeking in religious Hermeticism some way of toleration or union between warring sects ... There were many varieties of Christian Hermeticism, Catholic and Protestant, most of them avoiding the magic. And then come Giordano Bruno, taking full magical Hermeticism as his basis, preaching a kind of Egyptian Counter Reformation, prophesying a return to Egyptianism in which the religious difficulties will disappear in some new solution, preaching, too, a moral reform with emphasis on social good works and an ethic of social utility. As he stands in post-Reformation Oxford, the ex-Dominican has behind him the great ruins of the medieval past, and he deplores the destruction of the good works of those others, the predecessors, and the contempt for their philosophy, their philanthropy, and their magic.

> Where is there such a combination as this of religious toleration, emotional linkage with the medieval past, emphasis on good works for others, and imaginative attachment to the religion and symbolism of the Egyptians? The only answer to this question that I can this of is – in Freemasonry, with its mythical link with the medieval masons, its toleration, its philanthropy, and its Egyptian symbolism. Freemasonry does not appear in England as a recognisable institution until early in the seventeenth century, but it certainly had predecessors, antecedents, traditions of some kind going back much earlier, though this is a most obscure subject. We are fumbling in the dark here, among strange mysteries, but one cannot help wondering whether it might have been among the spiritually dissatisfied in England, who perhaps heard in

Bruno's 'Egyptian' message some hint of relief, that the strains of the Magic Flute [a euphemism for Freemasonry in reference to Mozart's Masonic-Egyptian opera] were first breathed upon the air.[37]

We shall examine such a connection between the Hermetic movement and Freemasonry in later chapters. Meanwhile it very much appeared, on that awful morning of February 1600, that Bruno's hopes for a great Hermetic reformation of the world, together with his dreams of an 'Egyptian' solar city somewhere in Europe, went up in smoke along with him in the Campo dei Fiori.

Or did they?

Enter Campanella

Around the time that the firewood was being heaped at Bruno's feet in Rome, another rebellious monk with much the same sense of mission was tried in Naples by the Inquisition and thrown in a dungeon. His name was Tommaso Campanella, the future author of *Civitas Solis*.

According to Frances Yates:

Tommaso Campanella was the last of the line of Italian Renaissance philosophers, of whom Giordano Bruno was the last but one. Like Bruno, Campanella was a magician-philosopher, in the line of the Renaissance Magi descending from Ficino. Campanella is known to have practiced Ficinian magic up to the end of his life. Like Bruno, too, Campanella was a Magus with a mission. This huge man ... had colossal confidence in himself as in touch with the cosmos and destined to lead a universal magico-religious reform. Unlike Bruno, Campanella was not burned at the stake, though he was several times tortured and spent more than twenty-seven years of his life in prison. Yet – also unlike Bruno – Campanella very nearly succeeded in bringing off the project of magical reform within a Catholic framework, or, at least, in interesting a number of very important people in it.[38]

But Yates could have been wrong on one important point. As we shall see in Chapter Twelve, it is possible that Tommaso Campanella did much more than 'nearly' succeed in 'bringing off' the magical reform.

We think that he may have succeeded even beyond Giordano Bruno's wildest dreams ...

Campanella spent the rest of his life trying to find the contemporary representative of the Roman Empire who would build his 'City of the Sun' ... In 1634, Campanella went to France, and transferred his whole scheme ... [to] the French Monarchy ...

Frances Yates, *Consideration on Bruno and Campanella on the French Monarchy*

Man lives in a double world: according to the mind he is contained by no physical space and by no walls, but at the same time he is in heaven and on earth, in Italy, in France, in America, wherever the mind's thrust penetrates and extends by understanding, seeking, mastering. But indeed according to the body he exists not except in only so much space as is least required, held fast in prison and in chains to the extent that he is not able to be in or to go to the place attained by his intellect and will, nor to occupy more space than defined by the shape of his body; while with the mind he occupies a thousand worlds.

Tommaso Campanella, *Metafisica*

CHAPTER TWELVE

ENVISIONING THE HERMETIC CITY

G iordano Bruno and Tommaso Campanella were both born in southern Italy – the former in 1548, the latter in 1568. Both entered the Dominican order at a young age. Both men had passionate and outspoken personalities. Both detested Aristotle and both were in continuous trouble with the Catholic Church. Both ultimately came to see themselves as Hermetic magi. And both, in their own ways, changed the world.

Campanella entered the Dominicans in 1583, when he was 15, but went absent without leave six years later in 1589. He settled in Naples where his first book, *Philosophia sensibus demonstrata* ('Philosophy Demonstrated by the Senses') was published in 1591. Its contents annoyed the Church but since the book did not contain sufficient grounds to justify a trial for heresy, charges were trumped up. Found guilty of harbouring a demonic familiar under the nail of his little finger, and denounced for showing a contemptuous attitude to the Church's power of excommunication, he was imprisoned for several months in 1592 at the Dominican convent in Naples.[1]

After his release later that year Campanella made his way to Padua. There in 1593 he was accused of sodomy (an indictment frequently cast at those the Inquisition wished to tarnish) but acquitted. Clearly a marked man by this point he was soon charged with other heretical acts: writing a sonnet against Christ; possessing a book of magic; and not accepting the rule and doctrine of the Church. Rather gravely he was also accused of debating matters concerning the Christian faith with a 'Judaiser' – who had lapsed from Christianity – without having denounced the man to the Inquisition.[2]

In February 1594 Campanella underwent his first bout of torture at the Inquisition's hands. He was tortured again, more severely, in July the same year and his case was handed over to Rome. On 11 October 1594 he was flung into the same dungeons as Bruno – but apparently not the same cell for there is no record of the two meeting there. Released seven months later in May 1595 while his case was being determined, Campanella was found to be in poor health and suffering from hernia, sciatica, consumption and partial paralysis.[3] He was rearrested in December 1596, imprisoned again, released in January 1597, rearrested in March 1597 and imprisoned again until December 1597 – on the latter occasion in the Inquisition's worst prison in Rome. His release came after he had abjured his heresies, accepted the prohibition of all his books, and agreed to reside for the remainder of his life in his native province of Calabria to the south of Naples.[4]

A new sort of republic and a heavenly city

It was not Campanella's destiny to live out his days quietly in Calabria. No sooner had he arrived home in July 1598 than he became embroiled in disputes with the local authorities. His writing began to take on a political tinge and also to hint that he possessed prophetic powers – given biblical sanction by Saint Paul in I Corinthians 14:31: 'For ye shall all prophesy one by one, that all may learn, and all may be comforted.'

What Campanella seemed to be prophesying, however – a revolution in Calabria against the authority of the kingdom of Naples[5] – did not comfort the Church. 'It occurred to me,' he wrote early in 1599, 'that revolution ought to happen soon.' To confirm this he consulted 'several astrologers' and they agreed 'that political revolution ought to occur for us.'[6] Elsewhere definitely with more in mind than just Calabria, he predicted:

> If a general transformation should impend for us, certainly it will happen on a crucial date, thus in the next seven-year period following the year 1600.[7]

Between February and April 1599 Campanella became an increasingly strident public preacher using the pulpit to forecast the imminence of 'grave upheavals' and apocalyptic events.[8] He began to attract a popular following amongst all social classes in Calabria, including powerful noblemen, and with incredible rapidity found himself at the centre of exactly what he had prophesied – a revolutionary conspiracy. He and his co-conspirators even planned to enlist the services of the Ottoman Turkish fleet in their rebellion and entered into negotiations to this end.[9]

But the uprising was doomed from the start, beset by poor coordination and grandiose but muddled objectives. At the political level these objectives involved the establishment of something very much ahead of its time, described by Campanella's biographer, Professor John Headley, as 'a new

THE MASTER GAME

sort of republic'.[10] Since it was to have been run along egalitarian principles and guided by benevolent scientist-priests,[11] we are reminded, irresistibly, of the actual conditions that the Cathar *perfecti* had succeeded in fostering in Occitania in the late 12th century before the Albigensian Crusades.[12] Additionally Campanella set out what sounds like a manifesto for the Hermetic idea of 'building the City of the Sun' in his proposed republic:

> And although some Fathers sustain ... that only in heaven will be realised the reconciled future community, nevertheless [others], with whom I agree, allow for a literal interpretation according to which *some sort of prelude of the heavenly city is already to be realised on earth.*[13] [Emphasis added]

This idea of building on earth an imperfect replica or 'prelude' of the City of God, the City of Heaven, the City of the Sun – or any one of a number of other celestial cities – is as old as the ancient Egyptian *Pyramid Texts* (roughly 2300 BC) as we saw in Chapter Nine. It is also, we know, central to the agenda of the Hermetic Texts (roughly 100 BC–AD 300). It was to become the dominant obsession of Campanella's life which, partly due to luck, and partly to his own resilience and quick-wittedness, did not end over a slow fire when his Calabrian 'revolution' failed.

In an insane world only the mad are sane

In August 1599 two defectors gave the conspiracy away. Campanella fled but was captured and imprisoned on 13 September in the castle at Squillace. At the end of October 1599 he was herded together with 155 of his co-conspirators into four galleys sailing for Naples. On arrival at the port of Naples sixteen of the prisoners were hanged – four from the yardarm of each of the galleys. Two more were ceremoniously slaughtered by quartering (being torn into four parts) on the wharf.[14]

As the mind behind the proposed revolutionary new republic with its sky-city to be built on earth, and as a man who had already come several times to the attention of the Inquisition, Campanella was now in imminent danger. One of several clerics to have participated in the conspiracy, he was investigated by a tribunal of inquisitors specially-appointed by Pope Clement VIII on 11 January 1600. The tribunal at once requested and was granted permission to use certain kinds of torture including week-long periods of underground isolation and sensory deprivation, as well as a nasty technique called the *polledro* that was 'designed to rupture veins and tissue'[15] without actually drawing blood.

After some weeks a partial confession was extracted from Campanella to the effect that he had indeed wanted to create a new sort of republic. But he realised that his best defence to the charges against him was to pretend to have been insane all along and thus not responsible for his actions. To help convince the Inquisition of this it seems that on 2 April 1600 he set fire to the contents of his cell.[16]

Three interrogations in quick succession, all accompanied by torture, followed on 17, 18 and 20 May 1600. Through these, and for the next 12 months of recurrent agonies, Campanella faultlessly maintained his charade of insanity. Then at the end of May 1601 an order was received from Rome requiring the inquisitors to prove once and for all whether he was really mad or just feigning madness – and to do so by means of a terrible torture device called *la veglia*, 'the awakener'. Campanella could stop the excruciating pain it would inflict upon him at any time simply by admitting that his madness was feigned. In that case he would be burnt at the stake as an impenitent heretic. If on the other hand he could withstand its pains for 40 hours then he was to be judged legally insane. This would mean that whatever else might happen to him, he could not be burnt by the Inquisition.[17]

Beating the awakener

Campanella's life-or-death duel with 'the awakener' took place on 4–5 June 1601 in the dungeons of Castel Nuovo, one of the great Neapolitan prisons.[18] The peculiar and horrible cunning of this torture, as Professor Headley describes, is that:

> The victim is suspended in such a way that only his arms and shoulder muscles prevent his body from coming to rest on a set of wooden spikes; eventually, however, he tires and must allow the spikes to gash his buttocks and thighs until he can once more raise himself. Thus between these positions he must move back and forth.[19]

It seems that several times during the hours of unremitting suffering that he endured – his diligent inquisitors taking notes all the while – Campanella cried out incoherently and uttered strange, usually meaningless phrases as though delirious: 'ten white horses'; 'I am slaughtered'; 'Enthrone and shut up'. In the midst of all this, pointing out that his body was plainly ruined and likely to die, his torturers suggested he should give thought to the salvation of his soul. He somehow found the energy and will to yell hoarsely back a four-word statement of his core belief:

The soul is immortal![20]

This was a belief that he shared with the Hermetic and Gnostic sages of ancient Alexandria, and with the Cathars. The same belief would also later be taken up and trumpeted by the French Revolution as we saw in Chapter One.

Ten hours passed, then 20, then 30. Finally, writes Professor Headley:

> After 40 hours, near death, yet spiritually unbroken, his simulation of madness undiscovered, our prisoner was cut down. According to canon law his insanity had been established; therefore he could not be executed.[21]

Campanella's jailer, who became his personal friend, records that as he lifted the broken body from the embrace of 'the awakener' to carry him back to his cell the supposed madman whispered the following question hoarsely in his ear:

> Did they really think that I would be enough of a blockhead to speak?[22]

The first European celebrity

He had escaped the fire, but he still remained very much in the frying pan. Legally mad or not, he was sentenced to life imprisonment in the dungeons of Naples without any hope of parole.

After everything he had already been through, such a grim prospect would have killed a lesser man but somehow the indomitable Campanella refused to abandon optimism and fade away. Instead, though he was kept for many years in a damp, dark, subterranean cell, he constantly made use of his brilliant mind. He composed poetry – some of which he managed to write down himself, some of which he dictated – and wrote countless letters to influential figures around Europe who he hoped might have the power to set him free. Most extraordinary of all, he somehow also managed to produce his great philosophical work *Civitas Solis* ('*The City of the Sun*'), with its magical 'natural religion' and its scientist-priests ruled by one of their number called 'Sun'. Not only that but Campanella successfully arranged to have the completed manuscript smuggled out of prison by one of his loyal disciples – a certain Tobias Adami, who we will meet again in Chapter Thirteen. Though it stirred great interest, and is widely recognised by historians of ideas as the inspiration for many of the great utopian schemes of the 17th and 18th centuries, no scholar seems yet to have seriously considered the possibility that Campanella's *Civitas Solis* could ever have been much more than just an idea – let alone that someone might actually have attempted to build it. Yet it is precisely this possibility that we intend to pursue.

Civitas Solis was by no means Campanella's only full-length work during his imprisonment. It is the most important, but much of his other output also proved to be exciting and provocative intellectual fare. All things considered his achievements were prodigious and after a little more than quarter of a century had passed, aged over 60 – and despite his sentence to perpetual imprisonment without parole – Campanella did win back his liberty. The final decade of his confinement until his release, first into house-arrest in 1627 and then at last to freedom in 1629, was spent in increasing comfort as mysterious friends in high places lobbied on his behalf.[23] Even before graduating to house-arrest he was already being allowed to hold tutorials, give full-scale lectures, and receive visiting VIPs in his cell – many of whom arrived with copies of his books which he would graciously autograph for them. He managed to transform himself, in a sense, into the Nelson Mandela of the Renaissance, 'one of the sights to see if visiting Naples', as John Headley puts it:

> Campanella had not only survived; he had become possibly the first European celebrity.[24]

After gaining his freedom in 1629, Campanella stayed for some years in Italy, much of the time in Rome. There he was drawn into the circle of the French ambassador, François de Noailles. In 1634 came reports of another uprising in the Naples area led by a certain Tommaso Pignatelli, once a disciple of Campanella. When captured Pignatelli wrongfully accused his former master of involvement in the conspiracy, placing him in immediate jeopardy of arrest. Now 66 years old, and understandably phobic about any idea of a return to prison, Campanella sought refuge in the French embassy. Soon afterwards, disguised and using the ambassador's personal carriage, he was smuggled out of Italy into France.[25]

France update: murders and plots

Things had changed in France since Giordano Bruno had enjoyed protection there. Henry III had died in 1589 a year after his domineering mother, Catherine de'Medici, and the throne had passed to Henry of Navarre, now crowned Henry IV of France. As we saw in Chapter Ten, Henry of Navarre, who belonged to the powerful Bourbon family, was a Protestant and had converted to Catholicism in 1593 in order to neutralise those who opposed his coronation as king of France. But not everyone was convinced of Henry's sincerity in this all-too-convenient 'conversion'. Certainly Bruno had not been – although his own theory, stated during his trial, was that Henry of Navarre was from the outset a Catholic at heart:

> When I praised the King of Navarre, I did not praise him because he was an adherent of the heretics [Protestants], but for the reason that ... he was not otherwise a heretic, but that he lived as a heretic from desire of ruling.[26]

Among those who most doubted Henry IV's 'conversion' were the Jesuits – the 'Society of Jesus', founded by Saint Ignatius of Loyola a century or so previously – whom the king had, in fact, distrusted all his life. 'They will kill me one day', he is reported to have confided in his close friends, 'I can see that they are putting all their resources into my death.'[27]

Sure enough, on 14 May 1610, Henry IV was assassinated by a religious fanatic, François Ravaillac. The official story told by the Church was that even under the most persuasive torture, Ravaillac had insisted that there were no accomplices to the crime and that he had acted entirely on his own initiative. But many, especially the Protestant Huguenots, believed that he had been put up to the murder by the Jesuits.

Others went so far as to suspect the involvement of Henry IV's Catholic queen, Marie de'Medici. Their marriage had been famously unhappy. It was also well known, and obviously suspicious, that barely two months before the assassination Marie had persuaded her husband to make her regent of France should he suffer an untimely death. Her official coronation as regent occurred on 13 May and Henry was murdered less than 24 hours later.[28] The coincidence was alarming, to say the least. But nothing could be proved against Marie and the blame, rightly or wrongly, fell entirely on the wretched Ravaillac. He suffered the ultimately penalty for regicide: first to be tortured with red-hot pincers, then seethed in hot oil, and finally, still alive, to be ripped apart by four farm horses tethered to his arms and legs.

The low libido of Louis XIII

Henry IV's eldest son Louis – the future Louis XIII – was only nine years old when his father was assassinated and Marie de'Medici's position as his regent was legally unassailable. He was crowned king in 1614 when he reached the required minimum age of 13 but was at first entirely dominated by his ambitious mother. He gradually began to assert his authority and in 1631, at the age of 30, he at last took full control of his throne and had Marie de'Medici banished forever from France.

Louis XIII had been married to the Spanish Infanta Anne of Austria, daughter of Philip III of Spain, when they were both only 14 years old, and the marriage remained unconsummated for many years. Of a very curious nature and disposition, Louis was more interested in his hobbies of repairing locks and making jams than in having sex with his wife. It was clear that the young man was very much unlike his father, Henry IV, who had seduced so many women during his short reign that it had earned him the nickname of *Le Vert Galant* ('the Green Gallant'), 17th century French slang for 'sexy'.

Louis' low libido wasn't the only problem. It was also obvious that he just plainly *disliked* his Spanish wife, even though she was openly affectionate to him, and perhaps even loved him. According to French historian Jean Duché, things had deteriorated so much that on a cold night in January 1619 Louis practically had to be dragged out of his own bed by leading courtiers and taken forcibly to the queen's chamber in order finally to consummate his marriage.[29] Two years later the queen – almost miraculously one could say in such circumstances – was found to be pregnant. Unfortunately she suffered an accident in the Louvre Palace and miscarried. The king's peculiar response to this was not sympathy but fury and he seems to have became even more reluctant to perform his marital duties after this tragedy.

As the years went by the desperation of the young and warm-blooded queen became so pronounced that she sought some affection by causally flirting with the dashing and very handsome Duke of Buckingham, the British ambassador in Paris. Rumours reached the ears of Louis XIII that his wife was having an affair with the duke, which in those days was an act of treason punishable by death. But being a very devoted and strict Catholic, it is unlikely that the queen would have taken such a risk. At any rate, and luckily for her, the king was persuaded of her innocence. And so, by the time Tommaso Campanella arrived in Paris 1634, a dark, cold and solemn mood had fallen over the royal couple, and everyone by then had given up on seeing them produce an heir for the Bourbon dynasty.

But then, as if by magic, something rather wonderful and strange happened …

Brief excursion to some buried Egyptian treasures

Since time immemorial a certain glamour of magic and mystery always surrounded the kings of France – whose origins were steeped in fabulous legends and myths. At the root of these were three successive royal houses, some even say races, known as the *Merovingians*, the *Carolingians* and the *Capetians*. All were bound by a very ancient Teutonic law, the so-called *Salic Law*, introduced by the Salian Franks who had invaded Gaul in the fifth century AD.

This *Salic Law* had been formalised by Clovis, the founder of the *Merovingian* dynasty, and was later repromulgated by the legendary Charlemagne, Carolus Magnus, founder of the *Carolingian* dynasty and first emperor of the Holy Roman Empire. The *Capetian* dynasty was founded in AD 987 when Hugh Capet became king of France. And through some oblique and rather dubious historical logic, the *Valois* and the *Bourbon* families also regarded themselves as linked, if not by blood then 'spiritually', to these ancient roots and, more directly, to the Capetians. The Capetian bloodline ended in 1328 with the death of Charles the Fair. The latter had left no sons or even brothers to succeed him and thus the throne of France had gone to his cousin, Philip of Valois, known as Philip VI 'the Fortunate'.[30]

In 1653 a mysterious treasure-trove was unearthed at Tournai (today part of Belgium), where the ancient Merovigian kings had set their capital. The discovery caused quite a stir at the time because the artefacts, mostly small items of gold and bronze, were believed to be from the tomb of King Childeric (c. AD 460), the father of Clovis. We note with interest that amongst the artefacts recovered was a golden Apis bull, a small statue of Isis and, in another nearby find at Saint-Brice, dozens of golden bees. In ancient Egyptian myths bees were the tears of the sun-god Ra while the hieroglyphic symbol of the bee was part of the royal titulary of the pharaohs (as in 'He of the Sedge and the Bee').[31] Interesting too is the fact that the Egyptian character of these artefacts was correctly identified by savants at this 17th century French court who went on to suggest a connection between the Merovingian dynasty and the Isis-Serapis solar cults of ancient Egypt.[32]

Predicting a Capetian miracle

Tommaso Campanella arrived at the French court in 1634. This was a full 20 years after the marriage of Louis XIII to the Spanish Infanta Anne of Austria and the royal couple remained without child. The prospects of a continuation of the Bourbon dynasty looked dim and it was the general view that there was not going to be a 'Capetian miracle' – the mocking term being used by this point to describe the likelihood of a royal successor.

The big problem, and the source of all sorts of rumours and gossip at court, was that Louis XIII flatly refused to have any sexual contact with his wife. The king was thought (variously) to be impotent, simply not interested in women, or perhaps a homosexual.[33] Reinforcing the latter speculation was the rather bizarre relationship, bordering on romantic love, which Louis was now publicly enjoying with his personal valet, the young Marquis of Cinq-Mars. Further complicating the matter, the king was unwell and suffered from tuberculosis. Last but not least, and notwithstanding the business with his (male) valet, he was also romantically in love with a young and very pious lady, Mlle Louise de la Fayette, who had entered a convent in Paris. Somewhat reminiscent of the pure Platonic love once promoted by the troubadours of Occitania, this affair of the king's had no sexual element to it whatsoever but was felt at court to be a distraction from any potential sexual encounters he might otherwise have had with the queen!

The queen herself, of course, was the one who felt most strongly about the matter. Hearing that the famous prophet and magus Tommaso Campanalla had recently arrived in France, she summoned him to her side. He had been highly recommended to her by Cardinal Richelieu, and she wanted to have his prophetic opinion on the matter of the succession.

There was nothing unusual about this. The queen and Richelieu, like most intelligent and highly-placed people of their epoch, were much influenced by prophetic and astrological predictions. Many European monarchs of the 16th and 17th centuries are known to have had their personal astrologers who were consulted regularly on matters of state, of marriage and even of war. Indeed, through intermediaries, Richelieu had already consulted Campanella on many occasions and, no doubt, the nerve-racking question of the succession must have been often raised and discussed.[34] The two men were to become close confidantes with Campanella dedicating a number of his new works to Richelieu and calling for the cardinal's assistance to 'build the City of the Sun' as expounded in the *Civitas Solis* which had just been reissued in Paris.[35]

Brokered by Richelieu, Campanella's meeting with the queen came quickly and, to the court's amazement, the magus boldly predicted that soon the French monarchy would be blessed with an heir.[36] The heir, moreover, would be a male child who, like the very Sun itself, would illumine the whole world and usher in a glorious and golden era for humanity:

> Everyone will acknowledge a single Father and a single God and love will unite them all ... Kings and nations ... will gather in a city which will be named *Heliaca*, The City of the Sun, which will be built by this illustrious hero [the future 'solar' king of France] ...[37]

As Jean Meyer delicately puts it, Campanella had taken a very dangerous, high-stakes gamble by proclaiming the imminent birth of a male heir to the French throne. If he were proved right he stood to gain much, if wrong his reputation would be ruined.

God sent

A flash thunderstorm over the city of Paris on a cold winter's day was to play in Campanella's favour, and his prophetic gamble would pay off. For early one afternoon in December 1637, Louis XIII left his small weekend residence at Versailles and made his way to the Château de Saint-Maur, where he intended to spend the night. *En route* he decided to make a stop in Paris at the convent of St. Marie on the Rue Saint-Antoine, where Louise de la Fayette, his platonic and very pious lady friend, lived.

With his bodyguards waiting outside, and an old nun serving as chaperone, the king and Sister Louise de la Fayette sat in a secluded part of the convent talking in whispers. When finally night fell, the king decided it was time to go, but he was informed by the captain of the guards, a man called Guitaut, who was deeply devoted to the queen, that there was a violent storm outside, making the trip to Saint-Maur imprudent. Guitaut strongly advised the king that it would be safer for him to spend the night at the Louvre Palace which was much closer.[38]

There was one small problem. The queen had her private apartments at the Louvre, and the king did not relish the prospect of spending the night in her company. But as the storm grew more violent, and with Guitaut constantly reminding the king that the queen would most certainly be overjoyed to receive him at the Louvre, Louis had not much choice by to agree. A guard was sent ahead to warn Anne of this wonderful opportunity that was presenting itself. A candlelit supper was quickly arranged, and a spare bed brought to the queen's chambers. The loyal Captain Guitaut had made sure that the news was sent to all the convents and churches in Paris to pray in unison for the long awaited event …

Sure enough, exactly nine months later, on 5 September 1638, Anne of Austria gave birth to a male child who was christened Louis – the future Louis XIV. As though as a reminder that this great miracle had been prophesied by Tommaso Campanella, it so happened that 5 September was also Campanella's 70th birthday. Now amidst great jubilations and prayers of thanks, the rapturous and very grateful queen summoned the magus and asked him to cast the natal horoscope for her son – who was already spoken of as the *Dieudonné*, the 'God-sent'. We know that Campanella paid at least two visits to the queen's private chamber, was present when she breastfed the infant, and was even given the immense honour of holding the future king in his arms.[39] Finally, after thoroughly examining the child, he announced, somewhat underwhelmingly, that the reign of Louis XIV would be long, happy, and glorious.[40]

But he had more to say in his Latin eclogue for Louis XIV, which appeared in print in January 1639.[41] Modelled on the messianic Fourth Eclogue of Virgil (which had prophesied the universal rule of Augustus Caesar), Campanella's expanded prophecy leaves no doubt about the future he saw for the French monarchy and the forthcoming reign of Louis XIV. Quite simply, it was divinely ordained to bring about the great universal 'Hermetic-Christian' reform that Bruno had dreamt of, and to build the 'City of the Sun' which he, Campanella, had promoted.[42]

So it is time to ask   what did Campanella really have in mind? What type of 'solar city' was he thinking of? Was it a real city or merely a symbolic vision of some utopian reform to be ushered in by the French monarchy?

A Hermetic signature

So far we can see that Campanella had succeeded in his Hermetic mission where Bruno before him had failed. True, Bruno had managed to gain some backing from Henry III of France and even had his chance to present his own Hermetic-Egyptian vision of universal reform to the scholars in Paris and Oxford. But what it all finally amounted to had been a heap of ashes in Rome's Campo dei Fiori. Campanella, on the other hand, thanks to his more cunning temperament and greater ability to deal with complex human relationships, now held the support of the French royal couple and their powerful minister, Richelieu. This, though it came very late in his life, gave him the almost unbelievable opportunity to plant the seed of his own vision of reform right in the heart of the French monarchy. Did not Campanella once boast, asks Frances Yates, that he could 'make a City in such a wonderful way that only by looking at it all the sciences may be learned'?[43] Now at last he was in a position to make good on his pledge.

Yates quite rightly sees in Campanella 'a more successful Bruno'[44] and writes that 'it does look very much as though a torch may have passed from Bruno to Campanella.'[45] She also points up another aspect of the mystery, something far more subtle and vague, that no one else seems to have seen before her. In her view Campanella's *Civitas Solis* was 'ultimately Egyptian in origin':

It is now clear that to the Roman ideal of universal empire returning in a new golden age, to the Platonic ideal of a state in which philosophers ruled, Campanella added a third ideal, that of the Egyptian state kept intact and eternal by priestly magic. The Sun ruler of the City of the Sun is both priest and king, supreme in both the spiritual and the temporal domains, in short he is Hermes Trismegistus, priest, philosopher and king. Campanella was thus in no sense a liberal revolutionary. His ideal was an all powerful theocracy like that of Egypt, so powerful that it regulated by scientific magic the celestial influences and through them the whole life of the people. Its apparently liberal side is that it encouraged scientific enquiry and invention ... but this advanced Solarian science was in the hands of the supreme priesthood and regulated by it – as in ancient Egypt.[46]

In our view it is not a coincidence that the 'liberal revolutionary' aspects of Campanella's utopia – to be based on the principles of truth, justice and brotherly love, and characterised by freedom of speech, equal rights for women, good health care, and universal education for children[47] – had already begun to be realised in Occitania hundreds of years before.[48] Nor is it likely to be an accident, as we saw in Chapter One, that they were to appear again, linked to the work of Voltaire, Rousseau and other leading lights of those times, in the philosophical and intellectual undercurrents of the 1789 French Revolution.

The strangest and most striking aspect of Campanella's scheme, however, and the one that Yates particularly draws attention to, is its Egyptianism. The Hermetic magus cleverly grafted it onto the French monarchy in the person of the future Louis XIV, thus ensuring it's acceptability within the existing systems of Europe. But at the same time there is no doubt that what Campanella ultimately had in mind was a revival of the ancient Egyptian 'golden age' when a 'solar' king and his wise and benevolent 'scientific-priesthood' had regulated and governed the land.

Were such thinking to be carried through to its logical conclusion then we would expect Louis XIV to have left a Hermetic signature on the landscape of France. We would expect him, in short, as Campanella had prophesied in the Latin eclogue, to have built, or to have attempted to build, the 'City of the Sun'.

Hidden magical springs

Of course it's always possible that the 'City of the Sun' was just a metaphor for an ideal type of society, rather than something that was intended to be realised in bricks and mortar. Yet there is much in Campanella's scheme, and in the Hermetic teachings, that that leads us to think otherwise. Most significant is the thoroughly 'astral' character of his model which constantly leverages the intimate feedback mechanisms between sky and ground, above and below, that are envisaged in the Hermetic texts.

The broad plan of Campanella's 'City of the Sun' as he sets it out in his great work *Civitas Solis*, looks like a diagram of the Copernican solar system. At its centre, on a raised mound, is a perfectly circular temple of gigantic size (representing the Sun) with its dome supported on soaring pillars. Ringing the temple are the seven concentric divisions of the city (one for each of the orbits of the then known planets) separated by walls penetrated by gates facing the cardinal directions – north, south, east and west. Two axial roadways traverse the city entirely, crossing, as it were, at the centre, one running due north-south and the other due east-west.[49]

Within the vast 'Temple of Sun' lying at the heart of all this geometrical perfection Campanella's text envisages an altar on which is to be found nothing except two huge globes, one showing 'all the heaven' and the other 'all the earth'.[50] On the ceiling of the dome are depicted 'all the greatest stars of heaven, with their names and the powers which they have over things below'; these representations are in correspondence with the globes on the altar. Seven eternal lamps also hang in the temple, called after the seven planets. The outer wall of the temple bears a representation of 'every star in its order'.[51]

Images and writings are inscribed on both the outer and inner faces of each of the seven sets of concentric walls and these seem primarily aimed to educate and inspire the citizenry. They include more world maps, cultural geographies of different peoples, representations of seas and rivers, knowledge about the animal, vegetable and mineral kingdoms, and images of 'inventors of sciences and laws' – an eclectic list including Hermes Trismegistus (in his Romanised disguise as Mercury), Jupiter (Zeus-Amun in the Graeco-Egyptian pantheon of Alexandria), the Prophet Muhammad, Jesus Christ and his 12 apostles, and, last but not least, Osiris.[52]

In summary, observes Frances Yates, the city that Campanella wanted, and prophesied that Louis XIV would in some way build, was to be 'a complete reflection of the world as governed by the laws of natural magic in dependence on the stars.'[53] It was to be carefully arranged 'so as to be right with the stars' – the source of 'all its happiness, health and virtue.'[54] Its ruler was to be priest who was to be 'head in all things, both spiritual and temporal',[55] while its governance was to be in the hands of great men who could understand and use natural magic: 'inventors, moral teachers, miracle workers, religious leaders, in short, Magi ...'[56] They were to be selected according to their ability, in the words of Marcilio Ficino, to 'draw down the life of heaven' for the benefit of mankind.[57]

The intellectual origins of Campanella's grand scheme, Yates shows, are not to be sought (except perhaps superficially) in contemporary or near contemporary works he might have known such as Thomas More's *Utopia*. 'To find the ultimate source,' she argues, 'one must dig deeper and uncover those hidden magical springs from which the Renaissance was fed.' She means the Hermetic texts and singles out particularly the *Picatrix* with its magical city of Adocentyn, reminding us that it featured:

> ... a castle with four gates, on which were images into which Hermes Trismegistus had introduced spirits. Compare this with the four gates and roads of the City of the Sun. On the summit of the castle was a lighthouse which flashed over the city the colours of the seven planets. Compare this with the seven planetary lamps always burning in the City of the Sun ... In the passage in *Picatrix* describing the City of Adocentyn Hermes Trismegistus is also said to have built a temple to the Sun ...[58]

In other words, Yates concludes, 'the deepest, the primary layer of influence behind the *City of the Sun* is, I suggest, Hermetic; and its first model, to which many later influences have been superadded, is, I believe, the magical city of Adocentyn described in the *Picatrix*, and the description in the *Asclepius* of the religion of the Egyptians.'[59]

In Chapter Eight we quoted at the length the famous *Lament* from the *Asclepius* in which we hear of the destruction by inimical forces of the magical, natural religion of the Egyptians, and its apparent disappearance from the earth for a long interval of time. But the reader will recall that the *Asclepius* also makes the prophecy: that the persecuted religion will one day be restored in 'a reformation of all good things, and a restitution most holy and most reverent of nature itself.' Most important of all, this restoration and restitution are to be triggered by the founding of a City aligned with the Sun.[60]

Could Louis have been influenced by Campanella to carry such thinking through to its logical conclusion and leave a Hermetic signature in the architecture of France? If so the old magus must somehow have found a way to reach out to him from beyond the grave – for he died in Paris on 21 May 1639, eight and a half months after the young 'Sun King' was born.

In matters of influence, however, as we shall see (and as the Hermetic texts themselves advise), it is best to presume that 'nothing is imposible.'[61]

CHAPTER THIRTEEN

THE INVISIBLE BROTHERHOOD

[Cardinal] *Richelieu did not receive the Rosicrucians, but when eleven years later Campanella came to Paris he had the powerful cardinal's support – an indication of Campanella's success in switching his ideas ... into channels acceptable to the powers that be.*
Frances Yates, Giordano Bruno and the Hermetic Tradition

The Rosicrucians, do they exist? Are you one? ...
Frances Yates, The Rosicrucian Enlightenment

In 1623, during the reign of Louis XIII and 11 years before Tommasso Campanella arrived at the French court, a subversive organisation made its presence known in Paris. Stealthily, by night, eye-catching placards were put up on the walls of public buildings and in all the main streets of the city, bearing the following announcement:

> We, being deputies of the principal College of the Brothers of the Rose Cross, are making a visible and invisible stay in this city through the Grace of the Most High, towards whom turn the hearts of the Just. We show and teach without books or marks how to speak all languages of the countries where we wish to be, and to draw men from error and death.[1]

Another poster contained a variant of the message with more specifically religious overtones:

> We deputies of the College of the Rose Cross, give notice to all those who wish to enter our Society and Congregation, that we will teach them the most perfect knowledge of the Most High, in the name of whom we are

today holding an assembly, and we will make them from visible, invisible, and from invisible, visible ...[2]

As it had certainly been intended to do, the poster campaign caused quite a stir in Paris. Contemporary reports speak of a 'hurricane' of rumour at the news that the mysterious Rose Cross fraternity – already believed to be active in Germany – had now come to France.[3] Pamphlets and further rumours (although of a rather concrete and specific nature) had it that the core of the brotherhood was formed by 36 'Invisible Ones' – implying that they were veiled, incognito, disguised – who were dispersed throughout the world in six groups of six.[4] They held their assemblies at the time of the summer solstice, the longest day of the year. And although the language of the pamphlets and posters seemed religious and obviously Christian it was said that adepts of the fraternity 'swore to abjure Christianity and all the rights and sacraments of the Church.'[5]

To understand the sort of moral panic, accompanied in many cases by a thrill of illicit excitement, which was generated by hints and rumours like these we need to keep in mind the general condition of Europe in 1623. For more than a century, bloody religious conflicts between Catholics and Protestants had been tearing the peoples of the Continent apart creating a climate of overwhelming fear and suspicion, and now the great struggle in central Europe that was to become the Thirty Years War had just begun, further inflaming the deep hatreds and passions of the time. So it was natural that everyone, particularly the court and the government of France, would feel disturbed and even a little threatened by these announcements that a clandestine brotherhood had set up shop in Paris and intended to save the people from 'error and death'.

Who was behind all this provocative propaganda? Who was responsible? Who were the 'invisible' people calling themselves brothers of the Rose Cross?

Although a mass of material supposedly stemming from these original 'Rosicrucians' has come to light, scholars still debate such questions today and have proposed no definitive answers. All that is clear – whoever they were – is that the self-styled 'invisible' brothers must have been cut from very much the same cloth as men like Bruno and Campanella. Though their methods were more guarded than those of the great Hermetic magi, they saw themselves in the same way as being endowed with special magical powers, or knowledge, or 'science' that could be used to bring about a religious and intellectual reform of the world.

The Rosicrucian Manifestos

If a secret society is successful – which means, by definition, that it is difficult to detect in its own epoch – then we may suppose that its traces are unlikely to be easily found by the historians of a later epoch. If we take the Rosicrucians at face value as a secret society, therefore, it follows that we really can't say for sure how long they may have existed undetected before they declared themselves. All we know is that the first direct and definite references to them were made in Germany during the 20 years before the 1623 poster campaign in Paris. From this early activity comes almost everything we know, or think we know, about the 'Invisible College' of the Rose Cross.

The name 'Rosicrucian' is derived from 'Christian Rosenkreutz', i.e. Christian Rose Cross or Rosy Cross, the hero of two small books, deep and most unusual in their contents, that were first published at Cassel in Germany in the years 1614 and 1615. The full title of the first is *Fama Fraternitatis, or a Discovery of the Fraternity of the Most Noble Order of the Rosy Cross*. Scholars generally refer to it as the *Fama*. The second, published in 1615 and usually known as the *Confessio*, is titled in full: *Confessio Fraternitatis, or the Confession of the Laudible Fraternity of the Most Honourable Order of the Rosy Cross, Written to all the Learned of Europe*. These two texts amount in English translation to a total of less than 25 pages and are known collectively as the 'Rosicrucian Manifestos'.[6]

The *Fama*

The *Fama* purports to be the work of a group of Rosicrucian adepts and tells the story of 'the most godly and highly illumined Father, our Brother, C. R. [Christian Rosenkreutz], a German, the chief and original of our Fraternity,' whose aim was to bring about a 'general reformation.' It seems that as a youth this C. R. had set out on a pilgrimage to the Holy Land but had stopped on the way amongst the 'wise men of Damascus'. Receiving him 'not as a stranger but as one whom they had long expected' they showed him secret things, 'whereat he could not but mightily wonder', and taught him knowledge of physics and mathematics. C. R. was so magnetised by his studies that he lost all interest in reaching Jerusalem – his original objective – and spent three years with the Damascene sages, undergoing what sounds very much like a Hermetic initiation.[7]

Finally, with their blessing, he began to make his way westwards again. First he journeyed into Egypt. Then he 'sailed across the whole Mediterranean Sea for to come unto Fez' (Morocco). There the 'Elementary Inhabitants', members of an occult society of 'magicians, Cabalists, physicians, and philosophers … revealed unto him many of their secrets.' However the knowledge that he had learned in Damascus seems to have been superior to theirs since he judged that 'their Magia was not altogether pure … their Cabala was defiled with their religion.'[8]

After two years in Fez, Brother C. R. moved on, this time to Spain and thence into the rest of Europe. He wished to share the great wisdom he had learned in the East and to teach the wise men of the West 'the errors of our [i.e. Western] arts, and how they might be corrected … also how the faults of the Church and the whole *Philosophia Moralis* was to be amended.' However he was ridiculed and attacked by the scholars to whom he unfolded his ideas because they 'feared that their great name should be lessened.'[9] We are reminded, inevitably, of the mission of Giordano Bruno to bring about the Hermetic reform of the world.

At last Christian Rosenkreutz returned to Germany. He built a home, meditated at length about his journey and his philosophy, 'and reduced them together in a true memorial'. He also intensified his studies of mathematics and made 'many fine instruments'. After five years 'came again into his mind the wished for reformation … and unwearying, he undertook, with some few who joined with him, to attempt the same.' We hear at this point of three other bretheren – 'Brother G. V.', 'Brother J. A.', and 'Brother J. O.' – who C. R. binds 'unto himself to be faithful, diligent and secret':

> After this manner began the Fraternity of the Rose Cross; first by four persons only, and by them was made the magical language and writing, with a large dictionary, which we yet daily use to God's praise and glory, and do find great wisdom therein …[10]

Soon afterwards these four founders were joined by four others – 'Brother B.', 'Brother G.', 'Brother P. D.', and 'Brother J. A.' – 'so in all they were eight in number, all bachelors and of vowed virginity.'[11] The group then 'collected a book or volume of all which man can desire, wish or hope for' – a system of guidance which 'shall unmovably remain unto the world's end' with the power to open the eyes of the masses of all lands and to make them less passive before 'the Pope, Mohamed, scribes, artists and sophisters.'[12]

Thus prepared 'and able perfectly to discourse of secret and manifest philosophy', the eight 'separated themselves into several countries' – there to draw aside from amongst the learned those who were worthy to receive their doctrines. Like Cathar *perfecti* who were renowned for their medical skills, these Rosy Cross brothers were to work as doctors curing the sick, and were to do so free of charge. The better to disguise themselves and blend in, they were not obliged to wear any particular habit 'but therein to follow the custom of the country'. Like Cathar *perfecti* they were celibate and, again like *perfecti*, each was to seek out and work with an apprentice, 'a worthy person who, after his decease, might succeed him.'[13]

In this way generations passed until 'none of us had in any manner known anything of Brother R. C. and of his first fellow bretheren,' than could be gathered from the books of the order. There began to be doubts as to whether the true teachings of the original eight had been properly passed down. At this time, however, and by chance, one of the brothers stumbled upon the long-lost tomb of Christian Rosenkreutz himself. It turned out to be a kind of Hermetic 'Hall of Records' containing all the wisdom necessary to restore the order:

> We opened the door, and there appeared to our sight a vault of seven
> sides and corners, every side five foot broad, and the height of eight foot.[14]

A permanent light, like 'another sun' glowed 'in the upper part in the centre of the ceiling.' Instead of a tombstone the vault contained a round altar covered with a brass plate on which was engraved the following mysterious epitaph:

> This compendium of the universe I made in my lifetime to be my tomb.[15]

Beneath the brass plate was the dead body of Christian Rosenkreutz, 'a fair and wise body, whole and unconsumed.' In his hand he held a parchment book, on the final page of which was this eulogy:

> A grain buried in the breast of Jesus, C. Ros. C. sprung from the noble
> and renowned German family of R. C.; a man admitted into the mysteries
> and secrets of heaven and earth through the divine revelations, subtle
> cogitations and unwearied toil of his life. In his journeys through Arabia
> and Africa he collected a treasure [of knowledge, not gold and worldly
> riches] surpassing that of Kings and Emperors, but finding it not suitable
> for his times he kept it guarded for posterity to uncover ... He constructed
> a microcosm corresponding in all motions to the macrocosm and finally
> drew up a compendium of things past, present and to come. Then, having
> now passed the century of years, though oppressed by no disease ... but
> summoned by the Spirit of God ... he rendered up his illumined soul ...[16]

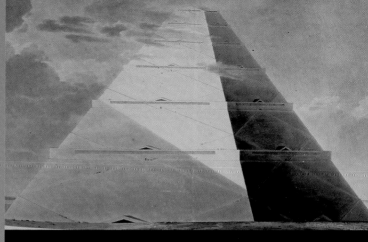

33. Pyramid project proposed by the revolutionary architect Étienne-Louis Boullée, in 1785: *Cénotaphe dans le genre égyptienne.*

32. The genie of Paris (or Liberty) on top of the Bastille Pillar. Compare to Picot's 'genie' in plate 2.

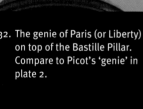

35. The glass pyramid at the Louvre.

34. The baroque 'pyramid' proposed for the Louvre for the centennial celebrations of the French Revolution of 1789. It is unlikely that I. M. Pei was unaware of this previous scheme when he designed the glass pyramid for the bicentennial in 1989. The link between the French Revolution and the 'pyramid' is, of course, the symbol of the *Être Suprême*, or 'Supreme Being', which appeared on the frontispiece of the Declaration of the Rights of Man and the Citizen in 1789 as the 'eye in the pyramid', an obvious Masonic symbol.

36. Aerial view of Paris and the Historical Axis from the Louvre to the Grande Arche. Compare the axis and the scheme to the aerial view of ancient Luxor, Egypt (see below).

OBELISK Luxor 2

Historical Axis to La Defense

26

River Seine

38. Aerial view of the Louvre and the Seine. Compare to aerial view of the Luxor temple and the Nile (see opposite). Note 'corresponding' position of obelisks in Paris and at Luxor.

37. Aerial view of the city of Luxor in Upper Egypt. Compare
the axis and general scheme to Paris (see above).

39. Aerial view of Luxor temple at Thebes. Compare to

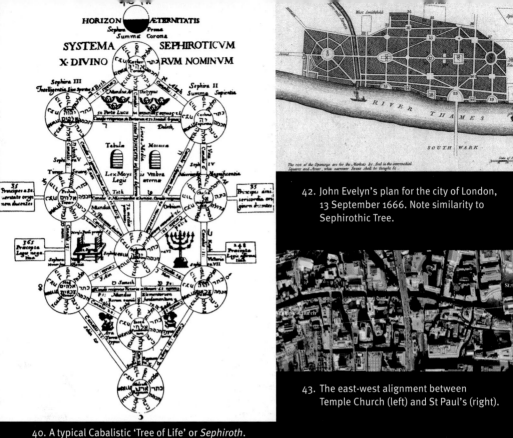

42. John Evelyn's plan for the city of London, 13 September 1666. Note similarity to Sephirothic Tree.

43. The east-west alignment between Temple Church (left) and St Paul's (right).

41. Plan proposed by Sir Christopher Wren for the city of London, 11 September 1666.

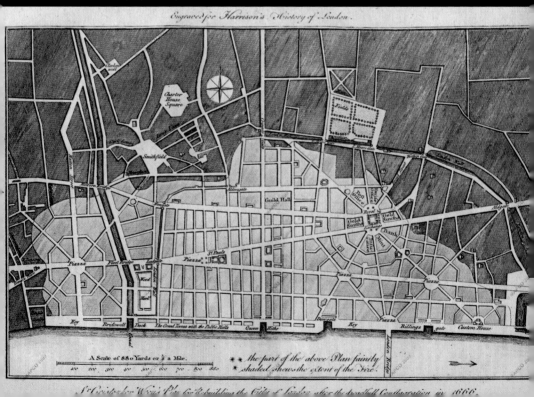

44. The obelisk of Thutmosis III on the Victoria Embankment, London, better known as 'Cleopatra's Needle'.

45. H. H. Gorringe, lecturing at a Masonic ceremony at the dedication of the New York Obelisk in 1881.

46. The alignment between St. Paul's Cathedral and Temple Church. It is clearly a deliberate scheme by Christopher Wren to 'connect', as it were, the 'new temple of Solomon' with the Knights Templar precinct in London. The hidden message is that it ghosted 'New Jerusalem' in England.

ple Church

St. Paul's Cathedral

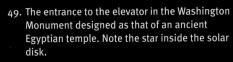

49. The entrance to the elevator in the Washington Monument designed as that of an ancient Egyptian temple. Note the star inside the solar disk.

50. Statue of George Washington in full Masonic regalia at the Washington Masonic Memorial.

47. The George Washington Masonic Memorial in Alexandria, Virginia.

48. A model of the Lighthouse of Alexandria (*Pharos*).

51. The Masonic foundation-laying ceremony for the New York Obelisk in 1880 during which the Grand Master linked Freemasonry to ancient Egypt.

52. Sun setting along the axis of Pennsylvania Avenue on 12 August, also the day of the heliacal rising of Sirius. In the reverse direction, looking east, the star would also align with the axis.

53. The interior of the Egyptian room in the Grand Lodge of Pennsylvania in Philadelphia.

54. George Washington in his Masonic outfit laying the cornerstone of the US Capitol.

55. The Freemasons of Washington, DC, parade towards the George Washington Masonic Memorial for the laying of the cornerstone.

The authors of the *Fama* claim that they 'have the knowledge of Jesus Christ' and that their philosophy 'is not a new invention':

Also our building (although one hundred thousand people have very near seen and beheld the same) shall forever remain untouched, undestroyed, and hidden from the wicked world.[17]

Finally, and in ringing tones, there comes this statement and prophecy of tremendous changes and the birth of a new order, which the Rosicrucians, with the treasures of knowledge at their disposal, stand ready to usher in:

Europe is with child and will bring forth a strong child, who shall stand in need of a great godfather's gift.[18]

The *Confessio*

Published in 1615 the *Confessio* presents itself as a sequel to the *Fama* and begins with a condemnation of 'the East and the West [meaning the pope and Muhammad] blasphemers against our Lord Jesus Christ.' It then promises that 'all learned who will make themselves known to us, and come into our brotherhood, shall find more wonderful secrets thereby than heretofore they did attain unto, and did know, or are able to believe or utter.'[19]

Using strange metaphorical language the *Confessio* next proposes what sounds like total revolution in Europe, wiping the slate clean, because 'posterity will be able only thereby to lay a new foundation and bring truth to light again.' This is argued to be preferable to endless renovations and repairs to 'the old ruinous building.'[20] The hoped for end result will be that:

... the World shall awake out of her heavy and drowsy sleep, and with an open heart, bare-headed, and bare-foot, shall merrily and joyfully meet the new arising Sun ...[21]

The text continues with an attack on the Church:

Like as the mathematician and astronomer can long before see and know the eclipses which are to come, so we may verily foreknow and foresee the darkness of obscurations of the Church ...[22]

We are told that 'the Romish seducers have vomited forth their blasphemies against Christ, and as yet do not abstain from their lies in this clear shining light.'[23] There are also repeated appeals for proper understanding of the scriptures.[24] Finally:

> We acknowledge ourselves truly and sincerely to profess Christ, condemn the Pope, addict ourselves to the true Philosophy, lead a Christian life, and daily call, entreat, and invite many more into our Fraternity, unto whom the same Light of God likewise appeareth.[25]

The *Confessio* for the first time provides the reader with the chronology within which the whole story is set: Christian Rosenkreutz is born in 1378 and lives for 106 years, dying in 1484. His tomb is rediscovered 120 years later – in other words in 1604, exactly 10 years before the publication of the *Fama*.[26]

Mystery of the Chemical Wedding

A third publication appeared in 1616 that added to the mystery of the Rosicrucian Manifestos. Its title is *The Chemical Wedding of Christian Rosenkreutz* and, like the Manifestos, it describes a secretive order which uses a red cross and red roses as its symbols.[27] Now, though, the focus has shifted to what might be called 'inner transformation' – as opposed to the social and religious transformation heralded in the Manifestos.[28]

The authors of the *Fama* and the *Confessio* have never been firmly identified. For some time, however, it has been the concensus of scholars – Frances Yates believed it to be a certainty – that the *Chemical Wedding* was the work of Johann Valentin Andreae, a young Lutheran pastor from Tübingen in Germany.[29] Recent research has begun to cast some doubt on this identification, primarily because the *Chemical Wedding* as it appeared in 1616 is distinctively different from all other surviving writings of Andreae. As the Hermetic scholar Adam McLean puts it:

> From what we know of Andreae as an orthodox and eminent Lutheran pastor and academic, it seems unlikely that he could have devised such a profoundly esoteric document, which in fact has as its basis many ideas heretical even in Protestant terms.[30]

The confusion enters in because Andreae lists a work called *The Chemical Wedding* amongst a number of short plays – 'first juvenile efforts as an author'[31] – that he wrote while studying at the University of Tübingen in 1602 and 1603. This early play has not survived. But Andreae moved in esoteric and Hermetic circles, as we shall see, and was very much involved with the nascent Rosicrucian movement of Germany,[32] so it was natural for scholars to identify his *Chemical Wedding* of 1602/3 with the anonymous *Chemical Wedding of Christian Rosenkreutz*, published in 1616. The latter contains references to the Rosicrucian Manifestos (1614/15) and to other contemporary matters and so cannot be identical to the lost 1602/3 text, but the general view is that Andreae must have updated it prior to publication.[33]

Born in 1586 Andreae would have been 17 in 1603, too young and inexperienced of the world, in our view, to have written a work as deep, dark and rich in complex symbols as *The Chemical Wedding of Christian Rosenkreutz*. By 1616, when it was published, he would have been 30 – a different matter altogether. Even so, if he was the author, he must not so much have 'updated' as completely rewritten the juvenile version of the play before bringing it out in print – for there is nothing at all of a 17-year-old boy to be seen in the finished work. And even accepting that he did completely rewrite it in his maturity, we still confront the problem of its 'heretical' undertones and its alleged incompatibility with the rest of Andreae's writings. The issue will probably never be resolved to everyone's satisfaction unless the lost manuscript of 1602/3 turns up. Meanwhile we find Adam McLean persuasive when he speculates that:

> Andreae did in fact write a version of the *Chemical Wedding*, perhaps a simple play or masque ... Some years later ... one of the 'Rosicrucian' fraternity ... with whom Andreae had some connections, might have decided to rework Andreae's early, unpublished play into the complex esoteric allegory we know today.[34]

A strange story

As to the content of the *Chemical Wedding*, there is simply not space here for us to do it justice. In English translation the printed text runs to about 90 pages, divided into seven chapters each representing a day's journey in a sort of pilgrim's progress. The narrator is Christian Rosenkreutz himself who, the reader will recall, was said in the Manifestos to have lived to the age of 106. In the *Chemical Wedding* his age must be 81 – for we know that he was born in 1378 and the story is set in the year 1459.[35]

The 'First Day' finds C. R. at his table, quietly meditating 'on the many great mysteries which the Father of Light, in his majesty, had allowed me to glimpse.'[36] We note in passing that the phrase 'Father of Light' never appears in the Christian Bible, either in the Old Testament or in the New Testament.[37] In the early centuries of the Christian era, however, it was in common usage amongst Manicheans and Gnostics as a reference to the God of Goodness, and there was a sect of Gnostic Christians whose members called themselves the 'Sons of Light'.[38]

Whilst in the depths of his meditation, C. R. is visited by the angelic, glowing, winged figure of 'a wonderfully beautiful female ... dressed all in blue, spangled like the heavens with golden stars.' She produces a 'small note', puts it on the table with a curtsey and immediately flies off into the upper atmosphere blowing loudly on a trumpet.[39] When C. R. opens the note he finds it contains an invitation to 'the wedding of the king' and a cryptic warning that he must study himself closely before deciding to accept:

If you're not clean enough, The wedding can work ill. Perjure here at your peril.[40]

What kind of wedding is it – one is inclined to ask – that can be perilous to guests who are impure or do not tell the truth? This is an early hint, one amongst many in the narrative, that we are not in any way dealing with an account of real events here, or even with pure fiction, but strictly and exclusively with what Adam McLean calls an 'esoteric allegory'. It may be said safely that the allegory of the wedding is meant to bring to mind something more of the nature of a quest or personal challenge than a 'marriage'. Very much in the same tradition as the quest for the Holy Grail, the ordeals and moral dilemmas that the guests confront over the coming 'Days', and in which they must cooperate to complete a complex alchemical operation, seem themselves to be part of a subtle process of purification and transformation.

Like the Grail Quest, the *Chemical Wedding* is often claimed as a document of esoteric Christianity. But as Adam McLean asks and observes:

Where is the Christian message? What is described seems more like an ancient 'mystery initiation' than a Christian religious experience.[41]

Still on the First Day of his quest, the octogenarian Christian Rosenkreutz does as the wedding invitation has warned him to do. He observes himself, both inwardly and outwardly, with absolute honesty and finds himself wanting:

THE MASTER GAME

The more I pondered, I could see that there was nothing in my head but a great want of sense and blindness in esoteric matters ... I also found that my physical life, outward conduct, and brotherly love towards my neighbour were far from being purged and pure enough. I was aware of fleshly desires, which aim only for reputation and worldly show, not for the well-being of others; I was always thinking how I could use my skills for my own immediate benefit, for building many splendid things, for making an everlasting name in the world, and other such materialistic thoughts ...[42]

It is interesting that the two matters for which C. R. reproaches himself are (1) his esoteric blindness and lack of inner *gnosis* and (2) his worldly and materialistic behaviour. Regardless he decides that he will attend the wedding. Dressed in a white linen coat with a blood-red belt bound crosswise across his shoulders, and wearing four red roses in his hat, he proceeds on his journey. Thus ends the First Day.

On the 'Second Day' Rosenkreutz enters a great forest and comes eventually to a clearing. There he is offered 'the choice of four paths, by all of which you may reach the royal castle, if you do not fall by the wayside.' One is short but dangerous, another long and winding – and so on. Eventually C. R. finds his way to the castle, where other guests are already gathered. A beautiful virgin appears and makes a portentous announcement reminding the guests that they are not supposed to be here unless properly prepared:

Tomorrow every one of you
Upon the balance will be weighed ...
He who dares beyond his powers
Would have done better not to come.
We wish you all the best.[43]

We will not take the reader step by step through the remaining 'Five Days' of the *Chemical Wedding*, which indeed feature (on the 'Third Day') a symbolic 'weighing of the guests' in which some are 'successful' and some are not. Varying degrees of punishment await those who prove 'too light in the balance' and the worst offenders ('who could not even outweigh a single weight') are slaughtered.[44] Many elements of this curious scene are strongly reminiscent of the stage in the afterlife journey known as the 'weighing of the soul' as it is described in the ancient Egyptian *Book of the Dead* – a text of the second millennium BC that no one in the 17th century is supposed to have been able to read. And other elements of the landscape of the *Chemical Wedding* also have ancient Egyptian resonances, to pick at random – a phoenix, the god Hermes, a royal staircase with 365 spiral steps, the 'House of the Sun', scenes of death, a rebirth ritual ('We had to drudge away on this island until we had done everything necessary for reviving the beheaded bodies'[45]), a pyramid, a pentagon, various pieces of equipment needed in the quest including a ladder, a rope and wings, an egg produced by alchemical processes, a bird that grows at miraculous speed, resurrection of the king and queen, and elevation of certain of the guests to the status of 'Knights of the Golden Stone'.

Towards the end of the 'Seventh Day' Christian Rosenkreutz writes his name in a great book above the following enigmatic motto:

The height of knowledge is to know nothing.[46]

Bruno, Campanella and the Rosicrucians

It seems to us to be beyond serious doubt that a great allegory of death, rebirth and spiritual transformation lies at the heart of the *Chemical Wedding* and that Adam McLean is right to compare the entire process to an ancient mystery initiation. At the successful completion of the Seventh Day we are perhaps to understand that the initiate, now an adept – literally a 'perfect' – has attained that *gnosis* by means of which 'the soul can escape its bondage to material existence.'[47] If so, no matter how different the mode of expression, the primary concerns of the *Chemical Wedding* can be seen to be essentially the same as those of the Alexandrian Hermetists, the Gnostics, the Manicheans, the Paulicians, the Bogomils, the Cathars – and all those on the great chain of heresy that we have traced in the preceding chapters. Since the *Chemical Wedding* can, in a sense, be regarded as the 'statement of faith' of the elusive Rosicrucian order, the clear implication is that their general reformation of the world was to be of a distinctly Hermetic nature.[48]

Reinforcing this is the fact that even a cursory examination of the *Fama*, the *Confessio* and the *Chemical Wedding* makes it quickly evident – whatever their identity – that our shadowy 'Rosicrucians' were using a strong mixture of Hermetic magic, Gnosis, Cabala and alchemy in a Christian framework. In short, these pamphlets that caused such a stir at the time were seeking not only to bring about a 'Rosicrucian' reformation of the world but also to do so with all the intellectual weaponry of the Hermetic magi such as Pico della Mirandola, Bruno and Campanella. Even more curiously, through their connection with Johann Valentin Andreae, the 'brothers' were also involved in the conception of a utopian city-society they called *Christianopolis* – a sort of microcosm of the world governed by Hermetic statesmen-priests[49] – that very much resembled Campanella's *Civitas Solis*. With such similar terminology, imagery and objectives, it is justified to ask whether this 'Rosicrucian' movement might not somehow have been rooted in Bruno's long sojourns in Germany between 1586 and 1591 (see Chapter Eleven) as well as the smuggling of advance copies of Campanella's *Civitas Solis* into that country – events that occurred in the years immediately *before* the Rosicrucian Manifestos first appeared.

During Bruno's Inquisition in Venice in 1592 (before his case was referred to Rome, see Chapter Eleven), his Venetian 'pupil' and betrayer, the faithless Mocenigo, reported that the Nolan had plans to found a new philosophical sect in Germany. Other witnesses said that the sect existed, that Bruno had named it the *Giordanisti* and that it much appealed to the Lutheran heretics in Germany. Such testimonies led Frances Yates to wonder whether these rumoured 'Giordanisti' could have had any connection with the unsolved mystery of the origins of the Rosicrucians who, she reminds us 'are first heard of in Germany in the early 17th century, in Lutheran circles.'[50] If such a connection exists at all, however, as Yates discovered, it is as yet far too murky and faint for us to be sure of. Nonetheless, sufficient hints and clues exist for her to suggest that 'Rosicrucian aspirations after a universal reform in a Hermetic context may well owe something to Bruno as well as to Campanella.'[51] And although no direct connection has so far been confirmed between Bruno and the Rosicrucian movement in Germany, there is at least strong circumstantial evidence of a connection between Campanella and the Rosicrucians.

The gradual unveiling of the City of the Sun

Campanella's great work, *Civitas Solis*, the 'City of the Sun', was written during his long years of incarceration between 1599 and 1627. The earliest printed edition, in Latin, was published in Frankfurt, Germany in 1623.[52] However Campanella's first draft of the manuscript – in Italian, not Latin – was complete as early as 1602, and has survived (although it was not published until 1904).[53] By 1613, and possibly as early as 1611,[54] the manuscript copy of another draft had been smuggled out of Campanella's prison by one of his disciples and regular visitors – the Lutheran Tobias Adami as we saw in Chapter Twelve. We know that Adami took the smuggled manuscript to the city of Tübingen in southern Germany,[55] where at the time lived Johann Valentin Andreae, a scholar with undeniable Hermetic and Rosicrucian connections and the possible author, or part-author of *The Chemical Wedding of Christian Rosenkreutz*.

Did Adami pass Campanella's manuscript to Andreae and to others in the proto-Rosicrucian circle in Tübingen? It seems highly likely. In which case – since the *Fama* and the *Confessio* did not appear until 1614 and 1615, while the *Chemical Wedding* appeared in 1616 – there is time enough to allow, as Yates suggests, for a Campanellan influence on 'Rosicrucian aspirations after a universal reform.' The link is tightened, Yates reveals, by the presence amongst Andreae's close friends of another of Campanella's German Lutheran disciples – a man called Wilhelm Wense.[56]

Dame Frances Yates has not been alone in noting the implications for our understanding of the Rosicrucian phenomenon of these behind-the-scenes connections involving Campanella, Adami, Wilhelm Wense and the enigmatic Johann Valentin Andreae. Christopher McIntosh similarly argues that Campanella's 'utopian work, *Civitas Solis*, which describes an ideal society ruled over by Hermetic priests … helped create the atmosphere in which the Rosicrucian Manifestos were produced.'[57] It would appear that Wense had even suggested to Andreae that the society the 'Christian Union' which Andreae wanted to create in Germany should be called *Civitas Solis*.[58]

In 1619, four years before the first (1623) publication of *Civitas Solis* but at least six years after the manuscript had reached Lutheran circles in Tübingen, Andreae was to publish a book of his own expounding the virtues of *Christianopolis* – a special kind of utopian city. There can be little doubt that Campanella's Hermetic-Christian vision of an ideal state was its inspiration.

The union of the Thames and the Rhine

The central image of *The Chemical Wedding of Christian Rosenkreutz* is the marvellous, magical wedding of a mythical king and queen. In February 1613, three years before the publication of the *Chemical Wedding*, a fabulous and almost mythical wedding did in fact take place …

The story begins on 24 March 1603 when Queen Elizabeth I of England died in Richmond Palace. Her life had been childless, and so the kingdom passed to her closest cousin, King James Stuart VI of Scotland, who was crowned James I of England at the age of 37. He was naturally followed into England by many loyal noblemen and gentry of his original Scottish court. With them they brought not only their traditional clannish sense of bonding in elite male fraternities but also the budding seed of what was eventually to become the most powerful and influential secret society of modern times.

James I was a staunch Protestant who, on the death of his illustrious cousin, found himself transformed from the king of a small, relatively poor country – Scotland – to the supreme head of one of the most powerful states in the world. His personality, it seems, was crude and ill-mannered, leaving much to be desired. Though married he apparently harboured an acute disdain for women, and preferred to spend his time in the company of men – with whom, it was inevitably rumoured, he was not averse to enjoying occasional sexual relationships.[59]

An all-out biblical fanatic of the worst sort, James I was fired by an adamant belief in his own 'divine right' to rule. In practice, however, he was to prove rather mediocre as a king and a statesman, some might even say, a failure. The English mistrusted the peace that he had struck with their traditional mortal enemy Spain, and were perplexed when he began to involve himself in an increasingly intimate relationship with the Spanish ambassador.

But all was forgiven in late 1612, when James I announced the marriage of his daughter, who bore the evocative name of Elizabeth, to the young and much loved German Protestant Prince Frederick V, the elector of the Lower Palatinate. As well as the high romance, the glamour, the excitement and the anticipation of the impending event (then, as now, the masses loved royal weddings) this move seemed to confirm James I's commitment to the Protestant cause. Many in England and elsewhere even began to hope that he might, after all, champion and defend the Protestants of Europe as Elizabeth I had before him. And such hopes, quite naturally, were focussed in particular on what might happen in Germany, the hub of the Protestant Reformation.

The elector of the Lower Palatinate was a sensitive, handsome and very gentle young man. He had received a refined French education at the famous University at Heidelberg, an enchanting university-city that was the seat of the Lower Palatinate, and in 1610 had succeeded his father, Frederick IV, a staunch Calvinist and one of the founders of the German Protestant Union. This was a coalition of German Protestant principalities whose objective was to resist the Catholic League and the power of the Hapsburgs by forging alliances amongst themselves in Germany and also with foreign sympathisers such as the French Huguenots under Henry of Navarre, and the English Protestants.

There were, in fact, two Palatinates, the Upper Palatinate in northern Bavaria and the Lower or Rhine Palatinate located on both sides of the middle Rhine. Since medieval times the Palatine rulers had served as stewards of royal territory in the absence of the Hapsburg emperors, and eventually obtained the right to be among the electors of new emperors, hence their title of 'electors'. When the Palatinate adopted Calvinism in the 1560s, these principalities suddenly became the bulwark of the Protestant cause in Germany. As elector of the Lower Palatinate, Frederick V symbolised Protestant resistance against the Counter-Reformation spurred by the Catholic League under the Hapsburgs, and quite naturally his marriage to the daughter of James I was perceived as a great strengthening of this resistance.

When Frederick arrived in England in the autumn of 1612 he made a huge positive impression on the English court. The young Princess Elizabeth fell deeply in love with him at first sight, and he, too, with her. It all promised to be the ultimate fairy-tale of the century. Frederick was invested with the Order of the Garter, and everyone in the realm rejoiced at the prospect of the fabulous wedding and of the great things that would come from this union.

The wedding took place on 14 February, St. Valentine's Day, 1613, amid lavish festivities along the River Thames near London. And two months later, on 25 April, the sparkling royal couple left for Germany, and set up court at the magnificent Heidelberg Castle in the Lower Palatinate.

Dee and Christian Rosenkreutz

We shall recall from Chapter Eleven that in 1583, the year Giordano Bruno arrived in England, the famous Elizabethan astrologer, conjuror and mathematician, John Dee, was preparing to leave. The Polish prince, Albert Laski, who had been amongst Bruno's audience at Oxford, had invited Dee and his family to join him at his home in Trebona, Poland, and Dee had accepted. Dee also took along his young clairvoyant assistant, Edward Kelly.

After leaving England in October 1583 Dee and his little party first stayed in Trebona for a year and then travelled extensively through Poland and Bohemia, from town to town, performing mystical séances and conjurations for the nobility until 1587. Dee and his family then returned to England, passing through Germany and Holland, but Kelly decided to stay in Poland. He was eventually killed in 1593 in an accident while trying to escape from a German prison where he had been jailed for heresy.

Back in England Dee feel into deep poverty, and was nearly destitute when Elizabeth I took pity on him and appointed him chancellor of St. Paul's Cathedral. A few years later Dee was appointed warden of Manchester College, where he stayed until the death of Elizabeth I in 1603. Under James

I, however, Dee lost all influence with the crown and all its support as well. He died in 1608, in an awful state of poverty, at the age of 81.

Curiously the character of Christian Rosenkreutz in the *Chemical Wedding* published eight years later, is also 81 years old. Remembering how the Rosicrucian Manifestos boast that the brothers communicate with one another in coded language, we suggest this may not be a coincidence. The author, whoever he was, may have been trying to express a deliberate, if cryptic, link between Dee and Christian Rosenkreutz, the legendary founder of the Rosicrucian movement.

This is speculation, of course. But what lends it some credibility is the fact that many scholars believe the roots of the Rosicrucian movement do go back long before the publication of the *Fama* and the *Confessio* in 1614 and 1615 – perhaps even all the way back to Germany and Bohemia in the 1580s, right after John Dee's visit to those countries. Dame Frances Yates, the greatest scholar of this field, certainly thought she could detect Dee's influence. This might have followed directly from his own travels in Germany and Bohemia. Or it could have come later and indirectly through the retinue of English scholars and artists, many of whom may have been influenced by Dee, who followed Elizabeth Stuart to her new home at Heidelberg Castle and then later on at Prague in Bohemia.[60]

Such influences were too well hidden for any scholar to expect to uncover them fully today. All we can say for sure is that the Rosicrucian phenomenon of 1614–16 followed closely on from the 'alchemical marriage' in 1613 of Frederick V and Elizabeth Stuart. Taken together with other signs of the times, these events conspired to raise hope of an end to the age-old system of religious and political intolerance that had ruled Europe for so long and seemed to offer the promise of a new dawn.

The Rosicrucian investment in Frederick V

To 'build the City of the Sun', in Hermetic parlance, requires the patronage and participation of powerful secular leaders. Without their support the great social, political and religious changes that the process requires – not to mention the architecture – are just impossible dreams. With this in mind it is, in our view, quite possible that Frederick of the Palatinate, head of the Protestant Union in Germany, was deliberately groomed by Rosicrucian and Hermetic thinkers to play the key secular role in their grand plan for Europe – the same role that they may also have had in mind for Henry IV of France before his assassination in 1610. The added frisson in Frederick's case was his marriage to the king of England's daughter – taken by many as a token of future English military intervention against the Hapsburgs and the Catholic League.

Frederick's most trusted chief advisor at Heidelberg was Prince Christian of Anhalt, a keen student of esoteric and mystical topics, particularly alchemy, Cabala and the occult. He was the patron of the German alchemist Oswald Croll, who was his physician, and he was a close friend of Peter Rosenberg, a wealthy landowner with estates around Trebona whose brother, Villem Rosenberg, had acted as host to John Dee during his stay there a few years before.[61] Even more striking is the fact that one of Prince Christian's closest relatives, Prince Augustus of Anhalt, is credited with having published – in 1605, nine years before the *Fama* – the earliest known reference to the Rosicrucian brotherhood.[62]

It was under Prince Christian's influence that the Heidelberg court, as well as Frederick and Elizabeth's later court in Prague, came to be frequented by many well-known Rosicrucian sympathisers – amongst them the famous English Hermetic philosopher Robert Fludd, a pupil of John Dee, and the German alchemist Michael Maier. Interestingly, Prince Christian is also known to have been in close contact with the great Italian reformer Paolo Sarpi, the latter a Venetian theologian and statesman who, other than his intensely anti-Catholicism sentiment, also wanted to turn Venice into an independent Protestant republic.[63] Sarpi was in turn a close friend of Galileo and is often credited with having been the first to introduce to this great astronomer the primitive optical long-distance sighting devices – telescopes – that were then being developed in Holland.

Prince Christian was 45 years old when the young Frederick, then barely 14, became elector of the Palatinate. Frederick and Elizabeth were still only 17 when they married and set up court in Heidelberg in 1613. Having previously served under Frederick IV, and with enormous experience of diplomacy, it was easy for Prince Christian to become a father figure to the impressionable royal couple – and there seems little doubt that it was he who promoted Frederick V as the figurehead of a great and imminent universal reformation. It is known that Prince Christian even harboured the hope that his protégée might become the first Protestant Holy Roman emperor after the anticipated overthrow of the Catholic Hapsburgs.

In August 1619 the throne of Bohemia, which the rebellious nobility of Prague considered to be an *elective* rather than a hereditary title, was offered to Frederick. Against the sound advice of the union of Protestant princes and the beseeching of his own mother he unwisely accepted the offer and late in September 1619 he and his English wife left Heidelberg Castle and headed for Prague. When the news reached England, it was greeted with huge enthusiasm by the public – almost as though a new or 'reincarnated Queen Elizabeth' had manifested herself in central Europe in defence of Protestantism. This time, moreover, a splendid young prince was to be found at her side bearing the title of head of the Protestant Union and protected by his powerful father-in-law, James I.

It was all a grave mistake, for James I had absolutely no intention of jeopardising the precarious peace that England then enjoyed with Spain and thus, indirectly, with the Catholic League and the Hapsburgs.

In these adverse political and military circumstances – which surely he must have been aware of – historians have often wondered why Frederick V accepted the crown of Bohemia at all? What was it that prompted him to take such a huge risk? Explaining this very matter to an uncle, Frederick himself stated in a letter that he believed it to be his 'divine calling which I must not disobey ... my only end is to serve God and his Church.'[64]

By God's 'Church' Frederick presumably meant the Bohemian or Calvinist-Reformed Church. But it is not altogether impossible that his idea of his 'divine calling' might have encompassed a much larger 'mission' extending beyond Bohemia, beyond Germany and even beyond Calvinism. Through Prince Christian of Anhalt, the Rosicrucian and Hermetic influences that are likely to have reached the young elector all envisaged a great and imminent religious and cultural reformation of the world – nothing less than a new Hermetic golden dawn for mankind that was about to break very soon. Those who promulgated such ideas believed that the instrument to bring this about was an ancient and secret knowledge that had recently been rediscovered – a knowledge that they had understood and that was to be found in the Hermetic writings, in the Cabalistic Hebraic texts, and in the old sciences of alchemy and natural magic.

All those who promoted such ideas – at high risk to their freedom and lives – were also seeking an enlightened monarch or prince to bring about this great universal reform and advancement of learning. It was expected that he would do so from the heart of a utopian republic or 'city' ostensibly named *Civitas Solis* (Campanella), *Christianopolis* (Andreae) or, as we shall soon see, *New Atlantis* (Bacon) or even *New Jerusalem*. It was visualised as a wonderful and magical Hermetic-Christian state ruled by a 'solar' king and governed by his wise and learned priest-scientists, priest-philosophers or *magi*, set at the very epicentre of the known world.

What better location, then, than the central European state of the Palatinate, ruled by an enlightened prince, a chivalrous knight of the Order of the Garter, who had just married a wonderful and sensitive princess of the blood royal of England? The latter, moreover, had been groomed in the sophisticated and enlightened Baconian and Shakespearian milieu of the Jacobean Renaissance. Better still, she brought with her the clout of her powerful father, James I, to buttress the great adventure and enterprise ahead.

After the unexpected death of Henry IV of France a terrible sense of loss and frustration befell free thinkers in central Europe until, it seems to us, a clever propaganda campaign using Hermetic-Christian-Cabala changed the direction of the movement. Now it was no longer France but Germany that offered the best vector for the great reform. As the leading Hermetic scholar Joscelyn Godwin puts it:

> The hopes of all whose outlook could be described as 'Rosicrucian' were pinned on Frederick: hopes that he could initiate the reform of which the *Fama* and the *Confessio* spoke ...[65]

The Battle of White Mountain

Days after Frederick V was crowned king of Bohemia, his rival, the deposed Ferdinand of Hapsburg, was immediately declared Holy Roman emperor – Ferdinand II – by the Catholic League. The league then mounted a ferocious crusade against the usurper Frederick and the Protestant cause in general. This was the start of the terrible Thirty Years War that was to scourge central Europe and kill half the population of Germany.

Through swift negotiations with his Catholic allies and even the 'heathen' Turks, Ferdinand II was able to form a powerful coalition against Frederick and his supposed Protestant allies. Badly organised and weakened by personal feuds, one by one the Protestant princes and the other foreign Protestant powers began to abandon the elector. The final blow came when it was gradually realised by all that James I, his powerful father-in-law, was not going to send any military support to him. The dismal end to Frederick's short reign was now imminent.

On 8 November 1620, a force of 26,000 Catholic soldiers belonging to Ferdinand II and placed under the command of the brilliant general, the Count of Tilly, marched against the 21,000 strong Protestant force of Frederick which was under the command of Prince Christian of Anhalt. The two armies met outside Prague on a gentle sloping field known as the *Bílá hora* – 'White Mountain'. Within a few hours Frederick's army had been smashed. Prince Christian was made prisoner of the Catholics, and

Frederick and Elizabeth barely managed to escape with their lives, leaving all their belongings behind.

Predictably Ferdinand II and the Catholic League took an abominable revenge on the rebellious Bohemian estates that had preferred Frederick, Protestantism, and perhaps a great deal more. Land and properties were confiscated, 27 leaders of the revolt were publicly beheaded and, to the horror of the Protestants, Catholicism was imposed as the only permitted faith in Bohemia. Those who refused to convert were ordered to leave the country and all their assets were confiscated.

It is estimated that over a quarter of million Bohemians chose to go into exile.[66] Many went to Holland, others to England and some even made it to the New World. The beautiful dream that Frederick's rule would be the vector for a Europe-wide 'Rosicrucian' reformation had been proved to be just that – a beautiful dream.

But this did not mean that the dream died. It simply shifted its location – to England, which many would argue was its natural home (if John Dee was indeed the Father of Rosicrucianism):

> The opportunity for general reformation and the advancement of learning that the Rosicrucian Manifestos had proclaimed ... had been lost in Germany through the collapse of the Frederickian movement. Those who had suffered from that bitter disappointment [came] to England, and those in England who bitterly regretted that the movement had not been supported, welcome[d] them.[67]

The previously 'Invisible College' of the Rosicrucian brotherhood was about to become very visible indeed ...

And after the decease of King David, Solomon that was son unto David
performed out the Temple his father had begun and had sent after Masons
into divers lands and gathered them together so that he had four score
thousand workers of stone and they were named Masons ...

The *Old Charges* of Freemasonry, circa 1583

The Legendary history of [Free]*masonry, of the actual art of building, is*
recounted in certain medieval poems [the *Old Charges*] ... *in these writings*
... *architecture is identified with geometry. One account maintains that*
geometry was discovered before the Flood; another states that Abraham
taught the Egyptians geometry. In yet another version ... geometry is said
to have been invented by the Egyptians ...

Frances Yates, *The Rosicrucian Enlightenment*

CHAPTER FOURTEEN

EMERGENCE OF THE INVISIBLES

Ｉf a Christian Gnostic of the fifth century AD and a Cathar of the 13th century were to encounter one another in a time-warp they would find that they had much in common. Their views of the Roman Catholic Church as a diabolical agency would be identical. Their basic beliefs and theology would be the same. Their ascetic lifestyles would be the same.

Were our time-travelling pair then to be transferred to an encounter with a 16th or 17th century European Protestant they would discover much less common ground. Although they would share with him a commitment to a simple and unostentatious form of religion, their basic beliefs and theology would be as different from his as they would be from those of a Roman Catholic.

But there's an old saying – 'my enemy's enemy is my friend.'

History shows, during their war to the death with the Roman Catholic Church in the 13th century, that the Cathars cooperated closely with another heretical sect, the Waldensians (or 'Vaudois') founded by one Peter Waldes in Lyons in the late 12th century.[1] In their simplicity and austerity, their distrust of sacraments administered by unworthy ministers, their opposition to the veneration of saints and relics, and many other aspects of their religion, these Waldensians were the true forerunners of the later Calvinist and Lutheran movements that came to define European Protestantism. Their argument, in other words, was primarily with the *behaviour* of the Roman Catholic Church but they accepted most of the tenets of Catholic doctrine that the Cathars vehemently rejected.[2] Even so the Waldensians were violently persecuted by the Catholic authorities and it was in this shared experience of persecution, coupled with their shared detestation of 'Romish' vanity and ostentation, that the Cathars and the Waldensians found common cause.

In this book we are tracing the course through history of two inter-related underground religions, Gnosticism and Hermeticism.

Having survived centuries of persecution following the triumph of literalist Christianity in the Roman Empire, Gnosticism underwent a renaissance in 12th century Europe when it found support amongst the ruling barons of the semi-independent state of Occitania. That renaissance, as we've seen, was brought to a bloody end by the Albigensian Crusades in the 13th century – although the Gnostic religion undoubtedly lingered longer in the Balkans until it was finally snuffed out there by Islam in the 15th century.

Meanwhile, Hermeticism – which might be described as Gnosticism's pagan twin – slept in the West for a thousand years before suddenly and spectacularly waking up again when the Hermetic texts were rediscovered and brought to Florence in the 15th century. It then enjoyed an amazing and highly enigmatic period of papal favour during the 16th century, documented in Chapter Eight, before the Vatican finally recognised it for what it was – a deadly heresy that would bring Catholicism to its knees if it could. The Inquisition's renewed interest in the matter, sending a clear signal of its intentions to all who sought to bring about a 'general reformation of the world', was marked by such acts as the torture and 27-year imprisonment of the Hermetic magus Tommaso Campanella, and the imprisonment, torture and savage burning in February 1600 of Giordano Bruno, the greatest magus of them all.[3]

Just as the Cathars had made common cause in the 13th century with the Waldensians, so too it was natural for the Hermetic and Rosicrucian visionaries who roamed Europe in the 15th, 16th and 17th centuries to make common cause with the Protestants of their time. The principle of my enemy's enemy being my friend still applied. And just as the Cathars had needed secular political support in order to become a force to be reckoned with – one that could actually change the world – so too the Hermetists and Rosicrucians of the 15th, 16th and 17th centuries needed secular political support, and for the same reason. Only in very exceptional cases – e.g. the ageing Campanella at the court of Louis XIII – were they likely to receive that support from Catholic rulers. Inevitably therefore we find key Hermetic and Rosicrucian figures turning up repeatedly in areas of Protestant influence – e.g. Bruno's travels in Germany between 1586 and 1591 – and congregating in large numbers around Protestant monarchs such as Frederick V, the elector of the County Palatine of the Rhine.

Bruno, for one, was as outspokenly honest with his wealthy and influential Protestant sponsors as he was with everyone else: he was not a Protestant and would not become one; he sought only their protection and simply wished to continue his studies in peace.[4] But we may confidently suppose that other Hermetic free-thinkers preferred to adopt a lower profile and to blend in, as perfectly as possible, amongst their Protestant hosts. These were uncertain, violent, highly volatile times and, since the terrible destruction of the Cathars, common sense had taught most heretics the wisdom of 'invisibility' – whether they found themselves amongst Protestants or Catholics.

Indeed was it not precisely this quality of 'invisibility' that was most emphasised in the Rosicrucian Manifestos? The reader will recall from Chapter Twelve that the *Fama* speaks of a 'magical language and writing' that had been developed by the early Rosicrucian brothers, presumably for secretive communications amongst themselves. The *Fama* additionally reports that the brothers are distributed about the world and, as a deliberate policy, wear no distinguishing garments but follow the custom of whichever country they find themselves in.[5] In other words they blend in – the way, perhaps Johann Valentin Andreae blended in as a straight-thinking Lutheran pastor whilst pursuing his Rosicrucian and Hermetic interests. It may be a mark of his success as a Rosicrucian 'invisible' that even today we cannot be one hundred per cent certain whether he was 'just' a Lutheran pastor and academic with some unconventional interests. Or was he, as most scholars believe, the author of the *Chemical Wedding* – the Rosicrucian statement of faith?

The Rosicrucian Manifestos speak, ultimately, of the existence of an 'Invisible College', working behind the scenes, through existing institutions for the moment, blending-in until the time comes when it can reveal itself to the world. What it seeks is a great general reformation of religion and society. And though the word 'reformation' in this context was itself perhaps chosen for its political correctness and acceptability in Protestant circles we are quite certain that it was not meant in the Protestant sense at all. It's very obvious from the Rosicrucian example that, veiled within Protestant religious bodies, organisations and power structures of the early 17th century, there were people whose agenda was much closer to Giordano Bruno's deeply heretical 'Egyptian' idea of the Hermetic reformation of Europe, and who might yet heed Tommaso Campanella's call to build the City of the Sun.

Eyes turn to England and the New World

We saw in the last chapter that on 8 November 1620 the Catholic forces of the Holy Roman Emperor Ferdinand II inflicted a devastating defeat on the Protestant forces of Frederick V, the elector of the Palatinate. The Bohemian estates were dragooned into Catholicism and a quarter of a million Protestant refugees fled, leaving all their worldly goods behind.

Amidst the massacres and the streams of refugees generated by this terrible ongoing conflict between Catholics and Protestants in central Europe, the opportunistic minds of some Hermetic thinkers would have turned naturally towards England, that great Protestant kingdom across the Channel. It would have stood out from the general background chaos of the Continent as a place where they still might hope to achieve universal reform based on advancement of learning.

Remember that Hermetic philosophers, conditioned by the characteristic sky-ground dualism of the Hermetic texts, were avid star watchers. We can therefore be sure that they would have been paying attention in December 1603, the year James I was crowned king of England, when there was an impressive conjunction of the planets Saturn and Jupiter, seen by astrologers to presage a new age.[6] It was in the following year, 1604, that the 'opening' of the tomb of Christian Rosenkreutz, described in the *Fama*, supposedly took place, ushering in a renewed cycle of Rosicrucian activity. That year also witnessed the strange appearance of two new stars in the constellations of Serpentarius and Cygnus giving rise to a combustible mixture of huge fears and tremendous hopes.[7]

It's not difficult to understand how Hermeticists and Rosicrucians taking shelter amongst Lutheran and Calvinist Protestants in the beleaguered war-zones of central Europe must have felt in this atmosphere. It should come as no surprise to learn, therefore, that for some the opening of the Stuart era in England was regarded as the foundation of a 'New Jerusalem', a land chosen by God that could lead the world into a new age of universal peace and enlightenment. We saw in the last chapter that such hopes were intensified by the widespread public perception – though it ultimately proved false – that a powerful alliance between the 'Rhine and the Thames', i.e. between Protestant England and Protestant Germany, had been cemented through the marriage of Frederick V of the Palatinate and Elizabeth of England.

But there was also another factor at work, one that must have loomed large in the collective subconscious of those seeking the great universal reform. This was the recent acquisition by England of vast and virgin territories in the Americas. A whole new continent had suddenly emerged

THE MASTER GAME

on the other side of the Atlantic, a sort of 'New Atlantis' ready to be colonised by a new breed of European. Might it not be easier and better, some of these reformers must have thought, to put aside Europe and its religious troubles altogether and to build instead, a *completely new society* on a clean slate in this untarnished 'new world' – a reformed society, furthermore, that could be dedicated to the pursuit of happiness, justice and the advancement of learning?

This was the context in which the great English visionary, Francis Bacon, was to publish a series of books that would galvanise the intellectuals of Europe.

Hermetic Bacon

Francis Bacon (1561–1626) was the son of the Lord Keeper of the Seal of Elizabeth I. At the age of 12 he was sent to Trinity College, Cambridge. At 18, finding himself virtually penniless after his father's death, he turned to law, and by the age of 23 Bacon had managed to win a seat in the House of Commons. Throughout his early career he was disliked by his peers and even distrusted by Elizabeth I, but after the queen's death in 1603 he found new royal favour and patronage under James I. With the king's support, Bacon quickly rose to fame and fortune, first as Lord Chancellor, then as Baron Verulam in 1618 and, finally, as Viscount St. Albans in 1621. However, Bacon's brilliant career in politics was to end in shame and dejection after he was accused of taking a bribe. He spent the rest of his life devoted to his writing.

It was in 1605, two years after the death of Elizabeth I, that Bacon published his epoch-making book *The Advancement of Learning*. Still hailed today as a cornerstone of education and science, this calm and measured work surveys the state of early 17th century knowledge and finds it wanting. If more attention were paid to research and experimentation, Bacon suggests, we could make much faster progress in understanding nature and thus improving the human condition. To this end, in his dedication of the book to his patron James I, he proposes the establishment of 'a fraternity in learning and illumination'[8] where scholars and the erudite of all countries could exchange knowledge and ideas for the benefit of humankind:

> Surely as Nature createth brotherhood in families, and arts mechanical contract brotherhoods in communities, and the anointment of God superinduceth a brotherhood in kings and bishops, so in learning

there cannot but be a fraternity in learning and illumination, relating to that paternity which is attributed to God, who is called the father of illumination or lights.[9]

Let's not forget this was written in 1605, nine years before the publication of the *Fama*, yet the language is plainly Rosicrucian. The 'fraternity in learning and illumination' that Bacon wishes for is precisely what the Rosicrucians (though 'invisible') later claimed to be. We also note with interest that Bacon refers to God as the 'father of illumination or lights'. The reader will recall from Chapter Thirteen that this same distinctive phrase – the 'Father of Light' – turns up in *The Chemical Wedding of Christian Rosenkreutz*, published in 1616. The phrase is not found anywhere in the Christian Bible. It was, however, in common usage in the early centuries of the Christian era amongst Manicheans and Gnostics as a reference to the God of Goodness. Likewise in the Hermetic texts of the same period we find frequent references to the spiritual, immaterial, first and greatest god as the God of Light. In the *Pimander* for example (a title that is itself derived from *Peime-n-Ra*, meaning the 'knowledge of Ra', the Egyptian sun-god) we may read:

That Light ... is I, even Mind, the first God, who was before the watery substance which appeared out of the Darkness.[10]

The above passage strikes an association not only between Light and the first God but also between both God and Mind. It likewise makes clear, in familiar dualistic terms, that all three (Light/Mind/God) are of a spiritual, non-material essence, different from, and preceding the 'watery substance', i.e. matter, that 'appeared out of Darkness.' These links are reinforced in the *Asclepius*:

Gross matter ... is the nutriment of bodies, and spirit is the nutriment of souls. But besides these, there is mind, which is the gift of heaven, and one with which mankind alone is blessed ... By the light of mind the human soul is illumined.[11]

It is precisely this illumination of the human soul by the light of mind that the Rosicrucians claimed to be devoted to and that Bacon sought to bring about through his proposed international 'fraternity in learning and illumination'. His choice of these particular words in his dedication to James

I must, moreover, be understood in the wider context of the times. As the Italian scholar Paolo Rossi points out, the view of Frances Bacon as 'a modern scientific observer and experimentalist emerging out of the superstitious past is no longer valid.'[12] Rossi's research, backed up by Frances Yates shows that:

> It was out of the Hermetic tradition that Bacon emerged, out of the Magia and Cabala of the Renaissance as it had reached him via the natural magicians ... Bacon's science is still, in part, occult science.[13]

The same science, natural philosophy and Hermetic magic were also advocated by Marsilio Ficino, Giovanni Pico della Mirandola, Giordano Bruno and the Rosicrucians. And what all sought to bring about was a universal revolution in learning promoted by an elite international fraternity of illuminati.

It can't be an accident that a fraternity fitting this description was soon to flourish in the British Isles and eventually to spread around the world: the fraternity of the Freemasons. Nor were we surprised to learn from our friend the Masonic historian Robert Lomas that both Francis Bacon and James I were, in all probability, Freemasons themselves – associated with the early formation of the so-called *Scottish Rite*. Indeed it seems that in addition to its obvious Hermetic and Rosicrucian content, the language used by Bacon in his dedication to James I is recognisably 'Masonic language' – i.e. a sort of allegorical system of communication used by Freemasons couched in symbolism and secret words and fully comprehensible only to initiates.[14] Such an idea is, of course, identical to the 'magical language and writing' spoken of in the Rosicrucian Manifestos.[15]

All in all there is, in our view, no doubt that Bacon's carefully chosen words of 1605 are resonant of Rosicrucian and Masonic influences, suggesting, at the very least, the presence of a proto-Freemasonic movement within the elite inner circle of the Stuart court.

A Rosicrucian Christmas card in the National Records of Scotland

At about the time that Francis Bacon was putting the finishing touches to *The Advancement of Learning*, the German alchemist Michael Maier (1568–1622), a renowned Rosicrucian thinker, was living in Prague and working as the private physician to Emperor Rudolph II. When Rudolph died in 1612 – the year before the marriage of Frederick V of the Palatinate and Elizabeth Stuart – Maier came to England. There he met Sir William

Paddy, the private physician of James I. It cannot be confirmed that Maier met the king, but he certainly felt comfortable enough to send him a personal Christmas card – one that, on face value, very much appears to associate James I with the Rosicrucian movement.

Maier's Christmas card to the king is kept today in the archives of the National Records of Scotland in Edinburgh. It depicts a large rose around which are written the words:

> Greetings to James, for a long time King of Great Britain. By your true protection may the rose be joyful.[16]

This weird card has lead many researchers to suppose that there might have existed in England some early form of the 'Rosicrucian movement' and that James I was seen as its protector by German Rosicrucians like Michael Maier.[17] It's very probable, while he was in England, that Maier would have met the Hermetic philosopher and Cabalist, Robert Fludd (1574–1637), who was then in his late thirties. Although Fludd had not yet published his own work on the Rosicrucian brotherhood, *A Compendium Apology for the Fraternity of the Rosy Cross* (1616), he nonetheless was a keen 'Rosicrucian in spirit.'[18]

It is certain that the German Rosicrucians must have noted Fludd's defence of their fraternity in England because later, in 1618, at the height of Rosicrucian furore, two more of Fludd's books, *History of the Macrocosm* and *History of the Microcosm* were published in the town of Oppenheim by the firm of Johann Theodor de Bry – who apparently paid handsomely for the privilege.[19] De Bry was also the publisher of one of Michael Maier's works, *Atalanta Fugiens*, likewise brought out in 1618,[20] and it seems probable that Maier was the link between Fludd and the Palatinate publisher.

Maier remained in England until 1616 and it would have been extraordinary if he had not met Bacon during this period since they moved within the same circle. What is known with certainty is that Bacon sat down to write a utopian book soon after Maier's visit which bears the unmistakable imprint of Rosicrucian thinking.

The New Atlantis

In 1627, a year after Bacon died, a manuscript he had been working on turned up amongst his personal papers. Its title was *New Atlantis*. And like Plato's original story of Atlantis (found in his dialogues, the *Timaeus* and the *Critias*) it had been left unfinished. It was also undated but scholars assume Bacon must have written it soon after the two Rosicrucian Manifestos and the *Chemical Wedding* had appeared in Germany – i.e. after 1616 – for it contains allegories and ideas that are distinctly reminiscent of those documents.

In brief, *New Atlantis* presents Bacon's utopian vision of a scientific and yet spiritually-oriented society that exists in secret on a far away island called 'Bensalem' which lies 'in the midst of the greatest wilderness of waters in the world'. This society is governed by an elite fraternity of scientist-priests who gather within a great college or lodge called *Salomon's House*. Members include accomplished astronomers and geometers, and – surprising in a 17th century document – the builders of aeroplanes and submarines ('we have some degrees of flying in the air; we have ships and boats for going under water'). They are also accomplished navigators and seafarers, but secretive and unwilling to reveal their existence: 'we know well most parts of the inhabitable world, and are ourselves unknown.'

Their quest, Bacon tells us, is for 'the knowledge of the causes, and secret motions of things' and it is their mission to 'nourish God's first creature, which was Light.' This mission they continuously spread abroad by means of:

... twelve that sail into foreign countries under the names of other nations, (for our own we conceal) ... These we call Merchants of Light.[21]

The travels of Bensalem's 12 invisible missionaries 'nourish the Light' by promoting the advancement of learning all around the world – very much the Rosicrucian method – and like the original eight Rosicrucians, and the Freemasons, they take an 'oath of secrecy' and proceed with discretion in all things.[22] They travel incognito, doing good deeds *gratis* like the Rosicrucians. They remain unnoticed and invisible because they wear the clothing and speak the languages of the countries they visit – for like the Rosicrucians they communicate easily in every language. At home in Bensalem they are distinguished by wearing a white turban emblazoned with a red cross – the eponymous symbol of the Rosicrucians – and their great 'seal' features a representation of 'cherubim's wings, not spread but hanging down'. The same emblem, Frances Yates has shown, was used in the Rosicrucian Manifestos.[23]

We digress for a moment to note that the image of 'cherubim's wings' also evokes the Judaic Ark of the Covenant, surmounted by the winged figures of two golden cherubim, which the Old Testament tells us once stood in the Holy of Holies of the fabled Temple of Solomon in Jerusalem. Bacon gives us a 'House of Salomon' located in a place called Bensalem – essentially the same idea. *Ben* in Hebrew and Arabic means 'son' or 'son of' – implying in this case, perhaps, a 'New Salem' or New Jerusalem.

Though the terms 'Rose Cross' or 'Rosicrucian' are not to be found anywhere in *New Atlantis*, Frances Yates believed it to be 'abundantly clear that [Bacon] knew the Rose Cross fiction and was adapting it to his own parable':

> New Atlantis was governed by R. C. [Rosicrucian] Brothers, invisibly travelling as 'merchants of light' to the outside world from their invisible college or centre, now called Salomon's House, and following the rules of the R. C. Fraternity, to heal the sick free of charge, to wear no special dress. Moreover the 'cherubim's wings' seal the scroll brought from New Atlantis, as they seal the *Fama*. The island has something angelic about it, and its official wore a red cross in his turban.[24]

Yates quite correctly pointed out that modern students of Bacon, unfamiliar with the Rosicrucian literature, would not readily recognise the similarity between *New Atlantis* and the Rosicrucian Manifestos. But this handicap would not have been applicable to the literati of the 17th century to whom the Rosicrucian literature was widely known. A case in point is an adaptation of Bacon's *New Atlantis*, entitled *Holy Guide*, published by the author John Heydon in 1662. On the island of 'Bensalem' they had a 'House of Strangers', a sort of quarantine or immigration point where new visitors were temporarily kept. In his adaptation, Heydon has Bacon's official of the House of Strangers speak as follows: 'I am by Office, Governor of this House of Strangers ... and of the Order of the Rosie Cross.' Heydon also refers to Bacon's 'wise men of the House of Salomon' as being 'wise men of the Society of the Rosicrucians', and speaks of this 'House of Salomon' as being one and the same as the 'Temple of the Rosie Cross.'[25]

A brief excursion to consider Freemasonry

The case for a link between the Rosicrucians and Bacon's fraternity of scientist-priests seems unassailable, yet we've seen that what Bacon tells us frequently supports a link with Freemasonry as well. Might it not be possible then that the elite brotherhood he had in mind was all along not the Rosicrucian brotherhood *per se*, but rather the up-and-coming 'speculative'

Masonic brotherhood which was beginning at exactly this time to insinuate itself into England?

Unquestionably, the term 'House of Salomon' in relation to an elite and 'wise' brotherhood is very suggestive of this, whether Bacon intended it to be or not. 'Salomon' is, in fact, the transliterated French form of 'Solomon', the well-known biblical 'wise king' whose famous 'temple' (or rather its reconstruction) is the epicentre of Freemasonic initiation and rituals. Indeed, as Masonic historians very well know, there is nothing more important and more symbolic to the ideal of Freemasonry that the Temple of Solomon and its 'rebuilding' in a supposedly spiritual manner. The Temple of Solomon is so intricately bound to Freemasonry that the entrances of many Masonic lodges are flanked by two columns representing the legendary original pillars of Solomon's Temple called *Boaz* and *Jachin* – meaning 'wisdom' and 'power'.[26] In the same way the architectural design of Freemasons' Hall in London, the headquarters of English Freemasonry, is almost certainly to be seen as an allegory of Solomon's Temple in Jerusalem. For example, the ceiling of the so-called *Grand Temple* is decorated with scenes and symbols of Solomon's Temple and reliefs on the main entrance door:

> ... are conventionally pictorial, depicting historical events. The three lower panels on each door show scenes connected with the building of King Solomon's Temple in Jerusalem, and the top left and right-hand panels together show the procession for the Dedication of the Temple. The inscription at the foot is God's promise to King Solomon as recorded in I Kings, 6:12.[27]

Here is the passage from I Kings 6:

> Then the word of the Lord came to Solomon, saying: 'As for this house which you are building, if you are obedient to my ordinances and conform to my precepts and loyally observe all my commands, then I will fulfil my promise to you, the promise I gave your father David, and I will dwell among the Israelites and never forsake my people Israel.' So Solomon built the Lord's house and finished it.[28]

Last but by no means least is the well-known fact that Scottish Rite Freemasonry sees itself as a revival in some form of the notorious medieval crusading order of the Knights Templar (so named because it established its headquarters in the 12th century on the site of Solomon's Temple in

Jerusalem). The Templars were contemporaries of the Cathars and like the Cathars they were ultimately persecuted for heresy, imprisoned, tortured and burnt at the stake. We will return to their mystery in the next chapter.

Isis in Virginia

When Frances Bacon placed his invisible island of Bensalem 'in the midst of the greatest wilderness of waters in the world' he was clearly signalling a location far away from his native England and Europe. Could he perhaps have been inspired by the idea of the Americas, still largely unexplored in the early 17th century? There, after all, lay a real 'new world', unburdened as yet by the deep-rooted religious and social traditions of the old world, where a great experiment modelled on Masonic or Rosicrucian ideals might have its best hope of successful implementation.

We note with interest that Bacon was a passionate exponent of Britain's colonisation and development of its recently acquired North American territory of Virginia. In 1606 the so-called *Virginia Company* was granted a royal charter by James I which allowed it virtually unlimited power of government in the colony. Bacon had been instrumental in the creation of the charter. Bearing this in mind, it is not surprising that in *New Atlantis*, Bacon refers to Bensalem as the 'Virgin of the World',[29] the latter a well-known allegory for Elizabeth I, the 'Virgin Queen', and by extension, her new domain of Virginia. But we saw in previous chapters that there also exists an important Hermetic text which is called the *Kore Kosmou* – literally the 'Virgin of the World' – in reference to the ancient Egyptian goddess Isis. In Chapter Eight we quoted a passage from the *Kore Kosmou* in which Isis makes the following astro-geographical statement:

> The earth lies in the middle of the universe, stretched on her back as a human might lie facing towards heaven ... Her head lies toward the south ... her right shoulder toward the east, and her left shoulder towards the west; her feet lie beneath the Great Bear [north] ... But the right holy land of our ancestors [i.e. Egypt] lies in the middle of the earth; and the middle of the human body is the sanctuary of the heart, and the heart is the headquarters of the soul; and that, my son, is the reason why men of this land ... are more intelligent [wise]. It could not be otherwise, seeing they are born and bred upon Earth's heart.[30]

Frances Yates makes the point that Elizabeth I, the Virgin Queen, was associated by her contemporaries with the constellation of Virgo, the latter identified by the Greeks as *Astraea*, a word meaning 'star'. This name *Astraea* appears to be connected to a number of ancient 'star' goddesses of the Middle East such as Astarte and Ashtoreth, all probably directly or indirectly stemming from *Ast*, the ancient Egyptian name for Isis, whose star was Sirius, the Dog Star.[31] Could this be a hint that, for some, the image of Elizabeth as the 'Virgin Queen' had contained a coded reference to the 'virgin' goddess Isis?

Such a possibility may not be as far-fetched as it at first appears. For, curiously enough, both 'Solomon's Temple' and the 'Temple of Isis' make appearances in the work of Sir Edmund Spenser, a contemporary of Francis Bacon. A close associate of the enigmatic Dr. John Dee,[32] Spenser was the author of the *Faerie Queen*, written between 1580 and 1590, a panegyric to Queen Elizabeth I and her imperial reform of the world. In it the celebrated poet refers to 'House of Alma', imagined as being an architectural allegory, in microcosm, of the macrocosmic world. The idea is strongly reminiscent of a statement made a generation later in the *Fama* (published in 1614) where we read that in the closing years of his life Christian Rosenkreutz 'constructed a microcosm corresponding in all motions to the macrocosm.'[33]

The whole notion of such correspondences between macrocosm and microcosm, sky and ground, above and below, is intensely Hermetic. Not surprisingly, therefore, Alastair Fowler, an acknowledged expert on Spenser, has discovered that the *Faerie Queen* contains a complex system of numerology as well as an 'astral' or planetary pattern within its central theme.[34] Frances Yates goes further to deduce that the mysterious 'House of Alma' encodes, by means of allegory and numerology, the proportions of the Temple of Solomon.[35] Another Elizabethan scholar, professor Angus Fletcher, sees a hint of Hermetic-Egyptian magic in Spenser's legend of the beautiful, noble and chaste lady-knight *Britomart* (an allusion to Elizabeth I), where the magician Merlin interprets the 'vision of Britomart' as being the 'Temple of Isis'.[36] Perhaps we should also note in passing that King Solomon is said in the book of Kings to have built a 'house' for his wife, an Egyptian princess, who, as a daughter of the pharaoh, would automatically have been identified by the ancient Egyptians with the goddess Isis:

Then Solomon brought Pharaoh's daughter up to the City of David [Jerusalem] to her own house which he had built for her.[37]

Antilian intrigues

The possibility that the newly colonised territories of Virginia were somehow part of the Rosicrucian and Hermetic dream of universal reform in a utopian setting may have been detected by the historian and researcher, Ron Heisler.[38] In an in-depth investigation into Michael Maier's sojourn in England between 1612 and 1616, Heisler discovered that 'in Maier's associations there is a pattern of an unexpected dimension.' This pattern emerges from a series of close contacts that Maier established in England with individuals who were all related in one way or another to the Virginia Company – a corporation of wealthy men whose royal charter, we saw above, had been drafted by Bacon.

Heisler's research reveals that when Maier published his first work in England, *Arcana arcanissima*, he personally sent copies to various notables, including Sir Thomas Smith and a certain Dr. Francis Anthony, both of whom were to become deeply involved with the running of the Virginia Company. Indeed Thomas Smith was its treasurer and Dr. Anthony became a member of its committee in 1619. Others involved with the company, such as its legal advisor John Selden, and the writer George Sandys, also seem to have had a special interest in Maier and his ideas.[39] All this led Heisler to suspect that the Rosicrucian reformer's *Atalanta Fugiens*, published in 1617, 'may have been deeply inspired by the utopian vision of America.'[40]

There is another connection with the Rosicrucian movement and the American colony of Virginia which might shed more light on this intriguing problem. In his remarkable study *The Tessera of Antilia*, scholar Donald R. Dickson presents evidence concerning the existence of a 'utopian brotherhood' known as Antilia (a name sometimes used in medieval times to refer to Atlantis). The brotherhood was apparently inspired by the Rosicrucian Manifestos and by 'Baconian beliefs in experimental science as a key to prosperity.'[41] To this end the brothers wished to purchase a small island in the Gulf of Riga in the Baltic on which to found their utopian society. Separately they also considered emigrating *en masse* to Virginia and establishing themselves there instead.[42] It is obviously not irrelevant that our old friend Johann Valentin Andreae, the suspected author of *The Chemical Wedding of Christian Rosenkreutz*, was a key participant in the Brotherhood of Antilia.[43]

All this very much suggests, if not actually confirms, that the utopian vision of the New World, and perhaps more specifically of Virginia in North America, was modelled or inspired by the Rosicrucian programme as set out in the Manifestos as well as by Francis Bacon's *New Atlantis*.

Also caught up in the blend was Freemasonry, that very real, visible and influential brotherhood, still with us today, that was launched on its present course on English soil in the early 17th century, right after the Rosicrucian scare ...

Before Freemasonry came out

The origins of modern Freemasonry are veiled behind such a mass of legends and pseudo-history that the subject has become a true nightmare for even the most dedicated of researchers. The problem lies in the fact that today Freemasons define themselves as a 'society with secrets' whereas once, and no one actually knows for how long, they were a secret society that went to great lengths to be 'invisible'. We've noted before that successful secret societies are, by definition, hard to trace in the historical record.

Freemasonry as a recognised institution originated in Britain in 1717 with the formation of the Grand Lodge of England, an event that is documented in the second edition of the *Constitutions of Freemasons* published by James Anderson in 1738.[44] But all this tells us is the moment when the former secret society publicly declared its existence, thereafter becoming visible – though still a society with secrets.

In 1722, sixteen years before Anderson's *Constitutions* appeared, a brother named J. Roberts helpfully published a compilation of the so-called *Old Charges* of Freemasonry, also known as the 'Gothic Manuscripts'. These, as the names suggest, are a collection of old manuscripts – some of which date from the late 14th century – in which is given a 'history' of the Craft of Freemasonry.[45] According to the manuscripts, the origins of Freemasonry go back to the antediluvian patriarch *Lamech* who lived before Noah's Flood. To Lamech's three sons – *Jabal, Jubal* and *Tubal* – and one daughter called *Naamah*, is accredited the invention of all the essential 'crafts' on which civilisation is based. We are told that *Jabal* was the inventor of geometry, *Jubal* invented music, *Tubal* invented the smelting trades, and *Naamah* was the inventor of weaving.[46] Knowing that one day God would punish humankind for its sins with a cataclysm of flood and fire they took precautions to write down all their learning on two huge pillars made of stone so that their discoveries would not be lost to mankind forever but could be recovered by the survivors. As the *Old Charges* inform us:

> The one stone was called marble that cannot burn with fire. The other was called lateras that cannot drown with water. Our intent is now to tell you

truly how and in what manner these stones were found whereon these crafts were written. The Greek Hermenes that was son unto Cush, and Cush was son unto Shem who was son unto Noah – this same Hermenes was afterwards called Hermes the Father of Wise Men, and he found out the two pillars of stone wherein the sciences were written and taught them forth ...[47]

The 'Greek Hermenes' is understood to be, of course, Hermes (the Thoth of the Egyptians and the Mercury of the Romans). As for 'Hermes the Father of Wise Men', there can be little doubt that this is reference to *Hermes Trismegistus*.

The rest of the 'history' in the *Old Charges* consists of a very convoluted and circuitous narrative that passes through Babylon, the coming of Abraham to Egypt (whence 'he taught the Egyptians the seven sciences') and finally brings us to the most important moment in the Masonic story – the building of Solomon's Temple in Jerusalem. We are told that through the construction of this magnificent edifice 'the worthy Craft of Masons was confirmed in the country of Jerusalem.'[48]

From there the *Old Charges* hop, skip and jump through space and time to try and show how this 'worthy Craft of Masons' was brought into Europe via France and finally to England in the 'time of St. Alban'.[49] Perhaps not totally unrelated is the curious fact that Francis Bacon, at the peak of his career, was granted the title of Viscount St. Albans by James I – thus linking him, in name at least, to this strange genealogy of Freemasonry in Britain.

We also note with interest that the *Old Charges* cast Hermes, the 'Father of Wise Men', as the finder and repromulgator of lost knowledge. Though the effect may not be intentional this is a scenario that does very much call to mind the rediscovery of the Hermetic writings in 1460 and their subsequent repromulgation. We saw in Chapter Eight that Marsilio Ficino and his intellectual successors, including men like Giordano Bruno and Tommaso Campanella more than a century later, really believed that the lost 'magical religion' or 'science' of the Egyptians had been rediscovered and felt strongly that it should be 'taught forth'.

An invisible college in dangerous times

Over two decades James I's extremely unpopular and confusing foreign policy, as well as his authoritarian attitude and contempt for Parliament, had created a deep and dark mood of discontent in England. When he died in 1625 he was succeeded by his cultivated but weak and somewhat unstable son, Charles I, who was destined to lead the monarchy into a headlong collision with Parliament and with the people. Disaster loomed ahead.

The new monarch pursued the same unpopular foreign policy as his father and proved to be even more tyrannical and dictatorial. His early marriage to the French Catholic Princess Henrietta Maria, the sister of King Louis XIII, did not go down well with the Puritanism that pervaded in the House of Commons. But most of all it was Charles I's mismanagement of the new war with Spain and France, and his abusive raising of funds through illegal taxations to finance a war in Scotland also, that finally brought the Parliamentarians to quasi-open revolt in 1640.

The unthinkable rumours of civil war in England were everywhere. These were extremely dangerous times for everyone. The Thirty Years War was still raging in central Europe, Spain and France were at war with England, and in England itself the monarchy and Parliament were at serious odds. Mistrust and treachery had become the norm, and one had to be exceedingly prudent even to survive, let alone to prosper, in this highly perilous and volatile environment. The state of generalised distrust and chaos also created a need amongst certain groups in society – intellectuals, the elite gentry and the military for example – for a neutral forum in which they could safely exchange views on politics, religion and science. It would much appear that the network and system of Masonic lodges, veiled by their multifarious rituals and screening system of recruitment and, above all, secrecy, may have provided just the right structure to satisfy such a need.

Operative, and possibly even a form of 'speculative' (i.e. esoteric, as opposed to strictly practical) Freemasonry had long existed in Scotland, probably since the late 15th century.[50] As time passed an *acception* system was introduced that allowed the recruiting of those men of stature and position in society who were not necessarily engaged in the operative stone-masonry, building and architectural trades.[51] This 'acception' system was almost certainly the precursor to the 'speculative', i.e. non-operative, enrolment system of the modern society of Freemasons. It would also much appear that acception was brought into England with the coming of the Stuart dynasty. Now, with the English Civil War looming ahead, it conveniently provided a ready-made network through the lodges in which the *accepted* English elite could meet in secrecy, in brotherly friendliness and within a liberal atmosphere – the whole veiled in rituals and symbolism that were intended to bond together men from different backgrounds but with similar social goals and spiritual aspirations.

Open parliamentary rebellion finally came in 1642. After a failed attempt to arrest five members of Parliament, Charles I and his Royalist supporters quit London and set up court-in-exile at Oxford, that traditional hub of elitist intellectuals and scholars. It was there, in the following years, that a strange fraternity of literati began to meet, calling themselves – evocatively – the 'Invisible College'. The earliest surviving written reference to this mysterious Invisible College comes from the celebrated physicist, Robert Boyle (1627–1691), in a letter he wrote to his tutor in France in 1646. In this letter Boyle states that he is now diligently applying himself to 'natural philosophy' based on the principles of 'our new philosophical college' and requests certain books from his tutor that 'will make you extremely welcome to our *Invisible College*.'[52] A few months later, in 1647, Boyle again mentions the Invisible College in a letter to a friend, saying that,

> The cornerstones of the Invisible or (as they term themselves) the Philosophical College, do now and then honour me with their company ... [These are] men of so capacious and searching spirits, that school-philosophy is but the lowest region of their knowledge ... [They are] persons that endeavour to put narrow-mindedness out of countenance, by the practice of so extensive a charity that it reaches unto everything called man, and nothing less than a universal goodwill can content it. And indeed they are so apprehensive of the want of good employment, that they take the whole body of mankind to their care.[53]

The term 'Invisible College', as well as the description of its activities and concerns given above, immediately brings to mind, of course, the Invisible College of the Rosicrucian brotherhood. Also the lofty intellectual and humane qualities of the college brothers, to which Boyle alludes, are, as we saw in the previous chapter, the very same qualities attributed to the Rosicrucian brothers – notably, for example, on the posters that sensationally appeared all over Paris in 1623.[54]

It turns out that Boyle had spent some time in Paris in his youth, during an educational tour of France and Geneva, and it is not impossible that he could have heard of the Rosicrucian Invisible College through his tutors or other acquaintances. Frances Yates observes that there is, on face value, an uncanny similarity in the terminology used by Boyle in his letters to his tutor and the terminology used by Francis Bacon in *New Atlantis*. Both authors speak of a learned and elite brotherhood that is 'invisible' and whose goal is the betterment of all mankind – which both hope to achieve through an enlargement of knowledge and by doing benevolent deeds.[55]

Many researchers agree that Theodore Haak and John Wilkins were probably the founders of Boyle's Invisible College.[56] Theodore Haak was a German immigrant who had settled in England in the 1620s, and John Wilkins was a vicar who later became bishop of Chester. At first there seems to be nothing in common between the two men, until it is realised that Haak was a refugee from the Palatinate and that John Wilkins acted as chaplain for Prince Charles Louis, the eldest son of Frederick V of the Palatinate and Elizabeth Stuart. Others who might have been connected to Boyle's Invisible College were the architect Christopher Wren and the alchemist Elias Ashmole. The Invisible College first met in London in 1645 then moved to Oxford in 1648. Let's look more closely at its activities and its members and at what it was trying to achieve.

Utopia on hold for the Civil War

While in England, Theodore Haak acted as an unofficial diplomat for the Palatinate and, more especially, as the representative and agent to the Bohemian bishop, Jan Amos Komenský, better known as 'Comenius' (1592–1670).[57] Comenius had been the bishop of the Bohemian Church of the Unity of Brethren until its fall in 1620 after the Battle of White Mountain near Prague. He was exiled with his fellow Protestants in 1628 and settled in Poland, where he became rector of the gymnasium at Leszno. There he developed a new Christian philosophy, a *pansophia* or 'universal knowledge' expressed in one common language to facilitate communication and understanding among scholars throughout the world. Comenius's ideas were published in 1631 in a work entitled *Janua Linguarum Reserata*, which attracted the interest of the great German philanthropist and educationalist Samuel Hartlib who had been living in England since the mid-1620s.

'Hartlib, in his whole life and work', wrote Frances Yates, 'was something like what an R. C. Brother, if real and not invisible, might have been.'[58] Dubbed the 'Great Intelligencer of Europe', Hartlib had set himself up as a human clearing-house, establishing a society known as the 'Office of Address' in order to promote a 'commonwealth of learning'. The office encouraged and facilitated the intellectuals of Europe to correspond and to exchange ideas, and bears comparison with Francis Bacon's 'House of Salomon'. Both concepts centre on an elite international brotherhood whose objective is to reform society and serve all mankind.

In 1640, two years before the Civil War broke out in England, the Long Parliament proposed radical reforms that, if implemented, would have bloodlessly stripped the Stuart monarchy of much of its power. Amidst a mood of great public excitement and enthusiasm there were those who began to believe that the utopian society they had so much dreamed of might perhaps be achieved in England. Zealous speeches were given in Parliament, amongst them one by special invitee Samuel Hartlib who presented his own vision of an 'English utopia'. He hoped that Parliament would adopt it and 'lay the cornerstone of the world's happiness'.

According to Frances Yates, the experience of addressing such a lofty crowd in such a lofty place went to Hartlib's head:

> In this thrilling hour when it seemed that England might be the land chosen ... to be the scene of the restoration of all things, when the possibility dawned that here imaginary commonwealths might become real commonwealths, invisible colleges real colleges, Hartlib wrote to Comenius and urged him to come to England to assist in the great work ... Comenius in far away Poland was overjoyed. He believed that he had a mandate from Parliament to build Bacon's New Atlantis in England.[59]

Comenius arrived in England in 1641, and was received by Haak and Hartlib. Among them was another of Hartlib's friends, the Scottish minister John Drury whom Hartlib had known since the 1620s. It was, in fact, Drury who had been instrumental in bringing Comenius to London. A staunch Protestant and outspoken reformer, Drury had just published a book in which he urged the restoration to the Palatinate of Prince Charles Louis, eldest son of the exiled Frederick V and Elizabeth Stuart. It will be recalled that Charles Louis's personal chaplain was John Wilkins, and we may well wonder, in view of such connections, whether Hartlib and Comenius might not have taken part in the activities of Haak and Wilkin's Invisible College. At any rate, while in England, Comenius wrote a book entitled *Via Lucis*, the 'Way of Light',[60] in which he calls for the formation of an elite fraternity of learned men. These brothers, moreover, are to be guided by some 'order' or 'sacred society' devoted to the welfare of humankind and they are to spread the light through the use of a universal language.

As well as the recurrent theme of 'Light' that seems to go right back to Manichean Gnosticism, the reader will note the similarity to Bacon's 'House of Salomon' with its learned fraternity that travelled the world and spoke many languages.[61] The Rosicrucians likewise claimed to be fluent in many languages and, in addition, to possess their own magical language and writing.

But all the great utopian ideas and expectations generated by Hartlib, Comenius and Drury came to nothing. A year after Comenius's arrival in England it was pretty obvious to everyone that the differences between Charles I and Parliament were irreconcilable and that civil war was inevitable. To Comenius especially, it became clear that the reformation he had hoped to bring about in England was definitely not going to happen. In 1642, Comenius prepared to leave England for Sweden, and John Drury took his leave for Holland.

It was in this manner that the dreams the utopian reformers had for Britain went up in smoke on 19 August 1642 when the king's banners were raised by the Royalist army at Nottingham, effectively marking the beginning of the English Civil War ...

The dashing cavalier of the Palatinate

At the start of the war, success for the Royalists – or *Cavaliers* as they were being called – seemed assured. Notable among the Cavaliers was the very dashing 23-year-old Prince Rupert, the younger son of the exiled Frederick V of the Palatinate and Elizabeth Stuart, the deposed king and queen of Bohemia. Rupert was to become the hero of the English Civil War, highly admired for his gallant cavalry charges against the parliamentarian forces, nicknamed the *Roundheads*. Rupert's heroic example did much to boost the morale of the king's forces, especially after he reclaimed Bristol in July 1643, relieved Newark and Nottingham in early 1644 and seized most of Lancashire by the summer of that year.

But his luck was soon to run out. The parliamentarian Oliver Cromwell, a 'brawny, flushed-faced MP from Cambridge', had trained an army of fanatics from the eastern counties and, with Sir Thomas Fairfax to command them by his side, Cromwell delivered the first serious blow to Prince Rupert's army at Marston Moor in Yorkshire on 2 July 1644.[62] It was the beginning of the end for the Royalists. But despite this terrible defeat, Rupert was appointed commander-in-chief of the king's army, and managed to pocket one more victory by recapturing the city of Leicester in May 1645. The following month he was severely beaten again by Cromwell at Naseby in Northamptonshire. When Rupert surrendered at Bristol to the Roundheads, an angry Charles I stripped him of his command. An odd career was to follow for Rupert. After the defeat of the Royalists at Torrington in 1646, he was banished by the Puritan Parliament. Somehow he managed to take charge of a small Royalist fleet stationed in Holland and became a dashing pirate of the seven seas, first preying on parliamentarian ships and eventually taking his swashbuckling to the Azores and the West Indies.[63] Only after the Restoration did Rupert return to England.

The end for the Royalists came in July 1646 when the king's stronghold at Oxford was surrounded and placed under siege by Cromwell and his Roundheads. Among those taken prisoner when the Royalists surrendered was a young man of 29 called Elias Ashmole, who had been serving as controller of the Ordnance Board for the king. Astrologer, alchemist and antiquarian *extraordinaire*, Elias Ashmole was destined to take a place of honour in the official history of Freemasonry ...

'I was made a Freemason'

Some four months after his capture by the Roundheads, Elias Ashmole made the following entry in his diary:

> 1646. Oct: 16. 4H 30' P.M., I was made a Freemason at Warrington, in Lancashire ...[64]

Most historians take this as the very first *recorded* Masonic initiation on English soil, but others reasonably argue that the honour should go to Sir Robert Moray. He was initiated into Freemasonry in 1641 at Newcastle-on-Tyne by members of the Edinburgh No. 1 Lodge who belonged to a Scottish regiment that had crossed into England. Thus the names of Moray and Ashmole are interlocked in Masonic history forever. And not only in Freemasonry. As we shall see, what also brings these two names together is the crucial role that both men were to play a few decades later in the conversion of the 'Invisible College' at Oxford into the very visible 'Royal Society' in London.

On 30 January 1649, amid an eerie silence followed by the roll of drums, Charles I was beheaded outside Whitehall Palace in London. England was renamed a 'Commonwealth and Free State', and, a few years later, Oliver Cromwell became Lord Protector of this new and morose Puritan dominion. It was the nearest that Britain was ever to get to a full-scale 'revolution'. But there was none of the wild jubilation that would be seen much later in France in 1789 to greet this odd and discomfited English 'Republic'.

In those turbulent and despotic years of Cromwell's rule, the Invisible College organised by Wilkins was moved to Cambridge and remained in low-key, semi-secrecy oblivious of the glorious future awaiting it. As for Wilkins himself, he had been appointed warden of Wadham College at Oxford and later was to become warden of Trinity College at Cambridge – the first and only scholar ever to head both these illustrious institutions. In 1656, by one of those odd twist of fate, Wilkins fell in love with and eventually married a widow, Mrs. Robina French, who was none other that the sister of Oliver Cromwell.

Even though many had bitterly opposed Charles I's tyrannical rule, the vast majority of the British population remained Royalists at heart and there was a deep nationwide yearning for a return to monarchy. In the autumn of 1658, less than ten years after the shocking regicide at Whitehall, Oliver Cromwell died in bed a much hated and despised man, and hopes were again raised for a full restoration of the monarchy. All eyes turned towards the English Channel, across which the legitimate heir to the British throne was somewhere roaming.

Restoration and the return to the promised land

When Oxford fell in 1646 Charles I had ordered his eldest son, Charles the Prince of Wales, to leave the country and take refuge in France. After a brief stay in the Scilly Islands Prince Charles headed for Paris, where he rejoined his mother, Queen Henrietta Maria, the sister of King Louis XIII of France. Louis XIII had died three years earlier, leaving the throne to his son, Louis, the future Sun King whose glorious reign, the reader will recall, had been predicted by the Hermetic magus-astrologer, Tommaso Campanella. The future Sun King was only eight years old when Charles arrived in Paris, and apparently did not much take to his older English cousin. Louis's mother, Queen Anne, and her trusted prime minister, the imposing Italian Cardinal Jules Mazarin, practically ran France, and it was widely believed that they were conducting an illicit romance, some even going as far as to suspect a secret marriage.[65]

The exile in Paris was to be a great disappointment and source of deep frustration for Charles, for not only was he completely dominated by his French mother, but also the French nobility snubbed him and ignored him. For several years he lingered in this state of limbo until the public execution of his father in London in 1649 jolted him back into action. Suddenly, at the French court, Charles was proclaimed Charles II, king-in-exile. Gradually he was lured to join and lead the Scottish Presbyterian forces in Perth who opposed Cromwell's regime. But this move proved to be disastrous, for the ill-organised Scots were no match for Cromwell's Roundheads and his parliamentarian cavalry, the *Ironsides*. When the two armies met at Dunbar on 3 September 1650 the Scottish forces under Charles II were decisively smashed. A final defeat at Worcester in 1651 was too much for Charles II, and he fled again to France. His life degenerated into a string of tempestuous love affairs,[66] and the small and poverty-stricken English court-in-exile became the laughing stock of Paris.

To make things worse, Mazarin came to terms with Cromwell and Charles II was booted out of France, left to wander around Europe and eventually southern Germany, where he sank further into a life of debauchery and idleness, siring at least three illegitimate children in the process.[67] Most of his time was spent hatching harebrained plots against Cromwell – on one occasion he even considered offering to marry the Lord Protector's daughter and to share the realm with him.[68] Finally, in the autumn of 1658 news was brought to Charles of Cromwell's death, and suddenly a new window of opportunity opened for him. He made haste for the port of Calais on the French coast and there waited to seize the moment.

At first it seemed as if the Protectorate and Puritan Republic left behind by Cromwell would prove too deep-rooted for the badly organised Royalists to wrench it back into their possession. But soon things began to fall apart for the Puritans, for Cromwell's son and successor, Richard, lacked the experience and character of his father. He was thus unable to contain the growing rift between the Roundhead army and Parliament, a conflict that quickly created a mood of uncertainty and discontent throughout the kingdom. The London taverns buzzed with talk of a possible 'restoration' of the Stuart monarchy and by early 1660 the whole country was fired up by Royalist supporters among the common folk.

An ex-Royalist soldier, George Monk, who was in control of Scotland for the Puritans, was now eager to avoid more anarchy and bloodshed, and decided to support the idea of a restoration. Monk arranged for an emissary, Sir John Grenville, to sail across the Channel in secret and meet with Charles II and his small court. A deal was struck that gave Charles full support from Monk and his powerful armed forces if he, Charles, would consent to certain conditions – mainly to uphold the Church of England but also to grant 'liberty to tender consciences' who practiced other faiths, and to leave important matters of state to Parliament. Charles II agreed, and Monk moved his huge army towards London. In April 1660 Charles issued his famous Declaration of Breda from Holland, where he promised a general amnesty to his enemies, 'liberty of conscience', equitable settlement to land disputes, full payment in arrears to the army and, most important of all, a free Parliament to run the affairs of the state. And on a breezy day in late May 1660, Charles II boarded the flagship *Naseby*, appropriately renamed the *Royal Charles,* and set sail for England.

The *Royal Charles* docked at Dover on 25 May. Monk was there on the quayside to receive Charles II in great pomp and in the midst of wild jubilation and emotional scenes. Huge spontaneous celebrations greeted the king all along the way to London, and the royal procession made a triumphal entry into the city on 29 May, the day of Charles II's 30th birthday. John Evelyn, the famous diarist and horticulturist, who was an eyewitness to the event, vividly described the scene:

> 20,000 horse and foot, brandishing their swords, and shouting with inexpressible joy; the way strewn with flowers, the bells ringing, the streets hung with tapestry, fountains running with wine ... myriads of people flocking even so far as from Rochester ... it was the Lord's doing, for such a restoration was never mentioned in any history, ancient or modern, since the return of the Jews from the Babylonian captivity ...[69]

Also the poet Andrew Marvell drew inspiration from the Bible, and described Charles II as being 'of a tall stature and sable hue, much like the son of Kish, that lofty Jew'.[70]

Such well-chosen analogies presenting Charles II as the 'son of Kish, that lofty Jew' and his restoration as a sort of 'return of the Jews from the Babylonian captivity' are most revealing, for they signal the incredible mood that had enveloped the return of this prodigal royal son to his 'Promised Land' – England. Such analogies also have a distinct 'Masonic' ring to them, for as we have seen, the name 'son of Kish' (or 'son of Cush', i.e. the biblical Nimrod) appears in the *Old Charges*, where he is said to be none other than 'Hermes the Father of Wise Men' who finds the two pillars upon which all the sciences were written. Nimrod, who was dark in complexion[71] like Charles II,[72] immediately evokes the Tower of Babel, which is another important 'Masonic' symbol[73] – one that was very significant to Comenius, Hartlib and Bacon in their search for a universal language. As for the 'return of the Jews from Babylonian captivity', this is one of the principle themes of Freemasonry, for it marked the events that lead to the rebuilding of Solomon's Temple in Jerusalem.[74]

And so here we have it, couched in symbolic language, the hope that London would soon become the epicentre of a far greater 'restoration' involving the 'sciences' and 'ancient wisdom' in a wonderful 'New Jerusalem' rising like a phoenix from the smouldering ashes of the Civil War. Little did anyone suspect that soon this euphoric vision would literally become true – not as they had intended but as a nightmarish satanic vision from the very gates of hell ...

From Invisible College to Royal Society

It says something for the character of Charles II that he spent the evening of his triumphal entry into London triumphantly entering into Barbara Palmer, the beautiful young wife of the Royalist Roger Palmer who he had recently met at the Hague in Holland.[75] She was the king's latest conquest, but many more were to follow. It was the start of an era of decadence at court that would soon disappoint those who had hoped for great things from the Restoration. Within four years England was again engaged in a disastrous and costly war, this time with Holland. And as if such a man-made calamity was not enough, London itself would receive two terrible blows in succession that would hit the city with such force that many came to believe they were witnessing divine retribution for the debauchery of Charles II. Meanwhile in these early days of the Restoration, with great changes and reformations still expected from the new king, the Invisible College decided to make its move.

In late November 1660 twelve members of this self-styled Invisible College met in a room at Gresham College in London. This was right after they had attended a lecture by Christopher Wren, the Gresham professor of astronomy, who was one of their number. There and then it was decided to found a '*College for the Promotion of Physico-Mathematicall Experimentall Learning*' which, very soon, would become the Royal Society. Among the twelve men that met at Gresham College were Robert Boyle, John Wilkins and Robert Moray. Christopher Wren was 28 at the time. John Wilkins, who had been in at the origins of the Invisible College with Theodore Haak, was appointed as chairman to this meeting. Robert Moray, the first Freemason to be initiated on English soil in 1641, advised the group that they should obtain a royal charter, and in early December Charles II gave his approval for the creation of the Royal Society. The society moved into premises at Gresham College, and it was decided immediately to draw up a list of suitable members.

A list of 40 was prepared, which included Elias Ashmole, Freemason *par excellence* and Rosicrucian enthusiast. Another on the list was the diarist and horticulturalist John Evelyn (1620–1706) who, as we will recall, had likened the return of Charles II and his court to the 'return of the Jews' to the Promised Land. According to Masonic historian and author Robert Lomas, John Evelyn was almost certainly a Freemason.[76]

Things were about to move very fast for many of these early members. Elias Ashmole was appointed by Charles II as Windsor Herald of Arms in Ordinary as well as Controller and Auditor of the Excise; Christopher Wren was made Savilian Professor of Astronomy at Oxford, although a far greater honour awaited him when later he shifted his career into the field of architecture. And the diarist John Evelyn was appointed to serve on several royal commissions. Robert Moray, possibly the most influential player in the formation of the Royal Society, acted as its first ad hoc president until the royal charter was granted by Charles II in 1662, after which Moray moved into permanent residence at the king's court at Whitehall.

Parallel developments in France

Although much praise and honour is bestowed on the Royal Society for being the first scientific academic body of its kind, it is often forgotten that another 'royal' society with even more illustrious royal patronage was already active in the city of Paris. In fact since the early 1640s, a group of scientists including the great mathematicians Blaise Pascal, Pierre Gassendi, René Descartes and Gilles de Roberval, had met informally in Paris, first at the residence of the famous theologian and mathematician Marin Mersenne and, after 1648, at the home of their sponsor Henri Louis Habert de Montmor.[77] This small but very powerful elite group was eventually to serve as the nucleus of the *Académie des Sciences* founded in 1666 under the patronage of Louis XIV.

Indeed, even earlier than the creation of this scientific body, the powerful Cardinal Richelieu, as 'prime minister' of France, had founded the *Académie Française* in 1638 under his own patronage and backed by letters of patent from Louis XIII. At the death of Richelieu in 1642 the patronage passed to the chancellor Pierre Séguier, the Count of Gien, and, after him, to Louis XIV – who himself became royal patron. Exactly like the Invisible College, the *Académie Française* sprung to life amongst a group of learned men who met informally. There were originally twelve members, then after the society was granted royal charter, the membership was expanded to 40. The reader will recall that the Royal Society in England was also to develop in the same way, with twelve informal founder members building up to 40 official members after December 1660.

The original objective of the *Académie Française* was to develop the French language into a format that would allow it to be understood by all, that is to become *universalised* into a *lingua franca*. This, of course, brings to mind the original ambitions of the Invisible College, with the universal-language schemes concocted by Hartib, Comenius and Wilkins. It also recalls the claim made by the Rosicrucian brotherhood, namely that its members could communicate with all the peoples of the world through a sort of 'natural language', appropriately dubbed the 'silent language' by modern Rosicrucian researchers.[78]

Had this natural, magical language anything to do with the Masonic secret sign language that also employs ancient symbols, particularly those used by Renaissance Hermetic-Cabalists and also Rosicrucian adepts? Whatever the answer to such a provocative question, it is nonetheless justified to a certain extent for us to wonder whether the developments of a philosophical-scientific group in Paris in the 1630s might not have had something to do with the Rosicrucian movement and, more particularly, the 'poster scare' of 1623 when it was alleged that emissaries of the Invisible College of the Rosicrucians had arrived in France, or were about to arrive, who could communicate in a universal or 'natural' language as a tool to reform and better the condition of the world.[79]

The Scottish connection

As regards the formation of the Royal Society in England in 1660, all historians agree that the initial driving force of this institution was Robert Moray. We've already seen how, in 1641, Moray was the first Freemason to be initiated on British soil. This event occurred two years after Cardinal Richelieu founded the *Académie Française* in 1638. In that same fateful year of 1638 the future Sun King Louis XIV was born and the Hermetic philosopher Tommaso Campanella, who had prophesied the unexpected birth, dedicated his famous *City of the Sun* to Richelieu.[80] The connection is that Robert Moray had spent many years in Paris where he had joined the Scots Guard of Louis XIII in 1633. In 1638 he had been elevated to the command of the guard by Richelieu who greatly admired this rather bold and refined young Scotsman.[81]

Twelve years later, in 1652, Moray married the lady Sophia Lindsay,[82] daughter of Sir David Lindsay, the first Earl of Balcarres. Lindsay was a learned man who enjoyed the private life. He had a keen interest in alchemy, and in his library were to be found many alchemical works which Lindsay himself had translated and copied in Scottish colloquial in his own handwriting, including some 'Rosicrucian literature'.[83] It was also in 1652 that Moray sponsored the very first English-language edition of the

Rosicrucian Manifestos which was published by the famous Welsh alchemist Thomas Vaughan (brother of the poet Henry Vaughan), who wrote under the pseudonym 'Eugenius Philalethes'.[84] Anthony Wood, a contemporary, was to describe Thomas Vaughan as 'a zealous brother of the Rosie-Crucian fraternity', and then also Moray, his sponsor, as a 'most renowned chymist [and] great patron of the Rosie-Crucians.'[85] With such keen sustained interest in all things Rosicrucian, one wonders if a contact did not take place between Moray and Campanella, both of whom were at the French court in 1638, both of whom were sponsored by Richelieu and, more importantly, both of whom had acted as patrons to the Rosicrucian movement.

There is yet another Royal Society founder to consider, the diarist John Evelyn, who also was no stranger to Paris in those troubled times. In 1643, after the outbreak of the Civil War in England, Evelyn left for Paris, then travelled to Rome, Venice and Padua. He was back in Paris in 1646, where a year later he married Mary Browne, the daughter of the British ambassador. Evelyn stayed in Paris till 1652. Was he, too, exposed to the 'Rosicrucian' and Hermetic ideas that hovered at the French court? It would be odd, indeed, if he was not.

According to Masonic historian Robert Lomas, the Jacobean court-in-exile in Paris was rife with Freemasons. Many of the Scots Guards, for example, were Masons from Scottish lodges including, of course, their leader, Robert Moray. The Masonic historian and Master of the famous Lodge of Antiquity, William Preston, who is known among Freemasons for having published the very popular book *Illustrations of Freemasonry* in 1772, even believed that Charles II himself might have been a member of the brotherhood.[86] Early Freemasons with a great appetite for illumination and arcane knowledge would have been particularly receptive to such 'Rosicrucian' ideas and the Hermetic-Christian utopian vision that Campanella preached. It is not impossible that these influences in Paris might have prompted Moray to seek out the Invisible College when he returned to England.

But we are now going to examine the connection of yet another Royal Society founder who deserves even closer scrutiny. For this particular English gentleman was to play a pivotal role in the events that were soon, quite literally, to reshape the old city of London …

Blazing star of doom

Towards the end of 1664 rumours spread that a 'blazing star' had been seen in the southeast sky from London. It was a comet. And these rare and impressive cosmic visitors were believed in those days to be the harbingers of 'famine and plague' and other such calamities.[87] Martin Luther, the German Protestant leader, even believed comets to be the signs of God's wrath or tokens of the Second Coming.[88] On 15 December 1664, Robert Hooke, a senior member of the Royal Society, reported the 'blazing star' to his colleagues. On 17 December Robert Moray spotted it from his observatory at Whitehall, and soon others saw it from other locations.

It vanished from view about the end of January 1665 but then just two months later in March 1665 a second comet appeared.[89] Amongst the general public and the erudite alike this was taken as the ultimate herald of doom. And they were not to be disappointed. In May 1665 the bubonic plague hit the city of London. The nightmarish disease was first noticed in the parish of St. Gilles in the Fields. With its narrow, dirt infested alleys, its virtually nonexistent drainage, and its total lack of public hygiene, London in the mid-1660s was the perfect environment for the Great Plague to strike and take hold. To make matters worse, the month of June that year was unusually hot, giving more impetus to the deadly epidemic. Within a few months people began to die in droves.

Predictably many attributed the Great Plague to the wrath of God. Henry Oldenburg, secretary of the Royal Society, went as far as to claim that 'when we have purged our foul sins this horrible evil will cease.'[90] Alarmed by the rising number of deaths, Charles II moved his court to Oxford in July, leaving the Londoners to their grim fate.[91] All those who could afford it followed suit, moving either into the country or, better still, across the Channel to the safety of continental Europe. It was at this time that Christopher Wren took the opportunity to travel to France ...

Christopher Wren's esoteric pedigree

Christopher Wren was educated at Westminster School and completed his studies at Wadham College, Oxford, where he attained the prestigious Fellowship of All Souls in 1653. Within a few years he was appointed professor of astronomy at Gresham College in London and, after the Restoration of Charles II in 1660, he was given the prestigious chair of Savilian Professor of Astronomy at the University of Oxford. He was only 29 when he took up this post, but even then was regarded by his peers as one of the most learned men in England.

Wren developed a close friendship with Prince Rupert of the Palatinate, who also held the title of Duke of Cumberland. Prince Rupert, like John Evelyn and Robert Moray, spent some time in Paris with Charles II during his exile. And like Moray, he had been very well received by Richelieu. On his return to England after the Restoration Rupert developed a keen interest in 'natural science' and became an active member of the Royal Society, often travelling to Oxford to visit Wren and see him at work in his laboratory.

It will be remembered that John Wilkins, one of the original founders of the Invisible College, was chaplain to Rupert's older brother, Prince Charles Louis, the elector palatine-in-exile. Wren, in fact, had probably known Prince Charles Louis in his childhood, when both were at the deanery at Windsor where Wren's father had been stationed as registrar of the Order of the Garter. In those early days Wren himself had been a protégée of Wilkins.[92] When we recall how much Frederick V of the Palatinate, the ill-fated father of Rupert and Charles Louis, had been indirectly entangled in the Rosicrucian movement in Germany, and also the many Rosicrucian connections that can be traced to the founding members of the Invisible College, it is tempting to consider the possibility that Wren too might have been influenced by the same Rosicrucian ideologies.

In 1663 Wren began to develop a keen interest in architecture, and it was becoming clear to him that this career, rather than one in mathematics or astronomy, was his true and natural vocation. Although Wren was a brilliant geometrician and had a talent for model-making and design, one cannot help but wonder if it was not his contact with the Invisible College in 1660, and more particularly the Masonic attachments of individual members of the Invisible College, that might have inspired him to make such a switch at this rather advanced stage of his academic career. We have seen how Freemasons hold architecture and geometry in the highest esteem. After all, the legendary hero of Freemasonry, Hiram Abiff, was allegedly the architect of Solomon's Temple. Likewise Freemasons also refer to God, who they prefer to call the Supreme Being, as the 'Grand Architect of the Universe'.

Since many, if not all, the protagonists who played a part in the formation of the Royal Society were Freemasons we ought not be too be surprised to find that Wren was a member of the brotherhood as well. According to Anderson's *Constitutions of Freemasons* (second edition) published in 1738, Christopher Wren was already a Master Freemason in 1673 and later, in 1685, became the Grand Master of all English Freemasons.[93] Other documents suggest that Wren may have joined the Freemasons by 1663, perhaps even earlier.[94] It is also thought that Wren was a regular member of one of the four original Masonic lodges that were amalgamated in 1717 to form the Grand Lodge of England.[95] This lodge was originally located at St. Paul's in London, and it is almost certain that Wren was at one time its Master.[96]

Pausing to deposit Wren in Paris we make an excursion to Rome to study a mysterious obelisk

When Christopher Wren arrived in Paris in late July 1665, he was in for a great treat.

Louis XIV was in the process of launching a massive revival in classical and baroque architecture in Paris and Versailles. He had invited the great Italian baroque architect, Gian Lorenzo Bernini to be advisor and witness to these events and, specifically, to design the new façade for the Louvre Palace. At the time Bernini, whose reputation in architecture had reached almost heroic levels, had just begun the design of the great plaza in front of the Vatican Basilica of St. Peter in Rome, at the centre of which still stands today an intact ancient Egyptian obelisk surmounted by a golden cross.[97]

We shall digress briefly to tell a little of the story of this 'Vatican Obelisk' and of Bernini's role in its final decoration, since these matters have a bearing on our primary theme – namely the survival of secret traditions that have carried ancient Egyptian religious concepts and symbolism through time and lodged them in the Western heartlands of orthodox Christian power.

The Vatican Obelisk, which stands more than 25 meters tall and weighs 320 tons, is hewn from a single block of solid granite. One of 13 original Egyptian obelisks that can still be seen in Rome today,[98] it is somewhat unusual in that none of its faces bear inscriptions telling us anything about its origins. We know for certain, however, that it was brought to Rome from Egypt on the orders of Emperor Caligula (AD 12–41). It was transported across the Mediterranean in a special ship and set in place in AD 37 in the 'Vatican Circus', which Caligula had built for chariot racing.

As to the ancient Egyptian provenance of the obelisk, we learn from the Roman historian Pliny, a contemporary of Caligula, that it had been made originally for one 'Nuncoreus, the son of Sesostris'.[99] The reference here is to the 12th dynasty Pharaoh Sesostris I (1971–1926 BC) who carried out extensive restoration at ancient Egypt's most sacred city, *Anu*, which the Greeks would later call Heliopolis – literally the 'City of the Sun'. Heliopolis was itself a sort of 'Vatican City' in the sense that it held the same powerful symbolic significance to the ancient Egyptians as the Vatican does to devout Roman Catholics today. But on the actual site of ancient Heliopolis, in the suburbs of modern Cairo, almost nothing is left to show of former glories. The magnificent Sun Temple that once formed the sacred heart of ancient

Egyptian spirituality is nowhere to be seen and the only remnant of any size is a lone obelisk raised by Sesostris I.[100] On this and other evidence scholars have concluded that the Vatican Obelisk also originally stood at Heliopolis and may perhaps even have formed one of a pair with the obelisk that remains on site.

Historian Christopher Hibbert, in his book *Rome: the Biography of a City*, asserts simply that 'the obelisk of Saint Peter's Square was transported by Caligula from Heliopolis in 37 AD.'[101] Likewise in their book *Roma Egizia* ('Egyptian Rome') Italian scholars Anna Maria Partini and Boris de Rachewiltz accept Pliny's statement that the Vatican Obelisk was originally from Heliopolis and belonged to a son of Sesostris. But they establish additionally that it was not brought directly from Heliopolis to Rome but was first taken by Emperor Augustus Caesar to Alexandria and raised there in the Julian Forum, where it remained until it was shipped to Rome by Caligula in AD 37.[102]

As we've seen Caligula had the obelisk raised in the Vatican Circus as the centrepiece of his private chariot-racing grounds. There it was to remain for the next 1600 years while the Vatican Circus – where Saint Peter was believed to have been martyred in AD 64 – was redeveloped to become the heart and centre of the Roman Catholic world. Begun in AD 334 by Constantine the Great (but not completed until the 16th century by the architects and sculptors Bramante, Raphael and finally Michelangelo himself)[103] the Basilica of Saint Peter was built half over the top of, and overlapping with, the Vatican Circus.

The result was that Caligula's obelisk ended up close to the south wall of the Basilica. It was observed in that spot in the 14th century by a certain Master Gregorius, an English prelate who made a journey to Rome and left us an account. He describes the obelisk as standing in a dark alley, its base and pedestal completely covered by rubbish, flanked by crumbling old houses up against the wall of the Basilica.

In the 15th century the plan was first conceived to move the ancient Egyptian relic to the position of honour it occupies today in the centre of Saint Peter's Square. The idea came from Pope Nicholas V (1447–1455) who intended that the base of the obelisk should stand on four life-size bronze statues of the Evangelists and that its tip should be surmounted by a huge bronze Jesus with a golden cross in his hand. Nicholas died before he could commission the work and the project lapsed.

It fell to Pope Sixtus V (1585–1590) to complete the plan. Dubbed the 'Last of the Renaissance Popes', Sixtus was:

... intent on making Rome Europe's finest city, and St. Peter's its grandest basilica. He was responsible for redesigning the city's entire layout, chiefly by the construction of immense avenues which opened up a series of vistas anchored in obelisks radiating from the core of the built-up area immediately across the Tiber from the Vatican towards the hills in the east.[104]

Sixtus dispensed with the four figures of the Evangelists proposed by Nicolas V for the base of the Vatican Obelisk and replaced them with four lions around a stone pedestal. He also dispensed with the idea of a statue of Jesus balanced on the tip of the obelisk. A bronze sphere, popularly believed to contain the ashes of Julius Caesar – the first 'divine' emperor of Rome and also 'pharaoh' of Egypt – had been positioned there by Caligula but proved on examination to be empty. Deciding to retain the sphere, Sixtus placed inside it fragments of Christ's supposed 'True Cross' that were in the possession of the Vatican. He then ordered that the heraldic symbol of his own family, a star over three small mountains, be placed above the bronze sphere, and, above the star, a golden cross. It was in this form, therefore, surmounted by a cross, that the ancient obelisk from Heliopolis was finally raised in the heart of the Vatican on 27 September 1588.[105]

The first thing Sixtus did after the obelisk was safely upright was to have it exorcised. With all the usual bells and incense a bishop stood before it and solemnly cried out:

I exorcise you, creature of stone, in the name of omnipotent God, that you may become an exorcised stone worthy of supporting the Holy Cross, and be freed from any vestige of impurity or shred of paganism and from any assault of spiritual impurity.[106]

To make sure that the point was properly driven home, Sixtus had the same formula carved permanently into the western and eastern sides of the base of the obelisk.

Ironically, however, the anti-pagan message was flatly contradicted by a secret or 'invisible' message that the obelisk itself had begun to pulse forth from the moment that a cross was fixed to its apex. The message was secret because it was written in three dimensions in ancient Egyptian hieroglyphs which no one in the 16th century is supposed to have been able to read. Whether by pure coincidence, or by design, however, it is a fact that an obelisk surmounted by a cross is a symbol that would have had a meaning for ancient Egyptian priests. The meaning is the name of the most sacred 'pagan' city of antiquity – *Anu*-Heliopolis – the ancient Egyptian 'City of the Sun'. Not only is the Sixtus arrangement of the obelisk meaningful in the ancient Egyptian language, in other words, but also, and much more impressive, the meaning is *correct* – since *Anu*-Heliopolis was the very place where this obelisk originally came from!

One small detail might spoil this otherwise intriguing picture. Although it is true that a hieroglyph showing an obelisk surmounted by a cross would have been understood as *Anu* (Heliopolis) by an ancient Egyptian priest, the symbol is nevertheless incomplete. It should normally be accompanied by a circle or ellipse divided into eight parts – the standard hieroglyphic indicator of a city. The failure of Sixtus and his architects to include such a circle in the plan for Saint Peter's Square seems to rule out any notion that some secret Hermetic game was being played here.

Or it would if things had been left the way they were when Sixtus died in 1590.

Instead, more than 70 years later, the architect Gian Lorenzo Bernini was commissioned by Pope Alexander VII (1655–1667) to redesign Saint Peter's Square. He chose to surround it with elegant freestanding colonnades, creating a huge elliptical space centred on the obelisk. Bernini's work on the project, as we noted above, was interrupted in 1665 when he took up Louis XIV's personal invitation to visit Paris. But he completed it on his return to Rome by marking out on the plaza, around the base of the obelisk, the beautiful geometrical pattern of a gentle ellipse divided into eight parts that can be seen there to this day.

Coincidence? Or could some secret group, capable of sustaining influence on the papacy over many decades, have understand ancient Egyptian hieroglyphs long before scholars learnt to read them in the 19th century?

Anu-Heliopolis was the archetypal 'City of the Sun' that Giordano Bruno and Tommaso Campanella had been determined to restore. And we have shown that Bruno and Campanella were not alone but were part of a larger network of Hermetic and 'Rosicrucian' thinkers spread across Europe who had become very influential – though still not unburnable – by the mid-1660s. The defiant act of writing the name of Heliopolis in 'invisible language' in the midst of the Vatican's proudest stronghold is precisely the sort of symbolic and talismanic guerrilla warfare that we would expect of the members of such a network.

But there is no proof. The reader must decide.

An English Architect meets his hero at the Court of The Sun King

Let's now return to Paris in July of 1665 where Christopher Wren had just arrived, fleeing the Great Plague in London, and where Bernini was then also in residence, invited by Louis XIV to design the new façade for the Louvre Palace.

At the court of Louis XIV Bernini mingled with France's leading architects such as Louis Le Vaux and Claude Perrault, as well as the great landscape architect André Le Nôtre. Born in 1613, Le Nôtre came from an illustrious family of royal gardeners – his grandfather had been in charge of the Tuileries Garden at the Louvre Palace, and his father had been the chief gardener of Louis XIII. At the birth of the Sun King Louis XIV, Le Nôtre was put in charge of the Tuileries and Luxembourg Gardens. Later, at the peak of Louis XIV's reign, Le Nôtre would design and engineer the famous Gardens of Versailles.

When Wren visited Paris, Le Nôtre was a mature man of 52 with an immense reputation at court. Since 1656 he had been in full control of all the king's buildings, and was on the verge of beginning one of his most ambitious – and least publicised – projects: the so-called *Grande Cours* or 'Great Course'. The central idea was a wide processional avenue, starting from the Tuileries, that would open the outlook from the Louvre towards the west. It had originally been proposed during the reign of Henri IV, the grandfather of the Sun King. But nothing was done about it until 1661, when Jean-Baptiste Colbert, Louis XIV's all-powerful minister of finance, appointed Le Nôtre to bring the idea to fruition.

Le Nôtre's scheme somehow manages to be grandiose yet exquisitely simple at the same time. A contemporary plan now kept in the *Archives des Hauts-de-Seine*, shows a vast straight avenue (the celebrated Champs-Élysées),[107] flanked on either side by rows of trees, running westward from the Tuileries all the way to the Pont de Neuilly. Roughly at the centre of the avenue there was a flat-topped hill, then known as the *Colline de Chaillot*, on which Le Nôtre proposed to situate a huge piazza in the shape of a 'star'.[108] In the fullness of time the latter was to become the Place de l'Étoile where, in 1815, Napoleon commissioned the famous Arc de Triomphe, today perhaps Paris's best known landmark.[109]

It was amidst illustrious men, therefore, in a Paris buzzing with new architectural concepts and idealistic city plans, that Christopher Wren was to spend six months of his life at the formative stage of his new architectural career. And aside from the obvious lure of the architectural revival then underway, a flurry of scientific activities also attracted the Englishman. He met with the topographer Melchisédech Thévenot, the astronomer Pierre Petit – a collaborator of Blaise Pascal – as well as the Huguenot philosopher Henri Justel. Both Petit and Justel would themselves eventually become fellows of the Royal Society.[110] Wren also befriended the physicist Adrien Auzout, who, like him, had cultivated a deep interest in architecture. Thévenot, Petit and Auzout belonged to the group of scientists we mentioned earlier who met, very much like a Parisian version of the Invisible College, under the patronage of Habert de Montmor. There was much talk of formalising this group under the charter of Louis XIV – again in the same fashion as the Royal Society – and members were thus naturally interested to meet Christopher Wren and to hear his views on the matter.

Wren also met Bernini, who had arrived in Paris just a month before he did. But at the time of this meeting, it is important to recall, Wren was to Bernini as a new undergraduate is to the head of a school of architecture. In short, Wren at this point was a nobody while Bernini was a giant who commanded the respect, the funds and even the patience of the pope and many kings and princes of Europe. In consequence the great Bernini was constantly swamped by his admirers while he was in Paris – so we may not suppose that he took much notice of the insignificant Wren.

For Wren himself, however, it was a life-changing encounter. To meet face to face, even briefly, with his architectural superhero, was an experience that affected him deeply. It is probable that from this moment on he was fired by the ambition that was to make him one of England's greatest architects. Here is how Adrian Tinniswood, Wren's latest biographer, sums up the meeting:

> With hindsight this meeting is one of the most momentous in the history of seventeenth-century architecture – the man destined to be England's greatest exponent of the Baroque in a face-to-face encounter with the most famous Baroque architect in Europe[111] ... The benefits Wren gained from his visit to France were considerable. They range from the experience of a more sophisticated architectural milieu than he knew in England, and a chance to exchange ideas in a less sophisticated, but still rewarding, scientific milieu, to the quantities of books he brought home with him – 'almost all France in paper'.[112]

But Christopher Wren may have brought back something else, something perhaps less tangible than drawings and papers but far more powerful: a 'vision' of the new role he had to play in the restored Stuart monarchy. We shall return to the city of Paris and its exciting scientific and amazing architectural renaissance in later chapters. Meanwhile things became uncomfortable there for Wren when Louis XIV declared war on Britain in January 1666 in support of the French alliance with the Dutch. It was time for Wren to go home. He arrived back in London in March 1666 and within a few months an incredible opportunity was to drop into his lap – one that no one could have imagined in their wildest dreams … or nightmares as the case would be.

Rising from the ashes

The Great Fire of London began on 2 September 1666, apparently sparked in a bakery at Pudding Lane, near London Bridge, when Thomas Farriner, the king's baker, forgot to dowse the fire of his oven before going to bed. Some embers fell on nearby kindling and soon his rickety wooden house was in flames. In those days the houses in the city of London were mostly built with timber frames and pitched roofs, which caused them to burn like big matchboxes. Within a few hours several streets were engulfed in a swirling inferno, with the fiery progress aided by a violent easterly wind that fanned the flames. By the time the Great Fire had abated five days later, 430 acres, that is nearly four fifths of the city, had been reduced to cinders. About 13,000 houses, 90 churches and 50 liveries had been destroyed, and even the great Cathedral of St. Paul's had been ruined.

Apparently Charles II himself worked heroically alongside the fire-fighters, which earned him back some public respect. Nonetheless, the king's enemies were quick to claim that this was God's wrath for the debaucheries at court and the ungodly foreign policies of Parliament. A pamphlet issued by the Dutch, who were at war with England, called it a vengeful act from the 'Almighty and Just God', and the Catholics in Britain promptly agreed with them. Even the *London Gazette* was to report that 'the heavy hand of God is upon us for our sins, shewing us his Judgement in raising the fire.'[113] One also wonders what the Jews of London must have thought with *Rosh Hashanah* (Day of Judgement) only ten days away, and *Yom Kippur* (Day of Atonement) a further ten.[114]

The rumour mill cycled wildly. Stories of a 'papal plot', or a 'foreign plot', or 'God's Wrath' were rife. Charles II did his best to persuade the angry population of London, now gathered at Moorfields, that their collective misfortune was due to nothing more than an accident. He vowed gallantly to take good care of all homeless Londoners and to rebuild their homes and their city immediately. But it is probable that the king was not entirely displeased at this opportunity, for he himself was a bit of dabbler in town-planning and design. Since the Restoration he had been bitterly frustrated by the lack of funds to transform London into a splendid metropolis that would eclipse the 'City of Light' that his cousin, Louis XIV, was turning Paris into. Now here, out of the blue, had come this amazing opportunity that might allow him to do just that.[115]

A new London, everyone hoped after hearing the king's emotional speech at Moorfields, was about to rise like a great phoenix from the smouldering ashes.

Or, better still, like a 'New Jerusalem', as we will see in the next chapter.

The major theme of the Knights Templar legend is its survival through the form of secret societies ... The Templars themselves were a secret society ... It has survived into Freemasonry ... Freemasonry, then, is the heir of the Templars [and] *purports to be the recipient of the ancient wisdom of the builders of Solomon's Temple coming down to them from the Crusades.*

Alain Demurger, *Vie et mort de l'ordre du Temple*

Even a brief survey will show that he [Charles II] *was dedicated to private alchemical experiments ... Such a king could indeed be expected to provide the long awaited 'Solomon's House'...*

Donald R. Dickson, *The Tessera of Antilia*

I will not cease from mental fight, nor shall my sword sleep in my hand, till we have built Jerusalem in England's green and pleasant land.

William Blake, Preface to 'Milton'

CHAPTER FIFTEEN

CABAL

A few days after the Great Fire had finally abated, Christopher Wren and John Evelyn, each man apparently acting independently, rushed to present Charles II with plans for the full reconstruction of London.[1] To be precise, Wren presented his plan on 11 September 1666 and Evelyn presented his on 13 September 1666.[2] The king is reported to have admired both designs greatly but in the end neither could be implemented because the pressing need of the time was not for grand architectural schemes but to re-house the tens of thousands of people made homeless by the Fire.

The abandoned plans of Wren and Evelyn would therefore amount to no more than a footnote to architectural history were it not for two very curious facts:

- Both men 'invisibly' incorporated esoteric symbolic devices into their proposed layouts for the streets and plazas of London, and can only have done so with the same purposes in mind.

- Exactly the same symbolic devices, again apparently used for the same purposes, turn up more than a century later on the other side of the Atlantic in the layout adopted for the streets and plazas of Washington, DC, the newly-built capital of the USA.

The first of these symbols is the simple octagon. The second is more complex, with multiple branches and terminals, and is known as the *Sephirothic Tree* or the 'Tree of Life'. It is derived from Hebrew Cabala, a system of Jewish mysticism that was elaborated in Occitania during the great period of intellectual and religious freedom that was ushered in there by the rise of Catharism in the 12th century.

The octagon and the Sephirothic Tree remain hidden in plain view in Washington to this day, as we will show in Chapter Nineteen, and can easily be seen by the prepared eye in Wren's and Evelyn's abandoned plans for London, which we will examine later in this chapter. In both cases the real issue is not so much demonstrating the use of the symbols but trying to find out *why* they were used in the first place. What was it that Wren and Evelyn, as well as their successors in the American Revolution, had in mind with these devices? Why would the octagon and the Sephirothic Tree have been significant to them?

The first clue that will help us to answer these questions does not lie in London in the 17th century or Washington in the 18th century, but in Occitania in the 13th century in an anomaly of the history of the Albigensian Crusades.

Mystery of the Knights Templar

We saw in Part I how the Albigensian Crusades that smashed the Cathars in the 13th century were mounted at the instigation of successive popes and fought by armies recruited from all over Europe, though principally from northern France. During the whole period of sustained warfare in Occitania, however, from the fall of Béziers in 1209 until the fall of Montségur in 1244, there were large numbers of seemingly obvious 'crusaders' permanently on hand in Provence and the Languedoc who took almost no part in the fighting at all. This is odd and what makes it odder is that these reluctant crusaders against the Cathar heresy were all members of an elite order of highly-trained warrior monks, sworn to papal service, who had already proved themselves in the Holy Land as valiant crusaders against the forces of Islam. Their full title was the 'Poor Knights of Christ and the Temple of Solomon', but they're much better known as the Knights Templar.

We do not propose to rehearse at great length here the familiar story of the Templars that has been told so many times before. But some background is unavoidable if we are going to work out why they abstained from the Cathar wars when we would have expected them to join in wholeheartedly on behalf of the Church.

The order was founded by nine French noblemen who travelled to the Holy Land in 1119 – twenty years after Jerusalem had been captured and occupied by the Christian powers in the First Crusade of 1099. The 12th century historian, Archbishop William of Tyre, tells us that 'foremost and most distinguished' amongst these nine men 'were the venerable Hugh de Payens and Godfrey de St. Omer.'[3]

When the nine arrived in Jerusalem they were received as VIPs by the 'Crusader King' Baldwin I. They requested and were granted the right to use as their headquarters the Al-Aqsa Mosque, which lies on the south side of the ancient Temple Mount and still survives today. Traditionally held to have been the site of the biblical Temple of Solomon, the Temple Mount also houses a second splendid Islamic shrine that the Templars now took control of as well – the Dome of the Rock. It too has survived the centuries and may be visited today. Its floor-plan forms a perfect octagon with all eight sides of equal length, its lofty walls rising to support a beautiful golden dome towering directly above the eponymous 'Rock'. This is the gigantic slab of exposed bedrock that is held in Judaic, Christian and Islamic tradition to have formed the original floor of the Holy of Holies of the Temple of Solomon. On it, the Old Testament tells us, once stood the Ark of the Covenant containing the tablets of the Ten Commandments given to Moses by God – the god in question being Jehovah who the Gnostics and their later successors the Cathars saw as the evil second-class deity who had created the material world as a trap for souls. A Jewish tradition says it was on this same rock that Abraham prepared to sacrifice his son, Isaac, on the instructions of Jehovah. For the Muslims it is the place from whence the Prophet Muhammad made his night journey into heaven.[4]

Solomon's Temple was the First Temple of the Jews, and biblical archaeologists today generally agree with the tradition that it was sited on the Temple Mount and most likely on the spot where the Dome of the Rock now stands. It was destroyed by the Babylonians when they sacked Jerusalem in 587 BC but the Second Temple was built on the same site between 537 and 517 BC after the return of the Jews from their Babylonian exile.[5] In its turn the Second Temple was destroyed by the Romans in AD 70 and there has never subsequently been a Jewish place of worship on the Temple Mount.

This is why the famous 'Wailing Wall' has been of such enormous importance to Jews down the ages and is today the single most important Jewish holy place. It dates back to the time of the Second Temple, being part of a retaining buttress built by Herod the Great in the late first century BC. It escaped demolition by the Romans in AD 70 (because, says the Midrash, the 'Divine Presence' hovered over it) and in later years it became a potent symbol of the nationalist aspirations of the Jewish people scattered in the diaspora.[6]

From AD 70, until Jerusalem was captured in AD 638 in the early Islamic jihads, we know little of the history of the Temple Mount. This is partly because of the confusion of the period that saw the collapse of the Roman Empire and the rapid expansion of Islam, and partly because the Islamic authorities controlling the site do not permit archaeological investigations (although some illicit digs have taken place).[7] Their reluctance is perfectly understandable since the Dome of the Rock and the Al-Aqsa Mosque represent respectively (after Mecca and Medina) the third and fourth most sacred sites in the Islamic world.[8]

Archaeologists believe that a Roman temple was built on the ruins of the Second Temple after AD 70. Six centuries later, in AD 670, Caliph Umar, the successor to Prophet Muhammad and at that point the absolute ruler of Jerusalem, ordered the Temple Mount cleared:

> ... and a Moslem house of worship to be erected there, on the spot where Israel's Temple had once stood.[9]

That same year a temporary wooden shrine was put up. Then in AD 691, during the reign of Caliph Abd al-Malik, the permanent structure of the Dome of the Rock that we still see today was built. Under its huge gilded cupola it represented a unique concept in Islamic architecture of the period with its striking octagonal floor-plan encompassing a circular central nave containing the sacred rock of the Temple of Solomon. Some decades later Abd al-Malik's son, Caliph Al-Walid, built the Al-Aqsa Mosque.[10] There then followed four centuries of relative peace under Islamic rule, rudely interrupted by the First Crusade and the capture of Jerusalem in 1099.

The Christian crusaders were utterly ruthless, and a bloodbath ensued. Only the Muslim governor of the Holy City, Iftikhar ad-Daula, and his personal bodyguard were allowed to leave in exchange for the city's treasure. 'They were the only Muslims to escape with their lives', reports author Piers Paul Read, in his extensive study of the Knights Templar:

> Intoxicated by their victory, and still charged with the passion of battle, the crusaders set about the slaughter of the city's inhabitants with the same indifference to their victims' age or sex ... they were all killed.[11]

Raymond of Aguilers, the chaplain of Count Raymond IV of Toulouse, the leader of the crusaders, was a witness to the event. When visiting the Temple Mount he had to wade through gore, flesh and blood that littered the streets:

> In all the streets and squares of the city, mounds of heads, hands and feet were to be seen. People were walking over dead men and horses ... what an apt punishment! The very place that endured for so long blasphemies against God was now masked in the blood of the blasphemers.[12]

At that point the Al-Aqsa Mosque, the Dome of the Rock and the whole of the Temple Mount came under Christian control and then, from 1119, under the exclusive control of the Knights Templar – hence, of course, their name.

The Rosy Cross and the Octagon

The Templars signalled their affiliation to Christ by wearing a blood-red cross in the distinctive style known as *croix pattée* stitched to the white background of their tunics – almost 500 years before the Rosicrucian Manifestos made a feature of a very similar 'Rosy Cross'. But their identification with the Temple of Solomon was equally strong, as they demonstrated from the outset by choosing the Temple Mount for their headquarters. Because the Dome of the Rock is an octagonal structure they adopted the octagon as their symbol of this affiliation and their *croix pattée* was cunningly designed so that an octagon with all eight sides of exactly equal length like the floor-plan of the Dome of the Rock was produced by joining all the exterior points of the cross.

One of the several puzzles surrounding the story of Templar origins is the speed with which King Baldwin I of Jerusalem handed over the keys of the Al-Aqsa Mosque to the nine founder knights when they turned up on his doorstep in 1119. It would be a puzzle under all circumstances, but perhaps particularly so in this case because, shortly before the Templars took possession, Baldwin had been lovingly renovating the mosque for use as his own palace.[13] No matter how heavily armed and battle-scarred these rather mysterious and impressive men were they were in no position to threaten the ruler of Jerusalem, who controlled far larger forces. So we may only suppose that he delivered the sacred precinct to them voluntarily – in which case they must have been able to furnish him with the most persuasive reasons why he should do so.

Once the Temple Mount was in their hands the knights lived, ate, slept and worked on this site sacred to three religions. They rarely left it during the next seven years. In public pronouncements they had declared that their mission to the Holy Land was 'to keep the road from the coast to Jerusalem free from bandits.' They don't seem to have done that. Indeed, in the words of one authority, 'the new Order apparently did very little' in this period.[14] Besides simple logic suggests that nine men could hardly have protected anybody on a highway almost 50 miles long – and their number stayed at nine until they were joined by the Count of Champagne in 1125. Moreover the members of an older and far larger military order – the Knights Hospitallers – were already doing the job of protecting pilgrims when the Templars arrived.[15]

Late in 1126 Hugh de Payens suddenly left Jerusalem and returned to Europe accompanied by André de Montbard, another of the founders. De Montbard's nephew was the renowned Catholic cleric Bernard (later Saint Bernard) of Clairvaux, who was about to become the sponsor of the Templars. A staunch opponent of the early Cathars, Bernard would subsequently lead a peaceful preaching campaign against them that took him deep inside Occitania in 1145 and subjected him to a number of humiliations. For example, though he was known as the greatest preacher of his age and was accustomed to being mobbed by adoring crowds of thousands, Bernard only managed to attract an audience of 30 when he preached in the Cathar city of Albi.[16] At Verfeil (northeast of Toulouse) mounted Cathar knights (they would, of course, have been *credentes*, not *perfecti* sworn to nonviolence) are reported to have pounded on the doors of a church where Bernard was attempting to preach and to have clashed their swords together so loudly that no one in the small congregation could hear a word he said.[17]

So if anyone had a reason to hate the Cathars and want to punish them it would surely be the Templars who owed so much to Saint Bernard. All the more difficult to understand therefore why the large numbers of Templars – who are known to have occupied fortresses and preceptories throughout the length and breadth of Occitania in the 12th and 13th centuries[18] – chose to step back from the Albigensian Crusades that raged after 1209. The reader will recall from Chapter Two that several times between campaigns the Catholic champion Simon de Montfort was able to retain only skeleton forces – sometimes down to as few as a dozen knights – with which to preserve crusader gains in Occitania. Never once, so far as we have been able to establish, did the Templars intervene on his behalf or help him in any way in these periods of dire need.

Why not?

If they were exactly what they very much seemed and claimed to be in 1209 – i.e. Catholic knights dedicated to the service of the pope and to the destruction of his enemies – then surely the Templars should have been the first, not the last, to raise the sword of wrath against the heretics of Occitania?

Hubris

Hugh de Payens and André de Montbard arrived in France in 1127 and in January 1128 participated in what was to be the most significant event in the early history of the Templars. That event was the Synod of Troyes, which had been convened with the explicit objective of procuring the Church's official backing for the Templar order. Bernard of Clairvaux presided over the synod and personally drew up the formal 'Rule of the Knights Templar' that, henceforth, was to guide the evolution and development of the order. Thereafter in a series of sermons and glowing panegyrics such as *De Laude Novae Militae* ('In Praise of the New Knighthood') he vigorously promoted the young order – thus using his own prestige and influence to guarantee its success.

The results were spectacular. New recruits flocked in from all over France and later from many other parts of Europe as well. Donations of land and money were received from wealthy patrons, and political power quickly followed. By the last quarter of the 12th century the order had become phenomenally rich, was operating a sophisticated international banking system (that made use of the first ever 'letters of credit') and owned fortresses and a vast range of properties in many different lands.

In the Holy Land the Templars' military might, violence and aggression were legendary, and their policy of 'no retreat, no surrender' often proved devastating. Not unexpectedly, the Muslim forces developed a deep hate for them and a profound mistrust for their unchivalrous, not to say highly un-Christian, behaviour towards their enemies and the civilian population.

There is also the matter of the foolhardy bravado and greed of the Knights Templar – characteristics that eventually played in favour of the Muslims. Take for example the siege of the stronghold fortress of Ascalon held by the caliph of Egypt. Because it was supplied by sea from Alexandria, and could not be starved or deprived of provisions, the fortress had to be taken by direct assault. On 15 August, the day of the Feast of the Virgin, forty Knights Templar led by Bernard de Trémélay placed a high tower against the walls of the fortress and managed to break into the Muslim stronghold. The rest of the Christian army failed to follow them, and the Templars were butchered – their heads cut off and their bodies thrown over the walls of the fortress.

From there on everything began to go horribly wrong. On 4 July 1187, in the full heat of the Levantine summer, the Knights Templar faced a large Muslim army in an arid and waterless region called the *Horns of Hattin*.

The political and religious balance in the Holy Land, and eventually in the whole of the Christian world, was about to change.

The Horns of Hattin

The leader of the Muslim army that the Templars were now about to engage on that fateful day was the legendary Salah-ad-Din Yusuf ibn-Ayyub, better known as Saladin.[19] This time the Templars were contending with a military genius of high intelligence and wide education and, most of all, with a cool mind and a perfect sense of timing.[20]

Saladin was born in the city of Tikrit, in Iraq. As an aside, the reader may be interested to note that Tikrit was also the birthplace of Saddam Hussein, the Iraqi leader deposed by the US in 2003, a connection across the ages that did not escape the attention of the Templar historian Piers Paul Read who commented,

> How many Arab leaders, one wonders, from Abdul Nasser to Saddam Hussein, have aspired to become a latter-day Saladin, defeating the infidel invaders at another Hattin or ... driving them into the sea?[21]

In his youth Saladin joined the service of Imad ad-Din Zengi, the ruler of Syria, and was appointed commander of Zengi's fortress in Baalbek in Lebanon. In 1146 Imad ad-Din died and was replaced by his son, Nur al-Din, under whom Saladin also served until he himself became vizier of Egypt in 1169 and, in 1171, proclaimed himself first Ayyubid sultan of Egypt.

According to his biographers Saladin was familiar with Euclid, the Almagest, mathematics, law and, more especially, the Koran. He also had an excellent knowledge of the history of the Arabs and was an expert on the pedigree of Arabian horses. What is generally remembered of this semi-legendary man, however, is his 'exquisite courtesy' and his clemency towards his enemies.[22] In his court, camp, or on the battlefield, Saladin was the epitome of chivalry, and his Arab roots imposed on him rules of hospitality and politeness that not only baffled his enemies but also earned him immense respect throughout the Muslim world and Christendom. In the aftermath of the Battle of Hattin, for example, his forces captured Guy of Lusignan, the young and handsome king of Jerusalem. Learning that Guy was close to death from exhaustion and thirst, Saladin had him brought to his tent and personally offered him a cup of cool water scented with roses, a gesture that also meant in Arab warfare that Guy's life would be spared and he would be treated in the manner appropriate to his high title. 'A king does not kill a king' Saladin told the bemused Christian leader.

In early 1187 Saladin was in command of a massive Muslim army with which he now felt ready to strike a death blow to the Christian crusaders who controlled Jerusalem and most of the Holy Land. On 1 July Saladin crossed the Jordan with 30,000 soldiers and 12,000 cavalry. In a swift assault he took the town of Tiberias, the stronghold of the prince of Galilee, the Christian knight Count Raymond III of Tripoli. This was a ruse to draw the Christian knights away from Jerusalem and into open battle near Tiberias. Raymond was in Acre with King Guy at the time; his wife, Eschiva, countess of Tripoli, who was still in Tiberias had taken refuge in the citadel and managed to send word to Raymond. Torn between saving the countess and saving the Latin kingdom of Jerusalem, Raymond advised King Guy not to march to Tiberias to engage Saladin in open battle, but to protect Jerusalem instead. Guy did not agree. Listening more to the advice of Reginald de Châtillon and Gérard de Ridefort, the Templar Grand Master, who accused Raymond of cowardice and screamed for revenge against Saladin, Guy foolishly ordered the knights and the army to march towards Tiberias.

In the heat of full summer, riding in the semi-arid region of the Negev desert wearing their heavy armour and laden with weapons, the Christians were already exhausted and parched when they reached the village of Lubia which had a water well. But the well was dry, and so the Christian army camped on the waterless plateau of the Horns of Hattin. To make matters worse, the Muslims set fire to the dry scrub upwind, sending smoke into the Templars' camp. At dawn Saladin ordered the attack. Frenzied by thirst, heat and the infuriating smoke, the Christians attempted a mad rush against the Muslim phalanx, resulting in all of them getting killed or taken prisoners. Raymond charged with his knights and managed to find himself on the other side of the Arab army. Realising the futility of his act, he fled to Tripoli. The remaining Christian forces made a circle around King Guy to protect him, and attempted several sorties against the Muslims, all of which failed.[23] With a few hours, after heavy losses, Guy and the rump of his army were taken prisoner.

As we saw earlier, Saladin showed clemency to Guy. The other knights were offered the choice of conversion to Islam or death by beheading. Most zealously opted for the latter, the gruesome task executed with glee by Sufi fanatics in Saladin's entourage. Saladin himself decapitated the insolent and very arrogant – not to mention bloodthirsty – Reginald de Châtillon in front of the horrified eyes of King Guy who now feared for his own life. This was the moment when Saladin uttered the famous words cited earlier: 'A king does not kill a king, but *that* man's [de Châtillon's] perfidy and insolence went too far.' Saladin also spared the life of Gérard de Ridefort, the Grand Master of the Templars – not out of compassion but to use him as leverage in his parleys with other Templar strongholds. Within weeks Saladin had taken the fortified towns of Acre, Nablus, Sidon, Ascalon, Jaffa, Beirut and Sidon. Only Tyre resisted. By mid-September Saladin was ready to go for the ultimate prize, the 'World Cup' of all crusading wars – *Jerusalem*.

We recall the great importance that Muslims everywhere accord to Jerusalem's Temple Mount (Al-Haram al-Sharif). This is because of the belief that in AD 621 Muhammad rode a winged-horse called the *Buraq*[24] and flew at night from Makkah (Mecca) to the Temple Mount. Known as *Lailat al-Miraj* (the 'Night of the Ascension'), this is regarded as one of the most significant events in Islam.[25] The 'Night' starts at Makkah, with the Prophet Muhammad resting in the Ka'aba, the cubical shrine that is regarded as Islam's most holy place. Here the Archangel Gabriel appears and gives Muhammad the *Buraq*. Muhammad then mounts the *Buraq* which takes him to the 'farthest mosque', which Muslims believe to be the Al-Aqsa Mosque in Jerusalem. There Muhammad prays. He then flies again on the *Buraq* to reach 'heaven', where he speaks to the earlier prophets such as Abraham, Moses and Jesus. The Archangel Gabriel then takes him to see Allah (God). Allah instructs Muhammad that Muslims must pray fifty times a day. Moses urges Muhammad to ask Allah for a 'reduction'. This Muhammad does several times until the number is reduced to five prayers a day. Muhammad then returns to Makkah and tells his story to a bemused population who go to Abu Bakr, Muhammad's loyal companion, and say: 'Look at what your companion is saying ... he went to Jerusalem and came back in one night!' Abu Bakr replies: 'If he said this, then it is true. I believe him ...' Because of this, Abu Bakr earned his celebrated epithet of *Al-Saddiq*, the 'Believer'.

With such a heritage to reclaim, we can imagine what Saladin and his men must have felt as they stood before the walls of Jerusalem in late September 1187 pitting their religious convictions against those of the whole of Christendom. Although no magical winged-horse had carried Saladin here, the Muslims held their breath and hoped with all their fervour that he, too, would soon pray on the sacred rock as did the Prophet Muhammad on that night of nights nearly six centuries before.

Tonight I will pray in Jerusalem!

A few weeks before the battle for Jerusalem, during the siege of Tyre, the Christian baron, Balian de Ibelin (whom the Arabs regarded as equal to a 'king'), asked Saladin for a safe conduit into Jerusalem so that he could bring his family out. Saladin agreed on condition that Balian swear an oath not take up arms against him and not stay more than a day in the city. The oath was sworn, but once inside Jerusalem, Queen Sibylla, (King Guy's ambitious wife), and Heraclius, the patriarch,[26] persuaded Balian to break his word to Saladin and stay to take control of the defence.

The conditions in the city were terrible. Hardly a handful of knights remained (some sources say only two, others say fourteen). Balian was forced to 'create' another sixty knights chosen from among his soldiers.

By 20 September 1187 Saladin was at the walls of Jerusalem. Through the mediation of an Eastern Orthodox Christian clergyman, Yussef Bateet, negotiations were opened between Saladin and Balian. Saladin said that he wanted to take the city without shedding any blood. Balian vowed to fight to the death rather than hand Jerusalem over to the Muslims.

A siege followed. Arab archers rained arrows down into the city. Huge catapults hurled heavy stones and Greek fire. Part of the city wall was breached on 29 September. The breach was strongly defended but the Arab numbers were overwhelming. Realising that end was near[27] Balian threatened to have the Dome of the Rock and the Al-Aqsa Mosque destroyed and the city burnt.

Further parley brought agreement from Saladin to be paid a ransom of 10 dinars for each man, 5 dinars for each woman and 1 dinar for each child. Funds from the city's treasury were used for those who could not pay, thus securing the freedom of a further 7,000 inhabitants. On 2 October came the formal surrender; Balian personally handed over the keys to the Tower of David, the citadel. A calm and disciplined evacuation of Jerusalem then took place, with the surviving Knights Templar and Knights Hospitaller leading two columns and Balian and Heraclius leading a third column. Saladin even allowed Heraclius to take a number of church treasures and reliquaries along.

That same evening, as the refugees still streamed away, Saladin entered Jerusalem in triumph amid shouts of a '*Allah'u Akbar*!' ('God is Great!')

A curtain had fallen on the crusaders' dream and Christendom's love affair with Jerusalem. A strange kind of hush, a dark mood of despair and confusion, fell over the Catholic pope in Rome and Catholic kings across Europe.

The Death Blow to the Templars in the Holy Land

The Templars clung on to some parts of the Holy Land for another century. Their final downfall came in the spring of 1290, when an Egyptian army led by Caliph Al-Mansur Qalawun and his son, Al-Ashraf Khalil, moved to lay siege to the city of Saint-Jean d'Acre (the modern Acre) which was in the hands of the crusading knights and regarded as the last bastion of the so-called *crusading* Christian states.

With its fortified wall and its back to the sea, Acre's reputation as a crusader stronghold was legendary. But now, after almost three centuries of warfare between Christians and the Muslims, the bulk of the crusading states had been severely weakened. Undermanned and drastically low on supplies, Acre was about to face the full brunt of the Muslim forces. There was a moment of hope when it was announced that Caliph Qalawun had suddenly died, as though felled by the hand of God, just before reaching the walls of Acre. But his son and successor Al-Ashraf Khalil, kept a cool head and immediately took control of the Arab army, By 6 April 1290 Acre was thoroughly under siege, with the only way out being from the sea.

Within the high walls the knights braced themselves for the worst, as it was now clear to all just how massively the Arabs outnumbered them. There were terrible scenes of panic as the populace scrambled for places on the few ships available, and many old people and children drowned in the mad scuffle to evacuate the doomed city. On 15 May the Arabs breached the walls and stormed inside. An awful carnage ensued, even by medieval standards. The Knights Templar fought to the last like mad lions, knowing full well the gruesome fate that awaited them if they were captured alive. Amazingly, they held on in a redoubt for a further twelve days and when the fighting was finally over the city looked like a giant butcher's floor.

Infuriated by the insane resistance of the Templars, Al-Ashraf Khalil ordered Acre razed to the ground and all prisoners – male and female, young and old, civilian or military – put to death 'under the Prophet's sword'. The Church of St. Andrew, renowned throughout Christendom, was demolished; its heavy Gothic door, weighing several tons, was taken as booty to Cairo to adorn the mausoleum of Al-Ashraf Khalil's brother. As the Arabs rode off from the smoldering stench and the terrible carnage, the already dark and somber mood of the Christian world deepened. The adventure of the crusades, of heroic tales and gallantry to 'protect' the Holy Land from the 'heathen', was finally over.

Nemesis

The fall of Acre marked the beginning of the end for the Templars. Within less than a decade of the disaster most of the knights had returned to Europe. Some went to England, where they were absorbed by the many long-established Templar preceptories there. The order's headquarters in England was located in London just north of the Thames to the east of Holborn in the district that is still called 'Temple' today. Some of the returning Templars went to Germany and to Spain. Many went to France, particularly to Paris and to the Port of La Rochelle where again, there were large numbers of existing Templar institutions to receive them. Thousands also chose to settle in Occitania which, by 1300, was increasingly being absorbed into France, and which had hosted a strong and continuous Templar presence for more than 150 years.

By the beginning of the 14th century the papacy's long and corrupt dependence on the French crown to provide a 'final solution' to the problem of the Cathar heresy had not only resulted in the annexation of Occitania into France but also in a steady diminution in the powers of the pope. So much was this the case that from 1309 until 1377 (a period referred to by Catholic historians as the 'Babylonian Captivity'), the papacy was not based in Rome but in Avignon where it was almost totally under the control of the French monarchy.

The pope who made the move to Avignon in 1309 was Clement V. Formerly Raymond Bertrand de Got, archbishop of Bordeaux, he was elected pope in 1305 and crowned at Lyons in the presence of King Philip IV of France, known as Philip the Fair. Two years later Clement laid grave charges of heresy against the Templars and authorized Philip to bring the knights to trial. The charges were in many cases identical to those that had been repeatedly brought against the Cathars by the Inquisition during the 13th century and included accusations of secret ceremonies in which initiates were required to spit on or break crosses – accusations that aroused feelings of righteous horror amongst orthodox Catholics.

Thus it was that on Friday 13 October 1307 all members of the order within reach of Philip's forces – including all the Templars in Occitania – were arrested. Since more than 15,000 of them were rounded up in this way it is clear that the operation must have been exceptionally well-planned and well-coordinated, and implemented by large numbers of the king's men. We know that simultaneous dawn swoops on hundreds of Templar properties were carried out and that in most cases the arrests were secured without a struggle.[28]

In the months that followed, the Templars were savagely tortured by the Inquisition. And as with the Cathars before them, and Bruno after them, this torture – which was of exceptional brutality, even by Inquisition standards – was specially authorized by the pope. Moving quickly to follow up the arrests in France, Pope Clement V also issued a bull, *Pastoralis praeeminentiae*, dated 22 November 1307, which ordered the arrest of all other Templars throughout the Christian world. Proceedings followed as far afield as England, Spain, Germany, Italy and Cyprus and, in 1312, another bull from the puppet pope, *Vox in excelso*, officially suppressed the order. Meanwhile thousands of Templars were subjected to the most gruesome tortures and many were subsequently burned at the stake.

The agonizing death of the last Grand Master of the Templars, Jacques de Molay, came on 18 March 1314, and was recorded for posterity by a monk who was an eyewitness to the event:

> At the hour of vespers [late afternoon], on a small island on the Seine
> situated between the gardens of the king and the church of St. Augustine,
> they [Grand Master Jacques de Molay and the Templar Preceptor
> of Normandy, Geoffroi de Charnay] were condemned to be burnt ...
> They were seen so resolute to endure the ordeal of the fire, with such
> willingness, that they gained the admiration and surprise of all who
> witnessed ...[29]

Such descriptions inevitably remind us of the calm fortitude of the Cathar *perfecti* when they faced similarly terrible deaths at the stake, and later of Giordano Bruno, the Hermetic magus who was burned for his beliefs in Rome in February 1600. But Jacques de Molay was a fighting man and he went out fighting. Twisting in horrible pain as he roasted in the midst of a slow fire, the last Templar Grand Master found the strength to call down a curse on the French monarchy for 13 generations and to prophesy that Clement V and Philip the Fair would both meet him for judgement before the throne of God within the year. Weirdly Clement V died just one month later, in April 1314, and Philip the Fair died inexplicably in November 1314.[30] The climax of the story comes many generations later with the outbreak of the French Revolution in 1789 and the public beheading by guillotine of the unfortunate Louis XVI in 1793. Allegedly as the king's head rolled into the basket a French Freemason darted forward, dipped his fingers in the blood and scattered it over the crowd, shouting: 'Jacques de Molay, thou art avenged!'[31]

Templar survivals and the long quest for Utopia

When Jacques de Molay was burned in 1314 many say that the Templars ceased to exist. This is true in the legal sense, for the order was suppressed. But practically speaking it did survive in a number of places. One was the Scotland of Robert the Bruce which liberated itself from English occupation at the Battle of Bannockburn in 1314. Another was Portugal where the Templars were tried but found to be free of guilt, and thus neither tortured nor imprisoned. There, though their order was officially dissolved in 1312 as elsewhere, it was able to reconstitute itself under a different name – the Militia of Jesus Christ (also known as the Knights of Christ or the Order of Christ).[32]

A persistent rumour down the centuries hints at a great mystery concerning the large and well-appointed Templar fleet that had been anchored in the French Atlantic port of La Rochelle on the night of 13 October 1307 when the mass of Templars were rounded up. Historians accept that the fleet was there the day before but gone the next morning, eluding the king's forces that came to take possession of it. Clearly, therefore, good numbers of Templars – enough at any rate to man and sail the fleet – did escape arrest in France.

But where did they go? On this there is no concensus. One theory has it that the Templars sailed to North Africa to join forces with their long-time enemies, the Muslims. Another theory has them discovering the Americas almost two centuries before Columbus. A third theory, not necessarily inconsistent with the latter as we shall see, has them sailing to Scotland and taking refuge amongst the large number of Templars already established in that country.[33] There according to 18th century Masonic sources such as the Chevalier Ramsay and the Baron von Hund, they formed the core of the underground movement that would eventually blossom forth again as Freemasonry.[34]

There is a particularly strong association linking the Templars in Scotland, Scottish Freemasonry and the ancient Sinclair family of Rosslyn near Edinburgh. A thorough study of the subject was published by Andrew Sinclair in 1991 under the title *The Sword and The Grail*.[35] It presents compelling evidence that Sir William Sinclair, who began construction of the spectacular Gothic chapel at Rosslyn around 1446, was himself secretly initiated as a Templar more than 130 years after the suppression of the order and was at the same time the hereditary Grand Master of Freemasonry in Scotland.[36]

Equally intriguing from our point of view is the evidence also presented in *The Sword and The Grail* of a voyage made to the northeast coast of America around 1398–9 by William's grandfather Prince Henry Sinclair, First Earl of Orkney and also an initiated Templar. This precocious voyage appears to have been partly memorialized in reliefs at Rosslyn Chapel, dated prior to 1450 (thus still more than 40 years before Columbus) that show American maize and aloe cactus.[37] Since 1991, so much new historical and archaeological evidence has been brought forward in support of this general thesis that it is no longer, so far as we are aware, seriously disputed by scholars.

What is more remarkable is the evidence that Andrew Sinclair managed to unearth regarding the *motive* for Prince Henry's transatlantic expedition:

There is little doubt that the Knights Templar wanted to create another Paradise and Temple of Solomon in the New World beyond the reach of Papal authority.[38]

Sinclair's research suggests that the underground remnants of the Templar order in Scotland at the end of the 14th century saw Prince Henry's pioneering voyage as the first step in the implementation of a long-term plan to establish a utopia. It was, in other words, a bold and very early attempt to put into action what would again be envisaged more than 200 years later by men like Campanella, Andreae and Bacon as the ideal solution to the repulsive corruption and entanglements of the Old World.

Of course it's possible that the actual adventure of a trans-Atlantic voyage in the late 14th century, and the philosophical adventures of the 17th century, could have occurred entirely independently of each other. But the involvement of powerful Templar symbolism in both periods makes us think otherwise. It is not only the recurrence of the Rosy Cross (which also appears on the tombstone of William Sinclair at Rosslyn).[39] Equally indicative of a link is the way in which the early explorers and the later philosophers were all inclined to express their mission in terms of exactly the same intent (whether symbolic or otherwise) – i.e. to rebuild the 'Temple of Solomon in the New World'.

For a variety of reasons which need not detain us here, Prince Henry Sinclair's voyage was not followed up in the way that the later voyages of Columbus were instantly followed up.[40] The chance was lost. But the big question is this. At the end of the 18th century, when the opportunity to create a genuinely new and revolutionary society built on new principles offered itself a second time with the American War of Independence and the vision of a free and independent United States, how can it possibly be an accident that Templar symbolism was once again involved?

We'll return to this problem in Chapter Nineteen. Meanwhile a more pressing and so far unaddressed issue demands our attention here.

How were the Templars transformed from the pope's chosen warriors in the 12th century into heretics who had to be burnt at the stake in the early 14th century?

The scholarly consensus, much of which makes a great deal of sense, is that the round-up of the Templars in 1307 was motivated almost entirely by King Philip the Fair of France, who trumped up the accusations of heresy against them, and had his puppet pope condemn them, so that he could steal their vast wealth. Since he did in fact steal much of their wealth, and since we know that Clement V did everything Philip told him, this is generally a very plausible scenario.

We disagree fundamentally on one point, however, which is the widely accepted idea that the accusations of heresy against the Templars were trumped up. Far from that, our proposal is that they very likely were heretics, guilty as charged, and that what had turned them into secret warriors against the Church was their long exposure to Cathar culture in Occitania and the return there from the Holy Land of many of the knights at the end of the 13th century.

Templars and Cathars

Looking at the dualist doctrines of the Cathars and at what is known about the initiations and beliefs of the Order of the Temple, Sir Steven Runciman notes:

> It may be that the secret practices of the Templars ... were partly based on Dualist ideas and usages ...[41]

It is generally accepted that the Templars were exposed to such ideas in the Holy Land – for example through their contacts with members of the ancient sect known as the Druze. Still extant today in Lebanon, Syria and Israel, the Druze are technically *Shi'a* Muslims but their beliefs have been characterised as 'a mixture of Judaism, Christianity and Islam [including] elements of Gnosticism.'[42] Other *Shi'a* splinter groups in the region such as the Nusayris also held beliefs identifiably tinged with Gnosticism.[43] The Templars would have been well-placed during their long stay in the Holy Land to encounter the descendants of the Sabians of Harran, the compilers of the great Hermetic text known as the *Picatrix* – which contains, as we saw in Chapter Eight, an early blueprint for the utopian Hermetic city.

Having absorbed esoteric 'Eastern' influences far more enthusiastically than any other crusading group it is difficult to imagine that the large numbers of Templars resident in Occitania from the 12th to the 14th century were unaware of the distinctly Gnostic and dualist flavour of the local Cathar religion. It also makes sense, if their own thinking was already tinged by dualism as Runciman speculates, that they might have been favourably predisposed towards the Cathar cause – particularly so if the noble families of Occitania who were united in their support for the Cathars were also supporters of the Templars. This is highly likely. Indeed, as a leading authority on the Templars, historian Martin Barber, points out, the great expansion that the Templars enjoyed in Occitania could not have been achieved without strong support from the nobles:

> The establishment of new communities, and the opening up of previously uncultivated territory which was common in the 12th century owed much to an alliance between the nobles' land and the Order's capital ...[44]

Simple logic suggests that if the Cathars were sponsored by the noble families of Occitania, as we know they were, and if the Templars were sponsored by the same noble families of Occitania, as we know they were, then the Cathars and Templars are likely to have been on friendly terms. This could explain why even at the outset of the Albigensian Crusades in 1209, called by a pope – Innocent III – who was known to favour the Templars and who had accorded them special privileges,[45] we find the Templars peculiarly reluctant to aid Innocent's cause.[46] There is no suggestion that the Knights had become heretics themselves by this stage, but it is obviously puzzling that one of the few duties these heavyweight fighters did during the Albigensian Crusades was very far from being a 'front-line' one. In 1212, to pay for the costs of the Crusade, the pope imposed a tax of three pence per household across the length and breadth of the Languedoc. The Templars collected it but otherwise, notes historian Aubrey Burl, they remained neutral.[47]

Such 'neutrality' amongst the pope's own chosen warriors in so crucial a holy war is highly anomalous and, in our opinion, significant. Several researchers pursuing this line of investigation have argued that as the Albigensian Crusades took their toll, and in particular after the fall of the last major Cathar fortress at Montségur in 1244, the Knights Templar became less 'neutral' and were increasingly influenced by Cathar doctrines. This happened says Andrew Sinclair, because:

> ... most of the Cathar knights who escaped the slaughter were received into the Military Order of the Temple of Solomon, which was itself permeated with oriental influences.[48]

Similarly Arthur Guirdham sees 'indications of some connection between the Cathars and the Templars' in the fact that:

> A large number of Templar knights were recruited from Languedoc. There was an influx of recruits in the mid-13th century when the Albigensian wars were to all intents and purposes over. It is significant that the immensely powerful and ubiquitous Order of the Temple took no part in the Crusade against the Albigensians.[49]

Evidence of this sort is irritatingly and elusively circumstantial – 'interesting, presumptive, but not conclusive', as Guirdham admits.[50] On the other side of the debate, however, historian Martin Barber is much more assertive:

> Romantics like to see connections between the two [i.e. between the
> Cathars and the Templars] but there were none: no fabulous treasure
> passed on to the Templars after the fall of the Cathar fortress of
> Montségur in 1244, no shared anti-Christian beliefs pervaded by esoteric
> cults ... Inevitably some of the accusations against the Templars derive
> from those against the Cathars – they were, after all, embedded in the
> minds of those who pursued dissent.[51]

Barber's argument, though reasonable, seems to us weakened by his evident desire *not* to be a 'romantic' and thus *not* to find a conspiracy in anything. In the case of organisations like the Templars and the Cathars, which were forced to be secretive and conspiratorial by the circumstances of the times, such a policy could be a mistake. If, for example, Cathar knights after Montségur had sought and been granted shelter by the Templars would we honestly *expect* to find records of this – let alone records of the transfer of any 'treasure'? Would these hypothetical fugitives, joining a religious military order that was already notorious for its secrecy and weirdness by 1244, have left a paper trail for the Inquisition, and later historians, to follow? It seems most unlikely.

On the other hand the hypothesis that the Templars were increasingly influenced by Cathar-dualist ideas from the mid-13th century onwards has much to recommend it – not least because it makes better sense than Barber's explanation of the charges of heresy that were brought against the order in the early 14th century. The reader will recall that one of the sensational indictments was that Templar initiates were required to spit on or break crosses. Such behaviour, though seemingly bizarre or diabolical, is entirely consistent with the Cathar religion which denied the physical incarnation of Christ, disbelieved in the Crucifixion, and regarded veneration of the cross as a form of idolatry and torture-worship.[52]

Seen from the perspective of the Inquisition – and of the French crown – the huge influx of heavily-armed and battle-proven Templars returning to the Languedoc in the last years of the 13th century after the loss of the Holy Land may well have looked threatening. Depending on the level of suspicion with which the permanent Templar population of the region was already regarded – fuelled perhaps by rumours that fugitive Cathars had joined Templar ranks – this quantum leap in the order's local military strength could well have been regarded as extremely dangerous by the secular and religious powers. Their suspicions, moreover, are likely to have been intensified by what they would have regarded as the most unwelcome signs of a Cathar revival led by the *Perfectus* Pierre Autier that began in 1299 (see Chapter Seven).

Once all these factors are taken into account, we propose that the perceived threat of a renascent Catharism supported by the armoured might of a Templar order now 'lost to heresy' is sufficient on its own to explain the sudden move that Philip and the Church made against the order in 1307. Whether there was any real substance to the perceived threat is another matter, but it is inconceivable that king and pope would have conspired to bring down the Templars at this exact moment when Catharism was in its death struggle without connecting the two matters together in their minds.[53] That is not to say that greed for the wealth of the Templars played no part in their decisions and actions. With a man like Philip, greed always played a part. But our point is that greed was not the only factor, nor perhaps even the main factor. What happened to the Templars between their arrest in 1307 and the burning of their last Grand Master in 1314 may be best understood as it was understood then – i.e. as yet another battle in the war against heresy and social revolution that the Church had waged since the time of Constantine the Great.

Elements of the Templar heresy

An argument can be made against any kind of secret association between the Cathars and the Templars on the grounds that their beliefs were fundamentally incompatible. While the latter took pride in the Old Testament symbolism of the Temple of Solomon, the former abhorred and opposed the Old Testament as the book of the evil demiurge.

This objection, though obvious, is irrelevant to the hypothesis being put forward here. We are *not* claiming that the Templars were influenced by Catharism in the early years of their existence – when they occupied the Temple Mount in Jerusalem between 1119 and 1187 and adopted the octagonal floor-plan of the Dome of the Rock as their fundamental symbol. Our proposal is that this influence may have *begun* to be felt during the 12th century, through the many Templar preceptories in Occitania, but that it did not have a significant impact until well into the 13th century when, as several historians believe, fugitive Cathar knights were absorbed into the order. We speculate that the process was accelerated after 1290, with the influx of returning Templars from the Holy Land, but that before it could reach critical mass it was interrupted by the pre-emptive strike of Philip the Fair and Clement V in 1307.

Another claim that we are *not* making is that the Templars had *become*

Cathars. Our hypothesis is that by 1307 Cathar dualism was one amongst a number of ingredients in a probably multi-faceted Templar heresy that had brought together a potpourri of seeming incompatible religious ideas. In a way the heretics who the Templars most remind us of are not so much the Cathars as the warrior sect of Christian Gnostics known as the Paulicians (see Chapter Five) who displayed the same fearlessness and willingness to kill. It is also widely recognised that the unique and idiosyncratic Templar religion was tinged with aspects of esoteric Islam and mystical Judaism that the order had picked up in the Holy Land.

The Judaic element meshed particularly well with the Knights' own original obsession with the Temple of Solomon and would have continued to be available to them in Occitania through the large and long-established Jewish communities that we know were also resident there at the time. These communities had an honoured place in Occitan society in the 12th and 13th centuries until the Albigensian Crusades destroyed the region's heterodox and tolerant way of life forever. Acclaimed schools of Talmudic law flourished at Narbonne, Lunel and Beaucaire and there is a report from 1160 that Jewish students travelled from 'distant lands' to study at them.[54]

In addition, as we saw in Chapter Two, the important branch of esoteric Judaism and mystical cosmic speculation known as the Cabala was developed amongst the scholarly Jews of Occitania's coastal cities between in the 12th and 13th centuries[55] – again overlapping with the Cathars and the Templars in the same area. We cited Benjamin of Tudela's 12th century description of a Jew at Lunel who had 'discarded all worldly business, studied day and night, kept fasts, and never ate meat'.[56] Since this suggests that Cathar ideas about how we should live in the world and what we are doing here had begun to influence the Occitanian Jews, why should not the occult philosophy of the Cabala, elaborated by Occitania's Jewish savants, have likewise influenced the Cathars – and the Templars?

Emanations and the Sephirothic Tree

Catharism was a revival, which took root in Occitania in the 12th century (and in the Balkans somewhat earlier) of Christian Gnostic heresies that had last flourished in Palestine and Alexandria in the first four centuries AD. It is a remarkable coincidence that Cabalism likewise is a revival, which took root in Occitania in the 12th century, of schools of Jewish mysticism that had last flourished in Palestine and in Alexandria in those same first four centuries.[57] And although the revival of Hermeticism did not come until the recovery of the Hermetic texts in the 15th century, those texts too had their origin in those first four centuries – and, moreover, in the same predominantly Alexandrian milieu that nourished Gnosticism and the schools of Jewish mystical speculation.

A central concept shared by all the dualist religions that we traced in Part I is that of *emanation*. In the simplest possible terms it is conceived of as a conscious or unconscious creative act of the pure and unassailable spiritual godhead forming manifestations of him/her/itself that then pursue an independent existence. The Gnostics of the first four centuries AD called these emanations *eons*. They were ranked in order of their degree of self-knowledge and they were frequently given abstract characters such as 'Silence', 'Intellect', 'Truth', 'Wisdom', and so on.[58]

Together the godhead and the *eons* formed the *Pleroma* – literally the 'Fullness' – the perfect group. The process that led to the creation of the world resulted from a fall within the Pleroma usually caused by curiosity or desire on the part of one of the *eons*.[59] The reader will recall that in some Gnostic schemes Jehovah, the God of the Old Testament, was portrayed as the fallen *eon*, in others he was even less than that, reduced to the status of an emanation of an emanation – smart enough to create the material world but too stupid to remember where he had come from and what his own small role really was in the scheme of things.[60] Likewise the Cathars saw Jesus not as the physical and material 'son of God', as the Christians did, but as a divine emanation.[61]

This concept of emanation is also fundamental to the Cabala. Here the text on which the 12th and 13th century Occitanian speculation was based was the *Sepher Yetzirah* ('Book of Creation'), a Hebrew treatise on cosmogony and cosmology originally compiled in the third century AD.[62] This work recounts a creative act on the part of the godhead manifesting 'in ten distinct stages of emanation' corresponding with the numbers one to ten.[63] These ten emanations, which combine alchemically with the 22 letters of the Hebrew alphabet – the 'language of God' – are known as the *Sephiroth*. Their order and qualities are as follows

(1) *Keter Elyon* (Supreme Crown) or *Ratzon* (Will); (2) *Chochmah* (Wisdom); (3) *Binah* (Intelligence); (4) *Chesed* (Love) or *Gedullah* (Greatness); (5) *Gevurah* (Power) or *Din* (Judgement); (6) *Tiferet* (Beauty) or *Rachamim* (Compassion); (7) *Netzach* (Lasting Endurance); (8) *Hod* (Majesty); (9) *Yesod Olam* (Foundation of the World) or *Tzaddik* (Righteous One); (10) *Malchut* (Kingdom) or *Atarah* (Diadem) or *Shekhina* (Feminine Divine Presence).[64]

As the Cabala was developed in the 12th and 13th centuries the Jewish mystics of Occitania organized these ten *Sephiroth* into 'a specific archetypal pattern' usually drawn as interlinked by a complex network of straight 'branches', or 'pathways', or 'columns' or 'pillars':

> The pattern thus called forth is the model on which everything that is to come into manifestation is based. It has been named the Image of God, but it is more generally known as the Tree of Life.[65]

One might think of it as a diagram of the DNA structure of reality – intended not as a literal 'map of reality' or representation of 'what reality is made of' but as a *mandala*[66] or talisman to be used for focused mental exercise through which knowledge of the true nature of things can be reached.

Sephirothic Tree and Temple of Solomon

Like other *mandalas*, the Sephirothic 'Tree of Life' is a geometrical pattern. It features three main vertical columns or pillars on which the ten *Sephiroth* representing the emanations of God are fixed like glass balls on a Christmas tree. There is a significant interpenetration of symbolism here with Freemasonry. As we saw in Chapter Thirteen, Freemasons generally represent the Temple of Solomon by two pillars or columns, known as *Boaz* and *Jachin* ('wisdom' and 'power') with the open corridor between the two pillars often considered as a 'third' pillar. Such imagery of two or three pillars, so close to the basic structure of the Tree of Life, is frequently evoked in Masonic illustrations and certificates.

It is also commonly found in Rosicrucian symbolism[67] and some researchers have even detected it on the engraved title-page of Francis Bacon's *The Advancement of Learning*.[68] This engraving, which appears in the 1640 edition, shows two pillars and beyond them the open ocean with a ship sailing away.[69] At the top of the left pillar is the symbol of the Sun and at the top of the right pillar is the symbol of the Moon – i.e. like the pillars in the Tree of Life they are surmounted by globes. But this is also, unmistakably, the same motif which is often seen in Masonic illustrations of Solomon's Temple, with the pillars *Boaz* and *Jachin*. One globe represents the visible world lit by the Sun, and the other globe the invisible or occult world under the glow of the Moon i.e. the secret world. Two hands, one extended from each of the globes, are clasped in what clearly seems to be a 'Masonic handshake'. We are not alone in noting that this whole arrangement is suggestive of a Sephirothic Tree of Life that branches out into 'Wisdom', 'Power', 'Intelligence' and so forth.[70]

This same general pattern using symbols to denote the various Masonic 'virtues' and the many paths to their attainment can be easily discerned in the so-called *tracing boards* used by Freemasons to this day in rituals likened to entry to the 'spiritual Temple of Solomon'. At the foot of these 'tracing boards' is to be seen a representation of the two pillars, *Boaz* and *Jachin*, beyond them some sort of shrine, probably symbolising the Holy of Holies of Solomon's Temple, and often represented by a pentagram or a 'Blazing Star'. Behind the pentagram/star device are spread a variety of Masonic symbols the whole culminating at the top of the tracing board where we find the Supreme Being represented either by a crown (*Keter* in the Cabalistic Tree of Life also means 'Crown'), or by the 'all seeing eye', or a glowing pyramid.

That such symbolism is to be directly associated with the Tree of Life is confirmed by the preparatory information given to Masonic candidates for the so-called *30th degree* of the Scottish Rite, also known as the *Knight Kadosh* degree, where a Sephirothic Tree is shown to the candidate along with a textual explanation of its symbolic use. According to Masonic historian Robert Lomas:

> In the preparatory section ritual of the Knight Kadosh, (the 30th degree of the Ancient and Accepted Scottish Rite and the first degree of the Chivalric Series), the Candidate is given this information. This division of the ten Sephiroth into three triads was arranged into a form called by the Kabbalists the Kabbalistic Tree, or the Tree of Life (as shown in the following Tracing Board) In this diagram the vertical arrangement of the Sephiroth is called – 'Pillars'. Thus the four Sephiroth in the centre are called the Middle Pillar the three on the right, the Pillar of Mercy and the three on the left, the Pillar of Justice.[71]

In chapter one of the *Sepher Yetzirah* it is stated that:

> Ten are the numbers of the ineffable Sephiroth, ten not nine, ten not eleven. Learn this wisdom and be wise in the understanding of it; investigate these numbers and draw knowledge from them; fix the design in its purity, and pass from it to its creator seated on his throne ...[72]

THE MASTER GAME

The *Sepher Yetzirah* also speaks of 'the 32 most occult and wonderful paths of wisdom' on which 'the Lord of Hosts engraved His Name'. These '32' paths, pillars or columns in the design represent the '10 Sephiroth' and the '22 letters' which are 'the foundation of all things'.[73] Thus the Sephirothic Tree, with its '22' paths and '10 emanations' also mystically connotes the number '32'. In Scottish Freemasonry this represents the 32 'degrees' that must be taken (i.e. 'pathways' that must be followed) in order to reach the door of full Masonic enlightenment – the ultimate 33rd degree. The link we make here is confirmed by the 33rd degree Scottish Rite author, Charles Sunmer Lobingier, who, in 1929, was commissioned by the Grand Commander of the Scottish Rite in Washington, DC to write an official history of this Masonic order:

> A later feature of the Kabala is the thirty-two paths of wisdom. The number is obtained by adding the letters of the Hebrew alphabet (twenty-two) to ten Sephiroth, and here we doubtless have the origin of the number of degrees as formulated by the Grand Constitution [of the Scottish Rite] ...[74]

The paradoxical Kircher

The belief that divine principles, emanations or archetypes can be made manifest in a 'temple' or 'house' of God – both in the material and in the spiritual sense – is at the very heart of the Tree of Life concept. But much earlier the ancient Egyptians also designed their temples with precisely such a purpose in mind – think, for instance, of the great sacred precinct of Amun at Karnak-Luxor.

The notion that the Egyptian esoteric design of temples could in some way be connected to the Sephirothic Tree was developed as early as the 17th century by the Hermetic-Cabalist and philosopher Athanasius Kircher in his book *Oedipus Aegyptiacus*. In this work Kircher, who was also (or seemed to be) a devout Jesuit, goes so far as to argue that all religions and all knowledge of the divine originally came from Egypt.[75] Joscelyn Godwin, professor of music at Colgate University in New York, is a world-renowned authority on Kircher and has this to say:

> Kircher derives all the wisdom of the Jews from Egypt, transmitted through the initiate Moses. In The Tree of the Sephiroth we have the primary metaphysical symbol of the Hebrew Cabalists. It shows ten invariable archetypes linked to each other by twenty-two paths corresponding to the twenty-two letters of the Hebrew alphabet. Since the

Tree is a diagram of the utmost universality, it may be used as a key to the working of every level of the Universe ... On the cosmological level, the lowest seven Sephiroth are the seven Chaldaean planets, and the upper triad, according to Kircher, the spheres of the fixed stars ...[76]

In 1621, Athanasius Kircher, then a young novice in the Jesuit order, was forced to flee Germany – his homeland – because of the outbreak of the Thirty Years War He eventually found his way into France and joined the Jesuit college at Avignon. A brilliant mathematician and accomplished linguist, Kircher developed an insatiable interest in all things Egyptian and in 1635 was given a post at the Jesuit college in Rome to study hieroglyphs. In 1638 Kircher was made professor of mathematics, but his scientific interests were wide and varied. His fame became such that scholars from all over the world corresponded with him and many came to see him in Rome, such as the English inventor William Gascoignes and the French painter Nicolas Poussin, to whom he taught perspectives.[77] Kicher was a keen collector of antiquities, and was to establish one of Europe's first museums, the *Museo Kircheriano* which some compared 'with Elias Ashmole's foundation in Oxford of the Ashmolean Museum.'[78]

Like Giordano Bruno before him Kircher was an all-out 'Egyptian' Hermetist who 'regarded Egyptian idolatry and polytheism as the source, not only of Greek and Roman religion, but of the later Hebrews.'[79] Kircher also believed that Egypt was the source of all civilisations and, more importantly, that all ancient philosophies, and especially Hebrew Cabala, had been 'derived from the Egyptian wisdom' handed down in the Hermetic writings.[80] Because of this, Frances Yates calls Kircher the 'most notable descendant of the Hermetic-Cabalist tradition'. Yates also comments that he was 'much preoccupied with Isis and Osiris as the chief gods of Egypt.'[81] In his *Oedipus Aegyptiacus*, Kircher reaches the following conclusion:

The divine Dionysius testifies that all created things are nothing else but mirrors which reflect to us the rays of divine wisdom. Hence the wise men of Egypt feigned that Osiris, having given charge of all things to Isis, permeated invisibly to the whole world. What else can this signify save that the power of the invisible God penetrates intimately into all?[82]

One of Kircher's closest friends was the great baroque architect Gian Lorenzo Bernini, who Christopher Wren met in France in 1665 at the court of Louis XIV.

Bernini, Like Kircher, was (or seemed to be) an ardent Jesuit, and all his life would attend Mass every morning at the small church of *Il Gesù* in Rome, where the founder of the Jesuit order, Saint Ignatius of Loyola, was buried. Kircher's vast knowledge of perspective and of the symbolic use of architecture gave him much in common with Bernini, and they collaborated on several architectural projects for the pope in Rome. Notable amongst these was an ancient Egyptian obelisk (not to be confused with the Vatican obelisk described in Chapter Thirteen) that they erected in the Piazza della Minerva where once had stood a Temple of Isis. It was in 1652, thus 13 years before Bernini met Christopher Wren in Paris, that Kircher published his *Oedipus Aegyptiacus*, a book that was a bestseller in its days and widely read throughout Europe.

Kircher's depiction of the Sepirothic Tree is identical to the portrayals in the Hebrew Cabala with ten emanations interlinked by 22 pathways. But unlike others, Kircher saw the original source of the Cabalistic knowledge enshrined therein as being 'Egyptian'. Could Kircher's 'Egyptianised' Hermetic-Cabalistic ideas of sacred and symbolic architecture and perspectives somehow have reached Christopher Wren and John Evelyn in England?

John Greaves, the Pyramids and Gresham College

In considering this question we note that there is another possible 'Egyptian' connection – again peculiarly involving Kircher – in Christopher Wren's background.

The reader will recall that Wren was appointed Savilian Professor of Astronomy at Oxford in 1661, right after the Restoration of Charles II.[83] Prior to Wren's appointment, the post had been occupied by Seth Ward, who held the position from 1649 to 1660. Before Ward the professor had been another eminent figure – John Greaves.

Like Wren, Greaves had formerly taught mathematics at Gresham College in London. His stint there was from 1630 to 1637, after which he took a sabbatical in order to make a rather unusual journey to Egypt, the main objective of which was to investigate the Pyramids of Giza. He hoped to find a 'universal unit' of measurement encoded into these great structures. To this end he teamed up with an Italian scientist, Tito Livio Burattini whose sponsor was none other than Athanasius Kircher.[84]

Burattini, although Italian by birth, was domiciled in Poland. He was a keen mathematician, astronomer and cartographer, but his real passion, like Kircher's, was ancient Egypt. Burattini was finally to travel there in 1637 with support from Kircher, a short while before Greaves himself arrived in

Egypt. In his book *Pyramidograhia*, published in 1646, Greaves refers to Burattini as 'an ingenious young man from Venice' and makes use of some of Burattini's drawings of the pyramids.[85]

It was when Greaves returned to England in 1639 that he was rewarded for his Egyptian endeavours with the post of Savilian Professor of Astronomy at Oxford – the same post that Christopher Wren would eventually occupy in 1661.

David Stevenson, professor of Scottish history at the University of St. Andrews, has discovered that Sir Robert Moray, the principal founder of the Royal Society and the first man to be initiated into Freemasonry on English soil, also had a connection with the ubiquitous Athanasius Kircher:

> In 1643 he [Robert Moray] was knighted by the king [Charles I] ... Later in that same year he was captured by imperial forces while fighting for the French, and was imprisoned in Bavaria. By 1645 he had been ransomed, having made use of his captivity to develop his scientific interests through conversations and correspondence with Jesuit scholars, including the remarkable Hermetic polymath Athanasius Kircher who was a leading authority on the mysteries of ancient Egypt.[86]

There is, too, another common denominator to consider: Gresham College itself. Many of the protagonists associated with the Invisible College, the Royal Society and the early London Masonic lodges were directly or indirectly involved with Gresham College. These included Robert Moray, John Wilkins, Christopher Wren and Robert Hooke. The origins of this college go back to Sir Thomas Gresham, the famous founder of the London Royal Exchange. In 1575 he bequeathed his home in Bishopsgate to serve as headquarters for the college and left provision in his will for it to be funded in the future through revenues accrued by the Royal Exchange. The idea of such a college seems to be somewhat 'Masonic', in the sense that Thomas Gresham decreed that seven 'readers' or scholars would be appointed to lecture on each of the seven liberal arts.[87] Indeed, according to Robert Lomas, Gresham College was 'the main centre for Freemasonry in Restoration London ... which Sir Thomas Gresham had set up to support his Masonic ideals of study.'[88]

Could all these circumstances, as well as the encounter with Bernini in Paris, have brought Christopher Wren into contact with Kircher's Hermetic-Cabalistic ideas and their application to geometrical design and structures such as the Sephirothic Tree of Life? And if they had, might they have influenced Wren's plan for the rebirth of London after the Great Fire? We can only surmise that the opportunity was there for this to happen.

Oddly enough, the same can also be said of John Evelyn, who presented his plan for a 'new' London just a couple of days after Wren. Evelyn, as we shall recall, had travelled to Europe between 1643 and 1652. He spent time in Rome during this period where he is known to have developed a keen interest in Bernini and his works.[89] It is by no means impossible that he might have seen or learnt something there, in the city where Giordano Bruno had been burnt at the stake less than half a century before, that sparked off Hermetic-Cabalistic ideas in his mind.

Many different streams converging

'After the disappearance of Catharism and the Temple at the beginning of the 14th century,' Arthur Guirdham asks:

> ... what outlet was there for those of a dualist tendency? One thing we can say with certainty. By this time the dualists of Europe had learnt that the open profession of their opinions was so hazardous as to be impracticable.[90]

In other words if religious teachings as contrary to Church dogma as those of the Cathars were in any way to survive the mindset of the Middle Ages they would have to go underground, and to follow whatever further course of natural evolution and development they could while remaining out of sight. We are convinced that this happened and that dualist beliefs were sheltered and nourished beyond the view of the Inquisition and historians long after 'Catharism and the Temple' had been officially destroyed. It seems to us that this process was dramatically catalysed and briefly brought out into the open again by the recovery of the Hermetic Texts in 1460 and that afterwards another period of incredible openness, progress and revolutionary thinking followed. But Hermetists like Bruno, who pushed the revolution too quickly, died for their beliefs while other less hot-headed thinkers waited patiently for a better time.

In the long years of waiting many different ideas, like many different streams converging, all become available to 'those of a dualist tendency'. Included in the mix were remnants of Cathar Gnosticism; Jewish mysticism and the Cabala; the recovered Hermetic revelations; Templar and Masonic notions about rebuilding Solomon's Temple; the Rosicrucian and 'New Atlantean' programme for an ideal utopian city designed to bring harmony between heaven and earth; and last but not least Tommaso Campanella's *Civitas Solis*, the Adocentyn of the *Picatrix*, to be made 'in such a wonderful way that only by looking at it all the sciences may be learned.'[91]

All these elements and influences, we suggest, were at work in the mysteriously similar city plans that Christopher Wren and John Evelyn prepared after the Great Fire of London in 1666.

Wren's plan to rebuild the Temple

The Great Fire swept over the city of London like a giant blowtorch, clearing an area one and a half miles long and half a mile wide. It destroyed almost everything from Tower Hill in the east to Temple in the west, where it finally burnt itself out in front of Temple Church, a distinctive round structure built of stone in the Gothic style.

The district where the Fire stopped – still known as 'Temple' and today inhabited mainly by lawyers – is so named because of its historical association with the Knights Templar. It lies roughly between St. Paul's in the east and Covent Garden in the west, and is bracketed by Fleet Street in the north and the Victoria Embankment in the south. The Templars built their great *preceptory* (headquarters) of the New Temple here in 1161, providing themselves in the process with a pier on the River Thames and inland access for their ships all the way to Newgate via the nearby River Fleet.[92]

Construction of Temple Church began in 1180. Like many other Templar places of worship, its core structure was a circular building with a domed roof, reminiscent of the Church of the Holy Sepulchre (the supposed tomb of Jesus) in Jerusalem. Let us note in passing that the Church of the Holy Sepulchre lies west of the site of Solomon's Temple in Jerusalem, an alignment, as we shall see later, that did not go unnoticed by the Templars in London. Dedicated to the Virgin, Temple Church was consecrated on 10 February 1185 by Heraclius, patriarch of Jerusalem, who was brought to London for the purpose. This was just two years before the dramatic fall of Jerusalem to the 'heathen' forces of the Arabs under Saladin in 1187.

The district of Temple and Temple Church remained under the order's control until its suppression in 1307. In 1312 all Templar properties in London, including the round church, were handed over to the rival military Order of the Knights Hospitallers. When the Hospitallers were in turn suppressed during the Reformation, the church and its surrounding buildings passed to the crown. The buildings were tenanted by lawyers – the *benchers* of the Inner Temple and the Middle Temple – who secured the freehold by royal charter from James I in 1608. These two 'Inns of Court' have remained the owners of Temple Church ever since and are under an obligation by terms of their royal charter to maintain it and its services forever.[93]

In the plans that Wren and Evelyn drew up for London's architectural rebirth after the Great Fire, both men paid inordinate attention the area around Temple Church.

Christopher Wren was first to get the king's attention. On 11 September 1666, with a blueprint tucked under his arm, he rushed to see Charles II at Whitehall. The blueprint was an amazingly detailed and professionally executed map for a new London, the sort of town-planning design project that should take weeks, if not months, to conceive and draft in final form. Yet barely a week had passed since the Fire and there were still dozens of smoke plumes hanging over the skyline of the charred city.

Wren's ideas combine a magnificent vision for a new capital city with an appreciation of sophisticated concepts in urban planning. His blueprint, which has survived, looks like the polished product of a highly-skilled team. Yet the evidence suggests that Wren did not consult his colleagues at the Royal Society and worked alone on the plan.[94] Was he trying to protect his ideas so that no one else could take the credit? Or was he just in a tremendous hurry – out of a natural desire to be 'first'?

He could have had many motives for secrecy and speed, but what interests us more are his motives and hopes for the new London.

Freshly back from his eight months in Paris where he had studied neo-classical architecture as well as new and daring city plans, Wren's dream was to replace the winding streets and courtyards of the old medieval city with new monumental avenues such as those he had seen in France. His plan is dominated by a main central avenue that runs virtually straight from one end of the city (Aldgate) to the other (the Strand), passing through a series of huge star-shaped plazas distributed along the way. From these plazas numerous straight roads emanate in all directions, linking up to smaller piazzas or *circuses* on either side of the main axis to form a closed network. Wren's plan also features a second monumental avenue running from the Tower of London, along Cannon Street and up to St. Paul's.[95] This second avenue merges with the main axis coming from Aldgate, and the whole is then prolonged to Ludgate to become Fleet Street.

It is at this point, just past Ludgate – and not far from Temple Church – that a major feature of Wren's plan stands out: a large open plaza in the form of an octagon with all eight sides of equal length. Wren's established Masonic connections make it more than likely that he would have known the significance of the octagon as the Templars' own symbol for the Temple of Solomon. He should also have known that the location he proposed for this distinctive octagonal plaza encroached physically on the site of the Templars' former London headquarters. But if there is any doubt over his deliberation in these matters it is settled for us by a final telling detail. Half a mile to the east Wren deliberately altered the east-west axis of the 'new' St. Paul's Cathedral by a few degrees to the south so that it would now align with Temple Church.[96]

We've noted that Temple Church was conceived of initially as a scale model of the Church of the Holy Sepulchre and that the latter stood west of the original site of the Temple of Solomon in Jerusalem. In Wren's London Temple Church stands west of St. Paul's in the same way. Could it be, therefore, that what the architect had in mind with all this was a scheme for building a 'hidden Jerusalem' in the heart of London?

The ghost in the plan

It is reported by Christopher Wren's own son (also called Christopher) that during his inaugural speech as professor of astronomy at Gresham College, Wren Senior described London as:

> ... a city particularly favoured by the celestial influences, a Pandora, on which each planet has contributed something ...[97]

This, it must be remembered, was a time when astrology and scientific astronomy overlapped seamlessly, and when many still believed in the influence of the stars and planets. But it is unlikely that Wren had in mind horoscopic astrology when referring to London. What is more likely is that he was thinking of influences of a more spiritual and mystical nature, such as the talismanic influences found in Hermetic magic and in Renaissance Christian-Cabala. Steve Padget, a professor of architecture at the University of Kansas, explains:

> Following the break with Papal authority, the 'cosmos' for the English no longer centred around Rome and St. Peter's, but London and the old Gothic St. Paul's. Its centre spire acted the role of *axis mundi* for this world, symbolising the centre of London, England and the universe ... When the spire was broken (felled in the Great Fire of 1666), it denoted a catastrophe of cosmic proportion. The symbolic connection between heaven/earth/underworld had been severed ...[98]

THE MASTER GAME

Charles II and the Anglican clergy were eager to dispel the rumour started by Catholics that the Great Fire had been the act of a wrathful God to admonish the English people for having broken away from the Church of Rome and the authority of the pope. The trick that the king and his advisers pulled off was to transform the Fire into a symbol of purification and regeneration for London and the realm, intended to bring to fruition a 'perfect Christian society'. And once that had been achieved, comments Professor Paget, 'the implication was that fulfilment of the *New Jerusalem* was possible.'[99] The king himself wrote a sermon in which, according to historian Vaughan Hart,

> ... the Bishop of London proclaimed St. Paul's at the centre of a royalist New Jerusalem for 'here hath the lord ordained ... the throne of David for judgement; and the charge of Moyses for instruction,' adding that 'this Church is your Son indeed, others are but synagogues, this is your Jerusalem, the mother to them all.'

> Following the Cabalistic theme within this sermon, the influence of Christian Cabala ... could be expected in ... subsequent work of the restoration of the seat of David and Moses ... The Christian Cabalist hoped that through such divinely inspired intellectual magic, pre-Christian or otherwise, the conditions on earth for nothing less than the Second Coming would be created, a necessary prelude to the Apocalypse and final establishment of the Heavenly Jerusalem.[100]

We shall return to Wren's design of the new St. Paul's and its full implications in due course. Meanwhile the longer we looked at his plan for London, the more we sensed something else was embedded in it, something 'ghosted', as it were, beneath the layout of the avenues and plazas. Standing back and viewing the design as a whole we realised that what the overarching vision reminded us of – albeit a little hazily – was the Sephirothic Tree of Life![101]

Naturally our first thought was that our eyes were just being tricked by a common optical illusion. And, indeed, a common optical illusion it might well have been were it not for the fact that two days after Wren had presented his plan to Charles II, yet another 'sephirothic' scheme for the redesign of London was proposed to the king by John Evelyn.

Evelyn's plan

On 13 September 1666, Evelyn secured his own audience with Charles II in – of all places – the queen's bedchamber in Whitehall.[102]

What immediately strikes the eye in Evelyn's plan, and must surely have struck the king's eye as well, is how strangely *similar* it is to Wren's. Yet on the face of things Wren seems to have done everything he could to keep his work secret.[103] We know, for example, that he did not take the advice of his colleagues at the Royal Society – much to the chagrin of Secretary Henry Oldenburg.[104] When the latter complained about the lapse Wren curtly replied that he had wanted to submit his design first, before anyone else had the chance to distract the king's attention and thus 'could not possibly consult the Society about it.'[105]

For his part Evelyn simply wrote in his diary: 'Dr. Wren had got a start on me.'[106] However historian Adrian Tinniswood is satisfied that there was much closer collusion between the two men than such remarks suggest:

> Striking similarities between the two schemes show that they [Wren and Evelyn] must have discussed their dream of an ideal London either before the fire brought those dreams a dramatic step closer to realization, or when they were both working on them in the second week of September. They both proposed that the area between Temple Bar and the Fleet should be given over to a piazza which would form the intersection of eight streets radiating out on the points of the compass. They both enclosed the buildings which fronted onto this piazza with an octagon of connecting streets. They both made the entrance to the northern end of London Bridge a focal point of their plan, and created a semicircular piazza as a grand introduction to it. They both sent main thoroughfares in from the east to converge at St. Paul's ... A passing reference in the explanatory discourse that Evelyn submitted along with his plan confirms some sort of collaboration, and suggests that he adopted some of Wren's ideas. He implied that the two men discussed their respective schemes on or immediately before 11 September, and says that the '*street from St. Paul's may be divaricated like a Pythagorian, as the most accurately ingenious Dr. Wren had designed it, and I willingly follow in my second thoughts.*' ...[107]

It cannot be a coincidence that the plans of Evelyn and Wren both incorporate the same meaningful Templar symbol of the octagon in exactly the same meaningful place: i.e. overlapping the old London headquarters of the Knights Templar close to Temple Church. We note also that on Evelyn's plan the octagonal plaza is placed directly west of St. Paul's Cathedral in such a way that its centre aligns with the axis of the cathedral – the two points being joined together by the wide avenue of Fleet Street.

Most intriguing of all, is the clear, purposeful definition with which Evelyn's plan is so obviously structured around the Sephirothic Tree of Life. If there is some ambiguity in Wren's case, Evelyn's plan certainly leaves no doubt as to his motive. For despite some minimal variations required for practicality, the similarity between Evelyn's geometrical pattern and that of the Sephirothic Tree of Life is *unmistakable*.

Presumably by firing their 'double salvo' on 11 and 13 September Wren and Evelyn must have hoped that the Sephirothic Tree of Life, as well as the other shared elements concealed in both their plans, would quickly be approved by the king. We suspect also that in the minds of both men must have been the well-known final verses from the book of Revelation which evoke the creation of the 'New Jerusalem' and the 'Tree of Life':

> Then I saw a new heaven and a new earth, for the first heaven and the first earth had vanished ... I saw the holy city, New Jerusalem, coming down out of heaven from God, made ready like a bride adorned for her husband ... It had a great high wall, with twelve gates, at which were twelve angels, and on the gates were inscribed the names of the twelve tribes of Israel ... the city had twelve foundation-stones, and on them were the names of the twelve apostles ... Then I was shown the river of the water of life, sparkling like crystal, flowing ... down the middle of the city's streets. On either side of the river stood a Tree of Life, which yields twelve crops of fruits ... Happy are those who wash their robes clean! They will have the right to the Tree of Life and will enter by the gates of the city ...[108]

It is quite obvious from this scheme of things in the book of Revelation that the design of the 'New Jerusalem' was to incorporate the number '12' and, more importantly, that the holy city should rest upon a matrix of 12 'foundation-stones' or *foci*. Interesting then, as historians Felix Barker and Ralph Hyde point out, that:

> Evelyn wanted *twelve* interconnecting squares and piazzas ... [and] a straight east-to-west thoroughfare [that would] cut its way for a mile and a half from 'King Charles Gate' [in the London wall, south of

Aldgate] to Temple Bar where there was a piazza with eight radiating roads like Wren's.[109]

Interesting, too, that if we superimpose Evelyn's obviously 'sephirothic' plan on the actual geometry of a Sephrothic Tree of Life, it can be seen that St. Paul's Cathedral corresponds to the one *sephirah*, the divine emanation known as *Tipheret*, which means 'Beauty'. Astrologically this *sephirah* represents the Sun, the centre of the universe, from which emanates all life and light. The analogy is obvious: St. Paul's was to be the spiritual centre of the regenerated city as it rose from the ashes like a solar phoenix to guide the restored Stuart monarchy on the true path of the reformed Christianity.

Corresponding to the large 'Templar' octagon in Evelyn's plan is the *sephirah* known as *Yesod*, which means 'Foundation'. Could this mean that the new world order which was to emerge from the 'New Jerusalem' had its foundations in the Order of the Temple or, more precisely, the new Masonic order which had emerged from Templar ideologies and to which the Stuart monarch had given his royal protection?

Another curious feature of Evelyn's plan is that he moved the Royal Exchange *away* from the centre of the city (whereas Wren had kept it there on the original site of Thomas Gresham's building).[110] Evelyn placed it nearer to the river, further upstream from London Bridge – most likely because he wanted to have at the heart of his planned 'New Jerusalem' another more relevant symbol which would correspond to the appropriate *sephirah* in the Tree of Life. This came in the form of the fountain he envisaged for the marketplace on Gracechurch Street, which may represent the so-called *11th hidden sephirah*, known as *Daat*, from which emanates the fountain of knowledge that irrigates the whole.[111]

Solomon's Temple veiled in Saint Paul's Cathedral?

In addition to serving as the spiritual centre and solar symbol of the regenerated London, logic suggests that Saint Paul's Cathedral also came to symbolise Solomon's Temple in the New Jerusalem that Wren and Evelyn had in mind. Christopher Wren was subsequently made surveyor of St. Paul's Cathedral in 1668 and surveyor general for the King's Works a year later. In this capacity he produced a design for the rebuilding of St. Paul's which, finally, in 1671 he presented to Charles II. Here is Tinniswood's assessment of the design:

The building was quite unlike anything seen in Britain before. A round central space more than 120 feet in diameter had four stubby arms of equal length projected out to north, south, east and west. The sloping sides of the octagon thus formed were concave, so that in plan the cathedral looked like a Greek cross. And inevitably, the central space was crowned with a monumental dome supported on a ring of eight pillars ...[112]

It is true that Wren's octagonal floor-plan for St. Paul's was something totally 'unseen in Britain before.'[113] But it most certainly had been seen by those who had visited the Holy Land and Jerusalem and studied the Dome of the Rock which the Knights Templar had much earlier adopted as their symbol for Solomon's Temple. Viewed in profile, Wren's design for the new St. Paul's does in fact bear an uncanny resemblance to the Dome of the Rock: both have the same octagonal floor-plan; both have the same rotunda or rounded central space; both have the massive cupola supported by eight pillars; both have been deliberately aligned to the four cardinal directions: north, south, east and west. Last but not least, from both the eight-sided Templar Cross can easily be derived.

What Masonic game was Wren playing in his plans for London and for Saint Paul's Cathedral? And why did it involve the symbols of an ancient heresy?

CHAPTER SIXTEEN

FROM SECRET SOCIETY TO SOCIETY WITH SECRETS

In February 1685 Charles II died peacefully at Whitehall, having made a deathbed conversion to Catholicism that left the nation somewhat confused. Since there were no legitimate sons the succession went to his autocratic brother, James, Duke of York, a devout and zealous Catholic. In 1673 James had married Mary of Modena, also a staunch Catholic. And not surprisingly, as soon as he was safely crowned he placed Catholics in important positions within the government. This raised fears, even amongst his Anglican supporters, that he was on the verge of reimposing Roman Catholicism as the state religion in Britain. The situation reached a crisis in 1689 when, on 22 February, James II was forced to abdicate in favour of William of Orange and his wife Mary, the heiress presumptive, who were both staunch Protestants.

This marked the end for the Stuarts as a ruling dynasty, but not yet for James II and his 'Jacobite' supporters (the latter being a name derived from the Latin version of 'James' i.e. *Jacobus*). As Charles II had done before him, James went into exile in France at the court of Louis XIV. He took along with him his whole family and a large band of Jacobites, and they all settled in the Château de Saint-Germain-en-Laye near Paris. It was there, according to some Masonic researchers, that the first official Masonic lodges on French soil began to emerge.

When James II died in 1701, his 13-year-old son, Prince James Francis Edward, was immediately recognised by Louis XIV as James III, the British king-in-exile. In 1713, however, Louis made peace with Britain, and the 'Old Pretender', as James III was now being called, left for Rome along with his family and his Jacobite court. In 1714 his half-sister, Queen Ann, died leaving no surviving children. But because of an act of Parliament that precluded

James from the succession on account of his Catholic faith, the British throne went to the Protestant elector of Hanover, who became King George I.

Within the small group of Jacobites in Rome making up the increasingly decrepit Stuart court-in-exile was a well-educated Scotsman called Andrew Michael Ramsay who served as private tutor of the children of the Old Pretender. Ramsay, who is better known to Freemasons as the 'Chevalier Ramsay', was soon to play a pivotal role in the evolution of Freemasonry.

Meanwhile in Britain the official 'coming out' of the Craft took place when the so-called *Grand Lodge of England* was created in London on 24 June 1717 – St. John's Day, the attested feast and 'new year' of the Freemasons.[1] In the New Testament, St. John the Baptist is depicted as the forerunner of Christ the Messiah, and in Eastern Christian tradition he is regarded as the most important saint after the Virgin Mary. Indeed, in the Gospel of Matthew Jesus himself is made to praise Saint John as follows:

> Truly, I say to you, among those born of women there has risen no one greater than John the Baptist.[2]

A prophet in his own right John the Baptist supposedly stepped aside to prepare the way for the Christ-Messiah by saying: 'He must increase, but I must decrease.'[3] In this apparently cryptic remark there is obvious solar symbolism which accomplished Freemasons will surely understand – for by 24 June the Sun's altitude in heaven does indeed decrease after passing the apogee of the summer solstice.

The celebration of St. John's Day traditionally began on the night of St. John's *Eve* i.e. 23 June, and was at one time called 'Bonfire Night' in parts of Europe and Ireland. But there was an inherent error in the Julian calendar relative to the true solar year (and thus also relative to the new, more accurate, Gregorian calendar). Accumulating year by year, the effect of this error was that '23 June Julian' was forever slipping further away from the summer solstice – such that it fell some 13 days *after* the solstice by 1717. At that time, Britain and its American colonies had not yet adopted the new Gregorian calendar (which they regarded as a Catholic, and thus tainted, innovation). The official calendar in Britain was therefore still the Julian calendar, which was 11 days *ahead* of the new Gregorian calendar.

St. John's Eve, 23 June 1717 on the Julian calendar corresponds with 4 July in the Gregorian calendar. Let us keep this curious conversion in mind since 4 July is clearly a date which would soon have a great symbolic resonance in the American colonies and in France.[4]

Recruiting from the ruling classes

On 24 June 1717 the formation of the Grand Lodge of England was achieved by the amalgamation of four older lodges in London. From this date onwards Freemasonry was no longer a secret society but began to operate very much out in the open, and in a manner that would certainly have attracted heresy charges in earlier, less enlightened, centuries.

A certain Mr. Anthony Sayer was appointed the first Grand Master of the new united body.[5] Very little is known of Sayer. He remained at his post for only a year and was succeeded by George Payne in 1718, then by the celebrated Dr. John Theophilus Desaguliers in 1719.[6] Of French birth, Desaguliers had been brought to England as an infant by his Huguenot parents who had fled from La Rochelle during the persecution of Protestants by Louis XIV. He grew up to become a brilliant scholar, and studied law at Oxford. In 1714 Desaguliers was elected a fellow of the Royal Society and eventually became its curator. There he befriended several famous scientists, including the great Isaac Newton. It was Desaguliers who was responsible for attracting into Freemasonry many men from the nobility, amongst them the Duke of Lorraine, the future Holy Roman Emperor Francis I, and Frederick Prince of Wales, the son of George II, to whom Desaguliers was appointed tutor.[7] It is thus that from 1721, and much thanks to Desaguliers, the Grand Lodge of England has always been headed by a member of the royal family.[8]

Such illustrious sponsorship and royal approval, as well as its policy of religious tolerance and freedom of thought and, paradoxically, its stringent oath of secrecy, made Freemasonry an exceedingly popular fellowship amongst the aristocracy and the educated middle classes. Masonic lodges began to flourish everywhere in Europe, and the first Parisian lodge of English origin, which went under the name of *St. Thomas*, was opened in 1726 by Charles Radclyffe, who belonged to an old Scottish family loyal to the Stuarts. It seems that Charles Radclyffe himself was the son of a natural but illegitimate daughter of Charles II.[9] Radclyffe unwisely attempted to return to England in 1746 where he was arrested as a Jacobite spy and executed.

Another illegitimate descendant of Charles II, who presided in the French lodge, *La Loge d'Aubigny*, was the Duke of Richmond, grandson of the Duchess of Portsmouth, Louise de Kérouaille, a favourite mistress of Charles II.[10] The Duke of Richmond had also put in a spell as Grand Master of the Grand Lodge of England in 1724.

The Jacobite community in Paris at the time also included the Duke of Wharton, who had likewise been Grand Master of the Grand Lodge of

THE MASTER GAME

England – in his case in 1722. The Duke of Wharton, who was expelled from the Grand Lodge in 1723 after a serious scandal, fled to Europe where he eventually settled in Paris to become the first Grand Master of French Freemasonry in 1728, later to be called the *Grande Loge de France*.[11] It was about this time that the Scotsman, Ramsay, who was also now in Paris, began to nurture radical ideas about how Freemasonry might be developed in France and in other lands.

The Knight Ramsay

Freemasonry's famous 'Scottish Rite' is often said to have originated in France in 1725, that is eight years *after* the formation of the Grand Lodge of England in 1717. The well-known Masonic historian Jasper Ridley has this to say:

> During the eighteenth century other Masonic rites developed in various parts of the world, of which the most important was the so-called *Scottish Rite*. It had never, in fact, existed in Scotland, but had originated in France, and was called the *Rite Écossais* – the Scottish Rite – because the Scotsman, the Chevalier Ramsay, was thought to have started it ...[12]

Other researchers think there's more to the story. It does seem almost certain that Andrew Michael Ramsay, better known as the Chevalier Ramsay, and indeed a Scotsman, was responsible for the *formation* of what became known as the Scottish Rite throughout the world. But there is much to suggest the that this rite was an amalgamation of older ideas that had circulated among earlier Scottish lodges in Scotland itself and that Ramsay had simply synthesised and brought to France.[13]

Andrew Michael Ramsay was born in 1686 in Ayr, a town about 40 miles southwest of Glasgow in Scotland, and not far from Kilwinning, 'the traditional birthplace of Scottish Freemasonry.'[14] Although the son of a lowly baker, Ramsay was to become a refined man of letters. Educated at the University of Edinburgh, he eventually received a degree in law from Oxford. After serving as an officer with the Duke of Marlborough in Flanders in 1706, Ramsay decided to remain in the Netherlands. There he met a Frenchman, Pierre Poiret, a disciple of Madame Guyon, a popular French Catholic mystic who was closely associated with the great French scholar and author, François de Salignac de la Mothe-Fénelon, the bishop of Cambrai. Fénelon was famous throughout Europe, and was particularly well known for having written *Les Aventures de Télémaque*, a very popular book at the time, in which he presented to the French court an allegory, set in historical locations such as ancient Egypt and Phoenicia, of the ideal utopian state.[15]

For a long time Fénelon had entertained excellent connections at the French court in Paris when he was tutor to the heir apparent and grandson of Louis XIV, the Duke of Burgundy. Indeed, Fénelon originally wrote the *Adventures of Télémaque* while he was at court – apparently for the benefit of the young prince, who he hoped would one day become king of France and put into practice the perfect state and the ideal government modelled on the golden age of the ancient world.[16] But Fénelon's unorthodox relationship with the Catholic mystic Madame Guyon eventually lost him the support of Louis XIV, who had him exiled to his diocese at Cambrai in 1709.

Now it seems that Ramsay may have acted as some sort of secretary for Madame Guyon, which might in turn explain why in 1710 he suddenly received an invitation to visit Fénelon at Cambrai.[17] There Ramsay and Fénelon developed a warm friendship which lasted until Fénelon's death in 1715. So influenced was Ramsay by Fénelon that he converted to Catholicism at his request.

In 1716, a year after Fénelon's death, Ramsay settled in Paris, where he circulated amongst the high aristocracy and became tutor to the young Duke of Château-Theirry. At the same time Ramsay befriended the powerful Philippe d'Orléans, nephew of Louis XIV and regent of France. The latter was the head of the Order of St. Lazarus, an old crusading order, akin to the Knights Templar, that had been founded in Jerusalem in the 12th century. Soon Ramsay was dubbed a knight of the Order of St. Lazarus by Philippe.

We know that Ramsay was initiated into Freemasonry by the Duke of Richmond at the Horn Lodge at Westminster[18] during a visit that he made to London in 1730. On his return to Paris, Ramsay joined Charles Radclyffe's Masonic lodge *St. Thomas*, and soon was appointed as Orator for the *Grande Loge* of France. It was in this capacity that he prepared a landmark speech in 1737, one that would have reverberations throughout the world in decades to come.

An ancient order and a dangerous whiff of Republicanism

Legend has it that Ramsay's speech, which is better known as Ramsay's Oration, was delivered on 21 March 1737 so that it would coincide with the spring equinox. There may be a reason for this date, as we shall see. However the evidence suggests that the Oration was not 'delivered' to an audience at all; instead, Ramsay had it printed and distributed to the lodge's members. By 1740 it was published in Paris, where it was widely and avidly read.[19]

Knowing that Ramsay was both a member of the Royal Society and a Freemason helps to put his Oration into context – for this remarkable document is resonant of 'republicanism' and of an ideal of global unity based on a new world order. Of particular note is the fact that the Oration was put before the general public as early as 1740 – a full 36 years before the outbreak of the American War of Independence in 1776 and 49 years before the outbreak of the French Revolution in 1789. We suspect that Ramsay's carefully-chosen words must have struck a worrying note with the French monarchy and royalists in general:

> The world is nothing more than a huge Republic, of which every nation is a family and every individual a child. Our society [i.e. Freemasonry] was at the outset established to revive and spread these essential maxims borrowed from the nature of man. We desire to reunite all men of enlightened minds, gentle manners and agreeable wit, not only by a love for the fine arts but much more by the grand principle of virtue, science, and religion, where the interests of the Fraternity [Freemasonry] shall become those of the whole human race, whence all nations shall be enabled to draw useful knowledge … Our ancestors, the Crusaders, gathered together from all parts of Christendom in the Holy Land, desired thus to reunite into one sole Fraternity the individuals of all nations …[20]

The last sentence gives an interesting and novel spin on the Crusades, or rather on those 'crusaders' who, we're told, desired 'to reunite into one sole Fraternity the individuals of all nations …' Since it is safe to say that 'a universal brotherhood of nations' was not uppermost in the minds of the vast majority of crusaders – who believed their job was to win the Holy Land for Christendom and to steal as much booty as possible – it is legitimate to ask *which* 'crusaders' Ramsay is talking about here?

We can only think of one group who might have been motivated by such an ideology and they are, almost inevitably, the Knights Templar – who are, moreover, frequently cited by Freemasons as their 'ancestors'. That it was indeed the Templars who Ramsay had in mind (though he did not wish to name them) is also made clear by several indirect allusions in the Oration:

> Because a sad, savage, and misanthropic Philosophy disgusts virtuous men, our ancestors, the Crusaders, wished to render it lovable by the attractions of innocent pleasures, agreeable music, pure joy, and moderate gaiety. Our festivals are not what the profane world and the ignorant vulgar

imagine. All the vices of heart and soul are banished there, and irreligion, libertinage, incredulity, and debauch are proscribed.[21]

It was well known throughout Europe that the Templars had been dissolved by papal decree and French military force after accusations of vice, debauchery and heresy. Here Ramsay is obviously defending the Templars and their alleged 'descendants', the Freemasons, against such accusations by claiming that what appeared as debauchery and heresy to the 'profane' was in reality nothing more that the display of innocent pleasures and moderate merry-making.

Ramsay also tells us that the order once enjoyed special royal protection in England:

After the deplorable mishaps in the Crusades, the perishing of the Christian armies, and the triumph of Bendocdar, Sultan of Egypt, during the eighth and last Crusade, that great Prince Edward, son of Henry III, King of England, seeing there was no longer any safety for his brethren in the Holy Land, from whence the Christian troops were retiring, brought them all back, and this colony of brothers was established in England. As this Prince was endowed with all heroic qualities, he loved the fine arts, declared himself Protector of our Order, conceded to it new privileges, and then the members of this Fraternity took the name of *Freemasons*, after the example set by their ancestors.[22]

The 'great Prince Edward, son of Henry III' evoked by Ramsay as the 'Protector of our Order' was the celebrated Edward I – famously nicknamed 'Longshanks' on account of his unusually tall stature. King of England from 1274, Edward I is best known for his war of oppression against the Scots first under William Wallace and later under Robert the Bruce – the latter long suspected to have been a patron of the Templars in the years after their persecution. But Ramsay's clear implication here is that Edward was *also* their patron. Presumably, therefore, he would have remained so until his death on 7 July 1307, three months before the mass arrests of Templars in France which, the reader will recall, took place on 13 October 1307.

In the years that followed it is notable that Edward I's son, Edward II, continued to favour the Knights Templar despite increasing pressure from the pope and King Philip IV of France as late as 1312, when Philip convinced the pope to issue his infamous *Vox in excelso* papal bull of 22 March (the spring equinox) officially suppressing the Templars. It seems that Edward

II's compliance was only half-hearted. He made a few token arrests while allowing most of the knights simply to melt into other chivalrous orders, such as that of the Knights Hospitallier.

Bearing this in mind, let's recall the legendary 'official date' of Ramsay's Oration – i.e. 21 March 1737, the spring equinox. Surely this must be a deliberate allusion to the papal bull that had suppressed the Templars on the spring equinox? Masonic historian Alexander Piatigorsky, who has made a special study of the Oration, notes how Chevalier Ramsay subtly managed to pack it with quite a number of controversial claims:

> The first places the origin of Masonic rituals 'at the time of the Crusades' and associates them with ... the Knights Templar and the esoteric traditions of other medieval Christian Orders. The second asserts that after the suppression of the Templars in the beginning of the fourteenth century and the decline of the other Orders, their esoteric traditions were originally grafted onto, or found shelter among, some Scottish Masonic Lodges e.g. the Mother Lodge of Kilwinning. And the third maintains that those Scottish Traditions (or Orders), which are Christian by definition ... were still continuing in Scottish Masonry, and that he [i.e. Ramsay] himself represented them in France as well as in England.[23]

It is interesting that Ramsay also goes on to state in his Oration that 'the famous festivals of Ceres at Eleusis, of Isis in Egypt, of Minerva at Athens, of Urania among the Phoenicians, and Diana in Scythia, were connected to ours [i.e. to the rites and festivals of Freemasonry].' He pauses to recognise that some fellow Freemasons attribute great antiquity to the brotherhood by ascribing 'our institution to Solomon, some to Moses, some to Abraham, some to Noah and some to Enoch who built the first city, or even to Adam.' But 'without making any pretences of denying these origins' Ramsay chooses to pass on 'to matters less ancient':

> This, then, is a part of what I have gathered in the annals of Great Britain, in the Acts of Parliament, which speak often of our privileges, and in the living tradition of the English people, which has been the centre of our Society [Freemasonry] since the 11th century.

> At the time of the Crusades in Palestine many princes, lords and citizens associated themselves to restore the Temple of the Christians in the Holy Land ... and to employ themselves in bringing back their architecture

... Our Order [which was amongst them] must ... be considered ... as an Order founded in remote antiquity, and renewed in the Holy Land by our ancestors in order to recall the memory of the most sublime truths ...

[After the Crusades were over] the kings, princes and lords returned from Palestine to their own lands, and there established diverse Lodges. At the time many Lodges were already erected in Germany, Italy, Spain, France, and from thence in Scotland, because of the close alliance between the French and Scots. James Lord Steward was Grand Master of a Lodge established at Kilwinning, in the west of Scotland ... This lord received as Freemasons into his Lodge the Earls of Gloucester and Ulster, the one English the other Irish.

By degrees our lodges and our rites were neglected in most places. This is why of so many historians only those of Great Britain speak of our Order. Nevertheless it preserved its splendour among those Scotsmen [the Scots Guards] to whom the kings of France confided during many centuries the safeguard of their royal persons.[24]

Whatever Ramsay's motives, and regardless of the vexed issue of the veracity of the Oration, most Freemasons agree that it was soon after its publication that the so-called *additional* or *higher degrees* of Freemasonry first began to appear. Ramsay may not have been involved directly in formulating any of these degrees but there can be little doubt that his ideas about the past – and future – of Freemasonry played an important role in bringing them into existence. These degrees are still very much part of the Masonic world today. They represent a set of goals towards which most Freemasons aspire, which may be attained by the right candidates through ever higher levels of initiation. Before returning to the story of Freemasonry in the years leading up to the French Revolution it will be useful to make a short excursion into these airy realms.

Excursion to the higher degrees (1) Schisms

When the Grand Lodge of England was founded in 1717, not all Freemasons wanted to accept its authority as a centralised Masonic body.

Even within Britain a powerful opposing faction eventually emerged which considered itself the 'true repository' of ancient Freemasonry. Those adhering to it called themselves the *Antients* and labelled all who joined the Grand Lodge of England disparagingly as *Moderns*. After nearly half a century of feuding between the Antients and the Moderns, both factions were finally 'united' in Britain under the banner of the 'United' Grand Lodge of England – a sort of Masonic mini-version of the 'United States'. This happened in 1813 when 21 articles of union were signed by both groups, the most important declaring and pronouncing that:

> ... pure Antient Masonry consists of three degrees and no more i.e. those of the Entered Apprentice, the Fellow Craft and the Master Mason, including the Supreme Order of the Holy Royal Arch. But this article is not intended to prevent any Lodge or Chapter from holding a Meeting in any of the Degrees of the Orders of Chivalry, according to the constitutions of the said Orders.[25]

What this means in practice, as we shall see, is that 'higher' or 'additional' degrees are available to Freemasons in English lodges exclusively through the Supreme Order of the Holy Royal Arch. However, in the world as a whole, there are other Masonic orders which also offer 'higher' or 'additional' degrees. Two that are particularly popular in the US are the so-called *York Rite*, and the *Ancient And Accepted Scottish Rite*, descended from Andrew Ramsay's original Scottish Rite. The York Rite offers three extra degrees, namely the *Royal Arch Masons* degree, the *Royal and Select Masters* degree and the *Knights Templar* degree. The Ancient And Accepted Scottish Rite, by far the largest and most important, offers a total of *33 degrees* and is considered by many as the most influential and supremely elitist of all the Masonic orders.

It is these rites that offer the 'degrees of the Orders of Chivalry' mentioned above. An important factor contributing to their formation and rapid proliferation was again the desire on the part of Freemasons *not* to be under the jurisdiction of United Grand Lodge of England – in this case often because they lived in countries that were in conflict with Britain. Since France remained Britain's traditional foe well into the 19th century, French Freemasons were determined to have a separate identity. While developing a completely independent type of Freemasonry of their own they also began to nourish close ties with Freemasons in the colonies during the build-up to the American Revolution.

This is why we find many of the higher 'degrees of the Orders of Chivalry' still enjoying active support in the US today. Moreover even the most cursory examination of the Scottish Rite and the York Rite leaves little doubt that the degrees they offer are heavily laced with Templar associations.

In the York Rite, which some Masons in the US call the 'American Rite', the symbolism, iconography and regalia used are all unambiguously 'Templar', and Templar symbols and links are openly flaunted. As noted above, the third 'additional' degree of the York Rite is called the *Knights Templar* degree.

As for the Scottish Rite, the chivalrous element of the Knights Templar is clearly seen in the names given to the various degrees offered – such as *Knight of the East, Knight of Jerusalem, Knight of Rose Croix, Knight Commander of the Temple, Knight Kadosh*, and so forth. In the US, the Scottish Rite also sponsors the very popular para-Masonic fraternity for young men, generally for sons of Freemasons, known as the 'International Order of DeMolay', so named in memory of Jacques de Molay, last of the true Grand Masters of the Knights Templar.[26]

Excursion to higher degrees (2) Holy Royal Arch

Regular or *Craft* Freemasonry, meaning that type of Freemasonry which is regulated by the united grand lodges and their various warrants around the world, offers three levels of initiation to the new recruits. These are often referred to as 'symbolic' or 'blue' degrees and are, respectively, *Entered Apprentice, Fellow Craft* and *Master Mason*.

Most Freemasons complete their Masonic education when they obtain the Master Mason degree. There are, however, a few others who want to take their initiation further and thus proceed to what are generally referred to as the 'additional degrees' or 'higher degrees'. These can be considered as emanating from Craft Freemasonry and can only be entered by those who have completed the third 'blue' degree of Master Mason. In Britain the only additional degree that is regulated by United Grand Lodge is the so-called *Royal Arch*. This is how the United Grand Lodge introduces the Royal Arch:

> Under the English Constitution, basic Freemasonry is divided into two parts, called the Craft and the Royal Arch. For Freemasons who really want to explore the subject in more depth there is a host of other ceremonies, which, for historical reasons, are not administered by the United Grand Lodge of England. All English Freemasons experience the three Craft (or basic) ceremonies unless they drop out from Freemasonry very early on. These three ceremonies (or degrees as we call them) look at the relations between people, man's natural equality and his dependence on others, the importance of education and the rewards of labour, fidelity to a promise,

contemplation of inevitable death, and one's duty to others. A fourth
ceremony – the Royal Arch emphasises man's dependence on God.[27]

The United Grand Lodge of England has its headquarters at Freemasons'
Hall in London. This huge neo-classical edifice is located at the crossroads
of Great Queen Street and Drury Lane. But few initiation ceremonies are
conducted there, with most of the three degrees being 'worked' in the 8,000
or so 'lodges' or 'temples' across the country. As one recent Grand Master
pointed out, there is an even wider 'spread from English origins throughout
the world' if we consider all the so-called overseas *warrants*.

Any Master Freemason, i.e. third degree Mason, can further his Masonic
career by taking one or more or all of the 'additional' or 'higher' degrees. In
England, this usually entails taking the supplementary degrees recognized
by the United Grand Lodge, meaning those administered by the Holy Royal
Arch under the jurisdiction of the Supreme Grand Holy Royal Arch Chapter
of Jerusalem instituted in 1766. Higher Royal Arch degrees are 'worked' not
in lodges but in *chapter lodges*. There are some 3,000 or so chapter lodges in
Britain alone, with an estimated combined membership of 150,000.

Excursion to higher degrees (3) Warrior-Masons of Zerubbabel

In Craft Freemasonry the themes of the rituals revolve around pseudo-
biblical events concerning the construction of Solomon's Temple. More
specifically, the third or Master Mason degree deals with the death and
raising of one Hiram Abiff, a pseudo-biblical character probably modelled
on the legendary Phoenician architect, Hiram of Tyre, who supposedly
designed or participated in the construction of Solomon's Temple around
950 BC.[28] In this ritual, the apotheosis is reached when the Master Mason-
elect is 'raised' from a symbolic death supposedly mimicking the death and
'raising' of Hiram Abiff who was himself brutally murdered by three 'Fellows'
for refusing to impart to them the 'secret' of the Master Mason's 'word'.
Presumably one of the messages of all this is that a Master Mason chooses
death rather than to break his Masonic oath – an act of ultimate loyalty
which is rewarded by him being 'raised' as a resurrected new Master.

In the Holy Royal Arch rituals, however, the so-called *Hiramic* theme is
replaced by a different focus, now concerning the *reconstruction* of Solomon's
Temple by *Zerubbabel* and his followers. In the Bible Zerubbabel was the
leader of the Jews exiled in Babylon who negotiated their freedom from
their Babylonian oppressors and heroically led them all back to Palestine.

Zerubbabel became governor of Jerusalem and ordered the reconstruction of the Temple which had been destroyed by the Babylonians. Interestingly some researchers believe that the particular obsession of the Knights Templar with Solomon's Temple might likewise have been focused, in a mystical sense, on its *rebuilding* rather than anything else:

> The Templars saw themselves as the Warrior-Masons of Zerubbabel, who persuaded King Darius to allow the rebuilding of the Temple of Jerusalem. They inherited the belief from the Gnostics and St. John that the Temple was the mystic centre of the world, and so they secretly resisted the power and authority of the Popes and Kings of Europe. The black and white devices of their order ... showed their Gnosticism and Manicheism, the belief in the continuing struggle of the devil's world against God's Intelligence. They bequeathed to the Masons the black-and-white lozenges and Indented Tassels of their Lodges.[29]

The alleged dualistic or 'Manichean' symbolism of the 'black and white devices' used by the Templars (which were numerous and included their checkered battle flag, the *beauséant*) are not matters that we need concern ourselves with here. What interests us more is this further hint of the continuity of interests, symbolism and ritual that seems to tie the Freemasons, who are still very much a force to be reckoned with in the world, to the Knights Templar who have supposedly been extinct for 700 years.

To return to the Royal Arch rituals of Freemasonry, there are usually three main 'actors' who assume the role of Zerubbabel and his two trusted colleagues, Joshua and Haggia. These protagonists re-enact the clearing of the site where once stood the 'Temple of Solomon' and while doing so discover a golden plate upon which are written the 'sacred and mysterious' names of God. These turn out to be the well-known name of Jehovah, correctly written as *Jahveh* (from the Latin consonants JHVH which are all that the Old Testament gives us) and also another, more mysterious name proclaimed to be *Jahbulon*.[30] The name *Jahveh* is split into three syllables, *Ja-h-veh*, and written inside a small circle. The same is done for *Jahbulon*, *Jah-bul-on*, but in this case inscribed on the corners of a triangle drawn inside the circle.

Thus combined, these obvious Pythagorean symbols also form the common alchemical device used to show the so-called *mystical relationship* of the square, the circle and the triangle. Masonic author and researcher Martin Short refers to a 'mystical lecture' that is sometimes given in Holy Royal Arch rituals in which it is explained that:

... In times of antiquity, names of God and symbols of divinity were always enclosed in triangular figures ... In the days of Pythagoras the triangle was considered the most sacred of emblems ... The Egyptians termed it the Sacred Number, and so highly was it prized by the ancients, that it became amongst them an object of worship. They gave it the sacred name of God ... This sacred *Delta* is usually enclosed with a square and circle ... the word on the triangle is that Sacred and mysterious Name you have just solemnly engaged yourself never to pronounce.[31]

Excursion to higher degrees (4) Much fuss about Jahbulon

Craft Freemasonry uses *epithets* for God such as the 'Grand Architect of the Universe', the 'Great Geometrician' or the 'Supreme Being'. But in the Royal Arch the adepts find it necessary actually to give God a name such as *Jahbulon*. We cannot be certain how long this name was used before it began to attract hostile attention in the early 1980s. In 1985, however, the Church of England and the Methodist Church urged Freemasonry to remove it from Royal Arch rituals on the grounds that they suspected it to be of pagan origins.[32] Many anti-Masonic researchers within the clerical establishments were convinced that the name *Jahbulon* veiled three ancient deities, namely the Hebrew *Jahveh* or *Yahweh*, the Phoenician *Baal* or *Buul*, and the patron deity of the ancient Egyptian city of *On* (*Anu*, or Heliopolis, the 'City of the Sun') who some took to be Ra, and some Osiris.[33]

The clerics protested that this sort of pagan syncretism was something 'which Christianity cannot accept' and that quite simply *Jahbulon*, whoever or whatever he was, had to go. The Freemasons retaliated by arguing that *Jahbulon* was not a name of God at all but merely a 'description of God'. The clerics, however, were unimpressed and fought a relentless battle over the matter in the media – causing much nervousness in Masonic circles inhabited by people who are normally accustomed to secrecy. In July 1989 the United Grand Lodge caved in under the pressure and announced that *Jahbulon* would henceforth be replaced by *Jahveh* alone, a name for God generally regarded as acceptable by Christians. This seemed to do the trick and the media lost interest in the story.

Not many clerics were convinced at this quick 'conversion' of the Masons. *Jahveh*, after all, was confirmed to have been associated with the first syllable of the name *Jahbulon,* and it seemed to some that the whole bizarre exercise merely amounted to more or less the same thing as replacing a name by its diminutive – such as 'Kat' for 'Katherine' and so forth.

Could there possibly be some fire behind all this smoke about Masonic 'paganism'?

Excursion to higher degrees (5) ancient Egypt and geometry

A 1901 aquarelle illustration made by artist R. F. Sherar of the original interior of the Supreme Grand Royal Arch Chapter of Scotland, designed by the architect Peter Henderson and located in Edinburgh, makes it immediately clear that this particular grand chapter at least was modeled on an ancient Egyptian pharaonic temple.[34] A closer examination of the various illustrations on the walls uncovers scenes taken from the ancient Egyptian *Book of the Dead* depicting the god Osiris on his heavenly throne like some monarch of the Solomonic age passing divine judgment on the neophyte brought before him. There is also a very similar pseudo-Egyptian temple at the Grand Lodge of Pennsylvania in Philadelphia, on the floor of which can be seen the winged-*uraeus* or solar-serpent, the supreme symbol of ancient Egypt. Many other Royal Arch chapters around the world are likewise designed or partly designed as 'Egyptian' temples, such as Freemasons' Hall in Dublin which, in Martin Short's, words boasts two sphinxes and other sculptures 'aping ancient Egypt.'[35] Short similarly draws attention to the modern Holy Royal Arch temple at Petersham, New South Wales in Australia which has an Egyptian room with murals showing scenes from the Egyptian *Book of the Dead* including images of Osiris.[36]

A colleague of Martin Short, the notorious anti-Masonic author Stephen Knight, had been one of the first – as early as 1981 – to take the Masonic name *Jahbulon* to task. In the refrain that the clergy would later echo he claimed that it was an allegory of pagan deities including the Egyptian god Osiris, the 'Lord of *On*'.[37] In 1987 Short reiterated Knight's view that the syllable *On* in *Jahbulon* denoted the ancient Egyptian holy city of *On*, i.e. Heliopolis or the 'City of the Sun' where had once stood the great sun-Temple of Atum-Ra, progenitor of Osiris. According to Martin Short:

> ... if *Jahbulon* means anything, it means 'God, the Lord of On', or possibly 'He Who is the Lord of On'. Whether that god is the sun-god Ra or Osiris, the God of the Dead, depends on which period of Egyptian history takes your fancy.[38]

Naturally most modern Freemasons vehemently deny all this, arguing that the ancient images and deities found in Masonic rituals are only used in a *symbolic* manner and then merely to emphasize or represent ideas that are entirely harmonious with Christianity.

But something that is rarely discussed remains unexplained about the name *Jahbulon*.

In Masonic Royal Arch iconography, the Pythagorean triangle is often shown alongside Masonic symbols such as the stonemason's block, the chisel and the mace. Now the pseudo-biblical setting in which the Royal Arch rituals unfold is derived from the so-called *Old Charges*, already discussed in Chapter Thirteen. The reader will recall that these *Old Charges* are a compilation of medieval manuscripts which provide an account of the ancient origins of Freemasonry. In one of these, the *Beswicke-Royds Manuscript* dating from the 16th century, there is a description of the so-called 'seven liberal arts and sciences' and the statement that all the sciences in the world are to be found in 'geometry'.[39]

Right across the whole spectrum of Masonic writings the discipline of 'geometry' continues to this day to be given a place of honour along with its ancient 'fathers' such as Euclid and, more especially, Pythagoras. Indeed Pythagoras' famous square-root-triangle theorem pops up in many Masonic illustrations and can even be seen on the frontispiece of the 1723 Masonic *Constitutions*. The curious sanctity and reverence that Freemasons give to geometry is such that the letter 'G' – commonly seen inside the symbol of the Masonic triangle or 'Blazing Star' where it denotes the 'Grand Architect of the Universe' – also apparently stands for 'geometry'. By the same logic, the Masonic 'Supreme Being' Himself is often called the 'Great Geometrician'.

Now the connections of Pythagoras and also of Euclid with ancient Egypt were well known to 18th and 19th century historians, who read the classics. Many classical chroniclers such as Cicero, Diogenes, Isocrates, Porphyry, Valerius, Strabo, Justinian and Clement of Alexandria, tell us that Pythagoras had long sojourned in Egypt, and Iamblichus even reports that Pythagoras stayed there for 22 years. All agree that it was in Egypt that Pythagoras learned the science of geometry from the ancient sages of Heliopolis. The Greek chronicler Isocrates even maintains that Pythagoras became a disciple of the Heliopolitan sages, and the historian Plutarch went as far as to assert that Pythagoras was initiated by the Egyptian priest Oenuphis of Heliopolis.[40] This almost mystical link between Pythagoras and ancient Egypt fascinated the scholars of the Renaissance and the Enlightenment, and led many to believe that much of the sacred and pristine 'science' or 'knowledge' of the ancient Egyptians had been somehow brought into Western tradition encoded in Pythagorean geometry.

In the *Old Charges* reference is made to a mysterious patriarch called *Jabal*, the 'descendent of Lamech',[41] who is known as the 'Founder of

Geometry' and is often called *Jabal of Geometry*.[42] The reader will recall from Chapter Thirteen that Jabal's geometry and the other antediluvian sciences were said to have been recorded on two stone pillars 'erected by the inhabitants of the ancient world to carry the knowledge of mankind over an impeding destruction which proved to be Noah's Flood.'[43]

After the Flood, the *Old Charges* go on to say that 'Hermes the Father of Wise Men' rediscovered the two pillars 'wherein the sciences were written and taught them forth'. We're told that the texts recording these 'sciences' were later taken out of Egypt by Moses during the Exodus and that in this way 'was the worthy Craft of Masons confirmed in the Country of Jerusalem.'[44] What is interesting about all this is that the *Old Charges* are adamant that the two stone pillars carrying this arcane knowledge were *not* those from Solomon's Temple, i.e. *Boaz* and *Jachin*, but much older ones somehow connected to the quintessential Egyptian sage 'Hermes the Father of Wise Men', i.e. Thoth or Hermes Trismegistus. A reasonable conclusion would be that these 'pillars' were thought to be *inscribed obelisks* from the great sun Temple of Heliopolis, where all the great sages of antiquity were taught the 'seven liberal arts and sciences.' As we have seen, in the Bible the city of Heliopolis is called *On*. So if the patriarch *Jabal* in the *Old Charges* was the 'founder' of geometry, then it is quite possible that the word *Jahbulon* is a cipher to denote the 'sacred geometry' or 'sacred science' of *On*, i.e. Heliopolis.

From Grand Lodge to *Grand Orient*

Having broached the subject of the higher degrees, and of the esoteric speculation that seems inevitably to arise from them let's now return to the more general story of Freemasonry in France in the years before the French Revolution.

Most historians believe that Freemasonry took root in France from the Scottish lodges that we know were set up in the 17th century by the Stuart Jacobites-in-exile, and thus well before the creation of the Grand Lodge of England in London in 1717.[45] This 'Jacobite' type of Freemasonry on the Continent was vehemently opposed by Masonic lodges later established in France under the warrant and jurisdiction of the Grand Lodge. In 1738, however, a general assembly of all lodges, both 'Jacobite' and 'English', voted that the powerful Duke of Antin, a cousin of King Louis XV, be elected as Grand Master of all Freemasonry in France.[46]

After the death of the duke in 1743, the French Freemasons elected another prince of the blood royal, Louis de Bourbon-Condé, the Count of Clermont, as the new Grand Master. Among other things, the Count of Clermont was also the lieutenant-general of the king's army, abbot of Saint-Germain-des-Prés in Paris, and a prominent member of the *Académie Française*.[47] More importantly, the Count of Clermont was the son of the Duke of Bourbon and Mlle de Nante, the latter a natural daughter of Louis XIV and his favourite mistress, the influential Mme de Montespan. But an even more powerful royal would be found. On 24 June 1772, a year or so after the death of the Count of Clermont, the *Grande Loge de France* elected as its new Grand Master, the Duke of Chartres, the future Duke of Orléans, first cousin of King Louis XVI. At his election the name of the *Grande Loge de France* was changed to the *Grand Orient de France*.[48] French Freemasonry under the *Grand Orient* quickly become very popular not only with the aristocracy but also, and perhaps more so, right across the middle classes amongst the military, academics, men of letters, the clergy and the bourgeoisie in general.

In these early formative years of the *Grand Orient* another important Masonic influence was to penetrate France – an influence that had the unmistakable hallmark of the Hermetic-Egyptian ideologies that Giordano Bruno and Tommaso Campanella had first imported a century before.

Cagliostro and 'Egyptian' Freemasonry

In the late 1770s there emerged from Italy, like a Bruno or Campanella reborn, yet another Hermetic-Egyptian reformist. He was to prove tenacious and determined and would become, in a most curious way, one of the political catalysts of the French Revolution.

Giuseppe Balsamo, a man who is better known as the 'Count' of Cagliostro, was born in the Italian city of Palermo in 1743.[49] Little is heard of Cagliostro until the 1760s, when we find him in Rome working as a restorer and copier of old paintings. There he married a ravishingly beautiful girl called Lorenza Feliciani, the daughter of a wealthy Roman coppersmith, and acquired some knowledge of medicine and alchemy. Along the way Cagliostro also managed to acquire a reputation of his own as a healer, an alchemist, and a very generous philanthropist.

By 1776, the year the American Revolution began, Cagliostro and the beautiful Lorenza were in England, having travelled there via Malta and Spain. They set up home on Whitcomb Street and Cagliostro began at once to introduce himself to Masonic circles in London. In this he had no difficulty since he carried impressive Masonic letters of recommendation from a certain Luigi Aquino, a Knight of Malta and brother of Prince Francesco Aquino, the Grand Master of Freemasonry in Naples.[50]

Within a year Cagliostro was raised to the rank of Master Mason at the Royal Tavern Lodge in Soho.[51] A very charismatic and well-spoken person, with an added touch of glamour thrown in by the constant presence of his beautiful wife Lorenza, Cagliostro's reputation as a healer and magician brought him amazing fame. It seems that he much impressed his English friends by guessing correctly the winning numbers of the lottery. This ability, quite naturally, created a huge stir, with everyone trying to buy winning numbers from him. So persistent were these demands that the Cagliostros had to close their home to all visitors except for a few personal acquaintances.[52]

An unfortunate incident involving an expensive diamond necklace that Lorenza was lured to accept from a cunning admirer in exchange for lottery numbers, was to bring charges of embezzlement against Cagliostro from the authorities in London.[53] After a very embarrassing trial that lasted several months, the Cagliostros left England in late December 1777 in the hope of making a better life on the Continent. They first went to Bavaria, staying in hostels recommended by fellow Masons, and were well received by the nobility of Leipzig. There Cagliostro is said to have encountered the French Hermetic alchemist, Antoine-Joseph Pernety.[54]

Pernety was a Benedictine monk from the Abbey of Saint-Germain-des-Prés in Paris. He had acquired some fame in 1766 for having founded a Masonic rite known as the *Hermetic Ritual of Perfection* for the so-called *Illuminati of Avignon*, an esoteric Masonic sect.[55] Persecuted by the Jesuits, Pernety had been obliged to flee Avignon, and had spent several years in Berlin under the protection of King Frederick II. The latter was a keen patron of Masonic orders and had himself been initiated into Freemasonry in 1738. Frederick II appointed Pernety curator of the Berlin State Library and granted him membership of the Prussian Academy of Sciences.[56]

In Berlin, Pernety practiced what he clearly believed to be Hermetic 'Egyptian' astral and talismanic magic. He frequently performed at séances attended by members of the German aristocracy for whom it was said he invoked the power of angels and spirits.[57] During these sessions Pernety addressed his new recruits with words reminiscent of the Renaissance magi:

> ... the science into which I am about to initiate you is the first and most ancient of sciences. It emanates from Nature, or rather it is Nature herself perfected by art and based on experience.[58]

Cagliostro reaches France by way of Germany and Russia

Germany in the 1770s was rife with exotic secret societies and Masonic orders. One of these was known as the 'African Architects'. It had been founded in 1767 by Karl Friedrich von Köppen, an officer in the Prussian army,[59] who is thought to have been behind a strange Masonic tract, the *Crata Repoa*, which purports to contain authentic reproductions of initiation rituals performed in the Great Pyramid by ancient Egyptian priests.[60] As odd as it may seem, this peculiar 'Egyptian' Masonic society of African Architects received the sponsorship of Frederick II, who even had a magnificent library built for its members in the region of Silesia in south Poland.[61]

There was also the so-called *Rite of Strict Observance* founded in 1756 by Karl Gotthelf, better known as the Baron von Hund, who had been initiated into Freemasonry in Paris in 1743 in one of the fashionable 'Templar' orders.[62] Baron von Hund, like the Chevalier Ramsay before him, claimed that Freemasonry was linked to the medieval Knights Templar, and his own Rite of Strict Observance was to enjoy astounding success in Germany and other parts of Europe. It was in one of the Strict Observance lodges, *Zur Wohltätigkeit*, that the composer Wolfgang Amadeus Mozart was initiated, and it is obviously from the influence of Hund's and Köppen's Masonic rite that Mozart was to develop the theme for his famous Masonic opera, *The Magic Flute*, which is set in a pseudo-Egyptian context highly charged with Masonic symbolism and virtues.[63]

But by far the most famous of all these exotic orders, and also somewhat connected to Hund's Strict Observance order, was an intensely anticlerical organisation called the *Illuminati of Bavaria*. It had been founded in 1776 in Ingolstadt by the lawyer Adam Weishaupt and was backed by the influential Baron Knigge, a Freemason and also a member of the Strict Observance.[64] Such German Masonic activity in the late 1770s was to have a great influence on American 'higher degree' Freemasonry and the Supreme Council of the 33rd Degree in Charleston, SC (later moved to Washington, DC).[65]

In 1777, a year after the start of the American Revolution and 12 years before the start of the French Revolution, Cagliostro arrived in Germany. He immediately involved himself with a wide variety of Masonic orders all of which had in common a distinctive blend of Hermetic-Egyptianism and neo-Templar ideologies.

And although most Masonic historians maintain that the 'Egyptian' type of Freemasonry was the invention of Cagliostro, it does very much appear that at least some of his ideas were cribbed from Köppen's *Crata*

Repoa. The basis of the Egyptian Rite can be summed up in Cagliostro's celebrated claim that:

> ... all light comes from the East and all initiation from Egypt.[66]

Cagliostro was the first Freemason to be aware of a huge and untapped source of Masonic recruits: women. And even though it is true that the idea of women's lodges had occurred to the *Grand Orient de France* as early as 1744,[67] it was nonetheless Cagliostro with his intriguing and attractive Egyptianised version of Freemasonry who, in practice, brought the ladies flocking in droves into the Masonic world.[68] It all began in 1775 when Cagliostro first set up an 'Egyptian Rite' lodge for women in the Hague, and where he was assisted by the beautiful Lorenza who would assume the role of 'Isis' in the rituals performed. From the outset what really seemed to appeal to women was the promise of a 'rejuvenation' ritual that Cagliostro and Lorenza performed in a pseudo-Egyptian setting. The course apparently took 40 days to complete, a period clearly modeled on the 40 days of embalming in ancient Egypt reported by classical authors such as Diodorus, who called this period the 'remedy which confers immortality.'[69] It is also said in the Bible when Jacob died in Egypt that:

> Joseph threw himself upon his father [Jacob], weeping and kissing his face. Then Joseph directed the physicians in his service to embalm his father [Jacob]. So the physicians embalmed him, taking a full forty days, for that was the time required for embalming.[70]

It was widely believed that the goddess Isis had invented the rites of embalming and rejuvenation, and therefore not surprisingly Cagliostro claimed that his own ritual was also the invention of the goddess Isis. Such claims, as well as Cagliostro's amazing reputation as a healer, did wonders for his new Masonic Egyptian Rite. But things started to go wrong when his travels brought him to Russia. At the court of Queen Catherine the Great, in the autumn on 1780, the queen herself accused him of being an imposter and a charlatan.

Fleeing Russia, Cagliostro travelled to France, entering through the Alsatian town of Strasbourg. There he met the immensely rich but also immensely naïve Louis René Édouard de Rohan, the French bishop of Strasbourg, known as the Cardinal de Rohan. He was fascinated by Cagliostro who performed a 'miracle' by curing Rohan's uncle, the Prince of

Soubise, from a near-fatal attack of Scarlet fever. The story of the 'miracle' went around France like wildfire, and from that moment on Cagliostro's reputation as a healer and magician began to open doors for him.

In the summer of 1784 he made his triumphal entrance in the city of Lyons. There hundreds of regular Freemasons willingly deserted their lodges to join Cagliostro's new 'Egyptian' lodge, *La Sagesse Triomphante*, which he hastily founded to receive them. On 24 December 1784, under the ecstatic gaze of his followers, Cagliostro proclaimed to the world the re-establishment of the 'true and ancient order of the *higher* rituals of Egyptian Freemasonry'. He would head it and hold the title *Great Copt*.[71] Funds were immediately raised by his enthusiastic disciples for the construction of a magnificent Egyptian temple, which, predictably, was to be in the form of a pyramid.

This was only the beginning of Cagliostro's meteoritic to rise to fame in France and his equally meteoric fall. His pyramidal 'temple' in Lyons was built and finally inaugurated in 1786, without the presence of Cagliostro who by that time was in Paris languishing in the Bastille for reasons that we'll explain in the next chapter. Afterwards his 'temple' remained a landmark in the district of Brotteaux in Lyons for many years. In 1788, the year before the Revolution, it was proposed that a second pyramid should be erected beside it – this one in honour of Joseph-Michel Montgolfier, the famous pioneer of the hot-air balloon, who was also a Freemason. Then in 1793 the idea was proposed yet again at the same location, only now the pyramid was to be a mausoleum for the 'martyrs' of the massacre of 1793, when the army of the Convention attacked Lyons. It is interesting that today, not far from this place, stands a high tower, the so-called *crayon*, shaped like an Egyptian obelisk with a huge glass pyramid at the top, owned by the Crédit Lyonnais bank. It was designed in 1977 by the New York architect, Araldo Cossutta. Oddly, Crédit Lyonnais owns another building at Lille which is designed as an inverted pyramid.

But we're getting far ahead of Cagliostro's story. On 30 January 1785, blissfully unaware of what lay in wait for him at the Bastille, he made his way to Paris.

We are now four short years from the French Revolution. For some it would be a cataclysm; for others an unprecedented opportunity …

Wonderful year! You will be the regenerating year, and you will be known by that name. History will extol your great deeds. You have changed my Paris, it is true. It is completely different today ... I nourish my spirit on it ...

Sebastien Mercier, 'Farewell to the Year 1789', as quoted in Lusebrink & Reichardt's
The Bastille: A History of a Symbol of Despotism and Freedom

Someone asked me if I would return to France in the case that those who attacked me [the king and the government] *would be removed? Surely, I replied, but only if the site of the Bastille* [where I was imprisoned] *becomes a public park ...*

Cagliostro, in a letter sent from London, 20 June 1786, where he
predicts the destruction of the Bastille after being exiled

Man is born free, but everywhere he is in chains.

Jean-Jacques Rousseau, *Le Contrat Social,*
the phrase that most inspired the French Revolution

CHAPTER SEVENTEEN

THE NEW CITY OF ISIS

C agliostro first took up residence in Paris in early February 1785 at the Hôtel de Strasbourg in the Rue Vieille-du-Temple, where his sponsor, the Cardinal de Rohan, resided. But then Cagliostro and Serafina (as he now called his wife Lorenza) moved to another small residence in the Rue Saint-Claude-au-Marais.[1]

There Cagliostro set up an 'Egyptian' Masonic lodge which very soon attracted many notables, among them the Duke of Montmorency-Luxembourg who, at the time, was Deputy Grand Master of the *Grand Orient*. Among the members was also the famous musician, Jean-Benjamin de Laborde, who had been the personal valet of Louis XV. The duke was appointed by Cagliostro as the Grand Master Protector of his new 'Egyptian' Freemasonry.[2] Then, in August 1785, Cagliostro, with the help of his wife, created his famous adoption lodge 'Isis' which immediately became a huge success with the ladies of the court. Among his recruits were the Countess of Polignac, the Countess of Brienne, the Countess of Choiseul (the wife of Louis XVI's finance minister), and many other ladies of the nobility.[3]

Cagliostro's Egyptian Rite rapidly became the craze of Paris, so much so that the ill-fated Queen Marie-Antoinette was to write in a letter to her sister: '*Tout le monde en est; on sait tout ce qui s'y passe*' ('Every one has joined; and everything that goes on is known to us').[4] Soon the sculptor Jean-Antoine Houdon, who was himself a keen adept of Cagliostro's Freemasonry, was to honour the maestro by fashioning a bust of him. It is reported that members of the famous *Philalethes* lodge, which studied the occult sciences, also fell under Cagliostro's spell and converted *en masse* into his new Egyptian Rite. Nothing, it seemed, could now stop this self-declared 'prophet of Isis'.[5]

Flashback (1) 15th–17th centuries: traditions of Paris as the city of Isis

There was, in fact, something about Paris itself that very much played in favour of Cagliostro's Egyptian Rite that conditioned citizens to respond enthusiastically to his claims regarding the ancient Egyptian goddess Isis.

Since the early part of the 15th century it is possible to document a persistent belief among Parisian historians that their city was somehow related to Isis. The belief probably goes back much further than that but is confirmed in a collection of manuscripts dating from around 1402 kept at the *Bibliothèque Nationale* in Paris. In these rare medieval documents we can find miniature drawings showing the goddess Isis dressed as a French noblewoman arriving by boat in Paris, where she is greeted by French nobles and clergymen[6] bearing the title 'the very ancient Isis, goddess and queen of the Egyptians.'[7] It is the 'boat of Isis' that is striking in these medieval miniatures for it bears an uncanny resemblance to the boat that was also placed on the medieval coat-of-arms of the city of Paris.[8] And during the same period we know that Parisians believed the name of their city to have been derived from the name of Isis. For example, a 14th century Augustine monk called Jacques le Grant wrote that:

> In the days of Charlemagne [eighth century AD] ... there was a city named Iseos, so named because of the goddess Isis who was venerated there. Now it is called Melun. Paris owes its name to the same circumstances, Parisius is said to be similar to Iseos (*quasi par Iseos*), because it is located on the River Seine in the same manner as Melun.[9]

In 1512, another French historian, Jean Lemaire de Belges, reported that an idol of the goddess Isis had been worshipped in a temple immediately outside the southern gate of Paris, where now stood the Abbey of Saint-Germain-des-Prés.[10] And the same was reported by many other contemporary writers, notably the 16th century Parisian historian Gilles Corrozet, who is reputed to be the first historian ever to produce a comprehensive guide to the city of Paris. In 1550 Corrozet also published a history of Paris titled *Les Antiquitez, Histoire et Singularitez de Paris*, in which he wrote that,

> ... coming to the imposition of the name [of Paris], it is said that there, where stands St. Germain-des-Prés, was a Temple of Isis of whom it is said was the wife of the great Osiris or Jupiter the Just. The statue [of Isis] having come in our times, of which we recall ... This place is called

the Temple of Isis and, for the nearby city, this was called Parisis ...
meaning near the Temple of Isis.[11]

The early 17th century French editors Pierre Bonfons and Jacques du
Breul republished Corrozet's book under their own names and titled *Les
Antiquitez et choses plus remarquables de Paris, recueillies par M. Pierre
Bonfons et augmentées par frère Jacques du Breul* in 1608. Jacques du
Breul was a Jesuit monk from Saint-Germain-des-Prés, and thus presumably
conversant with the records kept at that abbey. It is therefore of great
interest to find him writing as follows:

> ... at the place where King Childebert [fifth century AD] had constructed
> the church of St. Vincent now called St. Germain, and to which he
> donated his fief of Issy, the consensus was that there was there a Temple
> of Isis, wife of Osiris, also known as Jupiter the Just, and from whom the
> village of Issy got its name, and where can still be seen an ancient edifice
> and murals which are believed to be from the castle of Childebert.[12]

In 1612 yet another French historian, André Favyn, reported that the
church of Notre-Dame des Champs also once possessed an idol of Isis similar
to the one found in the nearby Abbey of Saint-Germain-des-Prés:

> I believe this was due to another idol, for the proximity that there is
> with [Notre Dame] and the Abbey of St. Germain-des-Prés where was
> venerated Isis, called by the Romans Ceres ...[13]

During the reign of Louis XIV an archaeological discovery was to add
even more fervour to this widely held set of beliefs linking Isis with Paris. In
1653, as we reported in Chapter Twelve, a worker digging the foundation
of a new vicarage in the city of Tournai stumbled across an ancient tomb
containing hundreds of golden ornaments. The tomb was thought to belong
to Childeric, a fifth century Frankish king and legendary ancestor of the
French monarchs.[14] Among the ornaments found within, and at a second
site discovered nearby, was a statue of Isis, the head of an ancient Egyptian
'Apis' bull (associated with the Osiris and later Serapis cults) and also some
300 golden bees. It was known, even at the time, that the symbol of the
ancient Egyptian pharaohs was the bee, which was immediately taken to
mean that there was a link between the ancient solar pharaohs of Egypt and
the ancient solar kings of France.

Flashback (2) 1665: the mystery of the deviated axis (1)

In 1665 the Childeric treasures were sent to Louis XIV who had them stored in his personal *Cabinet des Médailles*. We saw in Chapter Fourteen that the same year also witnessed a gathering in Paris of a powerful cabal of architects and city planners, including the stellar figure of Gian Lorenzo Bernini from Italy, Christopher Wren from England, and France's own André Le Nôtre. Wren was there to learn and listen. Bernini was designing the new façade of the Louvre Palace, and Le Nôtre was planning the Tuilleries Garden on the west side of the Louvre.

The central axis of the Louvre is set roughly east-west, running more or less parallel to the River Seine, which flows immediately to the south, and the Rue de Rivoli, which runs immediately to the north. If we follow the axis west today (i.e. towards the Tuilleries Garden) we will find that it passes through the apex of a huge glass Pyramid installed in the courtyard of the Louvre in 1984 and then, further west, through the centerline of the Arc du Carrousel (a triumphal arch built by Napoleon in 1806). At this point something strange happens – and it is the result of Le Nôtre's work in the 17th century. Instead of extending the 'axis of the Louvre' further to the west along its existing alignment, Le Nôtre made a deliberate decision, whilst developing the Tuilleries Garden, to deviate it a few degrees to the north – such that it now runs precisely at 26° north-of-west.[15] At first glance, it would appear that Le Nôtre may have wanted to adjust the alignment of the axis in order to have the Tuilleries Garden run more precisely parallel to the flow of the River Seine. That would seem a logical and practical decision for an urban architect to make. But still, why did he opt for exactly 26° and not, a rounded value such as, say, 25° or even 30°? We might suppose that the choice was arbitrary but for one very important point …

A few hundred yards downriver from the Louvre is the famous Cathedral of Notre Dame on the Île de la Cité, a small and peculiarly boat-shaped island in the River Seine. Here we find the alignment of 26° north-of-west incorporated into the axis of the cathedral itself.[16] Our point is that not only that Notre Dame's axis was established centuries before Le Nôtre but also that there is no obvious practical reason, in the case of the cathedral, that could account for this 26° alignment. It is not likely to be a coincidence that two major monuments within a few hundred yards both have the same axial alignment. If the angle is meaningful, however, then what does it mean?

The clue, we suggest, is the *Sun*. Let's not forget that Le Nôtre was planning a programme of monumental works for the Sun King. It should hardly be surprising, therefore, if solar symbolism were to be incorporated into such schemes. Further evidence that this is probably the right approach comes, yet again, from the anomalistic alignment of Notre Dame. As the Parisian historian Jean Phaure has observed, the axis of this great cathedral starts at an angle of 23.5° north-of-west but incorporates a deliberate deviation to the final figure of 26° north-of-west.[17] Why?

Readers with even a basic education in astronomy will recognize as we did that the angle of 23.5° has solar significance since it represents exactly the positive and negative declinations of the Sun at the summer and winter solstices respectively. But if this is to be the explanation for the axis of Notre Dame then why the deviation to 26°? Is it another solar alignment?

Let's first understand the significance of the angle of 23.5°.

The sun's altitude in the sky, measured at noon, changes throughout the year. It is at its highest at mid-summer (the summer solstice) and at its lowest at mid-winter (the winter solstice). These regular annual changes occur because the axis of the Earth is titled at an angle of 23.5° relative to the solar plane (referred to by astronomers as the ecliptic). Like a cosmic skewer passing through the north and south poles, this oblique axis governs our relationship to the Sun at all times and is, of course, the true *axis mundi* of our planet. The reader will recall from Chapter Fifteen how the spire of St. Paul's Cathedral in London was taken to symbolise the *axis mundi* and also how John Evelyn sought to equip St. Paul's with intense solar symbolism through his sephirothic scheme. We suggest that the angle of 23.5° in the axis of Notre Dame may have been intended to express a similar solar connection.

The sun's position changes throughout the year not only at noon (the astronomical 'meridian' or mid-line of the sky) but also at all other points along its arc – including, of course, at its rising and setting points on the horizon. At the latitude of Paris (48°, 51' north), an observer looking west (the general direction of Notre Dame's alignment) will note that the Sun sets at about 38° *north*-of-west at mid-summer and at about 38° *south*-of-west at mid-winter. On other days of the year the Sun sets at points in between these two extremes moving from north to south for six months and then travelling back from south to north again in the next six months. Obviously, with this pendulum-like swing, the Sun will set at any selected point within the range twice in the year (once on its journey from north to south and a second time on its journey from south back to north).

According to researcher and author Jean Phaure the second angle incorporated into the axis of Notre Dame Cathedral – i.e. the angle of 26° north-of-west – is to be explained by this pendulum swing of the Sun along the horizon. It turns out that the two days of the year when an observer at Notre Dame would see the Sun setting at 26° north-of-west are 8 May and 6 August – both dates of important Roman Catholic religious festivals.

The first, 8 May, marks *Saint-Michel de printemps*, a very popular feast in medieval times commemorating the miraculous apparition in the fourth and fifth centuries AD of the Archangel Michael on various mounts in Europe – for example on Mont Saint-Michel on the Brittany coast of France and on St. Michael's Mount in Cornwall, Britain. Michael the Archangel is the guardian prince of God's people, revealed in the Bible to be the 'captain' of God's army (Daniel 12:1, Joshua 5:14) – a role which many European monarchs were keen to project upon themselves.

The second date, 6 August, marks the *Transfiguration of Christ*, which remains an important feast in all of Christendom to this day. It commemorates the occasion, described in the New Testament, when Jesus was accompanied by his disciples Peter, James and John to the top of a mountain; there Moses and Elijah appeared and transfigured Jesus, making his face and clothes become white and shining as light (Mark 9:2–13; Matthew 17:1–13; Luke 9:28–36). We can understand, then, why Roman Catholicism has frequently associated 'shining' solar symbolism with the figure of Christ (for example his iconographical representations as a Sol Invictus in the early Roman Church).[18] It's obvious, too, that many Christian festivals track the solar cycle – such as Christmas (winter solstice), the Feast of St. John (summer solstice), Easter (the spring equinox), and so forth.[19]

Now in the Bible Elijah is prophesied to appear before the coming of the Jewish messiah, but Jesus maintains that this prophecy had already been fulfilled when Elijah appeared as John the Baptist (Matthew 17:9–13). Another biblical prophecy states that at the time when the messiah is about to appear: 'Michael will stand up, the great prince who mounts guard over your people.' (Daniel 12:1). Many Christians took this second prophecy as an indication that Michael the Archangel was to be the harbinger of Christ's Second Coming. For just as God sent Elijah in the form of John the Baptist to herald the first coming of the Christ on earth, so too will He send Michael at the end to proclaim Christ's Second Coming. And this appearance, the traditions leave no doubt, is to take place on a 'mount'. The Jews are clear that the setting is to be Mount Zion where Solomon's Temple stood. But for Christians the location of the Second Coming was for grabs – hence the many claims of St. Michael's appearance on mounts all over Europe in medieval times.

Flashback (2) 1665: the mystery of the deviated axis (2)

It seems obvious that complex interconnecting solar symbolism was at work in the choice of the angle of 26° north-of-west for the final axis of the medieval Cathedral of Notre Dame and thus in its linkage to the Feasts of *Saint-Michel de printemps* (8 May) and the *Transfiguration* (6 August). But let's not forget that this same axial alignment of 26° north-of-west was also much later adopted by Le Nôtre for the Tuilleries Garden and the Champs-Élysées (along what was to become the 'historical' axis of Paris). So it is interesting that in Le Nôtre's epoch – the epoch of the Sun King Louis XIV – the date of 6 August which commemorates the Transfiguration could boast not one but two significant sky events linked to the angle of 26°.

The first event, we already know, was *sunset* at 26° north-of-west, in line with the axis of Notre Dame Cathedral and the Historical Axis of Paris. The second event was the so-called *cosmic rising* of Sirius (i.e. the rising of the star at the same time as the sun).[20] This also occurred on 6 August, but, impressively, *in the exact opposite direction* – i.e. at 26° south-of-east, in direct line with the reverse view along the axis – and, of course, not at sunset but at *sunrise*.

Another matter also beckoned for attention. With the benefit of hindsight, we knew that along the Historical Axis of Paris would one day be raised a huge solar talisman: an obelisk from ancient Egypt. The reader will recall from Chapter One that this obelisk came from Luxor, the 'Heliopolis of the South' and a 'City of the Sun' *par excellence* of the ancient world. One of a pair that had stood outside the Luxor temple (the other still remains there *in situ*), the 'Paris' obelisk belonged to Pharaoh Ramses II, ancient Egypt's most powerful sun-king whose very name means 'son of the Sun'.[21] This obelisk thus creates an obvious symbolic link across the ages between two powerful solar kings – i.e. Ramses II and Louis XIV.

Furthermore, as we've seen in Chapter Ten, Luxor was an integral part of the much larger sun temple complex of Amun-Ra at Karnak. And here we find something very interesting indeed – for it turns out that just like the Historical Axis of Paris, the axis of the Temple of Karnak was set out by its architects along an alignment 26° south-of-east in one direction and 26° north-of-west in the other ...

Flashback (2) 1665: the mystery of the deviated axis (3)

No adjective in the English language can adequately describe the great sun temple complex of Amun-Ra at Karnak. But 'grandiose', 'breathtaking' and 'awe-inspiring' all apply. Known in ancient times as *Ipet-isut*, the 'most splendid of places', the central axis of this outstanding temple is over half a kilometer long, targeting the Theban hills and the Valley of the Kings in the west across the Nile where Egypt's mighty sun-kings were buried. The approach to the temple is also from the west along an impressive monumental avenue flanked by ram-headed sphinxes. As you pass the so-called *First Pylon* – massive inclined walls that serve to frame the gateway – and into a spacious open court, there looms ahead of you a huge statue of Ramses II. You then enter the Great Hypostyle Hall with its 134 massive rounded columns and cross beams that once supported a roof 25 meters above the floor. A series of other pylons finally takes you to the inner sanctuary of the sun-god Amun-Ra. When the distinguished British astronomer Sir Norman Lockyer visited Karnak in 1891 in order to measure the alignment of its axis, he was bedazzled by what he saw:

> This Temple of Amun-Ra is beyond all question the most majestic ruin in the world. There is a stone avenue in the centre, giving view towards the northwest, and this axis is something like 500 yards in length. The whole object of the builder of the great Temple of Karnak – one of the most soul-stirring temples which have ever been conceived or built by man – was to preserve that axis absolutely open; and all the wonderful halls of columns and the like, as seen on one side or other of the axis, are merely details; the point being that the axis should be absolutely open, straight and true. The axis was directed towards the west hills on the west side of the Nile, in which are the tombs of the kings ... There were really two temples [dedicated to the sun-god in his forms as Amun-Ra and Ra-Horakhti] in the same line back to back, the chief one facing sunset at the summer solstice, the other probably the sunrise at the winter solstice ... it is easy to recognise that these arrangements bear out the idea of an astronomical use of the temple ...[22]

Lockyer, who described this temple as a giant 'horizontal telescope' permanently aimed at the western horizon, calculated that its axis was aligned about 26° north-of-west, the place of setting sun at the summer solstice at the latitude of Luxor.[23] But, as he points out, the axis not only points towards the summer solstice sunset at its western end, but also towards the *winter solstice sunrise* at its eastern end. For it is an astronomical peculiarity that if an axis is aligned to the summer solstice *sunset* (looking westwards) this same axis will by necessity also be aligned in the opposite direction towards the winter solstice *sunrise* (looking eastwards).

THE MASTER GAME

So had the ancient builders wanted to aim the temple's axis at the summer solstice *sunset* or, the other way, at the winter solstice *sunrise*? The answer, as odd as it may first seem, is probably at both.

In ancient Egyptian texts we are told of a very important feast called *Mesora*, literally the 'birth of Ra' (the Sun). This feast took place on the New Year's Day of the civil (solar) calendar, the 1st day of the month known as *Thoth*. When the civil calendar was introduced in *circa* 2800 BC, the 'birth of Ra' festival was not far adrift from the summer solstice. But by the time the temple complex of Karnak-Luxor was begun in c. 2000 BC, the birth of Ra had 'moved' six months ahead to the *winter solstice*. This was because the Egyptian civil calendar was based around a 'idealised' year of 365 days that did not take into account the extra ¼ day in the true solar year, causing it to drift away from its original starting point at the summer solstice at the rate one day every four years. It can thus be seen that the great solar temple complex of Karnak-Luxor, which was begun in c. 2000 BC, was not merely dedicated to the Ra (the Sun) in general but, more specifically, to the 'birth of Ra' which fell on the 1st of *Thoth*. As provocative and controversial at it may be, this question must nonetheless be asked: Could André Le Nôtre, aided perhaps by the astronomers from the *Académie des Sciences* – who had been housed in the Louvre since 1663 – have consciously set out to create the same solar alignment for the Sun King of France as that of his ancient Egyptian counterparts?

Flashback (2) 1665: the mystery of the deviated axis (4)

There is a further curious astronomical fact to add to this already very intriguing collection of 'coincidences'. We have seen in Chapter Ten how a powerful celestial marker – the heliacal (dawn) rising of Sirius (represented by the goddess Isis in Egyptian and Hermetic mythology) was used by the ancient Egyptians to symbolise and sanctify the birth of their solar pharaoh-kings. The American astronomer Ronald Wells, a recognised authority on ancient Egyptian astronomical lore, has this to add:

> The goddess Isis, a daughter of *Ra* (the sun-god), was also identified with Sirius. The relationship came about astronomically not only because Sirius is the brightest body of the night (apart from the moon) like the sun is the brightest body of the day, but more particularly because *the place of its heliacal rising on the horizon is very close to the same point where Ra rises on the morning of his winter solstice birth*. Its yearly appearance at nearly the same spot coupled with the fact that

the river began to rise about the same time made the combined event sacrosanct.²⁴ [Emphases added]

The angle that Sirius makes with due east at rising is not the same when seen from different places on the planet. The further north one travels, the larger will be the angle. For example, from Paris, which stands very close to latitude 49° north, the angle today is 27.5°, whereas from Cairo (at latitude of 30° north) it is only 20°. A second factor also affects the angle at rising over very long periods of time. This is the phenomenon of precession – a very slow 'wobble' of the Earth's axis with a cycle of about 26,000 years. Calculations taking both these factors into account show that in 1637, the year Louis XIV was born, Sirius rose at 26° south-of-east, and thus *in direct alignment with Le Nôtre's axis*!

We know that since time immemorial the heliacal rising of Sirius, the star of Isis, was the cosmic sign that sanctified the supernatural 'birth' of the sun-kings of Egypt. We've seen how the cult of Isis was brought to Paris by the Romans. Indeed it may well be relevant that the Cathedral of Notre Dame itself stands over a very ancient sacred site which, according to some historians, was a shrine dedicated in Roman-times to Isis-Ceres.²⁵ We've also seen in Chapter Twelve how Louis XIV was supposedly conceived in Anne of Austria's private apartments at the Louvre on a stormy December night in 1637 – the so-called *Capetian miracle*. Putting all this together, how likely is it to be a coincidence that when the Le Nôtre's 'Sirius' axis of 26° is extended eastwards into the Louvre it passes *right through the apartments of Anne of Austria* where the 'Capetian miracle' took place in 1637? And is it also a coincidence that three centuries later, in 1989, an equestrian statue sculptured by Bernini for the Sun King Louis XIV depicting him as Alexander the Great (the quintessential classical solar king of antiquity), was brought from its former home at Versailles and carefully positioned in the open court of the Louvre in the *direct path* of this axis? ...

The reader will recall that the birth of Louis XIV on 5 September 1638 had been prophesied more than a year earlier by the Hermetic philosopher Tommaso Campanella in 1637. Campanella had also predicted that the future king would transform Paris into the 'Egyptian' City of the Sun. Intriguingly, Jean Phaure reports that when André Le Nôtre extended the 26° angle of the axis of the Tuilleries Garden further to the west to form the Champs-Élysées in 1665–67 he seems to have anticipated in his overall scheme the inclusion at a later date of certain other elements:

Le Nôtre ébauche en plan une croix, prévoit une étoile et projette soit un obélisque, soit une porte solaire analogue au portes Saint-Martin et Saint-Denis élevées sous Louis XIV. ('Le Nôtre placed in his plan a cross, foresees a *star* and projects either an obelisk or a solar gate. Similar to those of St. Martin and St. Denis built at the time of Louis XIV.')[26]

This is most interesting, not least because it was not until more than a century later, that two prominent monuments, one representing a 'star' and the other the obelisk of Ramses II brought from Luxor, would, in fact, be raised right on the axis of the Champs-Élysées as set out by André Le Nôtre.

Cagliostro and the affair of the queen's necklace

In Chapter Eighteen we'll pursue these matters further. But first we'll finish the strange story of the self-styled 'Count' of Cagliostro and see how his dramatic rise to fame and fortune in Paris after his arrival there in 1785 would be rudely stunted by his own mentor, the Cardinal de Rohan. For the latter was about to make one of the greatest blunders in history – a small folly that would set in motion untold consequences for France and the world ...

It all had to do with an obsession that the Cardinal de Rohan had concerning the queen, Marie-Antoinette. The latter had rebuked him at court, and the cardinal was desperate to make amends in whatever way he could. In the summer of 1785 a certain Countess de la Motte, who claimed to be an intimate friend and close confident of the queen, approached the cardinal and offered to help him in this delicate matter.[27]

The countess suggested that the cardinal should purchase on behalf of the queen an expensive diamond necklace, owned by the jewelers Boehmer & Bassenge. The queen dearly wanted this necklace, explained the countess. However, on account of the near bankruptcy of the country and the hostile attitude of the Parisian public towards the queen's extravagance, King Louis XVI had refused to buy it for her.

The jewelers wanted a staggering price – 1,600,000 livres, enough to have fed all the hungry of Paris for several months – but the foolish cardinal refused to be deterred. He was shown a very convincing – but forged – letter allegedly written by the queen, and the countess even arranged a nocturnal meeting in the Gardens of Versailles between the cardinal and an imposter disguised as the queen. The 'queen' confirmed to the cardinal that she could pay for the necklace out of her own pocket money if only the cardinal could pay the first deposit. So the over-excited cardinal rushed to the jewelers and bought the necklace on credit on behalf of the queen. He then gave it to the Countess de la Motte who assured him that it would be handed immediately to Marie-Antoinette.

The countess, of course, did nothing of the sort, but vanished with the necklace. When the jewelers presented the queen with the invoice for the next installment of the huge sum of money they thought she owed them an enormous scandal ensued. The queen, furious at how she had been so vilely implicated in this sordid affair, urged the king to press charges of fraud against the cardinal. The king reluctantly agreed.

It was a grave mistake, for it was obvious to all that the naïve cardinal had been the victim of a very clever embezzler. Knowing how unpopular the queen already was among the people, he made emotional appeals in court and managed to cause a huge political fuss. Matters got worse when the king tried to put pressure on the judges to condemn the cardinal. The net effect was to elevate the Cardinal de Rohan into a symbol of the oppression, despotism and financial profligacy of the monarchy. According to Masonic author, Jean-André Faucher, there was a widespread conspiracy behind all this involving many prominent Freemasons who were determined to have the cardinal, also a Freemason, released.[28] Among them was the Duke of Montmorency-Luxembourg together with other notables such as the Marquis de Lafayette and Honoré Gabriel Riqueti, better known as the Count of Mirabeau.[29] As a result the most the king was able to extract from an unsympathetic court was an order suspending the cardinal from office and exiling him to an abbey in the Auvergne.

Inevitably, Cagliostro, Rohan's colourful protégée, was dragged into the scandal and made its scapegoat. The king had him arrested, hastily tried and sentenced for fraud, and thrown into the Bastille in August 1785. There Cagliostro was to remain for nearly a year. Finally, in early June 1786, after much pressure from the Parisian public and behind-the-scenes manipulation by his Masonic friends, he was freed. It is reported that when Cagliostro walked out of the Bastille there was a huge Parisian crowd cheering him as a national hero.

Some historians have suggested that the trial of the Cardinal de Rohan and the unfair imprisonment of Cagliostro catalysed the growing discontent against the monarchy and led directly to the French Revolution. Rather than clear the queen's name in the scandal, the kangaroo courts set up to try Rohan and Cagliostro did the opposite. They highlighted the unpopularity and frivolity of the queen, the weakness of the king and his blatant abuse of the law. The German philosopher, Johann Wolfgang von Goethe, a Freemason, called the 'Affair of the Diamond Necklace' the 'preface of the French Revolution!'[30] The whole fiasco ended up making the Cardinal de Rohan and Cagliostro appear to be – as in a sense they were – the victims of a corrupt state ruled by a weak and pompous monarch.

Nonetheless, Cagliostro wisely decided to move to England. There he was at first greeted with much enthusiasm by the Masonic lodges but his 'Egyptian Rite' did not prove popular and he ended up being shunned and ridiculed.[31]

Prophet of Revolution plays with fire in Rome

Later in 1786, safely in London, Cagliostro published his famous *Letter to the French People* in which he urged them, with incredible premonition, to make a 'peaceful revolution', to destroy the Bastille and to replace it, perhaps, with a 'Temple of Isis'.[32]

But Cagliostro left his place of safety. In the spring of 1789 he made the same fatal error as Giordano Bruno almost two centuries before: he decided to return to Italy. He arrived in Rome in May 1789, two months before the Parisian mob would storm the Bastille. In Rome Freemasonry had officially been banned since 1738, and Cagliostro, who tried to set up an 'Egyptian Rite' lodge there was, quite literally, playing with fire.

When the news of the fall of the Bastille reached Rome, it caused pandemonium at the Vatican, where the cardinals were alarmed by the virulent anti-clerical tone of the French anarchists. Rumors of Masonic plots were rife. By then the Vatican had a complete file on Cagliostro's activities, and he was promptly accused of subversion and heresy. On 27 December 1789 Pope Clement XII signed the order for Cagliostro's arrest. He was at first sentenced to suffer the same awful fate as Bruno and the Cathar *perfecti* of earlier eras, but it was thought to be unwise to have yet another public burning in such unsettled times. Accordingly the pope showed 'clemency' by altering the death sentence to one of life imprisonment. Cagliostro was taken to a prison at San Leo near Naples, cast into a dungeon there, and never seen again. It was eventually discovered that he had died in 1795, at the age of 52, in what can only be described as very suspicious circumstances.[33]

Historians downplay Cagliostro's role as a catalyst for the French Revolution, and he is often presented – we have to say understandably – as some sort of embezzler, charlatan or con man. The attitude of many Freemasons seems to be that his activities were a brief and best-forgotten embarrassment. Yet the furore caused by his trial in Paris, and the fact that an estimated 8,000 citizens, many of them Freemasons, came to cheer him when he was released from the Bastille, seem to tell another story.[34] There is at least one Masonic historian, Manly P. Hall, who likewise seems to regard Cagliostro's career in a positive light:

> [Cagliostro] founded the Egyptian Rite of Freemasonry, which received into its mysteries many of the French nobility and was regarded favorably by the most learned minds of Europe. Having established the Egyptian Rite, Cagliostro declared himself to be an agent of the Order of the Knights Templars and to have received initiation from them on the Isle of Malta ... Called upon the carpet by the Supreme Council of France, it was demanded of Cagliostro that he prove by what authority he had founded a Masonic lodge in Paris independent of the *Grand Orient*. Of such surpassing mentality was Cagliostro that the Supreme Council found it difficult to secure an advocate qualified to discuss with Cagliostro philosophic Masonry and the ancient Mysteries he claimed to represent. Court de Gébelin – the greatest Egyptologist of his day and an authority on ancient philosophies – was chosen as the outstanding scholar. A time was set and the Brethren convened. Attired in an Oriental coat and a pair of violet-colored breeches, Cagliostro was hauled before this council of his peers. Court de Gébelin asked three questions and then sat down, admitting himself disqualified to interrogate a man so much his superior in every branch of learning. Cagliostro then took the floor, revealing to the assembled Masons not only his personal qualifications, but prophesying the future of France. He foretold the fall of the French throne, the Reign of Terror, and the fall of the Bastille. At a later time he revealed the dates of the death of Marie-Antoinette and the King, and also the advent of Napoleon. Having finished his address, Cagliostro made a spectacular exit, leaving the French Masonic lodge in consternation and utterly incapable of coping with the profundity of his reasoning. Though no longer regarded as a ritual in Freemasonry, the Egyptian Rite is available and all who read it will recognize its author to have been no more a charlatan than was Plato.[35]

The noble traveller

Antoine Court de Gébelin, the man who confirmed Cagliostro's knowledge of Egyptian esotericism, was himself a prominent member of the influential 'Nine Sisters' lodge as well as a proponent of the view that the Tarot card system was of Egyptian origin. Interestingly, Court de Gébelin believed that the 'Star' in the Tarot deck labeled XVI was, in fact, Sirius, the 'star of Isis'.[36] Later we shall see how his Tarot became interwoven with the 'higher degrees' of Scottish Rite Freemasonry. Meanwhile it is reasonable to conclude that whatever one's opinion of Cagliostro the man, it is clear that Cagliostro, the 'Great Copt' and founder of the 'Egyptian Rite', had an enormous psychological impact on the events that were slowly unfolding in Paris.

It is reported, for example, that while he was in that city, and at very height of his fame, Cagliostro had much hoped that his Egyptian Rite would receive official recognition from the Duke of Orléans, Philippe, the king's cousin, who was at the time the Grand Master of the *Grand Orient*.[37] Through the intervention of the Duke of Montmorency-Luxembourg, who was the official Protector of Cagliostro's Egyptian Rite as well as the chief administrator of the *Grand Orient de France*, it was arranged for Philippe d'Orléans to visit Cagliostro's *Isis* lodge in the Rue Saint-Claude. It seems that Philippe d'Orléans was duly impressed and offered his trust to Cagliostro.[38] Such a connection, as we will see, almost certainly had some repercussions on the dramatic events that were soon to implicate the Duke of Orléans in the 1789 Revolution.

Apparently during his trial in Paris in May 1786 the judge had bluntly asked Cagliostro, 'Who are you?' to which Cagliostro replied: 'I am a noble traveler'.[39] Indeed, Cagliostro had often claimed that he had traveled extensively in the East, particularly in Egypt and other Islamic countries. Bearing this in mind, the historian and esoteric researcher Joscelyn Godwin highlights something that may further explain Cagliostro's mysterious reply to his French judges:

> The initiatic journey to Islamic soil has been a repeated theme of European esotericism, ever since the Templars settled in Jerusalem and the mythical Christian Rosenkreuz learnt his trade in Damascus. We find it in the lives of Paracelsus and Cagliostro, then, as travel became easier, in a whole host that includes P. B. Randolph, H. P. Blavatsky, Max Theon, G. I. Gurdjieff, Aleister Crowley, René Guénon, R. A. Schwaller de Lubicz, and Henry Corbin. There was very likely some element of this in Napoleon's Egyptian campaign of 1797, when he announced to an astounded audience that he, too, was a Muslim ...[40]

Illuminated by Reason

Other researchers, however, have wondered whether Cagliostro's answer that he was a 'noble traveler' was not perhaps a coded message in Masonic language aimed at his judges in the hope that they would recognize him as an initiate of the anti-clerical and anti-monarchical Illuminati of Bavaria.[41]

Originally known as the 'Order of the Perfectibilists', we saw in Chapter Sixteen that these Illuminati of Bavaria were a very short-lived but controversial brotherhood known in particular for their radical anti-clerical stance. The Illuminati were founded in 1776 by Adam Weishaupt, an ex-Jesuit priest who was professor of law at the University of Ingolstadt, and given an official structure in 1779 by the Baron Knigge, a Freemason and member of the Templar Order of the Strict Observance founded by the Baron von Hund.[42] One of Weishaupt's remarks reveals the Illuminati's ambitious plans for social and cultural reform:

> Princes and nations will disappear without violence from the earth,
> the human race will become one family and the world the abode
> of reasonable men. Morality alone will bring about this change
> imperceptibly.[43]

According to Masonic historian Albert G. Mackey, the 'professed object' of the Bavarian Illuminati was:

> ... by the mutual assistance of its members, to attain the highest
> possible degree of morality and virtue, and to lay the foundation for the
> reformation of the world by the association of good men to oppose the
> progress of moral evil.[44]

In short, what the Illuminati were after was nothing less than a massively ambitious global reformation programme, a sort of 'new world order', calling for the eradication of monarchies under one universal power run by 'reasonable men'. It is therefore of great interest that in a rather curious statement made on the other side of the Atlantic by Thomas Jefferson, the name of Weishaupt crops up again in connection with the idea of rendering men 'wise and virtuous':

> As Weishaupt lived under the tyranny of a despot and priests, he knew
> that caution was necessary even in spreading information, and the

principles of pure morality. This has given an air of mystery to his views
... If Weishaupt had written here [i.e. in America], where no secrecy is
necessary in our endeavours to render men wise and virtuous, he would
not have thought of any secret machinery for that purpose.[45]

Although Jefferson does not specifically mention the word 'reason', it
is evident that it was very much in his mind when writing this statement.
Jefferson himself practically venerated 'reason' and was dubbed the 'man of
reason' *par excellence*, as another of his famous statements clearly shows:

It rests now with ourselves alone to enjoy in peace and concord the
blessings of self-government, so long denied to mankind; to show
by example the sufficiency of human reason for the care of human
affairs ...[46]

Indeed, 'reason' was to become the principal virtue of both the French
and American Revolutions, and in France, as we recall from Chapter One, a
'Cult of Reason' was even proposed as a substitute for Christianity.

The eye in the pyramid

Meanwhile, the ultra-radical Illuminati of Bavaria, that curious and
unholy progeny of Masons and Jesuits, began to send agents and emissaries
all over Europe – hence, perhaps, Cagliostro's definition of himself as
a 'noble traveller'. Like the Rosicrucians before them, the Bavarian
Illuminati were extremely secretive and preferred to travel incognito, often
assuming pseudonyms and code names. Weishaupt himself took up the
code name 'Spartacus'. The town of Ingolstadt, where the Illuminati had
their headquarters, was codenamed 'Eleusis' and the whole of Bavaria was
codenamed 'Egypt'. Perceived as highly revolutionary and anti-clerical, the
Illuminati were violently opposed by the Church and, more specifically, the
Jesuits, who eventually persuaded the elector of Bavaria, Karl Theodore, to
outlaw them in Germany in 1784.[47]

Anti-Masonic groups often claim that the insignia of the Illuminati was
the 'eye in the pyramid', and that the documents that bear proof of this were
confiscated by the elector of Bavaria, and are today (for reasons that need
not detain us) kept under lock and key at the British Museum.[48] The same
symbol, however, was well known long before the Illuminati came across it.
It was widely used, for example, by Hermetists and Cabalists from the 16th
to the 18th centuries.[49]

Weishaupt, it will be remembered, was a former Jesuit priest, and as such must certainly have been familiar with the works of Athanasius Kircher, the Hermetic-Cabalistic Jesuit we met in Chapter Fifteen – a magus, as the reader will recall, who had been particularly involved with Egyptian obelisks and, through a proxy, the exploration of the Giza pyramids in 1637. Kircher made profuse use of the 'eye in the pyramid' symbol. It can be seen, for example, on the cover of his book *Ars Magna Sciendi*, (the 'Great Art of Knowledge'),[50] and also on the top of an Egyptian obelisk surmounted by the so-called *Hapsburg double-eagle* that Kircher had designed specially for the German Emperor Ferdinand III.[51] Let us point out in passing that the same 'double-eagle' symbol, as well as the 'eye in the pyramid' symbol, are commonly used in the Supreme Council of the 33rd Degree, the Scottish Rite of Freemasonry.[52]

In July 1776, the same year that Weishaupt founded the Illuminati of Bavaria – and presumably by a curious fluke of history – the same 'eye in the pyramid' or 'eye in the triangle' symbol was proposed for the Great Seal of the newly created United States of America.[53] It was designed by Pierre-Eugène Simitière, a Swiss born artist who had emigrated to the colonies in 1766 and settled in Philadelphia. Benjamin Franklin and Thomas Jefferson, both signatories of the Declaration of Independence, were members of the committee set up to oversee the design, and a drawing of the Great Seal of the United States in the latter's own hand done in 1776 (preserved in the Library of Congress archives) clearly shows the 'eye in the triangle'.[54] We shall see later how also in that eventful July of 1776, Franklin left America for France as part of a congressional delegation to be based in Paris, and there was hailed as a hero of the American Revolution by the fashionable salons and the Masonic lodges.

The Illuminati and the Duke of Orléans

Historians of this period have noticed the coincidence of the nearly simultaneous events of the signing of the Declaration of Independence in America and the founding of Weishaupt's Illuminati in Germany. It is not known with certainty whether there had been any direct contact between Franklin, Jefferson and the Illuminati of Bavaria through the channel of French and German Masonic lodges, but it is nonetheless certain that both Franklin and Jefferson knew of Weishaupt's organisation – and we quoted above Jefferson's remarks on Weishaupt. Jefferson's own presence in Paris from 1784 to September 1789, makes direct contact between the two a strong possibility, as we shall see in Chapter Nineteen.

The general view is that the Illuminati of Bavaria simply died out after their persecution in Germany in 1784.[55] Not everyone, however, is convinced. Some believe that Illuminati members infiltrated Masonic lodges and stirred up political unrest in several European countries, most especially in France where the Revolution would finally break out in 1789.

One of the most prolific proponents of the 'Illuminati theory' was the distinguished 1920s British writer and historian Nesta Webster. Webster argued that a variety of secret plots hatched by the Illuminati and the French Freemasons combined with other factors to precipitate the Revolution.[56] Webster, and many others like her, see the Duke of Orléans, the Grand Master of the Masonic Order of the *Grand Orient*, as the main culprit and behind-the-scenes agitator of the Parisian revolutionary crowds and, more specifically, the crowd that would storm the Bastille on 14 July 1789.

That the Duke of Orléans played a vital role in the events of the Revolution cannot be denied; but to what extent, and how far-reaching was his influence, are matters that have long been debated by historians. There are records from the Masonic lodge *La Parfaite Union* in the city of Rennes, that leave little doubt that the Freemasons saw him as the main force driving the events that led to the Revolution:

> It is from our temples [lodges] and from those elevated into the holy
> philosophy [Freemasonry] that emanated the first sparks of sacred fire
> which, spreading rapidly from east to west and from south to north
> of France, embraced the hearts of all citizens ... None of us, my dear
> Brethren, can ignore that it was our Grand Master, the Duc d'Orléans, who
> has participated more than anyone else in the happy Revolution that has
> just begun ...[57]

If what this Masonic lodge says is true, then it is not impossible that the Duke of Orléans could have been in collusion with agents of the Bavarian Illuminati. French historian Jean-André Faucher shows that one of the Duke's closest associates and protégés, the Count of Mirabeau – the most outspoken of all the French revolutionaries, had in the year 1776, 'visited the city of Brunswick and met up with the Illuminati of Bavaria.'[58] And although some historians have raised doubts that Mirabeau was a Freemason, counter-evidence has surfaced that confirms Mirabeau's membership of the brotherhood from at least the year 1776.[59]

There are also telling statements made by two famous Masons of the time, the enigmatic Count of Saint-Germain and the hypnotic Franz Anton

Mesmer, that strongly suggest the presence of Illuminati agents in Paris in the years preceding the Revolution. Several researchers have suggested that the term 'noble traveller' used by Cagliostro during his court trial may have been a secret password of theirs.[60] It is surely also significant that Cagliostro, during his trial in Rome, admitted having been a member of the Illuminati.[61]

Out goes the Duke of Orléans, in comes Philippe Égalité

The Duke of Orléans was a descendent of Frederick V of the Palatinate and Elizabeth Stuart of England, that ill-fated royal couple of Bohemia who seem to have unsuspectingly catalysed the Rosicrucian fervour in Germany and the events of the Thirty Years War. The Duke's great-great-grandfather, also named Philippe d'Orléans, was the second son of Louis XIII and thus younger brother to the Sun King Louis XIV. In 1661 Philippe had married Henrietta of England, daughter of Charles I, and in 1671 he married again, this time to Elizabeth Charlotte, princess of the Palatinate and daughter of Elector Palatine Charles Louis, son of Frederick V and Elizabeth of Bohemia.[62]

No doubt because of his ancestry, the Duke of Orléans at the time of the French Revolution was an all-out Anglophile, and his obsessive affinity for all things English was directly responsible for the development of a bizarre fad in Parisian circles known as *Anglomania*. The Duke was a great admirer of the British Parliament and of the constitutional monarchy, and had openly opposed the despotic rule of his uncle, Louis XV, who had him exiled to England in 1771. He eventually returned to Paris only to begin at once opposing the new king of France, Louis XVI, who was his first cousin.

In 1786 the Duke of Orléans was elected Grand Master of the *Grand Orient de France*, and thus effectively the leader of all the Freemasons in the land. Immensely rich, as sole owner of much of France's choicest real estate, the Duke teamed up with the famous revolutionary orator, Mirabeau, and the vast grounds of his private residence at the Palais-Royal became a regular meeting place for the revolutionary crowds. Many believe that he used his great fortune to fund the revolutionaries and some even think he was the unseen force behind the storming of the Bastille in July 1789. Whatever the truth, it is absolutely certain that he vehemently opposed his cousin, Louis XVI, and that he was among those who voted for his execution in 1793. It is also certain that the Duke entertained the perhaps unrealistic hope that he could become king himself and form a constitutional monarchy such as in England.

So fervent was his support for the Convention and the *Commune de Paris* – the two principal revolutionary bodies that ruled France in the aftermath of the Revolution – that in 1792 Philippe d'Orléans changed his name to Philippe Égalité. Unfortunately, however, Philippe Égalité developed a great antipathy for the Marquis de Lafayette, the hero of both the French and American Revolutions. This, as well as other factors, led to his eventual downfall and, ironically, in November 1793 Philippe Égalité was to suffer the same fate as his royal cousin, when he lost his own head under the blade of the Guillotine. Nonetheless, his great ambitions for a constitutional monarchy in France would materialise with his eldest son, Louis-Philippe I, the so-called *Citizen King*, who was helped to the throne of France in 1830 by none other than his father's bitter enemy of old, the Marquis de Lafayette.

We shall now see how the very disturbing anti-clericalism that was to ensue after 14 July 1789 would send a shock wave across the whole of Christian Europe, as a new but also very old religion was about to be reborn from the womb of a goddess called 'Reason'. Ironically, this would certainly have been something that would have enthralled Cagliostro who, sadly, was now rotting in the papal dungeon near Naples. For the goddess Reason, as it turned out, would much resemble the Egyptian goddess Isis whom Cagliostro had so much extolled in Paris ...[63]

Behind the scenes of the Revolution

On the morning of the 14 July 1789 a crowd of about 800 people gathered in the city of Paris and marched in disorder towards the Bastille. Armed with an assortment of weapons they had plundered earlier from the arsenal at the *Invalides*, this unruly mob hurdled themselves on the poorly defended prison and, within hours, had 'liberated' its seven pathetic inmates.[64] Six of the Swiss mercenaries stationed to guard the Bastille were chopped to pieces. The head of the chief prison warden, Bernard-René Jourdan, the Marquis de Launay, was brutally hacked off with a blunt butcher's knife and paraded around Paris until late in the night.[65]

The clichéd images of the French Revolution that most of us learn in school depict oppressed Parisian citizens driven to revolt by famine, despotism and tyranny, marching in unison against the king's troops while chanting the *Marseillaise*. The truth, of course, was a great deal more complicated than that.

The economic and political conditions in France were certainly appalling, and thus ripe for revolutionaries to exploit. The winter of

1788–9 been terrible and very poor harvests followed. In addition King Louis XVI was an incompetent political player whose attempts to deal with the state's bankruptcy played into the hands of the agitators. All these factors created a context for the Revolution but we should not leap to the conclusion that any of them actually caused it.

History has shown that full-blown revolutions rarely take place without a great deal of covert intellectual and even financial activity going on behind the scenes. In France a subversive intellectual movement had been active amongst the educated classes and the liberal aristocracy for many years. By promoting the enlightened political visions of writers such as Voltaire, Jean-Jacques Rousseau, and the so-called *Encyclopédistes* – many of whom were Freemasons[66] – this at first loosely-organized movement did much to set the scene for the overthrow of the Old Regime.

The Duke of Orléans, having been rudely shunned by Queen Marie-Antoinette who bitterly disliked him, had developed a deep hatred not only for her but also for his cousin Louis XVI and for the entire court at Versailles. He soon began to use his great personal fortune to subsidize a variety of organizations, such as the infamous Jacobin Club, that were hostile to the king and queen. There is even evidence, somewhat downplayed by historians, that points to the existence of a sort of shadowy 'government-in-waiting', led by the Duke of Orléans and other agitators, which conducted subversive propaganda campaigns in many of the 600-plus Masonic lodges in France – of which 65 were in Paris. We've seen that the Duke was an avid admirer of Britain's constitutional monarchy. He was also the richest man in France and in direct line to the throne of France. All this would imply, if not prove, that the 'Revolution' may initially have been intended not to replace but to 'reform' the existing monarchy into a British-style constitutional system under the Duke of Orléans, and that the more radical idea of setting up an American-style republic came later.

When the Third Estate found its voice

Early in 1788, Louis XVI was coerced into agreeing to call a meeting of the Estates-General for May 1789. It was to prove a fatal mistake.

Traditionally, there were three so-called *Estates* in France: the nobility comprised the First Estate, the clergy comprised the Second Estate, the bourgeoisie and the nation in general comprised the Third Estate. In January 1789 Emmanuel-Joseph Sieyès, better known as the Abbé Sieyès, published a pamphlet that starkly highlighted how little say the Third Estate actually had in matters of politics even though it represented 98 per cent of the population.[67] Entitled *Qu'est-ce que le tiers-état?* ('*What is the Third Estate?*'), Abbé Sieyès pamphlet boldly proposed the immediate drafting of a *Constitution* and the formation of a *National Assembly* outside the nobility and the clergy. Thousands of copies of his article were sold and distributed all over France. And with this, the seeds of republicanism began to sprout.

It is not an accident that Abbé Sieyès was a Freemason, and a member of the powerful Nine Sisters lodge in Paris.[68] In Chapter One we discussed the origins of this important lodge, whose other members included thinkers such as Benjamin Franklin, the Marquis de Condorcet, anatomist Joseph-Ignace Guillotin, Tarot inventor Antoine Court de Gébelin, astronomer Jérôme Lalande, mathematician Charles-Gilbert Romme, and radical revolutionary leaders Camille Desmoulins and Georges Jacques Danton.[69]

Like Sieyès, Desmoulins had preached revolution and written a pamphlet entitled *La France Libre* ('*Free France*') which was followed in June 1789 by a violent attack on the monarchy. Desmoulins was chief among those who called for an armed uprising on the eve of the Revolution during a rally at the residence of the Duke of Orléans, which was at that time serving as the command headquarters for the revolutionaries.

Danton was the founder of the dreaded *Club des Cordeliers* which, like the Jacobin Club, was one of the most radical and influential organizations at work during the Revolution. The *Club des Cordeliers* was officially known as the *Society of Friends of the Rights of Man and the Citizen*, but it had inherited the name 'Cordeliers' from a former Franciscan monastery located on the Rue des Cordeliers, where its first meetings were held. The Cordeliers accepted members of all races, classes and creeds, and many were influential journalists and writers such as Jean-Paul Marat, Camille Desmoulins, Pierre-François-Joseph Robert and Nicolas de Bonneville.

The disastrous meeting of the Estates-General began on 5 May 1789. The Third Estate had 584 representatives compared to the 290 for the nobility and 292 for the clergy. Present were King Louis XVI and the Queen Marie-Antoinette. Many leading Freemasons and men of letters had been elected as representatives of the Third Estate and also had a strong presence in the other two Estates as well. Among them were the Marquis de Lafayette, Mirabeau, the Duke of Orléans and Robespierre.

As the days dragged on the king and his supporters appeared increasingly weak and confused, and it became obvious that they lacked any clear plan for solving the very real economic crisis in which the country by then found itself. Predictably, the negotiations between the Third Estate and the nobility broke down in chaos. In defiance, the Third Estate changed its name to the *Communes* (the 'Commons'), implying a constitutional monarchy by default, and Sieyès and Mirabeau took the helm. Mirabeau proposed that the *Communes* be called the 'Representatives of the French People'. Sieyès went one better, and had the name 'National Assembly' accepted. Immediately several members of the nobility, principal amongst them the Duke of Orléans and the Marquis de Lafayette, offered their support to the National Assembly. That had been expected but a shock wave hit the clergy and the nobility when Charles Maurice de Talleyrand-Périgord, a representative of the Second Estate, also crossed the fence to side with the National Assembly.

Born into the nobility, Talleyrand entered the clergy at an early age. In 1789, just before the fall of the Bastille, he was made a bishop by Louis XVI. As soon as he joined the National Assembly, he was among the first to propose the confiscation of all the assets of the Church in France.[70] With such radical views being increasingly flaunted as the weeks of discussions went by the king intervened on 20 June and ordered his guards to prevent the members of the National Assembly from entering the meeting hall. In response the outraged National Assembly met instead in another hall at Versailles – one that was used by the royals for playing tennis. Immortalized as the 'Tennis Court Oath', the members swore not to be moved until a constitutional monarchy was formed under a solid political and legal foundation.

Another meeting was called with the king on 23 June, but at this point Louis XVI threatened to exercise his divine right to rule and to act alone 'on behalf of the people'. He then ordered the delegates of the National Assembly to 'disperse forthwith' and stormed petulantly out of the hall. The delegates remained seated, refusing to budge. The Marquis de Dreux-Brézé, a staunch royalist and spokesman for the king, again ordered them to leave 'in the name of the King'. He was shouted down by Mirabeau, the Freemason who was sponsored by the Duke of Orléans: 'Sir, go tell to those who send you that we are here by the will of the people, and that we will not be moved except by the force of the bayonets'. When Dreux-Brézé reported this to the king, he is said to have replied: 'Damn them, let them stay!'[71]

The dye was cast, and from here on events rushed forward like a roaring tide. Louis XVI called in his troops to Versailles, sacked his finance minister, Jacques Necker, and formed a new government to 'oppose' the National Assembly. But it was all too late. At the Palais-Royal in Paris the National

Assembly, buttressed by the financial power of the Duke of Orléans, and with the whole of the Parisian population behind them, prepared for a full confrontation with the king's troops, and now the agitators were calling openly for an armed revolt against the Old Regime. Soon there began to be defections from the army to the side of the National Assembly. The point of no return was reached on 14 July 1789 when mobs of citizens took to the streets and the Bastille was stormed.

Impregnating the national conscience

It is, of course, not the purpose of this book, or indeed within its scope, to pass in review the full complexity of the political and cultural upheavals behind the French Revolution. Nor can we look at all the arguments and opinions that have been laid for *and* against the involvement and influence of Freemasonry on the Revolution. For not only are the historical events lost in the chaos of the times, but they have also suffered much distortion, bias and misinformation under the pen of factions wanting either to downplay the role of the Freemasons or to play it up. Not least amongst these factions, or course, is Freemasonry itself which seems to prefer to cloud the issue. In 1976, for example, Fred Zeller, Grand Master of the *Grand Orient de France*, had this piece of peculiar obfustication to offer on the subject:

> ... We can be assured that the Freemasons did not conspire against the throne, nor worked towards the formation of the Republic. In truth, no one had thought of this at the time. But they had slowly, patiently, during half-a-century of secret discussions (and forbidden by the laws of the time) impregnated the national conscience with the hope and will for change. In 1789 there were more than 70,000 Freemasons in France. Not surprisingly that in the revolutionary assemblies we note a majority of parliamentarians who were initiated in Masonic lodges![72]

Even such carefully chosen words cannot entirely disguise the obvious implication that the Masonic lodges played a major role in the events that led to the French Revolution! In a more candid manner in 1983, the Grand Master of the *Grand Orient*, Paul Gourdot, made a declaration similar to Fred Zeller's but then could not avoid adding that although it was the writings and examples of the *Encyclopédistes*, of Montesquieu, of Diderot, of Voltaire, that prepared the 'spirit' of the Revolution, it was nonetheless:

... those like Condorcet, Saint-Just, Danton [all Freemasons] who applied the principles of the formation of the First Republic with its immortal Declaration of the Rights of Man which was formulated in our lodges ...[73]

Besides there is another aspect of the French Revolution, in which Freemasons were also directly involved, that still requires explanation. This is the phenomenon of de-Christianisation that we introduced in Chapter One, and the attempt by the National Assembly to replace Christianity with the 'Cult of Reason' and the 'Cult of the Supreme Being' ...

2/100th of a second

On the cold morning of the 21 January 1793, a huge crowd gathered in Paris at the Place de la Révolution, today the Place de la Concorde, to watch the execution of King Louis XVI. With his hands tied behind his back, four executioners pounced on him, laid him flat facing down, and pushed his head into the crossbeam of the dreaded guillotine. To the surprise of the Parisian mob the king behaved bravely throughout the horrific ordeal, and even attempted a poignant farewell speech to the nation, but it was rudely interrupted by the thundering roll of drums immediately preceding his decapitation. Louis XVI's last audible words apparently were:

People of France, I am innocent, I forgive those who are responsible for my death. I pray God that the blood that will be spilt here never falls on France! And you, unfortunate people ...

The guillotine, which had been improved from an old design only a short while before by Joseph-Ignace Guillotin, was extremely efficient. Apparently painless, it is estimated that each beheading took just 2/100th of a second. Guillotin was a Freemason and member of the Nine Sisters lodge. He was also an active member of the National Assembly. He had developed this death machine specifically to cater for the anticipated high demand for executions after the fall of the Bastille. But no one, however bloodthirsty they might have been, could have predicted the thousands upon thousands of decapitations by guillotine during those early years of the Republic known appropriately to history as the 'Reign of Terror'.[74] After Louis XVI was beheaded, Marie-Antoinette was to wait a further nine months for her own appointment with the guillotine. But some years earlier, in 1790 when she had been under house arrest at the Tuileries

Palace, the queen had written these haughty words to her cousin, Emperor Leopold II of Austria:

> Take heed in your country of all Masonic associations. We already can see that all these monsters here have intentions to do the same in all other countries. Oh, that God saves my homeland, Austria, of such troubles.[75]

Isis of the Bastille

A few weeks before the guillotining of the queen, a very strange thing indeed had taken place in Paris. As if arising out of some inherent need for a matriarchal figurehead, a replacement in the form of a statue of the ancient Egyptian goddess Isis suddenly appeared on the scene. It was raised in the Place de la Bastille on 10 August 1793. As we saw when we introduced this mystery in Chapter One, it had been designed in haste by the artist Jacques-Louis David, who was an intimate friend of the revolutionary leader Robespierre and was acting as minister of propaganda for the National Assembly.

A coin was struck in 1794 to commemorate the occasion, and is described as being:

> ... the work of the famous engraver DUPRE ... which evokes the cult of Isis chosen to illustrate the goddess of Reason, and is also the first commemorative coin issued in France.[76]

The coin preserves the image of the so-called *Isis of the Bastille* or 'Fountain of Regeneration' which, along with its pedestal, stood some 20 feet high. The statue depicted the Egyptian goddess sitting on her throne flanked by two lions, and at her feet was placed a large bath emblazoned with the ancient Egyptian winged solar disc, a symbol of the pharaohs which was also much used by the Hermetics, the Rosicrucians and the Freemasons.[77]

Isis of the Bastille was naked from the waist up, her large breasts intended to evoke the idea of fertility and regeneration for the new republic of France. From her nipples gushed out water into a pool, and the people made their way to drink the 'water of regeneration' while an orchestra played popular revolutionary tunes.

Jacques-Louis David, who masterminded this curious festival, had been a hero of the people from the very start of the Revolution. Many of his paintings – depicting heroism and republican virtues – were treated as objects of worship by the Parisian crowds. A zealous revolutionary himself, David was famous not only for his art by also for the eloquent philosophical speeches he gave at the National Assembly. He had been the most outspoken participant in the 'Tennis Court Oath' and had been among those who had loudly demanded the death sentence for Louis XVI in December 1792. Some of the more radical revolutionary factions, such as the *sans-culottes* ('without culottes'), even regarded him as some sort of latter day messiah come to regenerate the spirit of France – a role which David took most seriously.[78]

Closing down the Church

The year before the guillotining of Louis XVI and Marie-Antoinette, the ultra-radical faction within the Revolution had begun a campaign to rid France of Christianity – the latter seen as an undesirable aspect of the Old Regime and thus unfit for the new Republic and its ideals.[79] The full meaning of this initiative was felt in October 1793, when priests and nuns all over France were forced to 'defrock' themselves in public while the assets of their churches and monasteries were taken over by the state.

The ultra-radical group within the National Convention – the new name for the 600 or so members of the National Assembly after it had been reshuffled in September 1792 – were called the *Hébertists*.[80] It was they who most directly and most often fanned the flames of de-Christianisation. Principal amongst them were Pierre Gaspard Chaumette, a prominent member of the *Commune de Paris*, and the eponymous Jacques-René Hébert, a popular journalist.

Hébert ran a radical newspaper, called *Le Père Duchesne* ('*Father Duchesne*'), which enjoyed a wide circulation during the Revolution. Both Hébert and Chaumette were staunch Freemasons.[81] In August 1792, Hébert had become the leader of the ultra-radical *Club des Cordeliers* – previously controlled by Maximillien Robespierre, Jean-Paul Marat and Georges Danton, the so-called *Triumvir*.

It seems that radicals like Chaumette and Hébert not only wanted to replace the 'head' of France, so to speak, but also the nation's very soul. An interesting account of these events is given by the 19th century author, the Baroness 'Emmuska' Orczy, made famous by her books *The Scarlet Pimpernel* and *The Elusive Pimpernel*. And although Orczy was a novelist, her stories are nonetheless based on historical accounts and succeed marvelously in capturing the mood in France during the Revolution:

56. The Statue of Liberty.

57. A typical Masonic symbolic rendition of 'Solomon's Temple'. Note the two pillars and the 'pentagram' in the centre.

58. The 'Ohio Historical Marker' showing the Masonic layout plan for Sandusky.

59. The original city plan of Sandusky, Ohio clearly showing the Masonic 'square and compass' emblem.

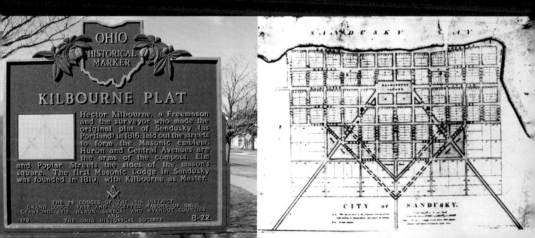

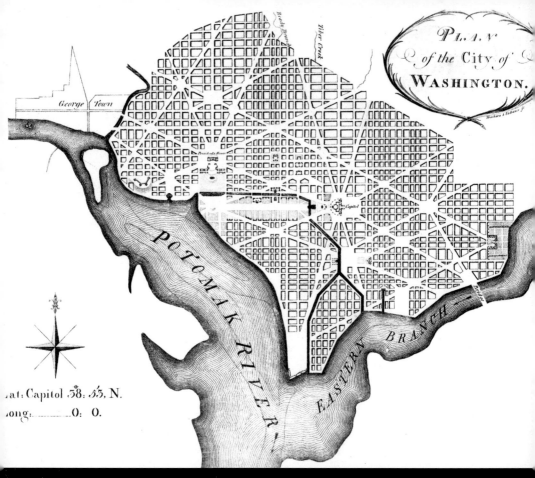

60. Pierre L'Enfant's plan for the city of Washington, DC (1791).

61. The pentagon symbol of the 32nd degree of the Scottish Rite.

62. The pentagon (at inner centre) of the 32nd degree showing the five 'Masonic armies'.

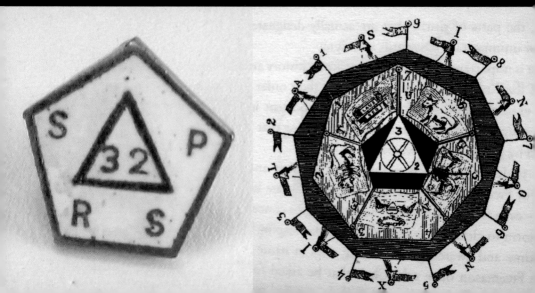

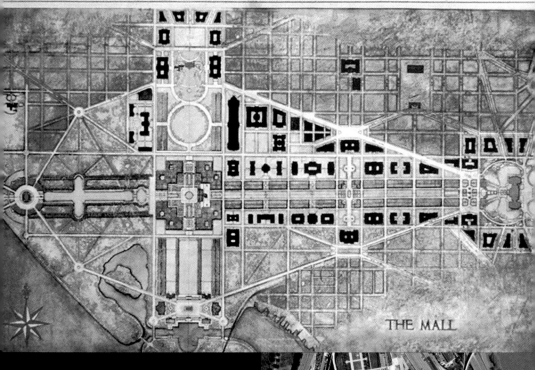

THE McMILLAN PLAN : 1901 - THE MALL

THE MALL

63. Aerial view of the Mall in Washington, DC.

64. Overhead view of the Pentagon building near Washington, DC. Note alignment of the entrance with the Capitol.

To Cap.

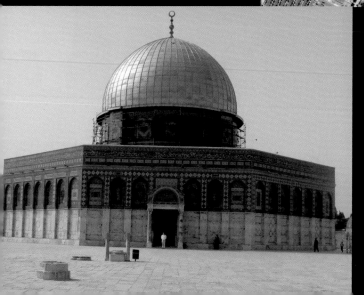

65. The 'Dome of the Rock' mosque on Temple Mount in Jerusalem.

Foreign Office,
November 2nd, 1917

Dear Lord Rothschild,

I have much pleasure in conveying to you, on behalf of His Majesty's Government, the following declaration of sympathy with Jewish Zionist aspirations which has been submitted to, and approved by, the Cabinet.

"His Majesty's Government view with favour the establishment in Palestine of a national home for the Jewish people, and will use their best endeavours to facilitate the achievement of this object, it being clearly understood that nothing shall be done which may prejudice the civil and religious rights of existing non-Jewish communities in Palestine, or the rights and political status enjoyed by Jews in any other country"

I should oe grateful if you would bring this declaration to the knowledge of the Zionist Federation.

66. The Balfour Declaration, 2 November 1917.

67. President Harry S. Truman in Masonic regalia.

68. Truman's letter recognizing the legitimacy of the state of Israel on 14 May 1948, just 11 minutes after it was announced by Ben Gurion in Tel Aviv.

69. The Twin Towers of the World Trade Center in New York City.

This Government has been informed that a Jewish state has been proclaimed in Palestine, and recognition has been requested by the provisional Government thereof.

The United States recognizes the provisional government as the de facto authority of the new State of Israel.

Harry Truman

Approved
May 14, 1948.

6.11

70. Accusation of a Masonic-Zionist plot for the millennium celebrations at the Giza pyramids in the (now banned) newspaper *Sawt al-Shaab*, December 1999.

71. A Masonic lodge in Cairo, Egypt, *circa* 1940.

72. The millennium celebration at the Giza pyramids, 31 December 1999.

73. The 'sacred rock' inside the Dome of the Rock mosque in Jerusalem.

74. The Knights Templar surrendering to Saladin after the Battle of Hattin.

75. The view along Pennsylvania Avenue towards the Capitol (Courtesy William Henry).

E

76. The rising of Sirius at Washington, DC.

77. The setting of Sirius at Washington, DC.

W

78. The Capitol (Courtesy Jason Weir).

79. The Washington Monument. (Courtesy Jason Weir).

80. DARPA's Information Awareness Office logo (now abandoned).

81. The headquarters of the Scottish Rite in Washington, DC (Courtesy Jason Weir).

Paris 1793: ... On! Ever on! In that wild, surging torrent; sowing the wind of anarchy, of terrorism, of lust of blood and hate, and reaping a hurricane of destruction and of horror. On! Ever on! France, with Paris and all her children still rushes blindly, madly on; defies the powerful coalition – Austria, England, Spain, Prussia, all joined together to stem the flow of carnage – defies the Universe and defies God! Paris this September 1793! ... Paris! a city of bloodshed, of humanity in its lowest, most degraded aspect. France herself a gigantic self-devouring monster ... That is thy reward, oh mighty, holy Revolution! Apotheosis of equality and fraternity! Grand rival of decadent Christianity ...

The man-eating tiger for the space of a sigh licked his powerful jaws and pondered! Something new! Something wonderful! We have had a new Constitution, a new Justice, new Laws, a new Almanack! What next? Why, obviously! How comes it that great, intellectual, aesthetic Paris never thought of such a wonderful thing before? A new religion!

Christianity is old and obsolete, priests are aristocrats, wealthy oppressors of the People, the Church but another form of wanton tyranny. Let us by all means have a new religion. Already something has been done to destroy the old! To destroy! Always to destroy! Churches have been ransacked, altars despoiled, tombs desecrated, priests and curates murdered; but that is not enough. There must be a new religion; and to attain that there must be a new God. 'Man is a born idol-worshipper.' Very well then! Let the People have a new religion and a new God. Stay! – Not a God this time! – for God means Majesty, Power, Kingship! Everything in fact which the mighty hand of the people of France has struggled and fought to destroy. Not a God, but a goddess. A goddess! An idol! A toy! ...

Paris wanted a new religion ... and grave men, ardent patriots, mad enthusiasts, sat in the Assembly of the Convention and seriously discussed the means of providing her with both these things which she asked for. Chaumette, I think it was, who first solved the difficulty ... it was Procureur Chaumette who first discovered exactly what type of new religion Paris wanted just now. 'Let us have a Goddess of Reason,' he said ... 'Let the People rejoice and dance around that funeral pile, and above it all let the new Goddess tower smiling and triumphant. The Goddess of Reason! The only deity our new and regenerate France shall acknowledge throughout the centuries which are to come!'

Loud applause greeted the impassioned speech. 'A new goddess, by all means!' shouted the grave gentlemen of the National Assembly, 'The Goddess of Reason! ... The goddess must be beautiful ... not too young ... Reason can only go hand in hand with the riper age of second youth ... she must be decked out in classical draperies, severe yet suggestive ... she must be rouged and painted ... Aye! The feast should be brilliant enough! Gay or horrible, mad or fearful, but through it all the people of France must be made to feel that there was a guiding hand which ruled the destinies of all, a head which framed the new laws, which consolidated the new religion and established its new goddess: the Goddess of Reason: Robespierre, her prophet!'

In those terrible years of 1793–4, all around France churches and cathedrals were violated and desecrated and, to the utter horror of the pope in Rome, the buildings were converted into 'temples' for the new *Culte de la Raison* ('Cult of Reason'), who was also called 'Liberty' or 'Nature'. Author Kathleen Jones, in her book *Women Saints*, gives a detailed account of these events:

In 'the Terror' ... priests and nuns went in danger of the guillotine, and many died when they refused to take an oath of loyalty to the new regime and to abandon their vocations. Churches were closed by troops who removed church bells, smashed altars and crucifixes, and made bonfires of vestments and confessional boxes. A popular spectacle was that of a priest abjuring his vocation, and a ceremony of 'debaptization' was invented for the laity. All public and private worship was forbidden. On 10 August 1793 the artist Jacques-Louis David, a strong supporter of the Revolution, organized a secular ceremony for the acceptance of the new Constitution. An enormous statue of the goddess Nature [Isis], spurting water from her breasts into a pool, was erected on the site of the Bastille, which had been razed to the ground. There was a new calendar, which began not with the birth of Christ but with the proclamation of the Republic. The months had new names [now surviving only on the names of Paris Metro stations] and there was a 10-day week, the *decadi*.

Christmas, Easter, Pentecost, and the harvest festival, together with saints' days, were abolished. In their place were substituted thirty-six new festivals, one every *decadi*, celebrating reason, courage, motherhood, temperance, hatred of tyrants, and similar ideals of the regime. On 10 November a great Festival of Reason was held in the Cathedral of Notre Dame in Paris, where sixteen Louis Capets had walked to their coronations as kings of France. The secularized Notre Dame was re-named the Temple of Liberty.

The rest of France varied in its expression of the new system: local administrators organized events varying from mildly pagan ceremonies to the active stirring-up of public hatred against religion of any kind. In Le Havre a girl of good morals was made the goddess Reason for a day, with floral tributes and dances; in Poitiers, farther south, there were grotesque ceremonies in which people dressed as sorcerers, priests, popes, monks, angels, and nuns were chased through the church of Saint-Porchaire.[82]

Cybele-Isis

Professor François Victor Alphonse Aulard (1849–1928), a highly respected historian of the French Revolution, somewhat downplays these events by arguing that the anti-clerical movement was not as pronounced and as radical as most historians would want us to believe.[83] But Aulard was himself militantly anti-clerical which may have blurred his judgement of the evidence under examination. There are other French historians and specialists of the Revolution such as Michel Vovelle, director of the *Insitut d'Histoire de la Révolution* in Paris, who have a completely different view:

> Between October 1793 and June 1794, a multi-faceted attack was mounted in France to eradicate [the Christian] religion. The goddess Reason triumphed: temples were opened to her, represented by living persons ... In tens of thousands the priests abdicated their sacerdotal role and many of them even married ...[84]

But by June 1794 the whole business of de-Christianisation had run completely out of control. Even the revolutionary leader Robespierre was horrified by the chaos and sought an alternative to this degrading carnage and mess. France was witnessing obscene pagan-like processions organized everywhere, often parading voluptuous women dressed as 'Liberty', 'Reason' or 'Nature' wrapped in blue and white veils and wearing the little red Phrygian cap (see Chapter One). The 'goddesses' were followed by wild crowds chanting and dancing, all very reminiscent of the ancient Greek

Bacchanals, the Roman Hilarias and the Isiaic processions. The image of these processions of 'goddesses' wearing the Phrygian cap also brings to mind the great pagan processions of the Phrygian mother goddess, Cybele, which took place in ancient France before the advent of Christianity. Cybele was often linked to Isis, as authors Anne Baring and Jules Cashford explain in their excellent book *The Myth of the Goddess*:

> Under the [Roman] Empire, the cult of Cybele became part of the Roman state religion. It existed side by side with the cult of Isis ... and both spread all over the Roman Empire ... An interesting image to follow through different civilizations is the 'Phrygian cap', which was worn by ... the priests of Cybele. This distinctive cap first appears in Crete ... Later, in Greece, it is worn by Hermes, messenger of the Gods ... Today similar caps are worn by the Sufi dervishes ... Mary was worshipped at sites once sacred to Cybele and Isis.[85]

In his book *Cybele and Attis*, the scholar Maarten J. Vermaseren gives a description of Cybele which clearly shows how this goddess was seen as the embodiment of Nature and all the cosmos:

> It is not only Nature that the goddess rules: her power reaches much further. She stands in the center of the Universe of Time, Sun and Moon, Earth, Water, the Sea and the Seasons. In front of her chariot stands the Tree of Life, stylized as an obelisk and entwined by a serpent ...[86]

The French scholar Jurgis Baltrušaitis in his book *La Quête d'Isis*, demonstrates the great extent to which Cybele and Isis were perceived as being the same entity by 17th century French historians. Baltrušaitis reports that in 1675 a priest called Berrier, while digging in the garden of the Saint-Eustache church, discovered a bronze statue of a female deity wearing a strange tower on her head. Details of this discovery were published in 1683 by Claude du Molinet, canon of the St. Genevieve church in Paris. Here is how Molinet describes the deity:

> The goddess that the Greeks called Io and the Egyptians called Isis is the same as the one the Romans honored under the name of Cybele, identified to the Earth or Nature, and the same as the Egyptians had married to Osiris ...[87]

Baltrušaitis goes on to say that the iconography of the Cybele and Isis figures that were found in France were 'identical ... Cybele is crowned with a tower; Isis also had a tower on her head ...'[88]

Cult of the Supreme Being veiling Isis again

By the end of spring 1794, Robespierre, now the undisputed leader of the National Convention in Paris, had began to turn against Hébert and Chaumette. Soon enough he accused them of being 'enemies of the Nation' and arranged their appointments with *madame guillotine*. He then decided to introduce his own idea of a 'republican religion'. This he named the 'Cult of the Supreme Being'. Its symbol was the 'eye in the pyramid', and Robespierre issued a decree stating that 'the French people recognize the existence of the Supreme Being and the immortality of the soul'. The 'Supreme Being' cult was largely modeled on the 'natural' philosophy of Jean-Jacques Rousseau, who Robespierre idolized.

It is clear that Robespierre considered the de-Christianisation of France as inevitable but that he also repudiated atheism and the wild excesses that had accompanied the Cult of Reason. What Robespierre sought to create was a new deist cult based on republican virtues to replace the spiritual vacuum left by the intense de-Christianisation activities of Hébert and Chaumette.

On 4 June 1794 Robespierre was elected president of the National Convention. He at once began to work closely with the artist Jacques-Louis David to prepare a grand celebration for Paris on 8 June 1794, the day of the Pentecost. The purpose of the celebration was to install the Cult of the Supreme Being as the new religion for France.

This curious event began in the Tuileries Garden in front of the Louvre, with Robespierre himself, draped in blue, standing next to a statue of the 'Supreme Being'. A huge makeshift amphitheatre was erected in order to seat the members of the National Convention. In front of the amphitheatre had been prepared a bonfire upon which, according to the programme written by Jacques-Louis David, were 'gathered all the enemies of the felicity of the people'. The 'enemies' were symbolized by a statue called 'Atheism' supported by figures called 'Ambition', 'Egoism', 'Discord' and 'False Simplicity'.

All over Paris houses were decorated with garlands and tricolor flags, and the streets through which the procession was to pass were lined with flowers. Pretty girls in white frocks carrying bouquets were placed along the quays of the Seine. The members of the National Convention, fully attired in their official costumes, filled the amphitheatre, each carrying a small bundle of wheat-ears, a symbol that Freemason and astronomer Jérôme Lalande associated at the time with the 'virgin' goddess Isis.[89] Lalande, as the reader will recall from Chapter One, was a prominent member of the Nine Sisters lodge in Paris and had been instrumental in introducing the new Republican calendar based on the Egyptian solar year which, in ancient times, was calibrated on the heliacal rising of the star of Isis, Sirius. Earlier, in 1731, Lalande had written:

> The Virgin is consecrated to Isis, just as Leo is consecrated to her husband Osiris ... The Sphinx, composed of a lion and a virgin, was used as a symbol to designate the flow of the Nile ... they put a wheat-ear in the hand of the Virgin, to express the idea of the months, perhaps because the sign of the Virgin was called by the Orientals ... *epi* or wheat-ear.[90]

The Nine Sisters lodge was founded by Lalande and the Abbé Cordier de Saint-Firmin, the godfather of Voltaire, in 1776 – the same year as the signing of the American Declaration of Independence. The following year, 1777, Benjamin Franklin, the most senior of the signatories to the Declaration, was appointed Grand Master of the Nine Sisters lodge in Paris. We'll return to this intriguing connection in Chapter Eighteen. Meanwhile let's continue to follow the progress of the Supreme Being on that balmy day of 8 June 1794.

Robespierre, with his hair powdered white and his whole body wrapped in a blue-violet mantle, delivered a prayer to the crowds from a high altar: 'The whole Universe is assembled here! O Nature, how sublime and delicious is your power!' He then evoked the Supreme Being and asked the congregation to pay homage to Him. But at the end of his very long sermon, rather than promise an end to the carnage or offer new hopes for curbing the excesses of the Revolution, Robespierre delivered instead a chilling warning to his political opponents: 'Tomorrow, when we return to work, we shall again fight vice and tyrants!' Then the large choir, brought from the national opera, sang a hymn by François Joseph Gossec entitled 'Father of the Universe, Supreme Intelligence'. Finally Robespierre stepped towards the veiled effigy representing 'Atheism' and set fire to it. Jacques-Louis David had designed it such a way that when the veil burnt a stone statue of 'Wisdom' was revealed beneath it, modelled on the ancient goddess 'Sophia' and meant to emerge 'like a phoenix from the flames'.

Widely used as a symbol in Freemasonry, Sophia has frequently been associated with Isis. According to the poet Gérard de Nerval, the statue that Robespierre 'unveiled' on that day was, in all probability, an effigy of Isis. In his book, *Les Illuminés* published in 1852, Nerval speaks of the ceremony performed by Robespierre and compares it to 'a remembrance of the practices of the *illuminés*', pointing out that the 'Veiled Nature' used for the 8 June 1794 ceremony was 'a statue covered with a veil which he [Robespierre] lit up and which represented either Nature or Isis.'[91]

At last when the effigy was revealed to the people and all the chanting stopped, Robespierre led a cortege at the helm of a massive chariot carrying the goddess and towed by eight oxen, their horns painted in gold. The cortege passed through the Place de la Révolution (now Place de la Concorde), Les Invalides and finally came to rest at the Champs de Mars where more celebrations, speeches and chanting took place.[92]

Notre Dame, Temple of the Goddess

Contemporary records confirm that the attacks on the clerical establishment in 1793–4 were not mere acts of sporadic 'revenge' against individual members of the clergy but rather a well-organised and systematic de-Christianisation campaign which resulted, in a matter of months, in the wholesale 'voluntary abdication' of some 20,000 Catholic priests, many of whom then gladly embraced the cult of the revolutionary goddess.[93]

French historian Michel Vovelle reports that the Cult of Reason first appeared during the trial of the Marie-Antoinette, and then took off with zest immediately after the queen's public execution on 16 October 1793.[94] It has been confirmed that the first signs of de-Christianisation were witnessed in the Allier and Nièvre departments on 2 October 1793 during the closing stage of the trial.

Then, on 7 October, a shockwave hit the country. It was reported that a representative of the National Convention, an ex-pastor called Philippe Rühl who was acting under the orders of Chaumette and Hébert, had taken the *Sainte Ampoule* – a glass chalice containing holy oil – from the Cathedral of Reims and smashed it in the public square. The *Sainte Ampoule* was said to contain the sacramental oil that had been used to consecrate the kings and queens of France since the time of Clovis in AD 496. When the *Sainte Ampoule* was smashed by Rühl, it is said that a priest, the Abbé Serrain of the village of Saint-Remi, rushed to the spot and managed to mop up some of the sacred oil.[95]

But Rühl's act was only a prelude. On 7 November 1793, a few weeks after the decapitation of Marie-Antoinette, the bishop of Paris, Jean-Baptiste-Joseph Gobel, was defrocked in front of a large audience at the National Convention. This charade too was orchestrated by Chaumette. The bishop, who was frightened out of his wits, promptly declared that he wanted to join the Hébertists and the Cult of Reason.

Three days later, on 10 November, the unthinkable happened: a large crowd, accompanied by a choir, stormed the Cathedral of Notre Dame de Paris. They carried in a makeshift throne upon which sat the 'goddess' personified by a beautiful Parisian actress, Mlle Aubry, who was dressed in the blue, white and red republican colors and wearing the Phrygian cap. The 'goddess', who was labelled 'Liberty, daughter of Nature', brandished a torch to signify that 'Liberty is the light of the world'.[96] The whole congregation was then led by Chaumette and the ex-Bishop Gobel to the National Convention. There it was decreed that the Cathedral of Notre Dame was henceforth to be known as the 'Temple for the goddess Reason'.[97]

City of Light

Let us note in passing that Chaumette was no ordinary Freemason. Like many Freemasons at the time, he had acquired a taste for 'Egyptian' symbols and rituals. He was, for example, a keen supporter of the astronomers Charles-François Dupuis and Jérôme Lalande, and it comes as no surprise that a contemporary critic was to exclaim: 'Messrs. Dupuis and Lalande see Isis everywhere …!'[98] It was fashionable in Masonic circles just before the Revolution to see ancient Egypt as the source of all Masonic enlightenment,[99] and we shall recall that the astronomer Dupuis was among those who argued that Isis was the original tutelary goddess of Paris. Indeed Dupuis in 1794 published the thesis that the Cathedral of Notre Dame was actually an *Iseum*, i.e. a former 'Temple of Isis', which had been converted or built upon by the Christians:

> This famous Isis was the goddess of the ancient French or the *Sueves* who joined to her cult the symbolic boat, known as the boat of Isis. This boat still exists on the coat-of-arms of Paris, the city of which Isis had become the tutelary goddess. It is Isis, mother of the God of Light, to whom the people [of Paris] make offering and light candles at the New Year and even during the rest of the year, in memory of the Feast of the Illumined Ones …[100]

Once again we note the epithet 'God of Light' which was used by the Gnostics and Manicheans in the first few centuries after Christ, and later by the Cathars. It also occurs in various forms in Freemasonry and in the Rosicrucian Manifestos as we have reported in earlier chapters, but never in the Christian Bible.

In support of Dupuis' position, the astronomer Lalande wrote:

M. Dupuis concluded in his research into the façade [of Notre Dame de Paris] that it is a crude copy of a frontispiece of an ancient Temple of Isis, the goddess whose cult was long ago established in Gaul [ancient France] and especially in Paris.[101]

With their clear Masonic penchant for the goddess Isis, whom they called 'mother of the God of Light' and also correctly identified as 'goddess of the year' (as she was known in ancient Egypt)[102] it is easy to understand the inspiration for the new Republican calendar that Dupuis and Lalande were closely involved in creating. The reader will recall from Chapter One that this so-called *Republican calendar* was built around the ancient Egyptian year of 365 days, which was divided into 12 months of 30 days each with 'five extra days' added to make up the full solar year.

But along with the goddess Isis-cum-Reason-cum-Nature, the revolutionaries of late 18th century Paris also made profuse use of other well-known Egyptian symbols: the pyramids and the so-called *Eye of Providence*. It was while trying to understand *why* such symbols were used that Robert Bauval stumbled on the key that would open a secret window looking out over Paris and allow us to see an enchanted, almost-magical landscape interwoven in the modern layout of this 'City of Light' …

CHAPTER EIGHTEEN

PARIS UNVEILED

In French Freemasonry the allegorical and metaphorical aspects [of architecture] *appear to have been invested with greater significance than in eighteenth-century England. Architectural history was equated with the development of society. And architecture was seen as a means of establishing a just and ordered system ...*

James Stephen Curl, The Art and Architecture of Freemasonry

O n 14 July 1792 a republican ceremony was held at the Champ-de-Mars in Paris at which a 'Pyramid of Honour' was erected to commemorate those who died during the storming of the Bastille.[1] An etching has survived of another republican ceremony that took place a little over a month later on 26 August 1792 in the Tuilleries Garden next to the Louvre. Again a pyramid was raised in honour of the martyrs of the Revolution. A third pyramid appeared in the Parc Monceau, this one commissioned by Philippe Égalité and designed by the architect Bernard Poyet, next to a pavilion that probably served as a Masonic temple. And there were many other pyramid projects that, though never built, still serve to show the peculiar obsession with the pyramidal form in the decades surrounding the 1789 Revolution.

There are, for example, the curious projects of the revolutionary architect Claude-Nicolas Ledoux,[2] a Freemason, who the architectural historian James Curl describes as being 'involved with Masonic and crypto-Masonic cults'. Indeed so involved was he with such interests that when a fellow Freemason from Britain, an architect, attended a Masonic meeting in Ledoux's home in Paris, he was put out by what he felt to be the excessively occult nature of the event. He commented afterwards: 'it would seem that Ledoux was more involved in the type of heretical Masonry of *Cagliostro*'.[3] Many architects have been intrigued by one of Ledoux's most ambitious designs, the so-called *Vue perspective d'une forge à canons* ('Perspective view of a forge cannon'), an iron smelting plant with massive pyramids and a layout that recalls 'various versions of the Temple complex in Jerusalem'.[4]

Then there are, of course, those most extraordinary pseudo-Egyptian designs by the revolutionary architect Étienne-Louis Boullée, the most famous of which was the so-called *Cénotaphe dans le genre égyptienne* ('Cenotaph in the Egyptian style'), which was a series of gigantic pyramids with their capstones missing – a design very reminiscent of the actual appearance throughout historical times of the Great Pyramid at Giza and of the truncated pyramid seen on the Great Seal of the United States.[5] James Curl, who is regarded as an expert on Masonic architecture, comments that 'in spite of its title *Cénotaphe*, the building was clearly a cemetery or a *centre for cults*, to judge from the processions going up and down the gigantic ramps.'[6]

Imaging the Supreme Being

Were Ledoux and Boullée thinking of the 'Supreme Being' in their designs? Perhaps. But both these men, like many architects of their generation, were much influenced by the famous architect and Freemason Antoine-Chrysostome Quatremère de Quincy. The latter was known for having presented a prize essay to the *Académie des Inscriptions et Belles-Lettres* in 1785 on ancient Egyptian architecture and, more specifically, on the pyramids.[7] According to James Curl, 'Quincy was not only a Freemason, but was very powerfully influenced by his Masonic convictions'.[8]

There is, too, an extraordinary project by Ledoux – Quatremère de Quincy's pupil – which is shown in his book *L'Architecture Considérée* published in Paris in 1804. There we can see a plan for the theatre of the city of Besançon in the form of a gigantic 'all-seeing-eye' which James Curl describes as 'an unquestionably Masonic allusion'.[9] The same idea was used by the revolutionary architect Poyet who had designed the Parc Monceau pyramid for Philippe Égalité. Another of Poyet's ambitious plans was for a public hospital in Paris, where a gigantic 'all-seeing-eye' can easily be discerned in the general layout.[10]

The 'Eye of Providence', the 'all-seeing-eye', the 'eye in the pyramid', and the 'eye in the triangle' were all symbols of the Supreme Being, the *Être Suprême* of Robespierre. Thus, for example, we have a poster dating from the Revolution, which depicts the hero-philosophers Voltaire and Rousseau pointing to a glowing solar disc within which is the 'all-seeing-eye' and a caption that reads: '*Être Suprême, Peuple Souverain, République Française*' ('Supreme Being, Sovereign People, French Republic').[11] The 'all-seeing-eye' is also prominent on a poster of the *Fête de la Fédération* at the Champ-de-

Mars dated to 1790, where the rays of the Sun shoot down to form a golden pyramid that engulfs two tricolor flags and a red Phrygian cap fixed on a 'pole of Liberty'.[12]

The association of the 'all-seeing-eye' with Voltaire on the first of these posters is particularly interesting. It is a very well-known fact among Freemasons that Voltaire was initiated on 7 April 1778 at the Nine Sisters lodge in Paris by the astronomer Jérôme Lalande and Benjamin Franklin.[13] When Voltaire died a month later, the lodge was converted into a 'Lodge of Sorrows', a sort of Masonic funerary service, and on 28 November 1778 a service was held there for his departed soul. In line with Masonic tradition, the whole interior of the lodge was draped in black veils. At the far end of the room was raised a stepped pyramid, also draped in black.[14] On the summit of this pyramid was a cenotaph, and at the place where the capstone would normally have been could be seen hovering a glowing triangle with the letter 'G' inscribed in it.

Such a pyramid with the same glowing capstone is, of course, to be seen on the Great Seal of the United States, the design of which was coordinated by Benjamin Franklin and Thomas Jefferson in 1776.[15] In Masonic symbolism the 'eye' representing the Supreme Being, is interchangeable with the letter 'G', and both symbols stand for 'God' i.e. the 'Grand Geometrician' or the 'Grand Architect of the Universe'. Author and professor, Michel Vovelle, also draws attention to a French revolutionary poster where the 'all-seeing-eye' is depicted over the breast of the 'goddess Reason'; she holds a victory wreath above a plaque on which appears a small 'glowing pyramid with the eye'.[16] Indeed, the same glowing triangle with the all-seeing-eye found it way to the top of the Declaration of the Rights of Man and the Citizen signed in August 1789 at the National Assembly. The text was modeled on essays written by the Marquis de Lafayette and the Abbé Sieyès, two very prominent Scottish Rite Freemasons. Perhaps we ought to recall the telling words of the Grand Master of the *Grand Orient*, Paul Gourdot, when he claimed that intellectuals such as Voltaire provided the 'spirit of the Revolution' and that the outcome of this – the First Republic – was based on 'the Declaration of the Rights of Man *which was formulated in our lodges*.'[17]

The cry of a dying tiger

Ironically, the extravagant ceremonies during the so-called *Festival of the Supreme Being* on 8 June 1794 were to lead to Robespierre's downfall. Not all who witnessed the event liked his spurious display of piety and reverence towards an effigy of a pagan deity, and even some of his closest allies were put off by what they saw as his increasing pompousness and vanity. Many worried that being at the helm of the National Convention had gone to his head.

The *Montagnards* (the 'Mountains') who were normally Robespierre's most ardent supporters, began to have doubts. And being mostly atheists, many of them were deeply embarrassed by the strange psuedo-religious shows he was now putting on. Amazingly, they found a way to accuse the previously invulnerable Robespierre of anti-republicanism and sent him to the guillotine on 28 July 1794. His jaw had been blown off by a pistol shot so he was bleeding profusely and unable to talk. All that the poor man could do was let out a frightening cry which, according to an eyewitness, sounded 'like that of a dying tiger'.

The Revolution had nearly run its course and, for a brief, tantalizing moment, the reigns of power were dangling free and there for the taking. A young Corsican officer who had been closely monitoring these grisly events and biding his time was slowly getting ready to make his move.

A new Alexander the Great was in the making ...

Napoleon's goddess

On the evening of the 5 March 1798, a date that, oddly, coincided with the well-known ancient Roman Feast of the *Navigium Isidis,* the Feast of the Boat of Isis, a carriage under heavy military escort left Paris for the port of Toulon. In it was the new hero of France, Napoleon Bonaparte, and his lovely wife Joséphine. They were on their way to meet up with the French fleet which was waiting to sail to Egypt.

In a mere two years Napoleon had risen from being an obscure artillery officer amidst the 'Terror' of 1794, to commander-in-chief of the army by early 1796. A week after his appointment as commander of the French army in Italy, Napoleon had married the exquisitely beautiful Joséphine de Beauharnais,[18] widow of Viscount Alexandre de Beauharnais, a Freemason and nobleman who, like many others of his Estate, had ended on the guillotine in 1794. Joséphine was the eldest daughter of Joseph-Gaspard de Tascher de La Pagerie, an impoverished nobleman who had settled in Martinique where Joséphine had spent the first 15 years of her life. She had come to Paris in 1779, a decade before the Revolution, and there had married the ill-fated de Beauharnais. It was an arranged marriage and never happy. When Napoleon met her in 1795, she was widowed with two children and on the verge of breaking up a turbulent affair with the Viscount Paul-François-Jean-Nicolas de Barras, the commander-in-chief of the Army of the Interior. Napoleon, who was deputy-general to Barras, was only 27 years old at the time.

Joséphine was 33 and the darling of Parisian high society, into which she had been introduced by the beautiful Thérésa Tallien. The latter was the wife of Jean-Lambert Tallien who, along with Barras, had plotted the downfall of Robespierre back in 1794. It was Thérésa, in fact, who had introduced Joséphine to her own lover Barras who, in turn, passed her on to Napoleon.

Joséphine seems to have been attracted to Freemasonry quite early in her career – perhaps partly because it was considered to be very fashionable among women of the aristocracy and partly because her first husband, the Viscount de Beauharnais had been a prominent Freemason who came from a family of illustrious Freemasons.[19] Joséphine was probably initiated in women's Freemasonry at Strasbourg while her husband, the viscount, was commander of the Rhine army.[20] Long afterwards, their son, Eugène de Beauharnais, who now was about to go to Egypt with Napoleon, would become Grand Master of the *Grande Oriente d'Italia* and also of the Supreme Council of the 33rd Degree in Italy.[21]

When she become empress of France in 1804 Joséphine was elected as the Grand Mistress and Patroness of women's Freemasonry in Paris.[22] Many ladies close to her also joined the Masonic sisterhood. Apparently Joséphine's lady-in-waiting, Madame de Canisy, was initiated into women's Freemasonry by the wife of the mayor of Strasbourg, Madame Dietrich, and to mark the event a commemorative medal was struck, showing a golden triangle at the tip of which was placed a star in a crown – almost a premonition of Joséphine's future role in France.[23] Joséphine's favourite niece, Émilie de Beauharnais, wife of Antoine Marie Chamans, Count of Lavalette and director-general of the Imperial Postal Office, was elected Grand Mistress of the adoption lodge *Anacreon* in Paris.[24]

Being a Freemason initiated in the ancient mysteries, and now with all this post-Revolution talk of deism, it may be possible that Joséphine had begun to take an interest in Islam and may even have privately encouraged Napoleon to bring it into the fold of Western Europe. For it is well known that her first cousin and closest friend, the beautiful Aimée du Buc de Rivéry, had been kidnapped by Arab pirates and sold to the harem of the sultan of Turkey, Abdul Hamid I, where she soon became his favourite concubine and bore him a son, the Emir Mahmoud. When the old sultan died, Aimée became the mistress of the heir-apparent, the young and glamorous nephew of the sultan, the Emir Selim, over whom Aimée was to wield enormous influence by turning him into a keen Francophile.[25] There thus existed a 'dynastic' link between Joséphine of France and her cousin the 'sultana' of Turkey, a connection which might have brought the Middle East and Islam within Joséphine's sphere of attention. At any rate, whatever was going on secretly in Joséphine's and Napoleon's minds, he would one day write to her from Egypt these curious words:

> I saw myself founding a new religion, marching into Asia, riding an Elephant, a turban on my head and in my hand a Koran that I would have composed to suit my needs.[26]

Whether or not such words were written in jest, we shall never know.

Inspirations for the invasion of Egypt

The idea for a French invasion of Egypt was not original to Napoleon. It was the brainchild of Talleyrand, the great French statesman and diplomat. We have already encountered Talleyrand when, in 1789, he resigned from his role as representative of the Second Estate – the clergy – and sided with the revolutionaries. But because he was in favour of a constitutional monarchy, he had to flee France in order to save his neck as the Revolution developed. He first went to England in late 1792 then, in 1794, to America where he stayed till September 1796, after the rise of Napoleon Bonaparte. Upon his return to France, he was made foreign minister by Napoleon.

In spite having reached the position of bishop in the Catholic Church, Talleyrand was a staunch Freemason who, during the early years of the Revolution, had been a supporter of the Duke of Orléans. Talleyrand had been a member of the prestigious lodge *Les Philalethes* in Paris, and of the lodge *Les Amis Réunis* (to which Marat, Sieyès and Condorcet also belonged).[27] *Les Philalethes* in Paris had been much involved with Cagliostro's Egyptian Rite back in 1784–5, where it was said that many of their members joined his lodge in Paris. The Freemason Henry Evans explains:

> The controversy between Cagliostro and the Lodge of *Philalethes* (or 'Lovers of Truth') is Masonic history. On February 15, 1785, the members of the *Philalethes*, with Savalette de Langes at their head, met in Paris to discuss questions of importance regarding Freemasonry, such as its origin, essential nature, relations with the occult sciences, etc ... among them being French and Austrian princes, councillors, financiers, barons, ambassadors, officers of the army, doctors, farmers, a general, and last but not least two professors of magic. M. de Langes was a royal banker, who had been prominent in the old Illuminati. A summons had been sent to Cagliostro to attend the convention, and he had assured the messenger

that he would take part in its deliberations. But he changed his mind and demanded that the *Philalethes* adopt the constitutions of the Egyptian Rite, burn their archives, and be initiated into the Mother Lodge at Lyons ['Triumphant Wisdom'], intimating that they were not in possession of the true Masonry. He deigned, as he said, to extend his hand over them, and consented 'to send a ray of light into the darkness of their temple.' The Baron von Gleichen was deputed to see Cagliostro and ask for more detailed information, and at the same time to request the presence of the members of the Mother Lodge at the convention. Renewed correspondence took place, but Cagliostro would not recede from his position. Finally three delegates from the *Philalethes*, among them the Marquis de Marnésia of French le-Comte, repaired to Lyons, and were initiated into Egyptian Masonry. In their report to the convention occur the following significant words: 'His [Cagliostro's] doctrine ought to be regarded as sublime and pure; and without having a perfect acquaintance with our language, he employs it as did the prophets of old ...'[28]

Could any of this 'Egyptian' hype have influenced Talleyrand in any way when he later began to push the idea of an 'Egyptian expedition' to Napoleon? It seems plausible, particularly since there were existing precedents for a French invasion of Egypt.

In 1249, five years after his army had captured the Cathar stronghold at Montségur, King Louis IX landing at the port of Damietta with a force of French knights and attempted to win control of Egypt. The king was defeated and captured by the Arabs at Mansoura, a small town on the road to Cairo, but was eventually ransomed for a huge sum. Undeterred Louis IX was to organize a second attempt to seize Egypt in 1270, this time approaching across the desert from a landing-point in Tunisia. But terrible diseases afflicted the French invaders and the king himself died on the desert trek.

A few centuries later, in 1672, the famous mathematician and philosopher, Gottfried Leibniz, presented Louis XIV with a secret plan for a full-scale invasion of Egypt.[29] Louis XIV was then at war with Holland and ultimately turned down the plan – the real object of which may have been to divert his attention from European conquests by getting him to focus instead on a 'universal mission' to unite East and West in the style of Alexander the Great.

Scholars suspect Leibniz to have been a member of the 'invisible' brotherhood of the Rosicrucians.[30] It is also known that he was for a long while in contact with the Jesuit and Hermetic-Cabalist, Athanasius Kircher, with whom he shared an interest in Egyptian hieroglyphs and obelisks.[31]

Kircher appears to have influenced Leibniz in his mathematical and philosophical research and especially in his studies of ancient languages which in due course would become a personal obsession.[32]

The idea of an invasion of Egypt still did not go away. Other similar plans were later proposed by the Duke of Choiseul, minister of foreign affairs under Louis XV.[33] Choiseul was among the very first of the high aristocrats of France to become a Freemason.[34] He was also a bitter enemy of the Jesuits whom he eventually managed to have banned from France in 1764. His wife, the Duchess of Choiseul, was a regular participant in the adoption lodge 'Isis' that Cagliostro had opened at Paris in 1785, and had even been nominated as the lodge's Grand Mistress at one stage.[35] Being the man responsible for the modernization of the French fleet, Choiseul was the authority on any naval invasion France cared to consider. But his project, too, was eventually shelved.

So when Talleyrand put forward his plan for the invasion of Egypt in early 1798, it was at first received with some hesitation. On the one hand Napoleon was wary of crossing the Mediterranean at a time when the British fleet under Horatio Nelson was actively seeking French prey. On the other hand the prospect of a glorious, and seemingly easy victory evoking the exploits of Alexander and Caesar was extremely tempting and Napoleon found it difficult to ignore. Intelligence reports had shown that the port of Alexandria was manned by a small and poorly-trained Arab garrison that was hardly a match for modern French battleships and Napoleon's elite troops.

Trouble with Joséphine

There were painful personal considerations bearing down on Napoleon when he took the decision to invade Egypt. These involved his wife, Joséphine. The couple had been married for barely two years and already Joséphine had been unfaithful with a young officer called Hippolyte Charles. Indeed a few months after their wedding in 1796 Napoleon – then away waging war in Italy – seems to have sensed that something was wrong with Joséphine's behavior and was prompted to write her this rather immature letter:

> I write you, my beloved one, very often, and you write very little. You are wicked and naughty, very naughty, as much as you are fickle. It is unfaithful so to deceive a poor husband, a tender lover! Ought he to lose all his enjoyments because he is so far away, borne down with toil, fatigue, and hardship? Without his Joséphine, without the assurance of her love, what is left him upon earth? What can he do? ... *Adieu*, adorable Joséphine;

one of these nights your door will open with a great noise, as a jealous person, and you will find me in your arms. A thousand loving kisses.[36]

In November 1796, Joséphine made a trip to Genoa with Hippolyte Charles, which provoked anger and emotional confusion in Napoleon. Although he now strongly suspected his wife of infidelity, his huge pride and obsessive love caused him to react paradoxically:

I do not love you anymore! On the contrary, I detest you. You are a vile, mean, beastly slut. You don't write to me at all. You don't love your husband ... Soon I will be holding you in my arms, then I will cover you with a million kisses, burning like the equator ...[37]

On 5 March 1798, amidst eloquent orations evoking France's 'universal mission' and the alleged need to thwart British trade with India, the Directory voted in favour of a military expedition to Egypt to be headed by Napoleon. The vote was kept secret until the fleet actually set sail from Toulon on 19 May 1798.[38] According to British historian Aubrey Noakes, Napoleon had wanted Joséphine to come along, probably to keep her away from mischief in Paris, but she had stubbornly refused.[39] But Vincent Cronin, in his biography of Napoleon, says the opposite, that it was Joséphine who desperately wanted to go to Egypt but that it was Napoleon who refused her.[40] Either way the result was that Joséphine stayed behind with strict orders from Napoleon not to see Hippolyte Charles ever again. Apparently a rather odd exchange of words took place between Napoleon and Joséphine as he prepared to board the flagship, *l'Orient*, bound for Egypt:

'When will you return?' She murmured.

'Six months, six years, perhaps never.' Bonaparte replied indifferently. As the boat pushed off from the quay, Joséphine stepped forward with one last message: 'Good bye, Good bye! If you go to Thebes [Luxor], do send me a little obelisk ...'[41]

And so, in this tense emotional mood, Napoleon set out for Egypt on his epic adventure of discovery and glory. In spite of Joséphine's disloyalty and frivolity, he was still madly in love with her, and fervently believed in their historical destiny together. Now, perhaps more than ever, he must have wanted to impress on her his heroism and unique sense of mission.

　　　　　　　　　　　　　　　　　THE MASTER GAME

'We who have destroyed the Pope ...'

When the French fleet reached Alexandria on 1 July 1798, an excited Napoleon issued a rather curious proclamation to the Egyptian people, who were under the supposedly oppressive rule of the Mameluks:[42]

> People of Egypt! You will be told that I come to destroy your religion. Do not believe it. Reply that I come to restore your rights and punish the usurpers, and that I venerate more than the Mameluks, Allah, his Prophet and the Koran ... There formerly existed in Egypt great cities, great canals, great commerce; by what means have they all been destroyed if not by the avarice, the injustice, and the tyranny of the Mameluks? ... Sheikhs! Imams! Go tell the people that we are the friends of true Muslims. Is it not we who have destroyed the Pope who preached that war must be made on Muslims? Is it not we who have destroyed the Knights of Malta because these madmen believed that God willed them to make war on Muslims? Is it not we who have been long friends with the Sultan and the enemies of his enemies? ...[43]

There is a very revealing color etching by the Parisian printer A. H. Basset dating from that time which shows what Napoleon might have had in mind.[44] In the top register Napoleon is seen in the center of the scene standing next to the pyramids of Giza and receiving the key of Egypt from two Arabs kneeling at his feet. Above Napoleon are two angels holding a wreath-crown; one angel represents 'Glory' and the other 'Renown'. In the lower register Napoleon is shown pointing to a large glowing triangle (the Supreme Being) hovering next to him, and seems to be inviting representatives of all the known religions to venerate the universal 'God' symbolized by the glowing triangle.

After Napoleon's capture of Cairo in late July 1798, the Arabs played along with his offer of a covenant between the new French Republic and Islam, all the while secretly hating him and his troops as much as they had hated the crusaders of bygone days. But it was a case of bargaining now with the devil until a way was found to throw him out. Meanwhile it must have been at about this time that General Jean-Andoche Junot, through a personal letter he had received from Paris, brought Napoleon irrefutable evidence that Joséphine had been seen staying at an inn with Hippolyte Charles immediately after he had left her in Toulon. Napoleon was devastated. In retaliation he began an open affair in Cairo with Pauline Fourès, the pretty wife of a young officer.[45]

The *folie égyptienne*, as historians would later call Napoleon's Egyptian campaign, was to cost France dearly: the complete destruction of the French invasion fleet at Abu Qir by the British under Nelson, and the loss of nearly 40 per cent of the expeditionary army which, at the outset, had totaled some 54,000 men. Worse still was the humiliating surrender of the survivors to the British forces under Ralph Abercromby at Alexandria.

Napoleon himself returned to France long before the surrender and somehow managed to survive this military and political disaster. Soon enough an effective propaganda campaign began to convert the reality of the defeat into the perception of a cultural victory.

The savants and the destiny of Napoleon

Napoleon had taken along to Egypt 167 'savants' – scholars and the erudite from many different disciplines – amongst them surveyors, mathematicians, astronomers, engineers, botanists, linguists, poets, artists and architects, all hand-picked from the newly formed *Institut National de France*. It had been the mathematician Gaspard Monge who had personally recruited them. Monge was one of Napoleon's closest friends and advisors, and considered the young general as his 'adopted son.'[46] The reader will recall that Monge was a prominent Freemason from the Nine Sisters lodge in Paris and had been directly responsible with Charles-Gilbert Romme for the introduction of the Republican calendar modeled on the Egyptian solar year. While in Egypt, Monge founded the *Institut d'Égypte* in Cairo, a scientific and *Encyclopédist* body modeled on its French counterpart, the *Institut National*. Monge acted as president of the *Institut d'Égypte* with Napoleon acting as his vice-president.[47] Many of the other savants and officers who accompanied Napoleon to Egypt were also Freemasons, notably his right hand man, General Jean-Baptiste Kléber, who is said to have founded the first modern Masonic lodge on Egyptian soil.[48]

Also among the savants was Dominique-Vivant Denon, an artist with an incredible talent for freehand sketching and the making of etchings. A highly educated man, Denon had been a diplomat in Russia and Sweden before the Revolution. He had been about to face the guillotine in December 1793 for his alleged royalist sympathies when he had been rescued from the blade by his friend, the painter Jacques-Louis David. A prominent member of the National Convention, David, had masterminded the celebrations of 'Isis of the Bastille' and in December 1793 was busy promoting the Cult of the Supreme Being with Robespierre.

Denon, who was talented, sophisticated and very handsome, was a favourite with the ladies of the aristocracy. He was highly admired by Catherine II of Russia and had no difficulty in winning the favour of the up-

and-coming Joséphine who introduced him to Napoleon. Joséphine urged Napoleon to take Denon to Egypt, but as the latter was not a member of the *Institut National*, Napoleon had at first resisted the idea. Eventually, however, as was often the case, he yielded to Joséphine's demands. It was a decision he would not regret, for it was Denon, through the publication of his spectacular drawings, who would find the magic to transform Napoleon's Egyptian fiasco into a cultural victory for him in person and for the French Republic as a whole.

Albeit tarnished a little by the defeat at Abu Qir and the humiliating surrender of the expeditionary army at Alexandria, Napoleon's 'conquest' of Egypt, allowed him to stand alongside history's most illustrious military heroes and empire builders: Alexander the Great and Augustus Caesar. And now here, in flesh and blood, was France's own Napoleon the Great. He had 'returned from Egypt' like some mythical solar hero ready to found a new French Empire modeled on the empire of Charlemagne. The famous *Description de l'Égypte*, which was published under the supervision of Denon, was dedicated to 'Napoleon le Grand', who is depicted on the front-cover as an Apollo-Sol Invictus, hero-king. There he may still be seen, riding the solar chariot under the protection of the Egyptian symbol of the winged solar disc – into which, in this case, has been placed a star.

Is it an accident that at about the same time, but on the other side of the Atlantic, the same symbolic representation of Apollo-Sol Invictus – including the same solar chariot and the same winged solar disk with the same star – would be used in connection with George Washington? We will return to this mystery in the next chapter.

Few historians would disagree that the driving force behind Napoleon's military conquests was his unshakable belief in his own destiny – the belief that he had somehow been chosen by history to unite all Europe, and perhaps even the whole world, under one, universal rule. Since his vision for this rule was based on French republican ideals, virtues and laws, Napoleon, by his own reckoning, had become *the embodiment of the Revolution* and its universal, almost sacred 'mission'.

After his return from Egypt in 1799 and now barely 30 years of age, Napoleon had the Directory proclaim him 'first consul' of the Republic, a term clearly drawn from republican Rome. In 1802 he was voted consul for life and soon, with his large and well-trained armies, he had annexed to France vast territories in Europe that included Germany, Austria and Italy. He was, by then 'emperor' of Europe in everything but title.

Then in 1804, now 35 years of age, Napoleon went for the ultimate prize.

The Holy 'French' Empire

On Christmas Day AD 800, Pope Leo III crowned the Frankish general, Charlemagne, as first emperor of the Holy Roman Empire. Charlemagne was in Rome with a large army to 'protect' the pope but the legend has it that he had merely entered the Basilica of St. Peter to take part in the Mass. When he approached the altar and kneeled to pray, the pope placed a golden crown on his head and caused the congregation to cry out:

> Life and victory to Charles the August, crowned by God, the great and pacific Emperor of the Romans![49]

It is said that the pope even prostrated himself before Charlemagne and paid him homage in the manner once accorded to ancient Roman emperors, which also included anointing him with sacred oil.

After Charlemagne's 'coronation', no other emperor or king had ever again been given the great honour of being physically crowned by a pope. A thousand years later, however, Napoleon Bonaparte decided it was high time to change all that.[50] To this end he had Pope Pius VII forcefully brought to Paris in late 1804. The coronation, meticulously planned by Napoleon himself, took place in the Cathedral of Notre Dame which, until very recently, had served as the 'Temple of the goddess Reason'. Just before the climax of the event, Napoleon stepped forward, took the crown away from the pope's hands and, in a grand symbolic gesture, crowned himself emperor. Under the bemused gaze of the pope, Napoleon then took a smaller crown and placed it on the head of the lovely and promiscuous Joséphine, making her empress.[51] David was to immortalize this moment in an appropriately huge painting that may be viewed today in the Louvre. Also marking the occasion, the sculptor Jean-Antoine Houdon, a Freemason, a member of the Nine Sisters lodge, and formerly a close friend of Cagliostro, made a marble bust of Joséphine.[52]

We may perhaps wonder if French artists such as Houdon, Denon and David were not somewhat bedazzled by Joséphine – who they went on to promote as the new Isis and thus the new tutelary goddess of continental Freemasonry and of the city of Paris. The reader will recall that in 1773, Court de Gébelin, Freemason, member of the Nine Sisters lodge and inventor of the modern Tarot, had written:

> No one ignores that Paris was originally enclosed in the island [the Île de la Cité]. It was thus, since its origins, a city of navigation ... As it was in

a river rife with navigation, it took as its symbol a boat, and as tutelary goddess, Isis, goddess of navigation; and this boat was the actual one of Isis, symbol of this goddess.[53]

The association with the 'Parisian' boat of Isis and the notion of 'empire' is explained by the early 19th century Parisian historian, François Noël:

The boat of Isis, a feast which was celebrated in Rome with great pomp, was known as *Navigium Isidis*; after it had been launched in the water, it was brought back to the Temple of Isis and prayers were made for the prosperity of the Emperor, for the Empire and for the Roman people ...[54]

Dates and words

In the brief period of Napoleon's occupation of Egypt, from 1798 to 1801, there were witnessed some events that gave a mythical sparkle to this otherwise doomed adventure.

First there is the matter of the date – 5 March 1798 – on which the Directory voted in favour of sending Napoleon to 'liberate' Egypt. Given the intense Masonic and Isiaic interests of some of the protagonists, it would be unusual if no one had realised that 5 March was the Feast of the 'Boat of Isis', the *Navigium Isidis*, widely popular during the Roman Empire and subsequently in ancient France (Gaul).

Second there are the confusing circumstances surrounding the naval Battle of Abu Qir, the shallow bay to the east of Alexandria where Nelson obliterated Napoleon's fleet on 1 August 1798. Abu Qir was the site of the ancient city of Canopus where legend has it that the ship carrying the Trojan lovers, Paris and Helen, long ago took refuge. Helen, as we recall from Chapter Ten, had been associated by Herodotus with an Egyptian deity who he called 'Aphrodite the Stranger'. The Alexandrians identified Aphrodite with Isis, and both Helen and Isis were well known to be protectors of mariners and ships. Moreover, the star of Isis – Sirius – was the *Stella Maris*, the 'Star of the Sea', also known as the 'Star of the East' or 'Star of the Orient'. Surely Napoleon and his erudite friends in Egypt would have been aware how highly evocative of all these mythical archetypes was the act of anchoring the flagship *l'Orient* at Abu Qir-Canopus?

We concede at once that the question is highly speculative, but Napoleon's mindset at the time does not exclude such links being made. Of Corsican origins, he remained all his life a very superstitious man, and considered Joséphine to be his 'lucky charm', a sort of human talisman. His extremely superstitious nature meant that he was always on the lookout for omens. French historian Jean Duché reports an occasion when Napoleon, having been openly criticized by a cardinal about his military campaigns, grabbed the cardinal by the sleeve, dragged him to a window, and, in broad daylight, asked him if he could see 'the star'. When the baffled cardinal retorted that there was no 'star' to be seen, Napoleon replied:

> Well, as long as I shall be the only one to see it, then I will follow my own destiny and will not permit anyone to criticize me![55]

To any French Freemason the word 'Orient' in the name of Napoleon's flagship would inevitably be reminiscent of the 'Mother Lodge' in Paris known as the *Grand Orient* i.e. the 'Great East'. In Masonic jargon to this day the word 'Orient' or 'East' denotes the name/place of the main Masonic temple in any town or city, and the term 'Grand Orient' or 'Great East' denotes the mother temple or lodge in a country.[56] For example, the *Grand Orient* denotes the main Masonic Temple of Paris in the Rue Cadet; likewise the 'Great East' denotes Freemasons' Hall of London.

Masonic Emperor Of The French?

There are no primary source documents that prove Napoleon was a Freemason; nor are there any that disprove this proposition. There has, however, been much learned speculation on both sides, with some scholars arguing vehemently that he was an initiated Mason[57] and some arguing equally vehemently that he was not.[58]

Many continental Freemasons in the 19th century certainly acted as though Napoleon was a member of the brotherhood. There were dozens of Masonic lodges in Europe that bore his name such as the *Saint Napoleon* lodge in Paris, the *Napoleomagne* lodge in Toulouse, the *Napoleone* lodge in Florence, *La Constellation Napoleon* in Naples, the *Étoile Napoleon* in Madrid and so on – with lodges usually choosing names that evoked Napoleon's military, social and cultural achievements.[59]

We know for sure that Napoleon's strategic entourage was filled with prominent Freemasons such as Talleyrand, Gaspard Monge, Jean Baptiste Kléber, André Masséna and others. We know too that most members of Napoleon's family were Freemasons, including his own father, Charles Bonaparte, his brothers Jérôme, Louis, and Joseph, his wife, Joséphine and his brother-in-law, Joachim Murat.[60] Historian and Masonic author, François Collaveri, asserts with confidence that:

> ... the initiation of Napoleon is not a legend; he was initiated into
> Freemasonry probably in Egypt as is expressly claimed by the *Grand
> Orient* of France.[61]

Other authorities go as far as to argue that Napoleon, as well as his
general, Jean-Baptiste Kléber, underwent their Egyptian Masonic initiation
inside the Great Pyramid of Giza at the hands of a Coptic sage.[62]

Kléber, the son of an operative Mason, had practiced architecture in
Paris long before joining Napoleon's army. In 1787, two years before the
French Revolution, he had designed an Egyptian-style temple for the Parc
d'Études in Paris.[63] Few had any direct acquaintance with ancient Egyptian
temples at that time and Kléber's design bears little resemblance to any of
the existing ancient temples in Egypt – though from the décor that he also
designed it is likely that he had a 'Temple of Isis' in mind.

According to historian Paul Naudon, Kléber founded Egypt's first
modern Masonic lodge which he predictably named *La Loge Isis*.[64] In June
1800, however, two years after arriving in Egypt, he was murdered by an
Arab fanatic. Kléber's corpse was embalmed and shipped back to France.
When the coffin arrived in Paris in late September, Denon made plans for the
construction of a replica of the Egyptian Temple of Dendera to be raised at
the Place des Victoires in Paris as a mausoleum for the great general.[65]

Napoleon researches Isis

After his return from Egypt Napoleon was to develop a rather curious
fascination with the goddess Isis. Indeed so strong was his interest that he
eventually set up a special commission, headed by the scholar Louis Petit-
Radelin, to confirm the ancient legend (reported by Corrozet, Dupuis and
others) that Isis was the true and ancient tutelary deity of the city of Paris.
Napoleon apparently expressed a specific interest in the so-called *boat of
Isis* and its alleged connection with the 'Boat of Paris' found in the coat-of-
arms of the city.[66] After a year or so of research into this matter, the special
commission was able to report to Napoleon that there was, in fact, much
evidence to support the claim that the boat of Isis was, indeed, the very same
as the Boat of Paris.[67] Highly impressed by these findings, Napoleon issued
instructions on 20 January 1811 that a figure of the Egyptian goddess and
her 'star' should now be included on the coat-of-arms of Paris:

> We have previously authorised and do also authorise now by these
> present signed documents by our hand, that our good city of Paris will

bear the coat-of-arms as shown and coloured on the attached drawing, at the front of the ancient ship, the prow loaded with a statue of Isis, seated, in silver on a sea of the same, and lead by a star also of silver.[68]

The drawing that was attached to Napoleon's letter is today kept in the *Bibliothèque Nationale de France*.[69] On this drawing can be seen the red, gold and silver coat-of-arms surrounded by a wreath of wheat. The whole is surmounted by a golden crown on which is perched the imperial eagle. The crown is transpierced by the Hermetic *caduceus*, the entwined winged-snakes. The main image is the silver boat floating on a silver sea. On its prow is the goddess Isis seated on a throne and guided by a five-pointed star hovering in front of the boat. Above the boat are three golden bees, symbolizing divine solar rule.

Interestingly, the same group of symbols also turns up in the *Description de l'Égypte* published by Denon – on the dedication of which Napoleon's name, denoted by the letter 'N', is seen surrounded by the Hermetic coiled snake surmounted by a crown and placed next to a pharaonic *cartouche* inside which is drawn a bee and a five-pointed star.

Napoleon appointed Denon as first director of the newly opened *Musée Napoléon* housed at the Louvre. At the same time he commissioned the architects Charles Percier and Pierre François Léonard Fontaine to design the Cour Carrée on the east side of the Louvre, and the artist Jean-Guillaume Moitte to decorate the eastern façade of the inner gateway. Moitte chose to have the most famous lawgivers of history, Moses and Numa, flank a statue of the goddess Isis seated on a throne. Next to Isis can be seen the legendary Inca solar emperor and lawmaker Manco Cápac.[70]

Three decades later, when Napoleon's body was repatriated from his place of exile in St. Helena and placed in the mausoleum at Les Invalides in Paris, the renowned sculptor and architect Louis-Tullis Visconti designed the final decorations on the circular walls surrounding the former emperor's large sarcophagus. In one of the scenes Visconti sculpted a representation of Napoleon as a solar god-king much resembling Manco Cápac and Sol Invictus, showing the revered French general seated on a throne, bare-chested and with the solar rays shooting out of his head, his arm outstretched handing the 'law' to the many nations of his empire …

The Place of the Star

The most famous monument of Paris, one that was commissioned by Napoleon himself in 1806, is, of course, the Arc de Triomphe at the western end of the Champs-Élysées.[71] The name of the location must have had a special resonance for Napoleon, for so long as anyone could remember it had been called *L'Étoile*, the 'Star'. Given his obsession with his own 'star of destiny' and his obvious interest in the connection between Isis and the city of Paris, it is not impossible that the 'star' in question was imagined by Napoleon to be Sirius. There is, moreover, a rather unusual depiction on the Arc de Triomphe that is highly implicit of Isis and her connection to Napoleon. On the east face of the monument is the commonly called 'Triumph of Napoleon' sculpted by the artist Jean-Pierre Cortot in 1833.[72] The scene shows 'Victory' (a naked woman) crowning Napoleon (who is wearing the toga of a Roman emperor) with a laurel wreath. A Roman goddess wearing a 'tower' on her head (supposedly symbolising a town surrendering to Napoleon) is seen kneeling at the emperor's feet.

The kneeling goddess is, in fact, Cybele, and had clearly been modelled by Cortot from the figure of a Roman goddess wearing a 'tower' on her head found in Paris in 1675 when the foundations of the church of Saint-Eustache were being excavated.[73] According to Claude du Molinet, the bishop of St. Genevieve who published the find in 1683, this effigy was:

> The one that the Greeks called Io and the Egyptians called Isis, and is the same as the one the Romans honored under the same of Cybele, being the Earth or Nature that the Egyptians married to Osiris who was the Sun, in order to make it fertile and mother of all productions that form within her breasts ...[74]

Thus in the minds of French historians of the 17th century, the goddess with the tower headdress was none other than a representation of Isis, for the latter, too 'had also a tower on her head'[75] (as indeed she does in ancient Egyptian hieroglyphs, although what looks like a 'tower' is, in fact, a throne).

In addition it would not be too farfetched to equate the kneeling figure on the Arc de Triomphe with the Empress Joséphine wearing the 'crown of Isis' in Paris – for this scene brings sharply to mind the famous painting by David of the coronation of Joséphine and Napoleon in December 1804 sanctioned by the presence of the pope.[76] In the painting Napoleon is shown wearing the laurel-wreath of Roman emperors while Joséphine is seen kneeling at his feet, herself wearing the empress's crown. The same scene is depicted on the Arc de Triomphe, where Napoleon is again garbed as a Roman emperor and crowned with laurel while Isis-Cybele kneels at his feet, herself wearing the crown-tower of the goddess.

We saw in Chapter Sixteen how the main axis of Paris (running through the monumental avenue of the Champs-Élysées) was aligned by Le Nôtre, either by coincidence or by deliberation, *26° north-of-west* towards the sunset on two religiously important days of the year (8 May and 6 August) and, also looking back, 26° south-of-east towards the *cosmic rising* of the star Sirius. We also saw that this arrangement correlates with the main axis of the great solar temple complex of Karnak-Luxor which is likewise directed 26° north-of-west towards the sunset and, looking back, 26° south-of-east towards the heliacal (dawn) rising of Sirius at the beginning of Egypt's civilization. We know that Sirius was the herald of the 'birth' of solar kings. And we've seen how Napoleon endowed the city of Paris with a new coat-of-arms blatantly displaying the goddess Isis and her star Sirius, and how he also commissioned a huge arch to be raised at the 'place of the star' right on the centerline of the axis of Paris. All these interlocking themes, when considered together, become even more intriguing when we add to them one further fact of history. In 1831, just as Napoleon's Arc de Triomphe was being completed, there was also brought to Paris an ancient Egyptian obelisk – the obelisk of Ramses II as the reader will recall, one of a pair that had originally stood outside the Temple of Luxor in Upper Egypt but now destined for a place of choice along the axis of Paris.

How France had a second revolution

The year 1831 was special for the French, for it followed the country's second great popular 'revolution', that of July 1830 when the restored monarchy under Charles X, a brother of Louis XVI, was toppled – never to return. This second revolution was engineered by France's and America's most famous Freemason, the Marquis de Lafayette, who personally masterminded the coup d'état that brought the 'Citizen King' Louis-Philippe d'Orléans, eldest son of Philippe Égalité, into power.

To French Freemasonry on both sides of the Atlantic it must have appeared as if the 'Blazing Star' or 'Star of the Orient' had finally risen over the horizon of Paris. Not surprisingly then, when the young Citizen King took charge of the completion of the Arc de Triomphe, it was proposed that the top of this monument should be decorated with a huge, golden five-pointed star.[77]

Let us see how the 1830 'Revolution' came to be.

After Napoleon's shattering defeat at Waterloo at the hands of the British on 18 June 1815, the emperor 'abdicated' and was exiled for life to the island of St. Helena. France was left with a terrible sense of failure, shame and utter confusion, and, in the chaos that followed, the people were coaxed to agree to the unthinkable – the restoration of the Bourbon monarchy.

In 1814 the Count of Provence, the younger brother of Louis XVI, became the newly restored king of France as Louis XVIII. Ironically, all was back to square one for the Republicans and the *Bonapartists*. But there was really no choice in this matter. A new Republic at that time would have been completely out of the question, let alone a 'successor' to Napoleon. It seemed to everyone that a constitutional monarchy *à l'anglaise* ('in the English manner') was the only realistic option. But the wellsprings of the Revolution were far from dry.

Tensions quickly began to develop between those who wanted the French Revolution to be an ongoing process and those others who wanted a return to the Old Regime of totalitarian monarchy. A group of zealous royalists, known as the *Ultras*, started a political movement which became known as the 'White Terror'. It aimed to eradicate all traces of the Revolution and to purge France of those who had supposedly 'betrayed' the monarchy before and after the fall of the Bastille.

Although the king secretly sanctioned the Ultras, publicly, at least at first, he wanted to be seen as a moderate. To this end he took as his prime minister the famous industrialist Élie Decazes, bestowed on him the title of Duke, and relied on the latter's high reputation as a reasonable and just man to win the support of the people. In this indirect manner Louis XVIII hoped to ride out the growing political storm that was brewing between Royalists and Republicans.

Decazes was a prominent Freemason. In 1818, the year before he was appointed prime minister, he had become the Grand Commander of the Supreme Council of the 33rd Degree of the Ancient and Accepted Scottish Rite. It is believed by some Masonic historians that even Louis XVIII was initiated into Freemasonry. This apparently was done in 1775 when he was still the Count of Provence. It is also said that Louis XVIII's brother, the Count of Artois (the future Charles X), was a Freemason and that both belonged to the lodge *Les Trois Frères*.[78]

It seems that Louis XVIII naïvely supposed that Freemasonry in France was still that quaint club frequented by aristocrats and the high bourgeoisie that he had known before the Revolution. But, of course, he was much mistaken. At first, with the influence of Decazes at court, everyone had hoped that the king would slowly be swayed towards a British-style parliamentary monarchy. But any chance of this happening was completely shattered on 13 February 1821 when a Republican fanatic, Louis Pierre Louvel, shot dead the young Duke of Berry, Charles Ferdinand d'Artois, who was the king's nephew.

The Duke of Berry had been the only hope of keeping the Bourbon dynasty going indefinitely, for it was well known that Louis XVIII had no children and that his brother was well past the age of producing more.[79] The assassin and, more specifically, those behind him, had figured that by eliminating the Duke of Berry they would, in effect, cut off the Bourbon bloodline to the throne of France. However, there was something that the assassins could not have known which ended up foiling their ingenious plot. The Duke of Berry's wife, the beautiful and intelligent Marie Caroline de Bourbon-Sicile, was pregnant. A few months later she bore a son, *l'enfant miracle* (the 'miracle child'), who was named Henry.

The assassination of the Duke of Berry gave the Ultras the excuse they wanted to start a witch-hunt against all anti-royalists. Louis XVIII now showed his true colors by allowing the Ultras a free hand in the affair. Louis dismissed the prime minister, Élie Decazes, who was suspected of being a Republican and Bonapartist. He was replaced by the Count of Villèle, a zealous royalist and Ultra ringleader of the worst sort.

Decazes's dismissal much alarmed the Republicans who now began to suspect strongly that Louis XVIII was about to restore the Old Regime, and plots began to be hatched against the king. Because Decazes and many of his supporters were Freemasons, the Ultras suspected that the lodges were behind these plots. Ironically, many Freemasons including Decazes were actually loyal to the king, but it is equally true that Masonic lodges became the cover for secret political gatherings and, as was clearly the case during the 1789 Revolution, an ideal breeding ground for radicals working against the monarchy.

By December 1821 members of an extremist secret society called the *Charbonnerie* (the 'charcoal burners'), whose aim was to launch an armed rebellion against the king, began to infiltrate Masonic lodges in Paris. The Charbonnerie had direct links to the Italian *Carbonari*, an ultra-radical, anti-clerical and anti-royalist group which, since the early 1820s, had been behind many armed uprisings against the joint papal and Austrian-Habsburg regime in Italy.

Much like the Freemasons, the Carbonari selected their members and had initiation ceremonies. These took place not in lodges but in *ventes*, an Italian word that means 'twenty'; each was limited to 20 members so as not to attract the attention of the police. The Carbonari's origins can be traced to the year 1812, and they were almost certainly a militant offshoot of the Masonic *Grande Oriente d'Italia* which, at that time, was headed by Joachim Murat, the king of Naples and brother-in-law of Napoleon.[80]

Indeed, Italian Freemasonry had flourished after the Napoleonic conquest of Italy, and by 1820 the Carbonari and the Freemasons in Italy formed a huge network of lodges and *ventes* that provided ideal meeting grounds as well as an effective system of secret communication for radical political groups plotting to liberate Italy from the detested Austrians.

The Carbonari, who symbolized the driving force behind Italy's independence movement, certainly did not hide the fact that they were staunch Bonapartists and, as such, opponents of all monarchies as well as enemies of the Catholic Church. In September 1821, after the death of Napoleon, they took to the streets causing serious unrest which forced Pope Pius VII to condemn them as well as Freemasons in general.[81] The days of burning at the stake were over, but in 1821 the Austrian police launched a massive operation in Italy to purge all radical elements from Masonic lodges and the *ventes* of the Carbonari. There were hundreds of arrests and many Masons and Carbonari were imprisoned. Others were deported or escaped into France, where they quickly began to infiltrate the Masonic lodges.

The 1822 Charbonnerie uprising in France immediately brought Masonic lodges there under intense scrutiny. To make things worse, it was also suspected by the Ultras that the notorious Marquis de Lafayette was the leader of the Charbonnerie. Lafayette was seen on both sides of the Atlantic as a great republican hero, and his reputation had become almost legendary among Freemasons. But even though Lafayette was staunch republican and also a very active Freemason, he was by no means a radical, and at heart almost certainly had favoured a constitutional monarchy rather than the chaotic 'Republic' he had witnessed first-hand in France after the 1789 Revolution. At any rate, whether Lafayette was sympathetic to the Charbonnerie or not became an academic issue, for the Charbonnerie was very poorly organized in France and heavily infiltrated by royalist spies. It was soon disbanded after the police arrested the Charbonnerie plotters *en masse* and also many Freemasons in the confusion that followed.

A series of death sentences were immediately passed. Among those executed were the famous 'four sergeants of La Rochelle', two of whom were found to be Freemasons belonging to the Egyptian *Rite of Memphis-Misraim*. According to the Masonic author Jean-André Faucher, the insurrection of 1821–22 was, indeed, largely blamed on the new Masonic *Rite of Memphis* and also the *Rite of Misraim*, both of which were believed to have originated in Italy in the early 1800s.[82] To make matters worse, Élie Decazes, the ex-prime minister, had become a member of the Rite of Misraim, as well as many other notable figures on the other side of the Channel in England who supported Decazes, such as the Duke of Leicester and the Duke of Sussex.[83]

In that troubled year of 1822 there were no less than 22 Misraim lodges in Paris plus about a dozen more elsewhere in France, mostly in Lyons and Metz. The pseudo-Egyptian character of the rites that were practiced in those lodges is evident in lodge names. For example there was one in Metz called *Heliopolis Reborn*, another in Lyons called *Memphis*, and yet another in Montauban called *The Flooding Nile*.[84]

The second revolution

It was the Rite of Misraim which, in 1822, was principally accused of harboring the Carbonari. In consequence it was banned in 1823. In the midst of these confusing and turbulent events Louis XVIII died in September 1824 leaving no offspring to take his place. He was succeeded by his brother, the Count of Artois, crowned as Charles X, who was now approaching his 70th year.

Like most aristocrats who had fled the 1789 Revolution, Charles had lived in exile until 1814, and this bitter and humiliating experience made him determined to restore the Old Regime with the divine right of kingship and also the full authority of the Catholic Church. At his coronation, Charles insisted that he should be anointed in accordance with the ancient rituals of kingship at Reims Cathedral with the few drops of sacred oil that had been saved when the *Saint Ampoule* had been smashed during the Reign of Terror of 1793–4.

Once crowned, Charles X became the leader of the Ultras and the Catholic revival began to gather pace, causing outrage among those who had supported the Revolution. Many anti-clericals as well as Republicans now joined Masonic lodges not for spiritual enlightenment but for political shelter. Charles X, who was a devout Catholic himself, began to revive the dreaded 'Society of Jesus', the Jesuits, and soon it was rumored that he had joined the order and might hand over power to them.

Political unrest reached boiling point in March 1830, when, in a naïve move to appease his critics, the king dissolved the *Chambre des Députés* and called a general election which he hoped the Ultras would win. The vote, however, went against the Ultras and Charles X now confronted two unsavory options: he could either agree to a constitutional monarchy or scoop the power already in his hands with a coup d'état by eradicating the Bonapartists and Republicans in his government. He unwisely opted for the latter, and by July 1830 the barricades were up again in the streets of Paris.

For the second time in less than 50 years a revolution had been unleashed against the Bourbon dynasty.

Lafayette seizes the day

Not unexpectedly, two factions quickly emerged, one made up of pure Republicans the other up of Constitutional Monarchists. Lafayette, that eternal compromiser, at first swayed between the two, even though the Republicans considered him their leader. In his view, however, the best option now was to oust the Bourbons altogether and replace them with a new monarchy who would 'constitutionalise' the Old Regime. He had in mind a young prince, the Duke of Orléans, whose father, Philippe Égalité, had sponsored the 1789 Revolution with his immense wealth and position – for which it eventually beheaded him!

Although Lafayette had been at odds with Philippe Égalité during the 1789 Revolution, he was now in very close contact with his son, Louis-Philippe d'Orléans. Lafayette's plan had the distinct advantage of offering a solution that might be acceptable to both the Republicans and the Constitutional Monarchists, and thus avoid the real risk of a civil war. It remained now to persuade the Republicans, the Bonapartists and, especially, the general population of Paris, that Louis-Philippe d'Orléans was the right man for the job. This, Lafayette achieved with the well-judged use of powerful symbolism – a technique that had so often worked with the rowdy Parisian mob.

In August 1830 Charles X was forced to abdicate. In a desperate bid to keep the Bourbon dynasty on the throne of France, he asked that his grandson, the 'miracle child' of the Duchess of Berry, be accepted as the new king. But both the Republicans and the Constitutional Monarchists rejected the proposal outright. This was the moment when Lafayette and his own candidate, Louis-Philippe d'Orléans, made their move. After three days of bloody street fighting in Paris, the crowds gathered at the Hôtel de Ville and, in a perfectly timed propaganda coup that only high initiates would know how to bring about, Lafayette grabbed a tricolor flag of the Revolution and wrapped it around Louis-Philippe d'Orléans, proclaiming him the 'Citizen King' of France.

Amazingly, the theatrical gesture worked. The Parisian mob cheered and Louis-Philippe won the day. The hard-line Republicans and Bonapartists were furious at having their 'revolution' snatched away from them by such trickery, but there was not much they could do.

Almost immediately King Louis-Philippe I began a series of projects supposed to demonstrate his love and support for Bonaparte and the Revolution. He ordered that the Arc de Triomphe, the construction of which had begun in 1809 but had been shelved ever since, should now be completed. He also ordered the construction of a huge pillar at the Place de la Bastille to commemorate the 1830 Revolution; on top of the pillar, as the reader will recall from Chapter One, was then placed the 'Genie of Paris', a winged youth much resembling the Greek Hermes.[85]

Also at about this time Louis-Philippe ordered that the obelisk brought from the Temple of Luxor in Egypt, and recently arrived in Paris, should now raised in the Place de la Concorde ...

Champollion

In 1822, a year and a half after Napoleon's death, an amazing scientific discovery was made which would not only stun the academic world but would also fulfill a promise that the emperor had made at St. Helena. For when asked why he had invaded Egypt, Napoleon had calmly replied:

I came to draw attention and bring back the interest of Europe to the center of the ancient world.[86]

This was a side of Napoleon that has often been neglected, namely that he was not only a military genius but also an accomplished scholar and a senior member of the *Institut National*. It was Napoleon who had the great forethought of taking the 167 savants to Egypt in 1798, and it was he who founded the first modern scientific institute in Egypt: the *Institut d'Égypte* in Cairo. It was therefore appropriate that his grand dream of restoring cultural interest in ancient Egypt was not fulfilled by a politician but rather by a quiet and studious young man living in the little town of Figeac near Grenoble – a young man who had never traveled out of France, let alone to Egypt.

On 17 September 1822 Jean-François Champollion, coughing and speaking with the weak voice of someone suffering from serious pulmonary problems, announced to a group of scholars at the *Académie des Inscriptions et Belles-Lettres* in Paris that he had an important statement to make regarding the mysterious ancient Egyptian hieroglyphs. Feeling awkward in front of such an illustrious and very skeptical congregation of learned men, Champollion slowly read a paper which he had addressed to the chairman of the *Académie Française*, Monsieur Dacier, and which was simply titled *Lettre à M. Dacier relative à l'alphabet des hiéroglyphes phonétiques*.

It was, in fact, a cultural and scientific bombshell on a scale rarely experienced in the world. For it became obvious to many of those listening to Champollion that day that the young man had solved the biggest mystery of the past: he had cracked the code of the ancient Egyptian hieroglyphic language. Indeed, Champollion's modest *Lettre à M. Dacier* was to mark the most prestigious moment of the *Académie Française* and provided the foundation stone upon which scientific Egyptology would be developed. Many Freemasons present on that day in September 1822 would also have thought it wonderful and most appropriate that this world-changing discovery had been announced in Paris, the city of Isis.

In the 1820s the area of Grenoble and Lyons where the Champollions lived was not only the haunt of Republicans and Bonapartists who opposed the monarchy, but also the hotbed of many innovative Masonic movements, especially those related to the 'Egyptian' type of Freemasonry started at Lyons by Cagliostro.[87] It is known that Champolion and, more especially, his older brother, Jacques-Joseph, were fervent Bonapartists, and so were most of their friends, many of whom were also Freemasons.[88] The question must arise, therefore, whether Champolion himself was not a member of the brotherhood and, more specifically, a member of one of the Egyptian-style lodges? Today some Masonic historians list Champollion as a 'famous Freemason', but there is no documented proof of his involvement.[89]

Champollion and his brother, Jacques-Joseph, had at one time been held under suspicion of political agitation and, in 1816, had even been placed under house arrest at Figeac. It is said that they gained the support of the influential Freemason, Élie Decazes, then the minister of interior, who ordered their release and allowed the two brothers to return to Grenoble in 1817.[90]

Decazes, as we shall recall, was to become Grand Commander of the Supreme Council of the 33rd Degree and one of the first notables to join the Egyptian Masonic Rite of Misraim.[91] Later also the prominent statesman, the Duke of Blacas, became the patron and protector of Champollion.[92] Paradoxically, the Duke of Blacas was a staunch Ultra and a favourite of both Louis XVIII and of Charles X. The duke had served as the French ambassador to the kingdom of Naples since 1815, then the hotspot of 'Egyptian' Misraim Freemasonry. Let us also note that there had been curious exchanges between Champollion and certain well-known adepts of these neo-Egyptian Masonic groups.

Champollion was a rival of Alexandre Lenoir, a staunch Freemason and once the superintendent of the king's buildings before the 1789 Revolution. Lenoir, who was a keen adept of the Scottish Rite,[93] and an 'initiate of the cult of Isis',[94] was also the publisher of *La Nouvelle Explication des Hiéroglyphes* in 1808. When Champollion began his own work on the Egyptian hieroglyphs he had condescendingly called Lenoir *un oison* ('a little goose') and stated that he only respected the older man because he was 'in the good books' of Empress Joséphine.[95] In 1814 Lenoir had published a book entitled *La Franc-Maçonnerie rendue à sa véritable origine* ('Freemasonry brought back to its true origins'), in which he linked the origins of the brotherhood to the 'cult of Isis', which may explain why Lenoir, as Champollion himself had dryly noted, was highly regarded by Joséphine.

There is, too, Champollion's relationship with an Italian-Greek beauty from Livorno, Angelica Palli, with whom Champollion had fallen desperately in love during a research trip to Italy in 1826. Livorno, which is on the Mediterranean coast near Pisa, had been the principal port of the Medici of Florence who, as we saw in Chapter Eight, played a great part in the Hermetic Renaissance. Angelica Palli, a poetess and writer, was very conversant with Hermetic and Neo-Platonic literature. Her evocative name (literally 'angel of the temples'), must have much stirred the fertile imagination of Champollion, who was to write of her to his friend, the Abbé Gazerra: 'I thank the great Ammon-Ra for meeting her.' She in return commented with delight on his 'philosophy' which she found to be imbued with 'Egyptian doctrines, fertile source from which drew Plato and … Pythagoras.'[96]

Many years later Angelica Palli became an active supporter of the famous Italian revolutionary, Giuseppe Manzini, a staunch Freemason who was head of the Italian Supreme Council of the 33rd Degree. Manzini was a close friend and colleague of the popular hero, Giuseppe Garibaldi, who was to become the first Grand Master of the Egyptian Masonic Rite of Memphis-Misraim.[97] There was, too, a curious connection between the city of Livorna, where Palli and Champollion had met, and a rather elusive Masonic society called the *Société Secrète Égyptienne*. It is thought that one of the founders of this society was Mathieu de Lesseps, father of the famous engineer, Ferdinand de Lesseps, who built the Suez Canal in Egypt.[98] The story goes that in 1818 the Austrian police raided a Masonic lodge in Venice. Amongst the confiscated documents was one revealing the existence of the secret society and implicating as one of its members no less a figure than Egypt's first modern ruler, Khedive Muhammad Ali.[99]

Mathieu de Lesseps was a staunch Bonapartist and also a keen adept of the Egyptian Rite of Freemasonry.[100] He was a very close friend of the khedive, and from 1803 to 1806 had been France's commercial attaché in Egypt, after which he had served as French consul in the city of Livorna.[101] We shall encounter the de Lesseps family again in the next chapter in connection with the Statue of Liberty that stands in New York Harbor. Meanwhile,

THE MASTER GAME

whether all this had any influence or bearing on Champollion whilst he was in Livorno is not clear, but it may explain his mindset as he began to plan there his first and only trip to Egypt …

'If you go to Thebes do send me a little obelisk …'

In Chapter One we saw that three years before his abdication in 1830, Charles X had commissioned the artist François-Édouard Picot to decorate the ceiling of his personal museum at the Louvre with an ancient Egyptian motif centred upon the goddess Isis.[102] The reader will recall that Picot had been a student of the radical revolutionary and Bonapartist Jacques-Louis David who, along with Robespierre, had masterminded the various celebrations in Paris of the goddess Reason and the Supreme Being and, more especially, the celebrations at the Bastille in August 1793 when a statue of Isis was displayed to the Parisian crowds. Bearing this in mind, the 'Isis' featuring on the large-format ceiling painting by Picot can be seen immediately to have been modelled on David's statue of 'Isis of the Bastille'. Indeed the painting itself contains independent confirmation of this connection – for seen flying above 'Isis', is the so-called *Genie of the Arts*, a naked youth with golden wings much resembling the Greek god Hermes. The 'genie' holds a torch in one hand in order to illuminate the landscape below for the benefit of the 'goddess Athena', at whose feet can be seen an owl, the symbol of wisdom acquired through initiation.

There is little doubt that the landscape beneath Isis in the painting is to be imagined not in Egypt but in Paris and, more precisely, at the Bastille – for the give-away is the 'genie' which, today, can actually be seen 'flying' over the Place de la Bastille. Where? It stands at the top of the huge pillar which was commissioned for the spot by the Citizen King Louis-Philippe I in 1830, three years after Picot completed the painting.

And there is one other point. In Picot's painting the goddess Isis is gazing at a tall obelisk in the distance. Could this obelisk be the *actual obelisk from Luxor* raised at the Place de la Concorde by Louis-Philippe I? Is the Picot painting suggesting some sort of connection or link between the city of Paris and the city of Luxor?

In 1828, a few months after Picot had completed the painting for Charles X, the latter offered to sponsor Champollion to undertake a feasibility study for bringing an obelisk from Egypt to Paris. The obelisk in question had been donated to France by Khedive Muhammad Ali.[103] Charles X cultivated a keen interest in ancient Egypt and, in 1828, had just inaugurated the Egyptian antiquities museum in the south wing of the Louvre.

In July that year Champollion headed a small team of scientists and artists, including the French archaeologist Charles Lenormant and the architect Antoine Bibent, and set sail from the port of Toulon towards Egypt. Champollion and his 'Argonauts' as he called his team, reached Alexandria on 18 August 1828 where, barely three decades earlier, Bonaparte had landed with his troops. Champollion was received by the French consul, Bernardino Drovetti, and a friendship quickly developed between the two.

Drovetti was from southern Italy, and since 1818 had also been the 'Great Copt' of the Egyptian Masonic lodges in Alexandria.[104] He had been appointed French consul in 1821, and had earlier served as assistant to Mathieu de Lesseps. And like de Lesseps before him, Drovetti had become a close friend of Khedive Muhammad Ali. This privileged connection gave Drovetti a rather free hand in dealing with ancient Egyptian relics, and he soon amassed a huge personal fortune. His British counterpart and rival was Henry Salt, the British consul in Alexandria, who, along with Giovanni Battista Belzoni,[105] the flamboyant Italian Freemason and Egyptologist, also traded in antiquities which he sold to private collectors and to the British Museum.

Champollion was totally enchanted by Egypt. He was to write of this ancient civilization:

> We in Europe are but Lilliputians, and no other ancient or modern people has developed the art of architecture on a scale so sublime, so huge, so grandiose as did the Egyptians ... I repeat yet again ... ancient Egypt taught the arts to Greece, the latter developed them into a more sublime form but without Egypt, Greece would probably not have become the home of the arts.[106]

So fascinated was Champollion with Egypt that he even entertained the notion that he had been somehow physically connected to it since his birth: 'It seems to me that I was born here', he wrote to his brother whom he had nicknamed *Ammon*, 'and the Europeans here think I look very much like a Copte'.[107]

During his 18-month visit to Egypt, Champollion manage to get an agreement with Muhammad Ali that he would take to Paris one of the two obelisks that stood outside the Temple of Luxor. The khedive would have been quite happy to let Champollion take both obelisks, but it seemed that one was all that the French engineers could cope with. The job of bringing the ancient monolith to France proved to be no easy task. As it weighed an estimated 230 metric tons and was 23 meters tall, there was some question

THE MASTER GAME

at first of slicing it into several manageable pieces, but Champollion would not have it, claiming that it would be a 'sacrilege'.[108]

On his way back to France, Champollion made the acquaintance of a young naval engineer called Raymond de Verninac Saint-Maur who would later receive the command of the *Luxor*, the special ship that was built to carry the obelisk down the Nile and across the Mediterranean. Verninac worked under the authority of the French minister of the navy, the Baron of Haussez, who much disliked Champollion on account of a feud he had with him in Grenoble, when Haussez had been the chief of police there. Not unexpectedly, Haussez pushed Champollion aside and took all the credit for securing the obelisk from the khedive of Egypt. Haussez was to write in his memoirs:

> As soon as it was known in the learned world how I dreamt of enriching France with a monument that only Rome owned, I was put in charge to try and obtain two obelisks much more precious ... than those of Alexandria [which ended up in London and New York], and also much more difficult to transport by reason of their location at Luxor.[109]

The operation was to take six years and Haussez was not to see it through. Hardly a year after he had come to office as minister of the navy, he was sacked during the chaos that followed the July Revolution of 1830. The responsibility for the project then passed to the distinguished Baron Taylor, the son of a naturalised Englishman. Taylor was a patron of the arts, and was himself an accomplished author. A friend of the geographer and archaeologist Jomard, Taylor had a keen interest in ancient Egypt and diligently took over where Haussez had left off. Supplied with letters of recommendation from the king, and a generous budget of 100,000 francs, he went to Egypt himself to meet the khedive and take charge of the shipping operation. Taylor quickly assigned the task of the engineering works to Jean-Baptiste Apollinaire Lebas, a stocky and rather short man whose small stature was to be the subject of much ridicule among the Egyptians, who could not believe that such a squat individual was given the mission of moving so tall an obelisk all the way to France.

It took from April to July 1831 for Lebas to get the purpose-built ship, the *Luxor*, from Toulon to Upper Egypt. It was summer, the heat at Luxor was insufferable – over 100 °F in the shade – and the whole affair was besieged by untold problems, including a terrible cholera epidemic. But at the end, Lebas proved to be the right man for the job. By October he had managed to have the obelisk lowered safely and in one piece to the sand.

Two further months followed while it was dragged the few hundred meters to the shore of the Nile and finally hoisted onboard the *Luxor*. Then Lebas had to wait till July of the next year for the inundation of the Nile in order to be able to sail downstream to Alexandria. After a delay of three months at Alexandria, the *Luxor* finally crossed the Mediterranean and arrived at the French port of Toulon on 11 May 1833. From there it was brought by river to Paris where it waited at the docks for three more years.

It was Louis-Philippe I who had personally long ago decided that the obelisk should be raised on the axis of Paris in the centre of the Place de la Concorde, immediately west of the Tuileries Garden between the Louvre and the Arc de Triomphe.[110] Now, at last, a date was set for raising the obelisk. On 25 October 1836, a crowd of 200,000 people gathered at the Place de la Concorde to witness the event – more than had assembled for the beheading of Louis XVI on the same spot 43 years earlier. Lebas personally supervised the difficult lifting operations which, to everybody's admiration and delight, went without any hitches. Amid cheers of jubilation and joy, Paris at long last had its very own solar talisman from ancient Egypt adorning its skyline. France now could fittingly claim for its capital the name of the *Cité de la Lumière* (the 'City of Light') – or should we say the 'City of the Sun'?

The beautiful obelisk standing in the Place de la Concorde was, and still is by virtue of its great antiquity, the oldest monument of Paris. It witnessed the story of Egypt from about 1500 BC and now in Paris it was to see the passing of the French monarchy and the creation of the Second Republic in 1848; the rise of the Second Empire under Napoleon III, the grandson of Napoleon Bonaparte, and its fall in 1871; the formation of the Third Republic under the 'Masonic' government of Léon Gambetta;[111] the First World War; and the Second World War; and finally, in 1958, the present Fifth Republic founded by General Charles de Gaulle.

But it was not until 1984 that it would be joined in Paris by a modern structure evoking the Great Pyramid of Giza …

Mitterrand's 'Great Works'

In 1981 François Mitterrand, then president of France, launched the so-called *Grands Travaux*, the 'Great Works', which involved the construction of a series of impressive architectural projects to the glory and culture of France. In eight years would come the bicentennial of the 1789 Revolution, and huge celebrations were being planned by Mitterrand who, with a zeal reminiscent of Louis XIV, wanted to furnish this event with great national monuments. Either intentionally or by coincidence the two monuments in which Mitterrand took great personal interest evoked ancient Egypt and the Masonic Supreme Being or 'Great Architect of the Universe'. These choices earned Mitterrand titles like *Sphinx, Dieu* ('God') and *Roi Soleil* ('Sun King') in France's satirical press.

Although François Mitterrand was not a Freemason,[112] he was nonetheless extremely sympathetic to the lodges – so much so that many in France remain convinced to this day that he was a clandestine Mason. Much has been made in recent years of the fact that Guy Penne, one of Mitterrand's closest political advisers, was a member of the Supreme Council of the *Grand Orient de France*.[113] There is also the scandal involving Mitterrand's son, Jean-Christophe, who, in 1982, joined the office of Penne and in 1986 took over Penne's job. Jean-Christophe was exposed by the French press for his embroilment in the so-called *Falcone Affair* involving shady arms deals in West Africa which also implicated some senior African politicians who were members of Masonic lodges.[114]

The two projects that most interested President Mitterrand were those that were to be readied for the bicentennial celebrations planned for July 1989. They involved the *Grand Louvre* project, which would ultimately feature a huge glass Pyramid, and the *Grande Arche de la Fraternité* project at La Défense on the extreme western end of the Champs-Élysées. Under the personal directive of Mitterrand, two institutions, provided with special budgets set up under the Ministry of Finance, were created to administer these projects, one being the EPGL, *l'Établissement public du Grand Louvre* and the other being the EPAD, *l'Établissement public pour l'aménagement de la région de la Défense*. Two renowned architects were then personally selected by Mitterrand: Ieoh Ming Pei, the celebrated Chinese-born American architect, for the Louvre,[115] and Johan-Otto Von Spreckelsen, a Danish architect for the Grande Arche.[116]

President Mitterrand was so keen to have I. M. Pei for the Louvre that he decided to bypass the normal requirements for an international tender and simply offered him the design commission.[117] According to Pei these were the circumstances:

> In July 1981, Paul Guimard asked to meet with me at the French Embassy in London ... He told me that President Mitterrand wanted me to come to Paris ... Only the President, Paul Guimard and myself were present at this meeting which took place on December 11, 1981 ...[118]

Pei claimed that at this first meeting with Mitterrand there was no specific mention of the Louvre Pyramid, and the president only spoke of 'the importance of architecture in French national life.'[119] It was later, in 1983, that Mitterrand sent his advisor, Émile Biasini, to New York with instructions to contract I. M. Pei directly for this project.[120] When asked by a journalist why a pyramid was chosen for the Louvre which was a classical baroque design, Pei replied:

> Architecture is geometry – it's geometry. The Louvre is also geometry. It's slightly tilted, but it's geometry ... The French opposed it at first, but never President Mitterrand. He never faltered in backing my idea ...[121]

I. M. Pei insists that he borrowed the idea for a pyramid from 'a garden trellis design of Le Nôtre, who laid out the vast gardens at Versailles for Louis XIV and also the gardens of the Tuilleries.'[122] Perhaps so. Yet the slope which Pei finally chose for his pyramid was 50.71°, only about a degree different from the slope of the Great Pyramid of Giza in Egypt. Was the similarity deliberate? We shall perhaps never know. But here is how Pei's senior architect, Yann Weymouth, replied when asked this question:

> Working with models and perspectives we studied form and site. We shaped the central skylight, studying it from ground level in perspectives and models. With a perfect equilateral triangle as side, the 54.74° slope felt aggressive, but as the slope approached 45° the form 'melted'. The 50.71° finally chosen is close to the slope of the Great Pyramid of Giza, so it is possible we were repeating studies made by the IVth Dynasty Egyptians.[123]

From the above statement it is clear that both Pei and Weymouth must in fact have studied the evolution of the fourth dynasty pyramids in Egypt with some care. According to Egyptologists the first true pyramids were those of Pharaohs Sneferu and, his celebrated son, Cheops (Khufu) – and it is a well-known fact that their three pyramids (two at Dahshur plus the Great Pyramid at Giza) had slopes starting near 54° (South Pyramid at Dahshur), then changed to 45° (North Pyramid at Dahshur) and finally settled for 51.85° (Great Pyramid at Giza)!

Given the historical importance of the project, the location of the site and the fact that it was to be a symbol for the bicentennial of the Revolution, Pei must also have been aware that several pyramid projects had been proposed for Paris in the past – such as those of Étienne-Louis Boullée and Claude-Nicolas Ledoux, mentioned at the start of this chapter. He should also have known that during the reign of Louis XIV a pyramid to the glory of the Sun King had been proposed for the Cour Carrée of the Louvre by the architect François Dubois,[124] and also that a weird baroque pyramid with a statue of Napoleon on its top had been designed by the architect Louis-Ernest L'heureux to stand precisely where Pei eventually placed his glass Pyramid.[125]

The *Grande Arche de la Fraternité* project, unlike Pei's, was the subject of an international tender, but the final decision was nonetheless taken by Mitterrand. Here is how the architect Von Spreckelsen described his design:

> An open cube, a window open to the world ... with a gaze towards the future. It is a modern Arc de Triomphe, to the glory of the triumph of humanity; it is a symbol of hope that in the future people may meet freely ...[126]

The Grande Arche is indeed a nearly perfect cubical structure 110 meters tall by 112 meters deep with a base that is just over one hectare in area. It is estimated that the Cathedral of Notre Dame would fit quite well in the void of the arch. In the official guide it is described as a monument that 'evokes the sense of the sacred ... which compares to the Egyptian pyramids.'[127] On the rooftop the artist Jean-Pierre Raynaud created a zodiac to inspire 'a real dialogue with the celestial vault, which is the true natural architecture',[128] and one might add on his behalf that his design was a sort of 'as above so below' concept.

On the top floor of the Grande Arche is the headquarters of the *Fondation l'Arche de la Fraternité*, the 'Foundation of the Arch of the Brotherhood', which includes Claude Cheysson, a former minister of foreign affairs, as a past president. The foundation dates from the 1970s when it was established as a human rights organisation headed by Edgar Faure, formerly president of France in the 1950s. When in the early 1980s President Mitterrand began to make it known that he wanted the Grande Arche monument to be a symbol of 'Fraternity and Liberty', Edgar Faure proposed to him that the foundation's headquarters in Paris should be moved to the Grande Arche building at La Défense.[129]

Mysteries of the axis

The *Grande Arche* project was completed on time for the bicentennial of the Revolution and was inaugurated with much fanfare by President Mitterrand on 14 July 1989. The final result is stunning. The Grande Arche can be seen from miles away, and, after the Eiffel Tower, it is unquestionably the most imposing landmark of Paris. Jean-Claude Garcias, who wrote the text for the official guidebook of the Grande Arche, described it as *the* monument of the 1980s that inspires the collective mind with the 'instinct of immortality'.[130] Moreover Garcias saw the Grande Arche not as a project that came out fully formed 'from the brain of its architect', but rather as 'the end product to a long and sinuous urban axis which was begun in the 17th century and which', he says, 'can be schematised as follows':

> Born in the open court of the Louvre, but deviated six degrees towards the north during the run through the Tuilleries, the great east-west axis of Paris has its origins in the avenue of trees planted by Le Nôtre at the beginning of the reign of Louis XIV, who opened the perspective towards the setting sun … It was followed by the development of the present Place de la Concorde under Louis XV, then the levelling of the slope on which today stands the Arc de Triomphe and the avenue of the Champs-Élysées. At the end of the Old Regime the engineer Perronet built the first stone bridge at Neuilly, taking the axis all the way to the hill of Chantecoq, our present area of La Défense …[131]

The Grande Arche, therefore, much appears to be the culmination an ongoing chain of ideas, an occult plan one might even venture to say, which began with the Sun King Louis XIV and ended with President François Mitterrand – who was jokingly referred to by the French as *Le Roi Soleil* because of the ambition of his *Grands Projets* scheme. Let us note in passing here that Mitterrand had also one more *Grand Projet* in store for La Défense: a skyscraper 400 meters tall called *La Tour Sans Fin*. This monster of a building was designed by the architect Jean Nouvel,[132] and, unlike most skyscrapers, was to feature varying levels of transparency acting as 'sky filters', such that at the top it would become fully transparent and disappear into the clouds.[133] What was intended, here, was an allusion to the biblical 'Tower of Babel', a universal talisman of the first magnitude that is also a popular Freemasonic pictogram often held to be a symbol for the origins of the Craft.[134] The *Tour Sans Fin*, however, was eventually scrapped due to lack of funds and the immense impracticality of the idea.[135]

Unquestionably, the Grande Arche occupies the place of honour on the western extremity of the axis of Paris. It is the final 'sunset' of a great plan whose 'sunrise', as we have seen, was the 'miraculous birth' of the Sun King Louis XIV at the Louvre – but whose *first sunrise*, we suggest, took place long ago and far away in ancient Egypt. The Grande Arche thus becomes an integral part of a monumental array of talismans strung out along the axis of Paris, notably the Arc de Triomphe at the Place de l'Étoile and the Luxor Obelisk at the Place de la Concorde. The axis then enters the precinct of the Tuileries Garden to make it way to the Louvre. When the axis is traced eastwards towards the Louvre, the reader will recall from Chapter Seventeen that it passes first through the bronze equestrian statue of Louis XIV represented as 'Alexander the Great', placed to the south of Pei's glass Pyramid. East again and we find that the axis transects the south wing of the Louvre and then enters the private apartments of Anne of Austria, Louis XIV's mother – the very place where the 'Capetian miracle' of Louis XIV's conception took place in December 1637.

Interestingly, the full effect of the ensemble of these 'Masonic' and 'Egyptian' monuments and, more specifically, of their alignments, was not to be unveiled on the bicentennial day of 14 July 1989, but exactly a year later when the French composer Jean Michel Jarre was commissioned to organise a special concert at the Place de la Grande Arche de la Défense for 14 July 1990. Why and how Jarre was chosen for this event is not clear, but it was to prove an amazing extravaganza of sound, light and fireworks the likes of which Paris had never seen before, not even during the Revolution when Jean-Jacques David and Robespierre had inaugurated the era of the Supreme Being near the Louvre.

Beginning at dusk on 14 July 1990, an estimated two million people filled the Champs-Élysées as if coming to attend some weird Hermetic Mass. On that strange night all the relevant monuments on the Historical Axis – Grande Arche, the Arc de Triomphe, the Luxor Obelisk and, of course, the Louvre Pyramid – were lit up as if to reveal a magical landscape for Paris.

The orchestra of Jean Michel Jarre, with the chorus wearing long, flowing white robes giving them a surreal appearance, were positioned at the foot of the Grande Arche inside a huge, makeshift metal-framed pyramid that was lit up with laser lights.

The lasers projected images onto the façades of adjacent skyscrapers. Many of these images were reminiscent of Hermetic-Masonic symbols, especially a set of large eyes projected on the sides of the Pyramid.

Eight years later, in May 1998, Jarre would be commissioned to perform a similar show, this time involving the Great Pyramid of Giza itself. While the show took place at Giza, President Hosni Mubarak of Egypt and other officials of his government attended a special ceremony at the Place de la Concorde in Paris at which a golden capstone was placed on top of the Luxor Obelisk.[136] During this ceremony Egypt's minister of culture, Dr. Farouk Hosni, announced that a golden capstone would also be placed on top of the Great Pyramid of

Giza at midnight on 31 December 1999 as a symbol for the new millennium. Weeks later Jarre was officially commissioned to organise that event.

Robert Bauval's Eureka afternoon (1)

On an afternoon in the early spring of 1992, Robert Bauval happened to be at the Louvre Museum bookshop and bought a copy of an archaeological journal containing a major pictorial on the city of Luxor. The journal was *Dossiers: Histoire et Archéologie*,[137] and the article in question was the work of a number of different authorities including Dr. Mohamad El-Saghir, director of antiquities at the Luxor Museum, and William J. Murnane and Lany D. Bell of the University of Chicago Epigraphic Survey.

Earlier that same day Bauval had also visited the Grande Arche at La Défense, and there, on the top floor, was an exhibition room featuring a superb aerial photograph of the city of Paris showing the whole length of the Historical Axis from the Bastille in the east all the way to the district of La Défense in the west. The photograph was several feet long, and showed every detail clearly: the distinctive crab-shaped layout of the Louvre, the Tuilleries Garden (even individual trees were visible), the Place de la Concorde and the Luxor Obelisk, the Arc de Triomphe, all the skyscrapers at La Défense and, of course, the Grande Arche. A security officer was standing nearby, and with his permission Bauval videoed the impressive aerial view, then took section shots of it with his still camera. A scale model of the axis of Paris, showing the main monuments and buildings, was also part of the exhibition so Bauval photographed and filmed this as well.

Bauval then left the La Defence area and travelled underground by Metro directly to the Louvre. All the way he pondered on the aerial photograph and scale model of the axis of Paris, refreshing his memory of the details by reviewing the footage he had shot with his video camera. Seeing the city as a whole from the air in this way, and scaled down in a three-dimensional model, gave a very special perspective – a high vantage point from which the metropolis seemed to reveal itself like some giant jigsaw puzzle that had been put together over the centuries.

Though one could be forgiven for not noticing it at all at ground level, what particularly stood out in the aerial view was the curious way that the axis of Paris slightly changed direction as it emerged from the Louvre and headed west. It seemed, on face value, that this had been done to have the Tuilleries Garden parallel to the course of the River Seine. But even so, it was clear that the axis could have been set true again as it emerged from the Tuilleries Garden into the Place de la Concorde. Here the Seine actually

THE MASTER GAME

took a slight turn to the south, whereas the axis was turned slightly in the opposite direction towards the north.

This curious anomaly bothered the structural engineer in Robert Bauval. He wanted to think that the deviation of the axis of Paris had been due to a practical problem, but somehow this explanation did not quite suffice in so ambitious a scheme where careful, coordinated deliberation was the obvious keynote throughout. One could see that deliberation, for example in the distances between the principal symbolic monuments placed along the axis and in the relative sizes of the three 'arches'. As the guide books like to point out:

> Curiously the distance between them doubles each time: 1 km from the Carrousel triumphal arch to the Concorde's Obelisk, 2 km from the Obelisk to the Arc de Triomphe at the top of the Champs-Élysées, and 4 km from there to the Grand Arche. Even more curiously, the size of the arches also doubles at each stage.[138]

So since everything else seemed to have been planned to produce a special symbolic effect wasn't it likely that the deviation of the axis was also part of the symbolic scheme?

Robert Bauval's Eureka afternoon (2)

As Bauval stepped out of the Metro station at the Louvre he decided on impulse to take a stroll along the nearby parts of the axis of Paris before visiting the museum. The aerial view of the axis, and the problems that it raised, were still vivid in his mind.

He first walked to the Luxor Obelisk at the Place de la Concorde, and there, placing himself with his back to the west face of the Luxor Obelisk, looked directly up the Champs-Élysées and along the axis of Paris. It shot straight as an arrow westward, past the Arc de Triomphe and all the way to Grande Arche six kilometers away.

He next placed himself on the east side of the Luxor Obelisk and looked back eastwards towards the Louvre. The axis shot straight along the centerline of the Tuilleries Garden and all the way to the Arc du Carrousel outside the Louvre's open court. But it was at this point that the troubling 'deviation' occurred for the eastwards extension of the axis did not merge, as one would have expected, with the central axis of the Louvre but instead crossed it and carried on along the Louvre's south wing.

Bauval now walked to the Arc du Carrousel, found the exact spot where the axis changed direction, and looked again east towards the Louvre. As he had thought, the axis of Paris did not extend through the glass Pyramid and the centerline of the Louvre, but instead ran to the right (south) of the Pyramid and neatly through the imposing bronze equestrian statue of Louis XIV in the style of Alexander the Great. Beyond the statue Bauval could see that the axis intersected with the Louvre at the second window of the façade of the Pavillon Sully. The window, by luck, was open. So Bauval decided to go there, figuring that he would be able to get a good shot with his camera of the whole axis of Paris looking west.

To reach the window, Bauval had to go to the first floor of the Pavillon Sully and pass through a series of rooms in which where displayed works from the Louvre's extensive Greek and Egyptian collections. On the ceiling of one of these rooms – number 30 on the guide map – was the mysterious painting by Picot that we described in Chapter One. Bauval had seen this painting before, of course, and remembered the curious scene of the Hermes-like 'Genie of Paris' witnessing the 'unveiling of Isis' to reveal an obelisk and pyramids in the distance. Now, with the Luxor Obelisk and Louvre Pyramid fresh in his memory, he could not help noticing how the obelisk and the pyramids in Picot's painting also appeared to be aligned in a perspective towards the distant horizon, just like those on the axis of Paris.

Realising that he was standing not far from where the axis of Paris crossed the Louvre, Bauval was startled by this strange coincidence but shrugged off the thought and made his way to the open window. From there, as he had hoped, he had a spectacular view westward along the axis of Paris, past the Luxor Obelisk, past the Arc de Triomphe and all the way to the distant Grande Arche. Now that he was attuned to it, the deviation of the axis was also quite unmissable. Bauval snapped a few photographs then made his way to the bookshop in the lower floor of the museum where, as noted earlier, he purchased an archaeological journal containing a detailed pictorial of the city of Luxor in Upper Egypt.

Robert Bauval's Eureka afternoon (3)

After browsing in the bookshop Bauval left the Louvre by the exit under the glass Pyramid. Outside in the courtyard, in bright sunshine, he found a seat and began to leaf through the pages of the journal he had just bought, *Dossiers: Histoire et Archéologie*. One of its double-page spreads featured a superb colour photograph of the Luxor temple from the air. The photograph was taken looking west towards the Nile with the temple sprawling from left to right (i.e. from south to north), and thus parallel to the course of the Nile. A single obelisk stood conspicuously in front of the temple's entrance on the north side. Next to it Bauval could clearly make out the empty plinth where once had stood the second obelisk that was now in Paris – and, weirdly, within his sight from where he now sat! How strange to think that these two distant points on the earth's surface, one in front of the Luxor temple in Thebes and the other in front of the Louvre Palace in Paris, had been brought together, as it were, by this ancient pair of solar talismans.

Bauval looked more closely at the photograph. Seen from this high altitude, it was funny how the crab-shaped outline of the Luxor temple and the way it was positioned along the River Nile, could easily be mistaken for the Louvre's same crab-like shape and the way that it, too, was positioned along the River Seine. With a mounting sense of excitement Bauval turned the pages of the journal and quickly found what he hoped it would contain – a second aerial photograph taken from much higher up that showed the whole layout of the city of Luxor, from the Temple of Luxor in the south to the Temple of Karnak in the north.

Now this was really strange!

Although he knew that he was looking at an aerial photograph of Karnak-Luxor, Bauval was overtaken by a powerful sense of visual *déjà vue*. He had seen the very same 'image' with the very same features just a short while before, but not in a photograph of Luxor. He played back the video film he had just taken at the Grande Arche – the video film of the aerial-view of Paris. Looking at it, and then again at the aerial photograph of Luxor in the archaeological journal, it was obvious that there were remarkable similarities between the layout of Paris from the Louvre to La Défense and the layout of the sacred Egyptian city from the Luxor Temple to Karnak!

The positioning and provenance of the obelisks were part of the puzzle. But even more stunning was the way that the axis of Paris and the axis of Luxor both *changed direction* at roughly the same place as they headed one towards La Défense, and the other towards Karnak. Bauval knew, however, that in Egypt, the Nile ran from south-north and that the Luxor temple faced north; whereas in Paris the Seine was directed east to west and the Louvre 'temple' faced west. Champollion and Lebas would have been acutely aware of these orientations. If they had really been participants in some mysterious game of symbolism, therefore, then surely they would have taken them into account?

An observation by the historian Jean Vidal in a Paris guidebook helpfully settled the matter:

> Let us note … that in the position that it occupies at the Place de la
> Concorde, the four sides of the obelisk have changed orientation: the

north side at Luxor is today turned to the west and directed towards the Champs-Élysées.[139]

Gazing back and forth from the aerial view of Paris to the aerial view of Luxor, it was as if both images had a will of their own, wanting to merge with one another. Bauval looked up and towards the distant Luxor Obelisk at the Place de la Concorde. It was as though a veil was slowly being lifted from the city of Paris just like the veil so tantalisingly lifted in Picot's painting ...

Architecture fulfilling prophecy

Remember how the Hermetic philosopher Tommaso Campanella predicted in 1638 that Paris would become an 'Egyptian' City of the Sun? Now Bauval had found what looked like an unmistakable architectural correlation between Paris and a 'City of the Sun' in Egypt – i.e. Thebes-Luxor. It was all very weird and yet at the same time strangely logical.

He imagined himself like the genie in Picot's painting, hovering over the Place de la Bastille to witness the unveiling of an Egyptian landscape. It was a secret landscape that had been slowly prepared and hidden in plain view in the streets of Paris. This had called for a *purposeful* multi-generational building and city-planning project that began when Le Nôtre first deviated the axis of the Tuileries Garden to 26° north-of-west in 1665 and was only completed in 1989 more than 300 years later.

Was it a conspiracy, or just a conspiracy theory? Were the similarities of the axis of Paris and the axis of Luxor just coincidences or something else?

What made it seem more likely to be 'something else', and indeed some sort of conspiracy, was the whole mysterious connection that had linked ancient Egypt and particularly the goddess Isis to the city of Paris for centuries. Nor – weird though it admittedly seemed – was it easy to set aside the matter of Campanella's prophecy, made at the birth of the 'solar-king' Louis XIV, that Paris was to become a 'City of the Sun' modelled on the golden age of ancient Egypt.

It was then that something else suddenly hit Bauval. At about the same time that the French Republicans were planning monumental urban projects to refurbish the city of Paris between 1789 and 1794, there was another group of 'brothers' and republicans planning to design a city from scratch on the other side of the Atlantic.

And there, too, strange geometrical layouts and alignments evoking Hermetic and Masonic ideas came to the surface ...

The extraordinary truth is that the very existence of the Washington Monument [an obelisk] *is intimately linked with the Egyptian star Sirius … How is it that the most important star of the ancient world should find itself, as it were, resurrected in the architecture of the United States?*

David Ovason, *The Secret Zodiacs of Washington DC*

If, as Thomas Jefferson argued, the Capitol represents 'the first temple dedicated to the sovereignty of the people', then the [Masonic] *brothers of the 1793 ceremony served as its first high-priests.*

Steven C. Bullock, *Revolutionary Brotherhood*

Washington DC can fairly be described as the world's foremost 'Masonic City.' Its centre was laid out according to a plan drawn up by the French Freemason Pierre L'Enfant.

Freemasonry Today, Issue 16

CHAPTER NINETEEN

THE CORNERSTONE

If a monument or a building – or even, as we now can see, a whole city – can become like a living heart, a talisman charged with powerful ideologies and meaning, then the 'pacemaker' of such a talisman must be its *cornerstone*.

In ancient times, and in many different cultures, the dedication ceremony for a new temple or stately monument often called for elaborate rituals performed by the ruler. During such ceremonies the objective was to call upon a god or goddess to cast his or her benevolent and protective powers on the building – or even to beseech the deity to descend from the heavenly world and reside within the temple. A crucial element was the placing of a permanent marker to commemorate the ceremony, generally in the form of the 'first stone' or 'cornerstone'.

In medieval Europe, in direct continuation of such ancient ideas, the laying of the cornerstone for a church or cathedral was understood to symbolise the 'raising of the building into the light of day, into consciousness or towards the heavens.'[1] In this respect it was vital that the most propitious moment be selected when participants could be assured that the influences of the stellar and planetary deities were at their very best. To that end a 'horoscope' was cast.

To modern Freemasons the cornerstone ceremony remains one of paramount importance. It serves not only as a link to their 'operative' ancestors who built temples and cathedrals, but also as a potent symbol of renewal and 'rebirth'. It expresses itself with particular force in the Masonic aspiration (whether taken literally or metaphorically) to 'rebuild Solomon's Temple' in Jerusalem and to lay its cornerstone. Indeed, for Masons and non-Masons alike, there are few other talismans that can evoke so much fervour – benevolent *or* destructive. Think of the Crusades, the 1967 Arab-Israeli War, the on-going Palestinian *intifada*, and you begin to feel the energy that this talisman is capable of unleashing. The finding and re-placing of the cornerstone of a renewed Temple of Solomon would set off an intellectual and spiritual explosion that would have huge ramifications for the Middle East and for the world.

In many ancient buildings we find that the cornerstone was embedded into the wall of a crypt or basement that had been carefully prepared prior to the ceremony. According to Masonic author David Ovason:

> Symbolically speaking, the crypt is the burial place. It is the earth into which the seed of wheat must be dropped, to grow and resurrect, emerging as a sprouting plant from the coffin. In Masonry, the crypt is the burial place of the Master Mason, under the Holy of Holies ... This idea of rebirth is continued even in modern times in the formal ritual of the Freemasonic cornerstone ceremonials, in which participants in the ritual scatter wheat upon the floor, and sometimes even link this seeding with the stars.[2]

It is known that from the earliest days of their civilisation the ancient Egyptians performed a 'stellar' ritual – a form of 'astral magic' – during the cornerstone ceremonies for their pyramids and temples. This ritual involved reference to the circumpolar stars in the northern sky, and, in the southern sky, to the stars of Orion and, more especially, the star Sirius.[3] In Ovason's view 'it was this promise of stellar immutability which first led the ancient Egyptian priests, and their pupils, the Greek architects, to orientate their temples to the stars'. The very same promise, says Ovason, leads Masonic architects to ensure that their buildings and city plans are 'also laid out with a geometry which reflect[s] the wisdom of the stellar lore.'[4]

The 'Raising' of Washington

On 18 September 1793, a little more than a month after the 'Isis' ceremony was held at the Place de la Bastille in Paris,[5] another ceremony laden heavily with specific symbolic referents took place on a high point known as Jenkins Hill on the other side of the Atlantic. At the climax of this ceremony, America's first president, George Washington, wearing a Masonic apron which had been presented to him by the Marquis de Lafayette, laid the cornerstone of the US Capitol in the presence of a congregation of high-ranking Freemasons.[6]

Surveyor, farmer, and Episcopalian, George Washington was born at Pope's Creek in Virginia. He grew up near the town of Fredericksburg on his father's plantation. As a young man he studied mathematics and surveying, and eventually joined the Virginia militia where he excelled. In 1775, at the age of 43, he was elected by the Continental Congress to serve as commander-in-chief of the Revolutionary army to fight the British. After the War of Independence was over, Washington retired from the army, and in 1789 the state of Virginia sent him to the Constitutional Convention where he was unanimously elected as president of the United States. He was re-elected without opposition in 1792, refused a third term in 1796 and died at Mount Vernon in 1799 from laryngitis at the age of 67.

George Washington became a Freemason in 1752 in Fredericksburg, and was 'raised' as a Master Mason the following year.[7] In 1777, when the Freemasons in the American colonies sought to form a 'United' Grand Lodge independent from England, they offered the position of Grand Master to Washington, but he modestly declined, saying that he was not qualified for this high office. In 1788, however, he did become Master of the Alexandria lodge, today known as the Alexandria-Washington Lodge No. 22, situated on the south side of the Potomac River near the city of Washington, DC. Since 1932 this famous lodge has been engulfed within a huge Masonic monument built around it. The monument is modelled on the ancient Lighthouse of Alexandria in Egypt,[8] the *Pharos*, and bears the official name of the George Washington Masonic National Monument.[9] According to Harvey Wiley Corbett of the New York firm Helmle & Corbett who designed this monument:

> ... the *Pharos* was erected to guide the ancient mariners safely to shore; what would be more appropriate than a facsimile of that Lighthouse in Alexandria, Virginia on top of the highest hill and overlooking the Potomac River?[10]

Isis of the Suez Canal

Both H. W. Corbett and Louis A. Watres – the latter representing the 'client' – were themselves Freemasons, and as such would have known that the ancient *Pharos* of Alexandria had been dedicated to Isis and also to her star, Sothis-Sirius. Nor was this the only time that Freemasons would evoke Isis and her star in a landmark monument in the United States. According to Bernard Weisberger, Isis was also in the mind of the designer of the Statue of Liberty that now stands in New York Harbor:

> The sculptor who made the great statue was Italian. His name was Auguste Bartholdi. His work was greatly influenced by the ancient sculptor Phidias who made gigantic statues of the ancient goddesses, particularly Athena, the 'goddess of wisdom' and Nemesis, a goddess who held a cup in her right hand. Before beginning the Statue of Liberty project, Bartholdi was seeking a commission to construct a giant statue of the goddess 'Isis', the

Egyptian Queen of Heaven, to overlook the Suez Canal. The statue of Isis was to be of 'a robed woman holding aloft a torch'.[11]

Frédéric Auguste Bartholdi was born in France, at the city of Colmar in Alsace. He had studied in Paris at the prestigious *Lycée Louis-le-Grand*, and, in 1855, when he was only 21, he embarked on a voyage to Egypt with three friends, the orientalists Léon Gerôme, Léon-Auguste-Adolphe Belly and Narcisse Berchère. There, while visiting the ancient temples of Thebes and Abu Simbel, Bartholdi became enchanted by the gigantic works of the ancient Egyptian sculptors. He spent eight months documenting the Colossi of Memnon and returned to France with numerous sketches and photographs.

It was during that first voyage to Egypt that Bartholdi met the celebrated French engineer Ferdinand de Lesseps, and thus began a friendship between the pair that was to last a lifetime. De Lesseps was negotiating funding with the authorities in France and Egypt for the construction of the Suez Canal to join the Mediterranean Sea with the Red Sea. Bartholdi was deeply impressed with de Lesseps's vision and began to think how he might complement it by creating a gigantic statue of a goddess holding a torch. Bartholdi imagined this statue positioned at the entrance to the canal and representing 'Egypt Enlightening the East' – a name, as most French Freemasons knew in those days, which was strangely reminiscent of Cagliostro's famous saying that 'All Enlightenment comes from the East, all initiation from Egypt'.[12]

Khedive Isma'il of Egypt, another Freemason, was much enamoured with the beautiful French Empress Eugénie, wife of Napoleon III, and indeed with all things French. Eugénie was a cousin of Ferdinand de Lesseps, and it was she who put in a good word to the khedive to look favourably on the Suez Canal project. We saw in Chapter Eighteen that de Lesseps's father, Mathieu, together with Muhammad Ali, Isma'il's grandfather, had founded the *Société Secrète Égyptienne* which practiced a form of Scottish Rite Freemasonry merged with Cagliostro's Egyptian Rite.[13]

It seems that Bartholdi did manage to discuss his idea of a giant statue for the Suez Canal with Khedive Isma'il, but nothing came of it, probably because of the financial crisis that had then struck Egypt due to over-borrowing from European bankers. But, Bartholdi was not disheartened in the least and took his project elsewhere.

Isis of New York, a Talisman to 'Liberty'

The idea of a similar monument to commemorate the friendship between France and the United States for the 100th anniversary of the Declaration of Independence was first discussed by Bartholdi and others at the home, near Paris, of Édouard René de Laboulaye, an authority on North American culture. It seems that Bartholdi simply 'converted' his original project for Egypt and proposed it instead as a 'Statue of Liberty enlightening the world' for New York. To this end the so-called *Union Franco-Américaine* (Franco-American Union) was established in 1875 to raise the necessary funds.

Not unexpectedly, several members of the Franco-American Union turn out to have been Freemasons, including Bartholdi's own cousin, who was the French ambassador to the United States. Other Freemasons also actively involved were Henri Martin, the Count of Tocqueville and Oscar de Lafayette. Bartholdi himself had been initiated into Freemasonry in 1875 at the Paris lodge *Alsace-Lorraine*, and was raised as a Master Mason in 1880.

Although Bartholdi was to be the designer of the Statue of Liberty, the actual task of building it fell on Alexandre Gustave Eiffel, the celebrated French structural engineer who would also design and build the Eiffel Tower in Paris. Eiffel, too, was a Freemason – so let us note in passing that the first two levels of his famous steel tower, according to French engineer Jean Kerisel, are shaped like a pyramid.[14] Eiffel would certainly have been aware that about a century before, in 1792, a pyramid had been erected on the very same spot on the Champs de Mars in Paris to commemorate the French Revolution.[15]

Here's what the *Reader's Companion to American History* has to say about the inspiration behind the Statue of Liberty:

> Sculptor Frédéric Auguste Bartholdi combined elements of the Egyptian pyramids he admired with his mother's face to serve as a model for the statue, which he finished early in 1884.[16]

There has been much dispute about whether the face of the Statue of Liberty was modelled on that of Bartholdi's own mother, and the matter, though trivial, has not been settled. What is more certain is that the statue was linked to the 'cult of Liberty' or the 'Cult of Reason' of the French Revolution, both of which, in the minds of Republicans, were intimately connected to Masonic ideals. It is certain, too, as we saw in Chapter One, that figures representing 'Liberty' and 'Reason' were often modelled on the Egyptian goddess Isis or her Greek and Roman counterparts.

Interestingly, according to French Egyptologist Bernard Mathieu, Bartholdi used to refer to the Statue of Liberty as the 'Pharos' before it was raised in New York, and he even designed a base for the statue just like the one believed to have been used for the ancient *Pharos* of Alexandria.[17] Bartholdi, who had spent much time in Egypt and had studied the origins of this ancient 'wonder of the world', would certainly have known the association of the *Pharos* with the goddess Isis – and, by extension, her star, Sirius – that we explored in Chapter Ten. In this respect, it seems highly likely that his giant statue of 'a robed woman holding aloft a torch' to serve as a sort of lighthouse for the Suez Canal and, later, for New York Harbor, may well have been imagined by him as Isis-Pharia and the Lighthouse of Alexandria.

Garibaldi, 'Hero of the Two Worlds'

There is, too, an aspect of Bartholdi's life that is rarely considered in this context but which, we think, had a bearing on his state of mind when he designed the statue.

Bartholdi was a close friend of the Italian revolutionary hero, Giuseppe Garibaldi, the leading military man behind the Italian Unification known as the *Risorgimento*. Along with the politicians Camillo Benso, the Count of Cavour, and Giuseppe Mazzini. Garibaldi is regarded as one of the founding fathers of modern Italy. It was said that Cavour was the 'intelligence' behind the *Risorgimento* and Mazzini its 'spiritual drive'. Garibaldi was the 'fighting force' that was essential to bring it to fruition. His famous quip, 'Give me the ready hand rather than ready tongue', encapsulates the spirit of this remarkable man. Not surprisingly, we find that for his heroic deeds in Italy and also in the revolutions in South America, Garibaldi – like the Marquis de Lafayette before him – earned the title 'Hero of Two Worlds.'

Garibaldi was born in Nice and served as a sailor in the merchant navy for many years. In 1833 while in Marseilles he met the great Italian patriot Giuseppe Mazzini who recruited him into the so-called *La Giovane Italia* ('Young Italy'), that spearheaded the Italian National Movement. The charismatic Mazzini was to have a deep and lasting impact on Garibaldi who, throughout his life, often referred to him as his 'Master.' Freemasonry was particularly active in the liberation movement,[18] and Giuseppe Mazzini, who was often called the 'apostle of the Italian Republic', was a staunch Freemason. He was elevated as a 33rd degree Mason of the Scottish Rite by the Grand Orient of Palermo in 1864.[19]

Garibaldi himself was initiated into the *Carbonari* secret society in 1833,[20] and then into regular Freemasonry in 1844. In 1862 he was made a 33rd degree Mason in Palermo, and in 1864 was elected in Florence as the Grand Master of all Italian Freemasonry. In 1870, when the Prussians put Paris under siege, Garibaldi, ever the hero, rushed to the rescue with a contingent of Italian volunteers to defend the newly declared Third Republic of France headed by France's first president, the Freemason Léon Gambetta.[21] For his military successes against the Prussians, Gambetta, invited Garibaldi to become a member of the National Assembly in Paris. In 1880 Garibaldi joined the 'Egyptian' Rite of Memphis and, a year later, he was appointed as the first General Grand Master of a 'united' Masonic order, the Ancient and Primitive Rite of Memphis-Misraïm.[22]

An 'admirable spot' for a global talisman

It was in France, during the military campaign of 1870, that Garibaldi was introduced to the sculptor Bartholdi, who was then a major in the French army. Bartholdi served for a while as Garibaldi's personal *aide-de-camp*, but a few months later went to America proposing 'to glorify the Republic and Liberty over there.' He arrived in New York in July 1871. Upon entering New York Harbor, he knew immediately where his gigantic statue of 'Liberty' should one day stand:

> The picture that is presented to the view when one arrives in New York is marvellous ... When one awakes, so to speak, in the midst of that interior sea covered with vessels ... it is thrilling. It is, indeed, the New World ... I've found an admirable spot. It is Bedloe's Island, in the middle of the bay ... just opposite the Narrows, which are, so to speak, the gateway to America.[23]

In the US Bartholdi made good use of the letters of introduction he had been given by high-ranking French Freemasons. He met with many notables and veterans of the Civil War, including Henry Wadsworth Longfellow, Horace Greeley, Senator Charles Sumner, and President Ulysses S. Grant. To each in turn he talked up his big idea while showing them drawings and a model of the statue which he now called 'Liberty Enlightening the World'.

The project, of course, was a success, and created the powerful global talisman that now stands in New York Harbor. Meanwhile the very intense Masonic involvement in the whole affair was made lucidly evident on 5 August 1984 when a bronze plaque was affixed to the pedestal of the statue. The plaque reads as follows:

> At this site on August 5th, 1884, the cornerstone of the pedestal of the statue of 'Liberty Enlightening the World' was laid with ceremony by William A. Brodie, Grand Master of Masons in the State of New York. Grand Lodge Members, Representatives of the United States and French

Governments, Army and Navy officers, members of Foreign legations, and distinguished citizens were present. This plaque is dedicated by the Masons of New York in commemoration of the 100th Anniversary of that historic event.

M. W. Calvin O. Bond, Grand Master of Masons
P. W. Robert G. Singer, Deputy Grand Master
M. W. Arthur Markwich, Masonic Anniversary Chairman

August 5, 1984[24]

At the original ceremony on 5 August 1884 Grand Master William Brodie was asked why the Masonic fraternity had been called upon to lay the cornerstone of the Statue of Liberty. He replied:

No other organisation has ever done more to promote liberty and to liberate men from the chains of ignorance and tyranny than Freemasonry.[25]

One could say the same down the ages of the Gnostics and the Hermeticists in their original Alexandrian context in Egypt and later in their Cathar and Renaissance incarnations of the Middle Ages. All along the object of these subversive religions, whether taught by Valentinus or Mani, Bruno or Campanella, has indeed been to liberate mankind 'from the chains of ignorance and tyranny'.

A short diversion: In God We Trust

We tend to forget, or not fully appreciate, the quasi-religious fervour of the Founding Fathers of the United States of America, acting as if they were inspired, indeed directly *guided*, by 'Divine Providence'. Through the whole sequence of events that led to the War of Independence and the signing of the Constitution there was a clear understanding among the main protagonists, especially George Washington and Benjamin Franklin, that they were working under 'Divine Providence' and that the creation of the new nation was to be under the 'patronage' of God. More specifically, they saw 'America' as part of a 'Divine Plan' for mankind.

The question, therefore, that needs to be asked – nay, begs to be asked – is *which* 'God' did the Founding Fathers have in mind? Because there has to be a very strong possibility that the god whose patronage they felt themselves to be under was not the Christian deity in any conventional sense, but rather the

'Grand Architect of the Universe' – that uniquely 'Masonic God' represented by the letter 'G' on the Masonic aprons of Washington, Franklin and others who played such a crucial role on the creation of the United States.

The notion that the American Republic and its people were under the direct protection and guidance of heaven is immediately apparent in the Great Seal of the United States – featuring the famous symbol of the pyramid with the 'Eye of Providence' set in the capstone hovering above it. Variants of this striking symbol have been used to invoke the presence of the Almighty since at least the time of the ancient Egyptians – for whom it was the eye of the sun-god watching over mankind. The motto on the Great Seal, *Annuit Cœptis*, 'He [God] favoured our undertakings', should be enough to confirm this point.

There are, too, the various inspirational speeches made by Washington, Franklin and other Founding Fathers which leave no doubt that they believed they were fulfilling God's Plan in the creation of the Republic and the drafting of the Constitution. For example, when the Constitutional Convention could not reach consensus on the draft, Franklin made an impassioned plea for divine help:

> God governs in the affairs of men. If a sparrow cannot fall to ground without His notice, is it probable that an empire can rise without His aid? I ... believe this and also that without His concurring aid, we shall succeed in this political building no better than the builders of Babel ... I therefore beg leave to move, that henceforth prayers imploring the assistance of Heaven and its Blessings on our deliberations be held in this Assembly every morning before we proceed to business.[26]

On 3 October 1789, just a few months after the French populace stormed the Bastille and set in motion the creation of the First Republic on European soil, George Washington issued a proclamation to 'assign Thursday the 26th Day of November next to be devoted by the People of these States to the service of that great and glorious Being ...'

> ... that we may then all unite in rendering unto Him our sincere and humble thanks for his kind care and protection of the People of this country ... to enable us all, whether in public or private sanctions ... to promote the knowledge and practice of true religion and virtue, and the increase of science among them and Us, and generally to grant unto all Mankind such a degree of temporal prosperity as He alone knows best.[27]

THE MASTER GAME

The day of 'rendering unto Him our sincere and humble thanks' became, of course, Thanksgiving Day which, since 1863, has been a national holiday celebrated by Americans each November on the fourth Thursday of the month. It is undoubtedly the case that ceremonies of this kind had been held before 1789, but the proclamation marked the first time that 'Thanksgiving' was sanctioned as official government policy. It is worth reiterating that Washington clearly did not have in mind a 'harvest festival', as many now mistakenly believe Thanksgiving to be, but a religious feast to give thanks to God for his 'kind care' and 'His Providence' to the nation and its people. Subsequently Washington's 1789 proclamation was echoed by several other presidents.[28]

The notion that the United States of America has been somehow selected by God for special care is also expressed in the motto 'In God We Trust', introduced in 1863 and approved to be stamped on 1 cent, 2 cents and 3 cents coins of the currency. Later in 1955 the motto was put on all currency coins and notes, and in July 1956 it was declared the official motto of the USA.

Admittedly, the notion of a nation favoured by God in accordance with some great divine plan is nothing new. Throughout history it has been the norm for kings and queens to believe that they had a divine right to rule and that their nations were under special divine protection. Such ideas were so entrenched in the European psyche that it literally took the beheading of King Louis XVI and Queen Marie-Antoinette of France to demonstrate to the masses that their rulers were mortals who could be subjected to the same law as the lowliest citizens.

Yet in America, despite the absence of a royal family, it seems that the concept of 'divine right' has been entangled in politics from the very beginning, and, more recently – from the Arab and Muslim point of view at least – in foreign policy. Even though the US's massive economic and military support for Israel may not seem unusual or problematic to some Americans, the fact is that most Muslims and Arabs see it as a 'crusading alliance' to retain the Holy Land under Judeo-Christian control. The more extreme Islamists, as we show in Chapter Twenty, go even further and characterise it as a 'Masonic-Zionist alliance'.

Now let's return to the 'talisman' of New York Harbor, that grand 'Lady Liberty', and see what else may be coaxed out of her ...

Another ancient Egyptian goddess lends her seven-pointed star

In view of the 'Isis' connection with Bartholdi's Statue of Liberty, we could not help noticing that there was something rather curious about the date of 5 August which was chosen for the important cornerstone ceremony.

Isis, we know, was identified with the star Sirius – a fact that was much discussed at the time of Bartholdi in Masonic circles and, especially, in lodges in France and the United States. In Chapter One we also saw that Sirius held a special fascination for French Freemasons and even more so for Masonic astronomers such as Lalande (who was a prominent member of the Franco-American Nine Sisters lodge in Paris). Lalande's interest had been focused on the mystique surrounding the heliacal (dawn) rising of Sirius which, to Freemasons, evoked ideologies of spiritual 'rebirth' and the 'raising' of the initiated into the mysteries.[29] Given that Bartholdi was a Freemason, had travelled extensively in Egypt, had worked closely with the Freemason Eiffel, had also been in close contact with Garibaldi and his 'Egyptian' type of Freemasonry, and had taken a keen interest in ancient Egyptian monuments, it would, we think, be perverse to imagine that he would have been unfamiliar with the heliacal rising of Sirius and its intense 'rebirth' symbolism. Indeed what better association than the heliacal rising of the star of Isis could be found to lock auspicious events in the sky to the construction on the ground of a 'temple' dedicated to freedom and intended to serve as the beacon of hope for a new life in a new land built on the lofty virtues of Freemasonry?

In the early days of ancient Egypt in the third millennium BC the heliacal rising of Sirius took place close to the summer solstice which (in our modern, 'Gregorian' calendar) falls on 21 June. When Egypt became a Roman province in 30 BC, however, the precession-cycle of our planet's axis had caused the heliacal rising of Sirius to 'slip' relative to the summer solstice so that it took place nearly one month later, that is around 20 July. When Bartholdi visited Egypt in the 1860s, the heliacal rising of Sirius had slipped even further behind the summer solstice, and from the latitude of ancient Heliopolis near Cairo would have been observed *on the morning of 5 August*.[30]

Now it is a well-established fact that in ancient Egypt, the cornerstone-laying ceremony of temples, known as the 'stretching of the cord', had been performed since time immemorial by a priestess impersonating the goddess *Seshat* – whose symbol was a seven-pointed star which she wore over her head. Seshat was known as the 'Lady of the Builders', a title that established her as the protector of temple-builders, architects and masons. Interestingly, she was also the wife of Thoth, the ancient Egyptian god of wisdom who provided the prototype of Hermes Trismegistus – the much revered patron of esoteric and occult traditions, including Freemasonry. *There is a very high probability that in ancient Egypt the stretching-of-the-cord ceremony was performed at dawn at the time of the heliacal rising of Sirius.*[31] Considering this, and Seshat's seven-pointed-star headdress, we have to wonder at Bartholdi's decision to place a seven-pointed star over the head of his statue of 'Liberty', and also at the choice of 5 August for the statue's cornerstone ceremony.

If we look even deeper into the symbolism that Bartholdi and others involved might have had in mind, the possibility must be considered that the seven-pointed star on the head of the Statue of Liberty is also there because it has esoteric connotations and sinuous links to the Egyptian goddess Isis. We have already seen how Scottish Rite Freemasons, particularly in France, variously associated the symbolism of Tarot card XVI, known as the 'Star', with the symbolism of the star of Isis i.e. Sirius. Is it not surprising, therefore, to discover that a seven-pointed star is often shown above the head of the woman who features on this card pouring water out of jug into a river – surely a clear metaphoric pictogram of the links between Isis, the star and the inundation of the Nile which took place at the heliacal rising of Sirius?

The 'Egyptian' Freemasonry that Bartholdi was especially associated with was introduced to France by Cagliostro who created the famous 'Isis' lodge in Paris (see Chapter Sixteen). Egyptian Freemasonry was immensely popular in Alsace, where Cagliostro spent much time with the local Masons and where, in Strasbourg, he met and was sponsored by the Cardinal de Rohan. It comes as no surprise, therefore, that in his celebrated 'Egyptian Rite' Cagliostro was particularly fascinated with the number seven which he directly equated with the 'Blazing Star' of the Masonic lodges and, consequently with the 'star of Isis' i.e. Sirius.[32] And although the Blazing Star of the Freemasons is usually five pointed, Cagliostro insists that the Masons are mistaken, and that this symbol should have seven points, exactly as seen on the head of the Statue of Liberty. When asked by one of his adepts about the meaning of the Blazing Star, Cagliostro replied:

> This star is the emblem of the Great mysteries revealed in supernatural philosophy and it is a new proof of the blindness and ignorance of modern Masons, because it ought to be terminated by 7 points or 7 angles, and you shall never see it represented in any lodge except by 3, 5 or 6 angles ...[33]

An obelisk for New York

At around the same time that the Statue of Liberty was being erected on Bedloe's Island an original ancient Egyptian obelisk was brought to New York's Central Park. This obelisk, which bears inscriptions dedicated to Pharaoh Thutmosis III (1479–1425 BC), is one of a pair that originally stood at Heliopolis in ancient times; the other stands today at London's Victoria Embankment. The obelisk eventually destined for Central Park was brought from Heliopolis to Alexandria in 12 BC, during the reign of Augustus Caesar, to adorn the entrance of the Caesarium temple near the great eastern harbour, right opposite the *Pharos* lighthouse on the northern side of the bay.[34] And from there, after a further eighteen centuries had passed, it was finally taken to New York.[35]

As was the case with the Statue of Liberty (as well as the 'London Obelisk'),[36] the whole complicated operation that brought the 'New York Obelisk' to New York was Masonic through and through. The man with overall responsibility for the project, a naval engineer, Henry Honychurch Gorringe, was a staunch Freemason who had been initiated in New York at the Anglo-Saxon Lodge No. 137.[37] Indeed, even Dr. Martina D'Alton, who wrote the official account of the New York Obelisk for the Metropolitan Museum of Art, could not avoid stating that:

> The Freemasons had a strong presence in New York. Almost to a man, all those involved in bringing [the obelisk] to America were members – Gorringe, Schoeder, Vanderbilt and Hurlbert, as well as the mayor, commissioner of police, and others in city politics ...[38]

It seems that the original idea of bringing an obelisk to New York had come from the Egyptian Khedive Isma'il himself. The occasion had been the inauguration of the Suez Canal in 1869. Finding himself next to William Hurlbert, the editor of the *New York World* newspaper, the khedive suddenly blurted out that he would like to send an obelisk as a gift to the government of the United States.[39] Hurlbert, a Freemason, would have immediately recognised in this gesture a sort of polite 'Masonic handshake' from the khedive, who also was a Freemason.[40]

Indeed, the Masonic influence went further than that. A few months before the opening of the Suez Canal, Khedive Isma'il's uncle, Prince Halim Pasha, had been elected Grand Master of the Rite of Memphis, which practiced pseudo-Egyptian rituals using a system of '92 higher degrees'.[41] Halim Pasha also served as the official Grand Master of the Grand Orient of Egypt.[42]

Gorringe arrived in Egypt in October 1879 with a Freemason colleague, Lieutenant Seaton Schroeder, to take delivery of the obelisk. The khedive had entrusted Solutore Avventure Zola (who had replaced Prince Halim Pasha as Grand Master of the Rite of Memphis in 1874)[43] with the task

THE MASTER GAME

of handing over the gift to the Americans.[44] It was reported at the time that when Gorringe finally had the obelisk lowered onto the sandy beach at Alexandria, there was great excitement. The many Freemasons in the party had noticed 'Masonic emblems' – a trowel, a builder's square and an architect's triangle – carved into the base of the ancient pedestal.[45] It seems that Gorringe was 'struck with the symbolism [and] decided to take the pedestal, steps, and foundation to the New World and reposition them as they had been.'[46]

Perhaps we should mention as well that Gorringe had only a few years before been 'struck' by something else. He was convinced that he had discovered 'Atlantis' in the Azores while working with the United States Coast Survey in 1876 – a 'discovery' which earned him a personal congratulatory message, no less, from President Ulysses S. Grant.[47]

The obelisk finally reached New York and:

On October 9th 1880, a parade of nine thousand Freemasons marched up Fifth Avenue, bands blaring, to Greywacke Knoll for a grand and solemn cornerstone ceremony.[48]

The ceremony itself took place the next day, 10 October 1880, when Jesse B. Anthony, the Grand Master of the New York Masons, did the honours to 'link the origins of Freemasonry to ancient Egypt.'[49]

We spoke earlier of the George Washington Masonic Memorial in Alexandria, Virginia. In its case the ceremony of the laying of the cornerstone was performed in May 1923 by President Coolidge using the same trowel that George Washington himself had used 130 years earlier when he had laid the cornerstone of the US Capitol in Washington, DC.[50]

The George Washington Masonic Memorial is thus the third of three significant Masonic monuments in the United States (the other two being the Statue of Liberty and the New York Obelisk) which all exhibit intense symbolic links to the ancient city of Alexandria in Egypt – a city which was universally associated in antiquity with the *Pharos* lighthouse and the goddess Isis-Pharia.

Philadelphia, the 'City of Brotherly Love'

Although the foundation of Washington, DC took place in 1793, the city was not occupied by the government until the end of President John Adams's term in 1801. During the two terms of George Washington's presidency, spanning the period from 1789 to 1797, the seat of government, and thus the capital of the young United States, were located in the city of Philadelphia – a name that literally means the 'City of Brotherly Love' or, perhaps more appropriately, 'City of the Love of the Brotherhood'. This name, to say the very least, has a strong Masonic ring to it. But then that is hardly surprising when we realise, as we shall see later in this chapter, that it was in Philadelphia that colonial Freemasonry first flourished in the Americas.

The story of Philadelphia, and its brief spell as the US's first capital, is the stuff that Hollywood producers dream of. It all began in England in 1681, when King Charles II was confronted with an old and nagging debt due to a certain Admiral William Penn and now payable to the admiral's son and heir, William.

William Penn was the visionary leader of the Quakers – Christian nonconformists who then happened to be causing a great deal of annoyance to the Church of England. So Charles II, who was unwilling to meet his obligations to Penn in cash, offered him instead a region in North America the size of England, on condition that Penn use it to develop a province where Quakers and other nonconformists could enjoy 'freedom of worship and self-government'. The name Pennsylvania was chosen by King Charles II himself, and means 'Forests of Penn', apparently in honour of Admiral Penn, William's father.

William Penn saw this, quite literally, as a God-sent opportunity to carry out what he called the 'Holy Experiment', and thus, to Charles II's delight, gladly accepted the offer and challenge. Yet not in his wildest biblical dreams would Penn have imagined the final outcome. As for Charles II, he thought that he had lumbered the irksome Quaker with a piece of useless real estate, not realising, of course, that he had in actual fact planted the seed of Britain's demise in the American colonies.

By the Rivers of Babylon

William Penn set sail for America in early 1682, his thoughts filled with dreams and visions of the great city he would found in the New World. Many contemporary documents show that Penn visualised what he constantly called 'my Greene Country Town' modelled on his rural properties back in England. But according to one of William Penn's most distinguished biographers, Susan Coolidge:

> ... the city of Babylon is said to have been in Penn's mind as a model for his proposed city.[51]

Much suggests that Coolidge is correct. It is known, for example, that Penn, was greatly inspired by the idea of placing his city between two rivers, the Delaware and the Schuylkill, in much the same way that ancient Babylon had been situated between the Tigris and the Euphrates Rivers. Another factor is the so-called *gridiron* layout adopted by Penn, which required an alignment of parallel avenues running east-west and crisscrossing with another set of avenues running north-south – a scheme that, according to some historians, was apparently used for ancient Babylon.[52] The third factor is, of course, the name that Penn chose for his city: Philadelphia, the 'City of Brotherly Love', in which people of different races and languages would be re-united.

In the Bible, Babylon was, of course, where the Tower of Babel had been built under Nimrod, when all men had spoken a single language. And for many Freemasons, the Tower of Babel serves as the ultimate talisman or symbol of their origins. In his celebrated essay *The Origins of Freemasonry*, Thomas Paine explained why:

> It is always understood that Freemasons have a secret which they carefully conceal; but from everything that can be collected from their own accounts of Masonry, their real secret is no other than their origin, which but few of them understand; and those who do, envelop it in mystery ... In 1730, Samuel Pritchard, member of a constituted lodge in England, published a treatise entitled 'Masonry Dissected'; and made oath before the Lord Mayor of London that it was a true copy: 'Samuel Pritchard maketh oath that the copy hereunto annexed is a true and genuine copy of every particular.'
> In his work he has given the catechism or examination, in question and answer, of the Apprentices, the Fellow Craft, and the Master Mason. There was no difficulty in doing this, as it is mere form. In his introduction he says, 'the original institution of Masonry consisted in the foundation of the liberal arts and sciences, but more especially in geometry, for at the building of the Tower of Babel, the art and mystery of Masonry was first introduced, and from thence handed down by Euclid, a worthy and excellent mathematician of the Egyptians; and he communicated it to Hiram, the Master Mason concerned in building Solomon's Temple in Jerusalem'.[53]

Thomas Paine correctly went on to point out that:

> Besides the absurdity of deriving Masonry from the building of Babel, where, according to the story, the confusion of languages prevented the

builders understanding each other, and consequently of communicating any knowledge they had, there is a glaring contradiction in point of chronology in the account he gives. Solomon's Temple was built and dedicated 1,004 years before the Christian era; and Euclid, as may be seen in the tables of chronology, lived 277 years before the same era. It was therefore impossible that Euclid could communicate anything to Hiram, since Euclid did not live till seven hundred years after the time of Hiram.[54]

What Paine, a pragmatist, failed to understand is that English Freemasonry does not have a 'history' in the sense scholars understand the term, but rather a 'symbolic history', where principles and ideologies of the Craft are elucidated or 'symbolised' by biblical, mythical and even historical events such as the building of Solomon's Temple and the Tower of Babel. To academic historians this sort of thing amounts to nothing more than pseudo-history – a yarn of absolutely no historical value concocted to glorify particular individuals or cultures by associating them with the biblical story. But Freemasons know better. Symbolic history – even though false or, at best, grossly distorted and exaggerated – is to be valued in itself for its effects on society and on mass human behaviour.

Within William Penn's vision of a 'New Babylon' between the rivers of the New World, was also a vision of a Mesopotamian-style 'Garden of Eden', whereby a huge area of 10,000 acres – of which 1,200 were reserved for Philadelphia – was to be developed in Penn's curious concept of a 'Greene Country Towne' with its 'gridiron' system of intersecting avenues. In this biblical 'theme park' each citizen would be allocated 'sizable areas of green'. Eighty acres in the centre of Philadelphia were specifically reserved for 'gentlemen's estates' with mansions set at least 800 feet apart from each other separated by lavish gardens and fields. The wide streets of the gridiron crisscrossed in perfect rectangular symmetry, and at each corner of the city-centre were 'squares' – forerunners of today's urban parks. In their midst was a fifth, larger 'square', with a wide avenue radiating from each side to form a giant *croisée* or 'cross'.

The whole city was circumscribed within a gigantic rectangle whose longer side ran east-west. Oddly, however, this great rectangle was not perfectly oriented to the astronomical cardinal directions (i.e. due north, south, east and west) but was instead fixed about 10° south-of-east. This may have been to keep the layout more or less parallel to the adjacent rivers. But a more esoteric purpose is by no means out of the question in such a 'City of Brotherly Love'. We note with interest, therefore, that the Sun aligns itself at rising with the axis of Philadelphia on two days of the year: 16 February and 13 October.[55] The latter date marks the anniversary of the suppression of the Knights Templar which took place, as we saw in Chapter Fifteen, on 13 October 1307. Whether by accident or by design, as we will show later, the same date of 13 October also crops up in connection with the cornerstone ceremony of the White House in Washington, DC.

Penn entrusted the design of Philadelphia to Thomas Holme, an accomplished urban architect, who published Penn's scheme in 1683.[56] Copies of Holme's design have survived, and the 'gridiron' principle can clearly be seen, with its four corners and central 'squares'. It was perhaps appropriate that such a geometrical city should not only serve as the capital of the newly-formed United States of America for the twelve years from 1789 to 1801, but should also have become the 'capital' of American Freemasonry. Today about 25 'Masonically related sites' are recognised in Philadelphia, not least the great Masonic Temple on Broad Street with it 'Egyptian' and 'Solomonic' rooms. On Fifth and Arch Street stands the Free Quaker Meeting House; it served as the Masonic Grand Lodge of Pennsylvania in the crucial years between 1775–1777. And let's not forget the National Memorial Arch dedicated to 'Brother' George Washington (rebuilt by the Freemasons of Pennsylvania in 1996).[57]

Such roots go deep. Just 40 years after William Penn's arrival in the New World, the utopian city that he created was to become the home of America's first Freemasons …

But before we investigate the intense Masonic character of the early history of the city of Philadelphia, it is worth emphasising that the idea of imbuing Masonic ideas and symbolism into the plans of a city is by no means fanciful thinking – as we will see in this 'brief deviation' …

A Brief Deviation: Kilbourne Plat

The surveyor Hector Kilbourne was responsible for designing the original plan of the city of Sandusky, Ohio (and in 1819 became the first Master of the Science Lodge No. 50, the first Masonic lodge in Sandusky). Being a Freemason, Kilbourne decided to integrate the 'square and compass', the best-known Masonic symbol, into the layout of the streets in the central downtown area now known as Kilbourne Plat. There can be absolutely no doubt that this was his intention, as not only one can very obviously discern the famous Masonic symbol in the original city plan, but just outside the city has been placed an 'historical marker' in the form of a large bronze plaque by the Ohio Historical Society which reads:

Hector Kilbourne, a Freemason and the surveyor who made the original plat of Sandusky (as Portland) in 1816, laid out the streets to form the Masonic emblem. Huron and Central Avenues are the arms of the compass. Elm and Poplar Streets the sides of the Mason's square. The first Masonic Lodge was founded in Sandusky in 1819, with Kilbourne as Master.

The 29 Lodges of the 16th District, Grand Lodge, Free and Accepted Masons of Ohio, Crawford, Erie, Huron, Seneca, and Wyandot Counties and The Ohio Historical Society[58]

Considering that this Masonic city design was hatched so soon after the design of Washington, DC in 1791, we feel entirely justified in looking for similar 'Masonic' influences in other major American cities which played a key role in the events that led to the creation of the USA.

The candle-maker's son

By the final quarter of the 18th century Philadelphia had grown to become the second largest English-speaking city in the world after London. And is its name implied its local culture was intensely Masonic. At the same time it was a rich commercial centre which, in direct contrast to its proclaimed 'brotherly love', was heavily engaged in the black slave trade. Tradition has it that it was in the city of Philadelphia that the first Masonic lodge in America was consecrated, the *St. John's No. 1 Lodge*.[59] It was also in Philadelphia that the most renowned of all American Freemasons, Benjamin Franklin, received his initiation.[60]

Born the son of a candle-maker in Boston, Benjamin Franklin left his home town in 1723 after losing his job because of the political tone of articles he had written for his brother's newspaper, the *New-England Courant*. The young Franklin settled in Philadelphia where he was encouraged by William Keith, the governor of Pennsylvania, to set himself up in the publishing trade. To this end, he was sponsored by Keith to go to England in order to acquire experience in the publishing business. Franklin stayed in London from 1724 to 1726 then returned to Philadelphia where he eventually founded the *Pennsylvania Gazette*. This was the newspaper in which appeared the first published commentary on Freemasonry in America.[61]

In 1730 Franklin was made a Freemason at the *St. John's* lodge in Philadelphia, and by 1734 became its Grand Master.[62] From 1737 to 1753 Franklin was in charge of the Philadelphia post office. A deist and preacher of religious tolerance, Franklin was also a scientist and, in 1751, gained

THE MASTER GAME

fame and notoriety when he invented the lightning conductor after flying a kite in a thunderstorm.

Franklin revisited England between 1757 and 1762, this time as the representative of the colony of Pennsylvania. He was to return again two years later, staying until 1775. During this last sojourn in London, Franklin entered into lengthy negotiations with the British government, and was instrumental in toppling the Stamp Act imposed by the British Parliament on the American colonies. As such, Franklin sowed the political and intellectual seeds that would lead to open opposition against the British in America and, ultimately, to the War of Independence. In 1775, when he heard that the colonists were preparing for an armed uprising against the British, Franklin felt that his position in England was becoming too dangerous and so made his way back across the Atlantic. He arrived in Philadelphia in May 1775, just two weeks after the first shots were fired against the British at Lexington. In June the Revolutionary army confronted the British forces at Bunker Hill, marking the beginning of a full-scale war.

Thomas Paine

It was from Philadelphia, too, that another popular journalist, Thomas Paine, a Quaker and staunch deist, began a violent attack on the British in his writings. Paine was born in Norfolk, England, and was the son of a Quaker and corset-maker. After repeated failures to forge a career, his luck began to turn when he met Benjamin Franklin in London in the early 1770s. Franklin advised him to seek his fortune in America and provided him with letters of recommendation. Paine arrived in Philadelphia in 1774 and two years later, in January 1776, published his celebrated pamphlet *Common Sense*, in which he put forward the notion of a 'Declaration of Independence'. It sold over half a million copies and some even believe it served as the basis of the formal Declaration of Independence that was eventually compiled by Thomas Jefferson in July 1776.

Aside from his great political impact, Paine is known in Masonic circles for promoting the same idea as the British archaeologist (and fellow and council member of the Royal Society), the Freemason William Stukeley – who claimed that Freemasonry took its rituals from the ancient Druids who, in turn, had inherited them from the ancient Egyptians.[63] In an article on this subject Paine informs us of his view that 'the ancient Druids ... like the Magi of Persia and the priests of Heliopolis in Egypt, were priests of the Sun'. Paine goes on to say:

The Christian religion and Masonry have one and the same common origin: both are derived from the worship of the Sun. The difference between their origins is that the Christian religion is a parody on the worship of the Sun ... And in what period of antiquity or in what nation this religion was first established, is lost in the labyrinth of unrecorded time. It is generally ascribed to the ancient Egyptians ... The religion of the Druids, as before said, was the same as the religion of the ancient Egyptians. The Priests of Egypt were the professors and teachers of science, and were styled priests of Heliopolis, that is of the City of the Sun ...[64]

In the same article, Paine supports his own claims by quoting Captain George Smith, inspector of the Royal Artillery Academy at Woolwich and Provincial Grand Master of Masonry in Kent, who had asserted that:

Egypt, from whence we derive many of our mysteries, has always borne a distinguished rank in history, and was once celebrated above all others for its antiquities, learning, opulence and fertility. In their system, their principal hero-gods, Osiris and Isis, theologically represented the Supreme Being and Universal Nature ... The Egyptians in the earliest ages constituted a great number of Lodges, but with assiduous care kept their secrets of Masonry from all strangers. These secrets have been imperfectly handed down to us by oral traditions only, and ought to be kept undiscovered to the labourers, craftsmen and apprentices, till by good behaviour and long study they become better acquainted in geometry and the liberal arts, and thereby qualified for Masters and Wardens ...[65]

We shall see later how Thomas Paine went to Paris during the French Revolution and befriended the astronomer Charles-François Dupuis who, as we shall recall, was an advocate of the view that the city of Paris owed its origins to the Egyptian goddess Isis. We shall also see how Paine developed a close friendship with the writer Nicolas de Bonneville, a Freemason, mystic and radical revolutionary, and with the mathematician and philosopher, the Marquis de Condorcet, likewise a revolutionary and a member of the Nine Sisters lodge.[66] Paine, who was to arrive in Paris at the height of Robespierre's reign, may have played a part in the attempt to induce the populace of Paris to adopt the new republican Cult of the Supreme Being, and perhaps even the cult of Nature-Reason-Liberty which was flaunted as a pseudo-Isis cult at the Place de la Bastille in August 1793 ...

Franklin in France

We saw in Chapter One that in late 1776, thirteen years before the French Revolution broke out, Benjamin Franklin was sent to France to serve as the first ambassador of the newly formed Republic of the United States. Being the most senior of the signatories of the Declaration of Independence, and also the inventor of the lightning rod, Franklin's huge fame had preceded him, and he was now hailed as a sort of cult hero upon his arrival in Paris. His primary mission was to gain support, both financial and militarily, for the American war against the British. This he succeeded in doing, largely through complex behind-the-scenes negotiations with Charles Gravier, the Count of Vergennes, Louis XVI's minister of foreign affairs.

Witty and wise, Franklin was taken by the pre-revolutionary French as a symbol of 'liberty in the New World'. He was the hero who opposed the British – and, by extension, the oppression and despotism of European monarchs in general. He was quickly to become the darling of the social salons in Paris and, invariably, the favourite of the elitist Masonic lodges. As we also saw in Chapter One, Franklin joined the famous Nine Sisters lodge while he was ambassador in Paris and, in 1777, was to become its Grand Master.

The Nine Sisters lodge was the natural successor of an older lodge, *Les Sciences*, founded in 1766 by the astronomer Jérôme Lalande and the philosopher and atheist, Claude Adrien Helvétius. In 1771, after the death of Helvétius, Lalande and Helvétius's widow, Mme Anne Catherine Helvétius, were instrumental in the founding of the Nine Sisters lodge. Mme Helvétius ran the famous elitist salon in the Rue Sainte-Anne in Paris, which was renowned throughout Europe for the intellectual excellence of its members.[67] She also hosted another salon at Auteuil near Paris, which maintained very close links with the Nine Sisters lodge.[68]

Franklin was a regular visitor to Mme Helvétius's salons, and so was the Marquis de Lafayette, who was then a young officer in the French army. Lafayette was also a member of the lodge, *Le Contrat Social*, itself linked to elitist lodges such as the *Société Olympique* whose members included other young officers, among them the Count de Chambrun, the Count-Admiral de Grasse, the Count-Admiral d'Estaing and the famous 'buccaneer' John Paul Jones. All these men would play important roles later in America in the War of Independence. Indeed it was almost certainly through these Masonic lodges and salons that Franklin's political and commercial agent in Paris, the American Silas Deane, recruited young French officers to help George Washington fight the British. One such officer recruited by Deane, probably through the intermediary of Pierre Beaumarchais, was the Marquis de Lafayette, who was only 19 years old at the time.[69]

'Why not?'

The importance of Lafayette in the American Revolution cannot be overstated. Indeed, many Americans today believe that were it not for Lafayette, Washington might have been unable to muster enough military support to defeat the British. Many have also wondered what prompted Lafayette to make such great personal sacrifices for the cause of America. Part of the answer can be found in the motto that he chose for his coat-of-arms: *Cur Non?*, ('Why Not?').[70] These two simple words perhaps reveal better than anything else the character of this enterprising and immensely courageous man.

Lafayette, whose full name was Marie-Joseph Paul Yves Roch Gilbert du Motier, was born on 6 September 1757 in Chavaniac, in the Haute-Loire in France. His father, an important general in the army, was killed in battle when Lafayette was only two years old, and his mother was to die eleven years later, leaving the adolescent Lafayette as the sole beneficiary of a huge fortune. True to his descent from a distinguished military family, he enrolled to study at the military academy in Versailles and by the age of 16 became a captain in the Dragoon guards of Louis XVI. At 19 he was introduced to the American agent Silas Deane who, thinking that Lafayette's influential position and financial fortune could be of great use to the American cause, immediately commissioned the young officer to join Washington's Revolutionary army in the colonies.

Lafayette was from the old nobility of France and enjoyed additional connections through his marriage. His father-in-law was the Duke of Ayen, who came from one of the country's wealthiest and most influential families, the Noailles. The Duke of Ayen's father and also his grandfather had held the highest military title, that of *Maréchal de France* ('Marshal of France'), and the Duke himself was the captain of Louis XVI's bodyguards. The Duke's brother, the Count of Noailles, was the French ambassador to England. Not surprisingly, in his letter of recommendation to the American Congress, Silas Deane described Lafayette as being 'of the first family and fortune [who] ... will do us infinite service'. He urged that 'a generous reception' be prepared for this young and dashing figurehead upon his arrival in America.

Fired by the excitement of defending 'Liberty' in the New Word, and hungry for military glory, Lafayette used his own money to purchase a ship, *La Victoire*, in order to sail to America with his companions. All this was done in secrecy, for Lafayette had not been granted the required permission from Louis XVI, nor had he received the approval of his powerful and influential father-in-law. However, the Atlantic crossing of *La Victoire* went without too much trouble, and Lafayette and his team arrived in Georgetown, South Carolina in mid-June 1777. He and six of his companions then made their way inland to Philadelphia, only to find Congress reluctant to endorse the military commissions they had received from Silas Deane in France. But in a passionate speech, Lafayette managed to persuade the congressmen that he would use his own funds and resources. Impressed with such zeal and commitment to their cause, Congress finally agreed to ratify his appointment and, a fortnight later, he was sent to the general quarters of George Washington north of Philadelphia. Legend has it that both men took to each other like brothers. Later, after the war, when Lafayette had returned to France, Washington was to write to him these famous words:

> Whether you come here in the character of commanding officer of a corps of gallant French, should circumstances lead to that event; whether as an American major general you come to retake command of a division of our army; or whether after the peace you come to see me simply as my friend and my companion, I shall receive you in every case with all the tenderness of a brother.[71]

In September 1777, riding at the side of Washington, Lafayette fought bravely against the British at the Battle of Brandywine. Wounded, Lafayette was evacuated to Philadelphia, and there witnessed the fall of the city to the British. He was to distinguish himself brilliantly at the Battle of Barren Hill seven months later. All in all Lafayette proved to be a superb officer in the field, and a wise advisor to Washington. His deep friendship with the future first president of the United States, who was 25 years his senior, turned to almost filial adoration. It was, however, Lafayette's catalytic role in the relationship between France and America, and his influence in persuading France to sign a treaty of alliance with Congress against the British early in 1778, that made him a crucial player in the War of Independence.

In 1781 he fought at Washington's side in the decisive Battle of Yorktown, and his brilliant actions largely contributed to the routing of British forces and their surrender to Washington. Now at 24, barely four years after he had arrived in America, the young and debonair Marquis de Lafayette was hailed as 'Hero of the Two Worlds' (as Garibaldi would be later) i.e. a hero on both sides of the Atlantic. The huge and lasting impression that Lafayette has had on the American people can be witnessed today with the hundreds of public places and streets that bear his name, including a whole county in Pennsylvania. When 42 years later, in 1824, Lafayette, by now a 33rd degree Freemason, visited America again, he was received as a national hero.

The immense and enduring sense of gratitude of the American people towards this remarkable Frenchman is immortalised in the words of Colonel Charles E. Stanton on behalf of General John J. Pershing, a 33rd degree Freemason, after the liberation of Paris in 1917: 'Lafayette, we are here!'

Stanton pronounced this 'brotherly homage' on 4 July, Independence Day, in the presence of hundreds of Freemasons in front of the tomb of Lafayette at the Picpus Cemetery in Paris.[72]

The House of the Temple

The 33rd degree system is regulated by the Supreme Council, 33°, Ancient and Accepted Scottish Rite, Southern Jurisdiction, USA. This elitist Masonic order, with its many ostentatious titles and impressive grades, seems to hold a strong appeal for high-ranking military men and for up-and-coming politicians. Today there are about 40 supreme councils as well as four national lodges around the world, all of which fall under the informal authority of this so-called *Mother Supreme Council*.

The Mother Supreme Council now has its headquarters in Washington, DC, located at 1733 16th Street, NW. Known as the 'House of the Temple', this imposing, neo-classical building is modelled on the Mausoleum of Halicarnassus, and was designed in 1911 by the famous architect and Freemason John Russell Pope. At the entrance are two imposing 'Egyptian' sphinxes symbolising 'wisdom' and 'power'.[73] The 'wisdom' sphinx has on its breast an image of an Egyptian goddess, probably Isis, and the 'power' sphinx has the ancient Egyptian *Ankh*, the so-called *key of life*, as well as the *uraeus* symbol designating the solar pedigree of the pharaohs.

The great door knob of the main entrance of the Supreme Council in Washington, DC is in the shape of a solar-lion, and inside the atrium, which is very reminiscent of an Egyptian temple, are two 'Egyptian' statues of seated scribes placed at the foot of a large ceremonial staircase. Each of these statues carries a hieroglyphic inscription which translates as 'Established to the Glory of God' and a dedication 'to the teaching of wisdom to those men working to make a strong nation.' The staircase leads to a bronze bust of Albert Pike, the most famous of all Scottish Rite Grand Masters to whom the 'House of the Temple' is dedicated. A plaque above the bust of Pike reads: 'What we have done for ourselves alone dies with us: What we have done for others and the world remains and is immortal.'

Another imposing pseudo-Egyptian motif in the Supreme Council in Washington, DC is the winged glowing triangle that hangs over the altar in the main room of the temple as well as on the ceiling. This is a motif which is, of course, modelled on the winged solar disc common to all ancient Egyptian temples. But more intriguing is the fact that it was Albert Pike himself who confirmed that the so-called *Blazing Star* that is often seen at the entrance of Masonic lodges, or associated with the Masonic glowing triangle, is none other than the star of Isis, Sirius:

The Ancient Astronomers saw all the great symbols of Masonry in the stars. Sirius still glitters in our lodges as the Blazing Star ...[74]

[This star is] an emblem of the Divine Truth, given by God to the first men, and preserved amid all the vicissitudes of ages in the traditions and teachings of Masonry.[75]

The Blazing Star in our Lodges, we have already said, represent Sirius, Anubis, or Mercury, Guardian and Guide of Souls.[76]

The Blazing Star or Glory in the centre refers us to that Grand Luminary the Sun, which enlightens the Earth, and by its genial influence dispenses blessings to mankind.[77]

The Blazing Star has been regarded as an emblem of Omniscience, or the All-Seeing-Eye, which to the Ancients was the Sun.[78]

He was Sirius or the Dog-Star, the friend and counsellor of Osiris, and the inventor of language, grammar, astronomy, surveying, arithmetic, music, and medical science; the first maker of laws; and who taught the worship of the Gods, and the building of temples.[79]

When coupled with the claims of Albert Pike regarding Sirius, the star of Isis, the intense pseudo-Egyptian quality of the House of the Temple in Washington, DC, especially the two sphinxes guarding the entrance, immediately brings to mind the two sphinxes and the Isis statue that were designed by Jacques-Louis David for the 1793 celebrations at the Place de la Bastille in Paris, as well as Picot's painting in the Louvre.

Before we examine this curious link further we need to know more about Albert Pike, and why the Washington, DC 'House of the Temple' was dedicated to him ...

The Blazing Star

Albert Pike is often described by Scottish Rite Freemasons as a poet, trapper, historian, revolutionary, lawyer, politician, army commander, orator, author and philosopher. In short, the Renaissance man *par excellence*. Born in Boston in 1809, he went to Harvard but dropped out to become a school teacher. He then became a trapper in Arkansas in 1831 but later was somehow admitted to the bar of the Supreme Court. He eventually moved to New Orleans to practice law, then joined the side of the South during the Civil War and was appointed a Confederate commissioner commander, leading Indian tribes. He was court-martialed on dubious charges of fraud, acquitted, and finally opened a law office in Washington, DC.

Pike is best remembered not so much for his colourful career but for having revived the Scottish Rite when he became the Grand Commander of this Masonic order in 1859. He has been dubbed the most 'famous (or infamous as the case may be) Freemason of his times'. He died peacefully in April 1891 while working at his desk at the Scottish Rite Temple in Washington, DC. Ironically, most of those who become Freemasons today know little, if anything, about him.

Pike joined Freemasonry in 1850 at the Western Star Lodge No. 2, Little Rock, Arkansas, and became a Master Mason in November that same year. In 1859, thus in less than a decade, he rose to the position of Sovereign Grand Master of the Supreme Council, 33°, of the Scottish Rite in the United States and, by definition, the whole world. When Pike joined the Scottish Rite he found the order in tatters, but by the end of his life 'he left it a stately temple to the dignity and rights of man' and made it the 'single most influential body of Freemasonry in the world.'[80] His first big task in this amazing reformation of the Scottish Rite was to rewrite and formalise the 33 degree rituals which had much degraded over the years. He then set about the task of providing a 'foundation literature' for the Scottish Rite, which entailed writing an opus of 860 pages entitled *Morals and Dogma of the Ancient and Accepted Scottish Rite of Freemasonry*, first published by the Scottish Rite Press in 1871.[81] This huge and somewhat baffling book was based on a series of lectures Pike had given, and is divided into 32 chapters to cover all the degrees except the last – the 33rd – which is not a degree as such, but more of a title.

It becomes evident on studying this book that Pike must have conducted an extensive investigation of comparative religion, Cabala, Hermeticism, mysticism, mythology, symbolism and speculative philosophy in general. For the first 60 years or so after it was published, *Morals and Dogma*, as it is known for short, was compulsory reading for all who joined the Scottish Rite. Yet in spite of its title, the book is not a Masonic manifesto at all, but rather an attempt to provide a historic and mythological framework for Scottish Rite Freemasons. Pike himself made it clear to his readers that they were free to accept or reject what he had written, although his immense reputation at the time meant that his research tended to be accepted without question. Besides, as one modern Masonic writer so correctly remarks about similar dubious historical claims, 'whether it is true is not the point; the point is that it is claimed to be true.'[82]

It was in *Morals and Dogma* that Pike made the association between the Masonic five-pointed 'Blazing Star' and the Egyptian star of Isis, Sirius, which is also often depicted as a five-pointed star. Pike strongly opposed the idea held at the time by some Masons that the Blazing Star represents the 'star of the East' i.e. the star of Bethlehem:

> To find in the Blazing Star of five points an allusion to Divine Providence is also fanciful; and to make it commemorative of the Star that is said to have guided the Magi is to give it a meaning comparatively modern. Originally, it represented SIRIUS, or the Dog Star.[83]

This was not the first time that Sirius had been equated with a Blazing Star. In Homer's *Iliad* (*circa* 800 BC) the wrath of the hero Achilles is described as the:

> ... blazing star that comes forth at harvest-time, shining forth amid the host of stars in the darkness of the night, the star whose name men call Orion's Dog [Sirius].[84]

We also find in Appolonius Rhodius's *Argonautica* that 'the Dog-star Sirius was scorching the Minoan Islands from the sky' Similarly there is a reference in the same text to 'Sirius rising from Okeanos [Oceanus], brilliant and beautiful but full of menace for the flocks.'[85] Aratus speaks of 'a star that keenest of all blazes with a searing flame and him men call Sirius.'[86] Finally Manilius referred to Sirius as 'the dog with the blazing face.'

So, whatever his faults, it seems that Albert Pike was a very meticulous scholar, and there can be little doubt that he consulted all these classical sources during his research for *Morals and Dogma*. Indeed, it is known that he had taught himself Latin, Greek and Sanskrit in order to study such ancient texts. We must also conclude that if Pike could easily make the obvious link between the Masonic 'Blazing Star' and Sirius, then quite clearly other educated Masons could have arrived at the same conclusion.

Did they?

Thomas Paine's Supreme Being

In 1782, after the surrender of the British at Yorktown, the Marquis de Lafayette returned to France to a huge hero's welcome. He was now ranked as a *Maréchal de Camp*, and served for a while as a diplomatic aide to Benjamin Franklin in Paris. In 1784 Franklin was joined by Thomas Jefferson, the new ambassador of the United States. In the same year Lafayette went on tour in Germany and met Frederick the Great. Meanwhile Thomas Paine was still in the United States, now poverty stricken and devoting his time to odd ventures like inventing the smokeless candle and designing a pierless iron bridge for the Schuylkill River near Philadelphia.[87]

Benjamin Franklin had been raised to the position of Grand Master of the Nine Sisters lodge in Paris seven years earlier, and had developed a large network of contacts in France and elsewhere in Europe. It is not so clear whether Thomas Jefferson was a Freemason but as James W. Beless, a 33rd degree Mason with an interest in this question, so aptly put it: 'Jefferson may not have been a card-carrying Mason, but his philosophy and actions certainly paralleled Masonic ideals and practices.'[88] A report from Dr. Guillotin, a member of the Nine Sisters lodge at the time when Jefferson was in Paris, confirms that Jefferson visited this lodge at least once.[89] There is also no doubt that Jefferson was often surrounded by prominent and very active Masons. According to Beless:

> His son-in-law, Governor of Virginia Thomas M. Randolph, his favourite grandson, Thomas Jefferson Randolph, and nephews Peter and Samuel Carr were all members of *Door to Virtue* Lodge No. 44, Albemarle County, Virginia. Freemasons such as Thomas Paine, Voltaire, Lafayette and Jean Houdon were some of his closest associates in Europe. Masons whom he admired in America included George Washington, Benjamin Franklin, Dr. Benjamin Rush, John Paul Jones, James Madison, James Monroe, Meriwether Lewis and William Clark ... He had marched in Masonic procession with *Widow's Son* Lodge No. 60 and *Charlottesville* Lodge No.

90 on October 6, 1817, at the cornerstone laying of Central College (now the University of Virginia) ... The Grand Lodges of South Carolina and Louisiana held funeral orations and processions for him following his death on July 4, 1826 and ... a Blue Lodge at Surrey Court House, Virginia, was named *Jefferson* Lodge No. 65 in 1801.[90]

While Jefferson was still in Paris, Paine returned to Europe in 1787. He first went to London where he hoped to get support for his iron bridge project. But after the fall of the Bastille in July 1789 he became interested in the French Revolution and began a regular correspondence with Jefferson in Paris.

In spring 1790 Paine travelled to Paris to advise Lafayette on constitutional matters, and during this first visit Lafayette presented him with the key of the (now nearly demolished) Bastille.[91] On the same trip, Paine made contact with the Freemason and writer Nicolas de Bonneville, who, with the Abbé Fauchet, had recently founded the so-called *Cercle Social* (the 'Social Circle'), a radical literary group that promoted deism and republican virtues and ideals. Later, in 1812, Nicolas de Bonneville would translate Thomas Paine's *Origins of Freemasonry* into French. In this work, Paine argues that the ancient Egyptian cult of the Sun and of Osiris are at the root of Masonic rituals.[92]

Among Paine's other Parisian friends and supporters was the Marquis de Condorcet, also a Freemason and a friend of Voltaire. A renowned mathematician as well as champion of human rights, Condorcet was a member of the Nine Sisters lodge – where fellow members included Benjamin Franklin, the occultist and inventor of the Tarot, Court de Gébelin, and the astronomer Lalande. Let us recall in passing that it was Court de Gébelin who, in 1781, had written in his celebrated book, *Le Monde Primitif analysé et comparé avec le monde moderne*, that:

> No one ignores that Paris was originally enclosed in the island [the Île de la Cité]. It was thus, since its origins, a city of navigation ... As it was in a river rife with navigation, it took as its symbol a boat, and as tutelary goddess, Isis, goddess of navigation; and this boat was the actual one of Isis, symbol of this goddess.[93]

The reader will recall from Chapter Seventeen that Court de Gébelin, who belonged to the 'Scottish Rite' and 'Templar' Freemasonry, had met the famous Cagliostro, inventor of 'Egyptian' Freemasonry, and admitted himself not qualified 'to interrogate a man so much his superior in every branch of learning'.[94]

It was Court de Gébelin who, along with Franklin, was given the ultimate honour of escorting Voltaire during the latter's Masonic initiation at the Nine Sisters lodge in 1778. Why, out of all the many illustrious members available, was Court de Gébelin selected to officiate in this most historic of initiations? The reason, we suspect, may well be in the alleged connection linking the Scottish Rite's 'degrees', the Tarot's 'cards' and the Cabalistic 'paths' – with the number 32 being the mystical common denominator for all three.

We saw in Chapter Fifteen, that the 33rd degree Scottish Rite author Charles Sunmer Lobingier, historian for the Grand Commandery of the Scottish Rite in Washington, DC, deduced that in the Cabala's 32 paths of wisdom[95] 'we doubtless have the origin of the number of degrees as formulated by the Grand Constitution' of the Scottish Rite.[96] It is well known that the modern esoteric Tarot is largely modelled on the ideologies of the Cabala and the Cabalistic Sephiroth. Even more interestingly in this context, we may recall that it was Court de Gébelin himself who had attributed to the Tarot an 'Egyptian origin' and furthermore had asserted that the so-called *Star* in the Tarot deck was none other than the star of Isis, Sirius. And even though Thomas Paine could not have met Court de Gébelin (the latter died several years before Paine came to Paris) all this goes to show the potent brew of Cabalistic and Hermetic ideologies that was bubbling amongst Paine's circle of friends in Paris at the precise time that he was preparing to publish his celebrated *Rights of Man*.

In early May 1790 Paine returned to London just as Edmund Burke published his *Reflections on the French Revolution* – a broadside attack on the uprising of the French people against the monarchy. Paine's outraged response was his celebrated *Rights of Man*, the first part of which he wrote and rushed into print before going back to Paris in early 1791 to establish the first 'republican' club there and to write his *Republican Manifesto*. By July 1791 the energetic Paine was once again in London where he wrote the second part of *Rights of Man* and dedicated it to Lafayette.[97]

It was during his visits to Paris that Paine met Thomas Jefferson who would become his friend and confidante.[98] Meanwhile in London he frequented an elite group of radical thinkers including the famous English poet William Blake. For all these radical intellectuals, as Professor David Cody has shown, the French Revolution in its early stages:

... portrayed itself as a triumph of the forces of reason over those of superstition and privilege ... [and] as a symbolic act which presaged the return of humanity to the state of perfection from which it had fallen away.[99]

Not unexpectedly Thomas Paine's *Rights of Man* was immediately banned by the British government and, rather disturbingly, effigies of Paine were burnt outside churches. Paine himself was indicted for 'seditious libel' which, in those dangerous days, carried the death penalty. He narrowly managed to escape arrest, however, through the timely intervention of his good friend, William Blake, who warned Paine not to return to his home and helped him flee immediately to France.

Upon arriving in Paris, Paine was hailed as a hero and friend of the revolutionaries and was promptly given honorary French citizenship and made a member of the National Assembly. But being a pacifist, Paine opposed the death penalty for Louis XVI and instead voted that the king be exiled. This stance infuriated the zealous Robespierre who had Paine thrown into prison in the old Luxembourg Palace. While incarcerated there, Paine managed to arrange for the publication of the first part of his most famous work, *The Age of Reason*.

In *Age of Reason* Paine makes clear that he was a deist and believed in a Supreme Being while opposing the established Church. Naturally he must have been aware that at precisely this time, Robespierre and Jacques-Louis David were pressing on with their own cults of 'Reason' and the 'Supreme Being'. And we know that 'Reason' and 'Liberty' – in the mind of at least David – were personified as the Egyptian goddess Isis during that strange ceremony that took place at the Bastille on 10 August 1793. In consideration of Paine's keen interest in Masonic origins, and his belief that Freemasonry owed its rituals to the Druids and the ancient Egyptians, it is not impossible that the personification of Paine's 'Reason' might also have veiled the same ancient goddess of the Nile ...

On 18 September 1793, barely five weeks after the 'Isis' ceremony in Paris, another republican ceremony was about to take place on the other side of the Atlantic on the summit of a low hill overlooking the Potomac River. But this time it was not to celebrate the demolition of a vilified national monument like the Bastille but rather to lay the cornerstone of a great 'Temple of Liberty' that would be built here – the brainchild of yet another adventurous Frenchman, Pierre-Charles L'Enfant.

Engineer, artist, soldier

On a warm and bright spring day in April 1909, D. H. Rhodes, the depot quartermaster of Digges Farm near Washington, DC, with the commissioners of the District of Columbia all present, supervised the disinterment of the remains of a man who had died 84 years previously, in 1825. The pitiful remains were gently gathered and placed in a metal-lined casket which was then covered with the American flag and taken to the Mount Olive Cemetery. Early in the morning of 28 April the casket was moved to the Capitol where it lay in solemn state until noon. Then, under military escort, it was finally taken to Arlington National Cemetery and buried in a permanent grave on sloping ground in front of the Custis-Lee Mansion and overlooking, in the distance, the city of Washington. A sum of $1,000 was allocated by Congress to erect a monument over the grave, featuring the street plan of the Federal City. Below the plan the name of the deceased may also be seen: *Pierre-Charles L'Enfant, engineer, artist, soldier.*

Pierre-Charles L'Enfant was born in Paris in 1754, the son of a painter of landscapes and battle-scenes.[100] Like his father before him, the young L'Enfant was educated at France's *Académie Royale de Peinture et de Sculpture.* There he learnt how to design military fortifications. He also studied the science of landscapes from the works of André Le Nôtre who, a century earlier, had designed the Tuileries Garden and the great Historical Axis of Paris. L'Enfant then joined the French army, and by 1776 when the American War of Independence began, he had reached the rank of lieutenant.

Like Lafayette and many other young Frenchmen of the time, L'Enfant was fired up with the new republican ideals of liberty and equality, and promptly offered his services to the American Revolutionary army. His knowledge of fortifications proved invaluable, and brought him to the attention of George Washington. L'Enfant was made 'captain of engineers', the embryo of what would later become the US Army Corps of Engineers. In March 1782 Washington was to write to L'Enfant:

> Your zeal and active services are such as reflect the highest honour on yourself and are extremely pleasing to me, and I have no doubt they will have their due weight with Congress in any future promotion in your Corps [of Engineers].[101]

Networking with the Cincinnati

We were intrigued to discover that L'Enfant had been associated with an organisation known as the Society of the Cincinnati.

Founded in 1783 for officers who had served in the War of Independence, to help them and their families in case of need, the society still exists today. Named after the fifth century Roman soldier Lucius Quintus Cincinnatus, it is a patriotic and elitist military organisation with the peculiarity of being based on hereditary membership and only open to the eldest male descendants of the original members. George Washington was its first president and, in 1790, the society gave its name to the city of Cincinnati.[102] Its membership would include America's first treasury secretary, Alexander Hamilton, first secretary of war, Henry Knox, and future president, James Monroe – the latter whose name is immortalised, of all places, in West Africa as 'Monrovia', the capital of Liberia.[103]

Although the Society of the Cincinnati is not a Masonic order as such, many of its founder members – Lafayette, Hamilton, Knox and Washington – were Freemasons, and thus not surprisingly 'the Cincinnati shared a rhetoric of fraternal affection and honour as well as a significant number of members with Masonry.'[104] In 1785 L'Enfant opened an architectural practice in New York, and through his Cincinnati connections, managed to land many lucrative design projects. When, in 1789, L'Enfant heard that plans were being made to establish a new federal capital for the United States in Virginia, he wrote directly to his old friend George Washington. According to Jean Jules Jusserand, author, historian and formerly French ambassador to the United States:[105]

> L'Enfant, with his tendency to see things *en grand*, could not fail to act accordingly, and the moment he heard that the Federal City would be neither New York nor Philadelphia, nor any other already in existence, but one to be built expressly, he wrote to Washington a letter remarkable by his clear understanding of the opportunity offered to the country, and by his determined purpose to work not for the three million inhabitants of his day, but for the one hundred of ours, and for all the unborn millions that will come after us. The letter is dated from New York, *11th of September, 1789*. 'Sir', he said, 'the late determination of Congress to lay the foundation of a city which is to become the capital of this vast empire offers so great an occasion of acquiring reputation to whoever may be appointed to conduct the execution of the business that your Excellency will not be surprised that my ambition and the desire I have of becoming a useful citizen should lead me to wish a share in the undertaking ...
> No nation, perhaps, had ever before the opportunity offered them of deliberately deciding on the spot where their capital city should be fixed

... And, although the means now within the power of the country are not such as to pursue the design to any great extent, it will be obvious that the plan should be drawn on such a scale as to leave room for that aggrandizement and embellishment which the increase of the wealth of the nation will permit it to pursue at any period, however remote. Viewing the matter in this light, I am fully sensible of the extent of the undertaking.[106] [Emphasis added]

'Templar' Octagons again, and the Tree of Life

In early 1791 George Washington asked Thomas Jefferson to instruct L'Enfant to proceed to Georgetown to join and give assistance to Andrew Ellicott, a Quaker and Freemason from Pennsylvania who was also the land surveyor for the District of Columbia. Ellicott, who was 37 at the time, was the son of a watchmaker from Bucks County in Pennsylvania and had grown up with a keen interest in astronomy. He had attained the rank of major during the War of Independence, and had somehow worked his way into a close friendship with Washington and Benjamin Franklin – the latter being particularly interested in Ellicott's by then very good knowledge of astronomy and of the techniques of stellar observation.[107]

In 1790 Washington appointed Ellicott as surveyor for the new federal capital – a job that he pursued with diligence over the coming year with the assistance of his younger brother Joseph. Ellicott had good reason to believe that he was Washington's chosen man for the job. L'Enfant, however, was to change all that. The strong-willed and pompous Frenchman simply barged in armed with Washington's instruction to 'assist' and practically took over from Ellicott.

L'Enfant's specific task was to 'have a drawing of the particular grounds most likely to be approved for the site of the federal town and buildings.'[108] L'Enfant worked closely with Jefferson to produce a preliminary plan by June 1791, and in September, he received a letter from the newly appointed commissioners responsible for the administration of the project informing him that the:

Federal district shall be called the 'Territory of Columbia' and the Federal City the 'City of Washington'.[109]

L'Enfant, described by many who knew him as hot-tempered and arrogant, soon began to antagonise the commissioners and refused to obey their instructions. The situation deteriorated rapidly, and in February 1792 George

Washington was forced to ask Thomas Jefferson to give L'Enfant a severe warning that he must recognise the authority of the commissioners. L'Enfant, however, was unwilling to compromise, and resigned from the project.

That same year Washington promoted Ellicott to surveyor general for the United States and gave him the task of completing the plan for Washington, DC based largely on L'Enfant's original design.[110] Within a month Ellicott had an engraving ready.

The suspicion has been raised that both George Washington and Thomas Jefferson participated directly in the evolution of this plan, here and there putting in their own specific ideas. For example, in their book *The Temple and the Lodge*, Michael Baigent and Richard Leigh point to curious octagonal patterns that seem to underlie the layout of Washington, DC, and argue that these were Templar symbols introduced by Washington himself. The octagons are huge and can be clearly made out in two distinct areas centred on the Capitol and the White House.[111]

The first printed edition of L'Enfant's plan, measuring 8.5 x 10 inches, is kept at the Library of Congress, Geography and Map Division, in Washington, DC.[112] The engraving was made by the artists James Thackara and John Vallance, and is thought to be the earliest surviving print of Washington, DC. Attached to the print is an article, published in the *Universal Asylum and Columbian Magazine* in March 1793, entitled *Description of the City of Washington, in the territory of Columbia, ceded by the States of Virginia and Maryland to the United States, by them established as the Seat of their Government.*[113]

The first observation to make about L'Enfant's plan is its grand ambition. For what the Frenchman had in mind was a splendid metropolis for 800,000 inhabitants, with classical buildings and monuments appropriate to the capital of an eventual gigantic republican empire of 500 million citizens. Now at the time, the entire population of the United States could not have then been much more than four million. The population of the whole of Europe was, in fact, less than 200 million and the world's population would have been around 900 million. Today there are more than 300 million people in the United States, a figure that is expected to double by the next century.[114] If it does, the US population would meet up with L'Enfant's staggering projection nearly 300 years later.

The plan itself is as ingenious as it is intriguing. Immediately one is struck by the similarity – or more precisely the *combined* similarity – to the city plan of Paris, to the plan of Versailles and, even more intriguing, to Wren's and Evelyn's aborted plans for London. But this is perhaps not so surprising. Apparently Jefferson, who was himself an accomplished architect and who had visited and studied many European urban centres, had supplied L'Enfant with plans of several European cities to serve as a guide.[115]

Like Paris and London, L'Enfant's plan features a dominant east-west layout, emphasized by the alignment of the Mall (which he called *Grande Avenue*) that runs from the US Capitol to the (future) Washington Monument. This would understandably lead a casual observer to conclude that the main axis of the city was fixed, whether by intent or by coincidence, to the equinox sunrise and sunset.[116] A closer examination of the map and contemporary accounts, however, makes it clear that the principal axis that L'Enfant had in mind was a presidential avenue (Pennsylvania Avenue), which joined the US Capitol to the presidential palace (the White House).

It does not take much to see that L'Enfant's plan was heavily inspired by the layout of Paris and, perhaps even more so, by the 'unexecuted' layouts of the city of London made by Wren and Evelyn after the Great Fire.[117] Most notable is the diamond-shaped design that evokes the Sephirothic Tree of Life; although not as evident as on Evelyn's plan for London, it can easily be discerned in the layout scheme which emanates from the Capitol in the east and culminates at the Washington Monument – a gigantic obelisk – in the west.

In Robert Cameron's excellent book *Above Washington*,[118] a series of stunning aerial photographs show that, in the main, the modern city has stayed fairly true to L'Enfant's scheme. Starting with the Capitol as the node of the plan looking west, two major avenues shoot at an angle, one to the southwest (Maryland) and to the other to the northwest (Pennsylvania) forming the classical upper portion of the Sephirothic Tree of Life which has as its node the first *sephirah* (divine emanation) representing the godhead. And although it may seem strange to equate the Capitol with the godhead, we note that in 1830 Congress commissioned a massive statue of George Washington seated on a throne in the style of Zeus, the godhead *par excellence* of the classical world. Initially placed in the forefront of the Capitol, the statue, sculpted by Horatio Greenough, was then moved to a less ostentatious location on the east side of the Mall, and today can be seen in the Smithsonian Museum.[119]

Continuing with the hypothetical sephirothic scheme of L'Enfant's Washington, DC, we note that the location of the gigantic obelisk of the Washington Monument corresponds to the *sephirah* known as *Tipheret*, which means 'Beauty'. This *sephirah*, as we saw in Chapter Fifteen, represents the Sun, the centre of things, from which emanates all life and light. The analogy intended by the 'Egyptian' obelisk that stands in Washington therefore seems obvious. Towering more than seven times as high those in Rome, Paris, London and New York, this powerful solar talisman is today the emblem of the capital city of the new world order.

Echoes

If we overlay Christopher Wren's plan for London with L'Enfant's for Washington we find that the Royal Exchange in the former corresponds with the US Capitol in the latter. Since we know that the laying of the cornerstone of the US Capitol was an intensely Masonic affair involving George Washington himself, the juxtaposition of the Capitol and the Royal Exchange raises an obvious question: was any similar Masonic ceremony ever held in London for the Royal Exchange?

The Royal Exchange was founded as the *bourse* by Sir Thomas Gresham in 1566 and received its present name by royal proclamation in 1571. On 3 September 1666 it was engulfed by the Great Fire and totally destroyed. Soon afterwards, however, Charles II commissioned new plans from the architect Edward Jarman for the rebuilding of the Royal Exchange[120] and work began in mid-1667. Just as Washington, Freemason and president of the United States, participated in the Capitol ceremony in 1793, so too, as we shall see, did Charles II, suspected Freemason and king of England, participate at the equivalent ceremony at the Royal Exchange 126 years earlier.

Thomas Gresham, the founder of the Royal Exchange, died in 1579. But his name has been persistently linked to Freemasonry and his legacy continued to play a role in its development long after his death. In 1660 his London residence, Gresham's house at Bishopsgate – by then Gresham College – became the first home of the Royal Society. The reader will recall that many of the original protagonists linked with Gresham College such as Sir Robert Moray, John Wilkins, Christopher Wren, Elias Ashmole and John Evelyn were, in some way or other, associated with either the Invisible College, the Royal Society or the early Masonic lodges in London. Though harder to specify there was also a strong Masonic 'ambience' at Gresham College, as Robert Lomas shows in his study of the Royal Society. This 'ambience' can be sensed in Gresham's own decree that 'seven readers' or scholars should be appointed there to lecture on each of the 'seven liberal arts'.[121] Indeed Lomas goes so far as to argue that the college was 'the main centre for Freemasonry in Restoration London ... which Sir Thomas Gresham had set up to support his Masonic ideals of study'.[122]

We have also seen in Chapter Fifteen how Christopher Wren, unlike John Evelyn, had retained the original location of the Royal Exchange in his plan for London, giving it a pre-eminent position in his overall layout. This is what historian Adrian Tinniswood has to say about Wren's decision:

> The real pride of place went to the [Royal] Exchange piazza with its radial vistas and its surrounding complex of commercial buildings. The absolutist ideology underlying the planning of Sixtine Rome, which Louis XIV and André Le Nôtre were currently putting to such good use in the laying out of Versailles, was here called into service to pay homage to mercantilism. *Trade was to be the new religion.*[123]

The 'new religion', in Wren's mind, might well have been a concoction of the new scientific ideologies coming from Royal Society, Freemasonry and Templarism – all of which extolled the virtues of commerce and trade. For all their possible dualism at a late stage of their history let's not forget that the Templars were at the very root of the banking and investment systems of Europe. As for the Freemasons, they would eventually insinuate themselves into the trade guilds and into the banking, investment and insurance institutions of the city of London. Thus the Royal Exchange becomes the symbol or talisman of mercantilism and all it stands for.

The confirmation that Masons and their rituals were involved in the rebuilding of Gresham's Royal Exchange after the Great Fire comes in the diary of Elias Ashmole where a cryptic note reads as follows:

> King Charles his position of the first stone at the Royall Exchange uppon its Restauration October 23rd, 1667, 23h. 7m. a.m. P. Esq. Ashmole et Dm. Bernard [sic].[124]

Elias Ashmole's pre-eminent role in the origins of Freemasonry in England requires no further emphasis. It should not surprise us, therefore, that according to historian C. H. Josten, a specialist on Elias Ashmole who examined this enigmatic entry, it is perhaps telling us that King Charles II laid the 'first stone' i.e. the cornerstone of the Royal Exchange 'in true Masonic form, and that for this reason Ashmole, the Freemason, was asked to determine the most propitious time for the ceremony.'[125] It is known that Ashmole was frequently asked by Charles II to 'cast horoscopes' for various stately functions and, more particularly, after the Great Fire of 1666, to select favourable dates for the laying of the cornerstones of important buildings. We know he did precisely this in 1675 when, for example, he participated in the cornerstone ceremony for St. Paul's (see next section). Indeed, the tradition of casting horoscopes or selecting propitious astrological dates for the laying of cornerstones of important buildings and monuments was then, and remains today, a common practice in Freemasonry. So we may well ask what was so 'favourable' about the date of 23 October selected by Ashmole?

We've already pointed out that in 1667 England was still using the Julian calendar which, at that time, lagged behind the Gregorian calendar by 10–11 days. A scholar like Ashmole would have known that the Gregorian calendar must soon be adopted in Britain – since it was obviously based on far more precise scientific realities than the Julian. Should this happen, then 23 October Julian would align to 13 October Gregorian. In other words, in most of continental Europe and, more particularly, France, the date of the ceremony for 'the first stone of the Royal Exchange' was not 23 October but *13 October*. To continental Freemasons, this date is immediately recognisable as a 'Templar' date, since, as we know, it marked the infamous suppression of the order on 13 October 1307. Ashmole was a Freemason with a keen penchant for heraldic chivalry. It is by no means out of the question that some sort of 'Templar' message was his hidden intent.

If this hypothesis is correct then similar 'Templar' symbolism might be expected to turn up in other cornerstone ceremonies where Elias Ashmole was involved. This should be especially be the case for St. Paul's Cathedral which we will now show to be an intensely 'Templar' talisman.

The Cornerstone of St. Paul's

There ceremony for the laying of the cornerstone of the new St. Paul's is surrounded by a riddle. According to one diary entry by Elias Ashmole, the event was supposed to have taken place on 21 June 1675. It would also appear that it was Ashmole who decided the date by a horoscope cast.[126] There is another entry in Ashmole's diary, however, that categorically states:

> *23 June 1675* 6h. 30' a.m. The foundation of St. Paul's Church London, layd. [sic].[127]

Historian and astrologer Derek Appleby believes that the different dates (21 June and 23 June) for the ceremony were due to a change of plan caused by bad weather.[128] This is possible. But there is another explanation. The prevailing calendar in England was still the Julian one, so that the date of 21 June – although evoking the summer solstice in the new Gregorian calendar

– actually fell 10–11 days *after* the solstice in the Julian calendar and thus had no special significance in that respect. What 23 June Julian did denote, however, was St. John's Eve, the herald to the Masonic and Templar New Year celebrated on 24 June. There is no question at all that Elias Ashmole would have been acutely aware of the meaning of this date. The reader will also recall that when British Freemasons created the Grand Lodge they chose to do so on 24 June *because it was* St. John's Day. But then, in 1814, the Gregorian calendar had been long previously been adopted (since 1752 in fact). In Ashmole's day, however, the Julian calendar was still very much in force.[129]

So what did Ashmole really have in mind – a Julian date or a Gregorian one? ...

If we convert 23 June Julian to its Gregorian counterpart we get 4 July.[130] How likely is it to be an accident, therefore, that in all history books on the Knights Templar, the date of 4 July is particularly highlighted. It is the date of the Templars' massive defeat by Muslim armies in the Holy Land at the Horns of Hattin on 4 July 1187 which was followed by the loss of Jerusalem to Christendom. There could therefore hardly be a more evocative 'Templar' or 'Solomonic' date than 4 July – evocative, that is, of the aspiration to rebuild Solomon's Temple in Jerusalem. The reader will also be aware, of course, that 4 July is Independence Day in the US, commemorating the signature of the Declaration of Independence and converting the date forever into a powerful talisman that spells out 'independence' and 'freedom' for the New World and, now by and large, for a new world order.[131]

It would be almost perverse in these circumstances to fail to examine more closely the dates of the cornerstone ceremonies of powerful talismanic monuments such as the US Capitol and the White House – and even the Pentagon – for possible astrological, Masonic and 'Templar' symbolism.

The Virgin and the Star

Masonic author David Ovason points out that when the cornerstone laying ceremony of the US Capitol took place on the morning of 18 September 1793, the Sun was in the constellation of Virgo, which, he argues, had special significance in the scheme of things.[132] According to Ovason:

> The imagery of Virgo as ruler of Washington DC is reflected in the considerable number of Zodiacs and lapidary symbols which grace the city. The Virgoan connection has also been emphasized in a number of foundation charts which are of fundamental importance to Washington

DC. The foundation of the city itself, and the three corners of the triangle which L'Enfant had marked out for its centre (the Capitol, the White House, and the Washington Monument) were each set down on the earth at a time when the constellation Virgo had a particular importance in the skies.[133]

Not being astrologers or Freemasons ourselves, we cannot vouch for certain on Ovason's theory. What we can support, however, is the hunch that *astronomy* had an important part to play in the planning and symbolism of cities such as Washington, DC.[134] Ovason goes on to make a particularly strong case that much of the symbolism surrounding events and monuments related to the Declaration of Independence and the foundation of the United States can be linked to the ancient heraldic star Sirius, whose pictogram was the well-known five-pointed star.[135] With this in mind, there is, we think, another astronomical matter to consider in connection to the Capitol.

Astronomical software such as *Starry Night* or *SkyMap Pro*, makes it a relatively easy matter to reconstruct ancient skies for any epoch and any location with a high level of precision and realism. We can thus, quite literally, observe events that were going on 'invisibly' in the sky (invisible because they were obscured to the naked eye by the light of the Sun) when the cornerstone of the Capitol was laid on the morning of 18 September 1793.

At Jenkins Heights, the location of the future Capitol, preparations had been going on through the night for the arrival of George Washington and his retinue of important guests. The White House (which had undergone its own Masonic cornerstone ceremony a little less than a year earlier on the now familiar 'Templar' date of 13 October 1792)[136] was to be the starting point of the procession. From there the presidential party would travel in horse-drawn carriages along Pennsylvania Avenue to Jenkins Heights.

The alignment of Pennsylvania Avenue between the White House and Jenkins Heights is 22° south-of-east. Looking along this alignment it cannot be an accident that a few hours before sunrise on 18 September 1793 (cloud conditions allowing) observers would have been able to see the bright star Sirius rising directly over Jenkins Heights. It would slowly have gained in altitude as the world turned, so that by dawn it would have been positioned, quite alone, over the spot where the Capitol would stand. That such portentous astral symbolism could have gone unnoticed by the group of important Freemasons and astronomers who planned Washington and decided the locations of its principal structures, seems most unlikely. But if this is so, it would mean that the axis of Pennsylvania Avenue must have been *deliberately* set by Pierre L'Enfant and/or by his colleague Andrew Ellicott so that it would be directed towards the rising of the star Sirius.

Is there anything to suggest that this is likely?

We have already seen how Pierre L'Enfant, while a student of architecture and city planning in Paris, had been much influenced by the work of the 17th century landscaper André Le Nôtre. It was Le Nôtre who had been directly responsible for the famous axis of Paris running from the Tuileries Garden, on the west side of the Louvre, along the Champs-Élysées and all the way to Chaillot Hill – where today stands the Arc de Triomphe. This axis, as the reader will recall, was directed by Le Nôtre 26° north-of-west and 26° south-of-east such that it aligned, whether by coincidence or intent, to the rising-point of Sirius – also 26° south-of-east – as observed from Paris during the reign of Louis XIV. Because there is a difference of 10° of latitude between Paris and Washington, DC, the rising point of Sirius as observed from Washington is also different. We have seen calculations show that the star rose 22° south-of-east, and thus in line with Pennsylvania Avenue,[137] when observed from Washington in the epoch of L'Enfant.

It makes sense to suppose that L'Enfant would have been well-aware of this fact. And so would the respected surveyor and astronomer, Andrew Ellicott, the man responsible for physically setting out the axis of Pennsylvania Avenue. Being a Freemason as well, he could hardly have ignored the alignment with the rising of Sirius, the five-pointed 'Blazing Star' of the Scottish Rite Masons, which would have been very obvious for much of the year to anyone standing at the White House and looking southeast towards the site of the future Capitol …[138]

So let us venture a little further in this direction and see what else comes up.

Hidden in the sky

While researching his book, *The Secret Zodiacs of Washington DC*, David Ovason noticed that when he looked back from the US Capitol westwards along Pennsylvania Avenue towards the White House from 6 to 12 August he would see the Sun setting in alignment with this avenue:

> For a period of about one week, the sunset viewed from the Capitol seems to take place directly over the western end of Pennsylvania Avenue. From 6 to 12 August the disc of the sun cuts into the horizon above the avenue, with almost magical precision. Anyone who watches the sunset, on any of

those days, cannot fail to realise that the designers of this city intended this period – or perhaps *one* day in this period – to be an important element in the city's design.[139]

Ovason goes on to note that:

In terms of the spherical geometry of astronomy, and the computerised programs available in modern times, there is no problem to establish a 'theoretical' date for the significant sunset. The Capitol is at longitude W 77° 01', latitude N 38° 53'. The azimuth for Pennsylvania Avenue proposed by Ellicott and L'Enfant was 290 degrees. This points to sunset around 11 and 12 August.[140]

If we use similar computer software to recreate the sky for the epoch of 1793 as seen from Washington, DC, and focus our attention on the period of 11–12 August, we will notice something most interesting not only regarding the Sun, as Ovason has observed, but also regarding the star Sirius. For on these very days Sirius rose *heliacally*, i.e. shortly before the Sun. The reader will recall that the heliacal rising of Sirius in ancient Egypt was the astro-solar event marking the beginning or 'birth' of the New Year and seems to have been the focus of much attention in Masonic esoteric lore. Let us recall also that the heliacal rising of Sirius was incorporated into the myth of the 'solar' birth of Alexander the Great and, if our theory is correct, into the myth of Louis XIV's 'Capetian miracle', and also into the very axis of Paris itself.

If you were both a land surveyor as well as a Freemason, like Andrew Ellicott (or, indeed, like George Washington himself), it would have been difficult under these circumstances *not* to associate the event of the heliacal rising of Sirius as viewed from Washington in 1793 with the 'birth' of the new Federal City and capital of the world's first true republic since Rome. It is perhaps pertinent also to note that the world's first 'republic' had been founded by Julius Caesar who, as it turns out, commemorated the republican era with the founding of the Julian calendar in 48 BC which had been calibrated for him in Alexandria in Egypt by an Egyptian astronomer who made use of the heliacal rising of Sirius.

Can it be a coincidence, therefore, that on 15 April 1791 at 3:30 p.m., a congregation of Freemasons gathered in *Alexandria* near the future site of Washington, DC and enacted the Masonic ceremony of the 'first stone' presided over by the Master of Alexandria-Washington Lodge No. 22?[141] Let us also note in passing that the Sun was in Pisces, a Christic symbol, when the constellation of Leo (a 'kingly' symbol) was on the rise in the east.

Next let's consider the heliacal rising of Sirius as seen from the city of Paris in that same year of 1793. There, because of the change of latitude, it would have occurred not on 11–12 August but on 20 August. In plain observational terms, this means that when looking from the Place de l'Étoile towards the Louvre just before dawn on 20 August 1793, an observer would have see the star Sirius rising over the Louvre Palace's south wing, right above the apartments where the 'Capetian miracle' had taken place. Also at this precise moment the Sun would have been in conjunction with the star Regulus, *Alpha Leonis*, the star of the 'solar-kings'. Indeed, this is why in ancient times the official 'birthday' of Alexander the Great was celebrated on 26 July Julian – because on that day the same conjunction of the Sun and Regulus likewise accompanied the heliacal rising of Sirius in Alexandria.

Such occult and astrological considerations seem in place in Alexandria in 332 BC, but we found it quite eerie and unsettling to be obliged to suspect that they also determined the positioning and alignments of major avenues and monuments in the great modern cities of the West.

And still the clues kept on presenting themselves ...

An obelisk for Washington

In 1799, five years after the founding of Washington, DC, George Washington died. The Freemasons of the United States organised his stately funeral, and all the lodges both in America and in France were temporarily turned into 'lodges of sorrow'.

In that same year of 1799 Napoleon's army occupied Egypt. To all Republican Masons, this must have seemed like a great historical moment when the ancient 'home' of Freemasonry was finally drawn into the new Masonic-cum-republican world order initiated by the United States and France.

Soon after Washington's death, plans were prepared to raise a great 'national monument' in Washington, DC due west of the US Capitol in commemoration of the first president of the Republic. In May 1800, the congressional committee formed for this purpose expressed itself in favour of building a pyramid, 100 feet square at the base and 'of proportional height', but lack of funds and, eventually lack of interest, meant that the project was shelved.[142] In 1833, however, a group of patriots created the Washington National Monument Society, which was successful in raising funds. Approval was obtained from Congress for the design and construction of an edifice appropriate to the memory of the 'Father of the Nation'.

The first design proposed was by Peter Force, an influential Freemason and one of the founding members of the society. His idea, too, was a pyramid, but this time even more enormous than the one envisaged in 1800.[143] In 1836 a design was put forward by Robert Mills, a Freemason and architect, which consisted of a circular colonnaded temple with a statue of Washington in Graeco-Roman garb riding the solar chariot of Apollo with a huge obelisk rising above it adorned with an enormous 'blazing five-pointed star' at the top. The design that was finally retained, however, was that of a lone giant obelisk with a tapered pyramidal apex – the Washington Monument that we know today. The obelisk, which is slightly taller than 555 feet, had to be placed slightly offset from the centerline of the Mall due to poor ground-bearing conditions in the ideal spot.

The notion of a pyramid (and an obelisk is simply a pyramid on a pillar) rising symbolically above the new Republic has a background. It had previously been proposed in 1776 when Benjamin Franklin and Thomas Jefferson designed the Great Seal of the United States (which can still be still seen today on the back of the US one-dollar bill, introduced in 1931 by Franklin D. Roosevelt, a 32nd degree Scottish Rite Freemason). In 1789 the same symbol was placed on top of the Declaration of the Rights of Man and of the Citizen signed in Paris under the guidance of the Freemasons Benjamin Franklin and the Marquis de Lafayette.

The cornerstone ceremony for the Washington Monument took place on Independence Day, 4 July 1848. We have already discussed the curious 'Templar' symbolism of this date, and also how it 'converts' to the St. John's Day of the Freemasons according to the Julian calendar. Appropriately, therefore, the cornerstone ritual for the Washington Monument was organised by the Freemasons of America, hundreds of whom attended in full Masonic regalia.[144] The ceremony was conducted by a prominent Mason, Benjamin French, the Grand Master for the District of Columbia, who donned the Masonic apron and sash that George Washington had worn for the 1793 ceremony of the Capitol. According to author David Ovason,

> The moment of the ceremonial cornerstone laying of the Monument has been preserved, and from this it is possible to reconstruct the foundation chart ... In many ways it is a remarkable horoscope, for it reflects precisely the same sort of stellar magic as was practiced in ancient Egypt, millennia ago.[145]

Due to lack of funds and political shenanigans, construction was delayed for several decades after the cornerstone had been laid, and it was not until 1880 that work began again at the site. A 'second' cornerstone ceremony was therefore arranged for 7 August 1880 at 'one minute of 11 o'clock.' Sensing that this curiously precise timing (10:59 a.m.) was for astronomical rather than astrological reasons, David Ovason worked out that the intention might have been to make a link with the rising of a particular star which, in this case, turned out to be *Spica*, the brightest star in the constellation of Virgo. The inspiration may have perhaps come from the Masonic astronomer Lalande who had been a founding member of the Nine Sisters lodge in Paris and who was present, along with Benjamin Franklin and the Tarot astrologer Court de Gébelin, at the initiation of Voltaire in 1778. Lalande had written that:

> The Virgin is consecrated to Isis, just as Leo is consecrated to her husband Osiris ... They put a wheat-ear in the hand of the Virgin, to express the idea of the months, perhaps because the sign of the Virgin was called by the Orientalists ... *epi*, or wheat-ear.[146]

It is likely that such ideas were entertained by those involved in the cornerstone ceremony of the Washington Obelisk which, after all, is a blatant 'Egyptian' symbol selected by Freemasons.

The final dedication of the obelisk took place on 21 February 1885, which was, curiously enough, just one day after George Washington's birthday. On that cold and snowy day, 21 Masonic lodges of the District of Columbia, as well as Masonic delegations from Massachusetts, Delaware, Pennsylvania, Maryland, Virginia, Texas, South Carolina and Georgia, along with a vast number of 'brothers', formed a huge procession. The president and members of Congress joined the Freemasons while a huge crowd of onlookers cheered and the US Marine Band played a 'number of rousing marches.' Ovason's calculations show that this ceremony, which took place in the afternoon, occurred at the moment of the rising of Sirius over the Capitol.[147] 'The extraordinary truth', he concludes:

> ... is that the very existence of the Washington Monument is intimately linked to the Egyptian star Sirius ... that the ancients represented in their sacred hieroglyphics as an obelisk-like form as well as a star. How is it possible that this most important star of the ancient world should find itself, as it were, resurrected in the architecture of the United States?[148]

In 1998 Robert Bauval visited the Washington Monument, which had been completely shored up with scaffolding for repair and embellishments in preparation for the millennium celebration planned for Washington, DC. Inside the monument's entrance, right over the door lintel, Bauval noticed a bronze plaque on which the face of George Washington had been sculpted by the French artist Jean-Antoine Houdon, a Freemason, and member of the Nine Sisters lodge in Paris, whose other subjects had included Cagliostro and Empress Joséphine.[149] Above the plaque was the unmistakable motif of the ancient Egyptian winged solar disc with a star prominently positioned at its centre.

We can now safely guess which star is represented here ...

The Pentagon and Sirius

In 1941, fifty-six years after the final dedication ceremony of the Washington Monument, another cornerstone was laid in Washington, DC, this time for a gigantic five-sided, star-shaped edifice: the Pentagon. The notables attending were not in Masonic regalia but instead wore the uniforms, spangled with gold five-pointed stars of the highest-ranking US military personnel.

Before the attack on Pearl Harbor in 1941, the 24,000 civilian and military personnel of the US War Department in Washington, DC were scattered amongst 17 buildings throughout the District of Columbia. In view of the forthcoming entry of the United States into World War II, it was hastily decided to place all these personnel together into one gigantic, centralised headquarters.[150] The job was given to the construction division of the US Army Quartermaster Corps, which produced a design for the future Pentagon in July 1941. The plans were approved by President Franklin D. Roosevelt who, on 1 December 1941, signed legislation transferring the whole project to the US Army Corps of Engineers. The first section was completed in April 1942, and the full edifice was completed on 15 January 1943 at a total cost of $85 million.[151]

In view of the great importance of the project, all the major decisions were approved by President Roosevelt himself.[152] It is often claimed that the distinctive and eponymous pentagonal shape of the building was derived from the fact that the first location proposed near Arlington cemetery was a five-sided plot of land. But if so, the question arises why the pentagonal design was retained even though another site was eventually chosen further to the south.

It is, of course, entirely possible that the prosaic explanation is the truth. But it is also true that Franklin Delano Roosevelt was raised as a Master

Freemason in 1911 at the Holland Lodge No. 8 in New York and, in 1929 became a 32nd degree Scottish Rite Mason at the Albany Masonic Temple.[153] He would have been acutely aware, as were all high ranking Scottish Rite Masons who had read Albert Pike's *Morals & Dogma*, that the pentagonal shape, or *pentacle*, was associated by Pike with the Masonic Blazing Star and, in turn, identified with the five-pointed star of ancient Egypt, Sirius.

In Robert Cameron's book *Above Washington*,[154] there is a remarkable photograph taken by NASA with infrared film, which 'demonstrates the ultimate refinement in aerial photography'. The photograph was taken by a U-2 spy plane from an altitude of 65,000 feet. Although the 'technical reading' for images of this sort is very specialised, even lay viewers can easily see that the positioning of the Pentagon on the west side of the Potomac seems to be guided by the general axis that leads southeast – and more or less parallel to Maryland Avenue across the river – straight towards the US Capitol.

Turning the observation around Robert Bauval calculated that the Pentagon lies some *24° south-of-west* when viewed from the Capitol. Reconstructing the skies over Washington, DC for the epoch 1941 with *Starry Night*, and directing his attention to 24° south-of-west he typed the command to 'run' the sky. As he had half-expected the star Sirius positioned itself right over the spot where the NASA photograph shows that the Pentagon is situated. Naturally Bauval wondered if here, too, a cornerstone ceremony had taken place in 1941 …

The True 'New Jerusalem' in Israel?

Every American, indeed almost everyone in the world, is acutely aware of the date of 11 September 2001. This was the 'day of infamy' when Arab terrorists crashed a commercial plane into the US Pentagon and two other planes into the Twin Towers of the World Trade Center in New York.

It was therefore very strange, indeed almost surreal, to discover that the date of the ground-breaking ceremony for the Pentagon was also 11 September – in its case 11 September 1941. Little has been made of this, although the coincidence can hardly be said to be obscure since President George W. Bush himself drew attention to it in a speech he gave to Pentagon staff exactly a month after the attack. According to the *Army Link News*:

> President George W. Bush, Lt. Gen. John Van Alstyne and First Lady Laura Bush joined a joint-service chorus and thousands of flag-waving Pentagon personnel in singing 'God Bless America' during the memorial ceremony

at the Pentagon Oct. 11, 2001 ... He [the president] listed a number of victims: three school children travelling with their teacher on the hijacked jet, an Army general officer, a Department of the Army civilian who had worked 30 years in the Pentagon, and a naval reservist. The President recalled how construction on the Pentagon, 'a symbol of America's freedom and confidence' and 'a symbol of our strength in the world,' began 60 years ago *on Sept. 11, 1941* ... [Emphasis added]

At this point we ask the reader to recall two things: (1) the intense 'Templar' and 'Judaic' characteristics of the Scottish Rite ceremonies to 'rebuild Solomon's Temple' in the context of the lodges; and (2) the root of the Islamic terrorists' grievance against the US – which is the oppression of the Palestinian people and the political and military support that the superpower extends to the state of Israel.

Could there have been more to President Roosevelt's – and President Truman's – involvement in the affair of the US Pentagon and the date of 11 September than at first meets the eye?

Is it a coincidence, for example, that the principal symbol used in 32nd degree Scottish Masonry is, in fact, a *pentagon*? And is it also a coincidence that in the same Masonic order, and same 32nd degree, the symbol of the pentagon is divided into five 'military' divisions of the 'Scottish Rite Army' in the same way the US Pentagon is divided into the five branches of the US Military?[155] More to the point, the Masonic author Christopher Knight, when investigating this very matter of the strange similarity between the US Pentagon and 32nd degree Scottish Rite rituals and symbolism, wrote,

... We could hardly believe our eyes. The 32nd degree is known as the degree of 'The Sublime Prince of the Royal Secret'. It comprises of three separate parts. These are the Opening Ceremony, the Ceremonial Section and the Allegory. This particular ceremony is very elaborate, as befits someone who has climbed as high on the Freemasonic ladder as it is possible to go under one's own effort. A great deal of play-acting takes place and the various characters all have fictional names. It suggests that the 32nd degree relates to the fight for Jerusalem ... The ceremony takes place in what appears to be a fictitious military camp ... [which] is a five sided figure or pentagon ...[156]

We know, of course, of the many harebrained conspiracy theories that followed the 11 September 2001 attacks, and we don't want to add more fuel to the fire. But it is also obvious that the foreign policies of Presidents Roosevelt and Truman greatly contributed to the creation of the state of Israel in the second half of the 1940s, and this made us wonder about their common affiliation to the Scottish Rite.

There is also the bizarre fact that President Roosevelt was both a 32nd degree Scottish Rite Mason as well as the 32nd president of the United States, while President Truman – who had been Roosevelt's vice-president – was both a 33rd degree Scottish Rite Mason and the 33rd president of the United States. In Scottish Rite Freemasonry, the four final degrees, from the 30th to the 33rd are the stage of initiation at which the candidate is thought to achieve the sublime objective of the Masonic enlightenment (or, some would say, 'experiment'), which – allegorically – is the 'rebuilding of the Temple of Solomon in Jerusalem'.

We've seen that the 'tracing board' provided in the rituals of the Scottish Rite's 30th degree makes use of the Sephirothic Tree of Life – which can be taken as the 'spiritual' representation of Solomon's Temple. As noted above, all such rituals are supposed to be purely allegorical, and we are assured by Masons that their meaning is simply that the candidate has achieved a level of spiritual perfection within himself as the human 'temple', and is thus compared, in a sense, to the perfection of the 'Temple of Solomon'.

Nonetheless we can hardly avoid posing the obvious question: is it possible that the Roosevelt and Truman administrations took the 'Masonic experiment' all the way and actually 'rebuilt' the Jewish Solomonic state in Palestine? As farfetched and incredible as it seems, there is something else in the background that justifies such an outrageous question – and this is the actual 'degrees' that both these presidents were linked to.

From the 30th to the 33rd degree

Several years ago while visiting a friend in Egypt, Robert Bauval was shown a Scottish Rite Masonic certificate issued at a lodge in Cairo in 1918 by the Supreme Council of the 33rd Degree. The certificate had belonged to the friend's maternal grandfather. Freemasonry is practically unknown in Egypt today, having been declared illegal by President Gamal Abdel Nasser in 1964. But in the early part of the 20th century it was extremely popular and many high-ranking government officials and even members of the Egyptian royal family were Freemasons.[157]

The certificate was printed in French and Arabic. Bauval, who is fluent in both languages, could not help noting not only that the location of the

Supreme Council was specified as 'Cairo', but also that the precise latitude was given as 'under the celestial vault at the zenith by 30° 2' 4" ...' which would pinpoint the location to somewhere in central Cairo near Abdeen Palace.

Here is a curious fact. The modern state of Israel extends from latitude 30° north to 33° north. When carried west into Egypt, the former latitude passes almost through the Great Pyramid of Giza.

We are reminded of the historical statement sent by President Truman to the provisional government of Israel on 14 May 1948. It reads simply:

> This Government has been informed that a Jewish state has been proclaimed in Palestine, and recognition has been requested by the provisional government thereof. The United States recognizes the provisional government as the de facto authority of the State of Israel.[158]

Two decades later, in June 1967, Israeli forces stormed Jerusalem and recaptured the city from the Arabs after eight centuries of Muslim occupation. The Star of David had finally risen again. The 'cornerstone' of the New Jerusalem and, by extension the New Temple, had been laid.

As has several times been the case during our years of research for this book, we felt the ghostly lifting of a veil brush against our faces. Yet this time the revelation of what lay behind the veil was so sinister, so worrying and so misunderstood by so many, that at first we thought it best to let it be, to ignore it, to delete it from our thoughts lest we be branded as 'conspiracy theorists'.

Only after much consideration have we reached the conclusion that we *must* bring this strange and frightening issue to attention.

Epilogue:
The Master Game

May 14th [1948], David Ben Gurion is creating history. At 4 o'clock this afternoon when he reads these words aloud he will change world politics forever. In this simple text lies a dream of the Jewish People that has endured two thousand years of exile. It is the Declaration of the Establishment of the State of Israel. Yet the nation may not survive the day. All around him powerful forces are working to obstruct or destroy his fledgling nation. In neighbouring Jordan, King Abdullah heads an alliance of five Arab nations to strangle Israel at birth. He [Ben Gurion] is defying the United Nations who have their own plans for the Middle East. Civil war rages across the country. The British Empire which has played peacekeeper for thirty years is leaving. His only hope lies in Washington. With the backing of President Truman, Israel might have a chance to survive.

BBC2, 'The Birth of Israel, May 14th 1948', *Days that Shook the World*

At the center of contemporary Islamism is an anti-Semitic conspiracy theory, the roots of which lead back to Europe at least a century ago. The basic theme (i.e., that the Jews control, or are attempting to control, the world's governments and media, and generally work to promote Zioism, Israel, etc.) is well known, and is often referenced in regard to the statements and actions of Hamas as well as other Islamist organizations. However, that the Jews are linked to the Freemasons (often regarded as a 'secret society') in this conspiracy has gone largely unexplored by observers of Islamism.

A. Miller, 'Freemasonry in the Mind of the Islamist'[1]

Those damned mystics with a private line to God ought to be compelled to disconnect. I cannot see that they have done anything save prevent necessary change.

Harold Laski, 1919

CHAPTER TWENTY

THE DAY THAT SHOOK
THE WORLD

In February 1998, almost exactly fifty years after David Ben Gurion read the Declaration of the Establishment of the State of Israel to the Jewish National Council in Tel Aviv, another 'Declaration' was read by one Osama Bin Laden: the 'Declaration Of The World Islamic Front For Jihad Against The Jews And The Crusaders'. Bin Laden called upon all Muslims to wage a 'Holy War' against Jews and 'Crusaders', i.e. Americans and their allies, 'until the Aqsa Mosque (in Jerusalem) and the Haram Mosque (in Makkah) are freed from their grip.'

Three years later, on 11 September 2001, Bin Laden's organisation, the dreaded Al Qaeda, masterminded the destruction of the Twin Towers of the World Trade Center in New York and severe damage to the Pentagon in Washington, DC by having suicide volunteers hijack four commercial airlines and fly three of them into those buildings. This abominable event has gone down in history as 9/11.

On 20 November 2003 the British consulate and the HSBC bank in Istanbul, Turkey, were destroyed by suicide bombers. A man claiming to be from the Turkish Great Orient Raiders of the Eastern Front (TGOREF) telephoned the semi-official Anatolian News Agency and coldly informed them that the TGOREF and Bin Laden's Al Qaeda group had jointly carried out the attacks. The mysterious voice then added these sinister words:

Our attacks against *Masonic* targets will continue. Muslims are not alone.[2]

And on 22 January 2003 the controversial north London Muslim spiritual leader, Sheikh Abu Hamza al-Masri, expressed these strange views to the *Independent*:

I am not saying every American government figure knew about this [September 11th]. But there are a few people [in the US government] who want to trigger a third world war. They are sponsored by the business lobby. Most of them are Freemasons, and they have loyalty to the Zionists.[3]

On 10 March 2004, BBC News reported that,

A suicide attack on a Masonic lodge in the Turkish city of Istanbul has left one person dead and five injured ... the highly secretive international society of Masons is seen by radical Islamic groups as a supporter of the policies of Israel and the United States.[4]

And the *Guardian* reported on the same day:

One of the bombers reportedly chanted 'God is great' before detonating his device ... [another] assailant, who identified himself as Abdullah Islam, shouted 'Down with the Israeli lodge' ...[5]

Accusations

Accusations of Masonic and/or Zionist or Jewish manipulations backed by America are not uncommon in the Arab World. In 1978 the most influential body in promulgating and interpreting Islamic law and ideologies, the Islamic Jurisdictional College (IJC) located at Al-Azhar University, condemned Freemasonry as an evil organization. Seventeen years later the same condemnation of Freemasonry was repeated in Saudi Arabia in the *Saudi Gazette* of 13 January 1995, 'The Curse of Freemasonry: In Questions of Faith', which reprinted the text issued in 1978 by the IJC at its meeting in Makkah. We show here only items 7, 8 and 10 which are self-evident:

7. It [Freemasonry] is a Jewish Organization in its roots. Its secret higher international administrative board are Jews and it promotes Zionist activities.

8. Its primary objectives are the distraction of all religions and it distracts Muslims from Islam.

10. It has branches under different names as a camouflage so people cannot trace its activities, especially if the name of Freemasonry has

opposition. These hidden branches are known are Lions, Rotary and others. They have wicked principles that completely contradict the rules of Islam. There is a clear relationship between Freemasonry, Judaism, and International Zionism. It has controlled the activities of high Arab Officials in the Palestinian Problem. It has limited their duties, obligations and activities for the benefit of the Judaism and International Zionism. Given that Freemasonry involves itself in dangerous activities, it is a great hazard, with wicked objectives, the Jurisdictional Synod determines that Freemasonry is a dangerous, destructive organization. Any Muslim who affiliates with it, knowing the truth of its objectives, is an infidel to Islam.[6]

Such condemnations are now commonplace on the Internet. For example, in a popular website, 'Islam online', we also found the following statement regarding Freemasonry and Islam:

The Society of Freemasons aims to rebuild the Temple of Solomon in Jerusalem after destroying Al-Aqsa Mosque because the Jews allege that the mosque has been built on the site of the destroyed temple. Everything that furthers the interest of the Jews and promotes their position in the world is undertaken by the society. The cover of absolute secrecy and its strict hierarchy enables it to make use of the positions and influence of its non-Jewish members to serve the Jewish cause. We have to understand that many of its members work for the society trusting that they only serve the causes of liberty, equality and justice. They remain unaware that they simply serve the cause of giving the Jews supremacy in world affairs. Islam respects other religions. Freemasonry deceives its members into thinking that they further the cause of a better humanity when they are actually furthering the interests of those who seek to give the Jews supremacy over all peoples of the world. Islam is the final message from Allah to man. It is the religion that supersedes all past divine messages, including Judaism. Freemasonry seeks to destroy Al-Aqsa Mosque in order to rebuild the Temple of Solomon in its place.[7]

In an article entitled 'The New Islamic Fascism' published in November 2001 in the *Jerusalem Post*, Robert S. Wistrich, professor of modern European and Jewish history at the Hebrew University of Jerusalem, wrote:

This Middle Eastern radicalism is a distinctly modern movement, though it also has indigenous Islamic roots. The conspiracy theory at its heart, which links plutocratic capitalism, international freemasonry, Zionism, and Marxist Communism, is almost identical with the mythical structure of Nazi anti-Semitism. For contemporary jihadists, a 'Judaized' America and Israel, together with heretical, secular Muslim regimes are the godless spearhead of these dark occult forces that seek to destroy Islam and undermine the cultural identity of Muslim believers.[8]

The perception that some Islamic militants have about the imaginary collusion between Freemasonry and Zionism needs to be carefully understood, not least because Islam is insinuating itself more and more deeply into the Western world where Freemasonry is widely practiced, especially in Britain and the US. We have noted how Islamic terrorists broke into a Masonic lodge in Turkey in March 2004 spraying bullets and detonating several bombs. Fortunately the only person to die in the attack was one of the terrorists. The second terrorist, Engin Vural, who survived was eventually tried in a Turkish court in August 2004. Vural confessed that he, as well as many other militants received their training in Pakistan and Afghanistan, and their network had planned more such attacks. On 13 March 2004, *Al-Jazeera* published an English translation of a statement purported to be from Al Qaeda:

> *Jund al-Quds* [Soldiers of Jerusalem] targeted a Jewish Masonic lodge in Istanbul. Three top Masons were killed in the operation, and if it was not for technical failure all the Masons would have been killed. Thanks to God anyway.[9]

More recently, CNN reported an aborted attack by a Muslim student on a Masonic temple in Atlanta, Georgia.[10]

The Lie that would not die

Unfortunately in the Muslim world the term *Massoony* ('Freemason') in the Arabic language is often used synonymously with 'Zionist' and vilified as one and the same thing. Indeed the term *Massoony* is also often used as a generic name for a multitude of organizations supposedly secretly colluding or working for the Zionists, the Israelis, the CIA and so forth, and believed to manipulate banks, military institutions, the media, educational bodies, governments and even the United Nations! To be more specific, many Arabs believe that the Muslim World and more specifically the Middle East is threatened by a secretive satanic force masterminded and manipulated by Freemasons and Zionists with the US branded as the 'Big Satan' and Israel the 'Small Satan'.

THE MASTER GAME

But where and why did such ideas originate?

The Masonic-Zionist conspiracy theory has its roots in the so-called *Protocols of the Elders of Zion*. This slim document, first published in Russia in 1903–5, purports to unmask a Zionist-cum-Masonic plot to take control of the world, and was used in anti-Semitic propaganda in Russia and later in Nazi Germany in the 1930s and, more recently, among radical Muslims.[11] Although long shown to be a hoax,[12] the *Protocols* have nonetheless been widely circulated and believed throughout the Middle East and are now used as a major propaganda tool in the spread of Islamism in the Western world. In 2002 Steven Simon,[13] assistant director of the International Institute of Strategic Studies, told the British House of Commons:

> The texts [the *Protocols*] that are very influential among al-Qaeda types and recruits to the organization, texts that can be found on the Internet or in broadsheets or in bookstores in the Middle East, already postulate a worldwide infidel conspiracy against Islam. The United States may bear the brunt of responsibility, but it is seen as part of a larger challenge, consisting of, depending on what you read, the UN, the EU, NATO and the Freemasons for that matter. As odd as that sounds, they have a prominent role in much of this conspiracy thinking.[14]

Although the supposed Masonic-Zionist conspiracy is generally seen in the Islamic world as a secular evil, Freemasons are often associated with the mysterious and satanic figure of the *Masih ad-Dajjal* (roughly translated as the 'false prophet' or 'false messenger') who, in Muslim lore, is supposed to appear before the *Yawm al-Qiyamah* or 'Day of Judgment'. According to *hadith* the *Dajjal* has one eye which, as to be expected, is often linked to the single eye in the pyramid on the US one-dollar bill and, of course, the 'eye in the triangle' symbol used extensively in Freemasonry. The Internet is rife with websites that connect Freemasonry with the *Dajjal*. According to many of these websites, Freemasonry was behind the Gulf War, the invasion of Afghanistan, the Iraq War, the oppression in the Gaza strip and the turmoil in Pakistan.

Experts on anti-terrorism are gradually coming round to realise that there is a growing and dangerous paranoia about Freemasonry in some Islamic quarters that is extremely worrying, not least because it is drummed into the young minds, often even as part of school curricula. For example, in Saudi Arabia a lesson for tenth grade boys on the Zionist Movement included in a schoolbook on Islamic culture is 'a curious blend of wild conspiracy theories about Masonic lodges, Rotary Clubs, and Lions Clubs with anti-Semitic invective. It asserts that the *Protocols of the Elders of Zion* is an authentic document and teaches students that it reveals what Jews really believe.'[15]

The Semblance of a 'Masonic-Zionist Conspiracy'

Many US presidents were Freemasons, including George Washington. But more relevant here are those two presidents who are known to have been involved in the creation of the modern state of Israel[16] – Franklin D. Roosevelt and, more directly, Harry S. Truman. As we saw in the last chapter, Roosevelt was the 32nd president of the United States as well as a 32nd degree Scottish Rite Mason. Harry Truman was the 33rd president of the United States and a 33rd degree Scottish Rite Mason. It may not be too far-fetched to speculate that the 32nd degree could bear a relevance to Solomon's Temple. As has often been suggested there is, at the very least, a curious similarity with the Cabbalistic Sephirothic Tree of Life formed by the 22 paths plus the 10 'emanations' of Jehovah. Moreover, some Scottish Rite certificates show the location of the issuing lodge by giving the geographical latitude in degrees – and this has been taken to suggest a mystical connection between degrees of latitude and the Masonic 'degrees' of initiation. It is perhaps more than a coincidence that the geographical latitude of the Temple Mount in Jerusalem lies just south of the 32nd parallel while the 'Mother Lodge' of the Scottish Rite was originally located in the city of Charleston in South Carolina just off the 33rd parallel. The York Rite Freemasons of America run a periodical called *Knight Templar*, with the seal of the so-called *Grand Encampment of Knights Templar of the USA*.[17] The front cover of the August 2010 issue of *Knight Templar* shows the Temple Mount in Jerusalem, with the Wailing Wall and the Dome of the Rock and an Israeli flag dominating the scene.[18]

Radical Arabs perceive a conspiracy in all this involving, at the very least, American Freemasons and the World Zionist Organization.[19] And the recent discovery of the diaries of former Secretary of the Treasury Hans Morgentau has added fuel to this political fire. The diaries report a meeting between Morgentau and Roosevelt on 3 December 1942 at which President Roosevelt made these extraordinary comments regarding the eventual creation of a Jewish state in Palestine:

> I actually would put a barbed wire around Palestine, and I would begin to move the Arabs out of Palestine ... Each time we move out an Arab we would bring in another Jewish family ... 90% of them should be Jews ... It

THE MASTER GAME

would be an independent nation just like any other nation – completely independent. Naturally, if there are 90% Jews, the Jews would dominate the government.[20]

The letter that stunned the world

During the early hours of 14 May 1948, according to the BBC2 programme cited at the beginning of this chapter, the Zionist leader David Ben Gurion put the finishing touches to the Declaration of the Establishment of the State of Israel which he would soon read. Let us note in passing that the population of Palestine at that time was just over two million souls of whom thirty per cent were Jews, while the remaining majority were mostly Muslims and a small number of Christians. Civil war between Muslims and Jews had broken out, and at first it looked like the Jews would be overwhelmed by an Arab military alliance formed by Jordan, Syria, Egypt, Iraq and Lebanon.

At 4 p.m. Ben Gurion read the Declaration which started with the words:

The land of Israel was the birthplace of the Jewish people. Here
their spiritual, religious and national identity was formed. Here they
achieved independence and created a culture of national and universal
significance. Here they wrote and gave the Bible to the world.[21]

The Declaration goes on to state that,

Accordingly, we, the members of the National Council, representing the
Jewish people in Palestine and the Zionist movement of the world, met
together in solemn assembly today, the day of the termination of the
British Mandate for Palestine, by virtue of the natural and historic right of
the Jewish people and of the Resolution of the General Assembly of the
United Nations. We hereby proclaim the establishment of the Jewish State
in Palestine, to be called ISRAEL ... The State of Israel will be open to the
immigration of Jews from all countries of their dispersion; will promote
the development of the country for the benefit of all its inhabitants;
will be based on the precepts of liberty, justice and peace taught by
the Hebrew Prophets ... our call goes out the Jewish people all over the
world to rally to our side in the task of immigration and development
and to stand by us in the great struggle for the fulfilment of the dream of
generations – the redemption of Israel. With trust in Almighty God, we
set our hand to this Declaration, at this Session of the Provisional State

Council, in the city of Tel Aviv, on this Sabbath eve, the fifth of Iyar, 5708, the fourteenth day of May, 1948.[22]

The Declaration announced that the Jewish state would officially come into existence at midnight on 14 May 1948 which marked the end of the British Mandate for Palestine. In Washington this would be 6 p.m. EST on 14 May.

At about the same time that Ben Gurion was in the process of reading the Declaration in Tel Aviv, Eliahu Epstein, head of the Jewish Agency for Israel, now calling himself, 'agent to the provisional government of Israel', received a phone call from Clark Clifford,[23] the special counsel to President Truman. Clifford, who was in his early forties at this time, urged Epstein to write at once to President Truman to 'welcome Israel into the community of nations'. Then at 11 minutes after the proclamation of a Jewish state in Palestine became effective, President Truman recognized the provisional government as the 'de facto authority of the State of Israel'.[24]

It seems inconceivable, at least in our opinion, that President Truman gave his personal approval within minutes, presumably without having seen the details of the constitution of this new 'Jewish state' claiming biblical rights to modern Palestine! At any rate, David Ben Gurion was immediately made Israel's first prime minister and Chaim Weizmann, the 'guiding spirit behind the Zionist Organization [now called the World Zionist Organization]' who was at the time living in New York, was to become it's first 'president'.

But what really happened at the White House on that fateful and confusing day of 14 May 1948?

An Insider's Account

In his memoirs, Clark Clifford revealed some rather shocking aspects of how and why President Truman so hastily recognized the Jewish state of Israel.[25]

A little background information is necessary at this stage. All who understood this vexed issue knew that the United Nations Partition Plan for Palestine of 29 November 1947 was,

... patently unfair, it awarded 56 percent of Palestine to its 650,000 Jewish inhabitants, and 44 percent to its 1,300,000 Muslim and Christian Arab inhabitants. Partition was adopted only after ruthless arm-twisting by the US government and by 26 pro-Zionist US senators who [sent] in telegrams to a number of UN member states.[26]

Making matters worse was Truman's famous statement regarding the Zionist lobby in America, in which he bluntly gave this explanation of his position:

> I'm sorry, gentlemen, but I have to answer to hundreds of thousands who are anxious for the success of Zionism: I do not have hundreds of thousands of Arabs among my constituents.[27]

As predicted by many, no sooner was the UN Partition Plan adopted than widespread armed fighting broke out between Jews and Arabs, as the latter rejected wholesale the partition arrived at by 'foreigners' for what was clearly a piece of Arab real estate. Nonetheless well-armed and experienced Jewish militias seized Arab villages that were given to Arabs by the UN, easily crushing badly armed and untrained Arab villagers. At this point, Secretary of State George C. Marshall, a highly respected five-star general and staunch opponent of the UN plan, asked Truman in no uncertain terms to reconsider his support for a Jewish state.

When the British announced their withdrawal from Palestine to be effective at midnight on 14 May 1948 (without even waiting for the final outcome of events in the UN) the conflict had already spread all over Palestine, and five Arab countries, including Egypt and Jordan, now openly threatened to send their armies across the border to 'kill the new born Jewish state at birth'. The State Department strongly urged Truman not to recognize Israel, at least not immediately, but rather to support the prevailing view at the UN for a UN 'trusteeship'. So why didn't he listen to such wise advice? To understand this, it is important to appreciate the pivotal role played by Clark Clifford, then Truman's political adviser for domestic affairs, in counteracting and eventually overriding Secretary Marshall's opposition. In Clark Clifford's own words:

> Marshall firmly opposed American recognition of the new Jewish state; I did not. Marshall's opposition was shared by almost every member of the brilliant and now legendary group of presidential advisers, later referred to as the 'wise men', who were then in the process of creating a post-war foreign policy that would endure for more than 40 years. The opposition included the respected Under Secretary of State Robert Lovett; his predecessor, Dean Acheson; the No. 3 man in the State Department, Charles Bohlen; the brilliant chief of the Policy Planning Staff, George Kennan; (Navy Secretary James V.) Forrestal; and ... Dean Rusk, then the director of the Office of United Nations Affairs ...

Officials in the State Department had done everything in their power to prevent, thwart, or delay the president's Palestine policy in 1947 and 1948, while I had fought for assistance to the Jewish Agency.[28]

Clifford then narrates the specific mood and happenings in early May 1948, and more specifically his own involvement:

At midnight on May 14, 1948 [6 p.m. in Washington], the British would relinquish control of Palestine. One minute later, the Jewish Agency, under the leadership of David Ben-Gurion, would proclaim the new state. I had already had several serious disagreements with General Marshall's protege, Dean Rusk, and with Loy Henderson, the director of Near Eastern and African Affairs ... He [Rusk] had no use for White House interference in what he saw as his personal domain in American policy in the Middle East. A number of Middle East experts in the State Department were widely regarded as anti-Semitic.

On May 7th, a week before the end of the British Mandate, I met with President Truman for our customary private day-end chat ... I handed the president a draft of a public statement I had prepared, and proposed that at his next press conference, scheduled for May 13th, the day before the British Mandate would end, he announce that it was his intention to recognize the Jewish state. The president was sympathetic to the proposal, but, being keenly aware of Marshall's strong feelings, he picked up the telephone to get the Secretary's views ...

I could tell that Marshall objected strongly to the proposed statement. The president listened politely, then told Marshall he wanted to have a meeting on the subject ... On ending the conversation, the president swivelled his chair toward me. 'Clark, I am impressed with General Marshall's argument that we should not recognize the new state so fast,' he said. 'He does not want to recognize it at all – at least, not now. I've asked him and Lovett to come in next week to discuss this business. I think Marshall is going to continue to take a very strong position. When he does, I would like you to make the case in favor of recognition' ...

President Truman had asked me to debate the man he most admired, a man whose participation in the administration was essential to its success. I was 41 years old, in my third year at the White House as a

THE MASTER GAME

presidential aide. Virtually every American regarded General Marshall, then 67, with a respect bordering on awe …

At 4 p.m. on Wednesday, May 12 … seven of us joined President Truman in the Oval Office … President Truman did not raise the issue of recognition; his desire was that I be the first to raise it, but only after Marshall and Lovett had spoken, so that he would be able to ascertain the degree of Marshall's opposition before showing his own hand. Lovett began by criticizing what he termed signs of growing 'assertiveness' by the Jewish Agency …

Marshall interrupted Lovett. He was strongly opposed to the behavior of the Jewish Agency, he said. He had met on May 8th with Moshe Shertok [future Israeli prime minister Moshe Sharett], its political representative, and had told Shertok that it was 'dangerous to base long-range policy on temporary military success.' Moreover, Marshall said, he had told Shertok that if the Jews got into trouble and 'came running to us for help … there was no warrant to expect help from the United States, which had warned them of the grave risk which they were running' … The United States, he said, should continue to support those resolutions in the United Nations which would turn Palestine over to the UN as a trusteeship, and defer any decision on recognition.[29]

At that point Clifford presented his own 'case', speaking of the 1917 Balfour Declaration which promised a homeland for the Jews to the Zionist Federation, the terrible events of the Holocaust, and now the chance to have a Jewish nation that would uphold democracy in the Arab world. However as Clifford made his argument he had noticed:

… Marshall's face reddening with suppressed anger as I talked. When I finished, he exploded.

'Mr. President, I thought this meeting was called to consider an important and complicated problem in foreign policy. I don't even know why Clifford is here. He is a domestic adviser, and this is a foreign-policy matter.' I will never forget President Truman's characteristically simple reply: 'Well, General, he's here because I asked him to be here.' Marshall, scarcely concealing his ire, shot back, 'These considerations have nothing to do with the issue. I fear that the only reason Clifford is here is that he is pressing a political consideration with regard to this issue. I don't think politics should play any part in this.'

Lovett joined the attack. 'It would be highly injurious to the United Nations to announce the recognition of the Jewish state even before it had come into existence and while the General Assembly is still considering the question. Furthermore, such a move would be injurious to the prestige of the President. It is obviously designed to win the Jewish vote, but in my opinion it would lose more votes than it would gain.' Lovett had finally brought to the surface the root cause of Marshall's fury: his view that the position I presented was dictated by domestic political considerations ...

When Lovett concluded his attack, Marshall spoke again. Speaking with great and barely contained anger and with more than a hint of self-righteousness, he made the most remarkable threat I have ever heard anyone make directly to a president. He said, 'If you follow Clifford's advice and if I were to vote in the election, I would vote against you.'

Everyone in the room was stunned. Here was the indispensable symbol of continuity, whom President Truman revered and needed, making a threat that, if it became public, could virtually seal the dissolution of the Truman administration and send the Western Alliance, then in the process of creation, into disarray before it had been fully structured. Marshall's statement fell short of an explicit threat to resign, but it came very close.

Clifford further recounts that in the 12 May 1948 meeting:

Lovett and I both tried to step into the ensuing silence with words of conciliation. We both knew how important it was to get this dreadful meeting over with quickly, before Marshall said something even more irretrievable ... he [Truman] rose and turned to him and said, 'I understand your position, General, and I'm inclined to side with you in this matter' ... Marshall did not even glance at me as he and Lovett left.

Clifford claims that after this meeting, Secretary Mashall never mentioned his name again. He also eventually found out that, at day's end on 12 May 1948, Marshall:

... did something quite unusual, which the president and I were unaware of at the time. Certain that history would prove him right, he wanted his personal comments included in the official State Department record of the meeting. His record, exactly as he wanted historians to find it when it was declassified, almost three decades later, reads as follows:

'I remarked to the president that, speaking objectively, I could not help but think that the suggestions made by Mr. Clifford were wrong. I thought that to adopt these suggestions would have precisely the opposite effect from that intended by Mr. Clifford. The transparent dodge to win a few votes would not in fact achieve this purpose. The great dignity of the office of the president would be seriously diminished. The counsel offered by Mr. Clifford was based on domestic political considerations, while the problem which confronted us was international. I said bluntly that if the president were to follow Mr. Clifford's advice and if in the elections I were to vote, I would vote against the president.'[30]

At this point it is noteworthy that President Truman, judging from his owns accounts and that of his biographers, shows that he was undecided over the issue and confused as to what was best to do. Lobbied on the one hand for the recognition of the Jewish state by his White House adviser, David Niles, and Truman's old army colleague and business partner, Eddie Jacobson, and on the other hand by the 'wise men' at the State Department, Truman, on face value, seems to have hesitated. Clifford, however, give the impression that, quite to the contrary, Truman position was set on recognition of the Jewish state. In other words, his position was inflexible and adamantine. At any rate, everyone, it seems – Clifford, Niles, and even the State Department – were in direct communication with Eliahu Epstein, the Washington representative of the Jewish Agency for Israel (which later was to convert itself into the government of new state of Israel). As for Clifford himself, here, in his own words, is his involvement on that day of 14 May 1948:

Even without a clear signal from Lovett and Marshall, I felt, we had to set in motion the machinery for recognition, in the event that a favorable decision was made. At 10 a.m., I made a different call – one that I looked on later with great pleasure ... I told the Jewish Agency representative [Epstein], 'we would like you to send an official letter to President Truman before 12 o'clock today formally requesting the United States to recognize the new Jewish state. I would also request that you send a copy of the letter directly to Secretary Marshall.'

Epstein was ecstatic. He did not realize that the president had still not decided how to respond to the request I had just solicited ... It was particularly important, I said, that the new state claim nothing beyond the boundaries outlined in the UN resolution of Nov. 29, 1947, because those boundaries were the only ones that had been agreed to ... A few minutes later, Epstein called me. 'We've never done this before, and we're not quite sure how to go about it,' he said ...

With my knowledge and encouragement, Epstein then turned for additional advice to two of the wisest lawyers in Washington, David Ginsburg and Benjamin Cohen, both of whom were great New Dealers and strong supporters of the Zionist cause. Working together during the rest of the morning, he and they drafted the recognition request ...[31]

Clifford then narrates how a staff member of the Jewish Agency for Israel drove to the White House with the request for recognition of the 'Jewish state' but was intercepted by another member because Epstein had heard on shortwave radio that the new state was not to be called the 'Jewish state' but the 'state of Israel' and thus instructed that the letter be corrected in ink before handing over the request for recognition to the White House! At any rate, when it became known to the American delegation at the UN (the latter then pushing for voting for continued trusteeship), the US ambassador to the UN, Warren Austin, walked out of the UN building so as not to be there when US recognition of Israel was announced. Dean Rusk thus had to quickly go to the UN Headquarters to persuade the US delegation members there not to resigning in protest!

Marshall did not resign as was previously feared. Lovett had apparently talked him out of it. According to Clifford,

Lovett remained adamant for the rest of his life, however, in his view that the president and I had been wrong. So did most of his colleagues. Nothing could ever convince him, Marshall, Acheson, Forrestal, or Rusk that President Truman had made the right decision ... Because President Truman was often annoyed by the tone and fierceness of the pressure exerted on him by American Zionists, he left some people with the impression that he was ambivalent about the events of May 1948.

THE MASTER GAME

This was not true. He never wavered in his belief that he had taken the right action.[32]

Truman's fateful decision led to a situation in which three quarters of a million Arab-Palestinians were forced to flee their own country as refugees during the 1947–9 fighting, and subsequently caused five Arab-Israeli wars in 1948, 1956, 1967, 1973 and 2006. Had a different decision been taken it seems probable that there would have been no 'Middle East Crisis', nor the formation of the various terrorist groups such as the PLO, Hezbollah and others that have resulted in modern times in the dreaded Al Qaeda of Osama Bin Laden, 9/11 and the wars in Afghanistan and Iraq.[33]

Flash forward to 1978: Jerusalem Day

In 1978 Ayatollah Khomeini arrived in triumph in Qom, the holy city of the *Shi'a* Muslims, and pronounced to an ecstatic and frenzied multitude that the Islamic Revolution had begun. A year later, now almost deified by his followers, he announced the creation of *Al-Quds* Day, Jerusalem Day:

> I invite Muslims all over the globe to consecrate the last Friday of the holy month of Ramadan as *Al-Quds* Day and to proclaim the international solidarity of Muslims in support of the legitimate rights of the Muslim people of Palestine. For many years, I have been notifying the Muslims of the danger posed by the usurper Israel ... I ask all the Muslims of the world and the Muslim governments to join together to sever the hand of this usurper and its supporters [America] ... and through a ceremony demonstrating the solidarity of Muslims worldwide, announce their support for the legitimate rights of the Muslim people. I ask God Almighty for the victory of the Muslims over the infidels.[34]

In solidarity with the Palestinians, Khomeini declared the liberation of Jerusalem a religious duty to all Muslims. The Ayatollah then added:

> In the Name of God, the Compassionate, the Merciful. *Quds* Day is an international day, it is not a day devoted to *Quds* alone. It is the day for the weak and oppressed to confront the arrogant powers, the day for those nations suffering under the pressure of America ... The oppressed should arm themselves against the oppressors and rub their noses in the dirt ... all the nations should rise up and throw these germs of corruption into the rubbish bin too ...

Quds Day is the day when the superpowers should be warned to stay at home and leave the oppressed alone. Israel, the enemy of mankind, the enemy of humanity, which is creating disturbances every day and is attacking our brothers ...

Quds Day is the day for announcing such things, for announcing such things to the Satans who want to push the Islamic nations aside and bring the superpowers into the arena. *Quds* Day is the day to dash their hopes and warn them that those days are gone ...

Quds Day is the day of Islam; it is the day when Islam should be revived, so let us revive it and implement Islamic laws in the Islamic countries. *Quds* Day is the day when we must warn all the superpowers that they can no longer keep Islam under their control by means of their evil agents. *Quds* Day is the day to give life to Islam. The Muslims must awaken, they must come to realise the power they have, the material power and the spiritual. What are the Muslims, who form a population of one billion, enjoy divine support and have Islam and their faith behind them, afraid of? ...

The governments in the world should know that Islam will not be defeated. Islam and the teachings of the Qur'an should prevail in all countries. Religion should be the religion of God and Islam is the religion of God so it should advance on all regions of the world. *Quds* Day is the day to announce such a matter, the day to announce 'Muslims, advance!' Advance on all the regions of the world ...[35] with our cries and shouts of *'Allah'u Akbar'* ['God is Great'] ...[36]

Flash forward to 2001: Masonic Oath?

We recall that in 1740 the Chevalier Ramsay, a Scotsman and Jacobean, created a Masonic order in France which he claimed had its roots in the Crusades and which, some believe, was the precursor to Scottish Rite Freemasonry – today headquartered in Washington, DC. Meanwhile Bin Laden's rhetoric, and the threats, accusations and attacks against Freemasons cited leave little doubt that Islamic fundamentalists regard America as a Masonic-crusading power whose ally in the Middle East is Israel.

Such perceptions could only have been heightened in January 2001 when the following newspaper article was circulated by the Associated Press:

A Bible that George Washington used to take the oath of office as the nation's first president will be used by George W. Bush. Three officials of the Manhattan-based St. John's Lodge of the Free and Accepted Masons will board an Amtrak liner for Washington, DC, tomorrow. They'll be carrying the nine-pound, 234-year-old King James Bible in a special case. For the sixth time in history, the Bible will be used on Saturday for the swearing in of a US president. George Washington was the first, in 1789. The last was George H. W. Bush, who used the Bible in 1989. Other presidents who have placed their left hand on the Masonic Bible were Warren Harding in 1921, Dwight Eisenhower in 1953, and Jimmy Carter in 1977. The Bible was also displayed at the New York World's Fair in 1964–65.[37]

When we consider the symbolic implications of all this for Muslims already paranoid about a supposed Masonic-Zionist plot, a new and extraordinary possibility presents itself.

It is the norm for the entrances to Masonic temples and lodges to be flanked by two pillars representing the twin pillars of Solomon's Temple, namely *Boaz* and *Jachin* – meaning 'wisdom' and 'power'. The so-called *Plan of Lodges* also incorporates these pillars as well as a five-pointed star or pentagon symbolising the Holy of Holies of Solomon's Temple. Indeed the Temple of Solomon, and its rebuilding in a spiritual manner, is probably the most important symbol representing the ideal of Freemasonry in the world today.

Could it be that the attacks on the Twin Towers at the 'entrance' of America, i.e. New York, and on the Pentagon – the 'Holy of Holies' of US military power – were intended, at least in part, as a coded symbolic *message* aimed at imagined Templar-crusaders or Zionist-Masons ... or both?

Was 9/11 the latest move in the millennia-old 'Master Game' – a move that demonstrates, more than any other, that all the players have now utterly lost their way?

'Jihad' or 'Crusade'?

At a press conference given on the south lawn of the White House on 16 September 2001, five days after the attack on the Twin Towers and Pentagon, President George W. Bush said:

We need to go back to work tomorrow and we will. But we need to be alert to the fact that these evil-doers *still* exist. We haven't seen this kind of barbarism in a long period of time ... This is a new kind of evil. And we understand. And the American people are beginning to understand. This *crusade*, this war on terrorism is going to take a while. And the American people must be patient. I'm going to be patient. But I can assure the American people I am determined, I'm not going to be distracted, I will keep my focus to make sure that not only are these brought to justice, but anybody who's been associated will be brought to justice ... It is time for us to win the first war of the 21st century decisively, so that our children and our grandchildren can live peacefully into the 21st century.[38]

On 16 February 2002, the president used the same rhetoric:

I want to tell you something, we've got no better friends than Canada. They stand with us in this incredibly *important crusade* to defend freedom, this campaign to do what is right for our children and our grandchildren.[39] [Emphasis added]

On 7 September 2002, *Counterpunch* editor Alexander Cockburn published an article titled 'The Tenth Crusade' in which he wrote:

Islamic fanatics flew those planes a year ago and here we are with a terrifying alliance of Judaeo-Christian fanatics, conjoined in their dreams of the recovery of the Holy Lands of the West Bank, Judaea and Samaria. War on Terror? It's back to the late thirteenth century, picking up where Prince Edward left off with his ninth crusade after St. Louis had died in Tunis with the word 'Jerusalem' on his lips.[40]

And James Pinkerton, a columnist in *Newsday* commented on 4 December 2003,

And now, in 2003, the Americans, the *Twelfth Crusaders*. The West is no longer 'Christendom,' but we, as first cousins to the Europeans, retain the old faith and bring new kinds of idealism, such as democracy and human rights. But the Crusader spirit is still there; it's still about bringing civilization and salvation of a backward people. As the born-again George W. Bush says, 'This is about good vs. evil.'[41]

From the Crusades to Al Qaeda

In November 2010, a spine-chilling statement was made on Internet by the self-styled Islamic state of Iraq (ISI), Al Qaeda's front in Iraq:

[ISI] declares all Christian centers, organizations and institutions, leaders and followers, are legitimate targets for *Mujahideen* [Muslim holy warriors] wherever they can reach them ... The killing sword will not be lifted from the necks of the [Vatican leaders] and their followers until they declare their innocence from what the Egyptian Church is doing.[42]

Al Qaeda's allegation was that Muslim women 'were being held against their will in Coptic Christian monasteries in Egypt'.[43] Although the charge sounds most improbable, the gruesome inevitable soon happened. On 31 October 2010, just hours after the 'statement' was put on the Internet, a group of fanatical SIS 'Muslim Warriors' stormed into the Our Lady of Salvation church in the Karrada neighborhood of central Baghdad. A hundred hostages were taken and the whole bizarre incident ended with the death of 58 people. Threats were then made directly towards Christian churches in Egypt and elsewhere in the Middle East.

In a garbled 'good-cop, bad-cop' reaction, the official Muslim Brotherhood in Egypt (ironically, the root organization from which Islamic Jihad, Hamass and Al Qaeda all sprang) quickly issued a statement:

The Muslim Brotherhood is stressing to all, and primarily Muslims, that the protection of Holy Places of all monotheistic religions is the mission of the majority of Muslims ... The Brotherhood rejects all stupid threats against Christian places of worship in Egypt by anyone and under any pretext.[44]

On face value the Muslim Brotherhood must be lauded for its swift condemnation of such threats and attacks on Christian establishments. Yet it is well known that for the past 60 years the Copts (Christians) of Egypt, have suffered almost continuous persecution at the hands of the Muslim Brotherhood. An exodus of almost biblical proportions has taken place and huge numbers of Copts have fled Egypt to settle in the Western world.[45]

Meanwhile in Baghdad a series of booby-trap bomb attacks on Christian families took place in November 2010 in the days after the terrible massacre at the Our Lady of Salvation church. According to the *Guardian* newspaper, Christians in Iraq now regret the downfall of Saddam Hussein, saying that 'for all his atrocities, the dictator left the Christians alone'. According to one Christian Iraqi woman, Linda Jalal:

We didn't suffer under him [Saddam Husein]. But now I am terrified to live in this society. We are being slaughtered like sheep. Yet we are civilians in our country.[46]

And on 31 December 2010, as hundreds of Copts were coming out of a church in the Sidi Bishr district of Alexandria, a powerful car-bomb exploded killing twenty-one people and injuring dozens of others. Unconfirmed reports indicated that Al Qaeda was behind this murderous act following its recent threat against Christians.

Infuriated by this act of senseless terrorism, Christian youths in Alexandria went on a rampage and attacked a nearby local mosque. Mayhem followed as sectarian tension was pushed to breaking point. And although the riot police was able to restore calm, a very uneasy mood fell across the whole of Egypt.[47]

Not only in Iraq and Egypt, but across the Middle East and indeed in the Muslim world as a whole, Christians increasingly live in fear, not knowing when some fanatic might decide to see them as a 'legitimate target'. The corollary is that in the predominantly Christian West, Muslims are now regarded with ever growing suspicion as they go about their daily lives. If there was any doubt that what is going on is a modern religious crusade, these recent troubling incidents have settled the matter.

Yet this is not the end; and in the famous words of Winston Churchill, 'It is not even the beginning of the end.' There will unfortunately be more such gruesome attacks, perhaps not only by Muslim fanatics on Christian 'targets' but also by Christian (or Jewish) fanatics on Muslim 'targets'.

Unless the 'crusading' undercurrent to these events is understood, and successfully defused, the root of the problem will persist, and will continue to create new factions, even if Al Qaeda is totally eliminated. In the somber words of Dr. Lucy-Anne Hunt, head of the School of History of Art and Design at Manchester Metropolitan University:

The motif of the crusader is an integral element of the historical memory. Among the Muslims, it will evoke reminiscences of crimes committed by the West in the past within seconds. On both sides, it has a reliably polarizing effect and demonizes the enemy. And it suggests that aggressive action is justified since it is willed by God … President Bush referred to it when opting for the recent war in Iraq. This appeal to God-given authority fits in with the simple choice given here: if you're not with us, you're against us. Conversely, in their attacks on Western targets, extreme Muslim groups have also accepted casualties among Muslims, as in the London bombings ... This polarization demonstrates that the need for ongoing dialogue and negotiation, albeit a painstaking and slow process, is ever more crucial.[48]

In other words, God must be made to step aside in this ever-growing conflict, and secular moderate heads of state must begin to speak out and drum some sense into the religious leaders and radical groups on both sides. This is the first and major step in stopping this runaway train that is slowly but surely leading us all into a world conflict which no nation, no religious group, nor even the human race as a whole can win.

THE GREAT PYRAMID AND FREEMASONRY

(Publisher's note: much of the information in this appendix is culled from Robert Bauval's book, Secret Chamber: The Quest for the Hall of Records, *Chapter 8).*

Millennium Madness and the Great Pyramid

Amid accusations of a 'Zionist' plot and 'Masonic' machinations, the Egyptian government cancelled the placing of a golden capstone on top of the Great Pyramid of Giza scheduled for the eve of the new millennium at midnight on 31 December 1999.

Oddly enough, the strange circumstances that led to this bizarre scandal had their origins in France on 14 May 1998 when a golden capstone was unveiled on top of the ancient Egyptian obelisk at the Place de la Concorde in Paris.

Guests of honor at the ceremony included Egypt's ambassador to France, Dr. Maher el Sayed, French minister of culture and communication, Catherine Trautmann and other dignitaries. The event took place during an official visit of Egyptian President Hosni Mubarak to France, with Egypt's minister of culture, Farouk Hosni, and the antiquities' chairman, Dr. Ali Gaballah in attendance. A commemorative plaque was fixed on the base of the obelisk which reads:

> This obelisk, offered by Egypt to France in 1830, to serve eternally as a
> bond between the two countries, has been dressed by its pyramidion
> of origin on 14 May 1998, under the presidency of Jacques Chirac in the
> presence of Catherine Trautmann, minister of culture and communication,
> and Dr. Maher El Sayed, ambassador of Egypt for the occasion of the
> Year France-Egypt 'Shared Horizons' and the visit of the president of the

Arab Republic of Egypt, Hosni Mubarak. The monument thus restored
is dedicated to Jean-François Champollion, founder of Egyptology, who
chose it from the temple of Luxor. This pyramidion is realized thanks to
the support of Yves Saint Laurent, Pierre Bergé and the House of Yves
Saint Laurent.[1]

The name of the famous fashion designer Yves Saint Laurent and his
ex-lover Pierre Bergé naturally attracted our attention. There was much
controversy on the internet surrounding Yves Saint Laurent regarding a
very weird publication he was involved with in 1967, namely a type of
comic book for children titled *La Vilaine Lulu* which has be described
as a Satanic-cum-Masonic manual by advocates of conspiracy theories
and the so-called Illuminati. The book concerns a young girl called Lulu
who, among other warped actions, goes around decapitating, hanging
and burning people. As for Pierre Bergé, we discovered a very intriguing
connection with Zionism that, to say the very least, makes his name on the
obelisk's plaque most disturbing. Bergé is one of France's most notorious
billionaires and philanthropists, as well as having once been a keen and
active supporter of François Mitterrand during his presidential campaigns.
Co-founder of the Yves Saint Laurent empire and one-time director of the
Paris Opera, Bergé is a well know patron of the arts and, partly because
of his Jewish faith, a staunch crusader against anti-Semitism. Bergé is the
founder of the Musée Dreyfus at the Maison Zola, opening in 2012.

The Musée Dreyfus, as the name implies, is dedicated to Alfred Dreyfus,
a French artillery officer of Alsatian Jewish origins who, in 1894, was
condemned to life imprisonment by a military court for allegedly spying for
Germany. This famous 'Dreyfus Affair' exposed the obvious anti-Semitism
in France at the time and split the nation into a huge controversial debate
when the writer Émile Zola published his celebrated open letter '*J'accuse* ...!'
in the French newspaper *L'Aurore* in January 1898. It is also well-known
that the Dreyfus Affair was the catalyst that was to give birth to Zionism.
This happened when Theodore Herzl, then a young journalist and the Paris
correspondent for the German newspaper *Neue Freie Presse*, followed
the story of Alfred Dreyfus and was so incensed with the anti-Semitism
that surrounded the affair and the French crowd's chanting 'death to the
Jews' that he organized the First Zionist Congress in Basel, Switzerland,
in 1897. The connection of Pierre Bergé with the Dreyfus Affair, and his
involvement in 1998 with the bizarre ceremony at the Place de la Concorde
in Paris when a golden capstone was placed on the Egyptian obelisk makes

the choice date, i.e. 14 May 1998 (the 50-year jubilee of the State of Israel), unlikely to be a 'coincidence'.[2]

This authentic ancient Egyptian obelisk, as we have seen in Chapter 1, was taken from the temple of Luxor in Upper Egypt in 1831 under the orders of Charles X, and raised in the Place de la Concorde in 1836 in celebrations attended by a crowd of more than 200,000 people. Charles X was a staunch Freemason, and it was (and still is) suspected it was the Masonic lodges that were really behind the bringing of the obelisk to France, as was also the case with those obelisks later taken out of Egypt to London and New York by British and American Freemasons.

The 'London' obelisk, or *Cleopatra's Needle* as it is more commonly known in Britain, was commissioned and paid for by a prominent Freemason, Sir Erasmus Wilson, and the raising ceremony was attend by hundreds of Freemasons in September 1878 under the auspices of the Prince of Wales, the Grand Master of the United Grand Lodge of England.

That same year former US President Ulysses S. Grant[3] and General William T. Sherman suggested, during a trip to Egypt, that America should also have an ancient Egyptian obelisk.[4] Henry Honychurch Gorringe,[5] a prominent American Freemason, was selected for the task of bringing the obelisk to New York. The obelisk was raised in October 1880 outside the newly built Metropolitan Museum of Art, with nearly ten thousand Freemasons attending the ceremony in full Masonic regalia.[6]

It is one of those strange coincidences of history that on 14 May 1998, when President Mubarak and his retinue attended the capping of the obelisk in the Place de la Concorde, huge celebrations were simultaneously underway in Tel Aviv marking the 50-year jubilee of the Declaration of the State of Israel. On the same day Egyptian culture minister Farouk Hosni told the French press that a ceremony similar to the capping of the obelisk would take place in Egypt for the millennial celebrations at which point a golden capstone would be placed on the Great Pyramid of Giza:

> We cannot rebuild the pyramids stone by stone, so we have chosen a symbolic event like the ancient Egyptians did when they used to cap obelisks [and] like what the French did at the Place de la Concorde.[7]

Later in October 1998 Farouk Hosni announced to the Egyptian press that French composer Jean Michel Jarre had been commissioned to organize this event at Giza. The Egyptian Tourist Authority announced that Jarre would compose an opera titled *The Twelve Dreams of the Sun* for the sum of 10 million US dollars and that,

> At midnight a helicopter will fly into the site and, hovering in a starburst of lasers and spotlights, will place a gigantic gilded capstone atop the Great Pyramid – all to the accompaniment of what is expected to be an unprecedented Jarre crescendo of electronic music. The gold cap, approximately 28 feet high (about the size of a two-story house) is being especially constructed to protect the pyramid structure. In place, it will catch the first light of the new millennium as the sun rises over Egypt. Capping pyramids with gold and timing important events to the setting and rising sun are very much part of the ancient Egyptian pharaonic tradition, making this piece of Jarre theatre particularly meaningful.[8]

Let us note that back in July 1989 Jean Michel Jarre had organized a somewhat similar event in Paris for the bicentennial of the French Revolution when he set up a large metal-framed pyramid as a stage for his band in front of the Grande Arche at La Defense at the western end of the Champs-Élysées. Another show by Jarre also took place a few years later in London's Canary Wharf which is topped by a glowing glass pyramid apparently having the same geometrical proportions as the Great Pyramid in Egypt like the one that stands in the courtyard of the Louvre Museum in Paris, built by the architect I. M. Pei.

It would appear that the idea of placing a golden capstone on the Great Pyramid originated with Dr. Zahi Hawass, at the time director-general of the Giza monuments. It seems that a few months before the May 1998 celebrations Hawass had unearthed two limestone blocks with ancient inscriptions and drawings depicting workers moving a capstone for a royal pyramid amid scenes of dancing and celebrations. Inspired by this, Hawass proposed that Egypt should celebrate the millennium in a similar fashion. At first three million people were scheduled to attend the event but the Egyptian authorities put a limit of 250,000 for security reasons. A massive worldwide promotional campaign was organized including New York, Los Angeles, Sydney and various cities in Europe. Preparations then began for a huge stage to be erected in the desert south of the Great Pyramid with seating capacity for VIPs.

All was apparently going to plan until, in September 1999, senior members of the Egyptian Parliament began to complain of the costs involved and also that the millennium celebrations coincided that particular year with the holy month of Ramadan when devout Muslims fast from dawn to dusk. To counteract such criticism, culture minister Farouk Hosni stated that a ban would be placed on alcohol during the celebrations and that no music would be played until after the official end of the fast was announced.

To add fuel to this political fire, the radical Egyptian press, notably the newspaper *Sawt al-Shaab* ('*Voice of the People*') reported that Jean Michel Jarre was Jewish and also that he intended to project an 'eye' among many other images on the Great Pyramid using laser beams. The upshot was that *Sawt al-Shaab* accused the organizers of staging a 'Masonic' event in collusion with the 'Jews'. The newspaper claimed that the 'eye in the pyramid' planned for this ceremony was intended to evoke the well-known Masonic symbol of the 'eye in the triangle' and, more specifically, the 'Eye of Providence' seen on the US one-dollar bill (and also in the 'Great Seal of the United States', suspected to be of Masonic significance).

More such accusations of 'Masonic-Zionist' infiltration of the millennium party at Giza ensued in the Arab press, although hotly denied by Farouk Hosni as 'groundless', and by Dr. Hawass who stated that 'the celebration has nothing to do with Masonic beliefs. The design on the US dollar is a faulty imitation of the Pyramids of the Middle Kingdom.'[9]

Adding to the growing hype was another bizarre twist to this strange story. This involved the so-called 'prophecies' made by American psychic Edgar Cayce known as the 'Sleeping Prophet', who died in 1945. It turns out that Cayce foretold the placing of a gilded capstone on the Great Pyramid and also associated the event with the establishment of a sort of 'new world order' based on Masonic principles:

> For with those changes that will be wrought, Americanism with the universal thought that is expressed and manifest in the Brotherhood of man into group thought as expressed in the Masonic Order, will be the eventual rule in the settlement of affairs in the world. Not that the world is to become a Masonic Order, but the principles that are embraced in the same will be the basis upon which the new order of peace is to be established ...[10]

It is well known in Egyptological circles that since 1973 the Edgar Cayce Foundation has been involved in various archaeological expeditions at Giza to find the fabled 'Hall of Records'.[11]

In 1996–7 much controversy surrounded the precise relationship of the Edgar Cayce Foundation and the Egyptian Supreme Council of Antiquities, with allegations that prominent members of the organization arranged for the university education of Zahi Hawass, then chief inspector of the Giza pyramids All these allegations and rumours reached a peak in early December 1999, and finally under heavy pressure from the Egyptian press and also from members of Parliament, the Supreme Council of Antiquities took a face-saving position by delegating the decision of placing the golden capstone to a scientific committee. Hawass stated that the capstone, which apparently was to be made from an 8-meter high light metal frame and covered in gold sheets, could not be lowered by a helicopter '... because it will hurt the pyramid. Therefore if we find out that putting this capstone will hurt the pyramid, then, we will not do it.' But some critics rightly pointed out a lightweight capstone on the 6 million ton stone pyramid would be like placing a flea on an elephant's back. Finally the Egyptian minister of culture caved in and, at the eleventh hour, admitted that due to public outrage over the 'Masonic' and 'Zionist' implications the placing of the golden capstone would be scrapped, but the show would go on just the same.

Ironically on the night of 31 December a thick fog settled over the Great Pyramid which would have anyway made it impossible for the helicopter to lower the capstone on its summit. Jean Michel Jarre did, however, manage to project his images on the Giza pyramids including 'eyes' until they, too, were engulfed by the fog and the thick smoke caused by the smoke of the huge firework display.

The one-eyed fiend

Although the alleged Masonic-Zionist conspiracy is generally seen as a secular evil, the Freemasons, as we saw in Chapter Twenty, are often associated with the mysterious and satanic figure of *Masih ad-Dajjal*, a supernatural entity akin to a 'false prophet' or a 'false messenger' who, in Muslim lore, is supposed to appear before *Yawm al-Qiyamah* (the 'Day of Judgment'). In the Koran the *Dajjal* has a single eye which is inevitably associated to the single eye in the pyramid on the US one-dollar bill and, of course, the 'eye in the triangle' in Freemasonry and also Judaic symbolism.

It was thus no surprise that a few days before the planned millennium celebrations at the Giza pyramids, *Sawt al-Shaab* accused culture minister Farouk Hosni of allowing the 'Jew' Jean Michel Jarre to present a 'Masonic-Zionist' event on the soil of Egypt to be seen live on television on a global scale by billions of viewers. The newspaper printed a large composite image showing a Freemason with a huge eye (clearly representing the *Dajjal*) on whose chest was pinned the Star of David and the Masonic triangle. Yet

Farouk Hosni and Zahi Hawass are themselves not immune to fictitious Israeli and Jewish plots against Egypt and the Arab World in general. In 1997 Farouk Hosni told the Arab press:

> The Israelis do not stop claiming that they built the pyramids, and this is why we need to stand firmly and respond courageously ... even if it leads to a crisis because those pirates are committing a robbery ... The Israelis want everything ... This is the way the Israelis took Palestine ... Now they use [this method] regarding the big pyramid. These are continuous projects – people come, steal your history and civilization. This proves that Israel has no history or civilization, since those who have history of their own do not need to rob the history of others ... Israel has many political goals ... First of all, they steal your civilization and history. Second, they do not have any civilization ... they do not have a country, and do not deserve a country. This is why they create a country by force ...[12]

To which Zahi Hawass added:

> A group of people are making an organized campaign. There are some people pushing them [Israel] ... These people are waging a big attack against us. I swore two years ago that I would not reveal their names, but I found out that I must mention them because it is becoming a threat.[13]

A few years later, on 17 September 2002, a small robot was used to explore narrow shafts in the Great Pyramid of Giza. The exploration was aired on a 'live' TV show by the National Geographic Channel with an estimated 300 million viewers watching. After the show Hawass told bemused journalists at a press conference at the Mena House Oberoi:

> The results of the robot's exploration refute the allegations reiterated by Jews and some Western countries that the Jews built the pyramids!

> ... and I will tell the public that everyone who tries to talk against the Egyptians should shut their mouths![14]

In a more recent television appearance in February 2009 Hawass seemed almost to be quoting from *The Protocols of the Elders of Zion*, those fake documents that claim to expose a Masonic-Zionist plot to control the Arab world, when he told the interviewer that,

> ... For eighteen centuries they [the Jews] were dispersed throughout the world ... they went to America and took control of its economy ... they have a plan: Although they are few in number, they control the entire world ... look at the control they have over America and the media![15]

Paradoxically, in view of the above, it was announced in early 2009 that Farouk Hosni was the prime candidate to be the new head of the United Nations Educational, Scientific and Cultural Organization (UNESCO.) Not unexpectedly worldwide protests ensued when it was revealed that in May of the previous year Hosni had told an Islamist politician that he would 'personally burn any Israeli books he found in an Egyptian library'. The French-based Reporters Without Borders wrote that 'Farouk Hosni has been one of the main forces for censorship in Egypt, trying unfailingly to control press freedom, as well as citizens' freedom of information'. The *Independent* of Ireland was even more forthright:

> To put such a creature in charge of the UN body for science, education and culture might seem rather like appointing a bull as manager of a china shop.[16]

Ultimately the UNESCO job went to Bulgarian ambassador to France, Irina Bokova. This decision, however, was seen by the Arab press as 'a sign of Western prejudice against Islam and the Arab world, the product of an international Jewish conspiracy.'

'America, Europe and the Jewish lobby brought down Farouk Hosni' was the headline in the Egpytian newspaper *Al-Masry Al-Youm*, while Egyptian foreign minister Ahmed Aboul Gheit accused 'international Judaism and Western powers' of plotting against Hosni. As for Farouk Hosni himself, he was quoted as saying: 'there was a group of the world's Jews who had a major influence in the elections and who were a serious threat to Egypt taking this position.'[17]

ENDNOTES

PREFACE: THE MASTER GAME
INTRODUCTION: THE GAME OF GAMES

1   Sir Walter Scott (trans.), *Hermetica: The Ancient Greek and Latin Writings Which Contain Religious or Philosophic Teachings Ascribed to Hermes Trismegistus*, Kessinger Publishing, Kila, MT, 1995, pp. 341–5.

PROLOGUE: THE SACRED CITIES
CHAPTER ONE: BEHIND THE VEILS

1   Jean Duché. *L'Histoire de France Raconté à Juliette*, Presses Pocket, Paris, 1954, p. 179.

2   Palloy made 83 'models' of the Bastille with the original stones which he had distributed to various towns in France. One of the 'Bastille' models can still be seen at the Musée de Valence. The rest of the stones were used for the building of the Pont de la Concorde. Some were pulverised and the fine powder sold in bottles.

3   Jean Kerisel, *La Pyramide à Travers les âges,* Presses des Ponts et Chaussées, Paris, 1991, p. 161.

4   Jurgis Baltrušaitis, *La Quête d'Isis*, Flammarion, Paris, 1985, p. 24. Ermanno Arslan, *Iside: il mito il mistero la magia*, Electa, Milano, 1997, pp. 642–4. See also Jean-Marcel Humbert, *L'Egyptomanie dans l'art occidental*, ACR, Paris, 1989, p. 36.

5   Arslan, op. cit., p. 643.

6   Michel Vovelle, *La Révolution contre L'Eglise: de la Raison à l'Etre Suprême*, Editions Complexe, Paris, 1988.

7   Ibid., p. 15.

8   Louis IX was canonised on 11 August 1297 and his feast day is 25 August; In AD 800 Charlemagne was unofficially 'beatified' by Pope Leo III but not actually canonised.

9   Vovelle, op. cit., p. 103.

10   Jean Starobinski, *1789: Les Emblèmes de la Raison*, Flammarion, Paris, 1979, p. 42.

11   *Grand Larousse Encyclopédique*, Paris, 1961, vol. 8, p. 1014.

12   The son of Louis XVI died in Temple prison in Paris in 1795 at the age of six. He was proclaimed king by the French nobility in exile in January 1793 after his father's death.

13   Originally offered as a gift to the French by Muhammad Ali in 1824. Champollion judged the Alexandria obelisks to be of poor quality due to their excessive corrosion by the sea air, and exchanged the 'gift' for a single obelisk from the Luxor temple.

14   Hunbert, op. cit., p. 44. Interestingly, at the top of the pyramid was to be place a statue of a goddess wearing a seven-pointed star on her head, much like the Statue of Liberty in New York.

15   Ibid.

16   Starobinski, op. cit., pp. 49 & 58.

17   Jacques Godechot, *La Prise de la Bastille*, Paris, 1965, p. 183.

18   Michael Baigent & Richard Leigh, *The Temple and the Lodge*, Jonathan Cape, London, 1989.

19   Steven C. Bullock, *Revolutionary Brotherhood*, University of North Carolina Press, Chapel Hill, NC, 1996, p. 50.

20   Fred Pick & G. Norman Knight, *The Pocket History of Freemasonry*, Frederick Muller, London, 1953, p. 272.

21   Ibid., p. 271.

22   Ibid., p. 275.

23   Pierre Chevallier, *Histoire de la Franc-Maçonnerie française*, Librairie Fayard, Paris, 1974, vol. I, pp. 272–88.

24   *Dossiers de l'histoire mystérieuse*, no. 7, part 2, ed. F., Carbonnel, p. 81.

25   Ibid.

26   *Dossiers de l'histoire mystérieuse*, no. 6, p. 64.

27   Chevallier, op. cit., vol. I, p. 275.

28   Jacques Debû-Bridel, *Lafayette: une vie au service de la liberté*, Editions Nouvelles de France, 1945, p. 27.

29   Quoted from Jean-André Faucher, *Les Francs-Maçons et le pouvoir de la Révolution à nos jours*, Librairie Académique Perrin, Paris, 1986, p. 46.

30   Faucher, op. cit., p. 47. Faucher, like many others, also points out that there were many Masons who supported the king and actually fought against the revolutionaries. This is true of the American Revolution as well.

31   John Lawrence, *Freemasonry: A Religion?*, Kingsway Publishing, London, 1987, p. 15.

32   Ibid., p. 109.

33   Ibid., p. 121.

34   Martin Short, *Inside The Brotherhood*, Grafton Books, London, 1989, p. 72.

35   Vovelle, op. cit., p. 187.

36   *Dossiers de l'histoire mystérieuse*, no. 6, p. 64.

37 Ibid.

38 Ibid.

39 Vovelle, op. cit., p. 274.

40 Ibid.

41 *Décret de la Convention*, 18 Floral An II, 7 May 1794.

42 Warren Roberts, *Revolutionary Artists*, State University of New York Press, Albany, 2000, p. 272.

43 *Grand Larousse Encyclopédique*, vol. 4, p. 784.

44 Roberts, op. cit., p. 270. The language used by Robespierre is intensely 'Masonic'. For example, he states that 'a system of well organised national festivals would offer at once the most gentle of fraternal ties and the most powerful means of regeneration'. This is almost like bringing out on a public scale the rituals performed in lodges.

45 The Republican calendar was introduced on 24 October 1793, just after the guillotining of Queen Marie-Antoinette.

46 Charles Sumner Lobingier, *Ancient and Accepted Scottish Rite*, Kessinger Publishing, Kila, MT, 1931, p. 24.

47 David Ovason, *The Secret Zodiacs of Washington DC*, Century, London, 1999, pp. 116–7.

48 Bessel deduced the existence of Sirius's super-dense companion by observing its the wave-like motion, but did not actually see the 'invisible' companion. The latter, known as Sirius B, was first 'seen' by telescope by Alvin Clark in 1862, and photographed by Lindenblad in 1970.

49 Ovason, op. cit., p. 117.

50 Baltrušaitis, op. cit., p. 31.

51 *Dossiers de l'histoire mystérieuse*, no. 7, p. 106.

52 Nigel Aston, *Religion and Revolution in France*, MacMillan Press, London, 2000, p. 272.

53 Kerisel, op. cit., p. 160.

54 Robert Bauval, *Secret Chamber*, Arrow, London, 2000, p. 507, n. 27.

55 Sylvie Legaret & Philippe Coutines, *Paris Story*, Editions Denoël, Paris, 1977, p. 83, plate 3.

56 Ibid.

57 Aston, op. cit., p. 271.

58 Ibid.

59 Ovason, op. cit., p. 87.

60 Short, op. cit., pp. 121–2.

61 Ibid., p. 122.

PART I: THE SECRET FAITH
CHAPTER TWO: LOST WORLD

1 Aubrey Burl, *God's Heretics: The Albigensian Crusade*, Sutton Publishing, Gloucestershire, 2002, p. 9. As early as 1198, as part of the virulent anti-Cathar propaganda of the time, Alan de Lille sought to promote an alternative derivation of the word 'Cathar' from 'cat's-arse' claiming that the devil appeared to the heretics in the form of a cat whose hindquarters they kissed. Similar acusations were later to be made against the Knights Templar – see Chapter Fifteen.

2 John 1:14.

3 F. L. Cross and E. A. Livingstone, (eds.), *The Oxford Dictionary of the Christian Christian Church*, Oxford University Press, Oxford, 1988, p. 1198.

4 St. Augustine, *City of God*, Penguin Classics, London, 1984, Introduction.

5 Chas S. Clifton (ed.), *Encyclopaedia of Heresies and Heretics*, ABC-Clio Inc., Santa Barbara, 1992, p. 49.

6 See Chapters Four, Five and Six.

7 Malcolm Lambert, *The Cathars*, Blackwell Publishers, Oxford, 1998, p. 4.

8 See Jonathan Sumption, *The Albigensian Crusade*, Faber & Faber, London, 1999, pp. 28–30. See also Arthur Guirdham, *The Great Heresy: The History and Beliefs of the Cathars*, C. W. Daniel Company Ltd., Saffron Walden, 1993, p. 23.

9 Jospeh R. Strayer, *The Albigensian Crusades*, University of Michigan Press, Ann Arbor, MI, 1995, p. 1.

10 Ibid., p. 3.

11 Gervase of Tilbury cited in Sumption, op. cit., p. 18.

12 Sumption, op. cit., p. 18.

13 Zoé Oldenbourg, *Massacre at Montségur*, Weidenfeld and Nicholson, London, 1997, p. 1.

14 Guirdham, op. cit., p. 15.

15 Lambert, op. cit., p. 62.

16 Guirdham, op. cit., p. 15; Lambert, op. cit., p. 62.

17 Oldenbourg, op. cit., p. 11.

18 Cited in Malcolm Barber, *The Cathars: Dualist Heretics in Languedoc in the High Middle Ages*, Longman, London, 2000, p. 51.

19 Lambert, op. cit., p. 62.

20 Guirdham, op. cit., p. 15.

21 Ibid.

22 Cited in Burl, op. cit., p. 21.

23 Barber, op. cit., pp. 65–6.

24 Ibid., p. 66.

25 Ibid., p. 25.

26 Malcolm Lambert, *Medieval Heresy: Popular Movements from the Gregorian Reform to the Reformation*, Blackwell, Oxford, 1992, p. 57.

27 Cited in Lambert, *The Cathars*, p. 39.

28 Cited in Ibid., pp. 39–40.

29 Steven Runciman, *The Medieval Manichee: A Study of Christian Dualist Heresy*, Cambridge University Press, Cambridge, 1999, p. 121; Sumption, op. cit., p. 39.

30 Ibid.

31 Stephen O' Shea, *The Perfect Heresy: The Life and Death of the Cathars*, Profile Books Ltd., London, 2001, p. 20.

32 For example, see Lambert, *The Cathars*, p. 155.

33 For example, see Oldenbourg, op. cit., p. 49; Runciman, op. cit., p. 160.

34 Oldenbourg, op. cit., pp. 21–2.

35 Cited in Lambert, *The Cathars*, pp. 142–3.

36 Lambert, *Medieval Heresy*, p. 121.

37 Lambert, *The Cathars*, p. 75.

38 Ibid., pp. 23 & 153; see also O'Shea, op. cit., p. 24.

39 Lambert, *The Cathars*, p. 75.

40 Runciman, op. cit., p. 160.

41 Ibid., p. 151.

42 Ibid., p. 160.

43 Lambert, *Medieval Heresy*, p. 120; Rion Klawinski, *Chasing the Heretics: A Modern Journey through Medieval Languedoc*, Ruminator Books, Saint Paul, MN, 2000, p. 68; Runciman, op. cit., pp. 159–60.

44 Lambert *Medieval Heresy*, p. 124, citing Guiraud. See also Sumption, op. cit., p. 50.

45 Testimony before the Inquisition of a woman of Puylaurens, cited in Sumption, op. cit., p. 52.

46 Lambert, *Medieval Heresy*, p. 109.

47 Runciman, op. cit., p. 158.

48 Ibid.

49 Lambert, *Medieval Heresy*, p. 108.

50 Lambert, *The Cathars*, pp. 240 & 242.

51 Ibid., p. 242.

52 Cited in Ibid., p. 139.

53 For example, see Strayer, op. cit., p. 247.

54 Lambert, *The Cathars*, p. 139.

55 Guirdham, op. cit., p. 24.

56 Lambert, *The Cathars*, p. 160.

57 Guirdham, op. cit., p. 23.

58 Ibid.

59 O'Shea, op. cit., p. 8.

60 Guirdham, op. cit., p. 95.

61 For example, see Oldenbourg, op. cit., pp. 283–4 and Lambert, *The Cathars*, p. 125.

62 Guirdham, op. cit., p. 95.

63 See Barber, op. cit., pp. 203–25.

64 All quotations from Weil cited in Ibid. Martin Barber (p. 207) dismisses Weil's argument for what he maligns as its 'cavalier disregard for evidence' and its 'fundamentally unhistorical' vagueness of approach.

65 Cited in Ibid., p. 206.

66 Oldenbourg, op. cit., p. 23.

67 Ibid., p. 24.

68 Ibid.

69 Burl, op. cit., p. 19.

70 See Sumption, op. cit., p. 90; O'Shea, op. cit., p. 20.

71 Geoffrey Wigoder (ed.), *The Encyclopaedia of Judaism*, The Jerusalem Publishing House, 1989, p. 514.

72 The report of Benjamin of Tudela, cited in Sumption, op. cit., p. 90.

73 Cited in Ibid.

74 *Encyclopaedia Britannica*, 15th edition, London, 1991, *Micropaedia*, 11: 946–7.

75 Ibid., 3:686–7.

76 Ibid., 11:946–7; 3:686–7.

77 Sumption, op. cit., pp. 29–30.

78 Oldenbourg, op. cit., p. 26.

79 Ibid., pp. 230–1.

80 For example, see Sumption, op. cit., p. 30; Lambert, *Medieval Heresy*, p. 83.

81 Guirdham, op. cit., p. 96.

82 Lambert, *The Cathars*, p. 149.

83 Oldenbourg, op. cit., p. 61.

84 O'Shea, op. cit., p. 41.

85 Oldenbourg, op. cit., p. 61.

86 Guirdham, op. cit., p. 16.

87 Barber, op. cit., p. 216.

88 Oldenbourg, op. cit., p. 51.

89 Ibid., p. 51.

90 Ibid., p. 69.

91 Ibid., p. 70.

92 Lambert, *The Cathars*, p. 160.

93 Technically the Albigensian Crusades ceased in 1229 with the Treaty of Paris; however military crusading was continued by French occupation forces in the Languedoc for a further fifteen years, culminating in the siege and massacre at the last Cathar stronghold of Montségur in 1244. See Chapter Seven for a more detailed discussion.

94 Oldenbourg, op. cit., p. 56.

95 Ibid., p. 310.

CHAPTER THREE: WHERE GOOD AND EVIL MEET

1 Cited in Oldenbourg, op. cit., Appendix C, p. 376.

2 F. L. Cross and E. A. Livingstone, (eds.), *The Oxford Dictionary of the Christian Christian Church*, Oxford University Press, Oxford, 1988, pp. 339 & 993.

3 For example, see Lambert, *Medieval Heresy*, p. 395: 'The Christian Church in the East as well as in the West was the heir to the assumptions of the pagan Roman Empire and of the whole ancient world, of the duty of the ruler to enforce right belief, and, with some hesitation, its leaders came to act on these assumptions … Byzantine chruchmen shared the horror of heresy and emperors took a direct part in the pursuit of heretics. Burning was a penalty imposed on the obdurate in the Byzantine Church as well – we have a vivid description by Anna Comnena of

the burning of the Bogomil leader Basil in Constantinople.'

4 For example, see Oldenbourg, op. cit., pp. 30–31; Lambert, *The Cathars*, p. 23; O' Shea, op. cit., pp. 22–3; Burl, op. cit., p. 9; Runciman, op. cit., p. 67; Lambert, *Medieval Heresy*, pp. 55–6.

5 Runciman, op. cit., p. 68; Lambert, p. 23; Barber, op. cit., p. 16.

6 Runciman, op. cit., p. 67.

7 Theophylact Lycapenus (AD 933–956), the patriarch of Constantinople, provides us with an earlier mention the heresy but, strangely, does not mention Bogomil himself. See Janet Hamilton & Bernard Hamilton, *Christian Dualist Heresies in the Byzantine World c. 650–c. 1405*, Manchester University Press, Manchester, 1998, pp. 98–101.

8 Runciman, op. cit., p. 68.

9 Cited in Ibid., p. 67.

10 Ibid., p. 68.

11 Oldenbourg, op. cit., p. 31.

12 Runciman, op. cit., pp. 69–70.

13 Hamilton & Hamilton, op. cit., p. 32.

14 Ibid., p. 36.

15 Ibid., p. 37; Runciman, op. cit., pp. 70–1.

16 Runciman, op. cit., pp. 70–1; Hamilton & Hamilton, op. cit., p. 38.

17 Hamilton & Hamilton, op. cit., p. 39; Runciman, op. cit., pp. 70–71.

18 Hamilton & Hamilton, op. cit., p. 40; Runciman, op. cit., p. 71

19 Runciman, op. cit., p. 72.

20 Barber, op. cit., p. 21.

21 Ibid., p. 21; see also Lambert, *The Cathars*, pp. 46–9.

22 Barber, op. cit., p. 22.

23 For example, see Runciman, op. cit., p. 170; Hamilton & Hamilton, op. cit., pp. 43–4.

24 Lambert, *The Cathars*, pp. 35 & 37.

25 Barber, op. cit., p. 71.

26 Lambert, *The Cathars*, p. 48.

27 Which was the view of most Orthodox and Catholic clergymen and monks of the period. In the East Euthymius Zigabenus definitely suspected a plot after interrogating the heresiarch Basil. See Hamilton & Hamilton, op. cit., p. 32. For other examples see Ibid., p. 266 and Lambert, *The Cathars*, pp. 22 & 31.

28 Cited in Barber, op. cit., p. 16; Hamilton & Hamilton, op. cit., p. 28.

29 Dimitur Anguelou, cited in Barber, op. cit., p. 16.

30 Obolensky, cited in Ibid., p. 16.

31 Lambert, *Medieval Heresy*, p. 116.

32 Cited in Lambert, *The Cathars*, p. 203.

33 See Lambert, *Medieval Heresy*, p. 118.

34 Zigabenus, cited in Hamilton & Hamilton, op. cit., pp. 39 & 204.

35 Lambert, *The Cathars*, p. 248.

36 Lambert, *Medieval Heresy*, p. 118.

37 Ibid., p. 118.

38 Ibid.

39 Ibid.

40 Runciman, op. cit., p. 171.

41 Barber, *The Cathars*, op. cit., p. 73

42 Oldenbourg, op. cit., p. 31.

43 Ibid.

44 Hamilton & Hamilton, op. cit., pp. 43–4.

45 Lambert, *The Cathars*, p. 33: 'The Cathar ritual of the consolamentum derives from the Bogomil form of the initiation of adepts ...'

46 The former Cathar turned inquisitor, Rainier Sacconi, cited in Ibid., p. 204.

47 Saccioni, cited in Ibid. Sacconi excepted the Albanensians and the Concorezzans from the otherwise general harmony, stating that they 'censure each other'.

48 *Oxford Dictionary of the Christian Church*, p. 1292.

49 Ibid.

50 Ibid.

51 The Cathar Pierre Autier, cited in Lambert, *The Cathars*, p. 251.

52 Ibid., p. 253.

53 Ibid.: 'The bodies of animals formed part of the chain of transmigration, though since they could not speak, no soul ... imprisoned there could reach salvation. It was a penitential process ... lasting till they reached the body of a man or woman who had "the understanding of God" and could be saved.'

54 Ibid.

55 Ibid.

56 *Oxford Dictionary of the Christian Church*, p. 997.

57 Hamilton & Hamilton, op. cit., p. 27.

58 See discussion in Lambert, *Medieval Heresy*, p. 121ff.

59 Lambert, *The Cathars*, p. 204.

60 Euthymius Zigabenus' debriefing of the Bogomil Basil, cited in Barber, op. cit., p. 19.

61 Cited in Lambert, The Cathars, p. 162.

62 Oldenbourg, op. cit., p. 35.

63 Ibid.

64 Pierre Autier, cited in Lambert, *The Cathars*, pp. 250–1.

65 For example, see Runciman, op. cit., p. 148; Barber, op. cit., p. 84.

66 Autier, in Lambert, *The Cathars*, p. 251.

67 Ibid.

68 For example, see Runciman, op. cit., p. 76.

69 Oldenbourg, op. cit., p. 35; see also Lambert, *The Cathars*, p. 25.

70 Cathar prayer, cited in Oldenbourg, op. cit., Appendix C, p. 376.

71 Runciman, op. cit., p. 75.

72 Ibid., p. 150: 'It was hoped when lives were pure the fragments of soul attached to them were able to catch on to the divine spirit which descended onto such perfected persons and thus won release.'

73 Robert Bauval & Adrian Gilbert, *The Orion Mystery*, William Heinemann Ltd., London, 1994; Robert Bauval & Graham Hancock, *Keeper of Genesis* (titled in the US: *Message of the Sphinx*), William Heinemann Ltd., London, 1996; Graham Hancock & Santha Faiia, *Heaven's Mirror*, Michael Joseph/Penguin, London, 1998.

74 E. A. Wallis Budge, *The Egyptian Heaven and Hell* (*Book of What is in the Duat*), Martin Hopkinson Co., London, 1925, pp. 240 & 258.

75 Ibid., p. 240.

76 Ibid., p. 258.

77 See note 73 above.

78 Cited in Runciman, op. cit., p. 75.

79 Barber, op. cit., p. 97.

80 Ibid.

81 Ibid., p. 98.

82 Lambert, *The Cathars*, p. 197.

83 Ibid.

84 Barber, op. cit., p. 86.

85 Ibid., p. 87.

86 Hamilton & Hamilton, op. cit., p. 28.

87 Oldenbourg, op. cit., p. 36.

88 Ibid., pp. 36–7.

89 Lambert, *Medieval Heresy*, p. 119.

90 Runciman, op. cit., p. 164.

91 Ibid., p. 173.

92 Ibid., p. 164.

93 Ibid., p. 171.

94 Ibid.

95 Ibid., p. 172.

96 Ibid., p. 171.

97 Ibid., p. 172.

98 Cited in Barber, op. cit., p. 11.

99 Ibid.

100 Strayer, op. cit., pp. 183–4.

101 Lambert, *The Cathars*, p. 23.

102 Hamilton & Hamilton, op. cit., pp. 98–101.

103 Everwof of Steinfeld, cited in Lambert, *The Cathars*, p. 22.

104 Ibid.

105 Everwin, cited in Barber, op. cit., p. 24.

106 Everwin, cited in Lambert, *The Cathars*, p. 22.

107 Lambert, *Medieval Heresy*, p. 119.

108 *Oxford Dictionary of the Christian Church*, pp. 285–6.

109 Lambert, *The Cathars*, p. 25.

110 Everwin, cited in Barber, *The Cathars*, op. cit., p. 24.

CHAPTER FOUR: CHAIN OF THE GREAT HERESY

1 Johannes Van Oort writing in Roelof van den Broek & Wouter Hanegraff (eds.), *Gnosis and Hermeticism From Antiquity to Modern Times*, State University of New York Press, Albany, 1998, p. 37.

2 *The Oxford Dictionary of the Christian Church*, pp. 357–8.

3 Genesis 1: 1–30.

4 Genesis 1: 28.

5 For example, see Lambert and Barber, whose works on the Cathars and Medieval Heresies have been extensively cited in previous chapters.

6 Runciman, op. cit., p. 88.

7 Hamilton & Hamilton, op. cit., p. 6.

8 Ibid., pp. 7–8.

9 Ibid., p. 8.

10 Ibid., p. 9.

11 Ibid.

12 Ibid.

13 Runciman, op. cit., p. 50.

14 Hamilton & Hamilton, op. cit., p. 9.

15 Ibid.

16 Ibid.

17 Ibid., p. 12.

18 Ibid.

19 See discussion in Barber, op. cit., p. 12.

20 Hamilton & Hamilton, op. cit., p. 9.

21 Ibid., pp. 12–13.

22 Ibid., p. 13.

23 Runciman, op. cit., pp. 32–3.

24 Ibid.

25 Hamilton & Hamilton, op. cit., p. 19.

26 Runciman, op. cit., p. 40.

27 Hamilton & Hamilton, op. cit., pp. 21–2.

28 Ibid., p. 23.

29 Cited in Hamilton & Hamilton, op. cit., pp. 6–7.

30 Ibid., p. 8.

31 Ibid., p. 10.

32 Ibid.

33 Runciman, op. cit., p. 21.

34 Ibid.: 'The Messalians were Gnostic in origin but they were less interested in intellectual speculation.'

35 Hamilton & Hamilton, op. cit., p. 30.

36 Runciman, op. cit., p. 90.

37 Ibid., p. 93

38 Ibid.

39 Ibid., pp. 91–2.

40 Hamilton & Hamilton, op. cit., p. 30.

41 Runciman, op. cit., pp. 21–2.

42 Ibid.; See also Francis Legge, *Forerunners and Rivals of Christianity From 330 BC to 330 AD*, University Books Inc., New York, 1965, vol. II, p. 313: 'Valentinus [2nd century AD], like many other Gnostics, divided Christians into two classes of

pneumatics and psychics, the first-named of whom were to enjoy a more distinguished position in the world to come than the other.'

43 Runciman, op. cit., p. 22.
44 Ibid.
45 Ibid.
46 Ibid.
47 Ibid.; Hamilton & Hamilton, op. cit., p. 30.
48 Runciman, op. cit., p. 22; Hamilton & Hamilton, op. cit., p. 30.
49 Runciman, op. cit., p. 22.
50 Ibid., p. 23.
51 Ibid. The Massalians were condemned by Flavian of Antioch who discovered their tenets by feigning a desire for conversion. 'Horrified by his discoveries, he began to persecute them with the full force of the newly-Christianised state.'
52 Encyclopaedia of Heresies and Heretics, p. 87.
53 Sumption, op. cit., p. 34; Legge, op. cit., p. 318.
54 Andrew Wellburn, Mani, The Angel and The Column of Glory: An Anthology of Manichean Texts, Floris Books, Edinburgh, 1998, p. 36.
55 Ibid., p. 25.
56 Ibid., p. 24.
57 Cited in Ibid.
58 Runciman, op. cit., p. 12.
59 Legge, op. cit., p. 279.
60 Ibid., p. 280.
61 Encyclopaedia of Heresies and Heretics, p. 87.
62 Wellburn, op. cit., pp. 12, 51, 86.
63 John R. Hinnels (ed.), The Penguin Dictionary of Religions, Penguin, London, 1988, p. 200.
64 Wellburn, op. cit., p. 87.
65 Ibid., p. 12.
66 Ibid.
67 Legge, op. cit., pp. 285–6; Wellburn, op. cit., p. 8off.
68 Cologne Mani-Codex, cited in Wellburn, op. cit., p. 83.
69 Ibid., pp. 83–4.
70 Encyclopaedia of Heresies and Heretics, p. 87.
71 Legge, op. cit., p. 279.
72 For example, Wellburn, op. cit., pp. 14–15 & 17.
73 Cologne Mani-Codex, cited in Wellburn, op. cit., p. 13.
74 Cited in Ibid., pp. 12–13.
75 Ibid., p. 11.
76 Cologne Mani-Codex, cited in Ibid., p. 16.
77 Legge, op. cit., pp. 280–1.
78 Encyclopaedia of Heresies and Heretics, p. 87.

79 Cologne Mani-Codex, cited in Wellburn, op. cit., p. 15.
80 Ibid., p. 15.
81 Ibid., p. 18.
82 Ibid., p. 15.
83 Oxford Dictionary of the Christian Church, p. 864.
84 Ibid.
85 Ibid.
86 Wellburn, op. cit., p. 67.
87 Ibid.
88 Encyclopaedia of Heresies and Heretics, p. 87.
89 Oxford Dictionary of the Christian Church, p. 864; Legge, op. cit., p. 281.
90 Legge, op. cit., p. 281; Wellburn, op. cit., pp. 67–8.
91 Encyclopaedia of Heresies and Heretics, p. 87; Penguin Dictionary of Religions, p. 201; Oxford Dictionary of the Christian Church, p. 864; Wellburn, op. cit., p. 108; Runciman, op. cit., pp. 6–17; Legge, op. cit., p. 281.
92 Legge, op. cit., p. 282.
93 Wellburn, op. cit., p. 68.
94 St. Augustine, op. cit., Introduction.
95 Legge, op. cit., p. 287.
96 Ibid.
97 Ibid., pp. 291–2.
98 Runciman, op. cit., pp. 12–13.
99 Legge, op. cit., p. 292.
100 Burl, op. cit., pp. 8–9.
101 Yuri Stoyanov, The Other God, Yale University Press, New Haven & London, 2000, p. 108.
102 Ibid.
103 Ibid., pp. 108–9.
104 Ibid., p. 109.
105 Ibid.
106 Ibid., p. 110; Runciman, op. cit., p. 14.
107 Stoyanov, op. cit., p. 110.
108 Ibid.
109 Ibid., pp. 117–8.
110 Ibid., p. 111.
111 Runciman, op. cit., p. 13; Barber, op. cit., p. 10.
112 Wellburn, op. cit., p. 149.
113 Lambert, p. 21.
114 See Legge, op. cit., pp. 221–2 & 317.
115 Runciman, op. cit., p. 15.
116 Ibid., pp. 15–16.
117 Hamilton & Hamilton, op. cit., p. 29.
118 Burl, op. cit. pp. 8–9.
119 Legge, op. cit., p. 318; Runciman, op. cit., p. 14.
120 Legge, op. cit., p. 320.
121 Ibid., pp. 278 & 337–8.
122 We have reported the beliefs of the Cathars and Bogomils on reincarnation in depth in

Chapters Two & Three; for an example of the Manichean belief in reincarnation see Legge, op. cit., p. 340.

123 Legge, op. cit., p. 278 for the Manicheans; the reader is already familiar from Chapters Two & Three with Cathar and Bogomil teachings on this matter.

124 Legge, op. cit., p. 278.

125 Cited in Ibid., p. 315.

126 Cited in Wellburn, op. cit., p. 51.

CHAPTER FIVE: KNOWLEDGE OF THE TRUE NATURE OF THINGS

1 Timothy Freke & Peter Gandy, *The Jesus Mysteries*, Thorsons-Element, London, 2000, p. 266.

2 For example, the actions of the Prefect Cynegius in Alexandria. See H. A. Drake, *Constantine and the Bishops: The Politics of Intolerance*, The John Hopkins University Press, Baltimore & London, 2000, p. 403–4 & 416.

3 Ibid., p. 408.

4 Ibid., p. 416.

5 Elaine Pagels, *The Gnostic Gospels*, Penguin, London, 1990, p. 13–5.

6 Ibid., p. 16.

7 Ibid.

8 Cited in Pagels, op. cit., p. 16.

9 Ibid., p. 16.

10 James M. Robinson (ed.), *The Nag Hammadi Library*, E. J. Brill, Leyden, NY, 1988, p. 73–89.

11 Ibid., p. 85.

12 Ibid., p. 121–2.

13 Ibid., p. 119.

14 Ibid., p. 387.

15 Ibid., p., 159.

16 Kurt Rudoph, *Gnosis: The Nature and History of Gnosticism*, Harper, San Francisco, 1987, p. 116.

17 *The Nag Hammadi Library*, p. 194. Compare Paul, *Ephesians* 6:12.

18 See discussion in Francis Legge, *Forerunners and Rivals of Christianity From 330 BC to 330 AD*, University Books Inc., New York, 1965, vol. II, p. 21.

19 Normandi Ellis, *Awakenng Osiris: The Egyptian Book of the Dead*, Phanes Press, Grand Rapids, MI, 1988, p. 84.

20 *Encyclopaedia of Heresies and Heretics*, p. 50.

21 *Nag Hammadi Library*, p. 165, 184.

22 Ibid., p. 185.

23 Ibid., p. 166.

24 Ibid., p. 352.

25 Ibid., p. 165.

26 Ibid., p. 340.

27 Joscelyn Godwin, *Mystery Religions In the Ancient World*, Thames & Hudson, London, 1981, p. 84

28 Ibid.

29 Runciman, op. cit., p. 173.

30 Ibid., p. 164.

31 Ibid., p. 173: 'There is one characteristic of any Dualist Church: Man, to escape from the vileness of his body, must seek to make himself spirit as far as may be. This is done by a *gnosis*, an experience that is usually won by an initiation ceremony. For the Early Christians Baptism was a kind of initiation and was often put off until late in life. The initiatory function declined in the Orthodox Church and the importance of Confirmation rose ... The Gnostic sects, however, by the stress they laid on their *gnosis*, retained the older practice.'

32 *Encyclopaedia of Heresies and Heretics*, p. 101–2.

33 R. van den Bruck, writing in *Gnosis and Hermeticism*, p. 96.

34 Hamilton & Hamilton, op. cit., p. 2.

35 *Gnosis and Hermeticism*, p. 102.

36 Runciman, op. cit., p. 7.

37 Legge, op. cit., p. 313; Runciman, op. cit., p. 7.

38 Legge, op. cit., p. 221.

39 Ibid., p. 207.

40 Drake, op. cit., p. 91; *The Oxford Dictionary of the Christian Christian Church*, p. 1108.

41 Freke & Gandy, op. cit., p. 277.

42 Ibid.

43 Tacitus, *Annals*, 15, 44:2–8, cited in Ken Curtis & Carsten Peter Thiede (eds.), *From Christ to Constantine: The Trial and Testimony of the Early Church*, Christian History Institute, Worcester, Pennsylvania, 1991, p. 50.

44 Freke & Gandy, op. cit., p. 278.

45 Drake, op. cit., p. 142; see also p. 164.

46 Dicoletian cited in Drake, op. cit., p. 142.

47 Freke & Gandy, op. cit., p. 278.

48 Eusebius, in *From Christ to Constantine*, p. 60.

49 *Oxford Dictionary of the Christian Church*, p. 338.

50 Drake, op. cit., p. 403.

51 Ibid. Further legislation in AD 392 comprehensively forbade everything non-Christian, even the worship of household gods. Other legislation stripped old priesthoods of their public endowments and privileges.

52 Ibid., p. 237.

53 Ibid.

54 In Eusebius, *Life of Constantine*, cited in Drake, op. cit., p. 389.

55 It is a curiosity, probably no more, that these 'Novatians' were also known by another name – the *Cathari*, or 'Pure Ones'. See Eusebiuus, *Life of Constantine*, Clarendon Press, Oxford, 1999, Commentary on Book III, p. 307.

56   Ibid., book III, p. 151–3.
57   Drake, op. cit., p. 349.
58   Ibid.
59   Ibid., p. 403.
60   Ibid., p. 420.
61   Ibid.
62   Ibid., p. 483.
63   Oldenbourg, op. cit., p. 28.
64   It was renounced by Emperor Gratian (AD 367–83), see Drake, op. cit., 403.
65   Drake, op. cit., p. 402–3; *Oxford Dictionary of the Christian Church*, p. 1108.
66   Irenaeus, cited in Elaine Pagels, op. cit., p. 68.
67   Freke & Gandy, op. cit., p. 299–300.
68   *Second Treatise of the Great Seth*, in *Nag Hammadi Library*, p. 366–7.
69   Drake, op. cit., p. 347–8.
70   Ibid., p. 350.
71   Ibid., p. 402–3.
72   Freke & Gandy, op. cit., p. 300.
73   Drake, op. cit., p. 404.
74   Legge, op. cit., Vol II, p. 21.
75   *Encyclopaedia Britannica, Micropaedia*, 10:447.
76   Drake, op. cit., p. 401, 404.
77   E. M. Forster, *Alexandria: A History and a Guide*, Peter Smith, Gloucester, Mass., 1968, p. 55, 160.
78   Ibid.
79   Drake, op. cit., p. 404.
80   Ibid.
81   Freke & Gandy, op. cit., p. 299.
82   *Nag Hammadi Library*, Introduction, p. 20.
83   Ibid.
84   Ibid.
85   Socrates Scholasticus, *Ecclesiastical History*, available: http://cosmopolis.com/alexandria/hypatia-bio-socrates.html.
86   Ibid.
87   Ibid.
88   From John, bishop of Nikiu, available: http://cosmopolis.com/alexandria/hypatia-bio-john.html.
89   Pagels, op. cit., p. 93.
90   Runciman, op. cit., p. 18: 'With Mani Gnostic Dualism reached its height of eminence ... Manichaeism absorbed the bulk of the Gnostically-minded public.'
91   Hamilton & Hamilton, op. cit., p. 2; Barber, op. cit., p. 12.
92   Hamilton & Hamilton, op. cit., p. 4; Barber, op. cit., p. 12.
93   Wellburn, *Mani*, op. cit., p. 35.
94   Legge, op. cit., Vol II, p. 356.
95   Ibid.
96   For a fuller discussion of the Inquisition see Chapter Seven.

CHAPTER SIX: THE RIVALS

1   Cited in Burl, op. cit., p. 66.
2   *Second Treatise of the Great Seth*, in *The Nag Hammadi Library*, p. 367. See also discussion by Roger A. Bullard & Joseph A. Gibbons, p. 362.
3   Ibid.
4   Ibid.
5   Ibid.
6   See Chapters Two & Three above for discussion of Cathar and Bogomil beliefs.
7   *Nag Hammadi Library*, p. 365.
8   Ibid., p. 362
9   For example, Henry Chadwick, *The Early Church*, Penguin, London, 1993.
10   Chadwick, op. cit., p. 43.
11   Ibid.
12   Ibid.
13   Ibid.
14   Ibid., p. 42.
15   Ibid., p. 43.
16   Ibid.
17   Ibid., p. 42.
18   Ibid., p. 45.
19   Oldenbourg, op. cit., p. 199–200.
20   Ibid., p. 4.
21   Ibid., p. 4–5.
22   Ibid., p. 5.
23   Cited in Barber, op. cit., p. 107; Oldenbourg, op. cit., p. 1.
24   *Chanson de la Croisade albigeoise*, cited in Oldenbourg, op. cit., p. 6.
25   Ibid., p. 8.
26   Ibid., p. 11–12.
27   Ibid., p. 12, 102–9.
28   Ibid., p. 104; Burl, op. cit., p. 35; O' Shea, op. cit., p. 71.
29   Oldenbourg, op. cit., p. 107.
30   Burl, op. cit., p. 36; Oldenbourg, op. cit., p. 106; O'Shea, op. cit., p. 71–2.
31   Oldenbourg, op. cit., p. 106.
32   Burl, op. cit., p. 36; O'Shea, op. cit., p. 71.
33   Burl, op. cit., p. 34.
34   See discussion in Pagels, op. cit., p. 15, 50–51.
35   *The Oxford Dictionary of the Christian Church*, p. 884.
36   O'Shea, op. cit., p. 80; *Oxford Dictionary of the Christian Church*, p. 884.
37   O'Shea, op. cit., p. 80.
38   Oldenbourg, op. cit., p. 111.
39   Ibid.
40   Ibid., p. 111–12.
41   Cited in O'Shea, op. cit., p. 83.
42   Cited in Oldenboutg, op. cit., p. 114.
43   Cited in Burl, op. cit., p. 44.
44   Oldenbourg, op. cit., p. 116; O'Shea, op. cit., p. 84; Burl, op. cit., p. 44.

45   Burl, op. cit., p. 42–6; O'Shea, op. cit., p. 85; Oldenbourg, op. cit., p. 115–16.
46   O'Shea, op. cit., p. 86.
47   Cited in Burl, op. cit., p. 46.
48   O'Shea, op. cit., p. 85; Burl, op. cit., p. 44–45.
49   Cited in Burl, op. cit., p. 45.
50   Cited in O'Shea, op. cit., p. 87.
51   Oldenbourg, op. cit., p. 119.
52   Cited in Burl,op. cit., p. 4.

CHAPTER SEVEN: THE SWORD AND THE FIRE

1   Barber, op. cit., p. 128–9.
2   O' Shea, op. cit., p. 109.
3   Oldenbourg, op. cit., p. 136
4   Sumption, op. cit., p. 227.
5   Cited in Oldenbourg, op. cit., p. 138.
6   Cited in O'Shea, op. cit., p. 115.
7   Ibid., p. 116.
8   Cited in Oldenbourg, op. cit., p. 141.
9   Ibid., p. 149; O'Shea, op. cit., p. 131.
10   *Chanson de la Croisade albigeoise*, cited in Oldenbourg, op. cit., p. 149.
11   Ibid., p. 149; O'Shea, op. cit., p. 131.
12   Oldenbourg, op. cit., p. 149.
13   Ibid., p. 166–7; Barber, op. cit., p. 3.
14   Oldenbourg, op. cit., p. 166–9.
15   Barber, op. cit., p. 130–31; Oldenbourg, op. cit., p. 198.
16   *Chanson*, cited in Oldenbourg, op. cit., p. 198.
17   Ibid., p. 202.
18   Cited in Ibid.
19   See Ibid., p. 204–7.
20   Ibid., p. 233.
21   Ibid., p. 234.
22   O'Shea, op. cit., p. 178.
23   Ibid., p. 176–7.
24   Ibid., p. 181.
25   Ibid., p. 184–5.
26   Ibid., p. 185–7.
27   Ibid., p. 187.
28   Oldenbourg, op. cit., p. 251, 267.
29   Barber, op. cit., p. 142.
30   Oldenbourg, op. cit., p. 234.
31   Cited in Ibid., p. 237.
32   Ibid., p. 236.
33   Ibid., p. 237–8.
34   Ibid., p. 239.
35   Ibid., p. 246.
36   Cited in Barber, op. cit., p. 143.
37   Ibid.
38   Ibid.
39   All decrees from translations by Zoé Oldenbourg, op. cit., pp. 269–71 and Appendix D: *Repressive measures and decrees promulgated against the Cathars by Councils between 1179 and 1246.*

40   Ibid., p. 269.
41   O'Shea, op. cit., p. 151.
42   Cited in René Weis, *The Yellow Cross: The Story of the Last Cathars, 1290–1329*, Alfred A. Knopf, New York, 2001, p. 12.
43   Ibid.
44   Oldenbourg, op. cit., p. 278.
45   Barber, op. cit., p. 146.
46   Ibid., p. 147.
47   Ibid.
48   Ibid.
49   Oldenbourg, op. cit., p. 284.
50   Lambert, *The Cathars*, p. 139.
51   Burl, op. cit., p. 187.
52   Lambert, *The Cathars*, p. 139.
53   Cited in Ibid.
54   Cited in Oldenbourg, op. cit., p. 291.
55   Ibid.
56   Cited in Ibid.
57   Strayer, op. cit., p. 149.
58   Oldenbourg, op. cit., p. 291.
59   O'Shea, op. cit., p. 192.
60   Cited in Lambert, *The Cathars*, p. 138; Oldenbourg, op. cit., p. 291.
61   Lambert, *The Cathars*, p. 139.
62   Cited in Burl, op. cit., p. 188.
63   Oldenbourg, op. cit., p. 286.
64   Barber, op. cit., p. 148.
65   Cited in Ibid., p. 149.
66   Cited in Ibid.
67   Ibid., p. 149.
68   Ibid.
69   Oldenbourg, op. cit., p. 300.
70   Ibid.
71   Ibid., p. 302–3.
72   Ibid.
73   Lambert, *The Cathars*, p. 127.
74   Oldenbourg, op. cit., p. 306.
75   Ibid., p. 286.
76   Ibid., p. 290.
77   Sumption, op. cit., p. 230; Oldenbourg, op. cit., p. 290; Barber, op. cit., p. 149.
78   Cited in Barber, op. cit., p. 149.
79   Oldenbourg, op. cit., p. 289–90.
80   Ibid., p. 289.
81   Ibid., p. 292.
82   Ibid., p. 290.
83   Strayer, op. cit., p. 156.
84   Oldenbourg, op. cit., p. 295.
85   Sumption, op. cit., p. 232.
86   Barber, op. cit., p. 154.
87   Cited in Ibid.
88   Cited in Oldenbourg, op. cit., p. 363.
89   Cited in Burl, op. cit., p. 207.
90   Sumption, op. cit., p. 232
91   Barber, op. cit., p. 169–70.
92   Strayer, op. cit., p. 158.

93   Ibid.
94   Ibid.
95   O'Shea, op. cit., p. 239–46.
96   Sumption, op. cit., p. 235.
97   Barber, op. cit., p. 167.
98   Hamilton & Hamilton, op. cit., p. 276–77.
99   Ibid., p. 47.
100 Ibid., p. 265.
101 Ibid.
102 Ibid., p. 54–55.
103 Runciman, op. cit., p. 114.
104 Ibid., p. 115.
105 Hamilton & Hamilton, op. cit., p. 29.

PART II: THE SACRED CITIES
CHAPTER EIGHT: THE OTHER SECRET RELIGION
1   *The Nag Hammadi Library*, p. 330ff.
2   *The Oxford Dictionary of the Christian Christian Church*, p. 1100.
3   W. K. C. Guthrie, *A History of Greek Philosophy IV: Plato: the man and his dialogues, earlier period*, Cambridge University Press, Cambridge, 1998, p. 22.
4   Ibid., p. 23.
5   Legge, op. cit., vol. II, pp. 92–3.
6   Freke & Gandy, op. cit., p. 141.
7   Pagels, op. cit., p. 62.
8   Forster, op. cit., p. 68.
9   Freke & Gandy, op. cit., p. 155.
10   See Chapters Two & Seven.
11   Margaret Starbird, *The Woman with the Alabaster Jar: Mary Magdalen and the Holy Grail*, Bear & Company, Rochester, Vermont, 1993, p. 75.
12   See Chapters Two, Six & Seven. See Oldenbourg, op. cit., pp. 269–71 & Appendix D: *Repressive measures and decrees promulgated against the Cathars by Councils between 1179 and 1246.*
13   Cistopher Hibbert, *The House of Medici: It's Rise and Fall*, Morrow Quill, New York, 1980, pp. 35–6.
14   Ibid., p. 63.
15   Ibid.
16   Ibid., p. 68
17   R. A. Schwaller de Lubicz, *Sacred Science*, Inner Traditions, Rochester, VT, 1982, p. 274.
18   Plato, *Timeus*, 22 A.
19   Schwaller de Lubicz, op. cit., pp. 279–86.
20   Frances Yates, *Giordano Bruno and the Hermetic Tradition*, University of Chicago Press, Chicago & London, 1991, p. 12.
21   Ibid., p. 13
22   By Johannes Getenberg in c. 1450 in Germany.
23   Yates, op. cit., p. 3
24   Roelof van den Broek & Cis van Heertum (eds.), *From Poimadres to Jacob Bohme*, In de Pelikan Press, Amsterdam, 2000, p. 372.
25   In Western and also in Eastern occultism and mysticism there is a belief that 'divine messengers' such as the Egyptian Thoth, the Greek Hermes, the Roman Mercury and the biblical Enoch, the Christian St. Michael or the Muslim Idris were reincarnations of the same divine entity. See Yates, op. cit., p. 48; Freke & Gandy, op. cit., p. 222; Chapter Nine, note 46. For the assimilation of Enoch to Idris and Hermes see Jean Daresse, *The Secret Books of the Egyptian Gnostics*, Inner Traditions, Rochester, VT, 1986, p. 315.
26   *From Poimadres to Jacob Bohme*, op. cit., p. 373.
27   Ibid., p. 374.
28   St. Augustine, op. cit., p. 814.
29   *From Piomandres to Jocob Bohme*, op. cit., p. 377.
30   Yates, op. cit., p. 42.
31   Ibid., p. 43.
32   Ibid.
33   Ibid.
34   Ibid., p. 39.
35   Ibid., p. 37, footnote 5.
36   Ibid., p. 86.
37   Ibid., p. 88.
38   Ibid., p. 89.
39   Ibid., p. 94.
40   Ibid., p. 95.
41   Frances Yates, The *Occult Philosophy in the Elizabethan Age*, Routledge & Keagan Paul, London, 1979, p. 22.
42   Cheistopher McIntosh, *The Rosicrucians*, Samuel Weiser Inc., York Beach, ME, p. 7.
43   Yates, *Giordano Bruno and the Hermetic Tradition*, p. 112.
44   Ibid., p. 114.
45   Erik Iversen, *The Myth of Egypt and its Hieroglyphs in European Tradition*, GEC GAD Publishers, Copenhagen, 1961, p. 62.
46   Ibid.
47   Ibid., p. 63.
48   Ibid.
49   Yates, *Giordano Bruno and the Hermetic Tradition*, p. 115.
50   Ibid., p. 49.
51   Ibid., pp. 49–50.
52   For a more detailed narrative, see Bauval, *Secret Chamber*, p. 163ff.
53   Atallah translation, Oourboros Press, 2002; Pingree translation as informed by Elizabeth Witchall, the Warburg Insititute, Aug. 2001.
54   Yates, *Giordano Bruno and the Hermetic Tradition*, p. 49.
55   Bauval, *Secret Chamber*, pp. 168–9.
56   Selim Hassan, *Excavations at Giza vol. VI –Part I*, Government Press, Cairo, 1946, p. 45. Hassan quotes from the Geographical Dictionary '*Moagam el Buldan*' by Yakut El

Hamwi vol. VIII (Cairo Edition), p. 457: 'To both of them (two pyramids) the Sabian made their pilgrimage.'

57 Yates, *Giordano Bruno and the Hermetic Tradition*, pp. 211–14.

58 Brian P. Copenhaver (trans.), *Hermetica: The Greek Corpus Hermeticum and the Latin Asclepius in a New English Translation, with Notes and Introduction*, Cambridge University Press, Cambridge, 1995, pp. 81–2.

59 Ibid., pp. 82–3.

60 Yates, *Giordano Bruno and the Hermetic Tradition*, p. 55–6.

61 Ibid., p. 52.

62 Ibid., p. 56.

63 Copenhaven, op. cit., p. 81.

64 Sir Walter Scott (trans.), *Hermetica: The Ancient Greek and Latin Writings Which Contain Religious or Philosophic Teachings Ascribed to Hermes Trismegistus*, Shambala, Boston, 1993, excerpt xxiv; pp. 501–3.

65 *Picatrix*, lib. IV, cap. 3; See also Yates, *Giordano Bruno and the Hermetic Tradition*, p. 54.

66 Yates, *Giordano Bruno and the Hermetic Tradition*, p. 55.

67 Ibid., p. 128.

68 Ibid., p. 54, footnote 1.

69 John Baines & Jalomir Malek, *Cultural Atlas of The World: Ancient Egypt*, Stonehenge Press, Alexandria, VA, 1991, p. 127.

CHAPTER NINE: TWO PHOENIXES

1 E. A. Wallis Budge, *The Book of the Dead*, Arkana, London & New York, 1985, p. 318.

2 Ibid., p. 628.

3 Ibid., pp. 492–3.

4 Tobias Churton, *The Hermetic Philosophy: A Primer*, Sabiot Truchon Books, London, 1998, p. 7.

5 Scott, op. cit., p. 43.

6 Copenhaver, op. cit., p. lix.

7 See discussion in Copenhaver, op. cit., pp. lviii–lix.

8 Churton, op. cit., p. 7.

9 See Chapters Five & Eight.

10 Cited in Yates, *Giordano Bruno and the Hermetic Tradition*, pp. 55–6.

11 R. O. Faulkner (ed.), *The Ancient Egyptian Book of the Dead*, British Museum Publications, London, 1989, p. 184.

12 R. O. Faulkner (ed.), *The Ancient Egyptian Pyramid Texts*, Oxford University Press, Oxford, 1969 (Aris and Phillips reprint), p. 101.

13 Cited in Yates, *Giordano Bruno and the Hermetic Tradition*, p. 394.

14 Faulkner, *Pyramid Texts*, pp. 240–41.

15 *The Emerald Tablet of Hermes Trismegistus*, Evanescent Press, Layton, California, 1988, p. 4.

16 Faulkner, *Book of the Dead*, p. 166.

17 Ibid., p. 44.

18 Faulkner, *Pyramid Texts*, pp. 67–8.

19 Ibid., p. 138.

20 Ibid., p. 227.

21 R. O. Faulkner, *The Ancient Egyptian Coffin Texts*, Aris and Phillips Ltd., Warminster, 1994, vol. I, p. 220.

22 Scott, op. cit., p. 181.

23 Ibid., p. 337.

24 Ibid., pp. 197–9.

25 Ibid., p. 241.

26 Ibid., p. 249.

27 For example, see Faulkner, *Pyramid Texts*, line 748, p. 138.

28 Thomas George Allen (trans.), *The Book of the Dead or Going Forth by Day*, The Oriental Institute of the University of Chicago, Chicago, 1974, p. 155.

29 Scott, op. cit., p. 123.

30 Ibid., p. 299.

31 Ibid., p. 301.

32 Ibid.

33 Ibid., p. 337.

34 Ibid., p. 305.

35 Ibid., p. 129.

36 Ibid., p. 193.

37 Ibid., p. 335.

38 Ibid.

39 Faulkner, *Coffin Texts*, vol. I, p. 31, footnote 4; and see Allan W. Shorter, *The Egyptian Gods: A Handbook*, Routledge & Keegan Paul, London, 1981, pp. 85 & 139.

40 Faulkner, *Coffin Texts*, vol. I, p. 186.

41 Ibid., vol. I, p. 30.

42 Ibid., vol. II, p. 254.

43 Budge, *The Egyptian Heaven and Hell* (*Book of What is in the Duat*), vol. III, p. 125.

44 Budge, *The Book of the Dead*, p. 298.

45 Faulkner, *Pyramid Texts*, p. 294.

46 The quoted words are from Yates, *Giordano Bruno and the Hermetic Tradition*, p. 55.

47 Scott, op. cit., p. 117.

48 Ibid., p. 327.

49 Ibid., p. 351.

50 Ibid., p. 433.

51 Ibid., p. 457.

52 Copenhaver, op. cit., p. 81.

53 Scott, op. cit., p. 429.

54 Ibid., p. 383.

55 *Vision of Isaiah*, cited in Barber, op. cit., p. 87.

56 For a full discussion and full supporting references, see Bauval & Hancock, *Keeper of Genesis* (in the US: *Message of the Sphinx*), p. 134ff.

57 Budge, *The Egyptian Heaven and Hell* (*Book of What is in the Duat*), vol. I, p. 258.

58 Ibid., vol. I, p. 240.

59 Ibid., vol. I, p. 258.

60 Ibid., vol. II, p. 21.

61 Ibid., vol. II, p. 39.

62 Ibid., vol. II, pp. 38–9.

63 Scott, op. cit., p. 419.

64 Ibid., p. 307.

65 Ibid., pp. 303–5.

66 Ibid., p. 295.

67 Ibid., pp. 301–3.

68 Ibid., p. 305.

69 For a full discussion of the concept of *Ma'at*, see Hancock & Faiia, *Heaven's Mirror*, p. 68ff.

70 Cited in E. A. E. Reymond, *The Mythological Origin of the Egyptian Temple*, Manchester University Press, Manchester, 1969, p. 309.

CHAPTER TEN: CITY OF THE GOD-KING

1 Joan Wynne-Thomas, *Proud-Voiced Macedonia*, Springwood Books, London, 1979, p. 34.

2 Herodotus, *The Histories*, Penguin Classics, London, 1996, book II, sections 55–56.

3 Wynne-Thomas, op. cit., p. 80.

4 Herodotus, op. cit., book II, section 42. It is known that a copy of Herodotus' *Histories* was kept by Alexander during his campaigns.

5 E. A. Budge, *The Mummy: Funereal Rites & Customs in Ancient Egypt*, Senate, London, 1995, p. 64.

6 Ahmed Fakry, *Siwa Oasis*, American University Press, Cairo, 1982, p. 167.

7 Budge, *The Mummy*, p. 64.

8 Diodorus, *Biblioteca Historica*, book I, sections xviii & xx.

9 Robert Bauval, 'Investigations on the Origin of the Benben Stone: Was It An Iron Meteorite?' in *Discussions in Egyptology*, vol. 14, 1989, pp. 5–16.

10 Plutarch, *Lives*, Harvard University Press, Cambridge, MA, 1985, chapter 'Alexander'.

11 Plutarch, *De Iside et Osiride*, University of Wales Press, Cardiff, 1970.

12 Jean-Michel Angebert, *Les Mystiques du Soleil*, Robert Laffont, Paris, 1971, p. 144.

13 Ibid., p. 161.

14 Sydney H. Aufrère, 'La Couronne d'Isis-Sothis, les Reines du Phare et la Lointaine' in *Egypt, Afrique et Orient*, no. 6, Avignon, Septembre 1997, pp. 15–18.

15 Plutarch, *Lives*, chapter 'Lysander'.

16 Fakhry, op. cit., p. 146.

17 Paul Faure, *Alexandre*, Fayard, Paris, 1985, p. 146.

18 Aristotle, *Politics*, quoted in Agnes Savill, *Alexander the Great and His Times*, Sterling, New York, 1990, p. 287.

19 Faure, op. cit., pp. 9 & 34. Also *Alexandrie IIIe siècle avant J. C.*, Editions Autrement, Paris, Série Mémoires, no. 19, p. 17.

20 Homer, *The Odyssey*, quoted in David Hatcher Childress, *Lost Cities and Ancient Mysteries of Africa and Arabia*, Adventures Unlimited Press, Kempton, IL, 1989, p. 91.

21 Herodotus, op. cit., book II, pp. 111–19.

22 Ibid.

23 Ibid. p. 42.

24 E. O. James, *Le Culte de La Déesse-Mère*, Le Mail, 1989, p. 196 (translated as *The Cult of the Mother-Goddess*, Thames & Hudson, London, 1960).

25 Sir James George Fraser, *The Golden Bough*, Wordsworth Editions, Ware, 1993, pp. 383–4.

26 Julia Samson, *Nefertiti and Cleopatra*, Rubicon Press, London, 1985, p. 127.

27 Bernard Mathieu, 'Le Phare d'Alexandrie', in *Égypte, Afrique et Orient*, no. 6, Avignon, September 1997, pp. 9–14.

28 E. M. Antoniadi, *L'Astronomie égyptienne*, Gauthier Villars, Paris, 1934, p. 77.

29 Aufrère, op. cit., p. 15–18.

30 Ibid.

31 Ibid.

32 Ibid.

33 Ibid.

34 Baltrušaitis, op. cit., p. 79.

35 Ibid.

36 Faure, op. cit., p. 479.

37 André Bernard, *Alexandrie la Grande*, Hachette, Paris, 1998, p. 66.

38 *Alexandrie IIIe siècle avant J. C.*, p. 44.

39 Jean-Yves Empereur, *Alexandria Rediscovered*, British Museum Press, London, 1999, p. 25.

40 Bernard, op. cit., p. 66.

41 Plutarch, *Lives*, chapter 'Alexander'.

42 According to Plutarch, for example, the night before Alexander's parents (Phillip of Macedon and his wife, Olympias) consummated their marriage 'she [Alexander's mother] dreamed that a thunderbolt fell upon her body, which kindled a great fire, whose divided flames dispersed themselves all about, and then were extinguished. And Philip, some time after he was married, dreamt that he sealed up his wife's body with a seal, whose impression, as be fancied, was the figure of a lion. Some of the diviners interpreted this as a warning to Philip to look narrowly to his wife; but Aristander of Telmessus, considering how unusual it was to seal up anything that was empty, assured him that the meaning of his dream was that the queen was with child of a boy, who would one day prove as stout and courageous as a lion.' Astrology was extremely popular in ancient Greece and, especially, in the Macedonian court where

Alexander was born. It is little surprise, then, that horoscopic astrology appears to have been created and nurtured in Alexandria. After Alexsander's invasion of Egypt an important school of astrology was established in the city of Alexandria. Here Babylonian and Greek astrology fused with the sky-religion of the Egyptian, and gave rise to type of astrology we know today as horoscopic (the influence of stars and planets on terrestrial matters and the lives of men). Although most of it was written in Greek, the *lingua franca* of that period, many of the authors were not Greeks but Egyptians. It is this Alexandrian type of astrology which would form the basis of Greek astrological writings which flourished in later centuries. For more on this, see Nick Campion, *Introduction to the History of Astrology*, chap. 'Mesopotamian Astrology'. Also Holden's *A History of Horoscopic Astrology* and Hand's *Chronology of the Astrology of the Middle East and the West by Period*.

43 George Hart, *A Dictionary of Egyptian Gods and Goddesses*, Routledge & Keagan Paul, London, 1988, p. 28

44 Herodotus, op. cit., book III, chapter 28.

45 Hart, op. cit., p. 30.

46 Ibid., p. 29.

47 Quoted from Lewis Spence, *Myths & Legends: Egypt*, Bracken Books, London, 1985, p. 285.

48 Faure, op. cit., p. 128.

49 Ibid., pp. 139–40.

50 Herodotus, op. cit., book II, 42.

51 Auguste Mariette, *Le Serapeum de Memphis*, Paris, 1858.

52 *Alexandrie IIIe siècle avant J. C.*, p. 45.

53 Bauval, *Secret Chamber*, p. 47.

54 Patrick Boylan, *Thoth, The Hermes of Egypt*, Oxford University Press, Oxford, 1922, p. 124.

55 Ibid., p. 94.

56 Bauval, *Secret Chamber*.

57 Christian Jacq, *Magic and Mystery in Ancient Egypt*, Souvenir Press, London, 1998, p. 19.

58 Ibid., p. 15.

59 Yates, *Giordano Bruno and the Hermetic Tradition*, p. 60.

60 Jill Kamel, *Coptic Egypt*, American University Press, Cairo, 1993, p. 15.

61 Ibid., p. 16.

62 See Alan K. Bowman, *Egypt After the Pharaohs*, British Museum Press, London, 1986.

63 Ibid.

64 Letter addressed by Hadrian to his brother-in-law, the Consul Servianus, in AD 134. See also Ahmed Osman's very good book on this topic, *Out of Egypt: The Roots of Christianity Revealed*, Century, London, 1999.

65 Kamel ,op. cit., p. 7.

66 Ibid., p. 8.

67 Ibid.

CHAPTER ELEVEN: THE PROPHET OF HERMES

1 Frances Yates, *Astraea: The Imperial Theme in the Sixteenth Century*, London, 1975, p. 184.

2 Ibid., p. 83.

3 The Sabaeans (Sabians) of Baghdad (modern Iraq) and Harran (modern Turkey) served as incubators and preservers of the Hermetic texts in the East during the long period that these texts were absent from the West. See discussion in Chapter Eight. Churton, op. cit., p. 31 notes: 'It is certainly strange that at the very time the Sabians seem to disappear from Baghdad, the Hermetic documents known to us as the Corpus Hermeticum appear in Constantinople after a 500-year interval.'

4 Giordano Bruno, *The Expulsion of the Triumphant Beast*, translated with introduction and notes by Arthur D. Imerti, Bison Books, University of Nebraska, Lincoln, NE & London, 1992, p. 4.

5 Ibid., p. 5.

6 Ibid., pp. 5–6.

7 Ibid., p. 6.

8 Ibid.

9 Frances Yates, *The Art of Memory*, Pimlico Press, London, 1996, p. 197.

10 Ibid., p. 198.

11 Yates, *Giordano Bruno and the Hermetic Tradition*, p. 203.

12 Ibid.

13 Yates, *Art of Memory*, pp. 212–20; See also Yates, *Giordano Bruno and the Hermetic Tradition*, pp. 197–9.

14 Hermann Kesten, *Copernicus and His World*, Roy Publishers, New York, p. 330.

15 Yates, *Giordano Bruno and the Hermetic Tradition*, p. 204.

16 Ibid.

17 Ibid.

18 Giordano Bruno, *La Cena de le ceneri*, 1584, dial. 4; See also Yates, *Giordano Bruno and the Hermetic Tradition*, p. 207.

19 Bruno, op. cit., dial. 5.

20 Yates, *Giordano Bruno and the Hermetic Tradition*, p. 209.

21 Cited in Frances Yates, *Giordano Bruno and the Hermetic Tradition*, p. 219.

22 Ibid., p. 215.

23 Ibid.

24 Ibid.

25 Bruno, *Spaccio della Bestia Trionfante*, 1584, dial. 3; See also Yates, *Giordano Bruno and the Hermetic Tradition*, p. 213.

26 Yates, *Giordano Bruno and the Hermetic Tradition*, p. 223.

27   Ibid., p. 215.

28   Ibid.

29   Ibid., p. 216.

30   *Kore Kosmou*, 48; see also Scott, op. cit., p. 485.

31   Bruno, *Spaccio*, dial. 1; Yates, *Giordano Bruno and the Hermetic Tradition*, pp. 231–2.

32   Yates, *Giordano Bruno and the Hermetic Tradition*, p. 232.

33   *The Corpus Hermeticum, Asclepius*, 27. See Scott, op. cit., p. 361; see also Copenhaver, op. cit., p. 83.

34   *Documenti della via di Giordano Bruno*, a curia di Vincenzo Spamanato, Florence, p. 44; see also Yates, *Giordano Bruno and the Hermetic Tradition*, p. 233.

35   Dorothea Waley Singer, *Giordano Bruno, His Life and Thoughts*, Henry Schuman, New York, 1950, chapter 7.

36   Giordano Bruno, *De Monade Numero e Figura*, Frankfort, 1591.

37   Yates, *Giordano Bruno and the Hermetic Tradition*, pp. 273–4.

38   Ibid., p. 360.

CHAPTER TWELVE: ENVISIONING THE HERMETIC CITY

1   John M. Headley, *Tommaso Campanella and the Transformation of the World*, Princeton University Press, Princeton, 1997, p. 26.

2   Ibid., p. 29.

3   Ibid., p. 30.

4   Ibid., pp. 30–32.

5   Which was then, to complicate matters, under the control of Spain.

6   Cited in Headley, op. cit., pp. 34–5.

7   Cited in Ibid., p. 40.

8   Ibid., p. 36.

9   Ibid.

10   Ibid., p. 38.

11   Ibid., p. 3: '… an effort to establish an ideal state, a democratic/theocratic republic as harbinger of a new aeon.'

12   See Chapter Two.

13   Cited in Headley, op. cit., p. 39. (Emphasis added.)

14   Ibid., p. 37.

15   Ibid., p. 38.

16   Ibid., pp. 38–9.

17   Ibid., p. 45–7.

18   Ibid., p. 47.

19   Ibid., p. 3.

20   Ibid., pp. 47–8.

21   Ibid., p. 3.

22   Ibid., pp. 47–8.

23   Ibid., p. 53.

24   Ibid.

25   Ibid., pp. 114–17.

26   Yates, *Giordano Bruno and the Hermetic Tradition*, p. 342.

27   Duché, op. cit., p. 66.

28   Ibid.

29   Ibid., p. 76

30   *Grand Larousse Encyclopédique*, vol. 2, p. 598; see also Jean Meyer, *La Naissance de Louis XIV*, Editions Complexe, 1989, pp. 12–13. In recent years some historians have attempted to attribute some sort of 'messianic' origin to the Merovingian lineage through various convoluted mystical links, involving among these a legendary Frankish king called *Pharamond* (c. AD 420), Mary Magdalena, the 'Holy Grail' and the small town of Rennes-le-Château (see M. Baigent, H. Lincoln & R. Leigh, *The Holy Blood and the Holy Grail*, Corgi, London, 1983; also L. Gardner, *Bloodline of the Holy Grail*, Element Books, Shaftesbury, 1996.

31   Ian Shaw & Paul Nicholson, *British Museum Dictionary of Ancient Egypt*, Book Club Associates, London, 1995, pp. 51 & 247.

32   Baltrušaitis, op. cit., pp. 86–93.

33   Duché, op. cit., p. 77.

34   Meyer, op. cit., p. 108.

35   Yates, *Giordano Bruno and the Hermetic Tradition*, p. 390.

36   Meyer, op. cit., p. 103.

37   Frances Yates, in 'Considérations de Bruno et de Campanella sur la monarchie française', *Actes du Congrès Leonardo de Vinci, Études d'Art*, no. 8, 9 & 10, Paris-Alger, 1954, p. 12

38   François Bluché, *Louis XIV*, Fayard, Paris, 1986, p. 29; also Duché, op. cit., p. 90.

39   Meyer, op. cit., p. 112.

40   Headley, op. cit., p. 130.

41   Ibid.

42   Ibid., p. 130–1.

43   Cited in Yates, *Giordano Bruno and the Hermetic Tradition*, p. 394, footnote 1.

44   Yates, *Giordano Bruno and the Hermetic Tradition*, p. 390.

45   Ibid. p. 366.

46   Ibid. p. 387.

47   Ibid. p. 369.

48   See Chapter Two.

49   Yates, *Giordano Bruno and the Hermetic Tradition*, p. 367.

50   Ibid., pp. 367–8.

51   Ibid., p. 368.

52   Ibid.

53   Ibid., p. 369.

54   Ibid., p. 370.

55   Ibid., p. 369.

56   Ibid.

57   Ibid., p. 370.

58   Ibid.

59 Ibid., p. 371.
60 See Chapter Eight and Yates, *Giordano Bruno and the Hermetic Tradition*, pp. 55–6, citing the *Asclepius*: 'The gods who exercised their dominion over the earth will be restored one day and installed in a city at the extreme limit of Egypt, a city which will be founded towards the setting sun, and into which will hasten, by land and sea, the whole race of mortal men ...'
61 Scott, op. cit., pp. 221–2.

CHAPTER THIRTEEN:
THE INVISIBLE BROTHERHOOD

1   Cited in F. Yates, *The Rosicrucian Enlightenment*, Ark Paperbacks, London, 1986, p. 103.
2   Cited in Ibid., p. 104.
3   Ibid., p. 103.
4   Ibid., p. 104.
5   Ibid.
6   Ibid., pp. 30, 238, 251.
7   *Fama*, in Ibid., p. 239.
8   *Fama*, in Ibid., pp. 239–40.
9   *Fama*, in Ibid., pp. 240–41.
10 Ibid., p. 242.
11 Ibid.
12 Ibid., p. 242–3.
13 Ibid., p. 243.
14 Ibid., p. 246.
15 Ibid.
16 Ibid., p. 248.
17 Ibid., p. 251.
18 Ibid., p. 244.
19 *Confessio* in Ibid., p. 252.
20 Ibid., p. 253.
21 Ibid., p. 257.
22 Ibid.
23 Ibid., p. 258.
24 Ibid.
25 Ibid., p. 259.
26 Ibid., pp. 248 & 255.
27 Ibid., p. 30.
28 Joscelyn Godwin (trans.), *The Chemical Wedding of Christian Rosenkreutz*, with Introduction and Commentary by Adam McLean, Phanes Press, Grand Rapids, MI, 1991, Introduction, p. 7.
29 Yates, Rosicrucian Enlightenment, p. 30.
30 Godwin, *The Chemical Wedding of Christian Rosenkreutz*, p. 10.
31 Yates, *Rosicrucian Enlightenment*, p. 31.
32 Ibid., p. 50: 'Andreae was certainly behind the scenes of the whole movement [the Rosicrucians] to which he frequently refers in his numerous works.'
33 Yates, *Rosicrucian Enlightenment*, p. 30–31.
34 Godwin, *The Chemical Wedding of Christian Rosenkreutz*, p. 10.
35 The full title is 'The Chemical Wedding of Christian Rosenkreutz in the year 1459', see Godwin, *The Chemical Wedding of Christian Rosenkreutz*, p. 13.
36 Ibid., p. 15.
37 Electronic Bible Search, *Franklin Electronic Bible*; for 'Father of Light'.
38 See Chapter Six.
39 Godwin, *The Chemical Wedding of Christian Rosenkreutz*, p. 15.
40 Ibid., p. 16.
41 Ibid., p. 107.
42 Ibid., pp. 16–17.
43 Ibid., pp. 33–4.
44 Ibid., pp. 46–8.
45 Ibid., p. 80.
46 Ibid., p. 102.
47 Stephan Holler, in *Gnosis: A Journal of the Western Inner Traditions*, The Lumen Foundation, San Francisco, Summer 1996, p. 26; See also Godwin, *The Chemical Wedding of Christian Rosenkreutz*, p. 145, Adam McLean's commentary on the symbolism of the death of the king and the queen in the *Chemical Wedding*: 'Now a physical death is actually a rebirth in the spiritual world, from when a being is released from its material envelope it returns to a more spiritual state.'
48 Yates, *The Rosicrucian Enlightenment*, p. 57.
49 Ibid., p. 147.
50 Yates, *Giordano Bruno and the Hermetic Tradition*, pp. 312–13.
51 Ibid., p. 414.
52 Ibid., p. 373.
53 Ibid., p. 367.
54 Ibid., p. 413.
55 Ibid.
56 Ibid.
57 McIntosh, op. cit., p. 21.
58 Yates, *Giordano Bruno and the Hermetic Tradition*, pp. 413–4, footnote 1. However, in Carlos Gilly's article '*Campanella fra i Rosacroce*' in *Tommaso Campanella e l'attesa del secolo aureo*, Fondazione Luigi Firpo, Florence, 1998, pp. 107–55, Carlos Gilly argues that Tobias Adami did not bring copies of Campanella's manuscripts to Germany till after 1610 when the Rosicrucian *Fama* manifesto (another work by Andreae) were already written. Gilly quotes Ole Worm's 'Laurea philosophica summa' published in Copenhagen 1619, where the author reports that he had known of the Manifesto in 1611, that is *before* it was publicly put to the press and thus could not have been influenced by Campanella's ideas. This argument, in my opinion is weak. *Civitas Solis* was written in 1602, and surely its content, if not actual physical copies, were probably known to Andreae and his entourage before the

writing of the Manifesto; otherwise why would Tobias Adami risk smuggling them out of the Inquisition prison in Naples to take to Andreae? And why would Wense suggest to Andreae to name his utopian book *Civitas Solis*?

59 J. P. Kenyon, *The Stuarts*, Fontana, London, 1966, p. 41.

60 Yates, *The Rosicrucian Enlightenment*, pp. 39–40: 'There can be no doubt that we should see the movement behind the Rosicrucian publications as a movement ultimately stemming from John Dee. The Dee influence could have come into Germany from England with the English connections of the elector palatine, and it could have spread from Bohemia where Dee had propagated his stirring mission in earlier years ...'

61 Ibid., p. 36–7.

62 McIntosh, op. cit., p. 24.

63 Yates, *The Rosicrucian Enlightenment*, pp. 134–8.

64 Ibid., p. 19.

65 Joscelyn Godwin, *Robert Fludd: Hermetic Philosopher and Surveyor of Two Worlds*, Phanes Press, Grand Rapids, MI, 1972, p. 11.

66 Hence the term 'Bohemian' to describe a roving or homeless person.

67 Yates, *The Rosicrucian Enlightenment*, p. 178.

CHAPTER FOURTEEN: EMERGENCE OF THE INVISIBLES

1 Oldenbourg, op. cit., p. 311.

2 Ibid., p. 78.

3 See Chapters Eleven & Twelve.

4 See Chapter Eleven.

5 *Fama*, cited in Yates, *The Rosicrucian Enlightenment*, p. 243.

6 McIntosh, op. cit., pp. 16–18.

7 Ibid., p. 18.

8 Yates, *The Rosicrucian Enlightenment*, p. 118.

9 Francis Bacon, *The Advancement of Learning*, book II, Macmillan & Co., London, 1895, Dedication to James I, section 13.

10 Scott, op. cit., p. 117.

11 Ibid., p. 321

12 Yates, *The Rosicrucian Enlightenment*, p. 119.

13 Ibid., p. 119.

14 Robert Lomas, *The Invisible College*, Headline, London, 2001, pp. 71–80 & pp. 85–6.

15 *Fama*, cited in Yates, *The Rosicrucian Enlightenment*, p. 243.

16 McIntosh, op. cit., p. 33.

17 Ibid.

18 Godwin, *Robert Fludd: Hermetic Philosopher and Surveyor of Two Worlds*, p. 11.

19 Ibid.

20 Yates, *The Rosicrucian Enlightenment*, p. 70.

21 Francis Bacon, *New Atlantis*, Kessinger Publishing, Kila, MT, 1992, p. 329.

22 Jerry Baker (ed.), *New Atlantis and The Great Instauration: Bacon*, Harlan Davidson, Arlington Heights, IL, 1989, p. xxx.

23 Yates, *The Rosicrucian Enlightenment*, p. 126; see also p. 55 for the R. C. 'seal'.

24 Ibid., p. 127.

25 John Heydon, *The Holy Guide*, London, 1662, sig. B6 recto.; sig. C7 recto.

26 Alexander Piatigorsky, *Freemasonry*, Harvill Press, London, 1997, p. 83.

27 Sir James Stubbs, *Freemason's Hall*, The Library Art and Publication Committee, London, 1983, pp. 53–5.

28 I Kings 6:11–14.

29 *New Atlantis and The Great Instauration: Bacon*, p. xxv.

30 Scott, op. cit., p. 501–3.

31 E. A. Wallis Budge, *An Egyptian Hieroglyphic Dictionary*, Dover Publications, New York, 1978, vol. I, p. 9a.

32 Yates, *The Occult Philosophy in the Elizabethan Age*, p. 96.

33 *Fama*, cited in Yates, *The Rosicrucian Enlightenment*, p. 248.

34 A. Fowler, *Spenser and the Numbers of Time*, Routledge & Keegan Paul, London, 1964.

35 Yates, *The Occult Philosophy in the Elizabethan Age*, p. 95.

36 Angus Fletcher, *The Prophetic Moment: An Essay on Spenser*, Chicago University Press, Chicago & London, 1971, pp. 157 & 275.

37 I Kings 9:24.

38 Ron Heisler, 'Michael Maier and England', *The Hermetic Journal*, 1989.

39 Ibid.

40 Ibid.

41 Donald R. Dickson, *The Tessera of Antilia: Utopian Botherhoods & Secret Societies in the Early Seventeenth Century*, E. J. Brill, Boston, 1998.

42 Ibid., pp. 114–5.

43 Ibid., p. 121.

44 Piatigorsky, op. cit., p. 38.

45 Fred Pick & G. Norman Knight, *The Pocket History of Freemasonry*, Frederick Muller, London, 1953, p. 30.

46 Piatigorsky, op. cit., p. 46.

47 Pick & Knight, op. cit., p. 32.

48 Ibid. p. 34.

49 Ibid. p. 35.

50 Lomas, op. cit., chapter 5.

51 Pick & Knight, op. cit., pp. 23 & 43.

52 Yates, *The Rosicrucian Enlightenment*, p. 182.

53   Ibid., p. 183.

54   Ibid.

55   Ibid.

56   Ibid., p. 182.

57   Ibid., p. 177.

58   Ibid., p. 176.

59   Ibid., p. 178.

60   First published in Amsterdam in 1668.

61   Yates, *The Rosicrucian Enlightenment*, p. 179.

62   Christopher Falkus, *Charles II*, Cardinal, London, 1975, p. 21.

63   After the Restoration, Charles II gave Prince Rupert various naval commands during the war against the Dutch. In the years before his death Rupert dabbled in scientific experiments and is said to have invented the art of mezzotint printmaking.

64   Pick & Knight, op. cit., p. 45. Present at Ashmole 'raising' ceremony was a certain Lord Henry Mainwaring, a colonel with the Roundheads, and by one of those strange twist of fate that can befall a person's life, Mainwaring's wife, after she was made a widow a few years later, would become Elias Ashmole's second wife in 1649.

65   For a saucy account of this romance see Guy Breton, *Histoires d'amour de l'fistoire de France*, Presse Pocket, Paris, 1960, pp. 14–15.

66   Falkus, op. cit., p. 38.

67   Ibid.

68   Ibid., p. 39.

69   Ibid., p. 46.

70   Ibid., p. 47.

71   He was presumably of Babylonian, i.e. dark, complexion.

72   Falkus, op. cit., p. 47.

73   Paul Naudon, *Histoire générale de la Franc-Maçonnerie*, Office du Livre, Paris, 1981, p. 49.

74   Lawrence, op. cit., pp. 92–100.

75   Antonia Fraser, *King Charles II*, Mandarin, London, 1993, p. 182.

76   Lomas, op. cit., p. 220.

77   Bluché, op. cit., p. 247.

78   For example, by Joseph Ritman and his colleagues at the Hermetic/Rosicrucian Library in Amsterdam. See *The Silent Language: The Symbols of Hermetic Philosophy*, In de Pelikaan Press, Amsterdam, 1994.

79   The origin of many of these sort of universalism or utopian movements in Europe stemmed from the growing rift between the papacy and the more purist factions of Christianity which eventually lead to the Protestant Reformation and the Catholic Counter-Reformation in the mid-16th and early 17th century. And there is no one person was more acutely aware of this dangerous rift between the Christian factions than Cardinal Richelieu

in Paris, who was in charge of both the religious as well as the affairs of state of France. Richelieu was constantly vigilant of the religious tension in France and the terrible civil war that this had cause in the not-too-distant past. And although the French court was intensely Catholic, especially after the union of Louis XIII and Anne of Austria, it was nonetheless well known that one of Richelieu's great ambitions was to end the papal-Habsburg-Spanish hegemony on central Europe. In his first years in office Richelieu surprised everyone with his ruthless determination to oppose these forces by taking quick and decisive military action against the papal forces in the Swiss canton of Grisons. This had sent a clear message to all those who were under the illusion that Richelieu was the unequivocal defender of Roman Catholicism and the Catholic League. His biggest political challenge came in 1630 when the Queen Mother, the hysterically staunch Catholic Marie de'Medici, incited her weak son, Louis XIII, to dismiss Richelieu. In a moment of uncharacteristic show of strength, Louis XIII refused to obey her and, instead, had her banished from court. This crucial decision that was to change the course of French history is known as the 'night of the dupes', an allusion to how Richelieu's astute political acumen had even duped the regents of France. Richelieu confused many with his shifting foreign policies, for on the one hand he dealt severely with Protestant Huguenot uprisings such as the one at La Rochelle after they sided with the English Protestants in 1628, and on the other hand he delivered equal severity towards the Catholic League when, for example, in 1635 he sided France with the Protestants during the Thirty Years War. Such acts earned him the hatred of both the Catholics and the Protestant extremists and generated an endless conflict between him and the pope in Rome. Immensely wealthy, Richelieu was an avid patron of the arts, and was himself a playwright and musician of some talent. The *Académie Française*, which he founded when he was fifty-three years old, was his pride and joy. Could Richelieu have been somewhat sympathetic to a new 'Christian' movement such as the Rosicrucian movement in Germany that sought to bring about a universal reform? Did he encourage individuals like Decarte to form a somewhat similar society in France to promote 'natural philosophy' as an antidote to the religious mania in Europe? These are extremely provocative and speculative questions that, nonetheless, require further investigation.

80   Yates, 'Considérations de Bruno et de Campanella sur la monarchie française', p. 12.

81   Lomas, op. cit., p. 114–6.

82   She died a year after they married, in

January 1653, while giving birth to a stillborn child; Moray was heartbroken and never remarried.

83 Data from *California Freemason*, 'The First Initiation on English Soil', October/November 2001, available at: www.cafreemason-digital.com.

84 Yates, *The Rosicrucian Enlightenment*, p. 185; the actual translation in English was not Vaughan's.

85 Dudley Wright, 'The First Initiation' in *The Builder*, 1921.

86 Lomas, op. cit. p. 250. For details on Preston see Pick & Knight, op. cit., p. 97.

87 Adrian Tinniswood, *His Invention So Fertile: A Life of Christopher Wren*, Jonathan Cape, London, 2001, p. 108.

88 Ibid., p. 109.

89 It might have been the same comet after it had passed the Sun; see Tinniswood, op. cit., p. 112.

90 Ibid., p. 115.

91 Fraser, op. cit., p. 237.

92 Lomas, op. cit., chapter 2.

93 Pick & Knight, op. cit., pp. 50–1.

94 Piatigorsky, op. cit., p. 209; Jasper Ridley, *The Freemasons*, Constable & Co., London, 1999, p. 23; Bernard Williamson & Michael Baigent, 'Sir Christopher Wren and Freemasonry: New Evidence', in *Ars Quatuor Coronatorum*, vol. CIX, pp. 188–90.

95 Pick & Knight, op. cit., pp. 68–70.

96 Ibid., p. 69.

97 For the story of the Vatican Obelisk see Christopher Hibbert, *Rome: The Biography of a City*, Penguin Books, London, 1985, pp. 175–8. See also E. A. Wallis Budge, *Cleopatra's Needle and Other Egyptian Obelisks*, Dover Publications, New York, 1990, pp. 255–7; also Labib Habachi, *The Obelisks of Egypt: Skyscrapers of the Past*, American University Press, Cairo, 1984, p. 131.

98 Today it is possible to be guided through churches and piazzas of Rome by the obelisks in decreasing size: Piazza San Giovanni in Laterano (32.18 m), Piazza San Pietro (25.37 m), Piazza del Popolo (23.20 m), Monte Citorio (21.79 m), Piazza Navona (16.54 m), Piazza dell'Esquilino (14.75 m), Piazza del Quirinale (14.64 m), Piazza della Minerva, Trinita del Monti (13.91 m), Monte Picio (9.25 m), Piazza della Rotunda (6.34 m), Piazza della Minerva (5.74 m) and Villa Celimontana (2.68 m).

99 Pliny, *Natural History*, vol. II, book xxxvi. See also Budge, *Cleopatra's Needle and other Egyptian Obelisks*, p. 255.

100 Baines & Malek, op. cit., pp. 173–4.

101 Hibbert, op. cit., p. 355.

102 A. M. Partini & B. de Rachewiltz, *Roma Egizia*, Edizione Mediterranee, 1999, pp. 105–6.

103 The Basilica was finally consecrated in 1626, on the 1300th anniversary of the original consecration by Constantine. The study of Michelangelo (who died before the work was fully completed) was carried on by Giacomo della Porta and Doenico Fontana. The new façade, erected by Carlo Maderno, was begun in 1607 and completed 1614. In 1650–67 Bernini added the famous Piazza and colonnade, which has the obelisk as foci.

104 Paul Johnson, *The Papacy*, Orion Publishing Group, 1998, p. 154.

105 Sixtus V then appointed Domenico Fontana to move the obelisk and raise it in front of the entrance of St. Peter's Basilica. The whole operation took nearly a year to complete. Fontana employed traditional methods, with the only real innovation over the ancient Egyptians being the use of horses instead of just sheer manpower. On the surface, the pope's motivation was the aesthetic improvement of the Vatican's Piazza, but a more profound purpose was the display of the growing power of the papacy in line with that of the ancient Roman emperors who had brought these Egyptian trophies to Rome more than sixteen centuries earlier. It is true that moving the obelisk to its new location was visually important to the Basilica; but the whole affair was an overt way for Sixtus V to draw the obvious parallel between the ancient emperors and the papacy. And like these emperors and pharaohs of old, Sixtus V granted Fontana extraordinary powers to commandeer any labour, any tools and any materials required for the task of raising the great obelisk. Fontana also had full papal authority to demolish any houses that happened to be in the way. And the pope made it clear that opposition or obstruction to the project by anyone could result in a huge fine and even the punishment of death. Indeed, during the final stage of raising the obelisk into place, Sixtus V gave strict orders that everyone in the huge crowd of spectators that had come to watch should remain totally silent. The penalty for breaking this order, the pope declared, was death. The story goes that at one stage the ropes holding the obelisk were about to break under the huge strain. And so a Genoese sailor bravely ignored the pope's command and shouted: '*Put water on the ropes!*', thus probably saving the monument from destruction. After the obelisk was safely raised into place, the crowds were finally allowed to cheer.

106 Peter Tompkins, *The Magic of Obelisks*, Harper & Row, New York, 1981, p. 36.

107 The name Champs-Élysées, i.e. the Elysian Fields (a concept which originated in ancient Egypt as the *Duat*), for the main avenue/axis of Paris can be traced to the epoch of Louis XIV, towards the end of his reign (see Marc Gaillard, *Les Belles Heures*

des *Champs-Elysées*, Editions Martelle, Paris, 1990, p. 11). This famous avenue is also known as the *Axe Historique*.

108 Gaillard, op. cit., pp. 10–11.

109 Marie-France Arnold, *Paris: ses mythes d'hier à aujourd'hui*, Editions Dervy, 1997; see map and preface. See also Jean Phaure, *Introduction à la géographie sacrée de Paris: Barque d'Isis*, Editions Du Borrego, Paris, 1985, pp. 20–21.

110 Tinniswood, op. cit., p. 122.

111 Ibid., pp. 125–6.

112 Ibid., p. 137.

113 *London Gazette*, 3–10 September 1666.

114 (Julian) 20 September 1666 = (Gregorian) 30 September 1666 = (Hebrew) 1 Tishri 5427.

115 Fraser, op. cit., p. 248.

CHAPTER FIFTEEN: CABAL

1 There were a few others, too, who prepared plans, but these were far less significant; see Tinniswood, op. cit. p. 151; Richard Hooke, curator and fellow of the the Royal Society as well as professor of geometry at Gresham College presented plans (Tinniswood, op. cit., p. 77).

2 Tinniswood, op. cit., p. 150.

3 William of Tyre, *A History of Deeds Done Beyond the Sea*, Octagon Books, New York, 1986, vol. I, pp. 524–5.

4 See the Koran, chapter XVII.

5 See discussion in Graham Hancock, *The Sign and Seal: A Quest for the Lost Ark of the Covenant*, Heinemann, London, 1992, p. 379–80.

6 Ibid., p. 385.

7 For example, see Hancock, *The Sign and the Seal*, p. 389ff.

8 Ibid., p. 94.

9 Dan Bahat, *Carta's Historical Atlas of Jerusalem*, Carta, Jerusalem, 1986, p. 46.

10 Ibid., pp. 46–7.

11 Piers Paul Read, *The Templars: The Dramatic History of the Knights Templar, The Most Powerful Military Order of the Crusades*, Phoenix Press, Sheffield, p. 83.

12 Ibid.

13 Hancock, *The Sign and the Seal*, p. 93.

14 John J. Robinson, *Born in Blood: The Lost Secrets of Freemasonry*, Century, London, 1989, p. 66.

15 Hancock, *The Sign and the Seal*, p. 93.

16 Oldenbourg, op. cit., p. 85.

17 O' Shea, op. cit., p. 29.

18 Barber, op. cit., p. 61: 'For Templars and Hospitallers, Languedoc was a major source of income and recruits ... During the 1130s the Templars appointed a regional Master or *bailli* over Aragon, Toulouse, and Provence, to oversee the increasing number of preceptories they were establishing in the region.'

19 Alain Demurger, *Vie et mort de l'ordre du Temple*, Editions du Seuil, Paris, 1989, pp. 152–8.

20 The Templars had once before faced Saladin Once Saladin. This was when they had joined King Baldwin's forces in 1177 and launched a surprise attack directly against Saladin and his bodyguard at Montgisard near Ramlah. Saladin's army was spread out and thus could not defend themselves and were forced to retreated back to the south.

21 Read, op. cit., p. xiii.

22 Ibid., p. 160.

23 An eyewitness account of this is given by Saladin's son, al-Afdal. It is quoted by Ibn al-Athir: 'When the king of the Franks [Guy] was on the hill with that band, they made a formidable charge against the Muslims facing them, so that they drove them back to my father [Saladin]. I looked towards him and he was overcome by grief and his complexion pale. He took hold of his beard and advanced, crying out "Give the lie to the Devil!" The Muslims rallied, returned to the fight and climbed the hill. When I saw that the Franks withdrew, pursued by the Muslims, I shouted for joy, "We have beaten them!" But the Franks rallied and charged again like the first time and drove the Muslims back to my father. He acted as he had done on the first occasion and the Muslims turned upon the Franks and drove them back to the hill. I again shouted, "We have beaten them!" but my father rounded on me and said, "Be quiet! We have not beaten them until that tent [Guy's] falls." As he was speaking to me, the tent fell. The sultan dismounted, prostrated himself in thanks to God Almighty and wept for joy.'

24 An excerpt from a translation of *Sahih al-Bukhari*, 5, 58.227, reads: 'I was brought by the Buraq, which is an animal white and long, larger than a donkey but smaller than a mule, which would place its hoof at a distance equal to the range of vision.'

25 In the 'chapter of the night journey', Sura al Isra, in the Koran it is written: 'Glory to (Allah) Who did take His servant for a Journey by night from the Sacred Mosque to the Farthest Mosque, whose precincts We did bless, – in order that We might show him some of Our Signs: for He is the One Who heareth and seeth (all things).'

26 Heraclius had great vested interest in the Templars. He is the one who had travelled to London with the Grand Master of the Templars in 1184–5, to consecrate the Temple Round Church which still stands today in Temple Bar in the British capital.

27 According to an eyewitness, a servant of Balian, the clergy organized a barefoot procession around the walls, emulating what the clergy on the First Crusade had done back in 1099 when they captured Jerusalem; women shrieked and cut off their children's hair after dipping them

THE MASTER GAME

28 Hancock, *The Sign and The Seal*, p. 154.

29 Demurger, op. cit., p. 322.

30 Robinson, *Born in Blood*, pp. 142–3.

31 Michael Baigent & Richard Leigh, *The Temple and the Lodge*, Arcade Publishing, New York, 1989, p. 91.

32 Hancock, *The Sign and The Seal*, p. 167.

33 For a full account, see Baigent & Leigh, *The Temple and the Lodge*.

34 Hancock, *The Sign and The Seal*, p. 166.

35 Andrew Sinclair, *The Sword and the Grail*, Crown Publishers, New York, 1992.

36 Ibid., pp. 48–9.

37 Ibid., plates section.

38 Ibid., p. 108.

39 Ibid., p. 75.

40 See discussions in Ibid.

41 Runciman, op. cit., p. 179.

42 Gaetan Delaforge, *The Templar Tradition*, Threshold Books, Putney, VT, 1987, p. 71.

43 See Albert Hourani, *A History of the Arab Peoples*, Faber & Faber, London, 1991, p. 184ff.

44 Barber, op. cit., p. 61. Barber shows that the same alliance was also established between the Knights Hospitaller and the Languedoc nobles.

45 Sinclair, op. cit., p. 76.

46 Guirdham, op. cit., p. 90.

47 Burl, op. cit., p. 38.

48 Sinclair, op. cit., p. 26.

49 Guirdham, op. cit., p. 89.

50 Ibid., p. 90.

51 Barber, op. cit., p. xiii.

52 See Guirdham, op. cit., pp. 90–91.

53 Ibid., p. 89.

54 The report of Benjamin of Tudela, cited in Sumption, op. cit., p. 90.

55 Ibid., p. 90; O' Shea, op. cit., p. 20.

56 Cited in Sumption, op. cit., p. 90.

57 Geoffrey Wigoder (ed.), *The Encyclopaedia of Judaism*, The Jerusalem Publishing House, Jerusalem, 1989, pp. 512–13.

58 Runciman, op. cit., pp. 6–7.

59 Ibid.

60 Ibid.

61 And again see Ibid.; the early Christian Gnostics held the same view.

62 *Encyclopaedia of Judaism*, pp. 740–41.

63 Z'ev ben Shimon Halevi, *Kabbalah: Tradition of Hidden Knowledge*, Thames & Hudson, London, 1988, p. 5.

64 An excellent article on the Sephiroth on the Web can be found at www.aril.org/Drob.htm.

65 Halevi, op. cit., pp. 5–6.

66 For a fuller discussion of mandalas see Hancock & Faiia, *Heaven's Mirror*, p. 122ff.

67 For a discussion see R. T. Prinke, 'Early Symbolism of the Rosy Cross', in *The Hermetic Journal*, no. 25, 1984, pp. 11–15.

68 See Francis Bacon Research Trust at www.fbrt.org.uk.

69 The printer was L. Lichfield of Oxford; Publishers were R. Young & E. Forrest; the engraving is by William Marshall, and the translation from Latin into English is by Rev. Gilbert Wats.

70 Ibid.

71 'The Ancient and Accepted Scottish Rite of Freemasonry containing Instructions in all the degrees' approved by the Supreme Council of the 33rd Degree of the Southern Jurisdiction, 1801.

72 William W. Westcott, *Collectanea Hermetica*, Part 1–10, 'Sepher Yetzirah', Samuel Weiser, York Beach, ME, 1988.

73 Ibid.

74 Lobingier, op. cit., p. 4.

75 See Joscelyn Godwin, *Athanasius Kircher*, Phanes Press, Grand Rapids, MI, 1991, p. 56.

76 Ibid., p. 61.

77 Ibid., p. 13.

78 Ibid.

79 Ibid., p. 15.

80 Ibid., p. 18.

81 Yates, *Giordano Bruno and the Hermetic Tradition*, p. 418.

82 Athanasius Kircher, *Oedepius Aegyptiacus*, Rome, 1652, p. 150; see also Yates, *Giordano Bruno and the Hermetic Tradition*, p. 418.

83 Wren had replaced Seth Ward, who had been holding this Savilian Chair since 1649. Ward was an intimate friend of John Wilkins, and together they were to write a controversial book in support of ancient universities in 1654 while at Oxford. In 1660 Charles II fired both Wilkins and Ward from their posts, and replaced the latter with Christopher Wren. Ironically, in 1661 Seth Ward was to become bishop of Exeter and, in 1668, Wilkins became the bishop of Chester. These were indeed strange times.

84 Peter Tompkins, *The Secret of the Great Pyramid*, Allen Lane, London, 1973, p. 30.

85 John Greaves, *Pyramidographia or a Description of the Pyramids in Aegypt*, London, 1646.

86 David Stevenson, *The Origins of Freemasonry, Scotland Century 1590–1710*, Cambridge University Press, Cambridge, 1988.

87 *The Last Will and Testament of Sir Thomas Gresham*, London, 1765.

88 Lomas, op. cit., pp. 154–64.

89 Hibbert, op. cit., pp. 179–86.

90 Guirdham, op. cit., pp. 91–2.

91 Cited in Yates, *Giordano Bruno and the Hermetic Tradition*, p. 394, footnote 1.

92 The Knights Templar first arrived in England in 1130 on the invitation of King Henry I. Initially they established their preceptory in High Holborn in the north, between Chancellor's Lane and Faitour Lane. In 1161 they moved it a mile southward to the more favoured site close to the Thames. Hugh Clout (ed.), *The Times History of London*, Times Books, London, 1991, p. 50.

93 David Lewer, *The Temple Church London*, Pitkin Pictorials, London, 1989, pp. 3–4.

94 *The Times History of London*, p. 150.

95 Felix Barker & Ralph Hyde, *London as it Might have Been*, John Murray, London, 1982, p. 22.

96 This point was also highlighted in Adrian Gilbert, *The New Jerusalem*, Bantam Press, London, 2002, p. 211: 'Wren changed the axis of St. Paul's so that it ran roughly 8° north-of-east ... this put it directly in line with the old Temple Church ...'

97 Christopher Wren (son), *Parentalia, or, Memoirs of the family of the Wrens*, Farnborough, Hampshire, 1995.

98 Steve Padget, 'Wren's St. Paul's: Axis Mundi of the New Jerusalem', paper read at Ball State University, Muncie, IN, 2000, p. 2.

99 Ibid., p. 4.

100 V. Hart, *Art and Magic at the Court of the Stuarts*, Routledge, London, 1994. See also V. Hart, *St. Paul's Cathedral: Christopher Wren*, Phaidon, London, 1995. Hart also added that 'in reflecting this 'Christianised' cosmology, Hermes was pictured in the pavement of Siena Cathedral and in frescos painted by Pinturiccio for Pope Alexander VI in the *Appartamento Borgia* in the Vatican ... the figure of Mercurius Trismegistus came to personify links between Christian magic and art in the Renaissance.'

101 The Sephiroth invited the initiate to pass between two 'pillars' on the pathway towards the godhead. Interestingly, according to Jewish author Z. Halevi, we find the same idea of passing between two 'pillars' in the design of Solomon's Temple, where one had to pass between two pillars known as *Boaz* and *Jachin* on the path towards the divine presence. See Halevi, op. cit.

102 Tinniswood, op. cit., pp. 150–2.

103 This tendency to secrecy was to be also the case when Wren designed new St. Paul's. See Barker & Hyde, op. cit., p. 31.

104 Tinniswood, op. cit., p. 150.

105 Ibid.

106 Barker & Hyde, op. cit., p. 23.

107 Tinniswood, op. cit., p. 152. See also John Evelyn, *London Revived*, Clarendon Press, Oxford, 1938, pp. 45–6.

108 Selections from Revelation 21:1–22:14.

109 Barker & Hyde, op. cit., p. 25.

110 In Wren's scheme, according to Adrian Tinniswood, 'the real pride of place went to the Exchange piazza with its radial vistas and its surrounding complex of commercial buildings. The absolutist ideology underlying the planning of Sixtine Rome, which Louis XIV and André Le Nôtre were currently putting to such good use in the laying out of Versailles, was here called into service to pay homage to mercantilism. Trade was to be the new religion.' That the Royal Exchange was Thomas Gresham's brainchild, and that his own home had probably served as a Masonic lodge prior to becoming the home of the Royal Society may also have had something to do with the symbolism intended in Wren's scheme.

111 This idea was first proposed by Adrian Gilbert in op. cit., p. 205. Gilbert also observes that it may not have been accidental that the *Daat sephirah* was brought close to Gresham College, home of the Royal Society.

112 Tinniswood, op. cit., p. 188.

113 Ibid.

CHAPTER SIXTEEN: FROM SECRET SOCIETY TO SOCIETY WITH SECRETS

1 Pick & Knight, op. cit., p. 68.

2 Matthew 11:11.

3 John 3:30.

4 4 July is, of course, US Indepedence Day.

5 Ibid., p. 69.

6 Ibid.

7 Ibid.

8 Ridley, op. cit., p. 37

9 Naudon, op. cit., p. 66.

10 Ibid., pp. 69–70.

11 Ibid., p. 72.

12 Ridley, op. cit., p. 72.

13 Lynn Picknett & Clive Prince, *The Templar Revelation*, Corgi Books, London, 1998, p. 481.

14 Lobingier, op. cit., p. 32.

15 Available at: http://www.gallica.bnf.fr/ark:/12148/bpt6k64393t.

16 The prince never became king, but died from illness in 1712.

17 Lobingier, op. cit., p. 35.

18 See Eliane Brault (ed), *Le Mystere du Chevalier Ramsay*, Editions du Prisme, Paris, 1973, p. 81; also *Transaction of the Qutuor Coronati Lodge*, 1934, vol. XLVII, p. 77. For a very good account of Ramsay's life and Masonic career, see Lobingier, op. cit., pp. 32–49.

THE MASTER GAME

19   Ridley, op. cit., p. 70.

20   The full 'Ramsay's Oration' can be found in Albert G. Mackey & H. L. Haywood, *Encyclopedia of Freemasonry*, Kessinger Publishing, Kila, MT, 2003. See also Cyril N. Batham, 'Ramsay's Oration: the Epernay and Grand Lodge Versions', in *Heredom: The Transactions of the Scottish Rite Research Society*, vol. 1, 1992.

21   The Chevalier Ramsay cited in Mackey & Haywood, op. cit., p. 831.

22   Ibid., p. 832.

23   Patigorsky, op. cit., p. 116–7.

24   Mackey & Haywood, op. cit., p. 832.

25   Pick & Knight, op. cit., p. 204.

26   The Order of DeMolay declares itself to be 'A young men's fraternal organization which was founded upon the basic principles of love of God, love of parents, and love of country. It tries to introduce these teachings to its members in various ways through the exercise of the seven cardinal virtues ... Love of parents, Love of God, Courtesy, Comradeship, Fidelity, Cleanness, Patriotism. The name "DeMolay" comes from a 13th century French hero and martyr named Jacques De Molay, who was the last Grand Master of a order of chivalric knights known as the Knights Templar ... Be between the ages of 12 and 21, believe in a Supreme Being (God), be of good moral character, Petition a DeMolay. Local groups of DeMolays are called chapters and are sponsored by a group of Masons or Masonic lodges.' In 1919, a Kansas City freemason named Frank S. Land, noticed a need for a young men's organization in the Kansas City area. After meeting with a local youth named Louis Lower, Land arranged a meeting with several other area youths at the Kansas City Scottish Rite building. With Land's guidance and the ambition of the young men, the Order of DeMolay was born. Almost instantaneously, the popularity of the new order grew and in no time at all, there were chapters in every state in the union and soon there were even chapters abroad. For over 75 years now, the Order of DeMolay has continued to teach it's member's the basic principles of life which will help prepare any young man for a good and clean manhood, and which will help them to develop a greater love and respect for their God, parents and country. In its history, the Order of DeMolay has boasted a strong membership and has long lists of successful and influential members.

27   'What is Freemasonry?', United Grand Lodge of England, text reproduced by the Lodge of Harmony, no. 1411 at www.harmony1411.cl/freemasonry.html.

28   I Kings 5–6; II Chronicles 2–6.

29   Sinclair, op. cit., p. 158.

30   For a detailed critical appraisal of these rituals, see Lawrence, op. cit., pp. 92–107.

31   Martin Short, *Inside the Brotherhood*, Grafton Books, London, 1989, p. 93.

32   Lawrence, op. cit., pp. 51–61.

33   Ibid.

34   Humbert, op. cit., p. 117.

35   Short, op. cit., p. 115.

36   Ibid., p. 123.

37   Stephen Knight, *The Brotherhood*, Grafton Books, London, 1985, pp. 236–9.

38   Short, op. cit., p. 104.

39   '*Geometry wherefore I thinke that science most worthy that fyndeth all others*', cited in Pick & Knight, op. cit., p. 32.

40   For a full account of Pythagoras in Egypt, see Schwaller de Lubicz, op. cit., p. 259.

41   See also Genesis 4–20.

42   Pick & Knight, op. cit., p. 32.

43   Ibid., pp. 32–3.

44   Ibid.

45   Naudon, op. cit., p. 64.

46   Ibid., p. 72.

47   Ibid., p. 74.

48   Ibid., pp. 74–6.

49   François Ribadeau-Dumas, *Cagliostro: homme de lumière*, Editions Philosophiques, Paris, 1981, p. 25.

50   Gérard Galtier, Maçonnerie égyptienne, *Rose-Croix et Neo-Chevalerie: Les Fils de Cagliostro*, Editions du Rocher, Paris, 1989, p. 29.

51   Ibid. p. 35; Masonic historians, however, still do not seem to be able to agree where had taken place Cagliostro initiation into Freemasonry. They venture two places, Malta in 1767 (Gastone Ventura, *Masonic Rites of Memphis and Misraim*, Atanòr, Rome, 1986) or London in 1777 (Galthier, op. cit., p. 30).

52   Ribadeau-Dumas, op. cit., p. 35.

53   Ibid., p. 39.

54   Pernety is often accredited for creating the so-called *Swedenborgian Rite* of Freemasonry. When he was fifty years old, Pernety left the Benedictine order and settled at Avignon. There he directed his earlier alchemical interests into Freemasonry and created the so-called *Rite Hermétique*. He then moved to Berlin and became librarian to Frederick II. In Berlin Pernety translate the works of Swedenborg, the Swedish theologian and alleged founder of the New Jerusalem Church.

55   Ribadeau-Dumas, op. cit., p. 50; Naudon, op. cit., p. 92.

56   In 1781, Fredrick II was initiated into the Order of The Golden Rose Cross, a German Rosicrucian order, by Johann Woller and Johann Bischoffwerder, two Rosicrucians who were to become Fredrick's closest advisors (McIntosh, op. cit., p. 95–6). The esoteric name given to Fredrick II during the initiation rituals was 'Ormesus Magnus'.

The Order of the Golden Rose Cross, according to the origins it gave itself, was allegedly created in Egypt, at Alexandria, by an Egyptian sage called 'Ormissus or Ormus' (Galtier, op. cit., p. 164), which is the 'second name' given to the imfamous Priere de Sion (M. Baigent, H. Lincoln & R. Leigh, *The Holy Blood and the Holy Grail*, p. 123). Ormus, as we shall see later, was also the name given to the founder of the Masonic Rite of Memphis. According to Masonic author Clara Miccinelli, the name 'Ormus' appeared as early as 1753 in a private letter written by Prince Raimondo di Sangre de Severo, a Freemason, to the Baron de Tchoudi in Paris (C. Miccinelli, *E dio Creo L'Uomo e la Massoneria*, ECIG, Genova, 1985, p. 73).

57 Ribadeau-Dumas, op. cit., p. 51.
58 Ibid. In 1758 Pernety had published a treatise with the ambitious title of 'The Egyptian and Greek Fables Unveiled and Linked to the same Principles, with an Explanation of the Hieroglyphs and the War of Troye', which gives us a fair indication what his 'science of Nature' was.
59 Galtier, op. cit., p. 36.
60 Ibid. See also Manly P. Hall, *Freemasonry of the Ancient Egyptians: Crata Repoa*, Philosophical Research Society, Los Angeles, 1965, pp. 81–102.
61 Galtier, op. cit., p. 36; see also Hall, op. cit., p. 73.
62 Naudon, op. cit., p. 91.
63 Ridley, op. cit., pp. 110–21.
64 Ibid., p. 129.
65 Naudon op. cit. p. 91
66 Galtier, op. cit., p. 19.
67 Naudon, op. cit., p. 229.
68 Pierre Chevalier, *Histoire de la Franc-Maçonnerie française*, Librairie Fayard, Paris, 1974, vol. I, pp. 258–9.
69 J. E. Manchip White, *Ancient Egypt in Culture and History*, George Allen & Unwin, London, 1970, p. 107. Herodotus gives 70 days (*Histories*, book II, section 85), which is more in line with ancient Egyptian practice.
70 Genesis 50:1–3. The duration of the Flood was also 40 days (Genesis 7:4, 8:6).
71 Chevalier, op. cit., pp. 256–62.

CHAPTER SEVENTEEN: THE NEW CITY OF ISIS

1 Ribadeau-Dumas, op. cit., p. 165.
2 Chevalier, op. cit., vol. 1, p. 261.
3 Ibid. See also Gisèle & Yves Hivert-Messeca, *Comment la Franc-Maçonnerie vint aux femmes*, Editions Devry, Paris, 1997, p. 148.
4 Naudon, op. cit., pp. 228–30.
5 An excellent article on Cagliostro can be seen in Henry Evans, 'Masonry and Magic in the Eighteenth Century', *The Master Mason*, June 1927.

6 *Bibliothèque Nationale*, ms. Fr. 12420 c. 1402 fol. XVI; ms. Fr. 598, c. 1403 fol. XVI.
7 Baltrušaitis, op. cit., p. 63.
8 L. M. Tisserand, *Les Armoiries de la ville de Paris*, Paris 1874, chapter 3, '*Formation du sceau ou des armoiries de Paris*', p. 61; also Baltrušaitis, op. cit., p. 63.
9 Jacques le Grant, *Sophologium*, Paris, 1475; also see Baltrušaitis, op. cit., p. 61.
10 Jean Lemaire de Belges, *Les Illustrations de Gaule et Singularitez de Troye*, Paris 1512; also see Baltrušaitis, op. cit., p. 59.
11 Baltrušaitis, op. cit., p. 58, plates 1 & 6.
12 Jacques du Breul, *Théâtre des Antiquitez de Paris*, Paris, 1612.
13 André Favyn, *Histoire de Navarre*, Paris 1612.
14 Baltrušaitis op. cit. p. 89
15 Phaure, op. cit., pp. 19–20 (map).
16 Ibid., p. 84 (map).
17 Ibid.
18 Ian Wilson, *Jesus The Evidence*, Pan Books, London, 1984, pp. 136–7. See also Freke & Gandy, op. cit., pp. 41–2.
19 From Edward Carpenter, *Pagan & Christian Creeds: Their Origin and Meaning*, BiblioBazaar, Charleston, SC, 2009, pp. 50–51:

The Jesus-story, it will now be seen, has a greater number of correspondences with the stories of former sun gods and with the actual career of the Sun through the heavens – so many indeed that they cannot well be attributed to mere coincidence or even to the blasphemous wiles of the Devil! Let us enumerate some of these. There are (1) birth from a virgin mother; (2) the birth in a stable (cave or underground chamber); and (3) on 25 December (just after the winter solstice). There is (4) the Star in the East (Sirius) and (5) the arrival of the Magi (the 'Three King's); there is (6) the threatened Massacre of the Innocents, and the consequent flight into a distant country (told also of Krishna and other sun gods). There are the Church festivals of (7) Candlemas (2 February), with processions of candles to symbolize the growing light; of (8) Lent, or the arrival of spring; of (9) Easter Day (normally on 25 March) to celebrate the crossing of the Equator by the Sun; and (10) simultaneously the outburst of lights at the Holy Sepulchre at Jerusalem. There is (11) [the Crucifixion and death of the Lamb-God, on Good Friday, three days before Easter; there are (12) the nailing to a tree, (13) the empty grave, (14) the glad Resurrection (as in the cases of Osiris, Attis and others); there are (15) the twelve disciples (the Zodiacal signs); and (16) the betrayal by one of the twelve. Then later there is (17)

Mid-summer Day, 24 June, dedicated to the birth of the beloved disciple John, and corresponding to Christmas Day; there are the festivals of (18) the Assumption of the Virgin (15 August) and of (19) the Nativity of the Virgin (8 September), corresponding to the movement of the god through Virgo; there is the conflict of Christ and his disciples with the autumnal asterisms, (20) the Serpent and the Scorpion; and finally there is the curious fact that the Church (21) dedicates the very day of the winter solstice (when any one may very naturally doubt the rebirth of the Sun) to St. Thomas, who doubted the truth of the Resurrection! ...

In the cathedral, the congregation faces the east in order to pray. It does not face Jerusalem but the east i.e. the direction of the sunrise. This direction of prayer is almost certainly derived from ancient pagan solar cults. In Christian worship the meaning is somewhat changed. Christ's has many attributes of the ancient sun-god, but he is also the Messiah who has come and who will return, another analogy of the death and rebirth of the sun-god in ancient myths. East is the place of sunrise, of solar rebirth, of the coming of light. In mystical religions the east symbolises spiritual enlightenment and divinity.

20   Norman Lockyer, *The Dawn of Astronomy*, Cassell & Co., London, 1894, p. 120.

21   Habachi, op. cit., pp. 155–6.

22   Lockyer, op. cit., pp. 98–106.

23   Much later, in 1973, the astronomer Gerald S. Hawkins disagreed with Lockyer and asserted that the Karnak Temple had not been aligned to the summer solstice sunset but rather to the *winter solstice sunrise* which took place 26° 55' south-of-east (See Gerald Hawkins, *Beyond Stonehenge*, Arrow Books, London, 1977, chapter 11 'Amon-Ra', pp. 193–218; see also Ronald L. Reese, 'Midwinter Sunrise at Karnak', in *Sky & Telescope*, March 1992, p. 276). Hawkins is best known for his work on the astronomical alignments of Stonehenge. Hawkins, however, did not carry out actual astronomical observations at Karnak as did Lockyer. He obtained his orientation angle from survey maps at the Franco-Egyptian Research Centre at Luxor and, like Lockyer before him, calculated the position of the sunrise/set at the solstice rather than actually observe it (Hawkins was in Egypt in May, a month before the summer solstice). A few years later the astronomer Ed Krupp confirmed Hawkins's values from actual observations of the sunrise at the winter solstice from the Karnak Temple (E. C. Krupp, *Echoes of Ancient Skies*, Oxford University Press, Oxford, 1994, pp. 253–7). Hawkins argued that Lockyer's conclusions were wrong, since the Theban Hills in the distance made it such that the setting sun at the summer solstice could not be properly seen through pylons of the temple. But although it is true to say that the Theban hills in the west present an obstacle to us from a *practical viewpoint*, this reasoning cannot be applied to the ancient Egyptians's *religious viewpoint*. To them such physical obstacles were not an impediment, viz., for example, the so-called *false door* made of solid stone often found in tombs and through which the soul of the deceased was imagined to pass. Egyptian astronomer-priests – and especially those assigned to the sun-cult – had been observing the sunrise and sunset at the solstices long before the construction of Karnak, and there is no question that they would have been acutely aware of its maximal and minimal declinations. And so the conclusion by Hawkins that the Theban Hills invalidates the alignment towards the summer solstice sunset is not tenable when placed in the religious context of the ancient temple builders (Hawkins, op. cit., p. 198). Hawlkins commends Lockyer's on the accuracy of his survey at Stonehenge, but says that 'his survey of the Amon-Ra temple was not.' Hawkins refers to the report by army engineer P. J. G. Wakefield, who performed a theodolite survey at Karnak for Locker on 21 June 1891. And although it is true that Wakefield reported that the Sun could not be seen from any of the points on the axis of the temple marked by Lockyer, he did add that he placed the theodolite at the entrance of Pylon 2 and that he was 'able to see a portion of the setting sun, the remainder being hidden behind the south wall of the great pylon (Pylon 1).' Now the Sun's diameter is about 0.5°, which means that it could be 'shifted' a further 0.5° to the north along the horizon, it would be seen between along that part of the axis running from Pylon 1 to Pylon 2. In c. 1500 BC the Sun was, in fact, 0.5° further north due to the obliquity of the ecliptic at the time. This suggests to me that the orientation of the Karnak Temple might be closer to 26° than the 26° 55' quoted by Hawkins which he got off the map of the Franco-Egyptian Centre. Indeed, Lockyer reported that according to Lepsius and other Egyptologists, the angle was '26° or 26° 30" north-of-west. When E.C. Krupp went to verify this, he did so on the winter solstice, and thus could only verify the alignment at the other end of the temple through the so-called *Temple of Ré-Horakhti* and the 'High room of the Sun'. In my opinion another survey should be made on 21 June to ascertain the statement of army engineer P. J. G. Wakefied. I did, in fact, observe the sunset on June 21, 2003; my conclusion is that the builders aimed at the sunrise on the winter solstice, but also knew that the sunset at summer solstice would take place in the reverse direction. And although it is true that the latter does

not fall on the axis alignment but a little short towards the west, it is obvious that the intention was there.

24 R. Wells, 'Ré and the Calendar' in A. J. Spalinger (ed.), *Revolution in Time: Studies in Ancient Egyptian Calendrics*, Van Siclen Books, San Antonio, TX, 1994, p. 19. Ron Wells calculated that at c. 3500 BC the star Sirius would have risen at exactly the same spot as the winter solstice sunrise. His computations assume a 'level horizon and no refraction'. My own calculations show that as seen from the latitude of Cairo today, it would have been seen rising about 29.5° south-of-east. However, in c. 3300 BC, at the foundation date of Dynastic Egypt, it would have risen some 28° south-of-east (Azimuth 118°). A simple calculation shows that at that epoch Sirius had the same declination as the Sun at winter solstice i.e. about −24° (that is, 24° south of the celestial equator), and thus performed exactly the same path at the Sun at the winter solstice. It was, quite literally, a 'second sun' seen at night in the place of the winter solstice sun.' The epoch 3300 BC is extremely significant in that it marks the historical begin of Dynastic Egypt, when the whole country was unified under one kingdom.

25 In Roman times the goddess Isis was closely identified and even merged with the Roman goddess Ceres, the Greek Demeter. See Batrusaitis, op. cit., p. 70. See also Fraser, op. cit., pp. 383 & 393. See also Marie-France Arnold, op. cit., pp. 87–8: 'The Romans did not call her [Isis] "mother of the wheat and of nature" as did the ancient Egyptians, but they venerated her and made offerings to her ... a shrine was built in the city of Paris at the exact spot where Christians would later build Notre Dame de Paris. In 1711, while digging a crypt under the cathedral destined for the burial of bishops this shrine was discovered ...' Anne Baring & Jules Cashford, in their book *The Myth of the Goddess: Evolution of an Image* (Arkana, London, 1993), showed that the concept of 'Notre Dame' in France, especially for the so-called *Black virgins*, has an esoteric association to the Egyptian goddess Isis (pp. 586 & 647). See also further Baltrušaitis, op. cit., pp. 24–40.

26 Phaure, op. cit., pp. 56–7.

27 Ribadeau-Dumas, op. cit., p. 167.

28 Fauche, op. cit., p. 32.

29 Ibid.

30 *Grand Larousse Encyclopédique*, vol. 3, p. 261a.

31 Naudon, op. cit., p. 95.

32 Faucher, op. cit., p. 27; see also Galtier, op. cit., p. 30.

33 Ribadeau-Dumas, op. cit., p. 294.

34 Ibid., p. 200

35 Manly P. Hall, 'Rosicrucian and Masonic Origins', in *Lectures on Ancient Philosophy and Introduction to the Study and Application of Rational Procedure*, The Hall Publishing Company, Los Angeles, 1929, pp. 408–9.

36 See Antoine Court de Gébelin, *Monde primitif analysé et comparé avec le monde moderne*, book 8, Paris, 1773–1783.

37 Ribadeau-Dumas, op. cit., p. 167–8.

38 Ibid. p. 168.

39 Ibid. p. 199.

40 Joscelyn Godwin, *The Theosophical Enlightenment*, State University of New York Press, Albany, 1994.

41 Ribadeau-Dumas, op. cit., p. 199.

42 Naudon, op. cit., p. 129.

43 Adam Weishaupt cited in Nesta H. Webster, *Secret Societies and Subversive Movements*, Book Tree, San Diego, CA, 2000, p. 215.

44 Mackey & Haywood, op. cit., p. 474.

45 Thomas Jefferson to Reverend James Madison, January 31, 1800, in Library of Congress, *The Thomas Jefferson Papers*, available at: www.memory.loc.gov/cgi-bin/query/r?ammem/mtj:@field(DOCID+@lit(tjo9oo5o)).

46 Noble E. Cunnigham Jr, *In Pursuit of Reason: the Life of Thomas Jefferson*, Ballantine Books, New York 1988, opening page.

47 Naudon, op. cit., p. 129. The order was apparently exposed in a most curious way. One of its leaders, Jacob Lang, while walking back home during a bad storm, was struck by lightning. Subversive documents were found on his body and taken to the elector of Bavaria, prompting him to launched an investigation into the Illuminati.

48 For source data see www. freemasonry.bcy.ca/anti-masonry/anti-masonryo2.html.

49 The 'eye' in a 'glowing triangle' was used in medieval times to denote 'God' and can be seen on the covers of many biblical manuscripts (see an example in Manly P. Hall's *The Secret Teachings of All Ages*, The Philosophical Research Society, Los Angeles, 1998, p. xcviii). Robert Fludd's works (1574–1637) is full of the glowing triangle-pyramid symbol, although he often replaces the 'eye' with other symbols or the words for 'god' (see Godwin, *Robert Fludd: Hermetic Philosopher and Surveyor of two Worlds*). German alchemists and Cabalists used the 'eye in the pyramid' symbol profusely in the early 18th century (J. Ritman (ed.), *The Silent Language, The Symbols of Hermetic Philosophy*, In de Pelikaan, Amsterdam 1994, pp. 59 & 75).

50 Godwin, *Athanasius Kircher*, p. 8.

51 Iversen, op. cit., p. 105, plate XIX.

52 Naudon, op. cit., p. 122.

53　The first design of The Great Seal was in July 1776 by Pierre-Eugène Simitière. A drawing made in 1776 by pencil on paper by Thomas Jefferson exists in the Library of Congress. The 'eye in the triangle' can clearly be seen on the top of the Seal. The first committee's choice for the Great Seal, which met on 20 August 1776, was: A shield with emblems of the six European cultures that migrated to America: three for Britain (English rose, Scottish thistle, Irish harp) and three for continental Europe (French fleur-de-lis, German eagle, Belgic lion). Supporting the shield: the Goddess of Liberty, who holds a spear and wears the Phrygian cap, and the Goddess of Justice with her balance. Crest: *'The Eye of Providence in a radiant Triangle* whose Glory extends over the Shield and beyond the Figures.' Motto: 'E PLURIBUS UNUM.'

54　The Great Seal First Committee was formed in the afternoon of the 4 July 1776. It comprised Benjamin Franklin, Thomas Jefferson, John Adams and Pierre-Eugène Simitière. Each member proposed various ideas. Franklin's idea was 'Moses standing on the Shore, and extending his Hand over the Sea, thereby causing the same to overwhelm Pharaoh who is sitting in an open Chariot, a Crown on his Head and a Sword in his Hand. Rays from a Pillar of Fire in the Clouds reaching to Moses, to express that he acts by Command of the Deity.' Motto: 'Rebellion to Tyrants is Obedience to God.' There were several 'committees' formed in the course of the next six years. The third and final committee was formed on 4 May 1782. Hardly a month before in Paris, on 12 April 1782, a series of peace talks had begun between the United States and Britain. America was represented by Benjamin Franklin. The US urgently needed an official sign of sovereignty and coat-of-arms for the signing of the peace treaty. The so-called *Third Committee* consisted of Chairman Arthur Middleton and John Rutledge, both of South Carolina, Elias Boudinot of New Jersey and Virginia's Arthur Lee. William Barton, a twenty-eight years old artist well-versed in the science of heraldry, came up with two complex designs which were graphic interpretation of the official written description that precisely defines the design as follows:

> *Obverse*: On the breast of the American bald eagle is a shield with thirteen vertical white and red stripes beneath a blue chief. In the eagle's right talon is an olive branch, and in his left a bundle. In his beak is a scroll inscribed with the motto 'E Pluribus Unum'. Over the head of the eagle, a Golden Glory is breaking through a cloud, and surrounds a constellation of thirteen stars on an azure field.
>
> *Reverse*: In the zenith of an unfinished pyramid is an eye in a triangle surrounded with a golden glory. Over the

eye are the words 'Annuit Coeptis'. On the base of the pyramid the numerical letters MDCCLXXVI, and underneath, the motto 'Novo Ordo Seculorum'.

55　See a very good article on this topic by Geoff Muirden, 'Conspiracy Theory and the French Revolution', in *The Journal of Historical Review*, vol. 9, no. 1, pp. 109–15.

56　See Nesta H. Webster, *The French Revolution*, Constable & Co., London, 1919. See also Webster, *Secret Societies and Subversive Movements*, A & B Publishers Group, New York, 1998 (1924), chapter 9.

57　Faucher, op. cit., p. 39.

58　Ibid., p. 24.

59　Ibid., p. 25.

60　Ribadeau-Dumas, op. cit., p. 199.

61　See Evans, op. cit. See also *Master Mason* magazine, vol.1, no.1, January 1924, to vol. 7, no. 3 & 4, March–April 1930.

62　*Grand Larousse Encyclopédique*, vol. 7, pp. 1009–10.

63　Galtier, op. cit., p. 37.

64　In July 1789 there were only seven prisoners in the Bastille. These were Jean de la Corrége, Jean Bèchade, the Count of Solages; Tavernier, Bernard Laroche, Jean-Antoine Pujade and DeWhitt, the latter an insane Irishman who was jailed as a spy; he was taken on the shoulders of the rioters that freed him from the Bastille, all the time shouting that he was Julius Caesar.

65　Captain Deflue had been moved to the Bastille earlier on July 7, 1789 along with 32 'Salis-Samade', a regiment of Swiss guards, to protect the Bastille. There were also 84 *invalides* at the time also appointed to defend the Bastille. All in all, a very poor match for the Parisian mob.

66　Chevallier, op. cit., vol. I, p. 272.

67　Out of the 25 Millions living in France at the time, 350,000 or so were 'nobility' and some 150,000 were 'clergy'. All the rest was considered the Third Estate.

68　Faucher, op. cit., p. 32.

69　Ibid.

70　In 1791 Talleyrand was excommunicated by the pope after he consecrated two 'constitutional' bishops. Talleyrand was to play a pivotal role a few years later in the rise of Napoleon Bonaparte and his daring military expedition to Egypt.

71　'*Et bien, f ..., qu'ils restent!*', see Faucher, op. cit., p. 172, plate 1.

72　Ibid., p. 34.

73　Ibid.

74　The first guillotining took place on April 25, 1792, when Nicolas Jacques Pelletie was executed in public at Place de Grève in Paris. The guillotine was still used in France well into the 20th century, and was finally officially banned in 1981. The last execution by guillotine in France was on 10 September 1977 in Marseilles, when the murderer Hamida Djambuti was beheaded.

75 Hivert-Messeca & Hivert-Messeca, op. cit., p. 124.

76 For source data see www.infomonnaies. com/fr/cnpr/v25/p2516.htm; also see Arslan, op. cit., p. 644.

77 This image can be seen, for instance, above the bronze image of George Washington on the Washington Monument (obelisk) in Washington, DC, east entrance, above the inner door.

78 *Grand Larousse Encyclopédique*, vol. 3, p. 910b.

79 Vovelle, op. cit., p. 28.

80 The Convention Nationale was essentially controlled by the 'Montagnards', the main political party to which the Hébertists also belonged. Its bitter rivals were the Girondins, a moderate and conservative faction, who were accused of secretly harbouring Royalist sympathies. When the Girondin were defeat at the Convention in June 1793 the Hébertists and the Montagnards lost a common enemy, a serious void, since their politics was mostly dependent on blaming another party and launching fiery verbal attacks on such 'enemy of the people'. Thus the momentum of accusation-styled politics was now deflected on each other, and soon the mood turned quite deadly. Robespierre, siezing an opportunity provided by a huge fraud and spy scandal which was construed to have involved the Hébertists, ordered the arrest of Hébert and Chaumette. They were hastily tried and sent to the scafold in March 1794. Now with no one left to blame and accuse for the problems that the Republic was facing, a terrible feud ensued between Robespierre and Danton – a feud that was to prove fatal for both men. Danton, who had been somehow mixed up in the scandal of the *Société Des Indes*, was accused of treason and sent to the guillotine in April 1794.

81 Faucher, op. cit., pp. 42–4.

82 Kathleen Jones, *Women Saints: Lives of Faith and Courage*, Orbis Books, Maryknoll, NY, 1999, p. 55.

83 See François Victor Alphonse Aulard, *Culte de la Raison*, Paris, 1892 and *Christianity and the French Revolution*, English edition, 1927). Aulard published many works of sources on the French Revolution. His best-known work is the *Political History of the French Revolution* (1901). In 1886 Aulard became the first professor of the history of the French Revolution at the University of the Sorbonne.

84 Vovelle, op. cit. Author K. Jones (op. cit.) reports the events of Sister Madeleine Fontaine (1723–1794), a nun who suffered the horrors of this persecution in 1794 and

was decapitated by the guillotine in June 1794 under the orders of Joseph Lebon, an apostate priest and a collaborator of Robespierre at the Convention. Sister Madeleine Fontaine, who was in her early seventies, was in charge of a small group of nuns in Arras where they ran a hospital and a school for children when the Revolution broke out. Apparently when she was dragged onto the scaffold, the old nun turned to the crowd and cried: 'Listen, Christians! We are the last victims. The persecution is going to stop. The gallows will be destroyed. The altar of Jesus will rise again gloriously!' Sister Madeleine Fontaine was beatified by Pope Benefict XV on 13 June 1920.

85 Baring & Cashford, op. cit., pp. 399–401. Apparently the wearing of the Phrygian cap by the revolutionary Sans Culottes, the most extremist faction of the French Revolution, had been popularized by Jacques-Louis David in *Les Amours d'Hélène et Paris* which he had painted in 1787 for the Duke of Artois, the future Charles X.

86 Maarten J. Vermaseren, *Cybele and Attis*, translated by A. M. H. Lemmers, Thames & Hudson, London, 1977, p. 10.

87 Baltrušaitis, op. cit., p. 80.

88 Ibid. Actually what Isis has on her head is not a tower but a 'throne'. Its upright shape, however, can easily be mistaken for a tower, indeed as it often was by the Parisian historians of the 18th and 19th century.

89 Ovason, op. cit., p. 87.

90 Jérôme Lalande, *Astronomie par M. de la Lande*, 1731, vol. IV, pp. 245ff.

91 Gérard de Nerval, *Les Illuminés*, Editions Folio, 1976; also see Cagliotro, *Les Païens de la République*, p. 1200.

92 Kerisel, op. cit., p. 160.

93 Vovelle, op. cit., p. 105.

94 Ibid., p. 271

95 *Grand Larousse Encyclopédique*, vol. 1, p. 365a.

96 Louis Blanc, *History*, vol. II, pp. 365–7.

97 *Grand Larousse Encyclopédique*, vol. 8, p. 1014c.

98 'MM. Dupuis et Lalande voient Isis par-tout ...!'; see Baltrušaitis, op. cit., p. 31.

99 Ibid., p. 35; Faucher, op. cit., p. 20.

100 Charles-François Dupuis, *Origine de tous les Cultes our Religion Universelle*, Paris, 1794, vol. III, p. 50; Baltrušaitis, op. cit., pp. 24–30.

101 'Histoire de l'Académie Royale des Sciences, année 1785, compte rendu de J. de Lalande', in *Le Journal des Scavans*, July 1788, pp. 475–8.

102 In the *Pyramid Texts*, which date from the third millennium BC, we read that 'Sothis [Sirius, the star of Isis]is your beloved

daughter [of Ra] who prepares yearly sustenance for you in her name of 'Year'. *Pyramid Texts*, line 965.

CHAPTER EIGHTEEN: PARIS UNVEILED

1   Kerisel, op. cit., p. 158.

2   Marcello Fagiolo, *Architettura e Massoneria*, Convivio/Nardini Editore, Florence, 1988, p. 44.

3   James Stephen Curl, *The Art and Architecture of Freemasonry*, B. T. Batsford, London, 1991, p. 118

4   Ibid.

5   Kerisel, op. cit., p. 161.

6   Curl, op. cit., p. 129.

7   Ibid., p. 129. For a detailed review on the pyramid design and the French Revolution, see J. P. Mouilleseaux, 'Les Pyramides éphémères de la Révolution Française', *Revue FMR*, 21, vol. VI, August 1989.

8   Ibid., p. 129.

9   Ibid., p. 117.

10 Fagiolo, op. cit., p. 53.

11 Legaret & Courtines, op. cit., p. 83, plate 3.

12 Ibid., plate 6.

13 Ovason, op. cit., p. 116.

14 Curl, op. cit., pp. 132–3.

15 See notes 47 & 48 of Chapter Twelve.

16 Vovelle, op. cit., frontispiece.

17 Faucher, op. cit., p. 34. It may be of interest to note that in 1819 Mme de la Villette, Voltaire's adored step-daughter, opened the so-called *adoption* lodge in Paris called 'Belle et Bonne' for the Rite of Misraim that practiced higher degrees of the Egyptian Rite (see *Dossiers de l'Histore*, no. 7, p. 98; also see Naudon, op. cit., p. 230).

18 Her real name was Marie Josèphe Rose. She was named 'Joséphine' by Napoleon after they married in 1796. Apparently the nickname was derived from Joseph, Napoleon's younger brother.

19 Hivert-Messeca & Hivert-Messeca, op. cit., p. 159.

20 Ibid., p. 160.

21 Ibid., p. 159.

22 Naudon, op. cit., p. 172.

23 François Collaveri, *Napoleon: empereur franc-maçon*, Editions Tallandier, Paris, 1986, pp. 26–27.

24 Ibid., p. 168.

25 The same had happened much later in 1867 when the Empress Eugénie, a great-grand-daughter of Joséphine, bedazzled the khedive of Egypt in one of the most exquisite and daring flirtations in history that eventually led to the construction of the Suez Canal by her cousin, the engineer Ferdinand de Lesseps (see Trevor Mostyn, *Egypt: La Belle Epoque*, Quartet Books, London, 1989, p. 17).

26 Mostyn, op. cit., p. 17.

27 Faucher, op. cit., p. 9 & pp. 32–3. Perhaps it should also be noted that Talleyrand's illegitimate son, the famous painter Eugène Delacroix, was among the core of agitators accused by the French police to have plotted with the Egyptian Masonic Rite of Memphis and the *Carbonari* against the restored king Louis XVIII in the failed coup d'état of 1822.

28 Evans, op. cit.

29 Iversen, op. cit., p. 125.

30 Yates, *The Rosicrucian Enlightenment*, p. 154.

31 Iversen, op. cit., p. 100.

32 Jean Lacouture, *Champollion: Úne vie de lumières*, Editions Grasset, Paris, 1988, p. 382.

33 Ibid., p. 34.

34 Faucher, op. cit., p. 18.

35 Chevallier, op. cit., vol. I, p. 261.

36 Napoleon cited in John S. C. Abbott (ed.), *Confidential correspondence of the Emperor Napoleon and the Empress Joséphine*, Mason Brothers, New York, 1858, p. 22.

37 Napoleon cited in John Eldred Howard (ed.), *Letters and documents of Napoleon*, Oxford University Press, Oxford, 1961, p. 165.

38 Lacouture, op. cit., p. 35.

39 Aubrey Noakes, *Cleopatra's Needle*, H. F. & G. Witherby, London, 1962, p. 1.

40 Vincent Cronin, *Napoleon*, Harper Collins, 1994, p. 146.

41 Noakes, op. cit., p. 1.

42 A military-political class made up of the descendents of freed slaves.

43 Alan Moorehead, *The Blue Nile*, Penguin, 1983, p. 65. Apparently Napoleon also told the Imams of Egypt: 'In the name of Allah ... tell your people that the French are also Muslims ... they have [occupied Rome and] ruined the papal See which was always urging the Christians to attack Islam ...'

44 Lauren Foreman & Ellen Blue Phillips, *Napoleon's Lost Fleet*, Roundtable Press, New York, 1999, p. 69.

45 Ibid., p. 159.

46 Ibid., p. 49.

47 Moorehead, op. cit., p. 124.

48 Naudon, op. cit., p. 224.

49 Thomas Hodgkin with Henry Ketcham, *The Life of Charlemagne (Charles the Great)*, A. L. Burt, New York, 1902, p. 261.

50 See Donald Bullough, *The Age of Charlemagne*, Paul Elek, London, 1973; also see Russell Chamberlain, *Charlemagne*, Grafton, London, 1986. Apparently Pope Leo III crowned Charlemagne as Holy Roman emperor in gratitude for having saved him and as well as Rome. In the *Frankish Royal Annals* (*Grandes Chroniques de France*) it

is reported that one of the Charlemagne's advisers suggested the idea to the pope. According to Einhard, his biographer, as well as other contemporary writers, the coronation actually took Charlemagne by surprise and made him angry. This, say modern scholars, is because Charlemagne considered the pope to be a mere subject of his vast empire.

51 Pope Pius VII, who had been forced to participate in this charade, was to take his revenge when Napoleon's empire began to crumble. Firstly in 1814, the pope restored the order of the Jesuits, which had been banned from France in 1764, and later, when the French had forced an earlier pope, Clement IX, to completely dissolve the Jesuit order in 1773. Perhaps not unrelated, in 1821, when Napoleon was dying a solitary death at St. Helen, Pius VII issued his famous bull, *Ecclessiam a Jesu Christo*, condemning Freemasonry and the *Carbonari* in all Christiandom (see Faucher, op. cit., p. 71).

52 Naudon, op. cit., p. 78.

53 Court de Gébelin, op. cit.

54 Noël, op. cit.

55 Duché, op. cit., p. 237.

56 Faucher, op. cit., p. 315.

57 See François Collaveri, *La Franc-Maçonnerie des Bonaparte*, Editions Payot, Paris, 1982; also see Galtier, op. cit., p. 139; see also Naudon, op. cit., p. 97.

58 Chevallier, op. cit., vol. II, pp. 17–30.

59 See Collaveri, *La Francs Maçonnerie des Bonapartes*, annex iv.

60 Ibid., p. 67.

61 Ibid., p. 68.

62 *The Kneph*, vol. III, no. 6, June 1883, p. 45; see Galtier, op. cit., p. 139–40.

63 Humbert, op. cit., p. 40.

64 Naudon, op. cit., p. 124.

65 Humbert, op. cit., p. 48; although the foundation stones were laid as well as the raising of a cardboard model of the building, the project was eventually abandoned due to lack of funds.

66 Lacouture, op. cit., p. 20.

67 Ibid., pp. 55 & 63.

68 Ibid., p. 54–5.

69 Baltrušaitis, op. cit., p. 55, see also plate III.

70 Arslan, op. cit., p. 645.

71 The architects were: Chalgrin (1806–1811), Joust (1811–1814), Blouet (1833–1836). The sculptors were: Cortot, Rude, Etex, Pradier, Lemaire.

72 Also known as *l'Apothéose de Napoléon*.

73 Baltrušaitis, op. cit., p. 80.

74 Ibid.

75 Ibid., p. 8.

76 Margaret Laing, *Joséphine and Napoleon*, Sidgwick & Jackson, London, 1973, pp. 131–2.

77 *Project d'Achèvement de L'Arc de Triomphe de L'Étoile, Monument des Victories, Sciences et Arts, ou de la Légion d'Honneur, offert au Roi des Français, Louis-Philippe 1er, et au Deux Chambres*. A photograph of this project can be seen in the museum of the *Arc de Triomphe*.

78 Naudon, op. cit., p. 78; Faucher, op. cit., p. 22 & pp. 62–3.

79 The Count of Artois had another son, Louis Antoine, but he was believed to be impotent.

80 Naudon, op. cit., p. 98.

81 Faucher, op. cit., p. 71.

82 Ibid., pp. 72–4.

83 Ibid., p. 73.

84 Galtier, op. cit., p. 121.

85 Jean-Marcel Humbert, 'Charles X et l'Égypte', in *Bourbons* magazine, no. 11, January–February 1998.

86 Lacouture, op. cit., p. 38; see also Emmanuel de Las Cases, *Mémorial de Sainte-Hélène*, Seuil, Paris, 1968, p. 67.

87 Lacouture op. cit., p. 333–74.

88 Ibid.

89 Ibid., p. 340.

90 Ibid., p. 324.

91 Faucher, op. cit., p. 73.

92 Lacouture, op. cit., p. 465.

93 Galtier, op. cit., p. 40.

94 Lacouture, op. cit., p. 33.

95 Ibid., p. 190.

96 Lacouture, op. cit., pp. 33 & 549.

97 Lacouture, op. cit., p. 550; Naudon, op. cit., p. 166.

98 Galtier, op. cit., pp. 150–1.

99 Ibid.

100 Ibid.

101 Ibid.

102 This painting can be seen in Room no. 30 in the Sully Wing of the Louvre Museum, the interior of which was designed by the architect Fontaine during the reign of Charles X.

103 Lacouture, op. cit. p. 727.

104 Galtier, op. cit., p. 151.

105 Belzoni is a character well known to British Freemasons. He had married a Englishwoman called Sarah and who, after Belzoni's death, was very active in promoting his Masonic thesis that the Egyptian god, Osiris, had been a 'Freemason' because he was 'clad in the distinctive Masonic apron' as was obvious, at least to Belzoni and his followers, from depictions on many Egyptian monuments (Short, op. cit., p. 118). It was Belzoni, of all people, who was to discover the magnificent tomb of Sethi I, the 'Sesotris' that had been the subject of much Masonic

controversy in England and France. Belzoni, with the help of Henry Salt, had made a full scale facsimile of this temple and had it shipped to Europe in 1818. First to Paris then to London in 1821, where it had made a sensation, especially in Masonic circles (see Morris Bierbrier (ed.), *Who Was Who in Egyptology*, Egypt Exploration Society, London, 1995, pp. 23–4). It is interesting to note, therefore, that Champollion, in March 1829, gave a party inside the Temple of Sethi I in honour of the birthday of his daughter, Zoraide, and also to the 'late Belzoni' (who died in 1825) whom Champollion apparently much admired (See Lacouture, op. cit., p. 661).

106 Lacouture, op. cit., pp. 636 & 668.

107 Ibid., pp. 613 & 618.

108 Ibid., p. 731.

109 Ibid., p. 734

110 Ibid., p. 742.

111 Five of the founders of the Third Republic were Freemasons, including their leader Léon Gambetta (see Faucher, op. cit., pp. 9 & 85.)

112 Faucher, op. cit., p. 8; François Mitterrand is often confused with Jacques Mitterrand who was a Grand Master of *Grand Orient de France* in the 1960s (see Ibid., pp. 169–70).

113 Ibid., p. 275.

114 Reported by BBC News, Africa, 22 December 2000, 16:01 GMT; see also www.ParisMatch.com/news/mit2812/s4page03_self.stm.

115 *The New Louvre*, Publications Connaissance des Arts, Paris, 1989, p. 36.

116 *La Grande Arche*, Publications Beaux Arts, Paris, 1990, p. 3.

117 *The New Louvre*, p. 38.

118 Ibid., p. 36.

119 Ibid.

120 Ibid., p. 38.

121 *Sunday Express*, 3 Feb. 1994, section 3, p. 7.

122 Ibid.

123 *The New Louvre*, p. 44.

124 Kerisel, op. cit., p. 157.

125 Ibid., p. 177.

126 *La Grande Arche*, p. 6.

127 Ibid., p. 19.

128 Ibid., p. 22.

129 Ibid., p. 31.

130 Ibid., p. 19.

131 Ibid., p. 11.

132 Jean Nouvel was born in 1945 at Fumel, a village in the southwest of France. He worked with an architectural firm while attending school. In 1975, he opened his own office and participated in several competitions. Since he opened his office, Nouvel has worked to create a stylistic language separate from that of modernism and post-modernism. Rejecting the strict obedience to Le Corbusier that had stifled much of modern architecture, Nouvel initiates each project with his mind cleared of any preconceived ideas. Although he may borrow from traditional forms, he creates a building that stretches beyond traditional constraints. Nouvel places enormous importance on designing a building harmonious with its site and surroundings. Although Nouvel relies on context to generate his designs, a certain continuum occurs from one design to the next. Within nearly all of his designs, Nouvel consistently presents an interplay of transparency, shadow, and light. In 1981 Jean Nouvel won the competition for a series of 'great projects' requested by François Mitterrand, the French president. In 1987 he was awarded the 'Grand Prix d'Architecture' for his whole body of work and the 'Equerre d'Argent' for his design work on minimalist pieces of furniture. Some of his well-known projects are: The Arab World Institute (Paris, 1987) and the Monolith (Morat, Switzerland, 2002).

133 See *The Guardian*, 21 May 2001: 'There are some buildings that deserve to have been built but never were. Jean Nouvel's Tour Sans Fin is one of them. Designed at the end of the 1980s, this Eiffel Tower-high glazed cylinder was to have risen up from the bombastic banality of La Défense, the vast office quarter at the western end of the Champs-Élysées, only to vanish as it kissed the sky.'

134 Quote from Thomas Paine, 'Origin of Freemasonry', in Moncure Daniel Conway (ed.), *The Writings of Thomas Paine*, G. P. Putnam's Sons, New York, 1896):

> In 1730, Samuel Pritchard, member of a constituted lodge in England, published a treatise entitled 'Masonry Dissected'; and made oath before the Lord Mayor of London that it was a true copy. Samuel Pritchard maketh oath that the copy hereunto annexed is a true and genuine copy of every particular. In his work he has given the catechism or examination, in question and answer, of the Apprentices, the Fellow Craft, and the Master Mason. There was no difficulty in doing this, as it is mere form. In his introduction he says, 'the original institution of Masonry consisted in the foundation of the liberal arts and sciences, but more especially in geometry, for at the building of *the Tower of Babel*, the art and mystery of Masonry was first introduced, and from thence handed down by Euclid, a worthy and excellent mathematician of the Egyptians; and he communicated it to Hiram, the Master Mason concerned in building Solomon's Temple in Jerusalem.'

135 See *New York Observer*, April 13, 2003.

136 Bauval, *Secret Chamber*, updated prologue and epilogue.

137 *Dossiers Histoire et Archéologie*, vol. 101, January 1986

138 Gérard Bauer, *Tableaux Choisis: Paris*, page 41

139 Lacouture, op. cit., Epilogue: 'L'absent Obélisque' by Jean Vidal, p. 731.

CHAPTER NINETEEN: THE CORNERSTONE

1 Ovason, op. cit., p. 76.

2 Ibid.

3 See E. C. Krupp, *In Search of Ancient Astronomies*, Chatto & Windus, London, 1979.

4 Ovason, op. cit., p. 5. For a fuller discussion on this, see also Lockyer, op. cit.

5 Although the 'Isis Fountain of regeneration' ceremony in Paris, which took place on 10 August 1793, was related to a political date, we cannot help being intrigued by the symbolism involved: Isis on throne flanked by lions, gushing water from her nipples. The star Sirius was, on that day, rising at dawn cosmically with the Sun which, at that time, was in Leo. In ancient Egypt the symbolism was clear: the goddess Isis brought the regenerative waters of the Nile's flood at about this time of year. It would seem unlikely that the organisers of this ceremony in Paris were unaware of this connection. As we have already noted elsewhere, the 'propaganda' artist Louis-David had taught symbolism to Picot who, in 1827, painted the Isis on the lion throne in the Louvre.

6 Bullock, op. cit., p. 137.

7 Pick & Knight, op. cit., p. 275.

8 William Adrian Brown, *History of the George Washington Masonic Memorial*, History House, Alexandria, VA, 1980, pp. 8–9.

9 Ibid., p. 56.

10 Ibid., p. 9.

11 Bernard Weisberger, *The Statue of Liberty: The First One Hundred Years*, Horizon Book Promotions, New York, 1988, p. 30; see also James Lloyd, *Beyond Babylon: The Last Week of the World*, Christian Media, Jacksonville, OR, 1995, p. 103.

12 Galtier, op. cit., p. 19.

13 Galtier, op. cit., p. 150.

14 Kerisel, op. cit., p. 176.

15 Ibid., p. 138.

16 Eric Foner & John A. Garraty (eds.), *The Reader's Companion to American History*, Houghton Mifflin, New York, 1991.

17 Mathieu, op. cit., p. 14.

18 Naudon, op. cit., p. 170.

19 Ibid., p. 167.

20 Naudon, op. cit., p. 171.

21 Chevallier, op. cit., vol. II, p. 487.

22 Garibaldi took over from Salvatore Zola, an Italian living in Egypt who was a relative of the famous French novelist Émile Zola. Salvatore Zola had fought with Garibaldi in the 1850s; Later in 1896 Zola resign from Freemasonry and ended his life in a mental hospital; see Galtier, op. cit., p. 153; also see *Dossiers de l'Histore*, 2117 RD 7, pp. 116–9.

23 Weisberger, op. cit., p. 28.

24 Transcipt of photograph available at: www.cobhammasons.org.uk/slplaque.htm.

25 *Freemasonry Today*, 19, January 2002, p. 12.

26 Robert Hieronimus, *Founding Fathers, Secret Societies*, Destiny Books, Rochester, VT, 2006, p. 67.

27 James Wasserman, *The Secrets of Masonic Washington*, Destiny Books, Rochester, VT, 2008, p. 70.

28 See, for example, the presidential Thanksgiving Proclamations by President Benjamin Harrison in 1890, 1891 & 1892 and also by President Grover Cleveland in 1893. Available at: www.pilgrimhall.org/ThanxProc1890.htm.

29 Bauval, *Secret Chamber*, epilogue. See also Robert Lomas & Christopher Knight, *The Second Messiah*, Arrow Books, London, 1998, p. 288. Also in his essay 'Origins of Freemasonry', Thomas Paine was to write these cryptic words: 'The Masons, in order to protect themselves from the persecution of the Christian Church, have always spoken in a mystical manner of the figure of the Sun in their lodges, or, like the astronomer Lalande, who is a Mason, been silent upon the subject.'

30 Skymap Pro 7 used for data source. 5–6 August is for the latitude of Heliopolis (30° north). In New York, which has a latitude of 44.5°, the heliacal rising in 1884 would have been around 12 August. Bartholdi may have opted for the original Egyptian latitude that marked this event. Oddly, we shall again encounter the date of 12 August as we examine the layout of Washington, DC.

31 Martin Isler, 'The Gnomon in Egyptian Antiquity', in *JARCE*, 28, 1991, pp. 167–8. Also M. Isler, 'An Ancient Method of Finding and Extending Directions' in *JARCE*, 26, 1989, pp. 201–2. See also Krupp, *In Search of Ancient Astronomies*, pp. 192–5.

32 Philippa Faulks & Robert L. D. Cooper, *The Masonic Magician: The Life and Death of Count Cagliostro and His Egyptian Rite*, Watkins, London, 2008, pp. 209–15.

33 Ibid., p. 215.

34 Budge, *Cleopatra's Needle and Other Egyptian Obelisks*, p. 166. The two obelisks had originally belonged to Thutmosis III (c. 1550 BC), the great warrior-pharaoh, who is often dubbed the 'Napoleon of 18th

dynasty Egypt' (Martina D'Alton, *The New York Obelisk*, Metropolitan Museum of Art, New York, 1993. p. 3), and had once adorned the Temple of sun-god Atum-Ré in the ancient Anu (On), the 'City of the Sun' (Habachi, op. cit., pp. 165–7). Three others belonging to Thutmosis III had also once stood at the Temple of Amun at Karnak (Budge, *Cleopatra's Needle*, p. 129). On the 'New York' obelisk (erroneously called 'Cleopatra's Needle') the hieroglyphic inscriptions confirm that Pharaoh Thutmosis III (his name literally means 'son of Thoth') was 'governor of Heliopolis' and it was he who had it made these two obelisk for his 'father', Atum-Ré, the 'Lord of Heliopolis' (Budge, *Cleopatra's Needle*, p. 172).

35   D'Alton, op. cit., pp. 42–4; also see Habachi, op. cit.; see also Budge's *Cleopatra's Needle and Other Egyptian Obelisks*.

36   Bauval & Gilbert, *The Orion Mystery*, epilogue.

37   Richard Noone, *5/5/2000, Ice: The Ultimate Disaster*, Three Rivers Press, New York, 1982, p. 19.

38   D'Alton, op. cit., p. 41–2.

39   Ibid., p. 12.

40   Pick & Knight, op. cit., p. 331; see also Bauval, *Secret Chamber*, p. 185.

41   Galtier, op. cit., 429–31.

42   Ibid., p. 153.

43   Ibid., p. 152.

44   Noone, op. cit., p. 19.

45   Ibid., p. 20; see also D'Alton, op. cit., p. 27.

46   D'Alton, op. cit., p. 27.

47   Ibid., p. 10.

48   Ibid., p. 42.

49   Ibid., p. 44.

50   Ibid., p. 25.

51   Susan Coolidge, *A Short History of the City of Philadelphia From its Foundation to the Present Time*, Arden Press, 1880, chapter 3. It has also been suggested that Penn was inspired by a utopic renaissance city plan by Cataneao in 1567, although this seems unlikely.

52   Ovanson, op. cit., p. 41.

53   See Thomas Paine, 'Origins of Freemasonry', in *The Writings of Thomas Paine*.

54   Ibid.

55   Using Starry Night Pro 4, for epoch 1683. The dates given are Gregorian. In Britain and the colonies they were still using the Julian calendar, even though it had been introduced in 1582 by the Vatican. It is possible that the Quakers also used the solar/Gregorian at that time.

56   Thomas Holme, *Portrait of the City of Philadelphia*, 1683.

57   *The Pennsylvania Freemason*, vol. 43, May 1996, no. 2.

58   Transcript of photograph available at: www.remarkableohio.org/HistoricalMarker.aspx?historicalMarkerId=152&fileId=128046.

59   Naudon, op. cit., p. 181. The St. John's Lodge in Boston is often cited as being the first to have formal documentation to prove its origin.

60   Pick & Knight, op. cit., p. 271.

61   Ibid.

62   Ridley, op. cit., p. 92.

63   Baltrušaitis, op. cit., pp. 201–8.

64   Paine, op. cit.

65   Ibid.

66   Naudon, op. cit., p. 32.

67   Ibid., p. 81.

68   Ibid.

69   Debû-Bridel, op. cit., p. 27.

70   Ibid., p. 29.

71   Connecticut Society of the Sons of the American Revolution, 'Washington–Rochambeau Revolutionary Route Newsletter', no. 38, available: at http://www.connecticutsar.org/about/rev-road/news38.htm.

72   Naudon, op. cit., p. 198.

73   See www.scottishrite.org/foundations/house-of-the-temple-foundation/about-the-temple.

74   Albert Pike, *Morals And Dogmas of the Ancient And Accepted Scottish Rite of Freemasonry*, prepared for the Supreme Council of the 33rd Degree for the Southern Jurisdiction of the United States, Charleston, SC, 1871, p. 486.

75   Ibid., p. 136.

76   Ibid., p. 506.

77   Ibid.

78   Ibid.

79   Ibid., p. 376.

80   Rex R. Hutchens, *Albert Pike – The Man Not The Myth*, address to the Supreme Council of the 33rd Degree for the Southern Jurisdiction, 17 October 1989.

81   Pike, op. cit.

82   Robert Temple, *The Sirius Mystery*, Century, London, 1998, p. 404.

83   Pike, op. cit., p. 18.

84   Homer, *Iliad*, book XXII.

85   Apollonius Rhodius, *Argonautica*, 2.518ff & 3.958ff.

86   Aratus, *Phaenomena*, 328.

87   *Encyclopaedia Britannica*, vol. 9, p. 65.

88   See *The Scottish Rite Journal* at: srjarchives.tripod.com/1998-03/beless.htm.

89   Ibid.

90   Ibid.

91   Paine eventually shipped the key to George Washington, and it is now displayed at Washington's home in Mount Vernon.

92 Baltrušaitis, op. cit., pp. 52–3.

93 Court de Gébelin, op. cit.

94 Hall, *Rosicrucian and Masonic Origins*, pp. 408–9.

95 The 'path' are obtained by adding the 22 letters of the Hebrew alphabet to the ten Sephiroth. See Chapter 14.

96 Lobingier, op. cit., p. 4.

97 *Theosophy Magazine*, vol. 27, no. 2, December 1938

98 Thomas Edison, 'The Philosophy of Paine', 7 June 1925, in Dagobert D. Runes (ed.), *The Diary and Sundry Observations of Thomas Alva Edison*, Philosophical Library, New York, 1948.

99 See article by David Cody, associate professor of English, Hartwick College available at: http://www.victorianweb.org/history/hist7.html. William Blake had just completed his poem 'The French Revolution' and was already nurturing his poetic vision of turning the England and the city of London into a 'New Jerusalem'. Although Blake himself was not a Freemason, he nonetheless produced the famous etching of the 'Supreme Being' as the 'Great Architect' of creation wielding his compass in the act of creation that Masonic publications are so fond of.

100 We are indebted to Ms Mimi Murray, a graduate of John Hopkins University, for making available to us her college major's thesis on Pierre-Charles L'Enfant.

101 Library of Congress, *The George Washington Papers*, available at: memory.loc.gov/ammem/gwhtml/gwhome.html.

102 The Society of the Cincinnati was formed on 13 May 1783 at the Verplanck House in Fishkill, New York. The first chapters were limited to the 13 colonies in America and France. The society was mostly the idea of Major-General Henry Knox, commander of the Continental army artillery and America's first secretary of war. Knox was secretary-general of the society under George Washington, who remained president until his death in 1799. Eligibility in the society was offered to officers who had served in the war. Of the 6,000 or so officers that were eligible, only 2,403 joined, mostly coming from the Delaware area. About 250 French officers also decided to join.

103 Tim Page, 'The Cincinnati: A Society That's In the Blood', *Washington Post*, 13 December 2001, p. C01; Later other presidents who have belonged to the Cincinnati include Jackson, Taylor, Pierce, Buchanan, Grant, Cleveland, Benjamin Harrison, McKinley, Theodore Roosevelt, Franklin D. Roosevelt, Taft, Wilson, Harding, Hoover and Truman. the organization's headquarters is at the splendid 50-roomed Anderson House at 2118 Massachusetts Avenue NW, Cincinnati. It's last original member died in New York in 1854, and today the society is still only open to direct descendants of the original members.

104 Bullock, op. cit., p. 130.

105 Jean-Jules Jusserand was also a Pulitzer Prize Winner for History in 1917.

106 From Jean Jules Jusserand, *With Americans of Past and Present Days*, Charles Scribner's Sons, New York, 1916.

107 See *The Journal of Andrew Ellicott*, Budd & Bartram, Philadelphia, 1803.

108 H. Paul Caemmerer, *The Life of Pierre Charles L'Enfant*, Da Capo Press, New York, 1950, p. 135.

109 Ibid., p. 167.

110 Ellicott did, however, change the alignment of Massachusetts Avenue and deleted some five short radial avenues. He also added two short radial avenues to the southeast and southwest of the US Capitol as well as participated in the naming of the streets.

111 Baigent & Leigh, *The Temple and the Lodge*, p. 262; Ovason, op. cit., pp. 42–3.

112 First printed edition of the L'Enfant plan, G3850 1792 L4 Vault.

113 *The Universal Asylum and Columbian Magazine*, March 1793, pp. 155–6; published in Philadelphia by William Young, Bookseller, No. 52 Second-Street, the corner of Chestnut-Street. A larger print of this map had, in fact, already been published several months earlier the November 1792 by Thackara and Vallance. The same map also appeared on facing the title page of *Observations on the River Potomack, the Country adjacent and the City of Washington* by Tobias Lear, and printed by Samuel Loudon & Son, No. 5 Water-Street in New York in 1793.

114 Available at: www.census.gov/population/www/popclockus.html & www.census.gov/population/www/projections/natproj.html.

115 Ovason, op. cit., p. 42.

116 Ibid., p. 83.

117 Although it is generally said that it was the André Le Nôtre design of Versailles and not Paris that influenced L'Enfant, the similarity of the main axial layout of Washington, DC with Paris is uncanny and too striking to be ignored. See *Washington Architecture 1791–1957*, prepared by a committee of the Washington-Metropolitan Chapter American Institute of Architects, Reinhold Publishing Corporation, New York, 1957, pp. 5 & 36.

118 Robert Cameron, *Above Washington: A Collection of Nostalgic and Contemporary Aerial Photographs of the District of Columbia*, Cameron & Company, San Francisco, 1979, plate on p. 81

119 Ibid., plate on p. 42.

120 This new Exchange was also destroyed by fire in 1838. The present Royal Exchange was built in 1842–44, and apparently cost

£150,000 at the time.

121 Taken from *The Last Will and Testament of Sir Thomas Gresham*, published in London 1765.

122 Lomas, op. cit., p. 292.

123 Tinniswood, op. cit., p. 150.

124 MS. Ashmole 242, f. 78; see C. H. Josten (ed.), *Elias Ashmole (1617–1692) His Autobiographical and Historical Notes, His Correspondence and Other Contemporary Sources relating to his Life and Works*, Oxford University Press, London, 1966, vol. 3, pp. 1 & 112. This entry by Elias Ashmole is accompanied by an astrological horoscope and inscribed notes by the astrologer William Lilly (see Annabella Kitson (ed.), *History of Astrology*, Mandala-Unwin Paperbacks, London, 1989, p. 200).

125 *Elias Ashmole*, vol. 4.

126 *History of Astrology*, pp. 199–204.

127 MS. Ashmole 1136, f. 53; cited in *Elias Ashmole*, vol. 4, pp. 1 & 432.

128 *History of Astrology*, p. 199–200.

129 It would not be until 1752 that the Gregorian calendar was introduced in England.

130 See: en.wikipedia.org/wiki/Conversion_ between_Julian_and_Gregorian_ calendars and converter at www.fourmilab. ch/documents/calendar.

131 Apparently the Declaration of Independence was voted by Congress on 2 July 1776 and only agreed unanimously on 4 July. It was then read out publicly on 8 July. See Ovason, op. cit., pp. 142–3. Note 23 June 1776 (Julian) converts to 4 July 1776 (Gregorian).

132 For a full discussion as to why Virgo was significant to Washington, DC, see Ovason, op. cit., appendix, pp. 357–91.

133 Ibid., p. 379.

134 A very critical review of Ovason's 'astrological' theory for Washington, DC has been published by the author Michael Baigent in *Freemasonry Today* (vol. 15, 1999). In a private conversation with Baigent during the writing of this book, he informed Bauval that Ovason's knowledge of astrology seemed very poor, and there were many mistakes in his book. There are, too, several astronomical errors. But in spite of this, Ovason's detailed and meticulous research into the documentation and records of the event surrounding the design and building of Washington, DC is excellent, and was most useful to us in the writing of this book.

135 Ovason, op. cit., p. 118.

136 The only surviving record of this very important Masonic ceremony is in a short unanimous letter printed in one of the Charleston newspapers when the Georgetown Lodge No. 9 of Maryland gathered on the site for the cornerstone ceremony on Saturday, 13 October 1792. The cornerstone was laid on the southwest corner of the president's house (later to be called the White House, by virtue of it being painted white after being scorched by fire in 1814 by the British artillery guns).

137 According to Ovason's observation of the setting sun on 12 August along Pennsylvania avenue, the axis would have to be between 20–22°, depending on the height of the observer. Ovason recognised this in his notes (see Ovason, op. cit., p. 456, note 69). This fact was verified for us on 11–12 August 2003 by David Hudgins, Ph.D., CFM, University of Oklahoma, who took a digital photograph of the event.

138 This happens almost every day of the year, except for about 2 ½ months when this star is not visible at night. David Ovanson thinks that the alignment from the White House to the Capitol (i.e. along Pennsylvania Avenue) was deliberately designed to point at the setting sun (Ovanson, op. cit., p. 337). Considering that Ovason makes a strong case that the five-pointed 'Egyptian' star symbol of Sirius was integrated into the fabric of the Declaration of Independence and the 'cornerstone ceremony' of the Washington Monument (the Egyptian-style obelisk), it is curious, to say the least, that he did not realise the significance of the stellar alignment to Sirius of the White House-US Capitol axis along Pensylvania Avenue.

139 Ovason, op. cit., p. 337.

140 Ibid., p. 456, note 69. Not knowing, however, from what vantage height Ellicott and L'Enfant made their observations, Ovason decided to establish his solar alignment by direct observations from 6–12 August.

141 Ovason, op. cit., pp. 47 & 58.

142 Ibid., p. 127.

143 Ibid.

144 Tompkins, *The Magic of Obelisks*, p. 322–9.

145 Ovason, op. cit., p. 129.

146 Quote in Ibid., p. 87 from Lalande, op. cit., vol. 1., p. 245.

147 According to StarryNight Pro 4, this event took place at about 4 p.m.

148 Ovason, op. cit., p. 137.

149 Naudon, op. cit., p. 79.

150 The Pentagon was conceived at the request of Brigadier-General Brehon B. Sommervell, chief of the Construction Division of the Office of the Quartermaster General, on a weekend in mid-July 1941. The purpose was to provide a temporary solution to the War Department's critical shortage of space. The building was dedicated on 15 January 1943, nearly 16 months to the day after the ground breaking.

151 See: pentagon.afis.osd.mil/construction. html and also: pentagon.afis.osd.mil/ facts-area.html.

152 Cameron, op. cit., p. 32.

153 Franklin D. Roosevelt's vice-president, Harry Truman, received the degrees in Belton Lodge No. 450; organized and became a charter member of Grandview No. 618. He served in France as a captain in the US Army in WWI. Served as both district lecturer and Deputy Grand Master for several years. He was elected Grand Master of Masons in Missouri in 1940. He always claimed this was the greatest honour that had ever come to him. He received the first Gourgas Medal of the Scottish Rite, NMJ, granted while he was serving as a Senator. He worked for servicemen and women through The Masonic Service Association during World War II. Elected vice-president in 1944 and became president on the death of Franklin D. Roosevelt (a Mason) on 12 April 1945. He died on 26 December 1972. On 28 December he was buried on his library's grounds with impressive rites. These included the only Masonic funeral service ever televised worldwide.

154 Cameron, op. cit., p. 117.

155 See C. Knight & A. Butler, *Before The Pyramids*, Watkins Publishers, London, 2009, p. 194.

156 Ibid., p. 247.

157 Bauval, *Secret Chamber*, chapter 7.

158 Available at: www.trumanlibrary.org/ photos/israel.jpg. Also see www. trumanlibrary.org/israel/palestin.htm.

EPILOGUE: THE MASTER GAME
CHAPTER TWENTY: THE DAY THAT SHOOK THE WORLD

1 A. Millar, 'Freemasonry in the Mind of the Islamist', Hudson New York, available at: www.hudson-ny.org/421/freemasonry-in-the-mind-of-the-islamist.

2 'Turkey blasts: Claims of al-Qaeda', *Mail & Guardian*, 20 November 2003, available at: http://www.mg.co.za/article/2003-11-20-turkey-blasts-claims-of-alqaeda.

3 Johann Hari, 'What I discovered inside Finsbury Park Mosque', *The Independent*, 22 January 2003, available at: www.independent.co.uk/opinion/commentators/johann-hari/what-i-discovered-inside-finsbury-park-mosque-602412.html.

4 'Istanbul bomb attack kills one', BBC News, 10 March 2004, available at: news.bbc.co.uk/2/hi/europe/3548433.stm.

5 'Al-Qaida 'not to blame' for Istanbul bombing', *The Guardian*, 10 March 2004, available at: http://www.guardian.co.uk/world/2004/mar/10/alqaida.turkey.

6 Available at: www.freemasonry.bcy.ca/anti-masonry/saudi_gazette.html.

7 'Can a Muslim Be a Freemason?', *Islam Online*, available at: www.islamonline.net/servlet/Satellite?pagename=IslamOnline-English-Ask_Scholar/FatwaE/FatwaEAskTheScholar&cid=1119503547288.

8 Robert S. Wistrich, 'The New Islamic Fascism', available at: www.jerusalem-en.sitecity.ru/ltext_2606062955.phtml?p_id ent=ltext_2606062955.p_2606064631.

9 Available at: http://english.aljazeera.net/archive/2004/03/20084914326902740.html.

10 'Ex-Georgia Tech Student convicted on terrorism charge', CNN, 10 June 2009, available at: http://edition.cnn.com/2009/CRIME/06/10/georgia.terror.trial/index.html.

11 There is still much popularity of the *Protocols of the Elders of Zion* in some nations of South America (recently published in Spanish in 2006 in Mexico) and Asia, but since the end of WWII political leaders in other parts of the world have rejected the notion that the *Protocols* represent a factual Jewish conspiracy. In the Middle East, however, many Arab and Muslim regimes and leaders have claimed them as being real. The *Protocols* were endorsed from Presidents Gamal Abdel Nasser and Anwar Sadat of Egypt, to King Faisal of Saudi Arabia and Colonel Gaddafi of Libya. Recently political and intellectual leaders in the Arab world who endorse the *Protocols*, and are supported by influential personages such as the Grand Mufti of Jerusalem, Sheikh Ekrima Said Sabri, and organizations such as Hamas, as well as the Ministry of Education of Saudi Arabia.

12 The history of the concepts found in the *Protocols* was traced back to the works of Herrmann Ottomar Friedrich Goedsche (aka Sir John Retcliffe) and Jacques Cretinéau-Joly by Lucien Wolf, and English journalist who published his findings in London in August 1921. A damning exposé was also given in a series of articles in the *Times* on 16–18 August 1921. The newspaper's Istanbul correspondent, Philip Graves, demonstrated clearly the plagiarism from Cretinéau-Joly's work. The *New York* Times also reprinted the articles on 4 September 1921.

13 Steven Simon is the award-winning co-author of *The Age of Sacred Terror* (Floris Books, Edinburgh, 2002) and author of *The Next Attack* (Times Books, New York, 2005). His current work examines the consequences of the American intervention in Iraq, Muslim and non-Muslim relations, and the role of religion in US foreign policy.

14 Cited in A. Millar, op. cit.

15 '2008 Update: Saudi Arabia's Curriculum of Intolerance', published by the Center for Religious Freedom of Hudson Institute with the Institute for Gulf Affairs, PDF available at: www.hudson.org/files/publications/saudi_textbooks_final.pdf.

16 The original thrust of the creation of the state of Israel in 1948 had begun with the so-called *Balfour Declaration* on 2 November 1917. Arthur James Balfour (1848–1930) was the British Statesman who maintained a position of great power

within the Conservative Party for 50 years. He was prime minister from 1902 to 1905 and foreign secretary from 1916 to 1919. Many Masonic researchers believe that Lord Balfour was a Freemason, but United Grand Lodge denies this. At any rate, After being prompted by Zionist leaders Chaim Weizmann and Nahum Sokolow, Balfour wrote to Baron Rothchild, leading finacier in England and head of the Zionist movement in UK. His famous letter from the Foreign Office is typed on plain paper:

Dear Lord Rothchild,

I have much pleasure in conveying to you. on behalf of his Majesty's Government, the following declaration of sympathy with Jewish Zionist aspirations which has been submitted to, and approved by, the Cabinet.

His Majesty's Government views with favour the establishment in Palestine of a national home for the Jewish people, and will use their best endevours to facilitate the achievement of this object, it being clearly understood that nothing shall be done which may prejudice the civil and religious rights of existing non-Jewish communities in Palestine, or the rights and political status enjoyed by Jews in any other country.

I should be grateful if you would bring this declaration to the knowledge of the Zionist Federation.

Yours, Arthur James Balfour

17   The Knights Templar is the final order joined in the York Rite. It does not deal with the Hiram Abiff legend. Unlike all other Masonic orders which accept members regarless of their faith, membership in the Knights Templar is open only to Freemasons who are Christians. This body is modeled off of the historical Knights Templar to carry the 'spirit of their organization'. It has been claimed that Freemasonry was founded by the Knights Templar or that the Knights Templar, after their persecution in 1312–4, took refuge in Freemasonry. The Grand Encampment of the United States, which regulates Masonic-Templars, acknowledges these theories but says there is no evidence to justify them. A local Knights Templar division is called a 'commandery' and is governed at state level by a Grand Commandery as well as the Grand Encampment of the United States. The Knights Templar confer three orders, and one passing order as opposed to the standard degree system found in regular Freemasonry:

The Illustrious Order of the Red Cross

The Passing Order of St. Paul, (or Mediterranean Pass)

The Order of the Knights of Malta (or simply Order of Malta)

The Order of the Temple

18   Available for download at: http://www.knightstemplar.org/KnightTemplar/Magazine/2010/0810.pdf.

19   The 'Father of Zionism' is regarded as Theodore Herzl (1860–1904). At the First Zionist Congress in Basel in 1897, which was masterminded by Herzl, he founded the World Zionist Organization. He died before seeing his vision of a Jewish state in Palestine become a reality. In 1949 his remains were brought to Jerusalem and buried in 'Mound Herzl' cemetery. Many Israeli leaders such a Golda Meir and Levi Eshkol are also buried in this cemetery. Herzl's family seemed to have been plagued by terrible tragedies: Herzl wife Julia suffered from mental instability; his eldest daughter, Pauline. was a heroine addict and died at the age of 40 from an overdose in a French hospital. His son, Hans, shot himself when he found out about his sister's death. His other daughter, Trude, was to die in the Nazi concentration camp. Her son, Stephen Theodore Norman (born Stephen Neumann), on learning of his family's extermination in the death camps, committed suicide in November 1946 by jumping off the Massachusetts Avenue bridge in Washington, DC. He was only 27.

20   See Robert Rockaway 'FDR's Plan For a Jewish State in Palestine', *Israel Insider*, 25 December 2002; see also Robert H. Abzug, *America Views the Holocaust 1933–1945: A Brief Documentary History*, St. Martin's, New York, 1999, pp. 134–5.

21   'The Declaration of The Establishment of The State of Israel', 14 May 1948, available at: http://www.mfa.gov.il/MFA/Peace%20Process/Guide%20to%20the%20Peace%20Process/Declaration%20of%20Establishment%20of%20State%20of%20Israel.

22   Ibid.

23   Clark Clifford is often said to have been the real influence on Truman on this matter. But in the words of Clifford himself, 'President Truman said he would like me to prepare the case for the formation of a Jewish homeland as if it were a case to be presented to the Supreme Court'.

24   Available at: http://www.trumanlibrary.org/photos/israel.jpg. Also see www.trumanlibrary.org/israel/palestin.htm.

25   Cliford's memoirs were written in two parts with Richard Holbrooke. The first part was published in the *New Yorker* magazine of 25 March 1991 and covered events from 1944 to Truman's recognize of Israel in May 1948. See Clark Clifford and Richard Holbrooke, 'Serving the President I –The Truman Years', *New Yorker*, 25 March 1991, archived at www.newyorker.com/archive/1991/03/25/1991_03_25_040_TNY_CARDS_000354728.

26   Richard H. Curtiss, 'Truman Adviser Recalls May 14,1948 US Decision to

Recognize Israel', *Washington Report on Middle East Affairs*, May/June 1991, p. 17, available at: http://www.wrmea.com/backissues/0591/9105017.htm.

27 Ibid.

28. Ibid.

29. Ibid.

30. Ibid.

31. Ibid.

32. Ibid.

33 Ironically, Clifford later served as lawyer for Arab businessmen and served as director of a bank (First American Banshares, but said to have been controlled by Bank of Commerce and Credit International – BCCI) they illegally took over, and has faced legal problems because of this in the 1980s. Indictment against him were put aside because of his failing health. Clifford died in October 1998.

34 Imam's message announcing *Quds* Day, dated 7 August 1979 (16 Murdad 1358 AHS), *Sahifa-yi Nur*, vol. 8, p. 229.

35 Imam's message dated 16 August 1979 (25 Murdad 1358 AHS), *Sahifa-yi Nur*, vol. 8, pp. 233–234.

36 Imam's remarks dated 9 August 1980 (18 Murdad 1359 AHS), *Sahifa-yi Nur*, vol. 12, p. 282.

37 In the event, the Masonic Bible was never used due apparently to a fear that it be damaged by bad weather conditions on the day George W. Bush took the presidential oath.

38 George. W. Bush, 'Remarks by the President Upon Arrival', 16 September 2001, available at: http://georgewbush-whitehouse.archives.gov/news/releases/2001/09/20010916-2.html.

39 George. W. Bush, 'President Rallies the Troops in Alaska', 16 Febraury 2002, available at: http://georgewbush-whitehouse.archives.gov/news/releases/2002/02/20020216-1.html.

40 Alexander Cockburn, 'The Tenth Crusade', *Counterpunch*, 7 September 2002, available at: http://www.counterpunch.org/cockburn0907.html.

41 James Pinkerton, 'Century In, Century Out – It's Crusade Time' *Newsday*, 4 December 2003, available at: www.newamerica.net/publications/articles/2003/century_in_century_out_its_crusade_time.

42 'Al-Qaeda Threatens Christians, Egypt's Muslim Brotherhood: Protect Churches', *Saudi Telegraph*, 3 November 2010, available at: www.sauditelegraph.com/news/newsfull.php?newid=434859.

43 'Al-Qaeda claims Iraq church attack', Al Jazeera, 2 November 2010, available at: english.aljazeera.net/news/middleeast/2010/11/201011134724982931.html.

44 'As deadline for Egypt's Coptic church expires Qaeda group says Christians *legitimate*

targets', Al Arabiya News, 3 November 2010, available at: www.alarabiya.net/articles/2010/11/03/124713.html.

45 Robert Fisk, 'Exodus. The changing map of the Middle East', *Independent*, 26 Oct 2010, available at: www.independent.co.uk/opinion/commentators/fisk/robert-fisk-exodus-the-changing-map-of-the-middle-east-2116463.html.

46 M. Chulov & E. Ibrahim, 'Christians in Iraq living in fear of 'pogrom' after bomb attacks', *Guardian*, 12 November 2010, available at: www.guardian.co.uk/world/2010/nov/12/christians-iraq-living-fear-pogrom.

47 Cam McGrath, 'Egyptian Government Shunts Responsibility For Attacks on Coptic Christians', Inter Press Service, 6 January 2011, available at: www.alternet.org/belief/149423/egyptian_government_shunts_responsibility_for_attacks_on_coptic_christians.

48 Interview with Lucy-Anne Hunt, 'From the Crusaders to Al Qaida', Humboldt Foundation website, available at: www.humboldt-foundation.de/web/1353.html.

APPENDIX: THE GREAT PYRAMID AND FREEMASONRY

1 Translated by author. Image available at: http://myblog.robertbauval.co.uk/__oneclick_uploads/2011/05/img_2757a.jpg.

2 Curiously, a relative of Émile Zola, a certain Salvatore Zola, was a prominent Freemason in Egypt in the 1800s and, of all things, was assigned by the Khedive Muhammad Ali to help the Americans remove an obelisk from Alexandria to New York's Central Park.

3 He was born Hiram Ulysses Grant, but always called Ulysses, his middle name, by his friends. Hiram was, and still is, a popular Masonic name (from Hiram Abiff, the legendary 'architect' of Solomon's Temple in Masonic rituals). This choice of name was clearly intended as a Masonic label, since Ulysses' father, Jesse Brant, had been Master Mason of a prominent lodge in Ohio.

4 Although there is controversy whether General William T. Sherman was a Freemason, his own father, Charles Robert Sherman, certainly was a senior Freemason, as confirmed by his Masonic apron located by the Ohio Historical Society. It is widely believed that Gen. Sherman spared prisoners who wore Masonic rings during the Civil War. The bringing of the Egyptian obelisk to New York's Central Park in 1880 was clearly a Masonic event. It is also interesting to note that it was Gen. Sherman who selected the site of Bedloe's Island (now Liberty Island) for the placing of the Statue Of Liberty in 1884, the latter clearly another Masonic event. William H. Herbert, the chief editor of the *New York World* newspaper, is often given credit for

being the first to suggest to Khedive Isma'il that the obelisk should be donated to the United States. He got the financial backing from a prominent Freemason, William H. Vanderbilt who, in turn got the political support from of Rep. Henry G. Stebbins, New York's commissioner of public parks. It was Stebbins who petitioned the US Secretary of State, William M. Evarts, to personally write to Elbert Farman, the American consul-general in Egypt, to persuade the Khedive of Egypt to donate the obelisk to the US. Let us note in passing that William M. Evarts was also chairman of the Committee for the Statue of Liberty in 1883–4 and it was he who sent a formal invitation to the Grand Masonic Lodge of New York to organize a ceremony "appropriate for the Occasion." See Willam C. Kiesel's article in the September 1983 issue of *The Masonic Philalesist*; also J. E. Bebrens's article in October 1983 issue of *Knight Templar* magazine.

5   On his way to the Mediterranean during a 2-year survey with the *Gettysburg*, Gorringe and a fellow Freemason, Lieutenant Seaton Schoeder, used equipment to measure depth and with 'snagged the top of a submerged mountain in the Atlantic Ocean which they claimed was the 'Lost Atlantis', and received a congratulatory telegram from President Grant for this 'discovery' (See D'Alton, op. cit., p. 10).

6   The important symbolic aspect of an obelisk is not its tall stem but its top which is shaped like a small pyramid, which feature very prominently in Masonic rituals.

7   See www.robertbauval.co.uk/articles/articles/hawass1.html.

8   Ibid.

9   Ibid.

10 Ibid.

11 See Bauval, *Secret Chamber,* Chapter 8.

12 Interview with *Ros al-Yusuf,* 'Israel is Robbing the Pyramids as it Robbed Palestine', 5 May 1997.

13 Ibid. Hawass was referring to Robert Bauval, Graham Hancock and John Anthony West.

14 See www.robertbauval.co.uk/articles/articles/hawass1.html.

15 Memri TV: Arabic Video, English Transcript. Rroadcast on 11 February 2009, available at: http://www.memritv.org/clip/en/2049.htm. During the writing of this book, the History Channel aired a five episode TV documentary titled *Chasing Mummies* featuring Dr. Zahi Hawass. Paradoxically, In episode 4 shown on 4 August 2010, former First Lady Barbara Bush introduced Hawass to an adoring American audience:"I'm thrilled to introduce the foremost scholar of Ancient Egypt ... it is my pleasure to welcome a great explorer."

16 Kevin Myers, 'The anti-Semite Farouk Hosni is, in fact, the forward-looking face of enlightened Arabia', *Independent,* 24 Sept. 2009.

17 Michael Slackman, 'Egypt Ponders Failed Drive for Unesco', *New York Times,* 28 Sept. 2009.

INDEX

George III, King of Great Britain and Ireland, 465

George Washington Masonic National Monument, 31–32, 497–498

Georgetown, 519, 530

German Protestant Union, 309, 312

Germany, 20, 37, 40, 64, 82, 159, 261, 264, 275–276, 297–299, 302–303, 307–315, 318, 320, 325, 340, 347, 368–369, 382, 402, 413, 433–436, 465, 524, 555

Gerôme, Léon, 499

Gesù, Il, 383

Giovane Italia (Young Italy), 501

Giza, 77, 196, 239, 251, 383, 434, 455, 463, 469, 484, 486, 489–490, 547

glass pyramid (Louvre), 17, 415, 420, 485, 487, 489, 492

Gleichen, Baron von, 460

Gnosis, 5–6, 39, 69, 76–77, 98, 102, 107–108, 112, 115–116, 118, 124, 168, 198, 213, 215, 218, 250–251, 258–259, 265, 305–306

Gnosticism, 40, 47, 70, 85, 88, 105–109, 111, 114–119, 127–128, 130, 137–138, 176–177, 220, 222, 256, 259, 318, 336, 373, 378, 385, 406 *see also* Bogomilism; Catharism

Gobel, Jean-Baptiste-Joseph, 452

God: God of Evil/Darkness; God of Good/Light, 3, 14, 24–25, 37–38, 46–48, 55, 59–62, 72–86, 89, 91, 93–97, 99–102, 104–105, 111–118, 120, 127–129, 133, 136, 141–145, 151, 161–162, 169, 175, 177, 185, 191–194, 199–200, 205–229, 232–235, 238–240, 243–247, 250–253, 257–258, 283, 290–291, 299–306, 313, 320–322, 325–327, 331, 346–347, 350, 354, 359–360, 366–370, 378–382, 389–391, 405–408, 422, 442–445, 452–453, 456, 463, 466, 481, 485, 496, 503–506, 520–521, 544, 550–554, 557, 565–566, 570–571 *see also* Cult of the Supreme Being; Jehovah

Godechot, Jacques, 19

Godwin, Joscelyn, 115, 314, 381, 431

Goethe, Johann Wolfgang von, 429

Golarian, William, 167

Gorringe, Henry Honychurch, 508–509, 574

Gospel of Philip, 110

Gospel of Thomas, 109–110, 134

Gospel of Truth, 110

Gospel to the Egyptians, 110

Got, Raymond Bertrand de, 369 *see* Pope Clement V

Gotthelf, Karl, 413 *see* Hund, Baron von

Gourdot, Paul, 441, 456

Gracechurch Street, London, 392

Grande Cours project, Paris, 352

Grand Lodge of England, 20–21, 24–25, 331, 347, 395–397, 402–405, 407–408, 410, 498, 536 *see also* United Grand Lodge of England

Grand Lodge of Pennsylvania, 408, 513

Grand Orient de France, 19, 410–411, 414, 417, 430–431, 435–436, 441, 456, 468–469, 485, 501, 508

Grand Royal Arch Chapter of Scotland, 407–408

Grande Arche de la Fraternité, 485, 487–493, 575

Grande Loge de France, 397 *see* Grand Orient

Grant, Jacques le, 418

Grant, President Ulysses S., 502, 509

Grasse, Count-Admiral de, 23, 517

Gravier, Charles, 517

Great Architect, 18, 24–25, 30, 102–103, 234–235, 348, 352–353, 382, 405, 455–456, 484–486, 488, 509, 512, 533, 540

Great Bear (Ursa Major), 201–202

Great Council of Florence (1439), 181–182

Great Fire of London, 354, 357, 385–389, 532–534, 545

Great Fire of Rome, 120

Great Seal of the United States, 30–31, 434, 455–456, 504, 541, 576

Greaves, John, 383–384

Greece/Greeks, 40, 52–53, 83, 96, 115, 137, 182, 203, 223–228, 230, 233–237, 239, 243, 249–250, 253, 255–256, 272, 329, 348, 448, 471, 482

Greek language, 182, 253, 256

Greeley, Horace, 502

Greenough, Horatio, 532

Gregorian calendar, 27, 395, 506, 535–536

Gregorius, Master, 349

Gregory IX, Pope, 159–160, 163, 170

Gregory XIV, Pope, 190,

Grenoble 478–479, 483

Grenville, John, 340

Gresham, Thomas, 384, 392, 533–534

Gresham College, London, 342, 346, 383–384, 388, 533

Guénon, René, 431

Gui, Bernard, 169

Guicciardini, Francesco, 180

Guillotin, Joseph-Ignace, 439, 442, 524

Guimard, Paul, 485

Guirdham, Arthur, 51, 56, 148, 374, 385

Guise, Count of 264, 275

Guitaut, 291

Gulf of Riga, 330

Gurdjieff, G. I., 431

Guyon, Madame, 397–398

Guzmán, Father Dominic de, 155 *see* Dominic, Saint

H

Haak, Theodore, 335–336, 342

Habert de Montmor, Henri Louis, 343, 353

Hadrian, Emperor, 255

Haggia, 406

Hague, the, 342, 414

Halicarnassus, 520

Halim Pasha, Prince, 508

Hall, Manly P., 430

Hamilton, Alexander, 529

Hamilton, Bernard, 89, 92, 104, 118, 170

Hamilton, Janet, 89

Hancock, John, 22

Hapsburgs, 264, 309–310, 312–313

Harding, President Warren, 567

Harran, 196, 203, 373

Hart, George, 245–246

Hart, Vaughan, 389

Hartlib, Samuel, 335–337, 341

Harvard University, 110

Hassan, Selim, 196

Hathor, 236, 251

Haussez, Baron of, 483

Headley, John, 282, 284–286

Hearers (Manichean), 103–104, 118

Hébert, Jacques-René, 444, 449, 451

Hébertists, 444, 452

Hebrew, 180, 189–192, 326, 357, 378, 381–383, 407, 557

Hebrew University of Jerusalem, 553

Hecataeus of Abdera, 228

Heidelberg, 309–312

Heidelberg University, 309

Heisler, Ron, 330

Heka, 250–251

Helen, Empress, 238

Helen of Troy, 234–236, 467

Halicarnassus, 520

Heliopolis (Anu; *On*), 204, 229, 232, 240, 244, 249–253, 274, 348–351, 407–410, 423, 476, 506–508, 515–516

Helios, 230, 238–239, 242

Helvétius, Anne Catherine, 23, 517

Helvétius, Claude Adrien, 23, 517

Helmle & Corbett, 498

Henderson, Peter, 408

Henrietta, Princess, 436

Henrietta Maria, Queen, 333, 339

Henry II, King of France, 262, 264, 314, 346

Henry III, King of France 262–264, 267–269, 275, 286–287, 292, 400

Henry IV, King of France (Henry of Navarre), 262–265, 275, 286–288, 309, 311, 314

Henry Sinclair, Prince, 371–372

Heracles, 243–244

Heraclius, Patriarch of Jerusalem, 366–367, 386

Herakleion, 243–244

Hermes, 3, 96, 102, 175, 182–198, 201–209, 212–213, 216–217, 250, 253, 257–261, 265–266, 271–274, 293–295, 306, 332, 341, 410, 448, 478, 481, 506

Hermes Trismegistus, 175, 182–198, 201–209, 212, 250, 253, 257–259, 265–266, 271–274, 293–295, 332, 410, 506

'Hermetic Ritual of Perfection', 214–215, 412

Hermetic texts 3, 175, 184, 198, 205–210, 213–215, 217–221, 256–259, 265, 270–272, 283, 293–295, 313, 318–320, 322, 377, 385 *see also* Bruno; Campanella; titles of individual works

Hermeticism, 107, 191–195, 259, 265–266, 278, 318, 377, 523

Hermopolis (*Kmun*; *Al Ashmunain*), 203–204

Herod the Great, 359

Herodotus, 183, 194, 224–226, 234, 236, 243–245, 247–248, 467

Heydon, John, 326

Hibbert, Christopher, 173, 349

Hieroglyphics, 183, 256, 289, 351, 479, 520, 542

Hieronymus of Cardia, 228

Hinduism, 39

Hippo, 100

Hippolytus, 176

Hiram of Tyre, 405

Historical Axis of Paris, 17, 423, 489–490, 528

Holland, 40, 310, 312, 315, 337–338, 340, 342, 460

Holland Lodge No. 8, New York, 544

Holme, Thomas, 513

Holy Land, 4, 13, 86, 141, 199–201, 298, 328, 358, 361, 363–364, 367–368, 373, 375–377, 393, 399–402, 505, 536

Holy Royal Arch, Supreme Order of the, 403 *see* Royal Arch

Holy Sepulchre Church, Jerusalem, 386, 388

Holy Spirit, 49, 69, 71, 75–76, 79, 114, 118, 192, 264, 568

Homer, 225, 234–235, 523

Honorius III, Pope, 153, 159

Hooke, Robert, 346, 384

Hormuzd, King, 99

Horn Lodge, Westminster, 398

Horns of Hattin, 363, 365, 536

Horus, 201–202, 222, 229, 238, 240, 243, 245–246, 273

Hosni, Farouk, 489, 572, 574, 576–579

Houdon, Jean-Antoine, 20, 417, 466, 524, 543

'House of Alma', 329

House of Commons, 321, 333, 555

'House of the Temple', Washington, DC, 520–522 *see* Mother Supreme Council

Huguenots, 261–263, 275, 287, 309, 353, 396

Hund, Baron von, 371, 413, 432

Hungary, 170

Hurlbert, William, 508

Hutchinson, Thomas, 21

Hyde, Ralph, 391

Hypatia, 130

I

Ignatius of Loyola, Saint, 287, 383

Île de la Cité, Paris, 16–17, 420, 466, 525

Île St. Louis, Paris, 17

Iliad (Homer), 225, 234–235

Illuminati, 323, 412–413, 432–437, 459, 573

Illustrations of Freemasonry, 345

Independence Day, US (4 July), 363, 395, 450, 520, 536, 541

India, 47, 53, 95–96, 99, 197, 462

Industrial Revolution, 86

Ingolstadt, 413, 432–433

Keith, William, 514
Kelly, Edward, 271, 310
Kerisel, Jean, 30, 500
Kérouaille, Louise de, 396
Khufu, Pharoah, 251, 486
Kilwinning, 397, 401–402
Kings, book of, 329
Kircher, Athanasius, 381–384, 434, 460–461
Kleber, Jean-Baptiste, 464, 468–469
Kmun (Hermopolis; *Al Ashmunain*), 203–204
Knigge, Baron, 413, 432
Knight, Stephen, 408
Knight Kadosh degree, 380, 404
Knights Hospitallers, 361, 386
Knights Templar (Templars), 327, 356, 358, 360–364, 366–371, 374–376, 386, 399–401, 406, 536
Knights Templar degree, 403–404, 413
Koester, Helmut, 110
Köppen, Karl Friedrich von, 413
Kore Kosmou, 201, 216, 273, 328

L

L'Enfant, Pierre-Charles, 474, 495, 527–533, 537–539
L'heureux, Louis-Ernest, 487
Laborde, Jean-Benjamin de, 417
Laboulaye, Édouard René de, 500
Lafayette, Marquis de, 23–24, 30–32, 428, 437, 439–440, 456, 472, 475, 477, 497, 501, 517–520, 524–526, 528–529, 541
Lafayette, Oscar de, 500
La Rochelle 264, 368, 370, 396, 475
Lagrange, Joseph-Louis, 28
Lalande, Jérôme, 22–23, 28–29, 32, 439, 450, 452–453, 456, 506, 517, 525, 542
Lambert, Malcolm, 48, 68, 80, 82–83, 170
Lamech, 331, 409
Lament of Hermes, 200, 218, 272, 295
Langes, Savalette de, 459
Langue d'oc (Occitan), 42
Langue d'oil, 42
Languedoc, 38, 41–43, 45, 50, 52–54, 64, 90, 120–121, 358, 374–375
Lao-Tsu, 102
Lauragais, the, 44
Lavaur, 150, 167
Lazzarelli, Ludovico, 186–188
Letter of Enoch, 186
Le Nôtre, André, 420, 423, 426
Le Vaux, Louis, 352
Lebanon, 364, 373, 557
Lebas, Jean-Baptiste Apollinaire, 483–484, 493
Leda, 235
Ledoux, Claude-Nicolas, 454–455, 486
Leibniz, Gottfried, 460–461
Leicester (city), 337
Leicester, Duke of, 476

Leicester, Robert Dudley, 270
Leigh, Richard, 531
Leipzig, 412
Lemaire de Belges, Jean, 418
Lenoir, Alexandre, 479–480
Lenormant, Charles, 482
Leo (constellation), 32, 243, 450, 540, 542
Leo the Great, Pope, 130
Leo III, Pope, 13, 466
Leonardo da Pistoia, 171, 175, 182, 184
Leopold II, Emperor, 443
Lesseps, Ferdinand de, 480, 499
Lesseps, Mathieu de, 480, 482
Leszno, 335
Letter to the French People (Cagliostro), 416, 429
Lexington, 21, 515
Libellus, 210–211
Library of Alexandria, Great, 129, 176, 183, 233, 249–253
Lille, 415
Lindsay, David, 344
Lindsay, Sophia, 344
Living Spirit, 73–74, 102–103, 213, 323
Livorno, 480–481
Lobingier, Charles Summer, 28, 381, 526
Lockyer, Norman, 424
Lomas, Robert, 323, 343, 345, 380, 384, 533
Lombardy, 64
London, 5–6, 21, 42, 56, 252, 269, 310, 327, 334–342, 345–348, 352–358, 368, 383–393, 395–398, 405, 410–412, 416, 421, 429, 468, 483–485, 508, 511, 514–515, 525–526, 531–535, 551, 571
London Gazette, 354, 514, 551
Longfellow, Henry Wadsworth, 502
Lorraine, Duke of, 396
Louis VIII, King of France, 153
Louis IX, King of France, 13, 153, 167, 460
Louis XIII, King of France, 287–289, 291, 296, 318, 333, 339, 343–344, 352, 436
Louis XIV, King of France (the Sun King), 208, 291–294, 343–344, 348, 351–355, 382, 394, 396, 398, 410–411, 419–420, 423, 426–427, 436, 460, 484, 486, 488–489, 492, 494, 534, 538–539
Louis XV, King of France, 15, 410, 417, 436, 460–461, 488
Louis XVI, King of France, 12, 15, 22, 27, 370, 410–411, 417, 427, 436, 438–440, 442, 444, 472–473, 484, 505, 517–519, 527
Louis XVIII, King of France, 15, 472–474, 476, 479
Louis-Philippe I ,16, 437, 477–478, 481, 484
Louvel, Louis Pierre, 473
Louvre, the 15–18, 30, 154, 288, 291, 348, 352, 420, 425–426, 449, 454, 466, 470, 481, 484–493, 521, 528, 538, 540 *see also* glass pyramid
Lunel, 54, 377
Luther, Martin, 261, 346
Lutherans, 302, 307–308, 317, 319–320
Luxembourg Palace, Paris, 527

Philadelphia, 20, 408, 434, 509–515, 519, 524, 529

Philae, 237

Philalethes, Les (Paris lodge), 417, 459–460

Philip Augustus, King of France, 153

Philippe Égalité, 436–437, 454–455, 472, 477 *see* Orléans, Philippe, d'

Philip II, King of Macedon, 225–227, 231, 233

Philip II, King of Spain, 264

Philip III, King of Spain, 288

Philip IV the Fair, King of France, 288, 369–370, 372, 376, 400

Philip VI the Fortunate, King of France, 289

Philolaus, 187

Philosophia sensibus demonstrata (Campanella), 281

Phrygian cap, 13–14, 447–448, 452, 456

Piatigorsky, Alexander, 401

Piazza della Minerva, Rome, 383

Picatrix, 195–196, 198, 202–204, 207–208, 267–268, 273–274, 295, 373, 386

Pico della Mirandola, Giovanni, 187, 190–197, 266, 306, 323

Picot, François-Édouard, 15–18, 481, 492, 494, 521

Pignatelli, Tommaso, 286

Pike, Albert, 520–524, 544

Pimander, 185–186, 189, 203, 211, 213, 215, 322

Pingree, David, 195

Pinturicchio, 194

Pisces (constellation), 540

Pius VII, Pope, 466, 475

Place de la Bastille, 12, 15–18, 31, 442–443, 478, 481, 489, 493–494, 497, 516, 521

Place de la Concorde, 15–18, 442, 451, 478, 481, 484, 488–491, 493–494

Place de l'Étoile, 352, 489, 540

Place des Victoires 469

Plague, Great (London), 352

Plato, 96, 102, 130, 176–177, 180–184, 187, 190, 203, 233, 235, 269, 324, 430, 480

Plethon, Gemistus, 181

Pliny, 348–349

Plutarch, 229, 231, 243, 409

Pneumatics, the, 93, 119

Poimandres, 189 *see* Pimander

Poiret, Pierre, 397

Poitiers, Diane de, 262

Poland, 269, 271, 275, 310, 335–336, 383, 413

Polignac, Countess of, 417

Polignac, François de , 223, 240

Pollux, 235

Pont Sully, 17

Pontifex Maximus, 120–122, 126

Pope, John Russell, 520

Portsmouth, 396

Portugal, 40, 370

Poussin, Nicolas, 382

Poyet, Bernard, 454–455

Prague, 311–314, 323, 335

Preston, William, 345

Pritchard, Samuel, 511

Proclus Diadochus, 183

Protestant Union, German, 309–313

Protestantism,190, 261–266, 275, 277–278, 286–287, 297, 302, 309–315, 317–320, 335–336, 346, 394–396

Proteus, Pharaoh, 236

Provence 15, 37, 42, 358, 473

Prussian Academy of Sciences, 412

Pseudo-Callisthenes, 227, 229, 231

Ptolemies, the, 222, 252, 254–256

Ptolemy I Soter, 129, 228, 240, 244–245, 252–253, 256

Ptolemy III, 232, 237

Puritanism, 333, 337–338, 340

Pyramids, Battle of the, 241

Pyramids, 16–19, 29, 77, 196–197, 232, 239, 383–384, 434, 453, 455, 463, 486–487, 492, 497, 500

Pyramid Texts, 208–211, 215, 251, 283

Pythagoras, 182, 187, 235, 407, 409, 480

Q

Quaestiones, the, 131

Quakers, 510, 513, 515, 530

Quatremère de Quincy, Antoine-Chrysostome, 455

Quispel, Gilles, 109

R

Ra, 214, 237–238, 289, 322, 407–408, 425

Rachewiltz, Boris de, 349

Radclyffe, Charles, 396, 398

Ramsay, Andrew Michael (Chevalier Ramsay), 371, 395, 397–403, 413, 566

Ramsay's Oration, 397–398, 400–402

Ramses II, Pharaoh, 423–424, 427, 472

Randolph, Thomas M., 524

Randolph, P. B., 431

Ravaillac, François, 287

Raymond of Aguilers, 360

Raymond of Alfaro, 167

Raymond III, Count of of Tripoli, 364–365

Raymond IV, Count of Toulouse, 360

Raymond VI, Count of Toulouse, 43, 140, 155–156

Raymond-Roger, Count of Foix, 43

Raynaud, Jean-Pierre, 487

Razes, 154

Reformation, 200, 260, 273–275, 278–279, 295, 298–299, 306, 309, 312–313, 315, 318–319, 337, 386, 432, 522

Regulus (star), 540

Reims Cathedral, 451, 476

Renaissance, 6, 14, 52–53, 171, 173, 181–183, 185, 187, 189–191, 194–195, 206, 219, 250, 252, 259–260, 274, 279, 286, 295, 314, 318, 323, 344, 349, 354, 388, 409, 412, 480, 503, 522

Republican Manifesto (Paine), 526

Rennes, 435

Restoration (Charles II), 338–342, 346–347, 355, 383–384, 389, 533

Revelation, book of, 391

Rhakotis, 231, 234

Rhodes, D. H., 528

Richelieu, Cardinal, 290, 292, 296, 343–345, 347

Richmond, Duke of, 396, 398

Ridley, Jasper, 397

Rights of Man (Paine), 526–527

Riquier of Narbonne, Guiraraut, 146

Risorgimento (Italian Unification), 501

Ritter, Helmut, 195

Robert, Pierre-François-Joseph, 439

Robert the Bruce, 370, 400

Roberts, J., 331

Roberval, Gilles de, 343

Robespierre, Maximilien, 13, 20, 24, 26–27, 30, 439, 443–444, 446–447, 449–451, 455–458, 464, 481, 489, 516, 527

Roger of Mirepoix, Peter, 167

Rohan, Cardinal de, 414, 417, 427–429, 507

Roman Catholic Church *see* Catholic Church

Roman Empire, 40, 52, 83, 94, 99–100, 121–122, 131, 144, 200, 207, 264, 280, 289, 293, 317–318, 359, 448, 466–467

Romans, 91, 238, 254–256, 332, 359, 419, 426, 448, 466, 471

Rome, 6, 9, 38–41, 48–50, 53–54, 60–61, 65, 94, 100, 106, 111, 117, 120–126, 131, 135, 140, 170, 180–181, 186–188, 197, 241, 254–258, 261–262, 276, 279, 281–286, 292, 307, 345, 348–351, 367–370, 382–385, 388–389, 394–395, 411, 429, 436, 446, 465–467, 483, 533–534, 539

Romme, Charles-Gilbert, 28, 439, 464

Roosevelt, President Franklin D., 541, 543, 545–546, 556

Rosenberg, Peter, 312

Rosicrucianism, 271, 296–298, 301, 306–307, 315, 318, 320, 322–326, 336, 344, 433, 443, 460

Rosicrucian Manifestos, 298, 302–303, 307–308, 311, 315, 319, 323, 325–326, 330, 345, 361, 453

Rosenberg, Villem, 312

Rosenkreutz, Christian (legendary), 298–306, 308, 310–311, 320, 322, 329–330, 431

Rossi, Roberto de', 180

Rossi, Paolo, 323

Rosslyn, 371–372

Roundheads, 337–339

Rousseau, Jean-Jacques, 1, 12, 26–27, 31, 293, 416, 438, 449, 455

Royal and Select Masters degree, 403

Royal Arch degree, 403–409

Royal Charles (formerly *Naseby*), the, 341

Royal Exchange, London, 321, 384, 392, 412, 533–535

Royal Society, 330, 338, 341–347, 353, 384, 386–387, 390, 396, 399, 515, 533–534

Royal Tavern Lodge, London, 412

Royalists (Cavaliers), 334, 337–340, 342

Rudolph II, Emperor, 323

Rühl, Philippe, 451–452

Rule of Faith (Catholicism), 135

Runciman, Steven, 51, 68, 80–81, 88, 92–93, 117, 373

Rupert, Prince, 337–338, 346–347

Russia, 413–414, 464, 555

S

Sabaeans, 196–197

Sacconi, Rainier, 79, 168

Sagesse Triomphante, La (lodge), 415

Saissac, Bertrand de, 43

Saint-Alexandre d'Écosse (lodge), 27

Saint-Brice, 289

Saint-Eustache church, 448, 471

Saint-Félix-de-Caraman, 64

Saint-Germain, Count of, 435

Saint-Germain-en-Laye, Château de, 394

Saint-Germain-des-Prés, Abbey of, 17, 411–412, 418–419, 435

Saint-Germain l'Auxerrois, Church of, 17

Saint-Jean d'Ecosse de la Vertu Persecutee, La Loge, Avignon, 26

Saint-Just, Louis Antoine de, 442

Saint-Hilaire, 239

Saint-Maur, Château de, 291

Saint Mary of Alet, monastery of, 44

Saint-Michel de Printemps, feast of, 422–423

Sainte Ampoule, 451, 476

Sais, 182, 240

Saladin, 363–367, 386

Salian Franks, 13, 289

Salt, Henry, 482

Samothrace, 226

Samson, Julia, 237

Samson of Rheims, Archbishop, 45

San Leo, 429

Sandys, George, 330

sans-culottes, 13, 444

Santa Maria degli Angeli, monastery of, 180

Saqqara, 240, 248–249

Sarpi, Paolo, 312

Sassanian Empire, 96

Satis, 237

Saturn (planet), 320

Sayer, Anthony, 396

Schopp, Gaspar, 260, 277

Schroeder, Seaton, 508

Schwaller de Lubicz, R. A., 431

Scots Guard, 344

Scotland, 308–309, 323–324, 333, 340, 370–371, 397, 402, 408

Scotland, National Records of, 323–324

Scottish Rite, 26, 323, 327, 380–381, 396–397, 403–404, 431, 434, 456, 473, 479, 499–501, 507, 520, 522–526, 538, 541, 544–546, 556, 566

TER GAME